MY GRAMMAR COACH

내신기출 N제 중3

정답과 해설은 EBS 중학사이트(mid.ebs.co.kr)에서 다운로드 받으실 수 있습니다.

교재 내용 문의	교재 내용 문의는 EBS 중학사이트 (mid.ebs.co.kr)의 교재 Q&A 서비스를 활용하시기 바랍니다.
교재 정오표 공지	발행 이후 발견된 정오 사항을 EBS 중학사이트 정오표 코너에서 알려 드립니다. 교재학습자료 → 교재 → 교재 정오표
교재 정정 신청	공지된 정오 내용 외에 발견된 정오 사항이 있다면 EBS 중학사이트를 통해 알려 주세요. 교재학습자료 → 교재 → 교재 선택 → 교재 Q&A

중학 내신 영어 해결사
MY COACH 시리즈

MY GRAMMAR COACH	기초편, 표준편
MY GRAMMAR COACH 내신기출 N제	중1, 중2, 중3
MY READING COACH	LEVEL 1, LEVEL 2, LEVEL 3
MY WRITING COACH 내신서술형	중1, 중2, 중3
MY VOCA COACH	중학 입문, 중학 기본, 중학 실력

MY GRAMMAR COACH

내신기출 N제 중3

이 책의 **구성과 특징**

＼첫째,

13종 교과서의 문법 요목 및 전국 중학교 시험 문제를 분석하여 구성 (p. 5~8 교과서 문법 연계표 참고)

＼둘째,

단원별 세분화된 요목으로 최대한 간단하게 문법 설명 제시

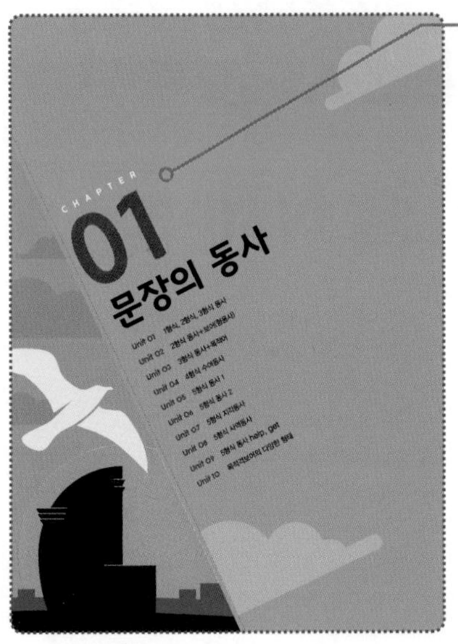

❶ 챕터별 세분화된 문법 요목

종합적인 이해에 앞서 세분화된 각각의 문법 요목에 대한 충분한 학습이 이루어지도록 유닛이 구성되었습니다.

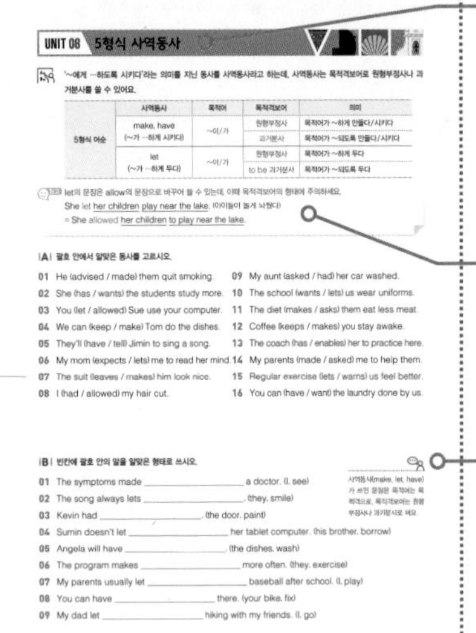

❷ 학습 지시 및 문법 핵심 정리

문법에 관한 긴 설명을 배제하고 어떻게 학습해야 하는지가 간단하게 제시되고, 해당하는 문법의 핵심만 한눈에 볼 수 있도록 정리되어 있습니다.

❸ 주의 및 참고

핵심 문법 정리만으로 부족할 수 있는 참고 사항 및 주의 사항이 세심하게 제시되어 있습니다.

❹ 문제 풀이 팁

막상 문제를 풀 때는 배운 내용이 기억나지 않거나, 배운 내용을 적용하기 힘든 경우들이 있습니다. 이를 위해 Coaching Tip을 통해 다시 한번 문법 설명이 제공됩니다.

STRUCTURE & FEATURES

\ **셋째,**

주관식 위주의 풍부한 드릴 문제 제시 및 세심한 코칭

\ **넷째,**

서술형 비율을 높인 중간고사 · 기말고사 실전문제

\ **다섯째,**

추가 연습할 수 있는 워크북 제공

\ **여섯째,**

문제 해결의 단서와 주의 포인트를 짚을 수 있는 정답과 해설

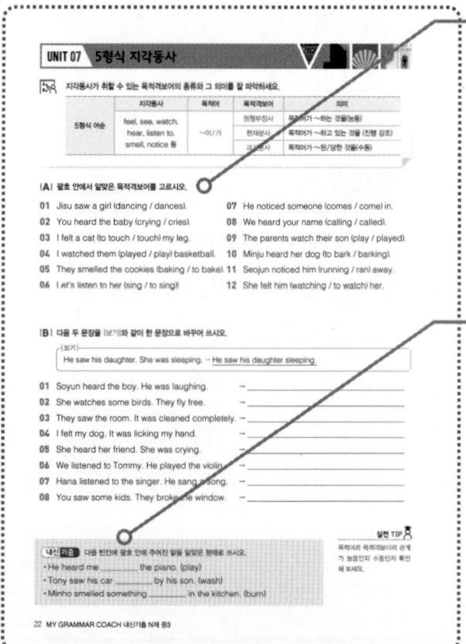

❺ 주관식 위주의 드릴 문제

해당 문법에 대한 집중적인 연습 및 완벽한 이해를 위해 해당 문법 요목에 가장 효과적인 주관식 위주의 연습 문제가 제시됩니다.

❻ 내신 기출 맛보기

챕터 끝에서 종합적인 실전 문제를 풀기 전에, 배운 내용을 바로 바로 실전형으로 풀어 볼 수 있게 구성되었습니다. 해당 문법이 내신 문제화 되었을 때 어떻게 나올 수 있는지를 미리 만나 보며, 학습에 대한 동기 부여가 될 수 있습니다.

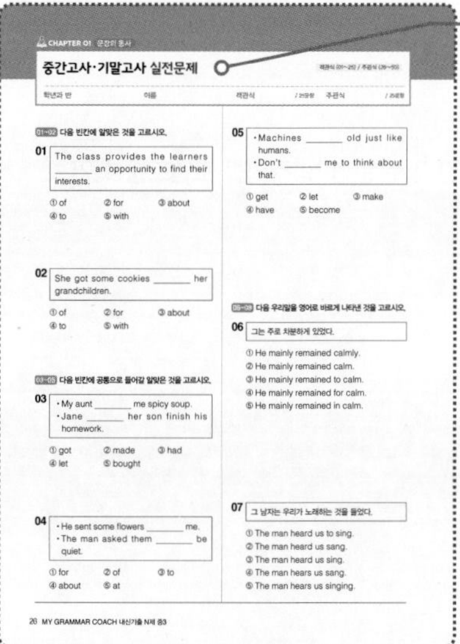

❼ 챕터별 중간고사 · 기말고사 실전문제

세분화된 유닛들로 충분한 학습을 한 후에 종합적으로 챕터별 실전문제를 풀 수 있습니다. 교과서별 중간고사 · 기말고사 시험 범위를 확인하여 시험 대비에도 도움이 될 것입니다. (객관식 25문항 + 주관식 25문항)

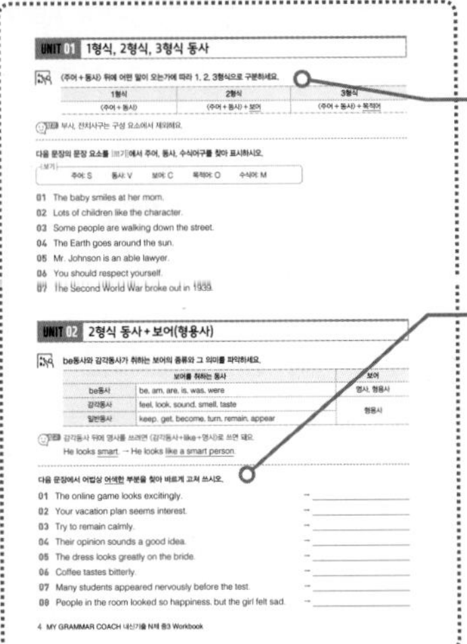

워크북

❽ 유닛별 문법 요약

본문에서 배웠던 각 유닛의 문법을 요약하여 배운 내용을 상기해 볼 수 있습니다.

❾ 유닛별 추가 연습 문제

유닛별 추가 연습 문제를 통해 부족했던 부분들을 확실하게 보충할 수 있습니다.

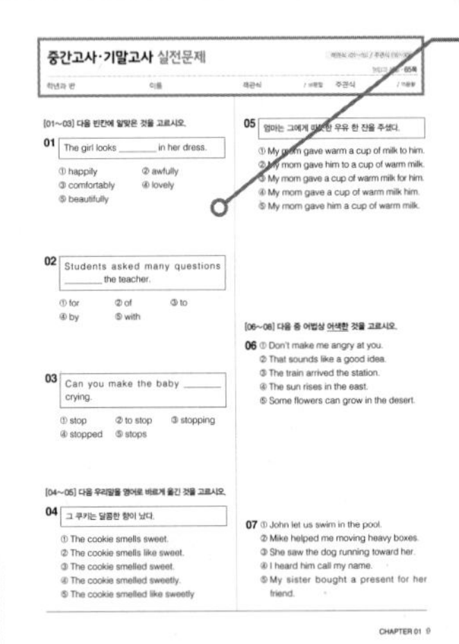

❿ 챕터별 중간고사 • 기말고사 실전문제

종합적인 문제 풀이를 할 수 있도록 워크북에도 추가적인 챕터별 실전문제가 수록되어 있습니다. 교과서별 중간고사 · 기말고사 시험 범위를 확인하여 시험 대비에도 도움이 될 것입니다. (객관식 15문항 + 주관식 15문항)

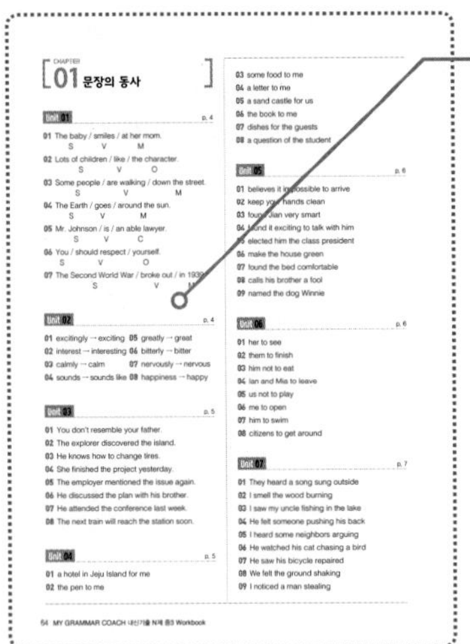

⓫ 정답과 해설

정답과 함께, 문제 해결에 필요한 필수 문법 및 주의할 포인트를 확인 학습할 수 있습니다.

중3 영어 교과서 문법 연계표

YBM(박)		GRAMMAR COACH	
단원	문법	Chapter	Unit
1	강조의 do	13	1
	관계대명사 what	10	6
2	현재완료 진행	2	7
	명사 수식 분사	6	7
3	It is ~ that ... 강조 구문	13	2
	have+목적어+과거분사	1	8
4	to부정사의 의미상 주어	5	2
	가정법 과거	11	1
5	과거완료	2	8
	so that+주어+동사 ~	8	5
6	관계대명사의 계속적 용법	10	9
	형용사+to부정사	5	7
7	관계부사 how	10	8
	the 비교급, the 비교급	7	6
8	분사구문	9	1
	worth+동사원형-ing	6	5
9	I wish 가정법 과거	11	4
	whether, if 사용	8	8

YBM(송)		GRAMMAR COACH	
단원	문법	Chapter	Unit
1	too ~ to부정사	5	8
	to부정사 부정	5	1
2	분사구문	9	1
	명사절을 이끄는 접속사 if	8	8
3	the 비교급, the 비교급	7	6
	It is ~ that ... 강조 구문	13	2
4	접속사 although	8	4
	seem to = It seems that ~	5	9
5	관계대명사 what	10	6
	현재완료진행	2	7
6	as+형용사/부사의 원급+as	7	1
	과거완료	2	8
7	가정법 과거	11	1
	so that ~ can	8	5
8	not only A but also B	8	11
	while 반면, ~하면서	8	6

천재(정)		GRAMMAR COACH	
단원	문법	Chapter	Unit
1	간접의문문	12	3
	관계대명사의 계속적 용법	10	9
2	과거완료	2	8
	비교급 강조	7	4
3	enough to	5	8
	not only A but also B	8	11
4	분사구문	9	1
	관계대명사 what	10	6
5	가정법 과거	11	1
	관계대명사 whose	10	4
6	the 비교급, the 비교급	7	6
	It is ~ that 강조 구문	13	2
7	간접화법	12	3
	if ~인지 아닌지	8	8
8	부정대명사	13	5
	to부정사 목적격보어	1	6

천재(이)		GRAMMAR COACH	
단원	문법	Chapter	Unit
1	관계대명사 what	10	6
	지각동사의 목적격 보어	1	7
2	명사 뒤에서 수식하는 분사	6	7
	since 이유, though 양보	8	3
3	현재완료 진행	2	7
	so ~ that	8	5
4	관계부사	10	8
	접속사 if/whether	8	8
5	과거완료	2	8
	It is ~ that 강조 구문	13	2
6	to부정사의 의미상의 주어	5	2
	가정법 과거	11	1
7	분사구문	9	1
	조동사 수동태	4	4
8	조동사 have p.p.	3	8
	관계대명사 계속적 용법	10	9

동아(이)		GRAMMAR COACH	
단원	문법	Chapter	Unit
1	to부정사의 의미상의 주어	5	2
	관계대명사 what	10	6
2	주어와 동사의 수 일치	12	1
	조동사가 포함된 수동태	4	4
3	사역동사+목적어+동사원형	1	8
	It is ~ that ... 강조 구문	13	2
4	the 비교급, the 비교급	7	6
	since ~이래로, ~때문에	8	6
5	가정법 과거	11	1
	의문사+to부정사	5	3
6	목적을 나타내는 so that ~	8	5
	형/부+enough+to부정사	5	8
7	소유격 관계대명사	10	4
	시간 접속사	8	1
8	분사구문	9	1
	과거완료	2	8

동아(윤)		GRAMMAR COACH	
단원	문법	Chapter	Unit
1	접속사 whether/if	8	8
	to부정사의 형용사적 용법	5	4
2	사역동사	1	8
	so that ~	8	5
3	관계대명사 계속적 용법	10	9
	It is ~ that ... 강조 구문	13	2
4	현재완료 진행	2	7
	의문사+to부정사	5	3
5	명사 수식 현재분사	6	7
	as+형용사/부사의 원급+as	7	1
6	과거완료	2	8
	관계대명사 what	10	6
7	분사구문	9	1
	as의 여러 의미	8	6
8	to부정사의 의미상 주어	5	2
	가정법 과거	11	1

능률(김)		GRAMMAR COACH	
단원	문법	Chapter	Unit
1	현재완료 진행형	2	7
	관계대명사 what	10	6
2	관계대명사의 계속적 용법	10	9
	명사 뒤에서 수식하는 분사	6	7
3	과거완료	2	8
	접속사 although, after, since	8	1
4	접속사 whether/if	8	8
	조동사의 수동태	4	4
5	to부정사의 의미상 주어	5	2
	관계부사	10	8
6	the 비교급 ~, the 비교급	7	6
	분사구문	9	1
7	가정법 과거	11	1
	목적을 나타내는 so that ~	8	5

YBM(양)		GRAMMAR COACH	
단원	문법	Chapter	Unit
1	to부정사의 의미상 주어	5	2
	관계대명사 who 계속적 용법	10	9
2	It is ~ that ... 강조 구문	13	2
	목적격 보어 명사, 형용사	1	5
3	관계대명사 what	10	6
	사역동사 make	1	8
4	과거완료	2	8
	분사구문	9	1
5	의문사+to부정사	5	3
	the 비교급 ~, the 비교급	7	6
6	직접 간접 화법 전환	12	3
	지각동사의 목적격보어	1	7
7	가정법 과거	11	1
	so ~ that	8	5

금성(최)		GRAMMAR COACH	
단원	문법	Chapter	Unit
1	사역동사	1	8
	동명사의 관용 표현	6	5
2	the 비교급 ~, the 비교급	7	6
	It ~ for ... to 구문	5	2
3	not only A but also B	8	11
	I wish 가정법 과거	11	4
4	과거완료	2	8
	동등 비교 구문 as ~as	7	1
5	so ~ that ...	8	5
	지각동사의 목적격 보어	1	7
6	It is ~ that ... 강조 구문	13	2
	분사구문	9	1
7	난이 형용사+to부정사	5	6
	So+동사+주어	13	4
8	접속사 whether	8	8
	It's time+가정법	11	7

미래엔(최)		GRAMMAR COACH	
단원	문법	Chapter	Unit
1	관계대명사 what	10	6
	접속사 although	8	4
2	It is ~ that 강조 구문	13	2
	관계대명사의 계속적 용법	10	9
3	〈관계대명사+be〉 생략	10	5
	강조의 do	13	1
4	과거완료	2	8
	간접의문문	12	3
5	분사구문	9	1
	not only A but also B	8	11
6	관계부사	10	8
	접속부사 however, thus 등	8	9
7	소유격 관계대명사	10	4
	가정법 과거	11	1

비상(김)		GRAMMAR COACH	
단원	문법	Chapter	Unit
1	관계대명사 what	10	6
	관계부사	10	8
2	to부정사의 의미상 주어	5	2
	현재완료 진행	2	7
3	명사절을 이끄는 접속사 if	8	8
	과거완료	2	8
4	분사구 후치수식	6	7
	가목적어 it, 진목적어 to ~	5	1
5	분사구문	9	1
	so that ~ can	8	5
6	It is ~ that 강조 구문	13	2
	have+목적어+과거분사	1	8
7	as의 여러 의미	8	6
	수의 일치 (긴 주어)	12	1
8	가정법 과거	11	1
	with+명사+분사	9	7

지학사(민)		GRAMMAR COACH	
단원	문법	Chapter	Unit
1	관계대명사 what	10	6
	지각동사의 목적격 보어	1	7
2	to부정사의 의미상 주어	5	2
	명사를 뒤에서 수식하는 분사	6	7
3	not only A but also B	8	11
	간접의문문	12	3
4	과거완료	2	8
	to부정사 감정의 원인	5	4
5	부정대명사 one	13	5
	분사구문	9	1
6	It is ~ that ... 강조구문	13	2
	however	8	9
7	가정법 과거	11	1
	5형식	1	5
8	too ~ to부정사	5	8
	No one 전체 부정	13	3

다락원(강)		GRAMMAR COACH	
단원	문법	Chapter	Unit
1	최상급	7	7
	이유 접속사 since	8	3
	관계대명사 what	10	6
2	to부정사 목적격 보어	1	6
	명사 수식 분사	6	7
	소유격 관계대명사	10	4
3	목적격 관계대명사	10	2
	조동사가 있는 수동태	4	4
	가정법 과거	11	1
4	현재 완료 시제	2	4
	to부정사 – 부사적 용법	5	6
	the 비교급, the 비교급	7	6
5	강조의 do	13	1
	대조 접속사 while	8	6
	과거완료 시제	2	8
6	be worth -ing (동명사 관용)	6	5
	접속사 whether	8	8
	to부정사 – 명사적 용법	5	1
7	관계대명사 – 계속적 용법	10	9
	the+형용사	12	1
	가목적어, 진목적어 to부정사	1	5
8	feel like -ing (동명사 관용)	6	5
	도치 구문	13	4
	some, others	13	5
9	It ~ that 강조 구문	13	2
	have(사역)+O+과거분사	1	8
	I wish 가정법 과거	11	4

이 책의 **차례**

연계표를 확인하여 나의 영어 교과서에 나오는 문법을 체크(✓)하고, 그 부분을 집중적으로 공부하세요.

CONTENTS

CHAPTER

01 문장의 동사

UNIT 01 1형식, 2형식, 3형식 동사

〈주어 + 동사〉 뒤에 어떤 말이 오는가에 따라 1, 2, 3형식으로 구분하세요.

	문장 요소	예문	참고
1형식	〈주어+동사〉	〈The train arrived〉 (on time). 〈She is sleeping〉 (on the sofa).	주어, 동사만으로 완전한 문장
2형식	〈주어+동사〉+보어	〈The train is〉 long. 〈She became〉 a nurse.	보어가 없으면 불완전한 문장
3형식	〈주어+동사〉+목적어	〈The train takes〉 us (to Busan). 〈She wants〉 some juice.	목적어(~을)가 필요한 문장

참고 부사(구), 전치사구는 문장 요소에서 제외해요.

|A| 밑줄 친 부분의 문장 요소를 |보기|에서 골라 쓰시오.

|보기| 목적어: O　　보어: C　　수식어: M

01 She goes to school. ________

02 They like online games. ________

03 The food smells good. ________

04 He plays with his brother. ________

05 I swim every weekend. ________

06 I like swimming. ________

07 A horse can run very fast. ________

08 You are a good runner. ________

09 Susie studies English. ________

10 She studies very hard. ________

11 He sings popular songs. ________

12 He is singing on stage. ________

|B| 다음 문장의 문장 요소를 |보기|에서 찾아 표시하시오.

|보기| 주어: S　　동사: V　　목적어: O　　보어: C　　수식어: M

01 My dad works very hard.

02 She wrote a letter to him.

03 The accident happened last night.

04 We went to the park last weekend.

05 He became an engineer.

06 They were standing in the rain.

07 Gina and Kevin came here by bus.

08 I saw a bird in the sky.

내신기출 다음 중 밑줄 친 부분을 생략해도 올바른 문장이 될 수 있는 것은?

① The dish became sour.　　② Some birds fly in the sky.

③ I had some pizza.

실전 TIP

전치사구나 부사(구)는 생략할 수 있지만, 목적어와 보어는 생략할 수 없어요.

UNIT 02 2형식 동사+보어

 be동사와 감각동사가 취하는 보어의 종류와 그 의미를 파악하세요.

보어를 취하는 동사		보어	의미
be동사	am, are, is, was, were	명사, 형용사	~(이)다
감각동사	feel, look, sound, smell, taste	형용사	~하게 느끼다/보이다, ~한 소리가 나다/냄새가 나다/맛이 나다

참고 감각동사 뒤에 명사를 쓰려면 〈감각동사+like+명사〉로 쓰면 돼요.
He looks smart. → He looks like a smart person.

그 외에 보어를 취하는 일반동사와 그 의미를 알아 두세요.

become	~이 되다, ~해지다	keep	~하게 유지하다	turn	~로 변하다, ~해지다
get	~해지다	remain	~한 채로 있다	appear	~인 것 같다

|A| 우리말과 같도록 괄호 안의 말을 활용하여 문장을 완성하시오.

01 날씨가 뜨거워졌다. (hot, turn) → The weather ______________________.
02 그 털은 거칠게 느껴진다. (rough, feel) → The wool ______________________.
03 그 음악은 좋은 소리가 난다. (nice, sound) → The music ______________________.
04 그 사과는 썩은 것 같다. (rotten, appear) → The apple ______________________.
05 그 피자는 좋은 맛이 난다. (taste, good) → The pizza ______________________.
06 그것은 달콤한 냄새가 났다. (smell, sweet) → It ______________________.
07 그것은 좋은 계획 같다. (a good plan, sound) → It ______________________.
08 그녀는 아름다워 보인다. (beautiful, look) → She ______________________.

|B| 다음 문장에서 어법상 어색한 부분을 찾아 바르게 고쳐 쓰시오.

01 Their new song is nicely. ______________________
02 They became very exhaustedly after work. ______________________
03 This bread doesn't smell well. ______________________
04 Tteokbokki may taste like spicy. ______________________
05 He always looks an actor. ______________________
06 People can feel relax at home. ______________________
07 This onion soup turned sourly. ______________________
08 This perfume smells wonderfully. ______________________
09 The leather of the bag feels smoothly. ______________________

UNIT 03 3형식 동사+목적어

동사 뒤에 오는 다양한 목적어들을 알아 두세요.

목적어로 쓸 수 있는 말	예문	해석
명사/대명사	I want a book. / I call him.	~을/를, ~에게
to부정사(구)	I want to read a book.	~하기를 / ~하는 것을
동명사(구)	I like reading books.	~하기를 / ~하는 것을
명사절	I know that you like books.	~라는 것을

동사 뒤에 전치사가 필요할 것 같지만, 그렇지 않은 3형식 동사에 주의하세요.

explain(~을 설명하다)	explain it to him	reach(~에 도달하다)	reach the beach
discuss(~을 논의하다)	discuss it	attend(~에 참석하다)	attend a wedding
enter(~에 들어가다)	enter the room	marry(~와 결혼하다)	marry her
mention(~을 언급하다)	mention it to me	resemble(~와 닮다)	resemble him

주의 위의 동사들은 explain about, discuss about, enter to와 같이 전치사와 함께 쓰일 것 같은 의미를 가졌으나, 바로 목적어만 써요.

|A| 다음 문장의 동사 뒤에 나오는 밑줄 친 부분의 문장 요소를 |보기|에서 골라 쓰시오.

|보기|
목적어: O　　보어: C　　수식어: M

01 I open the window in the morning. ______________

02 She finally accepted the invitation. ______________

03 He became a doctor. ______________

04 My mother added sugar to her coffee. ______________

05 They read the article very carefully. ______________

06 I can feel alive in woods. ______________

07 The author has written a dozen books. ______________

08 Anna does homework at home. ______________

|B| 다음 문장에서 목적어를 찾아 밑줄을 긋고 우리말로 해석하시오.

01 He likes playing soccer with his friends. ______________

02 The boy heard that an accident happened. ______________

03 Harry bought a very expensive car last month. ____________________

04 She forgot fighting with her friend yesterday. ____________________

05 I finished cleaning my room an hour ago. ____________________

06 They remember to wash their hands before a meal. ____________________

07 I found that the restaurant was open. ____________________

|C| 우리말과 같도록 괄호 안의 말을 활용하여 문장을 완성하시오.

01 그녀는 우리에게 그 규칙을 설명해 줬다. (the rules, explain)

→ She ____.

02 그들은 묻지도 않고 그 방에 들어갔다. (enter, asking, without)

→ They ____.

03 그녀는 그녀의 언니를 닮았다. (her sister, resemble)

→ She ____.

04 그는 독일 사람과 결혼했다. (a German, marry)

→ He ____.

05 우리는 그 문제에 대해 두 시간 동안 토론했다. (discuss, the problem, two hours)

→ We ____.

06 그녀는 한 장례식에 참석했어야 했다. (have to, a funeral, attend)

→ She ____.

07 그 배는 어두워진 후에 해안에 이르렀다. (reach, the boat, the shore)

→ ____ after dark.

08 그녀는 그것에 대해 내게 아무것도 언급하지 않았다. (mention, anything)

→ ____ about it.

3형식 문장은 〈주어 + 동사 + 목적어(+ 수식어)〉로 써야 해요.

내신 기출 다음 중 어법상 옳은 문장은?

① She attends at a middle school.
② You resemble with your grandpa.
③ Can you explain about the difference?
④ The airplane reached the airport one hour ago.
⑤ He will discuss about his future with his teacher.

실전 TIP

attend, explain, reach, discuss, resemble 등의 동사는 동사 뒤에 바로 목적어를 써야 해요. 전치사와 함께 쓰지 않는다는 것에 유의하세요.

UNIT 04 4형식 수여동사

목적어 두 개, '~에게(간접목적어)'와 '~을(직접목적어)'을 취하는 4형식 동사들과 그 어순을 알아 두세요.

	4형식 동사 (수여동사: ~에게 ~을 ~해 주다)	간접목적어	직접목적어
4형식 어순	give, make, show, send, ask, tell, lend, get, bring, teach, buy, cook 등	~에게	~을

주의 간접목적어(~에게)와 직접목적어(~을)의 순서를 바꾸어 쓸 수 없어요.

4형식 문장을 3형식 문장으로 바꾸어 쓸 수 있는데, 이때 어순과 전치사에 주의하세요.

3형식 어순	일반 수여동사(send, teach, tell, show 등)	직접목적어 (~을)	to	간접목적어 (~에게)
	get, make, buy, cook, build, find		for	
	ask, inquire	question, favor	of	

주의 다음과 같은 동사는 4형식 동사로 오해하기 쉽지만, 3형식으로만 써야 해요.

provide	~에게 …을 제공[공급]하다	provide A with B (A에게 B를 제공하다) provide B for A (A를 위해 B를 제공하다)
supply		supply A with B (A에게 B를 제공하다) supply B to A (A에게 B를 제공하다)

| A | **우리말과 같도록 괄호 안의 말을 활용하여 빈칸을 완성하시오.**

01 그는 내게 사진들을 보여 주었다. (show, pictures) → He _________ _________ _________.

02 그녀는 우리에게 이야기들을 말해 주었다. (tell, stories) → She _________ _________ _________ _________.

03 우리는 Jane에게 이메일을 보냈다. (send, e-mails) → We _________ _________ _________.

04 나는 그에게 충고를 했다. (give, advice) → I _________ _________ _________.

05 그는 그녀에게 꽃을 사 주었다. (buy, flowers) → He _________ _________ _________ _________.

06 그는 그들에게 수학을 가르친다. (teach, math) → He _________ _________ _________ _________.

07 나는 그녀에게 엽서를 썼다. (write, postcards) → I _________ _________ _________ _________.

08 그녀는 우리에게 저녁을 요리해 줬다. (cook, dinner) → She _________ _________ _________.

09 지민은 그들에게 물을 사 줬다. (buy, water) → Jimin _________ _________ _________.

10 그녀는 내게 피자를 만들어 줬다. (make, pizza) → She _________ _________ _________ _________.

11 Tom은 너에게 선물들을 줄 것이다. (give, presents) → Tom will _________ _________ _________.

12 소금을 내게 건네줄 수 있나요? (pass, the salt) → Could you _________ _________ _________ _________?

|B| 다음 4형식 문장을 3형식 문장으로 바꾸어 쓸 때, 빈칸을 완성하시오.

01 Hamin sent his friend a card. → Hamin sent ______________________.

02 Ms. Kim teaches us Korean. → Ms. Kim teaches ______________________.

03 My grandmother made me gloves. → My grandmother made ______________________.

04 We gave her a bunch of flowers. → We gave ______________________.

05 She will buy her son a computer. → She will buy ______________________.

06 Andy told everyone the news. → Andy told ______________________.

07 You must show me the ticket. → You must show ______________________.

08 She read her children the book. → She read ______________________.

09 My grandfather made me a kite. → My grandfather made ______________________.

|C| 우리말과 같도록 괄호 안의 말을 바르게 배열하시오. (단, 필요시 변형할 것)

01 그 도서관은 아이들에게 책을 제공한다. (to, the children, books, supply)

→ The library ______________________________________.

02 할아버지께서 나에게 새 시계를 사 주셨다. (buy, watch, new, a, me)

→ My grandfather ______________________________________.

03 그는 학생들에게 유용한 정보를 제공한다. (provide, information, students, useful, with)

→ He ______________________________________.

04 엄마는 지난 일요일에 우리에게 쿠키를 만들어 주셨다. (for, make, us, cookies)

→ My mom ______________________________________ last Sunday.

05 그는 환자들에게 의료 돌봄을 제공한다. (provide, patients, medical care, for)

→ He ______________________________________.

06 소는 우리에게 우유를 공급한다. (supply, milk, with, us)

→ Cows ______________________________________.

내신 기출 다음 빈칸에 알맞은 말로 바르게 짝지어진 것은?

- Hayun told her secret _________ me.
- Mina asked a favor _________ her teacher.
- I made a paper plane _________ my brother.

① to – to – for ② to – of – of ③ to – of – for
④ of – to – for ⑤ for – of – to

실전 TIP

4형식 문장을 3형식 문장으로 만들 때 어떤 전치사를 사용하는지 다시 한번 확인하세요.

UNIT 05 5형식 동사 1

목적격보어로 명사나 형용사를 쓰는 5형식 동사들을 알아 두세요.

5형식 어순	명사/형용사를 목적격보어로 쓰는 5형식 동사	목적어	목적격보어
	make, call, name, find, keep, elect, think, believe, consider 등	~을/를, ~이/가	명사, 형용사

참고 5형식은 〈주어+동사+목적어+목적격보어〉로 이루어지는 문장이에요.

만약, 목적어가 to부정사이면 목적어 자리에 가목적어 it을 쓰고, 진목적어 to부정사를 목적격보어 뒤에 써야 해요.

목적어가 (대)명사일 때 어순	목적어가 to부정사일 때의 어순
〈동사 + 목적어 + 목적격보어〉	〈동사 + 가목적어 + 목적격보어 + 진목적어〉
I think him difficult.	I think it difficult to talk to him.
I found the book easy.	I found it easy to read the book.
She made the work possible.	She made it possible to do the work.

|A| 괄호 안에서 알맞은 목적격보어를 고르시오.

01 I found their story (true / truly).
02 Keep your room (cleanly / clean).
03 They elected him (leading / the leader).
04 The speech made us (bore / bored).
05 Hot weather turns milk (sour / sourness).
06 The students found the test (hardly / hard).
07 That coat will keep you (warmly / warm).
08 We left the window (open / openly).
09 Sweet music can make me (happy / happily).
10 We call her (Dancing Queen / to dance).
11 My lie made my parents (anger / angry).
12 Leave the door (closed / closely), please.
13 A refrigerator keeps food (freshly / fresh).
14 Exercise can make you (healthy / health).

|B| 빈칸에 괄호 안의 말을 바르게 배열하여 문장을 완성하시오.

01 You'd better ______________________________. (the beverage, keep, cool)
02 I believe ______________________________. (impossible, persuade, it, to, her)
03 Please, ______________________________. (leave, alone, me)
04 He found ______________________________ the story. (hard, to, believe, it)
05 Coffee can ______________________________. (keep, awake, you)
06 Tests always ______________________________. (nervous, students, make)
07 He made ______________________________. (the job, it, finish, impossible, to)
08 The air conditioner ______________________________. (cool, the house, keeps)
09 The baseball game ______________________________. (made, excited, me)

5형식 문장으로 주어(The baseball game) 뒤에 〈동사(made) + 목적어(me) + 목적격보어(excited)〉의 어순이 되도록 배열해야 해요.

UNIT 06 5형식 동사 2

목적격보어로 to부정사를 쓰는 동사들을 알아 두세요.

	to부정사를 목적격보어로 쓰는 5형식 동사	목적어	목적격보어
5형식 어순	want, ask, tell, expect, enable, encourage, allow, advice, order, get, permit, force 등	~에게, ~이/가	to부정사 (~하기를/~하라고)

참고 to부정사의 부정형은 to 앞에 not을 쓰면 돼요.

|A| 다음 문장에서 동사(V), 목적어(O), 목적격보어(OC)를 찾아 표시하시오.

01 My parents want me to study hard.
02 The Internet enables us to contact them.
03 Sumi asked you to go shopping with her.
04 Sophia told her sister not to do so.
05 The doctor advised him not to smoke.
06 Mr. Choi allowed us to enter the room.
07 You want them to stay home after dark.
08 My mom told me to come home early.
09 Many fans expect the team to win.
10 They persuaded him to come to the party.
11 She always told students not to be late.
12 I encouraged Aiden to try again.
13 He warned us not to go there.
14 I asked Lily to play tennis with me.

|B| 빈칸에 괄호 안의 말을 알맞은 형태로 쓰시오.

01 I want ________________ my cousin. (you, meet)
02 My teacher persuaded ________________ English everyday. (I, study)
03 Good food enables ______________________ properly. (children, grow)
04 Olivia asked ______________________ the door. (I, close)
05 The guide told ______________________ pictures in the gallery. (the tourists, not, take)
06 We don't want ______________________ at night. (she, sing)
07 The doctor advised ______________________ alcohol. (the patient, not, drink)
08 Minju asked ______________________ her an umbrella. (he, lend)

내신 기출 다음 중 밑줄 친 부분이 어법상 어색한 것은?

① You'll never get him understand.
② We want him to come to the party.
③ The building makes the city famous.
④ Money enables us to do many things.
⑤ Parents should keep their children quiet here.

실전 TIP
목적격보어로 to부정사를 쓰는 동사들을 다시 한번 확인하세요.

UNIT 07 5형식 지각동사

지각동사가 취할 수 있는 목적격보어의 종류와 그 의미를 잘 파악하세요.

	지각동사	목적어	목적격보어	의미
5형식 어순	feel, see, watch, hear, listen to, smell, notice 등	~이/가	원형부정사	목적어가 ~하는 것을(능동)
			현재분사	목적어가 ~하고 있는 것을(진행 강조)
			과거분사	목적어가 ~된/당한 것을(수동)

|A| 괄호 안에서 알맞은 목적격보어를 고르시오.

01 Jisu saw a girl (dancing / dances).

02 You heard the baby (crying / cries).

03 I felt a cat (to touch / touch) my leg.

04 I watched them (played / play) basketball.

05 He smelled the cookies (baking / to bake).

06 Let's listen to her (sing / to sing)!

07 He noticed someone (comes / come) in.

08 We heard your name (calling / called).

09 The parents watch their son (play / played).

10 Minju heard her dog (to bark / barking).

11 Seojun noticed him (running / ran) away.

12 She felt him (watching / to watch) her.

|B| 다음 두 문장을 |보기|와 같이 한 문장으로 바꾸어 쓰시오.

|보기|
He saw his daughter. She was sleeping. → He saw his daughter sleeping.

01 Soyun heard the boy. He was laughing. → ______________________

02 She watches some birds. They fly free. → ______________________

03 They saw the room. It was cleaned completely. → ______________________

04 I felt my dog. It was licking my hand. → ______________________

05 She heard her friend. She was crying. → ______________________

06 We listened to Tommy. He played the violin. → ______________________

07 You saw some kids. They broke the window. → ______________________

08 Hana listened to the singer. He sang a song. → ______________________

내신기출 다음 빈칸에 괄호 안에 주어진 말을 알맞은 형태로 쓰시오.

- He heard me ________ the piano. (play)
- Tony saw his car ________ by his son. (wash)
- Minho smelled something ________ in the kitchen. (burn)

실전 TIP
목적어와 목적격보어의 관계가 능동인지 수동인지 확인해 보세요.

UNIT 08 5형식 사역동사

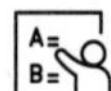

'~에게 …하도록 시키다'라는 의미를 지닌 동사를 사역동사라고 하는데, 사역동사는 목적격보어로 원형부정사나 과거분사를 쓸 수 있어요.

	사역동사	목적어	목적격보어	의미
5형식 어순	make, have (~가 …하게 시키다)	~이/가	원형부정사	목적어가 ~하게 만들다/시키다
			과거분사	목적어가 ~되도록 만들다/시키다
	let (~가 …하게 두다)	~이/가	원형부정사	목적어가 ~하게 두다
			to be 과거분사	목적어가 ~되도록 두다

let의 문장은 allow의 문장으로 바꾸어 쓸 수 있는데, 이때 목적격보어의 형태에 주의하세요.

She let her children play near the lake. (아이들이 호수 근처에서 놀게)

→ She allowed her children to play near the lake.

|A| 괄호 안에서 알맞은 동사를 고르시오.

01 He (advised / made) them quit smoking.

02 She (has / wants) the students study more.

03 You (let / allowed) Sue use your computer.

04 We can (keep / make) Tom do the dishes.

05 They'll (have / tell) Jimin to sing a song.

06 She (expects / lets) me to read her mind.

07 The suit (leaves / makes) him look nice.

08 I (had / allowed) my hair cut.

09 My aunt (asked / had) her car washed.

10 The school (wants / lets) us wear uniforms.

11 The diet (makes / asks) them eat less meat.

12 Coffee (keeps / makes) you stay awake.

13 The coach (has / enables) her to practice here.

14 My parents (made / asked) me to help them.

15 Regular exercise (lets / warns) us feel better.

16 You can (have / want) the laundry done by us.

|B| 빈칸에 괄호 안의 말을 알맞은 형태로 쓰시오.

사역동사(make, let, have)가 쓰인 문장은 목적어는 목적격으로, 목적격보어는 원형부정사나 과거분사로 써요.

01 The symptoms made ____________ a doctor. (I, see)

02 The song always lets ____________. (they, smile)

03 Kevin had ____________. (the door, paint)

04 Sumin doesn't let ____________ her tablet computer. (her brother, borrow)

05 Angela will have ____________. (the dishes, wash)

06 The program makes ____________ more often. (they, exercise)

07 My parents usually let ____________ baseball after school. (I, play)

08 You can have ____________ there. (your bike, fix)

09 My dad let ____________ hiking with my friends. (I, go)

UNIT 09 5형식 동사 help, get

help의 목적격보어로는 원형부정사나 to부정사 모두 쓰일 수 있어요.

	사역동사	목적어	목적격보어	의미
5형식 어순	help (~가 …하도록 돕다)	~이/가	to부정사	목적어가 ~하도록 돕다
			원형부정사	
			(to) be 과거분사	목적어가 ~되도록 돕다(수동)
	get (~가 …하도록 시키다)	~이/가	to부정사	목적어가 ~하도록 시키다
			과거분사	목적어가 ~되도록 시키다(수동)

주의 5형식의 get은 '시키다'라는 사역의 의미지만, 목적격보어로 to부정사를 쓰고, 수동의 의미를 나타낼 때는 과거분사를 써요.

She got her husband to take out the trash. (그녀의 남편에게 쓰레기를 내다 버리게)
She got the trash taken out (by her husband). (그녀의 남편에 의해 쓰레기가 내다 버려지게)

|A| 괄호 안에서 알맞은 목적격보어를 고르시오.

01 He helped me (do / doing) my homework.
02 She got them (go / to go) out immediately.
03 You must get the job (done / to do).
04 He must get the kids (be / to be) quiet here.
05 Jina helped him (to carry / carried) the box.
06 We need to get the television (fix / fixed).
07 He helps her (water / waters) the plants.
08 We help her (to solve / solves) the problem.
09 You have to get the paper (to sign / signed).
10 My dad got me (go / to go) to bed at 10.
11 Running helps me (lose / lost) weight.
12 The movie got us (to feel / feel) frightened.
13 Mina helps him (study / studying) math.
14 He got his car (to check / checked).

|B| 다음 문장에서 어법상 어색한 부분을 찾아 바르게 고쳐 쓰시오.

01 He got his dog stopped barking. ______
02 The book helps the reader understands other people. ______
03 I helped my aunt washed her baby. ______
04 Amy will get her hair to cut tomorrow. ______
05 You must get the error to correct. ______
06 Reading an English book can help us improving our English. ______
07 George has got his car to repair. ______
08 She helps Brian looks for his glasses. ______
09 My dad often gets me clean the living room. ______

UNIT 10 목적격보어의 다양한 형태

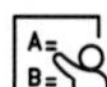

대표적인 5형식 동사들의 주요 목적격보어의 형태를 전체적으로 확인하세요.

동사	목적격보어
make, call, name, find, keep, elect, think, believe, consider	명사, 형용사
want, ask, tell, expect, enable, encourage, allow, advice, order, permit, force	to부정사
지각동사: feel, see, watch, hear, listen to, smell	원형부정사, 현재분사, 과거분사
사역동사: make, have, let	원형부정사, 과거분사
help	to부정사, 원형부정사
get	to부정사, 과거분사

|A| 괄호 안에서 알맞은 동사를 고르시오.

01 Danny (saw / asked) them dancing there.
02 Duna (heard / wanted) them to sing here.
03 The shirt (makes / enables) him look better.
04 The shirt (finds / helps) him to look better.
05 Gloves can (keep / allow) your hands warm.
06 He already (wanted / got) his hair cut.
07 He (had / told) the barber cut his hair.
08 He heard his name (call / called) at night.
09 He heard someone (call / to call) his name.
10 I must (order / get) the refrigerator repaired.

|B| 다음 문장에서 목적격보어를 찾아 어법상 바르게 고쳐 쓰시오.

01 I will have the person to fix my cellphone. ________________
02 I could expect the person fixed my cellphone. ________________
03 The people in the town wanted him leave there. ________________
04 The people in the town saw him left there. ________________
05 We'll listen to the band to sing their songs. ________________
06 We'll ask the band sing their songs. ________________

실전 TIP
다양한 목적격보어의 형태를 다시 한번 확인하세요.

내신 기출 괄호 안에 주어진 동사를 빈칸에 알맞은 형태로 쓰시오.

- The company got the package ________. (deliver)
- The doctor made the patient ________ smoking. (stop)
- She advised her children not ________ much salt. (eat)
- I watched my grandmother ________ dinner. (prepare)

중간고사·기말고사 실전문제

객관식 (01~25) / 주관식 (26~50)

학년과 반 이름 객관식 / 25문항 주관식 / 25문항

01~02 다음 빈칸에 알맞은 것을 고르시오.

01

The class provides the learners ________ an opportunity to find their interests.

① of ② for ③ about
④ to ⑤ with

02

She got some cookies ________ her grandchildren.

① of ② for ③ about
④ to ⑤ with

03~05 다음 빈칸에 공통으로 들어갈 알맞은 것을 고르시오.

03

• My aunt ________ me spicy soup.
• Jane ________ her son finish his homework.

① got ② made ③ had
④ let ⑤ bought

04

• He sent some flowers ________ me.
• The man asked them ________ be quiet.

① for ② of ③ to
④ about ⑤ at

05

• Machines ________ old just like humans.
• Don't ________ me to think about that.

① get ② let ③ make
④ have ⑤ become

06~08 다음 우리말을 영어로 바르게 나타낸 것을 고르시오.

06

그는 주로 차분하게 있었다.

① He mainly remained calmly.
② He mainly remained calm.
③ He mainly remained to calm.
④ He mainly remained for calm.
⑤ He mainly remained in calm.

07

그 남자는 우리가 노래하는 것을 들었다.

① The man heard us to sing.
② The man heard us sang.
③ The man heard us sing.
④ The man hears us sang.
⑤ The man hears us singing.

08

나는 그 소년에게 그 약을 먹으라고 말했다.

① I told the boy take the medicine.
② I told the boy taking the medicine.
③ I told the boy to take the medicine.
④ I told the boy took the medicine.
⑤ I told the boy must take the medicine.

09 다음 밑줄 친 부분을 어법상 바르게 고쳐 쓴 것 중 어색한 것은?

① She had her hair cutted yesterday. (→ cut)
② Dad doesn't let me ate too much fast food. (→ eat)
③ He helped his uncle washing his car. (→ wash)
④ Jessy had her brother to stay in his room. (→ stay)
⑤ I told him speak loudly. (→ speaking)

10 다음 중 어법상 어색한 것을 모두 고르면?

① My family watched the band play today.
② The cook smelled something burning.
③ He saw his food cooking in the kitchen.
④ She heard John talking to himself.
⑤ I felt someone stared at me.

11~12 다음 중 어법상 어색한 것을 고르시오.

11 ① The picture looked wonderful.
② The bouquet smelled good.
③ The temperature stayed high in summer.
④ Did you feel anxiously about the exams?
⑤ My teacher became angry during the class.

12 ① My grandfather paid $50 to the cashier.
② Please, bring the files to me.
③ They sometimes write letters to me.
④ Tim passed the salt to his sister.
⑤ Will you get newspaper to him?

13~14 다음 중 어법상 옳은 것을 고르시오.

13 ① She calls her grandmother 'granny.'
② They asked the boss for change the rule.
③ Teachers always get us read some books.
④ We heard the doorbell rang.
⑤ The storm made the tree falling down.

14 ① People found the book usefully for this job.
② They encouraged people wearing masks.
③ Let me to give some advice to you.
④ Would you lend me your bike?
⑤ Can you find the keys to me?

15 다음 중 밑줄 친 부분을 어법상 바르게 고쳐 쓴 것은?

① Don't expect me going there. (→ go)
② Doctors advised her take a walk every day. (→ taking)
③ We thought the boy very rudely. (→ rude)
④ She told the children polite. (→ be polite)
⑤ Nothing can make the prince happily. (→ is happy)

16 다음 중 어법상 옳은 것을 모두 고르면?

① Students discussed the topic for an hour.
② They resemble to each other.
③ Did you attend to the meeting last night?
④ Who entered the room a few minutes ago?
⑤ She will marry with my brother next week.

17 다음 4형식 문장을 3형식 문장으로 바르게 나타낸 것은?

① My aunt cooked me a delicious meal.
→ My aunt cooked a delicious meal to me.
② The company offered him a job.
→ The company offered a job for him.
③ Mr. Kim built his wife a small house.
→ Mr. Kim built a small house to his wife.
④ Mom always read their baby books.
→ Mom always read books to their baby.
⑤ The man asked them some questions
→ The man asked some questions to them.

18~20 다음 빈칸에 알맞은 말이 바르게 짝지어진 것을 고르시오.

18

- The lawyer asked a lot of questions ________ him.
- She asked me ________ go out.
- They can supply us ________ a lot of food.

① to – for – to
② of – to – with
③ to – to – for
④ for – of – to
⑤ of – of – with

19

- She had her cellphone ________ yesterday.
- They let the dog ________ at strangers.
- The waiter helped us ________ our meal.

① fix – bark – to choose
② fixing – barking – choose
③ fixed – bark – choose
④ fixed – barking – choose
⑤ fix – to bark – choosing

20

- We found the movie ________.
- The man kept ________ during the game.
- They considered his speech ________.

① boring – quiet – greatly
② bore – quiet – great
③ boring – quiet – great
④ boring – quietly – great
⑤ bore – quietly – greatly

21 다음 중 어법상 틀린 문장의 개수는?

ⓐ I tried to remain calmly when the baby began to cry.
ⓑ She made a sweater her husband.
ⓒ This medicine helped my grandfather recover from his illness.
ⓓ Please, keep me posting on any news.

① 없음 ② 1개 ③ 2개
④ 3개 ⑤ 4개

22 다음 중 어법상 옳은 문장의 개수는?

ⓐ The audience gave a big hand to us on our performance.
ⓑ I watched his bike stealing.
ⓒ The news made people scared.
ⓓ I found my neighbor friendly.

① 없음 ② 1개 ③ 2개
④ 3개 ⑤ 4개

23 다음 중 밑줄 친 단어의 쓰임이 나머지와 다른 것은?

① The detective got him to confess everything.
② We got our daughter a swimsuit to wear to the beach.
③ She always gets her son to clean his room.
④ The president didn't get anyone to come in his room.
⑤ I tried to get my friend to accept my apology.

24 다음 중 어법상 옳은 문장끼리 바르게 짝지은 것은?

ⓐ I felt sick after walking in the rain.
ⓑ The pasta I made tastes awfully.
ⓒ Many people appeared on the show.
ⓓ Can you show me the way to the station?
ⓔ Jack listened to people yelled at her.

① ⓐ, ⓒ
② ⓑ, ⓒ
③ ⓐ, ⓑ, ⓒ
④ ⓐ, ⓒ, ⓓ
⑤ ⓒ, ⓓ, ⓔ

25 다음 글의 밑줄 친 ⓐ~ⓕ 중, 어법상 어색한 것의 개수는?

My family went camping last week. ⓐ My dad let my brother drive the car because he turned 20 years old this month. While driving to the campground, ⓑ we saw a deer jump in front of our car. ⓒ My brother tried to avoid the deer, but he couldn't. ⓓ My dad called the police and explained about the situation. My brother got stressed out. ⓔ So my mom gave to him some encouraging words. ⓕ She told to him not worry, but he said he would never drive again.

① 1개 ② 2개 ③ 3개
④ 4개 ⑤ 5개

〈다음부터는 서술형 주관식 문제입니다.〉

26~28 다음 문장에서 어법상 어색한 부분을 찾아 바르게 고쳐 쓰시오.

26 Your accent doesn't sound like natural.

_______________ → _______________

27 The company provides with good health care for workers.

_______________ → _______________

28 The kind man found the lady's lost diamond ring to her.

_______________ → _______________

29~31 다음 문장의 밑줄 친 부분을 어법상 바르게 고쳐 쓰시오.

29 She didn't put the soup in the refrigerator to keep it warmly.

→ _______________

30 Ms. Kim had all the household chores do by her husband.

→ _______________

31 Chris found himself sticking somewhere in the middle.

→ _______________

32~33 다음 우리말과 같도록 빈칸에 괄호 안의 동사를 알맞은 형태로 쓰시오.

32

그녀가 우리에게 그녀의 노트북 컴퓨터를 쓰게 해 줄지도 모른다. (let, use)

→ She might ________ us ________ her laptop computer.

33

부모님은 그들의 딸이 가난한 남자와 결혼하는 것을 허락하지 않았다. (marry)

→ The parents didn't permit their daughter _______________ the poor man.

34~36 다음 우리말과 같도록 괄호 안의 말을 바르게 배열하여 문장을 완성하시오.

34 그 댄서들은 어제 무대 위에서 긴장한 것처럼 보였다.
(on, appeared, stage, nervous, yesterday)

→ The dancers ______________________
______________________.

35 그녀는 그의 마음을 바꾸는 것이 어렵다고 생각한다. (to, it, his mind, change, difficult)

→ She thinks ______________________
______________________.

36 너는 그 설명서를 읽는 것이 유용하다는 걸 알게 될 것이다.
(to, it, the instructions, helpful, read, find)

→ You will ______________________
______________________.

37~38 다음 주어진 문장과 의미가 같도록 문장을 완성하시오.

37 Her mom doesn't let her oversleep on weekends.

→ Her mom doesn't allow ______________________
______________________.

38 He had his secretary bring the document.

→ He got ______________________
______________________.

39~42 다음 우리말과 같도록 괄호 안의 말을 활용하여 문장을 완성하시오.

39 나는 비행기가 움직이는 것을 느낄 수 없었다.
(move, feel, the airplane, could)

→ ______________________

40 나의 아버지는 내가 그의 고장 난 카메라를 고치게 했다. (have, father, camera, repair, break)

→ ______________________

41 너는 그 회의에서 그의 이름이 언급되는 것을 들었니? (hear, mention, name)

→ ______________________
in the meeting?

42 의사는 그녀에게 따뜻한 물을 많이 마시라고 조언했다. (drink, advise, the doctor, warm, lots of)

→ ____________________

43~45 다음 글의 밑줄 친 ⓐ~ⓕ 중 어법상 어색한 것을 찾아 바르게 고쳐 쓰시오. (정답 3개)

The spring ⓐ is coming! My teacher encouraged us ⓑ going outside and look for some flowers. We found various flowers. They smelled ⓒ differently. The white flowers ⓓ resembled a wedding dress. Suddenly, a bee flew near me, so my teacher told me ⓔ to stay still. She had the bee ⓕ gone away. I felt relieved!

43 __________ → __________

44 __________ → __________

45 __________ → __________

46~48 다음 글의 밑줄 친 ⓐ~ⓕ 중 어법상 어색한 부분을 세 군데 찾아 바르게 고쳐 쓰시오.

ⓐ I had a busy day today because my mom had me do a lot of things. First, ⓑ I needed to get my dog wash. Then, ⓒ I had to do my homework for two hours. ⓓ I also wrote a letter for my grandmother. After that, ⓔ I helped my sister drew a picture. Finally, ⓕ my mom let me play computer games, but I couldn't. I was so tired.

46 __________ → __________

47 __________ → __________

48 __________ → __________

49~50 다음 우리말을 주어진 |조건|에 맞게 바르게 영작하시오.

49 이 기계는 우리가 그 일을 빨리 끝내는 것을 가능하게 할 것이다.

|조건|
1. This machine으로 시작할 것
2. 단어 enable, finish, the work, fast를 사용할 것
3. 10단어로 쓸 것

→ ____________________

50 그녀는 그녀의 지갑이 도난당한 것을 발견했다.

|조건|
1. She로 시작할 것
2. 단어 find, wallet, steal을 사용할 것
3. 5단어로 쓸 것

→ ____________________

CHAPTER

02 시제

UNIT 01 동사 변화형

주어가 3인칭 단수일 때, 동사의 현재형을 만드는 방법을 알아 두세요.

대부분의 동사	-s	rise – rises(올라가다, 뜨다) leave – leaves(떠나다, 남기다)	save – saves(구하다, 아끼다) prove – proves(증명하다)
-o, -s, -x, -sh, -ch로 끝나는 동사	-es	miss – misses(놓치다, 그리워하다) teach – teaches(가르치다)	finish – finishes(마치다) relax – relaxes(긴장을 풀다)
〈자음+y〉로 끝나는 동사	y를 i로 바꾸고 -es	cry – cries(울다) study – studies(공부하다)	try – tries(해 보다) worry – worries(걱정하다)
〈모음+y〉로 끝나는 동사	-s	pay – pays(지불하다) enjoy – enjoys(즐기다)	buy – buys(사다)
불규칙 동사	be	be – am/are/is(~이다, ~하다)	
	have	have – has(가지다, 먹다)	

동사의 과거형과 과거분사형이 같은 규칙 변화 동사들을 알아 두세요.

대부분의 동사	-ed	accept – accepted – accepted(받아들이다) add – added – added(더하다)
-e로 끝나는 동사	-d	disagree – disagreed – disagreed(동의하지 않다) believe – believed – believed(믿다) die – died – died(죽다) decide – decided – decided(결정하다) lie – lied – lied(거짓말하다)
〈단모음+단자음〉으로 끝나는 동사	마지막 자음 하나 더 쓰고 -ed	drop – dropped – dropped(떨어뜨리다) plan – planned – planned(계획하다)
〈자음+y〉로 끝나는 동사	y를 i로 바꾸고 -ed	carry – carried – carried(들고 있다, 나르다) marry – married – married(결혼하다) hurry – hurried – hurried(서두르다) study – studied – studied(공부하다) try – tried – tried(해 보다) worry – worried – worried(걱정하다)
〈모음+y〉로 끝나는 동사	-ed	delay – delayed – delayed(미루다, 연기하다) play – played – played(놀다) stay – stayed – stayed(머물다)

|A| 빈칸에 동사의 규칙 과거형과 과거분사형을 쓰면서 외우세요.

01 accept – ________ – ________
02 accomplish – ________ – ________
03 agree – ________ – ________
04 allow – ________ – ________
05 apply – ________ – ________
06 arrange – ________ – ________
07 believe – ________ – ________
08 borrow – ________ – ________
09 breathe – ________ – ________
10 bury – ________ – ________
11 carry – ________ – ________
12 classify – ________ – ________
13 collect – ________ – ________
14 copy – ________ – ________
15 cry – ________ – ________
16 decide – ________ – ________
17 delay – ________ – ________
18 demand – ________ – ________
19 deny – ________ – ________
20 depend – ________ – ________
21 destroy – ________ – ________
22 disagree – ________ – ________
23 display – ________ – ________
24 divide – ________ – ________
25 drop – ________ – ________
26 dry – ________ – ________
27 enjoy – ________ – ________
28 enter – ________ – ________
29 fail – ________ – ________
30 found – ________ – ________
31 grab – ________ – ________
32 guess – ________ – ________
33 hurry – ________ – ________
34 lie (거짓말하다) – ________ – ________
35 laugh – ________ – ________
36 learn – ________ – ________
37 maintain – ________ – ________
38 marry – ________ – ________
39 plan – ________ – ________
40 play – ________ – ________
41 prefer – ________ – ________
42 prove – ________ – ________
43 pull – ________ – ________
44 push – ________ – ________
45 raise – ________ – ________
46 regret – ________ – ________
47 remember – ________ – ________
48 share – ________ – ________
49 stay – ________ – ________
50 stop – ________ – ________
51 survive – ________ – ________
52 thank – ________ – ________
53 try – ________ – ________
54 worry – ________ – ________

동사의 불규칙 과거형과 과거분사형은 암기해야 해요.

정해진 규칙 없이 변하는 동사의 과거형, 과거분사형	am, is – was – been(~이다, ~하다) are – were – been(~이다, ~하다) become – became – become(~이 되다) begin – began – begun(시작하다) bind – bound – bound(묶다) bite – bit – bitten(물다) bleed – bled – bled(피를 흘리다) blow – blew – blown(바람이 불다) break – broke – broken(깨뜨리다) bring – brought – brought(가져오다) build – built – built(짓다, 건설하다) buy – bought – bought(사다) catch – caught – caught(잡다) choose – chose – chosen(선택하다) come – came – come(오다) do – did – done(하다) draw – drew – drawn(그리다) drink – drank – drunk(마시다) drive – drove – driven(운전하다) eat – ate – eaten(먹다) fall – fell – fallen(떨어지다) feed – fed – fed(먹이를 주다) feel – felt – felt(느끼다) fight – fought – fought(싸우다) find – found – found(발견하다) fly – flew – flown(날다) forget – forgot – forgotten(잊다) forgive – forgave – forgiven(용서하다) get – got – got/gotten(얻다, 사다) give – gave – given(주다) go – went – gone(가다) grow – grew – grown(자라다) have – had – had(가지다, 먹다) hear – heard – heard(듣다) hold – held – held(잡다) keep – kept – kept(간직하다, 유지하다) know – knew – known(알다) lay – laid – laid(놓다)	lead – led – led(이끌다) leave – left – left(떠나다) lend – lent – lent(빌려주다) lie – lay – lain(눕다, 누워 있다) lose – lost – lost(지다, 잃다) make – made – made(만들다) mean – meant – meant(의미하다) meet – met – met(만나다) pay – paid – paid(지불하다) ride – rode – ridden(타다) ring – rang – rung(울리다) rise – rose – risen(떠오르다) run – ran – run(달리다) say – said – said(말하다) see – saw – seen(보다) sell – sold – sold(팔다) send – sent – sent(보내다) shoot – shot – shot(쏘다) sing – sang – sung(노래하다) sit – sat – sat(앉다) sleep – slept – slept(자다) speak – spoke – spoken(말하다) spend – spent – spent(시간/돈을 쓰다) stand – stood – stood(일어서다) steal – stole – stolen(훔치다) swim – swam – swum(수영하다) take – took – taken(타다, 받다) teach – taught – taught(가르치다) tear – tore – torn(찢다) tell – told – told(말하다) think – thought – thought(생각하다) throw – threw – thrown(던지다) understand – understood – understood (이해하다) wake – woke – waken(일어나다) wear – wore – worn(입다) win – won – won(이기다) write – wrote – written(쓰다)
현재형, 과거형, 과거분사형이 같은 동사	bet – bet – bet(내기를 걸다) cost – cost – cost(비용이 들다) cut – cut – cut(자르다) hit – hit – hit(치다) hurt – hurt – hurt(다치게 하다)	let – let – let(두다) put – put – put(두다, 놓다) read[ri:d] – read[red] – read[red](읽다) shut – shut – shut(닫다) spread – spread – spread(퍼지다)

|B| 빈칸에 동사의 불규칙 과거형과 과거분사형을 쓰면서 외우세요.

01 am, is – ________ – ________
02 are – ________ – ________
03 become – ________ – ________
04 begin – ________ – ________
05 bet – ________ – ________
06 bind – ________ – ________
07 bite – ________ – ________
08 bleed – ________ – ________
09 blow – ________ – ________
10 break – ________ – ________
11 bring – ________ – ________
12 build – ________ – ________
13 burst – ________ – ________
14 buy – ________ – ________
15 catch – ________ – ________
16 choose – ________ – ________
17 come – ________ – ________
18 cost – ________ – ________
19 cut – ________ – ________
20 do – ________ – ________
21 draw – ________ – ________
22 drink – ________ – ________
23 drive – ________ – ________
24 eat – ________ – ________
25 fall – ________ – ________
26 feed – ________ – ________
27 feel – ________ – ________
28 fight – ________ – ________
29 find – ________ – ________
30 fly – ________ – ________
31 forget – ________ – ________
32 forgive – ________ – ________
33 freeze – ________ – ________
34 get – ________ – ________
35 give – ________ – ________
36 go – ________ – ________
37 grow – ________ – ________
38 have – ________ – ________
39 hear – ________ – ________
40 hide – ________ – ________
41 hit – ________ – ________
42 hold – ________ – ________
43 hurt – ________ – ________
44 keep – ________ – ________
45 know – ________ – ________
46 lay – ________ – ________
47 lead – ________ – ________
48 leave – ________ – ________
49 lend – ________ – ________
50 let – ________ – ________
51 lie (누워 있다) – ________ – ________
52 lose – ________ – ________
53 make – ________ – ________
54 mean – ________ – ________
55 meet – ________ – ________
56 overcome – ________ – ________
57 pay – ________ – ________
58 put – ________ – ________
59 quit – ________ – ________
60 read – ________ – ________
61 ride – ________ – ________
62 ring – ________ – ________
63 rise – ________ – ________
64 run – ________ – ________
65 say – ________ – ________
66 see – ________ – ________
67 sell – ________ – ________
68 send – ________ – ________
69 set – ________ – ________
70 shoot – ________ – ________

71 shut – ________ – ________
72 sing – ________ – ________
73 sit – ________ – ________
74 sleep – ________ – ________
75 speak – ________ – ________
76 spend – ________ – ________
77 spread – ________ – ________
78 stand – ________ – ________
79 steal – ________ – ________
80 sweep – ________ – ________
81 swim – ________ – ________

82 take – ________ – ________
83 teach – ________ – ________
84 tear – ________ – ________
85 tell – ________ – ________
86 think – ________ – ________
87 throw – ________ – ________
88 understand – ________ – ________
89 wake – ________ – ________
90 wear – ________ – ________
91 win – ________ – ________
92 write – ________ – ________

내신 기출 다음 동사의 변화형으로 옳지 않은 것은?

① spend – spent – spent
② delay – delayed – delayed
③ spread – spreaded – spreaded
④ overcome – overcame – overcome
⑤ understand – understood – understood

실전 TIP

동사의 불규칙 변화형은 무조건 반복해서 외워야 해요.

UNIT 02 기본시제 - 현재, 과거, 미래

다음 기본시제를 표현하는 동사의 형태 및 부정문, 의문문의 어순을 정확히 파악하세요.

시제	상황	긍정문의 동사 형태		부정문	의문문
현재	현재의 상태, 습관/반복, 진리	be동사	am, are, is	be동사(현재형)+not	Be동사(현재형)+주어 ~?
		일반동사	동사원형(+-s)	do(es)+not+동사원형	Do(es)+주어+동사원형 ~?
과거	과거의 동작, 상태	be동사	was, were	be동사(과거형)+not	Be동사(과거형)+주어 ~?
		일반동사	동사원형+-ed / 불규칙	did+not+동사원형	Did+주어+동사원형 ~?
미래	미래의 일	will+동사원형		will+not+동사원형	Will+주어+동사원형 ~?
		be going to+동사원형		be동사 뒤에 not을 씀	Be동사만 주어 앞에 씀

참고 시제를 판단할 때는 문맥이나 문장의 시간 부사를 파악해야 해요.

주의 시간, 조건의 부사절에서 미래는 현재시제로 표현하는 것에 주의하세요.
When he ~~will come~~ comes back, we will start.

|A| 빈칸에 괄호 안의 동사를 알맞은 형태로 쓰시오.

01 Water ____________ at 0°C. (freeze)
02 They ____________ tennis yesterday. (play)
03 The restaurant always ____________ at noon. (open)
04 It ____________ fine tomorrow. (be)
05 Edison ____________ the light bulb in 1879. (invent)
06 We ____________ swimming this coming Saturday. (go)
07 It ____________ not usually hot in October in Korea. (be)
08 I ____________ the book next week. (return)
09 My grandmother ____________ 70 years old last year. (be)

|B| 다음 문장의 밑줄 친 동사를 시제에 맞게 알맞은 형태로 고쳐 쓰시오.

01 They went skiing next week. ____________
02 Our solar system had eight planets. ____________
03 My sister go to school by bus every day. ____________
04 I will say hello to him for you when I will meet him. ____________
05 He makes a Christmas tree with his children last weekend. ____________
06 The great King Sejong invents Hangeul, the Korean alphabets, in 1146. ____________

UNIT 03 현재진행 & 과거진행

'~하고 있다'와 같이 진행 중인 동작을 나타낼 때는 진행형 〈be동사 + 동사원형-ing〉로 써야 해요.

현재진행	am/are/is+동사원형-ing	She is having breakfast now. They are not going to school now. I am leaving for Jeju-do tomorrow. (현재진행이 가까운 미래의 예정된 일을 표현하기도 함)
과거진행	was/were+동사원형-ing	She was having breakfast at that time. Were they going to school that day?

주의 소유나 상태를 나타내는 동사(have, want, know, like, believe 등)는 진행형으로 쓸 수 없어요. 하지만 have가 '먹다'라는 의미일 때는 진행형이 가능해요.

|A| 괄호 안에서 알맞은 것을 고르시오.

01 My dad (read / is reading) a newspaper now.

02 He (is leaving / was leaving) for Busan tomorrow.

03 She (was talking / is talking) on the phone an hour ago.

04 I (take / was taking) a shower when you called.

05 They (were going / are going) to San Francisco for business tomorrow.

06 Emily (was packing / is packing) her suitcase at that time.

|B| 괄호 안의 동사를 활용하여 진행시제 문장을 완성하시오.

01 Kevin ________________ a walk now. (take)

02 I ________________ lunch soon. (eat)

03 My aunt and cousins ________________ tomorrow. (come)

04 Anne ________________ the house when the neighbor visited. (clean)

05 What ________________ you ________________ then? (be, drink)

06 I ________________ television when my sister came home. (watch)

07 We ________________ homework yesterday at noon. (do)

내신 기출 다음 중 어법상 옳은 문장은?

① We are knowing who he is.
② I am loving my dog very much.
③ Anna was having lunch alone then.
④ He was believing what his son told him.
⑤ You were disliking spicy foods when you were younger.

실전 TIP

소유나 상태를 나타내는 동사는 진행형으로 쓰지 않는다는 데 유의하세요.

UNIT 04 현재완료 1 - 계속

과거는 과거에 끝난 일을, 현재완료는 과거의 일이 현재까지 영향을 미치는 일을 표현할 때 써요.

	과거	현재완료
긍정	주어+동사의 과거형	주어+have[has]+과거분사
부정	주어+did+not+동사원형	주어+have[has]+not+과거분사
의문	Did+주어+동사원형 ~?	Have[Has]+주어+과거분사 ~?
예문	He lived here last year. (작년에 살았음 / 현재와는 상관없음)	He has lived here for 5 years. (과거부터 현재까지 5년 동안 살아왔음)

for 또는 since가 있으면 '(과거부터 현재까지 계속) ~해 왔다'는 의미로 현재완료형으로 써야 해요.

뒤에 오는 말	for(~ 동안)+기간	since(~ 이후로)+과거 시점 / 과거 문장
예문	He has lived here for 5 years.	He has lived here since last year. He has lived here since he was born.

|A| 빈칸에 for와 since 중 알맞은 것을 쓰시오.

01 You've lived in Seoul __________ 10 months.

02 David has worked for the bank __________ it was established.

03 We've been friends __________ we were very young.

04 I haven't eaten anything __________ 2 days.

05 It has snowed __________ last Thursday.

06 He has known Bob __________ 5 years.

|B| 괄호 안의 동사를 활용하여 과거시제나 현재완료시제 문장을 완성하시오.

01 They ______________ in Vancouver since 2013. (live)

02 They ______________ in Vancouver in 2013. (live)

03 Joe ______________ my friend for 5 years. (be)

04 Joe ______________ my friend when we were elementary school students. (be)

05 My uncle ______________ chemistry since he graduated from university. (teach)

06 My uncle ______________ a science teacher a decade ago. (be)

내신 기출 다음 중 빈칸에 들어갈 말이 다른 하나는?

① She's studied German ________ August.

② They haven't smoked ________ half a year.

③ I haven't seen Sora ________ I moved here.

실전 TIP

'~ 동안'인지 '~ 이후로'인지의 의미를 파악해야 해요.

UNIT 05 현재완료 2 - 완료, 경험, 결과

현재완료 〈have[has] + 과거분사〉의 계속의 의미 이외의 다른 의미도 파악하세요.

완료	(과거에 시작한 일을 현재) ~했다	I have just finished the homework. (막 끝냈다) She's already heard the good news. (이미 들었다) He hasn't read the e-mail yet. (아직 읽지 않았다)
		참고 부사 just(방금[막]), already(벌써[이미]), yet(아직, 벌써) 등과 함께 씀
경험	(과거부터 지금까지) ~해 본 적 있다	She has tried Thai food before. (전에 먹어 본 적이 있다) I've never been to Paris. (가 본 적이 전혀[절대] 없다)
		주의 ever는 긍정문, never는 부정문에 사용함 참고 부사(구) before, often, once, twice, three times 등과 함께 씀
결과	(과거에 ~한 결과 현재) ~하다	She has lost her expensive bag. (잃어버려서 지금 가지고 있지 않다) He has gone to the hospital. (병원에 가서 (이곳에) 없다)

주의 〈have gone to+장소〉: (~로) 가 버려서 (이곳에) 없다(결과)
〈have been to+장소〉: ~에 가 본 적이 있다(경험)

|A| 다음 밑줄 친 현재완료의 쓰임을 |보기|에서 골라 쓰시오.

|보기|
완료　　경험　　결과

01 I've been to Busan. ____________

02 You've already done your homework. ____________

03 I've lost my smartphone. ____________

04 I've never been to Daegu before. ____________

05 My cousins have gone to Canada. ____________

06 We've been to Europe once. ____________

07 Has he already cleaned the house? ____________

08 They have just had lunch. ____________

09 It is not here. John has taken it. ____________

10 Have you discussed the matter yet? ____________

11 Have you ever seen any Disney movies? ____________

|B| 우리말과 같도록 괄호 안의 말을 활용하여 빈칸에 알맞은 말을 쓰시오.

01 그는 방금 집에 돌아왔다. (come) → He ________ ________ ________ back home.

02 그 비행기는 막 도착했다. (arrive) → The flight ________ ________ ________.

03 이 선생님은 전에 물리를 가르치신 적 있다. (teach) → Ms. Lee ________ ________ physics ________.

04 그들 모두 그 도시를 떠났다. (leave) → All of them ________ ________ the city.

05 그 팀은 게임에서 진 적이 두 번 있다. (lose) → The team ________ ________ a game ________.

06 Eva는 이미 그 책을 읽는 것을 끝냈다. (finish) → Eva ________ ________ ________ reading the book.

07 그녀는 그 일을 아직 다하지 않았다. (do) → She ________ ________ ________ the job ________.

08 그는 전에 방을 청소한 적이 전혀 없다. (clean) → He ________ ________ ________ his room ________.

|C| 우리말과 같도록 괄호 안의 말을 바르게 배열하시오.

01 그는 소윤이를 세 번 만난 적 있다. (met, has, three times, Soyun)

→ He ________________________________.

02 너는 벌써 점심 식사를 끝마쳤니? (you, finished, already, have)

→ ________________________________ lunch?

03 나는 그녀의 번호를 잊어버렸다. (her number, forgotten, have)

→ I ________________________________.

04 나는 전에 그 공원에 가 본 적 있다. (been, the park, to, before, have)

→ I ________________________________.

05 그녀는 아직 내게 전화하지 않았다. (called, yet, not, me, has)

→ She ________________________________.

06 너는 전에 스페인 음식을 먹어 본 적 있니? (tried, ever, you, have, Spanish food)

→ ________________________________ before?

07 나는 이미 그 영화를 봤다. (seen, already, the movie, have)

→ I ________________________________.

08 나는 무지개를 본 적이 전혀 없다. (never, seen, a rainbow, have)

→ I ________________________________.

09 그는 괌으로 가 버렸다. (gone, Guam, to, has)

→ He ________________________________.

〈have[has] gone to〉는 '~에 가 버렸다'라는 뜻의 현재완료의 '결과' 용법을 나타내요.

내신 기출 다음 밑줄 친 부분의 쓰임이 다른 하나는?

① Have you ever seen a lion?

② I've never heard his name before.

③ Have you been to the water park?

④ Somin has just completed the project.

⑤ Juwon has read the book several times.

실전 TIP

현재완료의 '계속, 완료, 경험, 결과 용법'인지는 해석을 통해 파악해야 해요.

UNIT 06 현재완료 3

자주 쓰이는 부사구와 함께 현재완료의 4가지 의미와 쓰임을 다시 한번 정리해 두세요.

계속	I have studied Chinese since last month. • for는 '~ 동안'의 의미로 지속된 기간 / since는 '~ 이후로, ~부터'의 의미로 시작된 기준 시점
완료	I have just finished the homework. • 주로 just, already, yet, finally 등과 함께 사용
경험	She has tried Thai food before. • ever, never, before, often, once 등과 함께 사용
결과	She has lost her expensive bag. • 〈have gone to+장소〉: ~에 가 버렸다(결과)(3인칭 주어에만 사용) *cf.* 〈have been to+장소〉: ~에 가 본 적이 있다, ~에 갔다 왔다(경험)

|A| 괄호 안에서 알맞은 것을 고르시오.

01 Has anyone (never / ever) seen a unicorn?

02 He hasn't done the laundry (already / yet).

03 She (worked / has worked) for the company last year.

04 I (lived / have lived) in this city since I was 4 years old.

05 The hospital (was / has been) here since the 1990s.

06 Some of the students have (yet / already) seen the show.

07 (Did / have) you (visit / visited) Ulsan in 2020?

08 Linda and Mina have known each other (since / for) a decade.

09 We have never played hockey (before / ago).

10 I (read / have read) the book the other day.

11 She has played the piano (since / for) she was 8.

12 The gardener has (just / yet) watered the plants in the yard.

13 Have you reviewed the report (for / yet)?

|B| 괄호 안의 말을 바르게 배열하여 문장을 완성하시오.

01 Sumi (just, written, has) the letter. → Sumi ______________________ the letter.

02 (hasn't, it, since, rained) March. → ______________________ March.

03 (have, you, already, finished) the homework. → ______________________ the homework.

04 We have (yet, completed, not, the course). → We have ______________________.

05 (has, lost, he) the tickets for the concert. → ______________________ the tickets for the concert.

06 (have, ever, you, been) to Los Angeles? → ______________ to Los Angeles?

07 Ron (never, has, visited) the museum before. → Ron ______________ the museum before.

08 (ever, have, heard, we) the song before? → ______________ the song before?

|C| **다음 문장의 밑줄 친 부분을 어법상 바르게 고쳐 쓰시오.**

01 He has been a soccer player since 15 years. ______________

02 We didn't see Jenny since last month. ______________

03 The flight from Sydney just arrives in Seoul. ______________

04 Did you try Indian food before? ______________

05 Susan hasn't slept well since 2 weeks. ______________

06 They never have smoked before. ______________

07 Where have you gone last Christmas? ______________

08 This is the best movie I ever saw. ______________

|D| **다음 두 문장을 현재완료시제와 괄호 안의 동사를 활용하여 한 문장으로 다시 쓰시오.**

01 I started studying English since 2015. I still study it. (study)

→ ______________

02 Amy began working for the company 2 years ago. She still works for it. (work)

→ ______________

03 Peter went to China to study. He is still there. (go)

→ ______________

04 Christina lost her pen. She doesn't have it now. (lost)

→ ______________

05 He didn't finish his homework. He is still doing it. (finish)

→ ______________

06 We were friends when we were little kids. We are still friends. (be)

→ ______________

실전 TIP

과거진행, 현재완료의 쓰임에 대해 알고 있어야 해요.

내신 기출 다음 중 어법상 어색한 문장을 찾아 틀린 부분을 바르게 고쳐 쓰시오.

ⓐ My brother was having breakfast when I got up.

ⓑ She has lived in Singapore since she left Korea in 2019.

ⓒ They have been to Sokcho for the holidays, so they are not here now.

____

UNIT 07 현재완료 진행

과거에 시작한 일이 현재까지 진행 중임을 강조할 때는 현재완료 진행형을 사용해야 해요.

	현재완료	현재완료 진행
형태	have[has]+과거분사	have[has]+been+V-ing
예문	He has lived here since 2000.	He has been living here since 2000.
의미	2000년 이후로 여기 살고 있다	2000년 이후로 여기 사는 중이다

참고 현재완료 진행형을 만드는 방법은 동사의 진행형(be동사+V-ing)에서 be동사만 완료형(have[has]+been)으로 만들고, 그 뒤에 진행형(V-ing)을 붙여요.

|A| 괄호 안에서 알맞은 것을 고르시오.

01 Yuna (has been reading a book / was reading a book) then.

02 Emily (has been staying / stayed) home all day yesterday.

03 They (have been climbing / are climbing) the mountain now.

04 Chris (waits / has been waiting) for them since 7:00 in the morning.

05 Robin (has been sleeping / was sleeping) when I called him.

06 He (has been visiting / has visited) Rome several times.

07 My grandparents (live / have been living) with us since last year.

08 Eugene (was cooking / have been cooking) when he smelled the smoke.

09 I (have been walking / walk) to school every day.

10 My brother (talks / has been talking) to his friend on the phone since then.

|B| 괄호 안의 말을 활용하여 현재완료 진행시제 문장을 완성하시오.

현재완료 진행시제는 〈have [has]+been+V-ing〉 형태로 써요.

01 I ________________ for 3 hours. (shop)

02 She ________________ the novel all day. (read)

03 It ________________ since yesterday. (not, rain)

04 Lisa ________________ her own dress for a week. (make)

05 I ________________ French for 3 years. (learn)

06 The kids ________________ in the pool all afternoon. (swim)

07 We ________________ for the test since 6:00 in the morning. (study)

08 All the students ________________ forward to the vacation. (look)

09 ________________ the mechanic ________________ the car since Monday? (repair)

10 Jinsu and Jina ________________ Taekwondo lessons for months. (take)

|C| 다음 두 문장을 현재완료 진행형을 써서 한 문장으로 쓸 때, 빈칸에 알맞은 말을 쓰시오.

01 Jian started playing the violin at 11 o'clock. She is still playing it.
→ Jian ______________ the violin ______________ 11 o'clock.

02 Tony started washing the dishes 20 minutes ago. He is still washing them.
→ Tony ______________ the dishes ______________ 20 minutes.

03 It began snowing last Saturday. It is still snowing.
→ It ______________________________.

04 We started playing the online game an hour ago. We are still playing it.
→ We ______________________________.

05 He began driving his car 5 hours ago. He is still driving it.
→ He ______________________________.

06 She started working for the law firm when she was 27. She is still working there.
→ She ______________________________.

|D| 다음 문장의 밑줄 친 부분을 어법상 바르게 고쳐 쓰시오.

01 We <u>have been knowing</u> each other for more than a year. ______________
02 Jiwon <u>was studying</u> in her room since 2 o'clock. ______________
03 They have been cleaning the store <u>for</u> this morning. ______________
04 I <u>have been wanting</u> to be a singer since I was a little girl. ______________
05 I <u>have been remembering</u> Ethan's number. I'll call him later. ______________
06 Have they been <u>watched</u> television since then? ______________
07 Jessica and her friends have been planting trees <u>since</u> an hour. ______________
08 Look at the flower in the vase. It <u>has been smelling</u> sweet. ______________

소유나 상태를 나타내는 동사(remember, know, want 등)와 감각동사(smell, look 등)는 진행형으로 쓰지 않아요.

내신 기출 다음 중 어법상 <u>어색한</u> 문장을 <u>모두</u> 골라 <u>틀린</u> 부분을 바르게 고쳐 쓰시오.

ⓐ They have been running for 2 hours.
ⓑ They have been meeting each other twice.
ⓒ The police have been looking for the missing child for days.
ⓓ She has been singing the same song since yesterday.
ⓔ Some of my friends usually have been playing soccer after school.

____

실전 TIP
현재완료 진행시제인지 아닌지 판단해야 해요.

UNIT 08 과거완료

과거 시점을 기준으로 더 먼 과거(대과거)부터 과거 시점까지에 걸친 일은 과거완료로 써야 해요.

	현재완료	과거완료
형태	have[has]+과거분사	had+과거분사
예문	He has lived here for 10 years.	He had lived here for 10 years when I met him.
의미	10년 동안 여기 살고 있다	내가 그를 만났을 때, 10년 동안 여기 살고 있었다

과거완료로 계속, 완료, 경험, 결과를 표현하거나, 단순한 대과거 표현이기도 하다는 걸 알아 두세요.

	과거완료	과거 – 대과거
계속	He had lived here for 10 years when I met him.	만났을 때 – 만나기 10년 전
완료	When I got home, they had fallen asleep.	도착했을 때 – 도착했기 전
경험	Until last week, he had never seen an elephant.	지난주 – 지난주 이전
결과	He couldn't come because he had lost his bike.	올 수 없었을 때 – 올 수 없기 이전
대과거	He had met my son before I came.	왔을 때 – 왔기 이전

|A| 괄호 안에서 알맞은 것을 고르시오.

01 I (had seen / have seen) the movie before I visited the city.

02 They (had been / were) hungry because they (hadn't eaten / haven't eaten) anything.

03 The movie (had started / has started) when you (are entering / entered) the cinema.

04 She returned the book that she (has borrowed / had borrowed) from the library.

05 He was brought to the hospital as he (had been injured / has been injured) in the accident.

06 When I (had came / came) home, I found out that I (hadn't locked / haven't locked) the door.

|B| 괄호 안의 말을 활용하여 과거완료시제 문장을 완성하시오.

01 Tim ________________ English for a long time before he went to America. (study)

02 She sold her coat that she ________________ a long time ago. (buy)

03 I couldn't brush my teeth because I ________________ up all the toothpaste. (use)

04 He found the wallet that he ________________ before. (lose)

05 Susan got up late because she ________________ the alarm. (not, set)

06 It was the best show we ________________. (see)

07 My sister ________________ the chicken when I came home that night. (eat)

08 We ________________ from him until this morning. (not, hear)

UNIT 09 과거완료 진행

대과거에 시작한 일이 과거까지 진행 중이었음을 강조할 때는 과거완료 진행형을 사용해야 해요.

	과거완료	과거완료 진행
형태	had+과거분사	had+been+V-ing
예문	He **had lived** here for 10 years.	He **had been living** here for 10 years.
의미	10년 동안 여기 살고 있었다	10년 동안 여기 사는 중이었다

|A| 괄호 안의 말을 바르게 배열하여 과거완료 진행시제 문장을 완성하시오.

01 Brian ________________ homework for 2 hours before Mina visited. (doing, had, been)

02 She ________________ to win the competition for years, but she couldn't. (trying, been, had)

03 It ________________ when we got up. (had, snowing, been)

04 I ________________ when my mom came home. (been, had, playing, the game)

05 We ________________ when you called. (the movie, had, watching, been)

06 Jane ________________ the house before the guests arrived. (cleaning, been, had)

|B| 괄호 안의 동사를 과거완료 진행시제와 과거시제로 써서 문장을 완성하시오.

01 We ___________ dinner when Sumin ___________ home. (have, come)

02 Jina ___________ for 8 hours when her mom ___________ her up. (sleep, wake)

03 I ___________ in Seoul before I ___________ from university. (live, graduate)

04 It ___________ for days, so the road ___________ wet. (rain, be)

05 They ___________ a sand castle when a big wave suddenly ___________ in. (build, wash)

06 He ___________ his passport for an hour before he ___________ it. (look for, find)

07 Because the boy ___________ in the rain, he ___________ all wet. (play, get)

08 We ___________ all day, so we ___________ to go out. (work, not want)

09 I ___________ exhausted because I ___________ all night. (be, study)

내신 기출 다음 빈칸에 알맞은 것은?

He had been waiting for the taxi for 30 minutes before it __________.

① arrives ② arrived ③ has arrived
④ has been arriving ⑤ had been arriving

실전 TIP
과거의 어느 때라는 기준을 나타내는 부사절이에요.

중간고사·기말고사 실전문제

객관식 (01~25) / 주관식 (26~50)

학년과 반 이름 객관식 / 25문항 주관식 / 25문항

01~03 다음 빈칸에 알맞은 것을 고르시오.

01

Peter and his roommate ________ the old air conditioner for ten years.

① used ② has used
③ use ④ using
⑤ have used

02

Judy ________ her science homework yet.

① does ② did
③ isn't done ④ has done
⑤ hasn't done

03

Victor ________ his office an hour before I visited him.

① leaves ② left
③ has left ④ had left
⑤ had been leaving

04~05 다음 주어진 문장의 밑줄 친 부분과 쓰임이 같은 것을 고르시오.

04

Have you ever seen an amazing landscape like this?

① She has been there once.
② Have you already read all the books here?
③ The painter has drawn this for years.
④ I think the bird has gone forever.
⑤ We haven't slept since last night.

05

The teacher has already forgiven us.

① The traveler has lost his passport.
② He hasn't delivered the letter to them yet.
③ I have tasted durian before.
④ It has snowed since last Monday.
⑤ She has taught math for ten years.

06~07 다음 우리말을 영어로 바르게 나타낸 것을 고르시오.

06

그녀는 10년 전에 산 코트를 버렸다.

① She threw away the coat she had bought ten years ago.
② She throws away the coat she had bought ten years ago.
③ She was throwing away the coat she had bought ten years ago.
④ She threw away the coat she has bought ten years ago.
⑤ She had thrown away the coat she bought ten years ago.

07

미나는 어젯밤부터 그녀의 역사 수업 에세이를 쓰고 있는 중이다.

① Mina wrote her essay for history class since last night.
② Mina was writing her essay for history class since last night.
③ Mina had written her essay for history class since last night.
④ Mina has been writing her essay for history class since last night.
⑤ Mina had been writing her essay for history class since last night.

08 다음 빈칸에 알맞은 것을 모두 고르면?

The graduate students have studied biology ________.

① for many years
② since then
③ last night
④ next year
⑤ five month ago

09~10 다음 중 어법상 어색한 것을 고르시오.

09 ① He will tell you everything tomorrow.
② The train is arriving at Busan station soon.
③ Thousands of people visit Seoul every year.
④ My friend seems to be happy at that time.
⑤ She isn't going to work next week.

10 ① He had bought a new phone last week because his old one had been broken.
② The girls have been friends since they were seven years old.
③ She had not arrived yet when we got there.
④ My mom said that she had met my dad at the festival.
⑤ I have never swum in a lake before.

11 다음 중 어법상 어색한 것을 모두 고르면?

① Has your son lived in Tokyo by any chance?
② Mr. Kim has just called you.
③ They already get the answer for the quiz.
④ She has never been to Europe.
⑤ He found out that I lose some weight.

12~13 다음 중 어법상 옳은 것을 고르시오.

12 ① They were having dinner when I arrived.
② They are wanting to live in the city.
③ The bag is belonging to my sister.
④ This candle is smelling like a flower.
⑤ Are you believing what he said?

13 ① She has been making pasta when I visited her.
② We have known this before it became well-known to other people.
③ I had been loving her ever since we met.
④ They had been waiting for an hour before the movie started.
⑤ He had forgotten the answer the teacher gave to him.

14 다음 중 어법상 옳은 것을 모두 고르면?

① He had cleaned his room before the guests arrived.
② After we finished eating, the chef had come out of the kitchen.
③ She has studied Korean since 2010.
④ Ben has gone to Africa twice.
⑤ Have you done your homework when the class started?

15 다음 밑줄 친 부분을 어법상 바르게 고쳐 쓴 것 중 어색한 것은?

① The sun is rising in the East every day. (→ rises)
② I am appreciating your efforts on this new research project. (→ appreciate)
③ Are you wanting the thing that you're looking at now? (→ Do you want)
④ The chef is tasting the new dishes they made right now. (→ tastes like)
⑤ My neighbor next door is making noises all the time. (→ makes)

16 다음 중 밑줄 친 부분을 어법상 바르게 고쳐 쓴 것은?

① She has cut all the vegetables before she put them in the refrigerator. (→ cuts)
② James becomes famous before he was 20 years old. (→ had become)
③ I realized that I don't turn off the stove when I left home. (→ hasn't turned off)
④ He had hidden the jewels right after he had stolen them. (→ hidden)
⑤ Why were you started eating dinner before the guests arrived? (→ have you started)

17~19 다음 두 문장을 한 문장으로 쓸 때, 빈칸에 알맞은 것을 고르시오.

17

> The alarm began ringing ten minutes ago. It is still ringing.
> → The alarm ______________ ten minutes.

① was ringing for
② has been ringing since
③ has been ringing for
④ had rung since
⑤ had been ringing for

18

> He has experience traveling in Canada. He lives in Seoul now.
> → He ______________ Canada before.

① is in
② has been to
③ has gone to
④ goes to
⑤ had gone to

19

> I used to ride a horse when I was young. I stopped riding it after I moved to the city.
> → I ______________ a horse before I moved to the city.

① rode
② was ridden
③ have ridden
④ have been riding
⑤ had ridden

20~21 다음 빈칸에 알맞은 말이 바르게 짝지어진 것을 고르시오.

20

> People ________ very quiet and calm ________ she came into the room an hour ago.

① had been – for ② have been – for
③ were – since ④ had been – since
⑤ have been – since

21

> • Terry ________ hiking on Saturdays.
> • We ________ fishing this coming weekend.
> • It ________ very hot for a month.

① went – went – was
② went – go – has been
③ goes – will go – has been
④ goes – went – was
⑤ will go – go – had been

22 다음 중 어법상 어색한 문장의 개수는?

> ⓐ The movie had already started when we got into the theater.
> ⓑ Were they having breakfast when you visited them?
> ⓒ My family has gone to America twice.
> ⓓ Have you been working on your assignment until now?

① 없음 ② 1개 ③ 2개
④ 3개 ⑤ 4개

23 다음 중 어법상 옳은 문장의 개수는?

> ⓐ He has been here a couple of minutes ago.
> ⓑ I am clearly remembering the day we had a car accident.
> ⓒ The government has forbidden the use of the drug for 5 years.
> ⓓ She had been waiting for the mail before the postman came.

① 없음 ② 1개 ③ 2개
④ 3개 ⑤ 4개

24 다음 중 어법상 어색한 문장끼리 바르게 짝지은 것은?

> ⓐ The judge was believing that the man was guilty of the crime.
> ⓑ Diana has been learning Chinese since she started living in Beijing.
> ⓒ She has never trust the man.
> ⓓ The leaves fell sooner or later.
> ⓔ We had stood there until someone picked us up.

① ⓐ, ⓒ ② ⓑ, ⓒ
③ ⓐ, ⓑ, ⓒ ④ ⓐ, ⓒ, ⓓ
⑤ ⓒ, ⓓ, ⓔ

25 다음 대화의 밑줄 친 ①~⑤ 중, 어법상 어색한 것을 모두 고르면?

> A: Jenny, ① why are you hating Dan so much?
> B: Because ② it turned out that he had been lying to me about everything.
> A: Really? ③ How long have you known him?
> B: ④ I have met him when I was twenty years old. ⑤ We are best friends since then, but I don't want to be friends with him anymore.

〈다음부터는 서술형 주관식 문제입니다.〉

26~29 다음 문장에서 어법상 어색한 부분을 찾아 바르게 고쳐 쓰시오.

26 What time have you taken the taxi yesterday?

__________ → __________

27 She bought the watch that she had been wanting to buy.

__________ → __________

28 Some countries have raised their tax rates in 2010.

__________ → __________

29 Teenagers are preferring texts to calls these days.

__________ → __________

30~33 다음 문장의 밑줄 친 부분이 어법상 맞으면 ○표 하고, 틀리면 바르게 고쳐 쓰시오.

30 It has been five years since they have started the entertainment business.

→ __________

31 The carpenter has built a small house for several months.

→ __________

32 The woman was mean to us since we became poor.

→ __________

33 The company had been making enormous profits so far.

→ __________

34~35 다음 우리말과 같도록 빈칸에 괄호 안의 동사를 알맞은 형태로 쓰시오.

34

그 감독은 지난겨울 이후로 북극곰에 대한 다큐멘터리 영화를 찍고 있는 중이다. (film)

→ The director ______________ a documentary movie about polar bears since last winter.

35

그 소녀는 아직 그녀의 친구를 위해 무엇을 살지 선택하지 않았다. (choose)

→ The girl ______________ what to buy for her friend yet.

36~38 다음 우리말과 같도록 괄호 안의 말을 바르게 배열하시오.

36

안 좋은 날씨는 얼마나 계속되었나요?
(how, continued, the bad weather, has, long)

→ ______________________________

37

우리가 버스 정류장에 도착했을 때, 그 버스는 이미 떠났다.
(we, left, already, when, had, arrived, the bus stop, at)

→ The bus ______________________________
______________________________.

38

김 씨 가족은 이 마을에서 30년간 거주하고 있는 중이다.
(living, been, in this town, for, has, thirty years)

→ Kim's family ______________________________
______________________________.

39~40 다음 두 문장을 한 문장으로 쓸 때, 빈칸에 알맞은 말을 쓰시오.

39

• Mary started keeping her diary two years ago.
• She is still doing it now.

→ Mary ________ ________ ________ her diary ________ two years.

40

• Steve used to write poems.
• He quit writing poems after graduating from high school.

→ Steve ________ ________ poems until he ________ ________ high school.

41~43 다음 우리말과 같도록 괄호 안의 말을 활용하여 문장을 완성하시오.

41

그들은 아직 경주를 시작하지 않았다. (begin, the race, yet)

→ ______________________________

42 너는 여전히 산타클로스를 믿고 있니? (believe in, still, Santa Claus)

→ ______________________

43 당신은 전쟁을 경험해 본 적이 있나요? (experience, ever, a war)

→ ______________________

44~46 다음 글의 밑줄 친 ⓐ~ⓕ 중 어법상 어색한 부분을 세 군데 찾아 바르게 고쳐 쓰시오.

ⓐ Jessica usually goes grocery shopping on Wednesdays. Last Wednesday, ⓑ she had gone to the supermarket she always goes to. ⓒ She was shopping as usual. After a while, she felt strange because ⓓ someone is following her. ⓔ She wasn't realizing it while she was shopping. When she got to the counter to pay, ⓕ she found out that her purse had been stolen.

44 ________ → ________

45 ________ → ________

46 ________ → ________

47~48 다음 글의 밑줄 친 ⓐ~ⓔ 중 어법상 어색한 것을 찾아 바르게 고쳐 쓰시오. (정답 2개)

I first ⓐ met Judy at the conference. She ⓑ has been the main speaker that day. My colleague ⓒ has been knowing her for a long time. Since he ⓓ introduced her to me, Judy and I ⓔ have been close friends.

47 ________ → ________

48 ________ → ________

49~50 다음 우리말을 주어진 |조건|에 맞게 바르게 영작하시오.

49 Jake는 이 마을을 떠난 후로 여기에 돌아온 적이 없다.

|조건|
- 완료시제를 사용할 것
- 단어 never, be back, here, leave, since를 사용할 것
- 문장 전체를 11단어로 쓸 것

→ Jake ______________________ this town.

50 우리가 그녀를 불렀을 때 Kate는 무언가를 숨기고 있는 중이었다.

|조건|
- 완료 진행시제를 사용할 것
- 단어 hide, something, call을 사용할 것
- 문장 전체를 9단어로 쓸 것

→ Kate ______________________ when ______________________.

CHAPTER

03 조동사

UNIT 01 can, could

조동사 can(~할 수 있다)은 다양한 상황에서 쓰일 수 있으므로 문맥을 파악하는 것이 중요해요.

능력	I can swim.	요청	Can[Could] you wait?
가능	I can help you.	추측	He can be busy.
허가	You can stay here.	금지	You cannot[can't] stay here.

주의 조동사 can의 부정형은 cannot 또는 can't로 써야 해요. *cann't (×)

참고 could는 can의 과거시제로도 쓰고, 정중한 요청을 나타낼 때도 써요.

can이 능력/가능을 의미할 때만 be able to와 바꾸어 쓸 수 있다는 것을 기억하세요.

능력/가능	I can swim. = I am able to swim.
허가	You can stay. ≠ You are able to stay.(×)

참고 able은 '~할 수 있는', '능력이 있는'이라는 의미로 '~해도 좋다'와 같은 허가의 의미로는 쓰지 않아요.
be able to는 be동사로 시제, 부정, 의문을 표현해요.

|A| 괄호 안에서 밑줄 친 조동사의 의미를 고르시오.

01 He can swim. (능력 / 허가)
02 You can borrow my book. (능력 / 허가)
03 The news can't be false. (능력 / 추측)
04 I can speak English. (능력 / 허가)
05 Dennis could win the game. (능력 / 허가)
06 You can take it if you need. (능력 / 허가)
07 We cannot eat here. (능력 / 금지)
08 Can you play chess? (능력 / 허가)
09 You can store data here. (히기 / 추측)
10 Could we enter the room? (추측 / 요청)
11 They could be right. (추측 / 허가)
12 Visitors cannot park here. (추측 / 금지)
13 Can it be true? (추측 / 허가)
14 Could I go home now? (능력 / 요청)

|B| 다음 문장을 be able to를 이용한 문장으로 바꾸어 쓰시오.

01 I can ride a bike. → ____________________
02 Can you sing it in French? → ____________________
03 They can speak Russian. → ____________________
04 Mary can run fast. → ____________________
05 He can't play the guitar. → ____________________
06 Chickens can't fly very high. → ____________________
07 She couldn't drive a car. → ____________________
08 Can she play the game? → ____________________

UNIT 02 may, might

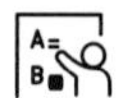

조동사 may의 다양한 의미를 기억해 두세요.

추측	~일지도 모른다	The story may[might] be true. The story may[might] not be true.
허가	~해도 된다	You may come in.
요청	~해도 될까요?	May I borrow your umbrella?
금지	~하면 안 된다	You may not come in.

주의 may의 부정형은 may not으로 쓰고, 축약하지 않아요.

참고 might는 may보다 더 불확실한 추측을 나타내요.

|A| 괄호 안에서 밑줄 친 조동사의 의미를 고르시오.

01 May I come in? (요청 / 추측)

02 You may be right. (허가 / 추측)

03 You may not smoke here. (금지 / 추측)

04 We may go home. (허가 / 추측)

05 Jisu may be sick. (허가 / 추측)

06 May I take your order? (요청 / 추측)

07 She might come to the party. (허가 / 추측)

08 May I use your computer? (요청 / 추측)

09 We may borrow the book now. (허가 / 추측)

10 May I sit here? (요청 / 추측)

11 They may be late. (허가 / 추측)

12 It might rain tonight. (허가 / 추측)

13 You may pay with cash. (허가 / 추측)

14 He might be home. (허가 / 추측)

15 What they said might be true. (허가 / 추측)

16 Ms. Park might help us. (허가 / 추측)

|B| 대화의 빈칸에 may나 may not 중 알맞은 것을 쓰시오.

01 A: I haven't seen Subin at school. Where's she?

B: I'm not sure. She ________________ be home.

02 A: May I take one of these?

B: Of course, you ________________. They're free.

03 A: Excuse me. May I park here?

B: No, you ________________. This spot is for the disabled.

04 A: What are you doing this Sunday?

B: I don't know. I ________________ go hiking.

05 A: May I play the online game now?

B: No, you ________________. You have homework to do.

UNIT 03 must

'~해야만 한다'라는 의무나, '~임에 틀림없다'라는 강한 추측을 표현할 때 조동사 must를 쓰세요.

의무	~해야만 한다	We must follow the rules.
강한 추측	~임에 틀림없다	She must be rich.
강한 금지	~하면 안 된다	You must not tell a lie.

주의 강한 추측을 나타내는 must의 부정형은 can't[cannot](~일 리가 없다)로 써요. The story can't be true.

|A| 괄호 안에서 밑줄 친 조동사의 의미를 고르시오.

01 I must be here by 9. (의무 / 추측)

02 Must I pay in advance? (의무 / 추측)

03 You must be very tired. (의무 / 추측)

04 We must obey the rules. (의무 / 추측)

05 All of us must attend. (의무 / 추측)

06 He must be interested in art. (의무 / 추측)

07 People must wear seat belts. (의무 / 추측)

08 You must not eat in the library. (금지 / 추측)

09 The news cannot be false. (금지 / 추측)

10 We must not be late tomorrow. (금지 / 추측)

11 They cannot be twins. (금지 / 추측)

12 His car must be expensive. (의무 / 추측)

13 You must be on the train by 6. (의무 / 추측)

14 He must be over 75 years old. (의무 / 추측)

|B| 괄호 안에서 알맞은 것을 고르시오.

강한 추측을 뜻하는 must의 부정형은 cannot, 의무를 뜻하는 must의 부정형은 must not으로 써요.

01 We (must / must not) keep the place clean.

02 You (must / must not) be noisy in the library.

03 You (must / must not) cross the street at the red light.

04 Matt has an expensive car. He (must / cannot) be rich.

05 You (must / must not) smoke anywhere in the building.

06 Amber is absent from school. She (must / cannot) be sick.

07 She looks so nervous. There (must / cannot) be something wrong.

08 All the students (must / must not) wear school uniforms.

09 He cleans his room every day. He (must / cannot) be lazy.

내신 기출 다음 중 밑줄 친 부분의 의미가 다른 하나는?

① All customers must report to reception on arrival.
② You must wear a mask when you go into the lab.
③ There must be something wrong with the elevator.

실전 TIP

must가 의무의 의미인지 추측의 의미인지 파악하세요.

UNIT 04 have to

have to는 의미상 must와 바꾸어 쓸 수 있지만, 부정형은 서로 다른 의미인 것에 주의해야 해요.

	must		have to	
긍정문	의무	We must pay.	~해야 한다(의무)	We have to pay.
부정문	금지	We must not[mustn't] pay.	~할 필요 없다(불필요)	We don't have to pay.
의문문	의무	Must we pay?	~해야 합니까?(의무)	Do we have to pay?

주의 주어가 3인칭 단수이면 has to로 써야 하며, 과거(~했어야 했다)는 had to로, 미래(~해야 할 것이다)는 will have to로 써요.

주의 have[has] to의 의문문은 〈Do[Does]+주어+have to+동사원형 ~?〉의 어순으로 써요.

|A| 괄호 안에서 알맞은 것을 고르시오.

01 We (did must / had to) go to bed early.
02 My parents (have to / has to) get up early.
03 You (don't / mustn't) have to do the dishes.
04 We (must / have) brush our teeth carefully.
05 You (mustn't / doesn't have to) run indoors.
06 She (have to / had to) take some medicine.
07 He (must / have / has) to finish the job now.
08 You don't (must / have to / has to) agree.
09 They (must / have to / has to) not argue.
10 Do I (must / have to / had to) pay for that?
11 (Must / Did) you have to prepare dinner?
12 He will (must / have to / has to) accept it.
13 (Must / Do / Does) I have to submit it now?
14 We (mustn't / doesn't have to) touch it.

|B| 다음 문장에서 어법상 어색한 부분을 찾아 바르게 고쳐 쓰시오.

01 I will must work out regularly. ______________
02 You do have not to keep it a secret. ______________
03 Mark have to see a doctor. ______________
04 I must helped my mom yesterday. ______________
05 He doesn't have to be late for school again. ______________
06 Do I have speak in English? ______________
07 Do she have to run to be on time? ______________
08 Minju doesn't has to go to school today. ______________
09 You must not to sing in the library. ______________

UNIT 05 should, ought to

'~하는 게 좋겠다, ~해야 한다'라는 의미의 충고나 제안을 할 때 should나 ought to를 쓰세요.

	should	ought to
의미	~하는 편이 좋겠다, ~해야 한다(충고)	~해야 한다 (should보다 강하고 must보다 약함)
긍정문	You should take the pill.	You ought to take the pill.
부정문/축약형	You should not[shouldn't] take the pill.	You ought not to take the pill.
의문문	Should I take the pill?	

주의 의문문에서는 ought to 대신 보통 should를 써요.

|A| 주어를 확인하고, 괄호 안의 말을 바르게 배열하여 문장을 완성하시오.

01 (take care of, my brother, should) → I ______________________.

02 (ought, my advice, listen, to, to) → They ______________________.

03 (tell, ought, the truth, to) → He ______________________.

04 (should, fasten, your seat belt) → You ______________________.

05 (to, ought, not, stay up, late) → Young children ______________________.

06 (not, should, stupidly, behave) → We ______________________.

07 (not, ought, to, hope, give up) → You ______________________.

08 (to, ought, careful, be) → We ______________________.

|B| 괄호 안의 말을 이용하여 문장을 완성하시오.

충고나 제안을 뜻하는 should와 ought to의 부정형은 각각 should not과 ought not to로 써요.

01 You ______________ like that. (not, talk, ought)

02 We all ______________ enough water. (drink, should)

03 ________ I ________ them to bring something? (ask, should)

04 I ______________ selfish. (not, be, ought)

05 You ______________ the new movie. (see, should)

06 ________ I ________ more vegetables? (eat, should)

07 You ______________ smoking right away. (quit, ought)

08 You ______________ about it too much. (not, worry, should)

09 We ______________ too much time on social media. (not, spend, ought)

UNIT 06 had better, would rather

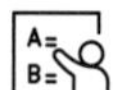

다음 조동사 표현들을 익히세요.

	had better	would rather
의미	~하는 게 낫다(should보다 강한 충고)	(차라리) ~하겠다
긍정문/축약형	You had better go now. (= You'd better)	I would rather stay (than leave). (= I'd rather)
부정문	You'd better not go now.	I would rather not stay.
의문문	* Should I go now?	Would you rather stay?

주의 had better는 의문문으로 잘 쓰지 않아요. 거의 should를 사용하여 의문문을 만들어요.

주의 would rather는 '~하기보다'라는 비교 대상을 자주 쓰며, than 뒤에 같은 동사원형을 쓴다는 것에 주의하세요.

|A| 괄호 안에서 알맞은 것을 고르시오.

01 You (had better / had better not / would rather not) be careful. The road is slippery.

02 I feel tired, so I (had better not / would rather / would rather not) stay home.

03 You (had better / had better not / would rather) go out. It's freezing cold.

04 I (had better / had rather not / would rather) ask him than wonder.

05 You (had better / had better not / would rather) be late again.

06 You (had better / had better not / would rather not) look after your sister.

07 I (had better / had better not / would rather) die than sing at the party.

08 You (had better / had better not / would rather not) hurry. The train is about to leave.

|B| 괄호 안의 말과 had better 또는 would rather를 이용하여 문장을 완성하시오.

01 You ______________________ a rest. I think you got a cold. (take, had)

02 I ______________________ my old pictures. (show, die, would)

03 ___________ you ___________ first or wait for them to come? (eat, would)

04 It's very cold today. You ______________________ gloves and boots. (wear, had)

05 You ______________________ snacks if you want to lose weight. (not, eat, had)

06 I ______________________ a book from the library. (not, get, would)

07 It's a boring movie. I ______________________ it. (watch, would, sleep)

08 I ______________________ with you. There is no room in the car. (go, would, not)

09 I have enough time. I ______________________ the bus. (walk, take, would)

UNIT 07 used to, would

'(과거에) ~하곤 했다'와 같이 과거의 반복하던 일은 used to와 would로 쓰세요.

	used to(~하곤 했다)	would(~하곤 했다)
예문	I used to go there on Sunday. (일요일에 거기에 가곤 했다)	I would go there when it rained. (비가 오면 거기에 가곤 했다)
주의	〈be used to〉는 완전 다른 의미가 돼요. be used to+명사/동명사: ~에 익숙하다 be used to+동사원형: ~하는 데 사용되다	과거의 상태를 나타낼 때는 would를 못 써요. There would be a tree. (×) → used to be He would live here. (×) → used to live

주의 과거의 습관적 행동을 나타내는 would는 상태 동사인 be, feel, taste, hear, have, live, love, like, want, understand, know, agree, believe 등과 같이 쓸 수 없고 used to를 써야 해요.

|A| 괄호 안에서 알맞은 것을 고르시오.

01 I (would / used to) live in a small house.
02 My mom (would / is used to) read novels.
03 The money (would / was used to) buy this.
04 We (would / used to) love playing outside.
05 You (used to / would) be curious about it.
06 It (would / is used to) make clothes.
07 She (would / was used to) staying up late.
08 He (would / is used to) walk every morning.
09 There (would / used to) be a cafe here.
10 We (would / are used to) meet on Sunday.

|B| 괄호 안의 말과 used to 또는 would를 이용하여 문장을 완성하시오.

01 Soyeon ______________________ going climbing. (like)
02 Jenny ______________________ long and curly hair. (have)
03 My grandfather ______________________ fairy tales. (tell)
04 Anna ______________________ glasses when she was little. (wear)
05 We ______________________ to the zoo every spring. (go)
06 She ______________________ in the countryside when she was young. (live)
07 My sister and I ______________________ all the time. (argue)
08 They ______________________ to school when they were kids. (walk)
09 My dad ______________________ the newspaper in the morning. (read)

used to는 과거의 습관이나 상태, would는 과거의 습관을 나타낼 때 써요.

내신기출 다음 빈칸에 would가 들어갈 수 있는 것은?

① Mark ________ live in India with his family.
② My dad and I ________ go fishing on weekends.
③ My uncle ________ know various kinds of flowers.

실전 TIP

would는 과거의 상태를 나타내는 문장에는 쓸 수 없다는 것을 기억하세요.

UNIT 08 조동사 + have + 과거분사

과거의 추측이나 후회를 나타낼 때는 동사를 〈조동사 + have + 과거분사〉의 형태로 쓰세요.

must + have + 과거분사	~했음에 틀림없다(강한 추측)	He must have forgotten. (잊었던 게 틀림없다)
cannot + have + 과거분사	~이었을 리가 없다(강한 부정 추측)	He cannot have known. (알았을 리가 없다)
may[might] + have + 과거분사	~했을지도 모른다(약한 추측)	He might have helped. (도왔을지도 모른다)
should + have + 과거분사	~했어야 했다(후회, 유감)	He should have called. (전화했어야 했다)
could + have + 과거분사	~할 수도 있었을 텐데(후회, 아쉬움)	He could have asked. (물어볼 수도 있었는데)

|A| 괄호 안에서 알맞은 것을 고르시오.

01 I didn't see Rick anywhere yesterday. He (may stay / may have stayed) home.

02 The road was wet. It (must rain / must have rained) last night.

03 They (cannot arrive / cannot have arrived) in Busan. They left an hour ago.

04 You drank a lot of water. You (must / should) have been thirsty.

05 Amy didn't call me back. She (forgets / may have forgotten) my number.

06 We (should / must) have come earlier. The show had already begun.

07 Laura finished the homework quickly. It (cannot / may) have been difficult.

08 Sam (must / cannot) have solved the problem. He's good at science.

09 Ronnie had a car accident. He (should be / should have been) careful.

|B| 우리말과 같도록 괄호 안의 말을 활용하여 문장을 완성하시오.

01 그는 세차를 했어야 했다. (wash) → He ____________________ his car.

02 너는 화낸 것을 사과할 수도 있었을 텐데. (apologize) → You ____________________ for being angry.

03 그는 그 영화를 봤을지도 모른다. (see) → He ____________________ the movie.

04 그들은 그 기사를 읽었음에 틀림없다. (read) → They ____________________ the article.

05 유주가 그 약속을 잊었을 리 없다. (forget) → Yuju ____________________ the appointment.

06 그녀는 그녀의 아이들과 더 많은 시간을 보냈어야 했다. (spend)

→ She ____________________ more time with her children.

〈should + have + 과거분사〉는 '~했어야 했는데 (하지 못했다)'라는 의미의 과거 사실에 대한 후회나 유감을 나타내요.

|C| 다음 문장의 밑줄 친 부분을 과거의 추측이나 후회를 나타내는 의미가 되도록 바르게 고쳐 쓰시오.

01 Andy <u>must broken</u> the window. ____________________

02 We <u>should have do</u> the homework first. ____________________

03 You <u>must had called</u> me when I was sleeping. ____________________

04 The rumor <u>can have not been</u> true. ____________________

05 Someone <u>could has warned</u> me about the disease. ____________________

06 She <u>may have be</u> sick for days. ____________________

07 They <u>have should been</u> more polite to elderly people. ____________________

08 There <u>might been has</u> a misunderstanding. ____________________

|D| 우리말에 맞게 영작했을 때, 어법상 <u>어색한</u> 부분을 찾아 바르게 고쳐 쓰시오.

01 너는 더 열심히 공부할 수도 있었을 텐데.

→ You should have studied harder. ____________________

02 나는 좀 더 부지런했어야 했다.

→ I could have be more diligent. ____________________

03 그는 학교에 결석했을지도 모른다.

→ He cannot be absent from school. ____________________

04 수미는 내가 그녀에게 준 그 가방을 잃어버린 게 틀림없다.

→ Sumi could lost the bag I gave her. ____________________

05 그들은 감기에 걸린 게 분명하다.

→ They must had catch a cold. ____________________

06 그 시험 결과가 틀렸었을 리 없다.

→ The test results might not be false. ____________________

07 언덕 위에는 탑이 있었을 리가 없다.

→ There can't be a tower on the hill. ____________________

08 재민이와 재윤이는 그 답을 알았음이 분명하다.

→ Jaemin and Jaeyun must know the answer. ____________________

내신기출 다음 빈칸에 알맞은 것은?

They ______________ her that they were going to be late. Then, she wouldn't be this mad.

① may have told ② must have told ③ could have told
④ couldn't have told ⑤ cannot have told

실전 TIP

'~할 수도 있었을 텐데, (하지 않았다)'는 의미를 파악할 수 있어야 해요.

중간고사·기말고사 실전문제

객관식 (01~25) / 주관식 (26~50)

정답과 해설 • 14쪽

학년과 반　　이름　　객관식　　/ 25문항　　주관식　　/ 25문항

01~02 다음 빈칸에 알맞은 것을 고르시오.

01

John is an honest man, so he ________ be a robber.

① cannot　② can　③ might
④ must　⑤ use to

02

Sometimes I ________ visit my grandparents on Sundays when I was young.

① may　② must　③ would
④ should　⑤ have to

03~05 다음 빈칸에 공통으로 알맞은 것을 고르시오.

03

• Everyone ________ follow the safety rules to prevent accidents.
• The ground is wet, so it ________ have rained.

① should　② ought to　③ has to
④ must　⑤ would

04

• ________ you leave a message for me?
• We ________ have given him money, but we didn't.

① Should[should]　② Might[might]
③ May[may]　④ Must[must]
⑤ Could[could]

05

• ________ I listen to what he tells me?
• You ________ have left some food for me. There's nothing to eat.

① Should[should]　② Might[might]
③ May[may]　④ Must[must]
⑤ Could[could]

06~08 다음 우리말을 영어로 바르게 나타낸 것을 고르시오.

06

너는 공공장소에서 소음을 만들면 안 된다.

① You ought not to make noise in public.
② You don't ought to make noise in public.
③ You ought not to making noise in public.
④ You don't ought to making noise in public.
⑤ You ought to not making noise in public.

07

나는 차라리 거기까지 걸어가는 게 좋겠다.

① I would rather walking there.
② I would rather walk there.
③ I had rather walk there.
④ I had better walking there.
⑤ I would better walk there.

08

그녀는 아마 그것을 잘 이해하지 못했을지도 모른다.

① She would not understand it well.
② She cannot have understood it well.
③ She may not have understood it well.
④ She may not understand it well.
⑤ She must not have understood it well.

09~10 다음 중 어법상 <u>어색한</u> 것을 고르시오.

09 ① Can you deliver the package by tomorrow?
② He speaks Korean. He can't be Chinese.
③ The counselor might be able to help them.
④ Do you turn down the volume, please?
⑤ We would rather take a bus than walk.

10 ① There used to be a big tree.
② He would be a cook, but he quit.
③ Mark ought to go to bed early tonight.
④ She would cry a lot when she was young.
⑤ It's too hard. I had better find another job.

11 다음 중 어법상 <u>어색한</u> 것을 <u>모두</u> 고르면?

① Sean didn't show up last night. He must have been sick.
② I'm certain she was there. She might have stayed there.
③ I made another mistake. I should have been more careful.
④ She has a beautiful voice. She can have sung this terrible song.
⑤ He could have had pizza for lunch, but he had a hamburger.

12~13 다음 중 어법상 옳은 것을 고르시오.

12 ① He won't be able to seeing his dog again.
② Will you able to attend the meeting?
③ The food tasted awful. He can be a good cook.
④ He has to take the class last night.
⑤ Lina has to apologize the teacher.

13 ① He bought her flowers. He has to like her.
② Joy might can speak another language.
③ Would you rather use this instead?
④ Don't worry. You must not finish it.
⑤ I would like listen to his songs.

14 다음 중 어법상 옳은 것을 <u>모두</u> 고르면?

① Judy looks happy. She must have passed the test.
② They could have won the game, but they gave up.
③ The man wasn't here yesterday. He might have stolen the money here.
④ She should have told me. I remember what she said clearly.
⑤ He lied again. I should have believed him.

15 다음 밑줄 친 <u>would</u>의 쓰임이 <u>다른</u> 하나는?

① We <u>would</u> fight a lot when we were young.
② My dog <u>would</u> bark loudly, so we trained him not to.
③ He said he <u>would</u> win the gold medal next.
④ I <u>would</u> play the piano a long time ago.
⑤ When I was little, my dad <u>would</u> take me to the playground.

16 다음 밑줄 친 <u>must</u>의 쓰임이 <u>다른</u> 하나는?

① He failed the test. He <u>must</u> be frustrated.
② Politicians <u>must</u> be honest with the public.
③ We <u>must</u> be quiet in the library.
④ Every child <u>must</u> be loved.
⑤ I don't like iced coffee; coffee <u>must</u> be hot.

17~18 다음 문장을 우리말로 바르게 나타낸 것을 고르시오.

17

The girl must have known them.

① 그 소녀는 그들을 알아야 한다.
② 그 소녀는 그들을 알았어야 한다.
③ 그 소녀는 그들을 아는 것이 틀림없다.
④ 그 소녀는 그들을 알았던 것이 틀림없다.
⑤ 그 소녀는 그들을 알았을 수도 있다.

18

I didn't have to meet the principal.

① 나는 교장 선생님을 만날 필요가 없다.
② 나는 교장 선생님을 만나면 안 된다.
③ 나는 교장 선생님을 만날 필요가 없었다.
④ 나는 교장 선생님을 만나지 않았어야 했다.
⑤ 나는 교장 선생님을 만나지 않으면 안 된다.

19~21 다음 빈칸에 알맞은 말이 바르게 짝지어진 것을 고르시오.

19

• I would ________ not tell you.
• He ________ have failed the test. He studied very hard.

① like – might
② like – can't
③ rather – can't
④ rather – might
⑤ better – can't

20

• James ________ have missed the bus. That was the last bus today.
• The bird will ________ to fly someday.

① must – be
② must not – be able
③ shouldn't – can
④ shouldn't – be able
⑤ must not – be

21

• You ________ the chocolate before it melted.
• She ________ comic books when she was little.
• ________ you be able to speak Korean by the time you graduate from college?

① should eat – used to reading – Are
② should eat – is used to reading – Will
③ should have eaten – used to read – Will
④ should have eaten – is used to read – Will
⑤ should ate – used to read – Are

22 다음 중 어법상 어색한 문장의 개수는?

ⓐ She was able to overcoming her difficulties.
ⓑ The doctor has to tell his patient the truth.
ⓒ He should come before she left.
ⓓ You had better wore sunglasses.

① 없음
② 1개
③ 2개
④ 3개
⑤ 4개

23 다음 중 어법상 옳은 문장의 개수는?

ⓐ She must be sad when she took this picture.
ⓑ We can get there on time last night.
ⓒ You may not like this news.
ⓓ I should have watched it by next week.

① 없음
② 1개
③ 2개
④ 3개
⑤ 4개

24 다음 중 어법상 옳은 것끼리 바르게 짝지은 것은?

ⓐ She should have read this first.
ⓑ She doesn't ought to keep the door open.
ⓒ You may be able to get this for free.
ⓓ It might have rained tomorrow.
ⓔ He's going to give a speech soon. He must have been nervous.

① ⓐ, ⓒ ② ⓑ, ⓒ
③ ⓐ, ⓑ, ⓒ ④ ⓐ, ⓒ, ⓓ
⑤ ⓒ, ⓓ, ⓔ

25 다음 대화의 밑줄 친 ⓐ~ⓕ 중, 어법상 어색한 것의 개수는?

A: May I take your order?
B: Yes, please. ⓐ I would like some beef. ⓑ What would you like to eat, Jin?
C: ⓒ I would rather have vegetables to meat.
B: I think ⓓ you should have had meat today. ⓔ You may not have eaten enough protein lately.
C: Okay. Then, ⓕ can I have chicken?

① 없음 ② 1개 ③ 2개
④ 3개 ⑤ 4개

〈다음부터는 서술형 주관식 문제입니다.〉

26~28 다음 문장에서 어법상 어색한 부분을 찾아 바르게 고쳐 쓰시오.

26 This museum is used to be a train station in the 1900s.

______ → ______

27 You ought not take photos here.

______ → ______

28 She must have been tired now because she walked a lot.

______ → ______

29~31 다음 두 문장의 의미가 같도록 알맞은 조동사를 이용하여 문장을 완성하시오.

29 I'm very sure that the store was closed yesterday.

→ The store ______ yesterday.

30 We regret that we didn't take an umbrella.

→ We ______ an umbrella.

31 It's impossible that Paul finished his homework by himself.

→ Paul ______ his homework by himself.

32~33 다음 우리말과 같도록 괄호 안의 동사를 활용하여 빈칸을 완성하시오.

32

그 소설은 여성에 의해 쓰여졌음이 틀림없다. (write)

→ The novel ______ ______ ______ ______ by a woman.

33

나는 무대에서 노래하느니 차라리 춤을 추겠다.
(sing, dance)

→ I would ________ ________ ________ ________ on stage.

34~36 다음 우리말과 같도록 괄호 안의 말을 바르게 배열하시오.

34

그 조수는 그녀의 실수에 대해 변명하지 말았어야 했다.
(not, the assistant, excuses, her, for, have, should, made, mistake)

→ ____________________

35

그가 우리 없이 떠났음에 틀림없다.
(without, have, he, us, left, must)

→ ____________________

36

나는 여동생을 돌보기보다는 차라리 설거지를 하겠다.
(take care of, would, my little sister, wash the dishes, than, rather, I)

→ ____________________

37~38 다음 주어진 문장과 의미가 같도록 빈칸을 완성하시오.

37

The astronaut couldn't breathe outside the spaceship.

→ The astronaut wasn't ________ ________ ________ outside the spaceship.

38

Jack earned a lot of money in the past, but now he is poor.

→ Jack used ________ ________ a lot of money.

39~42 다음 우리말과 같도록 괄호 안의 말을 활용하여 문장을 완성하시오.

39

우리는 미래에 북극곰을 볼 수 없을지도 모른다.
(may, see, polar bears)

→ ____________________ in the future.

40

오래전에 공룡들이 지구상에 살았었다.
(dinosaurs, use, live, on Earth)

→ ____________________ a long time ago.

41 Julie는 수영 선수가 될 수도 있었지만, 지금은 육상 선수이다. (can, become, a swimmer)

→ ________________________________, but she's become a runner.

42 너는 어디서도 마스크를 안 벗는 것이 좋겠다. (better, take off, your mask)

→ ________________________________ anywhere.

43~45 다음 대화의 밑줄 친 ⓐ~ⓕ 중 어법상 어색한 부분을 세 군데 찾아 바르게 고쳐 쓰시오.

A: Amy, have you seen my passport? I think ⓐ I may lose it again.
B: Again? That's why I keep telling you that ⓑ you should always keep it in a safe place.
A: Yeah, ⓒ I should have done that.
B: Have you checked your backpack? ⓓ Perhaps, you might left it inside the bag.
A: No, it isn't there.
B: Well then, ⓔ you would better get a new one for your trip next week.
A: Well, ⓕ I'd rather cancel the trip and stay home.

43 ______________ → ______________

44 ______________ → ______________

45 ______________ → ______________

46~48 다음 글의 밑줄 친 ⓐ~ⓕ 중 어법상 어색한 부분을 세 군데 찾아 바르게 고쳐 쓰시오.

I met an old friend from middle school. ⓐ He would be very short, but he is much taller than I am. ⓑ I shouldn't have teased him for being short. ⓒ He must been upset. ⓓ I think I had better to say sorry to him, but ⓔ he may not forgive me. What should I do? ⓕ Would you give me some advice?

46 ______________ → ______________

47 ______________ → ______________

48 ______________ → ______________

49~50 다음 우리말을 주어진 |조건|에 맞게 바르게 영작하시오.

49 지나는 그녀의 휴대폰을 그에게 빌려주지 말았어야 했다.

|조건|
- 조동사 should를 사용할 것
- 단어 cellphone, lend를 사용할 것
- 문장 전체를 7단어로 쓸 것

→ Jina ________________________________.

50 Brian이 그 회의에 결석했을 리가 없다.

|조건|
- 조동사 can을 사용할 것
- 단어 be absent from, the meeting을 사용할 것
- 문장 전체를 8단어로 쓸 것

→ Brian ________________________________.

CHAPTER

04 수동태

UNIT 01 수동태의 의미와 형태

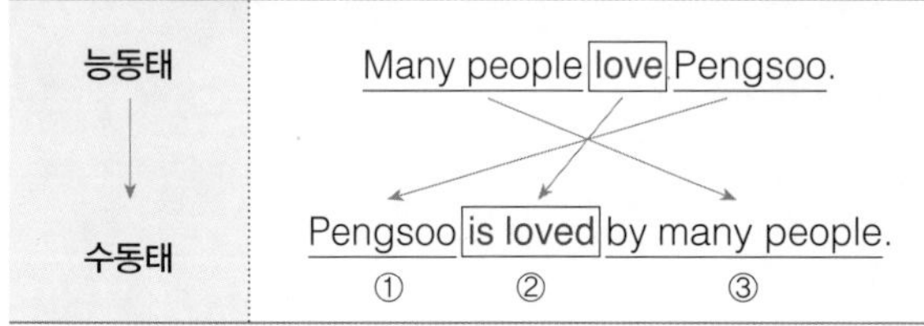

능동태
Many people love Pengsoo.
수동태
Pengsoo is loved by many people.
① ② ③

많은 사람들이 펭수를 사랑한다.
〈Many people에 초점〉

펭수는 많은 사람들에 의해 사랑을 받는다.
〈Pengsoo에 초점〉

아래 순서에 따라 수동태 문장을 만드세요.

Step ①	목적어를 주어 자리로 옮겨요.	인칭대명사라면 주격으로 써야 해요.
Step ②	동사를 〈be동사+과거분사〉로 써요.	be동사는 주어의 인칭, 수에 맞추고 시제도 표현해요.
Step ③	문장 끝에 〈by+행위자〉를 써요.	행위자가 인칭대명사라면 by 뒤에 목적격으로 써야 해요. 행위자가 일반인이거나 중요하지 않으면, 생략해요.

수동태로 쓸 수 없는 동사들을 기억하세요.

- 목적어(행위의 대상)가 없는 자동사: happen, occur, arrive, die, appear, smell, remain 등
- 소유나 상태를 나타내는 타동사: have, fit, lack, resemble, cost 등

|A| 다음 문장을 수동태 문장으로 바꾸어 쓸 때, 빈칸에 알맞은 말을 쓰시오.

01 I broke the window. → The window ________ by me.

02 He took a bottle of juice. → A bottle of juice ________ by him.

03 We flew kites in the yard. → Kites ________ in the yard by us.

04 My parents love me. → I ________ by my parents.

05 He found the key to the room. → The key to the room ________ by him.

06 She laid her glasses on the desk. → Her glasses ________ on the desk by her.

|B| 다음 문장의 밑줄 친 부분을 생략하여 수동태 문장으로 바꾸어 쓰시오.

01 <u>People</u> speak Spanish in Argentina. → ________

02 <u>Everyone</u> in Korea loves the pianist. → ________

03 <u>A thief</u> stole my bike yesterday. → ________

04 <u>They</u> built the town in 1980. → ________

05 <u>People</u> widely use rice cookers in Asia. → ________

06 <u>Someone</u> cleaned the room completely. → ________

07 <u>The host</u> welcomed the guests at the party. → ________

|C| 다음 문장에서 어법상 어색한 부분을 찾아 바르게 고쳐 쓰시오.

01 You were arrived at the airport on time. ____________

02 The car accident was occurred on the Madison Avenue. ____________

03 The picture is appeared on the screen when you press a button. ____________

04 He is resembled by his father. ____________

05 Apples and oranges was bought by my mom. ____________

06 Many people are died because of the disease last year. ____________

07 Corn is grown not by the farmer. ____________

08 The sun is risen in the east. ____________

|D| 다음 문장을 수동태 문장으로 바꾸어 쓰시오.

01 The poet wrote many poems.

→ ____________

02 Bell invented the telephone in 1876.

→ ____________

03 They don't prefer fast food.

→ ____________

04 Egyptians built the Pyramids a long time ago.

→ ____________

05 Only my sister understands my handwriting.

→ ____________

06 Many people recycle used bottles.

→ ____________

실전 TIP

수동태 문장의 동사는 〈be동사+과거분사〉로 나타내요.

내신 기출 다음 문장을 수동태로 쓸 때, 빈칸에 알맞은 말로 바르게 짝지어진 것은?

- I wore the shirt and jeans.
  → The shirt and jeans ____________ by me.
- The grocery store sells fresh vegetables.
  → Fresh vegetables ____________ by the grocery store.

① was worn – is sold
② are worn – are sold
③ were worn – are sold
④ were worn – were sold
⑤ were wearing – are selling

UNIT 02 by 이외의 다른 전치사를 쓰는 수동태

전치사 by가 아닌 다른 전치사와 자주 사용되는 수동태의 다음 관용 구문을 외우세요.

be made from	~로 만들어지다(재료 성질이 변함)	be worried about	~에 대해 걱정하다
be made of	~로 만들어지다(재료 성질이 안 변함)	be covered with	~로 덮여 있다
be known for	~로[때문에] 알려져 있다	be pleased with	~에 기뻐하다
be known to	~에게 알려져 있다	be satisfied with	~에 만족하다
be known as	~로서 알려져 있다	be tired of	~에 싫증이 나다
be filled with	~로 가득 차 있다(= be full of)	be surprised at	~에 놀라다
be excited about	~에 흥분해 있다	be interested in	~에 흥미가 있다

|A| 빈칸에 알맞은 전치사를 쓰시오.

01 He's known ________ his novels.
02 We're worried ________ your health.
03 I'm interested ________ classical music.
04 The mountain is covered ________ snow.
05 Luke is tired ________ frozen food.
06 Wine is made ________ grapes.
07 The jar is filled ________ coins.
08 He's satisfied ________ his new job.
09 She's known ________ an artist.
10 Everyone is surprised ________ the news.
11 They're excited ________ the festival.
12 The walls are made ________ brick.

|B| 다음 문장에서 어법상 어색한 부분을 찾아 바르게 고쳐 쓰시오.

01 We're covered of mud. ____________________
02 Sarah is pleased of the Christmas present. ____________________
03 The actor is known to his great performances. ____________________
04 The boss was surprised on the new employee's ability. ____________________
05 Many teenagers are worried with their futures. ____________________
06 The bowl is filled of water. ____________________
07 The book is read to many critics. ____________________
08 The shirt is made from cotton. ____________________

내신기출 다음 빈칸에 알맞은 말로 바르게 짝지어진 것은?

• Angela is pleased ____________ the test results.
• It's known ____________ many people as a great city.

① with – to ② with – for ③ with – as
④ from – for ⑤ from – to

실전 TIP
관용적 표현은 숙어로 외워 두면 편해요.

UNIT 03 수동태의 시제

수동태의 시제는 모두 be동사만을 이용하여 표현하는 것을 기억하세요.

현재	am/are/is+과거분사	Pengsoo is loved by many people.
과거	was/were+과거분사	The light bulb was invented in the 1880s.
미래	will be+과거분사	A lot of food will be prepared for the party.
진행	am/are/is/was/were+being+과거분사	The artificial lake is being built now.
완료	have/has/had+been+과거분사	The tower has been used as a prison.

참고 〈be동사+과거분사〉에서 be동사만 진행형으로 만들면 〈be동사+being+과거분사〉가 돼요.

참고 〈be동사+과거분사〉에서 be동사만 완료형으로 만들면 〈have/has/had+been+과거분사〉가 돼요.

|A| 빈칸에 밑줄 친 동사를 활용하여 괄호 안의 지시대로 바꾸어 쓰시오.

01 The letter deliver yesterday. (과거 수동태로) → The letter __________ yesterday.

02 The broken heater fix. (과거진행 수동태로) → The broken heater __________.

03 The warehouse clean tomorrow. (미래 수동태로) → The warehouse __________ tomorrow.

04 The lake pollute by tourists. (현재완료 수동태로) → The lake __________ by tourists.

05 The cathedral build. (현재진행 수동태로) → The cathedral __________.

06 The budget calculate. (미래 수동태로) → The budget __________.

07 He know as a chef for a long time. (과거완료 수동태로)
→ He __________ as a chef for a long time.

|B| 다음 문장을 수동태 문장으로 바꾸어 쓰시오.

01 I'm washing the cups.
→ ______________________________

02 My grandparents have raised me.
→ ______________________________

03 The students were making curry.
→ ______________________________

04 He has owned the car since 2020.
→ ______________________________

05 The researchers are developing a new medicine.
→ ______________________________

06 A new management team will run the company.
→ ______________________________

UNIT 04 조동사가 있는 수동태

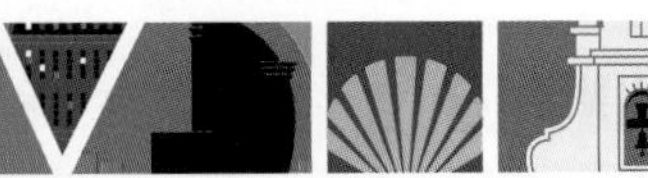

 수동태의 부정문과 의문문도 모두 be동사만을 이용하지만, 조동사가 있다면 조동사를 이용해야 해요.

	be동사 + 과거분사	조동사 + be + 과거분사
긍정문	The book is loved by all.	The book can be loved by all.
부정문	The book is not loved by all.	The book cannot be loved by all.
의문문	Is the book loved by all?	Can the book be loved by all?

|A| 괄호 안의 말을 활용하여 수동태 문장을 완성하시오.

01 The problem ________________ by me. (could, solve)

02 Many people ________________ by the infection. (may, affect)

03 ____________ the order ____________? (must, cancel)

04 Some plants ________________ as medicine. (might, use)

05 How ____________ the rainfall ____________? (must, measure)

06 The poor ________________ by the society. (should, help)

07 The rules ________________. (should, follow)

08 Cyber bullying ________________. (must, not, ignore)

09 ____________ the proposal ____________? (can, accept)

10 Personal information ________________ from the system. (may, not, remove)

|B| 다음 문장을 수동태 문장으로 바꾸어 쓰시오.

조동사가 있는 수동태는 〈조동사+be+과거분사〉로 써요.

01 Seoeun should send an e-mail.

→ ________________________________

02 He may cure the disease.

→ ________________________________

03 People under 18 must not drive a car.

→ ________________________________

04 You can plant the flowers next to the tree. (by 이하 생략)

→ ________________________________

05 Must we do our homework before dinner? (by 이하 생략)

→ ________________________________

06 We could buy many things with a hundred thousand won. (by 이하 생략)

→ ________________________________

UNIT 05 동사구 수동태

동사구를 수동태로 전환할 때는 동사구를 하나의 단어처럼 취급하여 항상 함께 붙여 써야 해요.

능동태	Some girls laughed at the boy.	몇몇 소녀들이 그 소년을 비웃었다.
↓ 수동태	The boy was laughed at by some girls.	그 소년은 몇몇 소녀들에 의해 비웃음당했다.

참고 다음의 동사구를 외워 두세요.

laugh at	~을 비웃다	hand in	~을 제출하다	put off	~을 미루다, 연기하다
take care of	~을 돌보다	turn on	~을 켜다	make use of	~을 이용하다
turn down	~을 거절하다	turn off	~을 끄다	look down on	~을 무시하다

|A| 괄호 안의 동사구를 활용하여 수동태 문장을 완성하시오. (단, 과거시제로 쓸 것)

01 The offer __________________. (turn down)

02 The game __________________. (put off)

03 The idea __________________. (laugh at)

04 The television __________________. (turn off)

05 The report __________________. (hand in)

06 The time __________________ well. (make use of)

07 The computer __________________ by Jeff. (turn on)

08 The plants __________________ by her. (take care of)

09 The country __________________ by other countries. (look down on)

|B| 다음 문장을 수동태 문장으로 바꾸어 쓰시오.

01 Parents should take care of children.

→ ____

02 I turned down the invitation.

→ ____

03 You can hand in the application.

→ ____

04 We put off the meeting to next week. (by 이하 생략)

→ ____

05 They will make use of Juwon's experience. (by 이하 생략)

→ ____

06 We should not laugh at other people's opinions. (by 이하 생략)

→ ____

UNIT 06 that절이 뒤에 나오는 수동태

주어가 일반적인 사람들이고 목적어가 that절일 때, 수동태 문장으로 바꾸어 쓰는 법을 알아 두세요.

능동태	People/They/We	say	that honesty is the best policy.
수동태	It	is said	that honesty is the best policy.

참고 일반적인 사람들 주어와 that절을 목적어로 쓰는 대표적인 동사들을 알아 두세요.
→ say, think, believe, know, consider, report, expect, suppose

that절의 주어를 문장의 주어로 수동태 문장을 쓸 때, that절을 to부정사로 바꿔야 해요.

능동태	People/They/We	say	that honesty is the best policy.
수동태	Honesty	is said	to be the best policy.

|A| 다음 문장을 수동태 문장으로 바꾸어 쓸 때, 빈칸에 알맞은 말을 쓰시오.

01 People say that you are honest. → You ______________ be honest.

02 We believe that he is 15 years old. → ______________ that he is 15 years old.

03 They suppose that I am right. → ______________ I am right.

04 Many think that she is rich. → She ______________ rich.

05 They reported that 5 people were killed. → ______________ 5 people were killed.

06 We expect that the lecture will be helpful. → The lecture ______________ helpful.

07 People consider that the device is necessary. → ______________ the device is necessary.

|B| 다음 문장을 두 가지 형태의 수동태 문장으로 바꾸어 쓰시오.

01 We know that global warming is serious.
→ ______________ / ______________

02 They consider that fire fighters are heroes.
→ ______________ / ______________

03 People say that French is hard to learn.
→ ______________ / ______________

04 They believe that he has a talent for teaching.
→ ______________ / ______________

05 Many think that she is the best player on the team.
→ ______________ / ______________

목적어가 that절일 때는 〈It is + 과거분사 + that ~〉이나 〈that절의 주어 + be동사 + 과거분사 + to부정사〉로 써요.

UNIT 07 4형식 문장의 수동태

4형식 문장의 목적어 2개(간접목적어, 직접목적어)를 주어로 수동태 문장을 쓸 수 있어야 해요.

	간접목적어(~에게)를 주어로 쓸 때	직접목적어(~을)를 주어로 쓸 때
능동태	She gave them a card.	She gave them a card.
수동태	They were given a card by her.	A card was given to them by her.
주의	직접목적어는 동사 뒤에 그대로 쓰고, 능동태의 주어는 〈by+행위자〉로 넣을 수 있어요.	능동태의 간접목적어(~에게)를 〈전치사+사람〉으로 써야 해요.

주의 직접목적어를 주어로 할 때, 간접목적어 앞의 전치사는 동사에 따라 다르므로 주의하세요.

give, tell, send, show, teach, sell, write, bring, offer	to	A card was given to them.
get, make, buy, cook	for	Curry was cooked for us.
ask의 직접목적어가 question이나 favor일 때	of	A question was asked of me.

주의 make, buy, get, send, bring, write, cook 등의 동사는 직접목적어만 주어로 써요.

|A| 빈칸에 알맞은 말을 |보기|에서 골라 쓰시오.

|보기|
to　　　for　　　of

01 A letter was written __________ you by me.

02 A question was asked __________ her by Minsu.

03 A camera was bought __________ you by your parents.

04 An invitation was sent __________ every attendee by him.

05 Chicken soup was cooked __________ the sick.

06 The car was sold __________ Jiho by the dealer.

07 A pen was given __________ me by Jumin.

08 A favor was asked __________ Brian by his brother.

09 An umbrella was brought __________ Lucy by her mom.

10 A secret was told __________ me by Mina.

11 Advanced chemistry is taught __________ some students by Mr. Lucas.

12 A copy of the report was made __________ me.

|B| 다음 문장을 주어진 단어로 시작하는 수동태 문장으로 바꾸어 쓰시오.

01 The client asked the lawyer a hard question.

→ The lawyer ________________________________.

→ A hard question ________________________________.

02 Her boyfriend gave her a ring.

→ She ________________________________.

→ A ring ________________________________.

03 Miso told me her address.

→ I ________________________________.

→ Her address ________________________________.

04 Hani bought me a cup of tea.

→ A cup of tea ________________________________.

05 We sent our mom some flowers for her birthday.

→ Some flowers ________________________________.

06 My aunt got me a rare book.

→ A rare book ________________________________.

목적어가 2개인 4형식 문장의 수동태는 간접목적어, 직접목적어를 주어로 하는 2개의 수동태가 가능하지만, buy, send, get 등의 동사가 쓰인 경우에는 직접목적어만 주어로 쓸 수 있음에 유의해야 해요.

|C| 우리말과 같도록 괄호 안의 말을 활용하여 문장을 완성하시오.

01 그 일은 그의 아버지에 의해 그에게 주어졌다. (get, his father)

→ The job ________________________________.

02 그 문자는 어제 그녀에게 보내졌다. (send)

→ The text message ________________________________.

03 다양한 요리들이 아빠에 의해서 우리를 위해 요리되었다. (cook, Dad)

→ Various dishes ________________________________.

내신기출 다음 문장을 수동태 문장으로 완성하시오.

You should show the staff your ticket.

→ Your ticket ____________________ the staff.

실전 TIP

4형식 문장의 수동태에서 직접목적어를 주어로 쓸 때, 동사에 따라 간접목적어 앞에 전치사(to, for, of)가 쓰임에 유의해야 해요.

UNIT 08 5형식 문장의 수동태

5형식 문장의 목적어를 주어로 수동태 문장을 쓰는 방법을 알아 두세요.

	목적격보어가 명사/형용사/to부정사일 때	
능동태	He made her happy / a doctor.	He told them to save money.
↓ 수동태	She was made happy / a doctor by him.	They were told to save money by him.

참고 능동태의 목적어를 주어로 쓰고, 수동태 동사를 쓴 후, 목적격보어를 그대로 써요.

|A| 다음 문장을 수동태 문장으로 바꾸어 쓸 때, 빈칸에 알맞은 말을 쓰시오.

01 My friends call me 'Genius.' → I am ____________ by my friends.

02 She told me to come. → I ____________ by her.

03 We asked him to move aside. → He was ____________ by us.

04 They elected Jim chairperson. → Jim was ____________ by them.

05 He encouraged me to write the book. → I was ____________ by him.

06 Pictures make the book interesting. → The book is ____________ by pictures.

07 I helped Hayun to choose new shoes. → Hayun was ____________ new shoes by me.

08 The students found the work boring. → The work was ____________ by the students.

|B| 다음 문장을 밑줄 친 부분을 주어로 하는 수동태 문장으로 바꾸어 쓰시오.

01 They call the boy 'Bookworm.'

→ ____________________________

02 My parents teach me to speak politely.

→ ____________________________

03 The journalist asked the politician to answer a few questions.

→ ____________________________

04 She made her friends very surprised.

→ ____________________________

05 The news made all of us disappointed.

→ ____________________________

06 The citizens elected him the mayor.

→ ____________________________

다양한 목적격보어를 취하는 5형식 문장을 수동태로 바꿀 때는 동사 다음에 목적격보어를 그대로 써요.

UNIT 09 지각동사, 사역동사의 수동태

지각동사나 사역동사의 5형식을 수동태로 쓸 때 목적격보어의 형태에 주의하세요.

	목적격보어가 원형부정사인 지각동사	목적격보어가 원형부정사인 사역동사
능동태	We saw the boys play soccer.	He made the driver stop.
↓ 수동태	The boys were seen to play soccer.	The driver was made to stop by him.
주의	수동태로 쓸 때는 목적격보어가 원형부정사일 때는 to부정사로 쓰고, 분사일 때는 그대로 분사를 써요. The boy were seen playing soccer.	

참고 사역동사 have와 let의 5형식 문장은 수동태를 쓰지 않고 be made to나 be allowed to를 써서 표현해요.
I had him clean the room. → He was made to clean the room.
I let him enter. → He was allowed to enter.

|A| **다음 문장을 수동태 문장으로 바꾸어 쓸 때, 빈칸에 알맞은 말을 쓰시오.**

01 The dentist made me brush my teeth 3 times a day.
→ I ____________________ my teeth 3 times a day by the dentist.

02 They saw some stars twinkle in the sky.
→ Some stars ____________________ in the sky.

03 We saw Chris playing the guitar.
→ Chris ____________________ the guitar.

04 The teacher had him read a book.
→ He ____________________ a book by the teacher.

사역동사 have와 let은 수동태로 쓰지 않아요. have는 be made to ~로, let은 be allowed to~로 쓸 수 있어요.

|B| **다음 문장을 수동태 문장으로 바꾸어 쓰시오.**

01 I saw you wave a flag.
→ ____

02 My mom won't let me go with you. (by 이하 생략)
→ ____

03 He heard a car stop suddenly.
→ ____

04 I felt something crawl on my arm. (by 이하 생략)
→ ____

05 We made a mechanic fix the washing machine.
→ ____

중간고사·기말고사 실전문제

객관식 (01~25) / 주관식 (26~50)

정답과 해설 • 18쪽

학년과 반 이름 객관식 / 25문항 주관식 / 25문항

01~03 다음 빈칸에 알맞은 것을 고르시오.

01

A big boat was got ________ them to cross the river.

① to ② for ③ with
④ by ⑤ of

02

A mysterious man ____________ in the fog.

① appeared
② was appeared
③ appearing
④ being appeared
⑤ has been appeared

03

Her devoted love for children will ____________ for a long time.

① remember
② remembered
③ be remembering
④ be remembered
⑤ been remembering

04~05 다음 빈칸에 공통으로 알맞은 것을 고르시오.

04

- Switzerland is known ________ its watches and chocolate.
- A teddy bear was bought ________ his daughter by him.

① to ② for ③ with
④ by ⑤ of

05

- The conductor cannot be pleased ________ his performance.
- The container was filled ________ grains.

① to ② for ③ with
④ by ⑤ of

06~08 다음 우리말을 영어로 바르게 나타낸 것을 고르시오.

06

그의 아이디어는 반 친구들에게 비웃음을 당했다.

① His idea laughed at his classmates.
② His idea was laugh at his classmates.
③ His idea was laughed at by his classmates.
④ His idea was laughed by his classmates at.
⑤ His idea was laughing at by his classmates.

07 마늘은 건강에 좋은 음식이라고 알려져 왔다.

① It has been known that garlic is a healthy food.
② It has known that garlic is a healthy food.
③ It has been known to garlic is a healthy food.
④ Garlic known to be a healthy food.
⑤ Garlic is known that is a healthy food.

08 Ross에 의해 새로운 일자리가 그녀에게 제안되었다.

① A new job offered for her by Ross.
② A new job was offered of her by Ross.
③ A new job was offered to her by Ross.
④ A new job was offered for her by Ross.
⑤ A new job was offered by her to Ross.

09~10 다음 중 어법상 어색한 것을 고르시오.

09 ① She is said to have a big fortune.
② They were told to go out and play.
③ Eating and drinking are prohibited in this place.
④ A number of problems are still remained in this organization.
⑤ The actress was asked about her new movie by reporters.

10 ① The girl was brought two kittens by her father.
② Clare wasn't allowed to travel abroad because she was under 18.
③ The patient will recover from the disease soon.
④ I was encouraged to help a friend with a disability.
⑤ We are supposed to consume at least 8 cups of water a day.

11 다음 중 어법상 옳은 것을 모두 고르면?

① His proposal was turned down by everyone.
② The song has being played for 10 minutes.
③ Our team was expected to win the game.
④ A favor was asked to him by his friend.
⑤ The wedding ceremony will held tomorrow.

12~13 다음 중 어법상 옳은 것을 고르시오.

12 ① The cream spaghetti was smelled very good.
② The boy was raised by one of his relatives.
③ He is resembled by his grandfather.
④ The balloon was risen up in the sky.
⑤ My new jacket is fitted me well.

13 ① That is known Van Gogh cut his own ear.
② The movie was translated to Korean by her.
③ Dan was made a sand castle by his brother.
④ My final essay has already been turn in.
⑤ She was forced participated in the event.

14 다음 문장을 수동태로 바꾸어 쓸 때, 어색한 것은?
① No one can look down on him for any reason.
→ He can be looked down on by no one for any reason.
② Everyone knows that he is a best-selling author.
→ He is known as a best-selling author by everyone.
③ His words encouraged me to try one more time.
→ I was encouraged to try one more time by his words.
④ The secretary arranged the president's schedule.
→ The president's schedule was arranged by the secretary.
⑤ My mom didn't let me buy the new tablet PC.
→ I wasn't let to buy the new tablet PC by my mom.

15 다음 중 어법상 어색한 것을 모두 고르면?
① Paper is made from trees.
② A postcard has been sent to the class by the teacher.
③ Were the citizens satisfied for the result?
④ The guard was watched patrol around the town by the thief.
⑤ He was told to stay away from the hot stove.

16 다음 문장을 수동태로 바르게 나타낸 것은?
① Jina must handle these fragile glass cups carefully.
→ These fragile glass cups are must handled carefully by Jina.
② The old woman has operated these hotels.
→ These hotels have been operating by the old woman.
③ The announcer reported that the economy would be better off next year.
→ The economy was reported to be better off next year by the announcer.
④ Anna bought her nephew a new bicycle.
→ Her nephew was bought for a new bicycle by Anna.
⑤ Ella heard someone laugh out loud in her living room.
→ Someone was heard laugh out loud in her living room by Ella.

17 다음 문장을 수동태로 바르게 나타낸 것은?

Alex saw the monkey climbing up the tree.

① The monkey was seen climbing up the tree by Alex.
② The monkey was seen climb up the tree by Alex.
③ The monkey was seen to climbing up the tree by Alex.
④ The monkey was seen climbed up the tree by Alex.
⑤ The monkey saw being climbed up the tree by Alex.

18~19 다음 문장을 수동태로 바르게 나타낸 것을 모두 고르시오.

18

Ally showed everyone pictures of her childhood.

① Everyone shown by pictures of her childhood to Ally.
② Everyone was shown pictures of her childhood by Ally.
③ Everyone was shown to pictures of her childhood by Ally.
④ Pictures of her childhood were shown everyone by Ally.
⑤ Pictures of her childhood were shown to everyone by Ally.

19

Many readers thought that his novel was a masterpiece.

① His novel was thought to be a masterpiece by many readers.
② His novel was thought to a masterpiece by many readers.
③ A masterpiece was thought to be many readers by his novel.
④ It was thought that his novel was a masterpiece by many readers.
⑤ It thought to be a masterpiece of his novel by many readers.

20~21 다음 빈칸에 알맞은 말이 바르게 짝지어진 것을 고르시오.

20

•His amazing artistic abilities are known ________ a lot of people. •Unfortunately, he ________ by a jellyfish in the sea last summer.

① for – was sting ② to – stung
③ to – was stung ④ for – sting
⑤ for – was stung

21

• The beautiful wall painting ________ by the painter at that time. • Can the broken printer ________? • The dog ________ 'Dory' by him.

① colored – fixed – named
② colored – is fixed – named
③ was colored – be fixed – named
④ was being colored – is fix – was named
⑤ was being colored – be fixed – was named

22 다음 중 어법상 어색한 문장의 개수는?

ⓐ Should the test finished by 2 o'clock?
ⓑ The bus has already been arrived.
ⓒ Tom is said that is very diligent.
ⓓ This shirt is made of pure cotton.

① 없음 ② 1개 ③ 2개
④ 3개 ⑤ 4개

23 다음 중 어법상 옳은 문장의 개수는?

ⓐ The fan has been turned on for five hours.
ⓑ The fight shouldn't be occurred here.
ⓒ The furniture was all covered by dust.
ⓓ We were made to make dinner for everyone by him.

① 없음 ② 1개 ③ 2개
④ 3개 ⑤ 4개

24 다음 중 어법상 옳은 문장끼리 바르게 짝지은 것은?

ⓐ It reported that over 100 people were injured from the accident.
ⓑ The artist is also known as an actor.
ⓒ She has been replaced by another player.
ⓓ The victim was died by a robber.
ⓔ She was bought a bunch of flowers by her boyfriend.

① ⓐ, ⓒ ② ⓑ, ⓒ
③ ⓐ, ⓑ, ⓒ ④ ⓐ, ⓓ, ⓔ
⑤ ⓒ, ⓓ, ⓔ

25 다음 글의 밑줄 친 ⓐ~ⓔ 중, 어법상 어색한 것의 개수는?

ⓐ She has to be hurried up now. The assignment is due today, and ⓑ the final essay needs to be turned in by 7. ⓒ The teacher is known that is very strict about the due date. ⓓ Still, the first page hasn't finished yet. ⓔ She has been given too little time.

① 없음 ② 1개 ③ 2개
④ 3개 ⑤ 4개

〈다음부터는 서술형 주관식 문제입니다.〉

26~28 다음 문장에서 어법상 어색한 부분을 찾아 바르게 고쳐 쓰시오.

26 The baby was lain on the bed by her father.

______ → ______

27 The river in this town has been polluting by factories.

______ → ______

28 Trainees taught how to use the facilities by the instructor.

__________ → __________

29~30 **다음 우리말과 같도록 괄호 안의 동사를 활용하여 빈칸을 완성하시오.**

29

대부분의 상품은 이미 다 팔렸다. (sell)

→ Most of the goods ______ already ______ ______ out.

30

그 고대 도시는 풍부한 문화로 알려져 있다. (know)

→ The ancient city ______ ______ ______ its rich culture.

31~34 **다음 문장을 밑줄 친 부분을 주어로 하는 수동태 문장으로 바꾸어 쓰시오.**

31 The committee put off <u>the Olympics</u> because of the pandemic disease.

→ ______________________________

32 Most people think that <u>Jeju Island</u> is the best vacation site.

→ ______________________________

33 The principal let <u>us</u> go outside the school during the lunchtime.

→ ______________________________

34 We have provided <u>free bread</u> since we opened this restaurant.

→ ______________________________

35~37 **다음 우리말과 같도록 괄호 안의 말을 바르게 배열하시오.**

35

세계에서 가장 높은 빌딩이 지금 서울에 건설되고 있다. (building, is, constructed, being, the highest, in the world)

→ ______________________________ in Seoul right now.

36

그녀는 지하철에서 소매치기를 당했던 것이 틀림없다.
(have, pickpocketed, been, must, she)

→ ______________________
______________ on the subway.

37

랍스터 요리가 요리사에 의해 손님들에게 요리되었다.
(cooked, the customers, the lobster dishes, for, were)

→ ______________________
______________ by the chef.

38~39 다음 주어진 문장과 의미가 같도록 빈칸을 완성하시오.

38

I was told a rumor about my boss by my colleague.

→ A rumor about my boss ______________
______________________.

39

How to get to the station was asked of a police officer by her.

→ A police officer ______________
______________________.

40~42 다음 우리말과 같도록 괄호 안의 말을 활용하여 문장을 완성하시오.

40

한 소녀가 나무 아래에서 자고 있는 것이 나에게 보였다. (see, sleep, under the tree)

→ A girl ______________________.

41

그는 지난달에 승진되었을지도 모른다. (might, promote, last month)

→ He ______________________.

42

숫자 4는 불운하다고 여겨진다. (believe, the number 4, unlucky)

→ It ______________________.

43~45 다음 글의 밑줄 친 ⓐ~ⓕ 중 어법상 어색한 부분을 세 군데 찾아 바르게 고쳐 쓰시오.

ⓐ Have you ever been laughed at by others? ⓑ When it was happened to you, how did you feel? And ⓒ how did you react? ⓓ You might have been dissatisfied by yourself. But, don't be. ⓔ Don't allow others to discourage you. ⓕ Your self-esteem should built on what you believe is right.

43 __________ → __________

44 __________ → __________

45 __________ → __________

46~48 다음 대화의 밑줄 친 ⓐ~ⓕ 중 어법상 어색한 부분을 세 군데 찾아 바르게 고쳐 쓰시오.

A: What's wrong? ⓐ What are you so disappointed at?
B: ⓑ The package I ordered hasn't been arrived yet. It's for my mom's birthday.
A: Oh, ⓒ you must be very worry for that. Have you contacted the store you ordered from?
B: Yes, they said ⓓ it had been sent to my old address and ⓔ it would be delivered by next week. But my mom's birthday is this weekend.
A: Don't worry. ⓕ Your mom will be pleasing with your gift even though it's late.

46 __________ → __________

47 __________ → __________

48 __________ → __________

49~50 다음 우리말을 주어진 |조건|에 맞게 바르게 영작하시오.

49 남극은 빙하로 덮여 있다고 말해진다.

|조건|
- It으로 시작할 것
- 단어 say, the South Pole, cover, glaciers를 사용할 것
- 11단어로 쓸 것

→ __________

50 이 건물은 창고로 사용되고 있다.

|조건|
- 현재완료 시제로 쓸 것
- 단어 building, use, as, a warehouse를 사용할 것
- 8단어로 쓸 것

→ __________

CHAPTER

05 부정사

UNIT 01 to부정사의 명사적 용법

동사를 명사(~하기, ~하는 것)처럼 사용하려면 〈to + 동사원형〉의 형태로 만들어야 해요.

명사적 to부정사의 역할		주의
주어	To become a scientist takes years. 과학자가 되는 것은 수년이 걸린다.	– to부정사 주어는 단수 취급 – 부정형은 〈not to-V〉
보어	Her dream is to become a scientist. 그녀의 꿈은 과학자가 되는 것이다.	
목적어	He promised not to be late. 그는 늦지 않을 것을 약속했다.	

참고 부정사란 정해진 품사가 없다는 뜻으로 명사, 형용사, 부사로 쓰여요.

to부정사 주어는 문장 뒤로 옮길 수 있는데, 이때 가(짜)주어 it을 주어 자리에 넣어야 해요.

to부정사 주어를 쓸 때	가주어 it을 쓸 때
To become a scientist takes years. 과학자가 되는 것은 수년이 걸린다.	It takes years to become a scientist. 과학자가 되는 것은 수년이 걸린다.

참고 주어 자리에 쓴 it을 가주어라고 하고, 뒤에 쓴 to부정사를 진주어라고 해요.

to부정사를 목적어(명사)로 쓸 수 있는 기본 동사들을 파악하세요.

want/would like(원하다)	hope(바라다)	plan(계획하다)	refuse(거절하다)
wish(소망하다)	promise(약속하다)	choose(선택하다)	learn(배우다)
expect(예상하다)	agree(동의하다)	decide(결정하다)	need(~할 필요가 있다)

|A| |보기|에서 알맞은 말을 골라 to부정사로 바꾸어 빈칸에 쓰시오.

|보기|
answer be build fight help prepare read win

01 It is a good thing ________________ the poor and the needy.

02 Her dream is ________________ an astronaut in the future.

03 The brothers promised not ________________ over the toys again.

04 I decided ________________ the author's new novel.

05 ________________ the next election is his goal.

06 It costs a lot ________________ a bridge over the river.

07 She refused ________________ the question.

08 ________________ a party is my present for Minju's birthday.

|B| 우리말과 같도록 괄호 안의 말과 to를 활용하여 문장을 완성하시오.

to부정사는 〈to+동사원형〉으로, 부정형은 to 앞에 not을 써요.

01 우리는 매일 30분 동안 산책할 필요가 있다. (need, take a walk)

→ We ______________________ for 30 minutes every day.

02 그는 다시는 늦지 않겠다고 약속했다. (promise, late, not, be)

→ He ______________________ again.

03 영어를 혼자 공부하기는 그다지 어렵지 않다. (English, difficult, study)

→ It isn't so ______________________ by yourself.

04 정기적으로 운동하는 것이 건강에 좋다. (your health, for, work out)

→ It is good ______________________ regularly.

05 당신에게 방해가 되지 않으면 좋겠어요. (disturb, not)

→ I hope ______________________ you.

|C| 다음 문장을 〈It ~ to ...〉 구문으로 바꾸어 쓰시오.

01 To hear people keep complaining is annoying.

→ ______________________________________

02 To order books online is simple.

→ ______________________________________

03 To use public transportation abroad is not easy.

→ ______________________________________

04 To pronounce some French words correctly is difficult.

→ ______________________________________

|D| 괄호 안의 말을 바르게 배열하여 to부정사가 포함된 문장을 완성하시오.

01 (retire, planned, at the age of 60) → She ______________________.

02 (sail, the ocean, across) → My dream is ______________________.

03 (agreed, our smart phone, use, not) → We ______________________ during mealtimes.

04 (deliver, a speech, people, in front of) → ______________________ is courageous.

05 (treat, students, differently, not fair) → It is ______________________.

06 (dangerous, at the red light, cross, the street) → It is ______________________.

내신기출 다음 밑줄 친 부분 중 문장 안에서의 쓰임이 다른 하나는?

① The team didn't expect to win the game.

② The best method is to prepare for all possibilities.

③ The man is planning to build a large castle on the hill.

실전 TIP

명사적 용법의 to부정사가 주어인지, 보어인지, 목적어인지 확인해 보세요.

UNIT 02 to부정사의 의미상 주어

to부정사의 행위를 하는 주체가 따로 있을 때는 그 행위의 주체자를 밝혀야 할 때가 있어요.

주어가 행위자	She was happy to see Paul. 그녀는 Paul을 보게 되어 행복했다.	She = to see의 행위자
일반적인 행위자	The book is hard to read. 그 책은 (사람들이) 읽기 어렵다.	to read의 행위자 → 사람들
특정 행위자	The book is hard for children to read. 그 책은 아이들이 읽기 어렵다.	to read의 행위자 → children

참고 for children과 같이 to부정사의 행위자를 의미상 주어라고 해요.

대부분 〈for + 행위자〉와 같이 to부정사 바로 앞에 쓰지만, of를 쓸 때가 있으니 주의하세요.

	사람의 성격이나 성품을 나타내는 형용사	의미상 주어	to부정사
It is	kind, wise, polite, honest, nice, clever, generous, foolish, silly, rude, careless 등	of you	to say that.
	~하다	네가	그런 말을 하다니

|A| 빈칸에 for나 of 중 알맞은 것을 쓰시오.

01 It's unusual _______ my mom to get angry.

02 It isn't safe _______ us to swim in the sea.

03 It's silly _______ us to make such a mistake.

04 It's wise _______ her to make the decision.

05 It's important _______ you to be on time.

06 It's nice _______ him to pick me up.

07 It's clever _______ you not to miss the chance.

08 It's hard _______ them to solve the problem.

09 It's better _______ her to be more careful.

10 It's dangerous _______ kids to jump on a bed.

|B| 다음 문장에서 어법상 어색한 부분을 찾아 바르게 고쳐 쓰시오.

01 It's nice for you to say hello to new students. _______________

02 The pants are too tight for me wearing. _______________

03 It's wise of him check the weather in advance. _______________

04 It's unhealthy of children to watch television till late at night. _______________

05 It's not polite for you to enter the room without knocking. _______________

내신기출 다음 중 빈칸에 들어갈 말이 다른 하나는?

① It's difficult _________ me to read the English book.

② It's generous _________ him to donate a lot of money.

③ It's impossible _________ me to get up at 5:00 in the morning.

실전 TIP
형용사가 어떤 성격인지 파악해 보세요.

UNIT 03 의문사+to부정사

의문사 뒤에 to부정사를 써서 하나의 명사처럼 쓸 때, 문맥에 맞게 알맞은 의문사를 써야 해요.

what+to부정사	무엇을 ~할지	when+to부정사	언제 ~할지
which+to부정사	어느 것을 ~할지	where+to부정사	어디에서 ~할지
who+to부정사	누구를 ~할지	how+to부정사	어떻게 ~할지, ~하는 법

참고 〈의문사+to부정사〉는 〈의문사+주어+should+동사원형〉으로 바꾸어 쓸 수도 있어요.

I don't know how to get there. (그곳에 가는 방법)

= how I should get there (내가 그곳에 어떻게 가야 하는지)

|A| 우리말을 참고하여, 괄호 안의 동사와 |보기|에서 알맞은 의문사를 골라 문장을 완성하시오.

|보기| what when where how

01 어떻게 사용해야 하는지 (use) → I don't know ______________ the dishwasher.

02 무엇을 입어야 하는지 (wear) → She didn't know ______________ for the party.

03 어디로 가야 할지 (go) → He didn't decide ______________ for the holidays.

04 언제 멈추어야 하는지 (stop) → We need to learn ______________ talking.

05 어디를 방문해야 하는지 (visit) → Dan decided ______________ in New York.

06 어떻게 해결해야 하는지 (solve) → The book explains ______________ the problems.

07 무엇을 해야 하는지 (do) → I wondered ______________ next.

08 언제 시작해야 하는지 (start) → The new employee didn't know ______________ working.

|B| 괄호 안의 말을 이용하여 두 문장의 뜻이 같도록 문장을 완성하시오.

〈의문사+to부정사〉는 〈의문사+주어+should+동사원형〉으로 바꿔 쓸 수 있어요.

01 They didn't tell me when I should turn off the lights. (when to)

→ They didn't tell me ______________.

02 You let me know where I should shop for Christmas. (where to)

→ You let me know ______________.

03 My parents told me when to go to bed. (when, should)

→ My parents told me ______________.

04 I didn't know how I should order a meal at an unmanned cafeteria. (how to)

→ I didn't know ______________ at an unmanned cafeteria.

05 She told me what to eat in Italy. (what, should)

→ She told me ______________.

UNIT 04 to부정사의 형용사적 용법

to부정사는 형용사처럼 명사를 꾸밀 수 있는데, 이때 어순에 주의하세요.

어순	형용사	명사	형용사	형용사 역할 to부정사
일반적인 명사의 경우	many	books		to read (~해야 할, ~할)
-thing/-one/-body의 경우		something	interesting	

to부정사가 수식하는 명사가 to부정사구의 전치사의 목적어일 때는 전치사를 함께 써야 해요.

수식하는 명사와 to부정사의 관계	명사	형용사 역할 to부정사	참고
단순 수식	friends	to like me (나를 좋아해 줄)	
to부정사 동사의 목적어		to trust (믿을 수 있는)	trust friends (동사의 목적어)
to부정사 전치사의 목적어		to talk with (같이 이야기할)	talk with friends (전치사의 목적어)

|A| 괄호 안의 말을 바르게 배열하여 문장을 완성하시오.

01 (a lion, to see, a chance) → I got ________________.

02 (to do, many things, right now) → You have ________________.

03 (to help, him, some friends) → Juwon has ________________.

04 (bought, to live in, a house) → She ________________.

05 (warm, something, to drink) → We need ________________.

06 (to show, us, old pictures) → My grandparents have ________________.

07 (in the park, chairs, to sit on) → There were ________________.

08 (new, nothing, to read) → The magazine has ________________.

|B| 다음 문장에서 어법상 어색한 부분을 찾아 바르게 고쳐 쓰시오.

01 I need a piece of paper to write. ________________

02 You got a couple of questions answer. ________________

03 He needs someone to depend. ________________

04 The girl looks for a fork and a knife to eat. ________________

05 She wants to buy warm something to wear. ________________

06 We have five classes attending today. ________________

07 The city has a plan of turn the vacant land into a park. ________________

08 He hasn't decided what do with the money. ________________

09 They have a child to take care. ________________

to부정사가 수식하는 명사가 전치사의 목적어이면 전치사도 꼭 함께 써야 해요.

UNIT 05 to부정사의 형용사적 용법 - be to용법

be동사의 보어로 쓰인 명사적 to부정사와 형용사적 to부정사의 의미 차이를 확인하세요.

	의미	예문	
명사적 to부정사	~하는 것	My plan is to visit the museum.	방문하는 것이다
형용사적 to부정사	예정	She is to visit the museum.	방문할 예정이다
	운명	Everyone is to die some day.	죽을 운명이다
	의무	We are to finish the project today.	끝내야 한다
	의도, 의지	If you are to get there, leave now.	도착하고자 하면
	가능	No one is to be left alone.	혼자 남겨질 수 없다

참고 표에 제시된 의미를 기억하여, 명사적 to부정사(보어)와 형용사적 to부정사를 문맥에 맞게 해석하세요.

|A| 〈be동사 + to부정사〉를 이용하여 두 문장의 뜻이 같도록 빈칸을 완성하시오.

01 He is going to arrive soon. → He ____________ soon.

02 You must not smoke in the restaurant. → You ____________ in the restaurant.

03 We were destined to be singers. → We ____________.

04 If you intend to succeed, do your best. → If you ____________, do your best.

05 Very little water could be found there. → Very little water ____________ there.

06 Jane is going to marry Tom next week. → Jane ____________ next week.

07 Passengers must fasten their seat belts. → Passengers ____________.

|B| 우리말과 같도록 괄호 안의 말을 이용하여 〈be동사+to부정사〉가 포함된 문장으로 완성하시오.

01 대통령은 다음 주에 워싱턴 D.C.를 방문할 예정이다. (visit, Washington D.C.)

→ The president ____________ next week.

02 그 영웅은 10년 안에 고향으로 돌아올 운명이었다. (come back, home)

→ The hero ____________ in 10 years.

03 훌륭한 피아니스트가 되고자 하면, 열심히 연습해야 한다. (a good pianist, be)

→ If you ____________, you must practice hard.

04 학생들은 그 시를 외워야 한다. (the poem, memorize)

→ The students ____________.

내신기출 다음 중 밑줄 친 부분의 쓰임이 다른 하나는?

① Are you to speak at the meeting? ② Do you have a friend to rely on?
③ They are to travel Jeju-do by car.

실전 TIP

to부정사의 형용사적 용법 중, 명사를 수식하는지 be to용법인지 확인하세요.

UNIT 06 to부정사의 부사적 용법

to부정사가 주어, 목적어, 보어가 아니라면, 부사의 역할을 하는 것으로 판단하세요.

부사적 to부정사의 의미	부사 역할 to부정사	같은 표현
~하기 위해서(목적)	I exercise to lose weight.	= in order to lose weight
		= so as to lose weight
~하지 않기 위해서(목적)	I try hard not to fail.	= in order not to fail
		= so as not to fail

'~하기 위해서(목적)' 이외에도 다음과 같은 의미로도 쓰이므로 문맥에 맞게 해석해야 해요.

부사적 to부정사의 의미	부사 역할 to부정사	의미
~하게 되어 …한(감정의 원인)	I'm happy to see you again.	너를 다시 만나서 행복한
~하기에 …한(형용사 수식)	This sentence is hard to understand.	이해하기에 어려운
~하다니 …한(판단의 근거)	She must be clever to solve it.	그걸 풀다니 영리한
~해서(결국) …하다(결과)	The girl grew up to be a star.	자라서 (결국) 스타가 되었다
	The turtle lived to be 188 years old.	188세까지 살았다

|A| 다음 문장을 밑줄 친 부분의 의미에 유의하여 우리말로 해석하시오.

01 I saved money to go to Europe. ______________________

02 I'm glad to see you again. ______________________

03 Mr. James is very hard to please. ______________________

04 She's smart to come up with such an answer. ______________________

05 He grew up to be a great musician. ______________________

06 People use a microwave to heat up food. ______________________

07 We're delighted to hear that you won the game. ______________________

08 The coffee machine is easy to use. ______________________

09 You were careless to ignore the risks. ______________________

|B| 우리말과 같도록 to부정사와 괄호 안의 말을 이용하여 문장을 완성하시오.

01 Tom은 금메달을 따게 되어 행복했다. (happy, the gold medal, win)

→ Tom was ______________________.

02 David는 매일 저녁 개를 산책시키기 위해 공원으로 간다. (his dog, so as, walk)

→ David goes to the park ______________________ every evening.

03 그 똑똑한 학생은 자라서 과학자가 되었다. (a scientist, grew up, be)

→ The smart student ______________________________.

04 미리 티켓을 예약해 두다니 Tony는 영리하다. (the tickets, reserve, in advance, clever)

→ Tony is ______________________________.

05 중국어는 외국인들이 배우기 어렵다. (for foreigners, learn, hard)

→ Chinese is ______________________________.

|C| 괄호 안의 말을 바르게 배열하여 문장을 완성하시오.

01 (our cousins, pleased, meet, to)

→ We're ______________________________.

02 (the lottery, lucky, win, to)

→ Kevin was ______________________________.

03 (understand, confusing, to, very)

→ The presentation was ______________________________.

04 (go, to, the theme park, to, excited, are)

→ The kids ______________________________.

05 (awoke, himself, to, find, famous)

→ He ______________________________.

|D| 다음 문장에서 어법상 어색한 부분을 찾아 바르게 고쳐 쓰시오.

01 He lived seen his dream come true. ____________________

02 Lucy practices every day in order improving her performance. ____________________

03 I studied hard so as to not disappoint my parents. ____________________

04 We are very sorry miss the concert. ____________________

05 The new movie is interesting for children enjoy. ____________________

06 You are very thoughtful remembering what I said. ____________________

07 Use the sunblock not in order to get burned. ____________________

내신기출 다음 중 밑줄 친 부분의 쓰임이 다른 하나는?

① She sets an alarm clock to get up early.
② I met my friend to see the movie together.
③ He goes to the gym every day to stay healthy.
④ Some leaders are to meet in Seoul next week.
⑤ Minho went to the station to meet his parents.

실전 TIP

to부정사가 부사적으로 쓰였는지 형용사적으로 쓰였는지 해석하면서 파악해 보세요.

UNIT 07 to부정사의 역할

to부정사가 문장 안에서 명사, 형용사, 부사 중 어떤 역할을 하고 있는지 파악할 수 있어야 해요.

to부정사의 품사	품사별 to부정사의 역할
명사	'~하는 것', '~하기'라는 의미로 주어, 보어, 목적어 자리에 쓴다.
형용사	앞의 명사를 수식하거나, be동사의 보어(be to 용법)로 쓴다.
부사	목적, 감정의 원인, 형용사 수식, 판단의 근거, 결과의 의미를 표현한다.

|A| 밑줄 친 부분이 문장 안에서 명사, 형용사, 부사 중 어떤 역할을 하는지 쓰시오.

01 To collect luxury cars is Tom's dream. ________

02 The book is difficult for them to read. ________

03 My plan for winter vacation is to visit Hawaii. ________

04 He was to be an artist from birth. ________

05 It is common to get lost in an unfamiliar city. ________

06 My mom went to the grocery store to buy some fish. ________

07 I want to buy a pen to write with. ________

08 I don't know what to do. What should I do? ________

09 She went to the library to get the book. ________

10 The police promised to investigate the cause of the accident. ________

|B| 우리말과 같도록 괄호 안의 말과 to부정사를 이용하여 문장을 완성하시오.

01 우리는 크리스마스에 부산에서 만날 예정이다. (be, meet)

→ We ________________ in Busan on Christmas.

02 나는 런던에서 어디에서 머물지 결정했다. (decide, stay)

→ I ________________ in London.

03 너는 뜨거운 마실 무언가가 필요하다. (hot, drink, something)

→ You need ________________.

04 그는 함께 이야기할 동료가 필요하다. (a colleague, talk with)

→ He needs ________________.

05 나는 감기에 걸리지 않으려고 채소를 많이 먹는다. (catch a cold)

→ I eat a lot of vegetables ________________.

06 그 영어책을 읽는 것은 너에게 어렵다. (it, difficult, for you, read)

→ ________________ the English book.

UNIT 08 too ~ to부정사 / enough to부정사

〈too ~ to부정사〉를 〈so ~ that ... can't〉 구문으로 바꾸어 쓸 수 있어야 해요.

too ~ to ... (너무 ~해서 …할 수 없다/ …하기에는 너무 ~하다)	I was too tired to study.	나는 너무 피곤해서 공부할 수 없었다.
so ~ that ... can't (너무 ~해서 …할 수 없다)	= I was so tired that I couldn't study.	나는 너무 피곤해서 공부할 수 없었다.

주의 〈so ~ that ...〉 구문에서 that 이하는 시제와 문맥에 맞게 쓰세요.

〈~ enough+to부정사〉 역시 〈so ~ that ... can〉 구문으로 바꾸어 쓸 수 있어야 해요.

~ enough to ... (…하기에 충분히 ~하다)	He is smart enough to solve it.	그는 그것을 풀기에 충분히 똑똑하다.
so ~ that ... can (매우 ~해서 …하다)	= He is so smart that he can solve it.	그는 매우 똑똑해서 그것을 풀 수 있다.

|A| 괄호 안에서 알맞은 것을 고르시오.

01 The runner is (enough fast / fast enough) to win.

02 One day is (too / enough) short to fully enjoy the city.

03 He's healthy enough (running / to run) a marathon.

04 I'm (too / enough) tired to walk.

05 The girl is tall (too / enough) to ride the roller coaster.

06 Nick is so smart that he (can / can't) solve it.

07 He is (careful / carefully) enough to carry the glass vase.

08 She was so excited (it / that) she couldn't sleep.

09 The air was (too / so) thin that they couldn't breathe.

10 The sweater is (too / very) delicate to wash in a washing machine.

|B| 우리말과 같도록 괄호 안의 말을 이용하여 문장을 완성하시오.

01 그녀는 그 모든 질문에 대답할 만큼 충분히 현명하다. (enough, clever, answer)

→ She is ______________________________ all the questions.

02 그는 너무 걱정이 되어서 잠을 잘 수 없었다. (sleep, anxious, so, couldn't)

→ He was ______________________________.

03 나는 너무 피곤해서 집을 청소할 수 없다. (clean, too, tired)

→ I am ______________________________ the house.

04 지용이는 너무 이기적이어서 다른 사람을 돕지 못한다. (help, others, so, can't, selfish)

→ Jiyong is ______________________.

05 우리는 너무 늦게 잠자리에 들어서 일찍 일어나지 못했다. (late, early, get up, too)

→ We went to bed ______________________.

06 수지의 점수가 아주 높아서 반에서 1등을 할 수 있었다. (be, so, high, could)

→ Susie's grades were ______________________ the top student in her class.

|C| 다음 두 문장의 의미가 같도록 빈칸에 알맞은 말을 쓰시오.

01 We were so exhausted that we couldn't go up the stairs.

→ We were ______________________ the stairs.

02 The rules are too complicated for them to follow.

→ The rules are ______________________ them.

03 The research project was so good that it could win the prize.

→ The research project was ______________________ the prize.

04 The lecture was clear enough for us to understand.

→ The lecture was ______________________ it.

05 She is so shy that she can't talk to her classmates.

→ She is ______________________ her classmates.

06 The tablet computer is light enough for me to carry everywhere.

→ The tablet computer is ______________________ it everywhere.

|D| 다음 문장에서 어법상 어색한 부분을 찾아 바르게 고쳐 쓰시오.

01 My brother is so young that can't get a driver's license. ______________

02 The soup was too spicy that we couldn't eat it. ______________

03 The weather is cold enough freeze the river. ______________

04 The web site is enough interesting to attract many visitors. ______________

05 The heroes were too brave to save the world. ______________

내신기출 다음 빈칸에 공통으로 알맞은 말을 쓰시오.

- The cheetah is fast enough __________ catch a zebra.
- My brother was too short __________ reach the top shelf.

실전 TIP

'~하기에 충분히 빠르다'와 '너무 작아서 닿지 못하다'는 표현을 생각해 보세요.

UNIT 09 seem + to부정사

look과는 달리, seem(~로 보이다)은 to부정사를 보어로 취할 수 있다는 걸 알아 두세요.

seem의 보어	예문 (~로 / ~하게 보이다)	look과의 비교
명사	He seems (like) a nice person.	= looks like
형용사	He seems nice.	= looks
to부정사	He seems to be nice / to be a nice person.	* look은 to부정사를 보어로 쓰지 않음

〈seem+to부정사〉를 〈It seems that ~〉 문장으로 바꿀 때 시제에 주의해야 해요.

〈seem + to부정사〉		〈It seems that ~〉 문장으로 전환하는 법	
seem(s) 현재	to+동사원형	seem의 시제 =that절의 시제	He seems to know me. (나를 아는 거로 보인다) = It seems that he knows me.
seemed 과거			He seemed to know me. (나를 아는 거로 보였다) = It seemed that he knew me.
seem(s) 현재	to have+과거분사	that절의 시제는 seem의 시제보다 과거	He seems to have known me. (나를 알았던 거로 보인다) = It seems that he knew me.
seemed 과거			He seemed to have known me. (나를 알았던 거로 보였다) = It seemed that he had known me.

|A| 다음 두 문장의 의미가 같도록 괄호 안에서 알맞은 것을 고르시오.

01 You seem (like / to like) him. → It seems that you (like / to like) him.

02 He (seems / seemed) to know you. → It seemed that he (knew / knows) you.

03 Minji seems to (have / has) studied hard. → It seems that Minji (studies / studied) hard.

04 The lady seems to (have / has) been rich. → It seems that the lady (is / was) rich.

05 The children seemed to have (break / broken) the window.
→ It seemed that the children (have / had) broken the window.

|B| 우리말과 같도록 괄호 안의 말을 바르게 배열하여 문장을 완성하시오.

01 너는 지금 긴장되어 보인다. (to, be, nervous, seem)
→ You ______________________________ now.

02 그는 어제 아파 보였다. (that, was, sick, seemed, he)
→ It ______________________________ yesterday.

03 그 도둑이 그림을 훔쳤던 것으로 보였다. (that, had, the thief, seemed, stolen)
→ It ______________________________ the picture.

04 그녀는 그 과제를 완수했던 것으로 보인다. (she, that, completed, seems)

→ It ______________________ the assignment.

05 그들은 합의에 이르지 못했던 것으로 보인다. (that, they, reach, didn't, seems)

→ It ______________________ an agreement.

06 하민이는 그 질문을 이해한 것으로 보이지 않는다. (the question, to, understand)

→ Hamin doesn't seem ______________________.

07 그녀는 결과에 실망했던 것처럼 보인다. (been, have, with, disappointed)

→ She seems to ______________________ the results.

|C| **다음 두 문장의 의미가 같도록 빈칸에 알맞은 말을 쓰시오.**

01 You seem to be interested in learning how to ski.

→ It ______________________ learning how to ski.

02 It seems that Harin has something to say.

→ Harin ______________________.

03 All the servers seemed to be busy at the restaurant.

→ It ______________________ at the restaurant.

04 It seems that the detective found the evidence.

→ The detective ______________________.

05 The teacher seemed to have known what to do for students.

→ It ______________________ for students.

06 It seems that she majored in economics.

→ She ______________________.

|D| **다음 문장에서 어법상 어색한 부분을 찾아 바르게 고쳐 쓰시오.**

01 Susan seemed to studied science yesterday. ______________________

02 She didn't seem that she ate breakfast. ______________________

03 It didn't seem that he tells a lie. ______________________

04 He seems being interested in learning how to swim. ______________________

05 He doesn't seem to sleep well last night. ______________________

내신기출 다음 우리말과 같도록 빈칸에 알맞은 것은?

그들은 이전에 그 장소를 방문해 본 적이 있었던 것 같았다.

→ It seemed that they ____________ the place before.

① visit ② have visited ③ had visited

실전 TIP

주절의 시제와 종속절의 시제가 다르다는 것에 유의하여 정답을 고르세요.

UNIT 10 목적격보어로 쓰이는 to부정사

목적격보어로 to부정사를 쓰는 동사들을 외워 두세요.

어순	주어	to부정사를 목적격보어로 쓰는 5형식 동사	목적어	목적격보어(to부정사)
예문	I	want, ask, tell, expect, enable, allow, advice, order, get, help	him	to come.
의미	나는	~한다	~가/~에게	~하라고/~하기를/~하는 것을

주의 help는 목적격보어로 to부정사와 원형부정사 둘 다를 쓸 수 있어요.
She helped the children (to) make paper boats.

|A| 다음 문장의 밑줄 친 부분이 어법상 옳으면 ○표 하고, 틀리면 바르게 고쳐 쓰시오.

01 I want you to make a choice. ____________
02 The system enables us work faster. ____________
03 I helped my sister do her homework. ____________
04 We expected you spending more time with us. ____________
05 My mom doesn't allow me to go to PC rooms. ____________
06 He ordered them not to tell anyone what had happened. ____________
07 The taxi driver couldn't get his taxi starts this morning. ____________
08 A cup of warm milk will help you to sleep well. ____________

|B| 우리말과 같도록 괄호 안의 말을 활용하여 문장을 완성하시오.

advise, tell, allow, want, ask 동사는 목적격보어로 to부정사를 써요.

01 의사는 그에게 체중을 줄이라고 조언했다. (advise, lose, some weight)
→ The doctor ____________________.

02 선생님은 우리에게 그 책을 주의 깊게 읽으라고 말씀하셨다. (tell, read)
→ The teacher ____________________ the book carefully.

03 그 호텔은 손님들이 호텔 안에서 담배 피우는 것을 허락하지 않는다. (not, allow, smoke, the guests)
→ The hotel ____________________ inside the hotel.

04 우리는 네가 우리 상황을 이해하기를 원한다. (want, understand)
→ We ____________________ our situation.

05 그는 그 아이들에게 너무 많은 정크 푸드를 먹지 말라고 조언했다. (advise, not, eat, the children)
→ He ____________________ too much junk food.

06 그녀는 내게 소리를 줄여달라고 부탁했다. (ask, turn down)
→ She ____________________ the volume.

UNIT 11 목적격보어로 쓰이는 원형부정사 1 - 사역동사

사역동사는 목적격보어로 to가 없는 원형부정사(동사원형)를 쓴다는 것을 알아 두세요.

어순	주어	사역동사	목적어	목적격보어(원형부정사)
예문	I	make, have, let	him	come.
의미	나는	~시키다 / ~(놔)두다	~가/~에게	~하라고 / ~하도록

|A| 괄호 안에서 알맞은 것을 고르시오.

01 The doctor has him (work out / works out) regularly.

02 She asked her dad (give / to give) her a ride to school.

03 I'll make him (tell / to tell) the truth.

04 My friends always makes me (laugh / to laugh).

05 He let me (made / make) my own decision.

06 Some parents let their kids (do / to do) whatever they like.

07 I'll have someone (show / to show) you the shirt.

08 We bought some oranges (make / to make) juice.

09 The jacket makes you (look / looking) thinner and taller.

10 Ms. Kim wants us (learn / to learn) 5 new words every day.

|B| 우리말과 같도록 괄호 안의 말을 활용하여 문장을 완성하시오.

사역동사 make, have, let의 목적격보어로는 원형부정사를 써요.

01 폭우는 내가 학교에 지각하게끔 했다. (make, be late for school)

→ The heavy rain ________________________.

02 그는 그녀가 그 제안을 받아들이도록 시켰다. (have, accept)

→ He ________________________ the suggestion.

03 선생님은 우리가 수업 중에 먹도록 시키지 않으신다. (not, let, eat)

→ The teacher ________________________ in class.

04 나는 네가 그를 다시 만나지 않기를 원한다. (not, meet)

→ I want ________________________ him again.

05 그녀는 그녀의 아들들에게 잔디를 깎도록 시킨다. (have, mow, her sons)

→ She ________________________ the lawn.

06 광고들은 우리가 더 많은 제품을 사게 한다. (make, buy)

→ Advertisements ________________________ more products.

UNIT 12 목적격보어로 쓰이는 원형부정사 2 - 지각동사

목적격보어로 원형부정사 또는 현재분사(-ing)를 쓰는 지각동사들을 기억하세요.

어순	주어	지각동사	목적어	목적격보어
예문	I	feel, see, watch, hear, listen to, smell 등	him	come / coming.
의미	나는	느끼다, 보다, 듣다, 냄새 맡다 등	~가	~하는 것을

주의 보거나, 듣거나(지각) 할 당시, 목적어의 행동이 진행되고 있음을 나타낼 때 현재분사(-ing)를 써요.

I saw him draw. 나는 그가 그림을 그리는 걸 봤다.

I saw him drawing. 나는 그가 그림을 그리고 있는 것을 봤다.

|A| 괄호 안에서 알맞은 것을 고르시오.

01 She felt someone (touch / to touch) her back.

02 The doctor made me (take / to take) the medicine.

03 They heard someone (screaming / to scream).

04 She ordered them (not leave / not to leave) the room.

05 She watched the stranger (stand / to stand) under the tree.

06 He saw lots of birds (fly / to fly) to the south.

07 He smelled something (to burn / burning) in the kitchen.

|B| 빈칸에 괄호 안의 말을 알맞은 형태로 쓰시오.

01 She asked me ________________ the dishes. (wash)

02 Junho felt something ________________ on his arm. (crawl)

03 Michael watched the cat ________________ into the garden. (sneak)

04 He heard the dog ________________ all of a sudden. (bark)

05 The doctor advised me ________________ my teeth 3 times a day. (brush)

06 We saw the boy and the girl ________________ a bike near the lake. (ride)

07 Bill let his sister ________________ the book. (return)

내신 기출 괄호 안에 주어진 말을 빈칸에 알맞은 형태로 쓰시오.

- We felt the ground ________________. (shake)
- My mom doesn't let me ________________ there. (go)
- They allowed the boys ________________ in the park. (dance)

실전 TIP

목적격보어의 형태를 판단하기 위해서는 문장의 동사에 주의해야 해요.

UNIT 13 독립부정사

독립적인 부사 역할을 하는 to부정사 표현을 기억하세요.

to be honest	사실은	to make matters worse	설상가상으로
to sum up	요약하면	to make a long story short	간단히 말해서
to begin with	우선	so to speak	말하자면
to be sure	확실히	strange to say	이상한 이야기지만
to tell the truth	사실을 말하자면	needless to say	말할 필요도 없이
to be frank with you	솔직히 말하면	not to mention ~	~은 말할 것도 없이

|A| 괄호 안에서 알맞은 것을 고르시오.

01 (To / It) be honest, I can't remember what you said.

02 To make matters (worst / worse), the fine dust problem is getting serious.

03 To (sum / say) up, you must start exercising.

04 (Needless / Need) to say, they were shocked by the decision.

05 To begin (with / up), we haven't finished the report yet.

06 (Strange / Honest) to say, I like hot and humid weather.

07 He is a great actor, (not / so) to mention a talented singer.

08 To be frank with (me / you), it seems that he failed the test.

|B| 우리말과 같도록 빈칸에 알맞은 독립부정사 표현을 쓰시오.

부사처럼 문장 전체를 꾸며 주는 다양한 독립부정사 표현들을 알아두세요.

01 말하자면, 나의 개도 가족의 일부이다.

→ My dog is, ______________________________, a part of my family.

02 확실히, 영어를 배우는 데 문법은 중요하다.

→ ______________________________, grammar is important in learning English.

03 간단히 말해서, 우리는 사업에서 성공을 거뒀다.

→ ______________________________, we succeeded in business.

04 설상가상으로, 태풍이 접근하는 중이다.

→ ______________________________, a typhoon is approaching.

05 이상한 말이지만, 우리 중 누구도 그 실수를 알아채지 못했다.

→ ______________________________, none of us noticed the mistake.

06 요약하자면, 그 문제를 해결하는 데 2가지 방법이 있다.

→ ______________________________, there are 2 ways to solve the problem.

중간고사·기말고사 실전문제

객관식 (01~25) / 주관식 (26~50)

정답과 해설 • 24쪽

학년과 반 이름 객관식 / 25문항 주관식 / 25문항

01~03 다음 빈칸에 알맞은 것을 고르시오.

01

It's impolite __________ the teacher.

① not answer ② not answering
③ not to answer ④ to not answer
⑤ to not answering

02

The director got the actor ________ into the sea.

① jump ② jumping ③ jumped
④ to jump ⑤ to jumping

03

Fiona and Sam seem ________ nothing yesterday.

① to eat ② ate
③ to ate ④ to have eaten
⑤ to had eaten

04~05 다음 빈칸에 공통으로 알맞은 것을 고르시오.

04

- The weather was ________ nice that we could go on a picnic.
- I love my dog. ________ to speak, he is like one of my brothers.

① that ② so ③ very
④ as ⑤ too

05

- My neighbor helped me ________ my backyard.
- Have you seen Mark ________ his room?

① clean ② to clean ③ cleaning
④ cleaned ⑤ to cleaning

06~08 다음 우리말을 영어로 바르게 나타낸 것을 고르시오.

06

좋은 아이디어를 제안할 창의적인 사람이 있나요?

① Is there suggesting good ideas creative anyone?
② Is there anyone to suggest good ideas creative?
③ Is there anyone creative to suggest good ideas?
④ Is there creative anyone to suggest good ideas?
⑤ Is there anyone creative suggest good ideas?

07

신호가 언제 경주를 시작할지 알려 준다.

① The signal tells you when start the race.
② The signal tells you when should start the race.
③ The signal tells you when you start the race.
④ The signal tells you when start to the race.
⑤ The signal tells you when to start the race.

08 그 젊은이는 행복하기 위해 열심히 노력한다.

① The young man try hard to be happy.
② The young man tries hard to happy.
③ The young man tries hard to be happy.
④ The young man tried hard to happy.
⑤ The young man tried hard to be happy.

09~10 다음 우리말을 영어로 바르게 나타낸 것을 모두 고르시오.

09 나는 너무 아파서 학교에 갈 수 없었다.

① I was too sick not to go to school.
② I was too sick to go to school.
③ I was too sick that I went to school.
④ I was so sick I could go to school.
⑤ I was so sick that I couldn't go to school.

10 그는 그 소파를 어디에 둘지 결정했다.

① He decided where to place the sofa.
② He decided where to placing the sofa.
③ He decided where should he place the sofa.
④ He decided where he should place the sofa.
⑤ He decided where should place the sofa.

11~12 다음 중 어법상 어색한 것을 고르시오.

11 ① It is hard for him to persuade the professor.
② It is fun for me to watch the movies.
③ It is good of you to get some fresh air.
④ It's rude of her to yell at her grandparents.
⑤ It's foolish of them to believe the story is real.

12 ① My teacher wants me stay in the classroom.
② To take care of a baby is not easy work.
③ His job is to listen to customers' complaints.
④ The reporters promised not to take pictures of her.
⑤ My sister got me to talk to the counselor.

13~14 다음 중 어법상 옳은 것을 고르시오.

13 ① I bought my dog a toy to play.
② Do you have a pen to write?
③ They have no house to live.
④ Elderly people need some friends to talk.
⑤ Eddie may have a serious story to tell.

14 ① He explained it too short to understanding.
② I'm not sure when I should to call her.
③ Homeless people are worried about where to sleep in winter.
④ She is to seeing a doctor at 6 o'clock tomorrow.
⑤ The room is large enough held an event.

15 다음 밑줄 친 부분의 의미로 가장 알맞은 것은?

<u>You are to wait here</u> until I come back. Don't go anywhere.

① You must wait here
② You can wait here
③ You want to wait here
④ You are planning to wait here
⑤ You might wait here

16~17 다음 중 밑줄 친 부분의 쓰임이 나머지 넷과 다른 것을 고르시오.

16 ① My family is to travel to Europe someday.
② Kids are to listen to their parents until they become adults.
③ He is to eat dinner after he finishes his homework.
④ Alan is to meet his friend this weekend to play baseball.
⑤ The store is to be closed this week because of the storm.

17 ① The boy I taught grew up to be a famous composer.
② Kate prepared some food to serve the guest.
③ My uncle stopped smoking to be healthy when he gets older.
④ He drank a lot of coffee not to fall asleep.
⑤ The girls are selling cookies to raise money.

18~19 다음 주어진 문장과 의미가 같은 것을 고르시오.

18

He is so tall that he can reach the ceiling.

① He is too tall to reach the ceiling.
② He is too tall that reach the ceiling.
③ He is tall enough to reach the ceiling.
④ He is enough tall to reach the ceiling.
⑤ He is tall to reach ceiling enough.

19

The detective seems to have known the thief.

① It seems that the detective knows the thief.
② It seems that the detective knew the thief.
③ It seems that the detective known the thief.
④ It seemed that the detective knew the thief.
⑤ It seemed that the detective had known the thief.

20~21 다음 빈칸에 알맞은 말이 바르게 짝지어진 것을 고르시오.

20

• Strange ________, I sometimes hear a voice out of nowhere. • The hallway is ________ to walk through. Even a small child can't pass.

① saying – so narrow
② saying – narrow enough
③ say – too narrow
④ to say – narrow enough
⑤ to say – too narrow

21

• It's polite ________ you not to speak loudly in public. • He will never find out how ________ the riddle. • Robert went to bed early last night. He seemed ________ tired.

① to – should solve – to be
② of – should solve – to have been
③ of – to solve – to have been
④ for – to solve – to be
⑤ for – to solve – was

22 다음 대화의 빈칸에 알맞은 것은?

> A: May I help you?
> B: Yes, I'm looking for a denim skirt.
> A: How about this one? You can try it on.
> B: I think ________________. Do you have this in a larger size?
> A: I'm sorry. This is the only size we have.

① it's small enough for me to fit in
② it's too small for me to fit in
③ it's so small that I can fit in
④ it's too big for me to fit in
⑤ it's so big that I can't fit in

23 다음 중 어법상 <u>어색한</u> 문장의 개수는?

> ⓐ There is an interesting topic to talk.
> ⓑ It's careless of her not to clean the dirt right away.
> ⓒ To memorize numbers are not easy.
> ⓓ He woke up early enough to eat breakfast.

① 없음　② 1개　③ 2개
④ 3개　⑤ 4개

24 다음 중 어법상 옳은 문장의 개수는?

> ⓐ They worked hard enough to achieve their goals.
> ⓑ It's generous of her to forgive her brother for his mistake.
> ⓒ What I like to do in summer is to lying on the beach.
> ⓓ He smelled something burning in the kitchen.

① 없음　② 1개　③ 2개
④ 3개　⑤ 4개

25 다음 중 어법상 옳은 문장끼리 바르게 짝지은 것은?

> ⓐ Could you tell me what to make pasta?
> ⓑ We will go slowly to begin with.
> ⓒ David chose to not go to college.
> ⓓ We are looking for the house to move.
> ⓔ It is nice of you to lend me your new laptop.

① ⓐ, ⓑ　② ⓑ, ⓓ　③ ⓑ, ⓔ
④ ⓑ, ⓓ, ⓔ　⑤ ⓒ, ⓓ, ⓔ

〈다음부터는 서술형 주관식 문제입니다.〉

26~27 다음 문장의 밑줄 친 부분이 어법상 맞으면 ○표 하고, <u>틀리면</u> 바르게 고쳐 쓰시오.

26 Tom invited me <u>come</u> to his birthday party.

→ ________________

27 The princess <u>was to die</u> of eating a poisoned apple.

→ ________________

28~30 다음 문장에서 어법상 <u>어색한</u> 부분을 찾아 바르게 고쳐 쓰시오.

28 The medical team had lots of patient to take care.

________ → ________

29 Ms. Brown told her students paying attention to her.

________ → ________

30 It's important of him to take his medicine on time.

_______________ → _______________

31~33 다음 우리말과 같도록 괄호 안의 말을 활용하여 빈칸을 완성하시오.

31

심판은 그가 경기장 밖으로 나가는 것을 허락했다. (go out)

→ The referee allowed him ________ ________ ________ of the field.

32

Jim은 잠에서 깨어 그것이 단지 꿈이었다는 것을 깨달았다. (realize)

→ Jim woke up ________ ________ it was only a dream.

33

그 토끼는 너무 빨리 달려서 잡을 수 없었다. (fast)

→ The rabbit ran ________ ________ ________ catch it.

34~36 다음 우리말과 같도록 괄호 안의 말을 바르게 배열하여 문장을 완성하시오.

34

감기에 안 걸리려면 더 따뜻한 옷을 입어야 한다. (should, get a cold, not, clothes, are, wear, to, you, warmer)

→ If you ______________________________.

35

다음에 무엇을 고를지 내게 알려 주세요. (know, next, to, let, what, me, choose)

→ Please, ______________________________.

36

매일 아침 일찍 일어나다니, 그는 틀림없이 성실하다. (to, early, get up, sincere, morning, every)

→ He must be ______________________________
______________________________.

37~39 다음 주어진 문장과 의미가 같도록 빈칸을 완성하시오.

37

To pronounce some French words is very tricky.

→ It is ______________________________.

38

The Iron Man was strong enough to save the world.

→ The Iron Man was so ______________________________
______________________________.

39

It seemed that he had pretended to like me.

→ He seemed to ______________________________
______________________________.

40~42 다음 우리말과 같도록 괄호 안의 말을 활용하여 문장을 완성하시오.

40 다른 사람을 돕지 않다니, 그는 이기적이다. (selfish, help, others)

→ It is ______________________.

41 Steve는 앉을 무언가를 찾고 있었다. (look for, sit, something)

→ Steve ______________________.

42 이 주스는 마시기에 너무 시다. (taste, drink, sour, too)

→ This juice ______________________.

43~45 다음 대화의 밑줄 친 ⓐ~ⓕ 중 어법상 어색한 부분을 세 군데 찾아 바르게 고쳐 쓰시오.

A: ⓐ Do you know how get to the hotel?
B: No, I don't. Let's look it up on the map.
A: Hmm. ⓑ It's too far to walk from the station. Why don't we take a taxi?
B: ⓒ It only takes 20 minutes walking there. You once told me ⓓ you wanted go on a diet. ⓔ You should walk more to lose weight.
A: Okay. ⓕ It's nice of you to remember what I said.

43 ____________ → ____________

44 ____________ → ____________

45 ____________ → ____________

46~48 다음 글의 밑줄 친 ⓐ~ⓕ 중 어법상 어색한 부분을 세 군데 찾아 바르게 고쳐 쓰시오.

ⓐ Peter is to give a speech at the graduation ceremony next month. ⓑ He seems to be a little nervous, but I believe ⓒ he is enough brave to speak in front of the crowd. Also, ⓓ there's still a lot of time left for him to practice. ⓔ His family will be very proud see him speak, ⓕ to not mention his parents.

46 ____________ → ____________

47 ____________ → ____________

48 ____________ → ____________

49~50 다음 우리말을 주어진 |조건|에 맞게 바르게 영작하시오.

49 그는 며칠 동안 아팠던 것처럼 보였다.

|조건|
- 〈seem+to부정사〉를 사용할 것
- 단어 sick을 사용할 것
- 문장 전체를 10단어로 쓸 것

→ He ______________________ for a few days.

50 너는 다음 주까지 그 과제를 제출해야 한다.

|조건|
- 〈be동사+to부정사〉를 사용할 것
- 단어 turn in, the assignment를 사용할 것
- 문장 전체를 10단어로 쓸 것

→ ______________________ by next week.

CHAPTER

06 동명사와 분사

Unit 01 주어, 보어, 목적어로 쓰이는 동명사

Unit 02 동명사 vs. to부정사

Unit 03 동명사의 의미상 주어 & 부정

Unit 04 동명사의 시제와 수동태

Unit 05 동명사의 관용 표현

Unit 06 현재분사 vs. 과거분사

Unit 07 명사를 앞뒤에서 수식하는 분사

Unit 08 보어로 쓰이는 분사

Unit 09 감정을 나타내는 동사의 분사

Unit 10 동명사 vs. 현재분사

UNIT 01 주어, 보어, 목적어로 쓰이는 동명사

동사를 명사처럼 쓸 때는 동사를 to부정사로 만들거나 동명사(V-ing)로 만드세요.

동명사의 역할		주의
주어	Becoming a scientist takes years. 과학자가 되는 것은 수년이 걸린다.	– 동명사 주어는 단수 취급 – 전치사 뒤에 쓸 수 ○
보어	Her dream is becoming a scientist. 그녀의 꿈은 과학자가 되는 것이다.	
동사의 목적어	He enjoys talking with us. 그는 우리와 이야기하는 것을 즐긴다.	
전치사의 목적어	Thank you for inviting us. 우리를 초대해 준 것에 대해 감사드립니다.	

참고 전치사 뒤에는 to부정사를 쓸 수 없고, 동명사만 쓸 수 있어요.

to부정사만 목적어로 쓸 수 있는 동사들이 있듯이, 동명사만 목적어로 쓰는 동사들을 파악하세요.

enjoy (즐기다)	keep (계속 ~하다)	imagine (상상하다)	practice (연습하다)
avoid (피하다)	quit (그만두다)	deny (부정하다)	give up (포기하다)
finish (마치다)	mind (신경 쓰다)	suggest (제안하다)	stop (~하기를 멈추다)

|A| 다음 문장의 밑줄 친 동명사(구)가 무엇에 해당하는지 |보기|에서 찾아 쓰시오.

|보기|
주어: S　　보어: C　　목적어: O　　전치사의 목적어: P.O.

01 Reading is my hobby. ______
02 My dream is writing a book. ______
03 He enjoys skating. ______
04 Driving a car isn't easy. ______
05 She imagined becoming a singer. ______
06 We are good at fishing. ______
07 She doesn't mind studying here. ______
08 I considered quitting the job. ______
09 Singing on stage is my wish. ______
10 He gave up buying the car. ______
11 Thank you for inviting me. ______
12 They finally quitted smoking. ______

|B| 다음 문장의 밑줄 친 부분을 동명사구에 유의하여 우리말로 해석하시오.

01 Jogging every morning is not easy. ______
02 He considered studying abroad. ______
03 Their dream is traveling the universe. ______
04 She denied telling a lie. ______
05 My job is writing articles. ______
06 We don't mind using public transportation. ______

07 Susie could imagine being the winner. ____________

08 We gave up trying to persuade you. ____________

09 The customers didn't quit complaining. ____________

|C| 다음 문장에서 어법상 어색한 부분을 찾아 바르게 고쳐 쓰시오.

01 Lucy is very poor at cook. ____________

02 His goal is get a job. ____________

03 I gave up learned French. ____________

04 Wearing safety goggles are a must. ____________

05 Some of them are good at to make crafts. ____________

06 My injury prevented me from played tennis. ____________

07 By go to the gym 3 times a week, I lost some weight. ____________

08 Without say goodbye, he left the room. ____________

|D| 우리말과 같도록 괄호 안의 말을 활용하여 문장을 완성하시오.

01 그 수술은 Sarah가 죽는 것을 막았다. (prevent, from, die)

→ The surgery ____________ Sarah ____________.

02 내 목표는 국가대표로 선발되는 것이다. (be, chosen)

→ My aim is ____________ as a national representative.

03 그들은 잠시 기다리는 것을 꺼리지 않았다. (not, mind, wait)

→ They ____________ for a while.

04 늦어서 죄송합니다. (sorry, for, be)

→ I'm ____________ late.

05 환경을 보호하는 것에 대해 이야기해 봅시다. (talk about, the environment, protect)

→ Let's ____________.

실전 TIP

동명사구가 주어인지 보어인지 목적어인지 파악해야 해요.

내신기출 다음 중 밑줄 친 부분의 쓰임이 다른 하나는?

① She practiced playing the violin.

② His hobby is drawing cartoons.

③ We finished cleaning the classroom.

UNIT 02 동명사 vs. to부정사

동사별로 목적어로 to부정사를 쓸지, 동명사를 쓸지, 아니면 둘 다 쓸 수 있는지를 파악하세요.

to부정사만 목적어로 취하는 동사	want, wish, expect, hope, promise, need, plan, choose, decide, refuse, learn, agree
동명사만 목적어로 취하는 동사	enjoy, keep, imagine, practice, avoid, quit, deny, give up, finish, mind, suggest, stop, admit, consider
둘 다를 목적어로 취하는 동사	like, love, hate, prefer, begin, start, continue

목적어가 to부정사일 때와 동명사일 때 의미가 달라지는 동사에 주의하세요.

	to부정사	동명사
remember	I remember to call him. (전화해야 한다는 걸 기억한다)	I remember calling him. (전화했던 걸 기억한다)
forget	I forgot to call him. (전화해야 하는 걸 잊었다)	I forgot calling him. (전화했다는 걸 잊었다)
try	I tried to call him. (전화하려고 노력했다)	I tried calling him. (전화를 (한번) 시도해 봤다)
regret	I regret to call him. (전화하게 되어 유감이다[안타깝다])	I regret calling him. (전화했던 걸 후회한다)

주의 stop은 동명사를 목적어로 취하며, 〈stop+to부정사〉는 '~하기 위해 멈추다'라는 의미로 to부정사는 목적어가 아닌, '~하기 위해'라는 목적의 의미인 부사적 용법으로 쓰인 것임을 알아 두세요.
I stopped calling him. (전화하는 걸 그만뒀다) / I stopped to call him. (전화하기 위해 멈췄다)

|A| 다음 두 문장의 의미가 같도록 |보기|와 같이 바꾸어 쓰시오.

|보기|
I hate to talk about others. → I hate talking about others.

01 They prefer to travel by car. → They prefer ________________.

02 Sunmi began learning Japanese. → Sunmi began ________________ Japanese.

03 The babies started crying. → The babies started ________________.

04 The prices continue to increase. → The prices continue ________________.

05 Jiyu loves reading books. → Jiyu loves ________________ books.

06 They continued working after the break. → They continued ________________ after the break.

|B| 빈칸에 괄호 안의 동사를 알맞은 형태로 쓰시오.

01 Many children enjoy ________________ outdoors. (play)

02 The architect finished ________________ the building. (design)

03 The reporter avoids ________________ confusing words. (use)

04 The government needs ________________ taxes. (reduce)

05 The student strongly denied ________________ on the test. (cheat)

06 The vegetarian refused ________________ any meat. (eat)

07 We agreed ________________ at 10:00 in the morning. (start)

|C| 우리말과 같도록 괄호 안의 말을 활용하여 문장을 완성하시오.

01 나는 너에게 이야기했던 게 전혀 기억나지 않는다. (not, remember, talk)

→ I ________________________ to you at all.

02 그는 사람들 앞에서 울지 않으려고 애썼다. (try, not, cry)

→ He ________________________ in front of the people.

03 그들은 쉬려고 멈췄다. (stop, rest)

→ They ________________________.

04 그녀는 문을 잠그는 것을 깜빡했다. (forget, lock)

→ She ________________________ the door.

05 그 개는 땅을 파는 것을 멈췄다. (stop, dig)

→ The dog ________________________ in the ground.

06 너는 식료품점에 가야 할 것을 기억했니? (remember, go)

→ Did you ________________________ to the grocery store?

07 나는 시험 삼아 시합에 나갔다. (try, take part in)

→ I ________________________ the game.

〈remember+to부정사〉는 '~할 것을 기억하다'라는 뜻이고, 〈remember+동명사〉는 '~했던 것을 기억하다'라는 뜻이에요.

|D| 다음 문장에서 어법상 어색한 부분을 찾아 바르게 고쳐 쓰시오.

01 They regret to quit school so young. ________________

02 Don't you remember to post the letter yesterday? ________________

03 Jimin wished staying there forever. ________________

04 It stopped to snow. ________________

05 Beth practices to drive nowadays. ________________

06 I regret informing you that they are sold out. ________________

내신 기출 다음 빈칸에 공통으로 들어갈 수 없는 것은?

- I __________ taking part in various sports activities.
- I __________ to take part in various sports activities.

① like ② started ③ began ④ consider ⑤ continue

실전 TIP

동명사와 to부정사 모두를 목적어로 취할 수 없는 동사를 찾아보세요.

UNIT 03 동명사의 의미상 주어 & 부정

동명사의 의미상 주어(행위자)가 문장의 주어와 다를 경우, 소유격이나 목적격으로 동명사 앞에 쓰여요.

소유격 의미상 주어	Do you mind my turning on the TV? (내가 TV를 켜는 것)
	I'm proud of my sister's passing the exam. (내 여동생이 시험에 합격한 것)
목적격 의미상 주어	Do you mind me turning on the TV? (내가 TV를 켜는 것)
	I'm proud of my sister passing the exam. (내 여동생이 시험에 합격한 것)

참고 to부정사와 마찬가지로, 부정의 의미는 동명사 앞에 not이나 never를 써야 해요.
I'm sorry for **not** coming on time. (시간에 맞추어 오지 못한 것)
Wisdom is not in **never** making a mistake, but in **never** making the same one again.
지혜는 실수를 절대 하지 않는 것에 있는 것이 아니라, 같은 실수를 다시 하지 않는 것에 있다.

|A| 괄호 안에서 알맞은 것을 고르시오.

01 We're sorry for (aren't be / not being) on time.
02 She was worried about (not to finish / not finishing) the report.
03 We don't mind (you / yours) leaving early.
04 They are proud of their son (winning / a winner) the race.
05 She suggested (going not / not going) out this weekend.
06 They don't like (he / his) being late.
07 (She / Her) being lazy annoys her parents.
08 Are you sure of (they / their) coming tomorrow?
09 Do you mind (I / my) opening the window?

|B| 우리말과 같도록 괄호 안의 말을 활용하여 문장을 완성하시오.

동명사의 부정형은 〈not/never+동명사〉이며, 의미상 주어는 소유격이나 목적격으로 써요.

01 우리는 네가 무례하게 구는 것이 싫다. (be rude)
→ We hate ________________.

02 Jerome은 돈을 가지고 있지 않다는 것을 부인했다. (not, have)
→ Jerome denied ________________ money.

03 그 캠페인은 공기를 오염시키지 않는 것에 대한 것이다. (not, pollute the air)
→ The campaign is about ________________.

04 나는 네가 그 과정을 끝마친 것이 자랑스럽다. (complete the course)
→ I'm proud of ________________.

05 몇몇 학생은 대학에 지원하지 않는 것을 고려하는 중이다. (not, apply to a university)
→ Some students are considering ________________.

UNIT 04 동명사의 시제와 수동태

동명사의 시제가 문장의 시제보다 과거이면, 〈having + 과거분사〉로 써야 해요.

시제	동명사의 형태	예문	의미
현재	+단순 동명사(V-ing)	She denies being there.	= She denies that she is there. (거기 있다는 것을 부인한다)
과거		She denied being there.	= She denied that she was there. (거기 있었다는 것을 부인했다)
현재	+완료 동명사(having +과거분사)	She denies having been there.	= She denies that she was there. (거기 있었다는 것을 부인한다)
과거		She denied having been there.	= She denied that she had been there. (거기 있었다는 것을 부인했다)

주의 동명사의 의미가 수동이면, 〈being + 과거분사〉로 써야 해요.

Happiness comes more from loving(능동) than being loved(수동). (사랑하는 것으로부터 / 사랑받는 것보다)

|A| 주어진 문장과 의미가 같도록 빈칸에 알맞은 말을 쓰시오.

01 He denies being married. → He denies that he ________ married.

02 He denies having been married. → He denies that he ________ married.

03 She regrets not having tried hard. → She regrets that she ________ try hard.

04 She regretted not having tried hard. → She regretted that she ________ tried hard.

05 He is accused of having stolen a car. → He is accused because he ________ a car.

06 He was accused of having stolen a car → He was accused because he ________ a car.

|B| 우리말과 같도록 괄호 안의 말을 활용하여 문장을 완성하시오. (단, 동명사 형태로 쓸 것)

01 그녀는 사진 찍는 것을 즐기는 것 같다. (enjoy, take pictures)

→ She seems to ____________________.

02 식당에서는 서비스를 빨리 받는 것이 중요하다. (serve)

→ ____________________ quickly in a restaurant is important.

03 사람들은 비웃음 받는 것을 싫어한다. (hate, laugh at)

→ People ____________________.

04 나의 목표는 그 경기에 참가하도록 선발되는 것이다. (choose)

→ My goal is ____________________ to take part in the game.

05 나는 남의 도움을 받지 않는 편을 선호한다. (prefer, not, help)

→ I ____________________ by others.

UNIT 05 동명사의 관용 표현

동명사와 자주 쓰이는 관용 표현은 외워야 쓸 수 있어요.

go -ing	~하러 가다	be worth -ing	~할 가치가 있다
How[What] about -ing?	~하는 게 어때?	have trouble -ing	~하는 데 어려움이 있다
be busy -ing	~하느라 바쁘다	feel like -ing	~하고 싶다
spend+시간[돈]+-ing	시간[돈]을 ~하는 데 쓰다	It is no use -ing	~해 봐야 소용없다
look forward to -ing	~하기를 기대하다	on[upon] -ing	~하자마자 (= as soon as)
when it comes to -ing	~하는 것에 관한 한	cannot help -ing	~할 수밖에 없다
be[get] used to -ing	~에 익숙하다[익숙해지다]	There is no -ing	~할 수 없다
keep[prevent] ... from -ing	…가 ~하는 것을 막다	never ... without -ing	…하면 반드시 ~하다

주의 〈be used to+동사원형〉 ~하는 데 사용되다 / 〈used to+동사원형〉 ~하곤 했다

|A| 괄호 안에서 알맞은 것을 고르시오.

01 We (went / came) shopping for Chuseok.

02 I spent most of the weekend (reading / to read) novels.

03 When it comes to (teach / teaching) English, they are experts.

04 He is (watching / looking) forward to seeing his family.

05 The article is well (worth / worthy) reading.

06 Many people have trouble (finding / to find) a job.

07 My uncle was busy (did / doing) the project.

08 It is no (useful / use) crying over spilt milk.

09 Upon (reading / to read) the letter, she started crying.

10 We (couldn't / wouldn't) help changing the schedule.

|B| 우리말과 같도록 괄호 안의 말을 활용하여 문장을 완성하시오.

동명사와 함께 쓰는 다양한 관용 표현을 알아두세요.

01 그 식당은 방문할 만한 가치가 있다. (worth, visit)

→ The restaurant ______________________.

02 나는 무언가 따뜻한 것을 마시고 싶다. (feel, drink)

→ I ______________________ something warm.

03 그들은 서로 사랑에 빠지지 않을 수 없었다. (help, love)

→ They ______________________ each other.

04 나는 다음 달에 파리에 가는 것을 고대하고 있다. (look, go)

→ I am ______________________ to Paris next month.

05 그녀는 아침 식사로 우유 한 잔을 마시는 것에 익숙하다. (be, used, drink)

→ She ______________________ a cup of milk for breakfast.

06 공원에 도착하자마자 우리는 동물원으로 갔다. (upon, arrive)

→ ______________________ at the park, we went to the zoo.

|C| 다음 문장에서 어법상 어색한 부분을 찾아 바르게 고쳐 쓰시오.

01 I look forward to being inviting by you. ______________________

02 Some visitors had trouble find the exit. ______________________

03 The music is worth to listen to. ______________________

04 Who it comes to speaking in public, he is the best person. ______________________

05 We are looking forward to stay in the hotel. ______________________

06 The team members were busy to prepare the conference. ______________________

|D| 우리말과 같도록 괄호 안의 말과 |보기|에서 알맞은 표현을 골라 문장을 완성하시오.

|보기|

It is no use -ing　　be worth -ing　　can't help -ing　　spend ~ -ing

feel like -ing　　go -ing　　be used to -ing

01 나는 비밀을 말하지 않을 수 없었다. (tell, the secret)

→ I ______________________.

02 우리는 오늘 나가고 싶은 기분이 아니다. (go out)

→ We ______________________ today.

03 그 다큐멘터리는 볼 만한 가치가 있다. (see)

→ The documentary ______________________.

04 나는 언니와 수영하러 갈 계획이 있다. (a plan, swim)

→ I have ______________________ with my sister.

05 몇몇 십 대들은 컴퓨터 게임을 하는 데 너무 많은 시간을 쓴다. (too much time, play)

→ Some teenagers ______________________ computer games.

06 우리 강아지는 많은 사람과 함께 있는 데 익숙하다. (be with)

→ My dog ______________________ many people.

07 그 아이를 진정시키려 하는 것은 소용없었다. (calm down)

→ ______________________ the child.

내신 기출 다음 중 어법상 어색한 것은?

① We got used to living in the countryside.

② Scratching two stones was used to producing fire.

③ The new animal keeper was not used to dealing with the animals.

실전 TIP

〈be used to -ing〉의 의미인지 〈be used to+동사원형〉의 의미가 되어야 하는지 파악하세요.

UNIT 06 현재분사 vs. 과거분사

동사를 형용사(명사 수식, 보어 역할)처럼 쓰기 위해서는 현재분사나 과거분사로 만들어야 해요.

		현재분사	과거분사
형태		동사원형+-ing	과거분사형(-ed 또는 불규칙 형태)
의미		~하는(능동)	~된, ~당한(수동)
역할	명사 수식	falling leaves(떨어지는)	fallen leaves(떨어진)
	보어	The news is shocking.(충격적인)	People are shocked.(충격받은)

참고 현재분사형(V-ing)과 과거분사형(V-ed)은 여러 용도로 사용되는 점을 기억하세요.

V-ing		V-ed	
진행형	He is singing now.(노래하는 중이다)	수동태	The car is fixed.(고쳐지다)
동명사	Singing is fun.(노래하기는)	완료형	He has already fixed it.(이미 고쳤다)
현재분사	a singing bird(노래하는 새)	과거분사	the fixed car(고쳐진 차)

| A | 다음 문장의 밑줄 친 부분의 쓰임을 |보기|에서 골라 쓰시오.

|보기|
진행형 동명사 현재분사 수동태 완료형 과거분사

01 Answering the question is not easy. ______________
02 I was injured in the car accident. ______________
03 The running man on the street looks healthy. ______________
04 We were surprised at her being absent. ______________
05 He is painting the wall. ______________
06 I have heard the story before. ______________
07 The kids eating snacks are my brothers. ______________

| B | 빈칸에 괄호 안의 동사를 알맞은 형태로 쓰시오.

명사처럼 쓰여 주어, 보어, 목적어로 쓰는 동명사와 형용사처럼 쓰는 분사를 구분하세요.

01 Are you afraid of ______________ the truth? (speak)
02 They have ______________ doing the laundry. (finish)
03 The movie was very ______________. (interest)
04 The driver was ______________ for drunk driving. (arrest)
05 Nancy found a ______________ taxi in front of the station. (wait)
06 ______________ a good book gives me pleasure. (read)
07 All the windows were ______________. (close)
08 We're ______________ forward to ______________ from you soon. (look, hear)

UNIT 07 명사를 앞뒤에서 수식하는 분사

분사는 목적어나 부사(구)를 취할 수 있고, 이때 명사를 뒤에서 수식하는 것을 알아 두세요.

현재분사	명사 앞	Do you know the running dog? (달리고 있는 개)
	명사 뒤	Do you know the dog running in the park? (공원에서 달리고 있는 개)
과거분사	명사 앞	My uncle will fix the broken window. (깨진 창)
	명사 뒤	My uncle will fix the window broken by the boy. (소년에 의해 깨진 창)

|A| 다음 문장의 밑줄 친 부분이 수식하는 명사를 찾아 쓰고, 그 뜻을 우리말로 쓰시오.

01 Don't wake up the sleeping baby. ______________

02 The damaged parts were replaced. ______________

03 I knocked on the closed door. ______________

04 The stolen car hasn't been found. ______________

05 There is a baby sleeping on the bed. ______________

06 We can see many flying insects in summer. ______________

07 Some herbs were used to treat burned skin. ______________

08 The police looked for the car stolen last week. ______________

|B| 괄호 안의 말을 알맞은 분사 형태로 바꾸어 쓰고, 분사가 수식하는 말을 찾아 쓰시오.

01 The man (lead) the group is George. ______________

02 They tried to restore the (delete) files. ______________

03 The fence (surround) the building is very tall. ______________

04 We carefully planned a (relax) vacation. ______________

05 The homework (make) us busy will be done tomorrow. ______________

06 People (gather) outside the City Hall building were reporters. ______________

07 The song (compose) by him is very popular. ______________

08 Anyone (interest) in science can come to the class. ______________

내신기출 다음 중 어법상 어색한 것은?

① Look at the kite flown in the air!

② They tried to open the door locked by you.

③ The bike damaged by the accident will be repaired.

실전 TIP

분사와 분사가 꾸며 주는 명사의 관계가 능동인지 수동인지 확인해 보세요.

UNIT 08 보어로 쓰이는 분사

분사를 형용사처럼 보어로 쓸 때, 주어나 목적어와의 관계가 능동인지 수동인지 파악하세요.

주격 보어	현재분사	The news is surprising. (놀라게 하는, 놀라운)	news = surprising 관계
	과거분사	We are surprised by the news. (놀람을 당한, 놀란)	We = surprised 관계
목적격 보어	현재분사	I heard someone calling my name. (부르는)	someone = calling 관계
	과거분사	I heard my name called. (불려지는)	my name = called 관계

|A| 다음 문장의 밑줄 친 보어가 설명하는 말을 찾아 쓰시오.

01 The new online game is exciting. ______________

02 He is known for his knowledge. ______________

03 I heard the song sung by them. ______________

04 She heard the boy playing the piano. ______________

05 We were excited about the trip. ______________

06 He heard someone knocking on the door. ______________

07 Our achievement is astonishing. ______________

08 They saw a tree fallen on the ground. ______________

09 We found one box covered with dust. ______________

10 She was surprised at his words. ______________

11 I saw some bees flying around the flowers. ______________

12 They became bored with the lecture. ______________

|B| 우리말과 같도록 괄호 안의 말을 알맞은 분사 형태로 고쳐 쓰고, 분사가 설명하는 말을 찾아 쓰시오.

01 나는 해변이 사람들로 붐비는 것을 보았다.

→ I saw the beach (crowd) with people. ______________

02 그들의 모험은 매우 짜릿했다.

→ Their adventure was very (thrill). ______________

03 증인은 용의자가 버스에 타는 것을 보았다.

→ The witness saw the suspect (take) a bus. ______________

04 나는 엄마가 전화로 이야기하는 것을 들었다.

→ I heard my mom (talk) on the phone. ______________

05 그 실종된 아이는 역에서 발견되었다.

→ The missing child was (discover) in the station. ______________

UNIT 09 감정을 나타내는 동사의 분사

감정 동사를 분사로 만들 때, 감정을 유발하는지, 느끼는지를 판단하여 분사의 형태를 결정하세요.

감정을 표현하는 동사	감정을 유발 → 현재분사	감정을 느낌 → 과거분사
interest(흥미를 끌다)	interesting(흥미를 갖게 하는)	interested(흥미를 느끼는)
excite(신나게 하다)	exciting(신나게 하는)	excited(신이 난)
tire(피곤하게 하다)	tiring(피곤하게 하는)	tired(피곤한)
shock(충격을 주다)	shocking(충격적인)	shocked(충격을 받은)
move(감동시키다)	moving(감동적인)	moved(감동한)
disappoint(실망시키다)	disappointing(실망스러운)	disappointed(실망한)
confuse(혼란시키다)	confusing(혼란스럽게 하는)	confused(혼란스러운)
frighten(겁먹게 하다)	frightening(겁먹게 하는)	frightened(겁먹은)
puzzle(당황하게 하다)	puzzling(당황하게 하는)	puzzled(당황한)
satisfy(만족시키다)	satisfying(만족시키는)	satisfied(만족한)
surprise(놀라게 하다)	surprising(놀라게 하는[놀라운])	surprised(놀란)
bore(지루하게 하다)	boring(지루하게 만드는)	bored(지루함을 느끼는)
please(기쁘게 하다)	pleasing(기쁨을 주는)	pleased(기쁜)
embarrass(당황하게 하다)	embarrassing(당황하게 하는)	embarrassed(당황한, 난처한)
amaze(놀라게 하다)	amazing(놀라운)	amazed(놀란)
fascinate(매료시키다)	fascinating(매력적인)	fascinated(매료된)
depress(우울하게 하다)	depressing(우울하게 만드는)	depressed(우울해진)
relax(느긋하게 쉬다)	relaxing(느긋하게 해 주는)	relaxed(느긋한, 편안한)

|A| 괄호 안에서 알맞은 것을 고르시오.

01 It is (tiring / tired) work.

02 The audience was (moving / moved) by the speech.

03 The (disappointing / disappointed) customers will never return.

04 They were deeply (shocking / shocked) by his death.

05 The results are (disappointing / disappointed).

06 The kid was (exciting / excited) about the birthday party.

07 The police delivered the (shocking / shocked) news.

08 We're (tiring / tired) after running.

09 Let's do something (exciting / excited).

|B| 빈칸에 괄호 안의 동사를 알맞은 형태로 쓰시오.

01 The rules are ___________. (confuse)

02 We were ___________ by the rules. (confuse)

03 The fans were ___________ with the baseball game. (bore)

04 The baseball game was ___________. (bore)

05 His answer was ___________. (amaze)

06 The teacher was ___________ by his answer. (amaze)

07 He was ___________ by driving to Busan. (exhaust)

08 Driving to Busan was ___________. (exhaust)

09 She was ___________ about the result. (depress)

10 The result was ___________. (depress)

|C| 우리말과 같도록 밑줄 친 동사를 알맞은 형태로 고쳐 쓰시오.

01 우리는 네가 곧 온다는 소식을 들어서 기쁘다.

→ We were please to hear you come soon. ___________

02 그 식당은 만족스러운 식사를 제공한다.

→ The restaurant offers a satisfy meal. ___________

03 그들은 그 배우의 연기에 감동을 받았다.

→ They were move by the actor's performance. ___________

04 우리는 그 충격적인 소문 때문에 깜짝 놀랐다.

→ We were surprise at the shock rumor. ___________

|D| 우리말과 같도록 괄호 안의 말을 바르게 배열하시오.

01 우리는 시험 결과를 받았을 때 당황스러웠다. (embarrassed, we, were, when, the test result, got)

→ We ___________________________.

02 이 책은 감동적인 이야기를 담고 있다. (has, stories, touching, this book)

→ ___________________________

03 여행이 취소되어서 우리는 실망스러웠다. (because, disappointed, were, the trip, was, canceled)

→ We ___________________________.

내신기출 다음 빈칸에 들어갈 interest의 형태가 다른 하나는?

① Her fashion is really ___________.
② She was always ___________ in arts.
③ The list includes many ___________ books.
④ The recently published book is ___________.
⑤ There are many ___________ places in the country.

실전 TIP

흥미를 갖게 하는 것인지, 흥미를 느끼는 사람인지를 구분해 보세요.

UNIT 10 동명사 vs. 현재분사

현재분사와 동명사는 형태가 같아서, 문맥상 그 쓰임과 의미를 구분할 수 있어야 해요.

	현재분사	동명사
명사 앞	running man (뛰고 있는 남자) washing woman (세탁하고 있는 여자)	running shoes (달리기 신발) *뛰고 있는 신발(×) washing machine (세탁기) *세탁하고 있는 기계(×)
be동사의 보어	The news is surprising. (소식은 놀랍다) The movie was boring. (영화는 지루하다)	My hobby is dancing. (취미는 춤추기이다) The plan is going to Jeju. (계획은 가는 것이다)

참고 용도를 나타내는 동명사에는 다음과 같은 것들이 있어요.
shopping bag(쇼핑백) / sleeping bag(침낭) / waiting room(대기실) / fitting room(탈의실)

|A| 다음 문장의 밑줄 친 부분이 동명사인지 현재분사인지 쓰시오.

01 She is swimming in the pool. ______

02 He held a sleeping baby. ______

03 The meeting room is on the 3rd floor. ______

04 He gave me a shopping bag. ______

05 Swimming is one of my hobbies. ______

06 I was running when you called me. ______

07 Look at the birds singing in the trees. ______

08 She usually goes shopping with her dad. ______

|B| 다음 문장의 -ing의 역할에 유의하여 밑줄 친 부분을 우리말로 해석하시오.

01 My dream is becoming a police officer. ______

02 Some passengers are in the waiting room. ______

03 The woman wearing a white jacket is my aunt. ______

04 You'd better bring drinking water. ______

05 He told me a fascinating story. ______

06 We listened to the shocking news. ______

07 I bought a pair of running shoes. ______

08 A few people were running to the bus stop. ______

내신 기출 다음 중 밑줄 친 부분의 쓰임이 다른 하나는?

① The dancing girls are ballerinas.
② You need a sleeping bag for camping.
③ She wants to buy a new swimming suit.

실전 TIP
밑줄 친 부분과 그 뒤에 나오는 명사와의 관계를 파악해 보세요.

중간고사·기말고사 실전문제

객관식 (01~25) / 주관식 (26~50)

학년과 반 　 이름 　 객관식 / 25문항 　 주관식 / 25문항

01~03 다음 빈칸에 알맞은 것을 고르시오.

01

The witness could remember ________ the robber at the crime scene.

① see ② seeing ③ to see
④ saw ⑤ seen

02

Do you think your new car was worth ________?

① buy ② bought ③ buying
④ to buy ⑤ to buying

03

Children are looking at their kites ________ in the sky.

① fly ② flew ③ flown
④ flying ⑤ to fly

04~05 다음 빈칸에 알맞지 않은 것을 고르시오.

04

No one ________ to do a dangerous job.

① likes ② enjoys ③ prefers
④ wants ⑤ hopes

05

All of them ________ learning how to drive a car.

① began ② kept ③ refused
④ quit ⑤ gave up

06~08 다음 우리말을 영어로 바르게 나타낸 것을 고르시오.

06

나는 그녀가 많이 아프다고 듣게 되어 유감이다.

① I regret to hearing that she is seriously ill.
② I regret hear that she is seriously ill.
③ I regret to hear that she is seriously ill.
④ I regret heard that she is seriously ill.
⑤ I regret hearing that she is seriously ill.

07

신나는 음악은 그를 거리에서 계속 춤추게 했다.

① The exciting music kept him dancing in the street.
② The excited music kept him dancing in the street.
③ The exciting music kept him dance in the street.
④ The excited music kept him from dancing in the street.
⑤ The exciting music kept him from dancing in the street.

08 그 배우는 사람들의 관심을 받는 것에 익숙하다.

① The actor used to getting people's attention.
② The actor used to get people's attention.
③ The actor is used to get people's attention.
④ The actor is used getting people's attention.
⑤ The actor is used to getting people's attention.

09~10 다음 중 어법상 어색한 것을 고르시오.

09 ① All of my classmates agreed to buy the teacher a present.
② Andy decided to become an architect.
③ Irene loves to take care of stray cats.
④ They began to run away from the monster.
⑤ He quit to drink alcohol after heart surgery.

10 ① Have you ever imagined traveling into space?
② She spent too much time shopping online.
③ The squirrels were busy to collect acorns in the woods.
④ Can you hear the sound coming from the roof?
⑤ The language he uses is spoken in a small region of China.

11 다음 중 어법상 어색한 것을 모두 고르면?

① Some children have trouble reading books.
② It's no use saying sorry to her. She won't forgive you.
③ A lot of people go to camp to the mountains on their holidays.
④ Did Andrew spend all of his money to buy a car?
⑤ We can't reach our goal, but it's still worth trying.

12~13 다음 중 어법상 옳은 것을 고르시오.

12 ① They looked forward to visit their relatives in London.
② What about drinking some tea and go to bed?
③ Upon taking a shower, Anne went to bed.
④ We cannot help to love this cute puppy.
⑤ Will you go to hike with me this weekend?

13 ① The woman was surprised at the news and screamed loudly.
② What was the most embarrassed moment in your life?
③ What an interested story you told me!
④ The concept he explained to us is still confused.
⑤ Dogs don't get boring with the same old toys.

14 다음 중 어법상 옳은 것을 모두 고르면?

① The man stood in the corner gave me this.
② The passengers couldn't read the sign writing in Chinese.
③ Watch out for the pieces of breaking glass on the floor.
④ I can't be friends with a person lying to me.
⑤ You should do the remaining homework tomorrow.

15 다음 중 우리말 해석이 잘못된 것은?

① She tried shooting the ball, but the ball didn't go into the basket.
→ 그녀는 공을 던져봤지만, 공은 바구니에 들어가지 않았다.
② She clearly remembers to call her daughter in Canada at 2 a.m.
→ 그녀는 새벽 2시에 캐나다에 있는 그녀의 딸에게 전화했던 것을 분명히 기억한다.
③ The police kept him from committing another crime.
→ 경찰은 그가 또 다른 범죄를 저지르는 것을 막았다.
④ The cars stopped to let the ambulance pass through the road.
→ 구급차가 도로를 통과하도록 차들이 멈췄다.
⑤ He regretted not participating in the group activity.
→ 그는 단체 활동에 참여하지 않은 것을 후회했다.

16~17 다음 중 밑줄 친 부분의 쓰임이 나머지 넷과 다른 하나를 고르시오.

16 ① Kids are talented at learning languages.
② The lecture was about recycling waste.
③ We have never seen his smiling face.
④ She stopped dating him because he lied.
⑤ Playing the guitar is one of my hobbies.

17 ① Can you see the boy saying hello to us?
② The company has achieved satisfying results.
③ The crying baby crawled to his mom.
④ The man performing on stage was my uncle.
⑤ Mary always likes helping other people.

18~19 다음 주어진 문장과 의미가 같은 것을 고르시오.

18

The man denies having cried alone.

① The man denies to cry alone.
② The man denies crying alone.
③ The man denies that he cries alone.
④ The man denies that he cried alone.
⑤ The man denies to have cried alone.

19 Do you mind him asking questions?

① Do you mind if I ask him questions?
② Do you mind if he asks you questions?
③ Do you mind if you ask him questions?
④ Do you mind to ask questions of him?
⑤ Do you mind asking him questions?

20~21 다음 빈칸에 알맞은 말이 바르게 짝지어진 것을 고르시오.

20 She often enjoys ________ on ________ leaves on the street in autumn.

① step – falling
② stepping – fallen
③ stepping – falling
④ to step – fallen
⑤ to step – fell

21
- Getting along with strangers ________ not very difficult for me.
- The girl imagined ________ by her favorite singer.
- There are some ________ goods to be repaired in the box.

① are – to be loved – damaging
② is – being loved – damaging
③ is – being loved – damaged
④ is – to be loved – damaged
⑤ are – loving – damaged

22 다음 대화의 빈칸에 알맞은 것은?

A: How can I get to City Hall?
B: Go straight, and turn left on Baker Street. You should ____________, or you will go in the opposite direction.

① remember turning left
② remember to turn right
③ remember not to turn left
④ remember not to turn right
⑤ remember not turning right

23 다음 중 어법상 어색한 문장의 개수는?

ⓐ Animal protection can be a fascinated subject to discuss.
ⓑ They were afraid of being caught by the enemy.
ⓒ He refused accepting the truth.
ⓓ She admitted copying someone else's design.

① 없음 ② 1개 ③ 2개
④ 3개 ⑤ 4개

24 다음 중 어법상 옳은 문장의 개수는?

ⓐ How often do you practice to play drums?
ⓑ Can you smell something burned?
ⓒ Athletes are usually exhausting after the race.
ⓓ We are fond of his making funny faces.

① 없음 ② 1개 ③ 2개
④ 3개 ⑤ 4개

25 다음 중 어법상 옳은 문장끼리 바르게 짝지은 것은?

ⓐ When it comes to deal with customers, no one can beat Jackson.
ⓑ The lady choosing among the many princesses will marry the prince.
ⓒ Why does everyone avoid working with Mr. Johns?
ⓓ Nora looked so shocked to hear about her husband's accident.
ⓔ He is considering changing the curtains in the living room.

① ⓐ, ⓑ　② ⓑ, ⓓ
③ ⓑ, ⓔ　④ ⓑ, ⓓ, ⓔ
⑤ ⓒ, ⓓ, ⓔ

〈다음부터는 서술형 주관식 문제입니다.〉

26~27 다음 문장의 밑줄 친 부분이 어법상 맞으면 ○표 하고, 틀리면 바르게 고쳐 쓰시오.

26 My colleague suggested <u>to take</u> a break during the meeting.

→ ____________

27 His wife doesn't like <u>his eating</u> at midnight.

→ ____________

28~29 다음 괄호 안의 말을 빈칸에 알맞은 형태로 고쳐 쓰시오.

28 We saw a woman ____________ to a hospital in an ambulance. (take)

29 Tim forgot ____________ his phone, so it will run out of power soon. (charge)

30~31 다음 문장에서 어법상 어색한 부분을 찾아 바르게 고쳐 쓰시오.

30 Do you know the title of the new song singing by Lady Gaga?

____________ → ____________

31 She regretted to open the box when she saw a pile of trash inside it.

____________ → ____________

32~35 다음 우리말과 같도록 괄호 안의 말을 빈칸에 알맞은 형태로 쓰시오.

32

그 아이는 불을 켠 채로 잠이 들었다. (turn on)

→ The child fell asleep with the light ________ ________.

33

아침을 먹자마자, 우리는 공항으로 출발했다. (have)

→ On ________ breakfast, we left for the airport.

34

그 변호사는 그녀가 벌을 받지 않을 것을 확신한다. (punish)

→ The lawyer is sure of her ________ ________ ________.

35

우리가 라디오 소리를 키워도 괜찮을까요? (turn up)

→ Would you mind us ________ ________ the volume of the radio?

36~38 다음 우리말과 같도록 괄호 안의 말을 바르게 배열하시오.

36

오전 11시 이전에는 여기에 주차할 수 없다.
(is, 11 a.m., parking, no, before, there, here)

→ ________________________________

37

엄마를 찾는 한 소년에 대한 이야기는 매우 감동적이었다.
(his mom, moving, about, really, finding, a boy, was)

→ The story ________________________________
________________________________.

38

그녀는 아들의 말을 무시했던 것에 대해 미안해하고 있다.
(words, sorry, ignored, she, is, having, about, her son's)

→ ________________________________

39~42 다음 우리말과 같도록 괄호 안의 말을 활용하여 문장을 완성하시오.

39

그는 내일 양로원에 방문하기로 한 것을 기억하고 있니? (remember, the nursing home, visit)

→ ________________________________ tomorrow?

40

Ted는 그의 아버지가 음악가라는 것을 자랑스러워한다. (be proud of, his father, be, a musician)

→ Ted ________________________________.

41

모든 사람들이 이국적인 풍경에 매료되었다. (fascinate, the exotic scenery, by)

→ Everyone ______________________.

42

경찰이 트럭 안에 숨겨진 단서를 발견했다. (the police, find, a clue, hide)

→ ______________________
in the truck.

43~45 다음 대화의 밑줄 친 ⓐ~ⓕ 중 어법상 어색한 부분을 세 군데 찾아 바르게 고쳐 쓰시오.

A: What's wrong? ⓐ You look embarrassing.
B: ⓑ I forgot to return this book to the library. It was due last Wednesday.
A: Oh, that book? ⓒ I remember you borrowing it 3 weeks ago. I recommended it. ⓓ Did you even finish reading it?
B: No. ⓔ I found it so bored after a couple of pages. So ⓕ I gave up to read it.
A: No way. That's disappointing! I really liked that book.

43 __________ → __________

44 __________ → __________

45 __________ → __________

46~48 다음 글의 밑줄 친 ⓐ~ⓕ 중 어법상 어색한 부분을 세 군데 찾아 바르게 고쳐 쓰시오.

ⓐ Not driving when you go to work give you many advantages. First of all, ⓑ you can enjoy reading books or to watch something fun. ⓒ You don't have to feel annoyed by other aggressive drivers. Also, ⓓ you don't need to be busy looking for a parking space. Finally, ⓔ you can save money spent on your car. Of course, it may be uncomfortable not to have a car for a while, but ⓕ you will get used to use public transportation soon.

46 __________ → __________

47 __________ → __________

48 __________ → __________

49~50 다음 우리말을 주어진 |조건|에 맞게 바르게 영작하시오.

49 그는 외식하는 것보다 집에서 요리하는 것을 선호한다.

|조건|
1. 동명사를 사용할 것
2. 단어 prefer, cook at home, eat out, to를 사용할 것
3. 8단어로 쓸 것

→ ______________________

50 우리는 그녀의 놀라운 공연을 보지 않을 수 없다.

|조건|
1. 동명사를 사용할 것
2. 단어 help, watch, amaze, performance를 사용할 것
3. 7단어로 쓸 것

→ ______________________

CHAPTER

07 비교 표현

UNIT 01 원급 비교

'~만큼 …한[하게]'은 〈as + 형용사/부사의 원급 + as〉로 표현하세요.

형용사	She is	as	kind	as	him[he is].
부사	She can swim		well		him[he can].

참고 〈as ~ as〉 뒤에는 목적격 대명사(him)나 〈주어(he)+동사(is[can])〉의 형태로 쓸 수 있어요.

부정문(~만큼 …하지 않은[않게])에서는 〈not as[so] + 형용사/부사의 원급 + as〉로 쓸 수 있어요.

형용사	She isn't	as[so]	kind	as	him[he is].
부사	She can't swim		well		him[he can].

|A| 우리말과 같도록 괄호 안의 말과 〈as ~ as〉 구문을 이용하여 문장을 완성하시오.

01 1월은 12월만큼 춥다. → January ____________________ December. (cold)

02 7월은 8월만큼 덥다. → July ____________________ August. (hot)

03 그는 Bill Gates만큼 부자가 아니다. → He ____________________ Bill Gates. (rich)

04 Tom은 Andy만큼 키가 크다. → Tom ____________________ Andy. (tall)

05 책상은 침대만큼 무겁지 않다. → The desk ____________________ the bed. (heavy)

06 너의 눈은 별만큼 빛난다. → Your eyes ____________________ stars. (bright)

07 민지는 David만큼 똑똑하다. → Minji ____________________ David. (smart)

08 그 책은 사전만큼 두껍지 않다. → The book ____________________ the dictionary. (thick)

|B| 다음 두 문장을 괄호 안의 말과 〈as ~ as〉 구문을 이용하여 한 문장으로 바꾸어 쓰시오.

'~만큼 …하다'는 의미는 〈as+형용사/부사의 원급+as〉로 나타내요.

01 The singer is popular. The actor is popular just like the singer.
→ The actor ____________________ the singer. (popular)

02 Rome is 20˚C now. Seoul is 10˚C today.
→ Seoul ____________________ Rome. (warm)

03 The gold ring is $100. The silver ring is $80.
→ The silver ring ____________________ the gold ring. (expensive)

04 A car can go 200 km per hour. A bike can go 30 km per hour.
→ A bike ____________________ a car can. (fast)

05 His first novel is not very famous. His second novel is really famous.
→ His first novel ____________________ his second novel. (famous)

06 Dogs are friendly. Cats are not very friendly.
→ Cats ____________________ dogs. (friendly)

UNIT 02 as+형용사/부사의 원급+as possible

〈as + 형용사/부사의 원급 + as〉를 이용한 다음 표현을 익혀 두세요.

as ~ as possible (가능한 한 ~하게)	Please call me as quickly as possible. (가능한 한 빨리)
	I tried to go there as often as possible. (가능한 한 자주)
as ~ as + 주어 + can[could] (주어가 …할 수 있는 만큼 ~하게)	Please call me as quickly as you can. (당신이 할 수 있는 만큼 빨리)
	I tried to go there as often as I could. (내가 할 수 있었던 만큼 자주)

주의 〈as ~ as〉 뒤에 〈주어+can[could]〉을 쓸 때 알맞은 주어와 시제로 쓰세요.

|A| 우리말과 같도록 괄호 안의 말을 바르게 배열하시오.

01 가능한 한 일찍 일어나다 (as, get up, early, as possible) → ______

02 당신이 할 수 있는 한 빨리 도착하다 (arrive, soon, as you can, as) → ______

03 가능한 한 많이 먹다 (much, eat, as, as possible) → ______

04 당신이 할 수 있는 한 빨리 걷다 (walk, as, as you can, fast) → ______

05 가능한 한 신속히 답장하다 (quickly, as, respond, as possible) → ______

06 당신이 할 수 있는 한 자주 방문했다 (as you could, often, visited, as) → ______

07 가능한 한 열심히 공부하다 (as possible, hard, as, study) → ______

|B| 다음 두 문장의 의미가 같도록 빈칸에 알맞은 말을 쓰시오.

01 Come home as early as possible.
→ Come home as early ______ ______ ______.

02 I made the riddle as easy as possible.
→ I made the riddle as easy ______ ______ ______.

03 Finish your homework as quickly as you can.
→ Finish your homework ______ quickly ______ ______.

04 She ran away as fast as possible.
→ She ran away as fast ______ ______ ______.

05 I help my parents as often as I can.
→ I help my parents ______ ______ ______ possible.

내신 기출 다음 우리말을 영작할 때, 어법상 어색한 부분을 찾아 바르게 고쳐 쓰시오.

그 외국인들은 할 수 있는 한 천천히 말했다.
→ The foreigners spoke as slowly as they can.

______

실전 TIP
시제가 일치되었는지 확인해 보세요.

UNIT 03 비교급과 최상급 만드는 법

형용사/부사의 비교급과 최상급을 만드는 방법을 알아 두세요.

형용사/부사의 형태		원급	비교급	최상급
대부분	-er / -est	tall	taller	tallest
-e로 끝남	-r / -st	nice	nicer	nicest
-y로 끝남	y를 삭제 -ier / -iest	early	earlier	earliest
〈단모음+단자음〉으로 끝남	끝자음 추가 -er / -est	hot	hotter	hottest
-ous, -ful, -ive, -ing 등으로 끝남	more / most+원급	famous exciting	more famous more exciting	most famous most exciting
〈형용사+ly〉 형태의 부사		slowly	more slowly	most slowly

〈명사+ly = 형용사〉는 y를 삭제하고 -ier / -iest를 붙여요.
friendly(친절한) – friendlier – friendliest / lovely(사랑스러운) – lovelier – loveliest

불규칙 변화하는 형용사/부사의 비교급과 최상급은 암기해야 해요.

원급	비교급	최상급
good(좋은) / well(잘)	better(더 좋은, 더 잘)	best(가장 좋은)
bad / ill(나쁜) / badly(나쁘게)	worse(더 나쁜)	worst(가장 나쁜)
many(수가 많은) / much(양이 많은)	more(더 많은)	most(가장 많은)
little(적은)	less(더 적은)	least(가장 적은)

A 빈칸에 단어의 비교급과 최상급을 쓰면서 외우세요.

01 능력 있는 able – ________ – ________
02 화난 angry – ________ – ________
03 나쁜 bad – ________ – ________
04 나쁘게 badly – ________ – ________
05 아름다운 beautiful – ________ – ________
06 큰 big – ________ – ________
07 따분한 boring – ________ – ________
08 용감한 brave – ________ – ________
09 밝은 bright – ________ – ________
10 바쁜 busy – ________ – ________
11 조심하는 careful – ________ – ________
12 주의 깊게 carefully – ________ – ________

13	(값이) 싼	cheap	–		–
14	깨끗한	clean	–		–
15	차가운	cold	–		–
16	편안한	comfortable	–		–
17	호기심이 많은	curious	–		–
18	위험한	dangerous	–		–
19	어두운	dark	–		–
20	깊은	deep	–		–
21	맛있는	delicious	–		–
22	어려운	difficult	–		–
23	근면한, 성실한	diligent	–		–
24	더러운	dirty	–		–
25	쉬운	easy	–		–
26	쉽게	easily	–		–
27	흥미로운	exciting	–		–
28	비싼	expensive	–		–
29	유명한	famous	–		–
30	빠른	fast	–		–
31	뚱뚱한	fat	–		–
32	유창하게	fluently	–		–
33	어리석은	foolish	–		–
34	신선한	fresh	–		–
35	상냥한	friendly	–		–
36	좋은	good	–		–
37	훌륭한	great	–		–
38	잘생긴	handsome	–		–
39	행복한	happy	–		–
40	어려운	hard	–		–
41	건강한	healthy	–		–
42	무거운	heavy	–		–
43	도움이 되는	helpful	–		–
44	높은	high	–		–

45	뜨거운	hot	– ______	– ______
46	아픈	ill	– ______	– ______
47	중요한	important	– ______	– ______
48	재미있는	interesting	– ______	– ______
49	친절한	kind	– ______	– ______
50	큰, 넓은	large	– ______	– ______
51	게으른	lazy	– ______	– ______
52	가벼운	light	– ______	– ______
53	양이 적은	little	– ______	– ______
54	긴	long	– ______	– ______
55	사랑스러운	lovely	– ______	– ______
56	낮은	low	– ______	– ______
57	운이 좋은	lucky	– ______	– ______
58	수가 많은	many	– ______	– ______
59	양이 많은	much	– ______	– ______
60	좋은	nice	– ______	– ______
61	시끄러운	noisy	– ______	– ______
62	나이 많은, 오래된	old	– ______	– ______
63	예의 바른	polite	– ______	– ______
64	가난한	poor	– ______	– ______
65	인기 있는	popular	– ______	– ______
66	예쁜	pretty	– ______	– ______
67	빨리	quickly	– ______	– ______
68	조용한	quiet	– ______	– ______
69	무례한	rude	– ______	– ______
70	슬픈	sad	– ______	– ______
71	안전한	safe	– ______	– ______
72	심각한, 진지한	serious	– ______	– ______
73	얕은	shallow	– ______	– ______
74	마른	skinny	– ______	– ______
75	느린	slow	– ______	– ______
76	천천히	slowly	– ______	– ______

77	작은	small	– ______	– ______
78	강한	strong	– ______	– ______
79	화창한	sunny	– ______	– ______
80	맛있는	tasty	– ______	– ______
81	끔찍한	terrible	– ______	– ______
82	두꺼운	thick	– ______	– ______
83	얇은	thin	– ______	– ______
84	못생긴	ugly	– ______	– ______
85	유용한	useful	– ______	– ______
86	약한	weak	– ______	– ______
87	잘	well	– ______	– ______
88	넓은	wide	– ______	– ______
89	현명한	wise	– ______	– ______
90	어린, 젊은	young	– ______	– ______

UNIT 04 비교급

비교 표현 '~보다 더 …한[하게]'은 〈비교급 + than〉으로 써야 해요.

비교 포인트	예문	의미
형용사 비교급 + than	She is taller than her mom.	그녀는 그녀의 엄마보다 더 키가 크다.
부사 비교급 + than	She can run faster than her dad.	그녀는 그녀의 아빠보다 더 빠르게 달릴 수 있다.

참고 '~보다 덜 …한[하게]'이라는 의미의 비교 표현은 〈less+원급+than〉으로 써요.

주의 비교급을 강조하여 '훨씬 더'라고 할 때, 비교급 앞에 much, even, far, still, a lot을 써요.
* very는 비교급이 아닌 원급을 강조하여 비교급에는 쓸 수 없음에 주의하세요.

|A| 다음 문장의 밑줄 친 부분이 어법상 옳으면 ○표 하고, 틀리면 바르게 고쳐 쓰시오.

01 Your attitude is much important than your intelligence. ____________________

02 You're even more diligent than Jisu. ____________________

03 He swims a lot of faster than her. ____________________

04 The actress is very more beautiful than others. ____________________

05 This car is far expensive than that. ____________________

06 We're much more interested in dancing than singing. ____________________

07 They ran faster than we can. ____________________

08 Going by subway is more cheap than taking a taxi. ____________________

|B| 괄호 안의 말을 활용하여 비교급 문장을 완성하시오.

01 His English is ____________________ mine. (well)

02 The accident ____________________ we expected. (bad)

03 You look ____________________ yesterday. (good)

04 I need ____________________ money than I have. (still, much)

05 Maggie is ____________________ Judy. (a lot, careful)

06 I am 170 cm. My friend is 165 cm. I ____________________ my friend. (tall)

07 The Amazon River ____________________ the Han River. (even, long)

08 Seoul ____________________ other cities in Korean. (far, crowded)

내신기출 다음 빈칸에 쓸 수 없는 것은?

Paper books are ________ more popular than e-books.

① much ② even ③ very ④ still ⑤ a lot

실전 TIP
원급 형용사를 강조하는지, 비교급 형용사를 강조하는지 파악하세요.

UNIT 05 배수사 비교

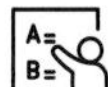

'~보다 –배 …한[하게]'은 〈as + 원급 + as〉 또는 〈비교급 + than〉 앞에 배수사를 붙이세요.

주어 + 동사	배수(사)	원급/비교급	비교 대상	의미
Regular pizza is	three times	as thick as	thin pizza.	얇은 피자보다 세 배 더 두꺼운
		thicker than		
Math is	a hundred times	as difficult as	history.	역사보다 백 배 더 어려운
		more difficult than		

참고 '배수사'란 〈숫자+times(~배)〉라고 배수를 나타내는 말이에요. three times(3배), ten times(10배) 등으로 표현해요. 단, '2배'는 twice라고 표현한다는 데 유의하세요.

|A| 괄호 안의 말을 활용하여 우리말에 맞는 표현을 완성하시오.

01 ~보다 두 배 더 많은 (many, as) → ____________________

02 ~보다 세 배 더 긴 (long, than) → ____________________

03 ~보다 열 배 더 큰 (large, as) → ____________________

04 ~보다 두 배 더 자주 (often, as) → ____________________

05 ~보다 백 배 더 쉬운 (easy, as) → ____________________

06 ~보다 다섯 배 더 많은 (much, as) → ____________________

07 ~보다 두 배 더 빠르게 (fast, as) → ____________________

08 ~보다 세 배 더 비싼 (expensive, than) → ____________________

09 ~보다 여섯 배 더 높은 (high, than) → ____________________

|B| 다음 두 문장의 의미가 같도록 괄호 안의 말을 이용하여 빈칸을 완성하시오.

01 The ruler is three times longer than the pencil. (as ~ as)

→ The ruler is ____________________ the pencil.

02 The table is five times as heavy as the chair. (than)

→ The table is ____________________ the chair.

03 The cartoon is four times as short as the documentary. (than)

→ The cartoon is ____________________ the documentary.

04 This jacket is $100 and that coat is $300. (more expensive)

→ That coat is ____________________ this jacket.

05 This fabric is ten times lighter than leather. (as ~ as)

→ This fabric is ____________________ leather.

UNIT 06 비교급 표현

다음 비교급을 이용한 유용한 표현을 알아 두세요.

형태	〈the+비교급 ~, the+비교급 ...〉	〈비교급+and+비교급〉
의미	~하면 할수록 더 …하다	점점 더 ~한[하게]
예문	The darker it is, the brighter stars shine. 어두울수록, 별은 더 빛난다.	It's getting colder and colder. 날씨가 점점 더 추워지고 있다.
	The sooner, the better. 빠를수록, 더 좋다. (뒤의 주어와 동사 생략 가능)	She will become more and more popular. 그녀는 점점 더 인기 있게 될 것이다.

|A| 우리말과 같도록 괄호 안의 말을 활용하여 문장을 완성하시오.

01 날씨가 점점 더 더워진다. (hot) → It's getting ______________.

02 나이 들수록 더 현명해진다. (old, wise) → ______________ they grow, ______________ they become.

03 작을수록 더 가볍다. (small, light) → ______________ it is, ______________ it is.

04 어릴수록 더 빨리 배운다. (young, fast) → ______________ we are, ______________ we learn.

05 집들이 점점 더 비싸진다. (expensive) → The houses are getting ______________.

06 신선할수록 더 맛있다. (fresh, delicious) → ______________ they are, ______________ they are.

07 그는 점점 더 빨리 달릴 것이다. (fast) → He'll run ______________.

08 많이 연습할수록 너는 더 잘한다. (much, well) → ______________ you practice, ______________ you play.

09 노트북이 무거울수록 더 싸다. (heavy, cheap) → ______________ a laptop is, ______________ it is.

|B| 우리말과 같도록 괄호 안의 말을 바르게 배열하시오.

01 일찍 일어날수록 나는 더 빨리 도착할 것이다. (I, get up, I'll, arrive, the sooner, the earlier)

→ ______________________________

02 더 많이 가질수록 더 많이 원한다. (the more, the more, you, you, want, have)

→ ______________________________

03 겨울에는 밤이 점점 더 길어진다. (are getting, the nights, longer and longer)

→ ______________________________ in winter.

04 아이들은 자라면서 점점 더 키가 큰다. (get, children, taller and taller)

→ ______________________________ as they grow.

05 더 자주 만날수록 더 가까워진다. (they, they, meet, become, the closer, the more often)

→ ______________________________

06 날씨가 좋을수록 더 많은 사람이 야외로 나간다. (go outside, the weather is, the finer, the more people)

→ ______________________________

UNIT 07 최상급

다음 최상급 표현을 알아 두세요.

형태	〈the+최상급〉	〈one of the+최상급+복수명사〉
의미	가장 ~한[하게]	가장 ~한 것들 중 하나
예문	Mina is the tallest student in the class. (미나는 반에서 키가 가장 큰 학생)	Seoul is one of the busiest cities in Asia. (서울은 아시아에서 가장 바쁜 도시들 중 하나)
	It's the most difficult of all the questions. (그 모든 문제들 중 가장 어려운)	Math is one of the most difficult subjects. (수학은 가장 어려운 과목들 중 하나)

참고 최상급 뒤에는 〈in+단수명사(장소나 집단): ~에서〉, 〈of+복수명사: ~들 중에서〉가 올 수 있어요.

|A| 괄호 안에서 알맞은 것을 고르시오.

01 The Burj Khalifa is (a tallest, the tallest) building in the world.

02 Autumn is (more beautiful, the most beautiful) season of the year.

03 *Parasite* is one of the most interesting (movies, movie).

04 It's the best cafe of all the (cafe, cafes).

05 Mt. Halla is (a higher, the highest) mountain in South Korea.

06 When was (the most cold, the coldest) winter in Russia?

07 This is (the fastest, the most fast) car of all the cars.

08 The earthquake was (the worst, the badest) disaster in the country.

09 My brother is the youngest one in my (family, families).

10 Sarah is (one, a person) of the smartest students in the class.

|B| 우리말과 같도록 괄호 안의 말을 활용하여 문장을 완성하시오.

'가장 ~한'이라는 의미를 나타낼 때는 〈the+최상급〉이나 〈one of the+최상급+복수명사〉를 써요.

01 나일강은 아프리카에서 가장 긴 강이다. (long)

→ The Nile is ______________________ in Africa.

02 기후 변화는 요즘 가장 심각한 문제 중 하나이다. (serious, issue)

→ Climate change is ______________________ nowadays.

03 이 장치는 내가 써 본 것 중 가장 유용한 것이다. (useful)

→ This device ______________________ one I've ever used.

04 그 박물관은 그 도시에서 가장 인기 있는 장소이다. (popular, spot)

→ The museum is ______________________ in the city.

05 Andy는 그 회사에서 가장 유능한 직원 중 한 명이다. (able, employee)

→ Andy is ______________________ in the company.

UNIT 08 최상급 표현

원급과 비교급을 이용하여 최상급의 의미를 표현하는 방법을 알아 두세요.

최상급	Tom is the fastest (boy) in his class.	Tom이 가장 빠르다
원급	= No (other) boy is as fast as Tom in his class.	= Tom만큼 빠른 소년은 없다
비교급	= No (other) boy is faster than Tom in his class.	= Tom보다 더 빠른 소년은 없다
	= Tom is faster than any other boy in his class.	= Tom은 다른 어떤 소년보다 빠르다
	= Tom is faster than all the other boys in his class.	= Tom은 다른 모든 소년들보다 빠르다

|A| 다음 문장의 의미가 같도록 괄호 안에서 알맞은 것을 고르시오.

01 He's the tallest student in the class.

→ No other student is (tall / taller) than him in the class.

→ No other student is (as tall / taller) as him in the class.

02 She's the smartest student in school.

→ She's smarter than any other (student / students) in school.

→ She's smarter than (some / all) the other students in school.

03 I can swim faster than any other member in the club.

→ I can swim (the faster / the fastest) in the club.

→ I can swim (faster / the fastest) than all the other members in the club.

|B| 우리말과 같도록 괄호 안의 말을 활용하여 문장을 완성하시오.

01 그 무엇도 음주운전보다 더 위험하지 않다. (dangerous)

→ Nothing is ______________________ than drunk driving.

02 어떤 사람도 그 군인보다 용감하지 않았다. (brave, no other, person)

→ ______________________ than the soldier.

03 너는 여기에 있는 다른 어떤 사람보다 스페인어를 유창하게 말한다. (fluently, any other, person)

→ You speak Spanish ______________________ here.

04 수학은 내게 모든 다른 과목들보다 더 어렵다. (difficult, all the other, subject)

→ Math is ______________________ to me.

05 어떤 의자도 저 소파만큼 편안하지 않다. (comfortable, no other, chair)

→ ______________________ as that sofa.

06 Baikal 호는 세상에 있는 어떤 호수보다도 크다. (large, any other, lake)

→ Lake Baikal is ______________________ in the world.

UNIT 09 원급 vs. 비교급 vs. 최상급

형용사/부사의 원급, 비교급, 최상급에 관한 기본 사항을 표에서 확인한 후 종합적으로 연습하세요.

구분	형태	의미	참고
원급	as ~ as ...	…만큼 ~한[하게]	as ~ as 사이에는 원급을 써요.
비교급	-er[more ~] than ...	…보다 더 ~한[하게]	than과 함께 써요.
최상급	the -est[most ~] of/in ...	…에서/중에서 가장 ~한[하게]	최상급 앞에 the를 붙여요.

|A| 괄호 안에서 알맞은 것을 고르시오.

01 We studied three times (long / longer) than them.

02 It's getting (as cold as / colder and colder) in November.

03 This television is (newest / the newest) one in the shop.

04 Today is (very / even) sunnier than yesterday.

05 I don't eat as (much / more) as I used to.

06 She sings (the best / better than) all the other people in the country.

07 (The tastier / The tastiest) the cookies are, (the happy / the happier) I am.

08 They try to solve problems as soon as they (will / can).

|B| 다음 문장에서 어법상 어색한 부분을 찾아 바르게 고쳐 쓰시오.

01 He is the one of the luckiest people in history. ____________________

02 The house is three times old than the school. ____________________

03 She ran twice as slowly like me. ____________________

04 No other spring was warm than this spring. ____________________

05 This lemon is sourer than all other lemon. ____________________

06 You play the piano better than I am. ____________________

07 Can you speak more louder, please? ____________________

08 Jiho ran as fast as he did. ____________________

내신기출 다음 중 밑줄 친 부분이 어법상 어색한 것은?

① My mom gets up the earliest in my family.
② No other person gets up as early as my mom in my family.
③ No other person gets up earlier than my mom in my family.
④ My mom gets up earlier than any other people in my family.
⑤ My mom gets up earlier than all the other people in my family.

실전 TIP

any 뒤에는 단수명사, all 뒤에는 복수명사가 온다는 데 유의하세요.

중간고사·기말고사 실전문제

객관식 (01~25) / 주관식 (26~50)

학년과 반 이름 객관식 / 25문항 주관식 / 25문항

01~03 다음 빈칸에 알맞은 것을 고르시오.

01

As the man began to exercise steadily, his illness got ___________.

① more and better
② more good
③ well and well
④ more well
⑤ better and better

02

He drove his little son to the hospital ___________ he could.

① as far as
② as long as
③ as quickly as
④ as fastly as
⑤ as short as

03

The girl _______________ her friend when she gives a presentation.

① cannot speak as loudly as
② can speak not as loudly as
③ can speak as not loudly as
④ can speak as loudly not as
⑤ can speak as loudly as not

04~05 다음 빈칸에 알맞지 않은 것을 고르시오.

04

Sharing used goods will be a ________ more reasonable choice than buying new ones.

① even ② very ③ a lot
④ much ⑤ far

05

This animation movie might become ________ popular than you have thought.

① less ② more ③ much less
④ least ⑤ more and more

06~08 다음 우리말을 영어로 바르게 나타낸 것을 고르시오.

06

수박은 멜론보다 더 저렴하지만 덜 달다.

① Watermelons are cheaper but sweeter than melons.
② Watermelons are cheaper but less sweeter than melons.
③ Watermelons are less cheap but less sweet than melons.
④ Watermelons are less cheap but sweeter than melons.
⑤ Watermelons are cheaper but less sweet than melons.

07 치타는 세계에서 가장 빠른 동물 중 하나이다.

① A cheetah is one of fast animals in the world.
② A cheetah is one of fastest animals in the world.
③ A cheetah is one of the fastest animal in the world.
④ A cheetah is one of the fastest animals in the world.
⑤ A cheetah is one of the fastest animals among the world.

08 어떤 성악가도 그보다 더 고음을 낼 수 없다.

① No vocalist can make a higher note than he can.
② No vocalist can make as high note than he can.
③ No vocalist can make the highest note of he can.
④ No vocalist can make high note than he can.
⑤ No vocalist can make a higher note so he can.

09~10 다음 중 어법상 어색한 것을 고르시오.

09 ① Which flavor do you think is more delicious, strawberry or mango?
② The coffee I drank today was less strong than the one I drank yesterday.
③ The baby cried loudlier when her uncle held her.
④ Have you ever heard a sadder story than this one?
⑤ People in a poor country can live happier lives than those in an advanced country.

10 ① The leaves of the small tree are much greener than that of the big tree.
② The waiting line for this restaurant is longer than before.
③ The king wanted to meet the wisest man in his country.
④ He works much faster than his colleagues.
⑤ She was younger than anyone else at the party.

11 다음 중 어법상 어색한 것을 모두 고르면?

① The man became kinder to people after he married.
② My mom was far angrier than I expected.
③ Please, speak so slowly as possible.
④ He offered the lowest price of all the bidders.
⑤ The author has very more curious stories to write.

12~13 다음 중 어법상 옳은 것을 고르시오.

12 ① The patient got more ill after the treatment.
② Hot air is more lighter than cold air.
③ This chocolate is less sweeter than ordinary chocolate.
④ My skin burns easilier than hers.
⑤ Fiona is the friendliest neighbor in my town.

13 ① The terriblest thing in my life happened the other day.
② David studied as hardly as Jonathan.
③ The cookies don't contain as much sugar as we think.
④ His pain gets more worse than yesterday.
⑤ Our final exam was very difficult than the mid-term.

14 다음 중 어법상 옳은 것을 모두 고르면?
① The AI technology becomes helpfuller and helpfuller.
② Picasso was one of greatest artists in modern art history.
③ She doesn't drink so much milk as she used to drink.
④ The salad was the freshest I've ever eaten.
⑤ Birds are not as smarter than mammals.

15~16 다음 중 문장의 의미가 나머지 넷과 다른 것을 고르시오.

15 ① He makes the most delicious sushi of all the chefs in this area.
② No chef in this area makes more delicious sushi than him.
③ He makes sushi as delicious as the chefs in this area.
④ He makes more delicious sushi than any other chef in this area.
⑤ No other chef in this area makes sushi as delicious as him.

16 ① Mercury is smaller than any other planet in the solar system.
② Mercury is smaller than all the other planets in the solar system.
③ No planet in the solar system is as small as Mercury.
④ No other planet in the solar system is less small than Mercury.
⑤ Mercury is the smallest planet in the solar system.

17~18 다음 주어진 문장과 의미가 가장 가까운 것을 고르시오.

17

The new theory was not as simple as the scientist explained.

① The new theory was so simple that the scientist could explain.
② The new theory was simpler than the scientist explained.
③ The new theory was less simple than the scientist explained.
④ The new theory was the simplest of what the scientist explained.
⑤ The new theory was the least simple of what the scientist explained.

18

Small insects can be more dangerous than any other animal on Earth.

① Small insects can be the most dangerous animals on Earth.
② Small insects can be as dangerous as any other animal on Earth.
③ All the other animals can be more dangerous than small insects on Earth.
④ No other animals can be less dangerous than small insects on Earth.
⑤ No small insects can be more dangerous than any animals on Earth.

19~20 다음 빈칸에 알맞은 말이 바르게 짝지어진 것을 고르시오.

19

> If you read the book I recommend, you can understand the class a lot ________ with ________ time and effort.

① easy – less ② easier – fewer
③ easier – few ④ more easily – fewer
⑤ more easily – less

20

> • Son is more famous than ________ other soccer player in Korea.
> • The new theater has ________ as many seats as the old.
> • Kevin lived in this village longer than ________.

① any – two time – me
② all the – twice – I did
③ any – twice – I did
④ all the – two time – I was
⑤ any – two – I was

21~22 다음 표에 대한 설명이 바르지 않은 것을 고르시오.

21

Ages of my family members				
Grandma	Dad	Mom	Brother	Me
75	46	46	18	15

① My grandma is the oldest in my family.
② My dad is more than twice as old as my brother is.
③ My mom is as old as my dad is.
④ My grandma is five times as old as I am.
⑤ My brother is three times older than I am.

22

	Distance from school to house
Andy	··········· 0.6km
Betty	······················ 1.2km
Clare	···· 0.2km

① Betty's house is the farthest from school.
② Andy's house is half as far from school as Betty's house.
③ Clare's house is closer to school than the other two students' house.
④ Andy's house is closer to school than both Betty's and Clare's house.
⑤ Betty's house is six times farther from school than Clare's house.

23 다음 중 어법상 어색한 문장의 개수는?

> ⓐ The cleaner the environment is, the healthier the wildlife will be.
> ⓑ To me, clowns are scary as the ghosts.
> ⓒ Only the luckiest person can win a lottery.
> ⓓ Her dancing skills got more and more good.

① 없음 ② 1개 ③ 2개
④ 3개 ⑤ 4개

24 다음 중 어법상 옳은 문장의 개수는?

> ⓐ Justin was one of the most talented applicants in the audition.
> ⓑ Does he have as more information as everyone does?
> ⓒ The better job you do, the more money you can earn.
> ⓓ The solution was not so effective as people hoped.

① 없음 ② 1개 ③ 2개
④ 3개 ⑤ 4개

25 다음 중 어법상 옳은 문장끼리 바르게 짝지은 것은?

> ⓐ The players on the ground became more competitive and competitive.
> ⓑ Skiing is even more exciting than hiking.
> ⓒ Finding correct answers is less important as understanding them.
> ⓓ My grandpa is ten times as old as my little sister.
> ⓔ One of the highest mountain in Korea is Mt. Seorak.

① ⓐ, ⓑ ② ⓑ, ⓓ ③ ⓑ, ⓔ
④ ⓑ, ⓓ, ⓔ ⑤ ⓒ, ⓓ, ⓔ

〈다음부터는 서술형 주관식 문제입니다.〉

26~27 다음 문장의 밑줄 친 부분이 어법상 맞으면 ○표 하고, 틀리면 바르게 고쳐 쓰시오.

26 The children became more lazy than ever as the vacation started.

→ ________________

27 My son moved the quickliest ever when he saw the new game console.

→ ________________

28~29 다음 괄호 안의 말을 빈칸에 알맞은 형태로 고쳐 쓰시오.

28 They needed a ________ place than the noisy coffee shop to discuss the issue. (quiet)

29 This leather jacket is the ________ item of all the clothes in this store. (good)

30~31 다음 문장에서 어법상 어색한 부분을 찾아 바르게 고쳐 쓰시오.

30 The kites are flying more and more highly into the sky.

________ → ________

31 My girlfriend is the loveliest woman of the world.

________ → ________

32~35 다음 주어진 문장과 의미가 같도록 빈칸에 알맞은 말을 쓰시오.

32

> Stand up as straight as possible.

→ Stand up as straight ________ you ________.

33

The highway is four times as wide as regular roads.

→ The highway is four ________ wider ________ regular roads.

34

Joseph is the most honest lawyer in this law firm.

→ Joseph is more ________ ________ ________ other lawyer in this law firm.

35

The new employee was not so diligent as the boss expected.

→ The new employee was ________ ________ than the boss expected.

36~38 다음 우리말과 같도록 괄호 안의 말을 바르게 배열하시오.

36

자원봉사자들이 더 자주 방문할수록 아이들은 더 행복할 것이다.
(happier, will, the volunteers, more, the, the, often, be, visit, the kids)

→ ________________________________

37

어떤 어머니도 Maria보다 아들에게 더 헌신적일 수 없다.
(be, other, to, her son, more, can, mother, no, devoted, than, Maria)

→ ________________________________

38

우정의 문제가 가족의 문제보다 훨씬 더 스트레스이다.
(friendship, than, even, family, are, stressful, of, of, more, those)

→ Matters ________________________.

39~42 다음 우리말과 같도록 괄호 안의 말을 활용하여 문장을 완성하시오.

39

Victor는 그의 친구보다 책이 두 배 더 많다.
(have, as, twice, many books, his friend)

→ Victor ________________________.

40

병 때문에 Henry는 점점 더 야위어져 갔다.
(become, thin, because of, his illness)

→ Henry ________________________.

41 어떤 개도 나의 개보다 더 똑똑하지 않다. (no, dog, clever, than, other)

→ ______________________________

42 그 호루라기는 내가 생각했던 만큼 소리가 크게 나지 않았다. (the whistle, so, sound, loud, think)

→ ______________________________

43~45 **다음 표를 보고, 괄호 안의 말을 활용하여 빈칸을 완성하시오.**

Time it took to solve the riddle			
Danny	Eva	Hannah	Ian
5 min.	15 min.	3 min.	13 min.

43 Out of the four, no other student solved the riddle ________ ________ Hannah did. (fast)

44 It took Eva ________ ________ ________ than Danny to solve the riddle. (long)

45 Ian didn't spend as ________ ________ ________ Eva to solve the riddle. (much time)

46~48 **다음 대화의 밑줄 친 ⓐ~ⓕ 중 어법상 어색한 부분을 세 군데 찾아 바르게 고쳐 쓰시오.**

A: Let's go back to the campsite. ⓐ It's getting darker and darker.
B: But ⓑ I'd like to enjoy the view more. ⓒ This is one of the most fantastic view I've seen.
A: That's true. ⓓ No other place as beautiful as here. But we should go now. ⓔ The more we stay, the dangerous it becomes.
B: Okay. ⓕ We've already spent twice much time here as we planned, actually.

46 ____________ → ____________

47 ____________ → ____________

48 ____________ → ____________

49~50 **다음 우리말을 주어진 |조건|에 맞게 바르게 영작하시오.**

49 여러분의 안전이 모든 것들 중 가장 큰 관심사이다.

|조건|
1. Your로 시작할 것
2. 단어 safety, great, concern을 사용할 것
3. 문장 전체를 8단어로 쓸 것

→ ______________________________ of all.

50 그녀는 그보다 세 배 더 높은 점수를 받았다.

|조건|
1. She로 시작할 것
2. 단어 score, high, than을 사용할 것
3. 문장 전체를 8단어로 쓸 것

→ ______________________________ he did.

CHAPTER

08 접속사

Unit 01 부사절 접속사 1 – 시간

Unit 02 부사절 접속사 2 – 조건

Unit 03 부사절 접속사 3 – 원인과 결과

Unit 04 부사절 접속사 4 – 양보

Unit 05 so that ~ & so ~ that ...

Unit 06 여러 의미를 지닌 접속사

Unit 07 명사절 접속사 1 – that

Unit 08 명사절 접속사 2 – whether / if

Unit 09 접속부사

Unit 10 명령문 + and / or

Unit 11 상관접속사

UNIT 01 부사절 접속사 1 - 시간

다음의 시간을 나타내는 부사절 접속사를 익혀 두세요.

시간 접속사	의미	예문	주의
when	~할 때, ~하면	The snow began to melt **when** the sun came out.	
while	~하는 동안, ~하면서	**While** I was waiting for a bus, I met some friends.	
as	~할 때, ~하면서	She listened to music **as** she was preparing food.	
until	~할 때까지	The female will sit on the eggs **until** they hatch.	will hatch (×)
since	~한 이후로	It has been three months **since** I met her.	
as soon as	~하자마자	He will give me a call **as soon as** he arrives.	will arrive (×)

주의 시간을 나타내는 부사절에서는 현재시제가 미래시제를 대신해요. 〈until, as soon as 예문 참고〉

A 우리말과 같도록 괄호 안에서 알맞은 것을 고르시오.

01 내가 점심을 먹는 동안에 그들이 도착했다. → They arrived (until / while) I was eating.

02 그녀가 잠들 때까지 그가 머물렀다. → He stayed (until / since) she fell asleep.

03 내가 서울로 이사했을 때 나는 8살이었다. → I was 8 (while / when) I moved to Seoul.

04 그녀는 떠나면서 작별 인사를 했다. → She said bye (as / until) she was leaving.

05 나는 5살 이후부터 그녀를 알아왔다. → I have known her (when / since) I was 5.

06 나는 그가 떠났을 때 그것을 열었다. → I opened it (while / when) he left.

07 그는 읽을 때 안경을 쓴다. → He wears glasses (when / since) he reads.

08 나는 버스에서 내리면서 너를 봤다. → I saw you (until / as) I was getting off the bus.

B 다음 문장의 밑줄 친 부분이 어법상 옳으면 ○표 하고, 틀리면 바르게 고쳐 쓰시오.

01 It's been a month since he left to Tokyo. ______________

02 I began to do my homework as soon as I came home. ______________

03 Wait here until we will pick you up. ______________

04 I've lived here when I was born. ______________

05 She cleaned the house while he was preparing for dinner. ______________

06 Do not leave here since I come back. ______________

07 Someone knocked the door as I came out of the bathroom. ______________

08 We will wait until we will hear from them. ______________

UNIT 02 부사절 접속사 2 - 조건

 앞뒤 문맥을 확인하여, if를 써야 하는지 반대의 의미인 unless를 써야 하는지를 판단하세요.

if	~한다면	If it rains tomorrow, we will not go on a picnic.	비가 오면, 안 간다
unless	~하지 않는다면 (= if ~ not)	Unless it rains tomorrow, we will go on a picnic. (= If it doesn't rain tomorrow, we will go on a picnic.)	비가 안 오면, 간다

주의 조건을 나타내는 부사절에서도 현재시제가 미래시제를 대신해요.

|A| 빈칸에 If와 Unless 중 알맞은 것을 쓰시오.

01 ________ it rains, we'll stay home.
02 ________ it snows, I'll drive to work.
03 ________ I see him, I'll let him know.
04 ________ she is foolish, she'll understand.
05 ________ I tell a lie, they can trust me.
06 ________ you need the book, I can lend it to you.

|B| 우리말과 같도록 괄호 안의 말과 if나 unless를 이용하여 문장을 완성하시오.

'~한다면'은 if로, '~하지 않는다면'은 unless(=if ~ not)로 표현할 수 있어요.

01 너무 많이 먹는다면, 너는 배탈이 날 것이다. (eat, too much)
→ ______________________, you'll have a stomachache.

02 지금 떠나지 않는다면, 나는 지각할 것이다. (leave, now)
→ ______________________, I'll be late.

03 규칙적으로 운동한다면, 너는 살을 뺄 수 있을 것이다. (work out, regularly)
→ ______________________, you can lose some weight.

04 네가 사과하지 않는다면, 그는 화를 낼지도 모른다. (apologize)
→ ______________________, he may get angry.

05 그들이 그 문제에 집중하지 않는다면, 그걸 풀 수 없을 것이다. (concentrate on)
→ ______________________ the question, they can't solve it.

06 우리가 밤에 큰 소리로 노래한다면, 이웃들이 불평할 것이다. (sing, loudly)
→ ______________________ at night, neighbors will complain.

내신 기출 다음 빈칸에 들어갈 말이 다른 하나는?

① ________ you drink too much coffee, you can't sleep at night.
② ________ the weather is fine, the game should be canceled.
③ ________ the weather is too hot, exercising outside can be dangerous.

실전 TIP '~라면'인지 '~이 아니라면'인지 의미를 먼저 파악해 보세요.

UNIT 03 부사절 접속사 3 - 원인과 결과

앞뒤 문맥에 맞게 접속사 so(그래서)를 쓸지, because(~ 때문에)를 쓸지 판단하세요.

so + 결과	그래서 ~	It was very dark, so we couldn't see anything.	
because + 원인	~ 때문에	She had to take a taxi because she was too tired.	= as[since]

주의 because[as, since]는 접속사로 뒤에 문장을 쓰고, because of는 전치사이므로 뒤에 (동)명사를 써야 해요.
The roads were slippery because[as, since] it snowed. (눈이 내렸기 때문에)
= The roads were slippery because of the snow. (눈 때문에)

|A| 괄호 안에서 알맞은 것을 고르시오.

01 It was rainy. (so / because) we didn't go on a picnic.

02 She can't go to the party (as / while) nobody invited her.

03 I went to bed early (because / because of) I was sick.

04 The child doesn't have to buy a ticket (when / since) she is under 6.

05 We were late (because of / since) the heavy traffic.

06 He wanted to enjoy the autumn. (so / because) he decided to go climbing.

07 Some people rushed to the store (as soon as / until) it opened.

08 He ran very fast. (since / so) he won the race.

|B| 괄호 안의 말과 알맞은 접속사를 활용하여 문장을 완성하시오.

01 그녀는 유명한 배우여서 많은 사람이 그녀를 알아본다. (recognize)
→ She is a famous actress. ______________________ her.

02 그는 머리를 잘랐기 때문에 달라 보인다. (have his hair cut)
→ He looks different ______________________.

03 나는 과학을 잘 못하기 때문에 그 기사를 이해할 수 없다. (be poor at)
→ I can't understand the article ______________________.

04 폭우 때문에 도로가 물에 잠겼다. (the heavy rain)
→ The road was flooded ______________________.

05 어제가 엄마 생신이어서 나는 꽃 한 다발을 사드렸다. (buy a bunch of flowers)
→ Yesterday was my mom's birthday. ______________________ for her.

06 신약 때문에 그 병은 치료될 수 있다. (the new medicine)
→ The disease can be cured ______________________.

UNIT 04 부사절 접속사 4 - 양보

'비록 ~이지만, 비록 ~일지라도'라는 양보의 표현은 접속사 though를 쓰세요.

though	비록 ~이지만, 비록 ~일지라도	Though she failed several times, she never gave up.
		= Although[Even though] she failed several times, ~.
but	하지만	= She failed several times, but she never gave up.

주의 because(~하기 때문에 …한다) 〈순접〉 vs. though(~할지라도 …한다) 〈역접〉

|A| 빈칸에 알맞은 것을 |보기|에서 골라 쓰시오.

|보기|
but though because

01 ___________ I studied very hard, I didn't get good grades.

02 You can't watch the game ___________ you have a lot of things to do.

03 They invited more than 20 people, ___________ only 10 people came.

04 She drank water a lot ___________ she wasn't thirsty.

05 He arrived there on time ___________ he left home early.

06 I feel good ___________ I didn't sleep well last night.

|B| 다음 두 문장을 괄호 안의 접속사를 이용하여 한 문장으로 쓰시오.

01 I tried hard. I couldn't do it. (although)
→ I couldn't do it ______________________________.

02 It rained a lot. We went to the beach. (though)
→ ______________________________, we went to the beach.

03 We were tired. We didn't stop running. (even though)
→ We didn't stop running ______________________________.

04 It was very cold. We decided to take a walk. (although)
→ ______________________________, we decided to take a walk.

05 The house is not big. It is very expensive. (though)
→ The house is very expensive ______________________________.

내신 기출 다음 빈칸에 들어갈 말이 다른 하나는?

① ________ he was tired, he worked hard.
② ________ she was sick, she didn't go to work.
③ They lost the game ________ they played well.

실전 TIP
부사절과 주절이 순접의 관계인지 역접의 관계인지 확인하세요.

so that ~ & so ~ that ...

⟨so that ~⟩과 ⟨so ~ that ...⟩의 쓰임과 의미를 혼동하지 마세요.

so that ~	~하도록	He saved money so that he can buy the house. (그 집을 살 수 있도록 돈을 저축했다)
so 형용사/부사 that ...	매우 ~해서 …하다	He became so rich that he can buy the house. (매우 부자라서 그 집을 살 수 있다)

참고 ⟨so that ~(~하도록)⟩은 의미상 ⟨in order that ~ / in order to / so as to⟩로 바꾸어 쓸 수 있어요.
He save money in order that he can buy the house. (= in order to[so as to] buy the house)

참고 ⟨so ~ that ...(매우 ~해서 …하다)⟩는 의미상 ⟨too ~ to ...⟩ 또는 ⟨~ enough to ...⟩로 바꾸어 쓸 수 있어요.
He became rich enough to buy the house.

|A| 괄호 안에서 알맞은 것을 고르시오.

01 We studied hard (so that / in order to) pass the test.

02 Read the book carefully (so that / so as to) you can understand it.

03 The house is too large (to be cleaned / in order to be cleaned) every day.

04 She drinks warm milk (so that / because) she can sleep well.

05 The book was (so interesting that / so that) I read the book in a day.

06 It was (so foggy that I couldn't / so foggy in order to) see clearly.

07 He exercises every day (that / so that) he can stay healthy.

|B| 다음 두 문장을 ⟨so that ~⟩이나 ⟨so ~ that ...⟩을 이용하여 한 문장으로 완성하시오.

01 I'll give you my e-mail address. You can contact me.
→ I'll give you my e-mail address ______________________________.

02 The sofa is comfortable. I can sit on it all day.
→ The sofa is ______________________________.

03 The road is slippery. The drivers must be careful.
→ The road is ______________________________.

04 They listened to the lecture. They could understand the problem.
→ They listened to the lecture ______________________________.

05 We saved a lot of money. We could travel to Europe.
→ We saved a lot of money ______________________________.

06 The shelf was high. The child couldn't reach it.
→ The shelf was ______________________________.

UNIT 06 여러 의미를 지닌 접속사

다음 접속사들은 한 개 이상의 의미를 지니므로 그 의미를 문맥상 잘 판단하세요.

as	~함에 따라, ~할수록	As we climb higher, the air becomes colder.
	~하는 대로	We did exactly as you had asked.
	~ 때문에	As it was late, they had to go back home.
	~할 때, ~하면서	As she left the room, she locked the door.
since	~한 이후로, ~한 때부터	He has lived in Seoul since he was born.
	~ 때문에	We don't see beavers since they are active at night.
while	~하는 동안, ~하면서	While the pasta was cooking, she prepared the sauce.
	~하는 반면	While my sister is good at math, I am hopeless.

|A| 괄호 안에서 알맞은 것을 고르시오.

01 We'll do it (as / while) we planned.

02 You can have tea (while / even though) you are waiting.

03 He spilled the coffee (as / unless) he was getting up.

04 (As / Although) we go up, the air grows thinner.

05 (While / But) some people think he's funny, others think he's rude.

06 She had to stay home (so that / as) she didn't feel good.

07 We have learned English (as / since) we entered the elementary school.

|B| 우리말과 같도록 괄호 안의 말과 접속사 as, since, while을 활용하여 문장을 완성하시오.

01 그녀는 사무실을 나갈 때 그를 보았다. (come out of)

→ She saw him ______________________ the office.

02 그는 나이가 들어감에 따라 더 현명해진다. (get older)

→ He gets wiser ______________________.

03 나는 어린아이였을 때부터 화가가 되고 싶었다. (a child)

→ I've wanted to be a painter ______________________.

04 그녀는 유학하고 싶었던 반면, 그녀의 부모님은 반대했다. (want, study abroad)

→ ______________________, her parents were against it.

05 쇠는 뜨거운 동안 쳐라[쇠뿔도 단김에 빼라]. (it, hot)

→ Strike the iron ______________________.

06 그들은 스포츠에 흥미가 있었기 때문에 축구 클럽에 가입했다. (be interested in)

→ ______________________ sports, they joined the soccer club.

UNIT 07 명사절 접속사 1 - that

접속사 that(~하다는 것) 뒤에 하나의 절(주어 + 동사)을 써서 하나의 명사처럼 사용하세요.

that절	의미: 그가 늦게 일어난다는 것	주의
주어	That he gets up late is unbelievable.	that절은 단수 취급
목적어	No one knows (that) he gets up late.	목적어 that절의 that은 생략 가능
보어	The truth is that he gets up late.	

참고 주어 자리에 쓰는 that절은 가(짜)주어 It을 주어 자리에 쓰고, 진(짜)주어는 문장 뒤로 옮길 수 있어요.
→ It is unbelievable that he gets up late.

|A| 다음 문장의 밑줄 친 부분의 문장 요소를 쓰시오. (주어: S, 보어: C, 목적어: O)

01 That the sun is larger than the moon is true. ________

02 I thought that you told me a lie. ________

03 It is true that the moon goes around the earth. ________

04 The truth is that we don't have enough money. ________

05 They never believe that he stole the money. ________

06 The important thing is that you did your best. ________

|B| 우리말과 같도록 접속사 that과 괄호 안의 말을 활용하여 문장을 완성하시오.

접속사 that은 명사처럼 주어, 보어, 목적어 자리에 올 수 있어요.

01 네가 그 해결책을 생각해 냈다는 것은 사실이다. (the solution, come up with)
→ ____________________ is true.

02 놀라운 소식은 그들이 금메달을 땄다는 것이다. (the gold medal, win)
→ The surprising news is ____________________.

03 나는 내가 긴장했다고 말한 적이 결코 없다. (nervous)
→ I've never said ____________________.

04 사실은 기름이 물에 뜬다는 것이다. (oil, float, on water)
→ The fact is ____________________.

05 피카소가 스페인에서 태어났다는 것은 널리 알려져 있다. (Picasso, be born, in Spain)
→ It's widely known ____________________.

내신기출 다음 중 밑줄 친 that을 생략할 수 있는 것은?
① The reason for my absence was that I had a fever.
② It is known that the earth is larger than the moon.
③ Some people don't agree that a pet is a part of family.

실전 TIP
목적어 역할을 하는 접속사 that은 생략할 수 있다는 것을 다시 상기하세요.

UNIT 08 명사절 접속사 2 - whether / if

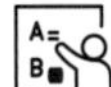

'~인지 아닌지'라는 명사절을 만들 때는 접속사 whether 또는 if를 쓰세요.

whether/if절	의미: 그가 늦게 일어나는지 (아닌지)	주의
주어	Whether he gets up late is unknown.	주어 자리에는 if를 쓰지 않아요.
목적어	No one knows whether[if] he gets up late.	if를 문장 중간에 쓸 때, 명사절 접속사 if와 조건절의 if를 혼동하지 마세요.
보어	The questions is whether[if] he gets up late.	

참고 whether는 부사절 접속사로 사용될 때는 '~이든 아니든 간에'의 양보의 의미를 지니기도 해요.
Whether you like it or not, you must do it. (네가 좋아하든 아니든)

참고 whether는 의문사처럼 뒤에 to부정사를 쓸 수 있어요.
Let's decide whether to go or stay. 갈지 있을지 결정하자.

|A| 빈칸에 if와 whether가 모두 가능하면 I/W, if만 가능하면 I, whether만 가능하면 W를 쓰시오.

01 I wonder ____________ you have a twin sister. ____________

02 I don't know ____________ they have been to Busan. ____________

03 ____________ you study hard, you can pass the test. ____________

04 ____________ it is true or not doesn't matter. ____________

05 Do you know ____________ Jack likes Mina? ____________

06 ____________ they know each other is not sure. ____________

07 ____________ it rains tomorrow, the game will be postponed. ____________

|B| 우리말과 같도록 괄호 안의 말과 접속사 if나 whether를 활용하여 문장을 완성하시오.

01 네가 내일 떠나는지는 중요하지 않다. (will, leave)
→ ________________________________ doesn't matter.

02 나는 네가 한국에서 태어났는지 알고 싶다. (be born)
→ I want to know ________________________________.

03 우리가 성공하는지 실패하는지는 우리의 노력에 달려 있다. (fail, succeed)
→ ________________________________ depends on our effort.

04 우리는 새로운 자원이 필요한지 고려해 봐야 한다. (need, new sources)
→ We should consider ________________________________.

05 우리가 준비가 됐든 안 됐든 간에 우리는 시험을 볼 것이다. (be ready)
→ ________________________________, we'll take a test.

UNIT 09 접속부사

문장 앞에 접속부사를 쓸 때, 앞의 문장과의 관계를 파악하여 알맞은 의미의 접속부사를 쓰세요.

앞 문장과의 관계		접속부사
앞 문장에 대한	예시를 들어줄 때	for example, for instance(예를 들어)
	반대의 이야기를 할 때	however(하지만) on the other hand(다른 한편으로는, 반면에) otherwise(그렇지 않으면) nevertheless, nonetheless(그럼에도 불구하고)
	결과를 말할 때	thus(그래서) therefore, hence(그러므로) as a result(결과적으로) in conclusion(결론적으로)
	추가적인 이야기를 할 때	in addition, besides, moreover(게다가)
	다른 이야기로 전환할 때	anyway, by the way(어쨌든, 그런데)

|A| 빈칸에 however, thus, besides 중 알맞은 것을 쓰시오.

01 It was very hot. ____________, we went hiking.

02 I like doing sports. ____________, I decided to join the tennis club.

03 The food was free. ____________, it tasted good.

04 You studied very hard. ____________, you got good grades.

05 It was sunny. ____________, it wasn't so warm.

06 He was thirsty. ____________, he drank water a lot.

07 You are smart. ____________, you are very polite.

|B| 다음 문맥에 맞게 괄호 안에서 알맞은 접속부사를 고르시오.

01 You're good at Korean. (Therefore / On the other hand), I'm good at English.

02 The ticket is hard to get. (In addition / Nevertheless), it is expensive.

03 Vegetables are good for health. (Thus / However), I try to eat vegetables a lot.

04 His idea sounded good. (Thus / However), I disagreed with him.

05 My friends have various hobbies. (For example / By the way), Jimin likes playing basketball.

06 The price of the shoes was not reasonable. (Nonetheless / Otherwise), I bought it.

내신기출 다음 빈칸에 들어갈 말이 다른 하나는?

① They were tired. _________, they kept walking.

② She was sick. _________, she didn't see a doctor.

③ He got up early. _________, he wasn't late for school.

실전 TIP

앞뒤 문장 관계가 역접인지 아닌지 확인하세요.

UNIT 10 명령문 + and / or

 명령문 뒤에 and를 쓸 때와 or를 쓸 때 반대의 의미가 되는 것에 주의해야 해요.

명령문 + and	~해라, 그러면 ~할 것이다	Hurry, and you will not be late. (서두르면 늦지 않을 거다)
명령문 + or	~해라, 그렇지 않으면 ~할 것이다	Hurry, or you will be late. (서두르지 않으면 늦을 거다)

〈명령문 + and/or〉는 의미에 맞게 조건문 if/unless 문장으로 바꾸어 쓸 수 있어야 해요.

Hurry, and you will not be late.	= If you hurry, you will not be late.
Hurry, or you will be late.	= Unless you hurry, you will be late.

|A| 빈칸에 and와 or 중 알맞은 것을 쓰시오.

01 Hurry up, __________ you'll get there in time.

02 Close the window, __________ you'll catch a cold.

03 Don't tell her a lie, __________ she'll get angry with you.

04 Wear a helmet, __________ you'll be safe.

05 Leave right now, __________ you won't miss the plane.

06 Don't be late, __________ we will get disappointed with you.

|B| 다음 두 문장의 의미가 같도록 빈칸에 알맞은 말을 쓰시오.

01 If you listen to relaxing music, you'll sleep well.
→ Listen to relaxing music, __________ you'll sleep well.

02 Unless you read the manual carefully, you won't understand it.
→ Read the manual carefully, __________ you won't understand it.

03 Work out regularly, and you'll stay healthy.
→ __________ you work out regularly, you'll stay healthy.

04 Turn off the heater, or your eyes will get dry.
→ __________ you turn off the heater, your eyes will get dry.

05 If you tell your parents the truth, they will help you.
→ Tell your parents the truth, __________ they will help you.

내신 기출 다음 빈칸에 들어갈 말이 다른 하나는?

① Take a break regularly, ________ you'll be exhausted.
② Be kind to your friends, ________ they'll be nice to you.
③ Don't eat too much, ________ you'll have a stomachache.

실전 TIP
앞뒤의 관계가 '그러면'인지 '그렇지 않으면'인지 확인하세요.

UNIT 11 상관접속사

서로 상관이 있는 것들을 묶어 주는 상관접속사의 종류와 의미를 알아 두세요.

상관접속사	의미	상관접속사	의미
both A and B	A와 B 둘 다	not A but B	A가 아니라 B
either A or B	A 또는 B	not only A but (also) B = B as well as A	A뿐만 아니라 B도 = A와 마찬가지로 B도
neither A nor B	A도 B도 아닌		

참고 〈not only A but also B〉는 〈B as well as A〉로 쓸 수 있어요.

상관접속사로 이루어진 말이 주어일 때 주어와 동사의 수 일치에 주의하세요.

상관접속사	수 일치	예문
both A and B	복수 취급	Both Tom and Sara are busy.
either A or B	B에 수 일치	Either I or she has to go.
neither A nor B		Neither his brothers nor his sister knows you. 〈*모른다(부정)〉
not A but B		Not Tom but his parents have a car.
not only A but (also) B = B as well as A		Not only Tom but also his sisters are coming. = His sisters as well as Tom are coming.

|A| 우리말과 같도록 빈칸에 알맞은 접속사를 쓰시오.

01 나는 수영하기와 스키 타기를 둘 다 좋아한다. → I love ___________ swimming and skiing.

02 우리는 수학뿐만 아니라 영어도 공부한다. → We study ___________ math but also English.

03 너는 초콜릿도 사탕도 싫어한다. → You like ___________ chocolate nor candy.

04 그는 한국어뿐만 아니라 중국어도 배운다. → He learns Chinese as ___________ as Korean.

05 그들과 우리 모두 틀렸다. → Both they ___________ we were wrong.

06 내가 아니라 그녀가 대답해야 한다. → Not I ___________ she has to answer.

07 우리는 닭고기나 소고기를 먹을 수 있다. → We can have either chicken ___________ beef.

|B| 문장의 주어를 확인하고, 빈칸에 괄호 안의 말을 알맞은 형태로 쓰시오. (단, 현재시제로 쓸 것)

01 Not the boss but they ________________ attend the meeting. (have to)

02 Both my uncle and my aunt ________________ English at school. (teach)

03 Not only I but also you ________________ meet Adam. (be going to)

04 Either she or her brothers ________________ by bike. (go to school)

05 Neither you nor Tom ________________ the book. (have)

06 Both the judge and the lawyer ________________ in the courtroom. (be)

07 Either I or she ________________ give a presentation. (be supposed to)

08 You as well as I ________________ to blame for it. (be)

|C| 우리말과 같도록 빈칸에 알맞은 말을 쓰시오.

01 나도 그도 노래를 잘하는 사람은 아니다.

→ Neither I ___________ he ___________ not a good singer.

02 너와 나 둘 다 이 사건에 책임이 있다.

→ ___________ you and I ___________ responsible for this accident.

03 그녀는 요리뿐만 아니라 제빵도 잘한다.

→ She's good at baking ___________ ___________ ___________ cooking.

04 그 기계는 옷을 세탁할 뿐만 아니라 건조하기도 한다.

→ The machine ___________ ___________ washes clothes but dries them.

05 우리 집이나 도서관에서 숙제하자.

→ Let's do homework ___________ at my home ___________ in the library.

06 그들은 돈을 벌기 위해서가 아니라 다른 사람들을 도우려고 시간을 썼다.

→ They spent their time ___________ to make money. ___________ to help others.

|D| 다음 문장의 밑줄 친 부분이 어법상 옳으면 ○표 하고, 틀리면 바르게 고쳐 쓰시오.

01 They like both singing and dance. ________________

02 Not only her parents but she speaks Korean. ________________

03 Either he or I has to water the trees. ________________

04 I drink neither juice or soda. ________________

05 The job requires both intelligence and strong. ________________

06 Both English and French is spoken in Quebec. ________________

내신 기출 다음 빈칸에 들어갈 말이 바르게 짝지어진 것은?

- We can ________ take a bus or walk.
- The present is not mine, ________ yours.
- Helen Keller could neither hear ________ see.

① either–but–nor ② either–but also–or ③ both–but–nor

실전 TIP

상관접속사의 의미뿐만 아니라 짝을 이루는 단어로 알아야 해요.

중간고사·기말고사 실전문제

객관식 (01~25) / 주관식 (26~50)

학년과 반　　이름　　객관식　　/ 25문항　　주관식　　/ 25문항

01~03 다음 빈칸에 알맞은 것을 고르시오.

01

The hen will sit on the eggs ________ they hatch.

① since　② when　③ until
④ because　⑤ as soon as

02

The obvious fact is ________ there are still many people suffering from the war.

① whether　② unless　③ which
④ that　⑤ thus

03

Get permission to come in here, ________ the guards will stop you.

① and　② or　③ but
④ so　⑤ while

04~05 다음 빈칸에 알맞지 않은 것을 고르시오.

04

This book has a lot of good points: a perfect plot, attractive characters, and so on. ________, it's a good book to read.

① Thus　② Hence　③ Otherwise
④ Therefore　⑤ In conclusion

05

People started shouting for joy ________ the comedian came up to the stage.

① since　② when　③ as soon as
④ as　⑤ unless

06~07 다음 빈칸에 알맞은 것을 모두 고르시오.

06

He couldn't understand the process ________ it was too complicated.

① since　② while　③ though
④ as　⑤ until

07

They needed to cooperate ________ win the game.

① since　② that　③ so as to
④ as　⑤ in order to

08~09 다음 두 문장의 빈칸에 공통으로 알맞은 것을 고르시오.

08

• Mia always listens to the radio ________ she works.
• ________ it rained, the baseball game today was cancelled.

① as[As]　② because[Because]
③ though[Though]　④ when[When]
⑤ since[Since]

09

> • The mother wanted to rest ________ the baby was taking a nap.
> • ________ whales are mammals, sharks are fish.

① when[When] ② if[If]
③ until[Until] ④ while[While]
⑤ as[As]

10~12 다음 우리말을 영어로 바르게 나타낸 것을 고르시오.

10

> 네 여동생이 숙제를 마칠 때까지 간식을 먹지 마라.

① Not eat snacks when your sister finishes her homework.
② Don't eat snacks while your sister finishes her homework.
③ Not eat snacks as your sister finishes her homework.
④ Don't eat snacks since your sister will finish her homework.
⑤ Don't eat snacks until your sister finishes her homework.

11

> 사람이 태어날 때부터 악하다는 것은 너의 의견일 뿐이다.

① Humans are evil from birth is just your opinion.
② That humans are evil from birth is just your opinion.
③ That humans are evil from birth are just your opinion.
④ Those humans are evil from birth is just your opinion.
⑤ Those humans are evil from birth are just your opinion.

12

> 그가 한국 입국을 허가 받을지 아닐지는 여론에 달려 있다.

① That or not he will be allowed to enter Korea depends on public opinion.
② Unless or not he will be allowed to enter Korea depends on public opinion.
③ If or not he will be allowed to enter Korea depends on public opinion.
④ Whether or not he will be allowed to enter Korea depends on public opinion.
⑤ Otherwise or not he will be allowed to enter Korea depends on public opinion.

13~14 다음 중 어법상 <u>어색한</u> 것을 고르시오.

13 ① I think either he or you is telling the truth.
② People rushed into the department store as soon as it opened.
③ You will probably go to prison if you commit a crime.
④ It was so cold that I needed to put on my cardigan.
⑤ Because of what he has done, his coworkers don't like him.

14 ① What do you usually do when you have free time?
② The mole will grow bigger unless you get rid of it.
③ She went to sleep early because her flight schedule the next day.
④ Dave woke up early in order not to be late for school.
⑤ The problem is whether it has side effects or not.

15~16 **다음 중 어법상 옳은 것을 고르시오.**

15 ① Julie did her best so that could recover from her illness.
② If she invites me or not, I will be at her birthday party.
③ That he found the solution was a lie.
④ It is a mistake I didn't turn off the stove.
⑤ Marine life is dying because of a huge amount of trash was thrown away.

16 ① Both pie and ice cream is my favorite dessert.
② Either John or his brothers is going to receive the fortune.
③ Not only the player but also the spectators is angry at the referee's decision.
④ Not students but their teacher have the answer for the question.
⑤ The pilot as well as the flight attendants takes the service training.

17~18 **다음 밑줄 친 접속사의 의미가 나머지 넷과 다른 것을 고르시오.**

17 ① What can I do if she doesn't forgive me?
② It was checked if there were any errors.
③ Do you know if he has married?
④ Let's test if his theory really works.
⑤ How can I find out if someone offered a better price than our company?

18 ① Why don't you listen to music as you exercise?
② The man couldn't access the file as he didn't know the password.
③ Please drop in and see us as you pass by my neighborhood.
④ Sally asked her uncle a present as he came back from his business trip.
⑤ As she went to school, she carried an umbrella with her.

19~20 **다음 주어진 문장과 의미가 같은 것을 고르시오.**

19

Spend more time with your parents, or you will regret not doing so later.

① If you spend more time with your parents, you will regret not doing so later.
② If you don't spend more time with your parents, you won't regret not doing so later.
③ Unless you spend more time with your parents, you will regret not doing so later.
④ Unless you don't spend more time with your parents, you will regret not doing so later.
⑤ Unless you spend more time with your parents, you won't regret not doing so later.

20

Though we are different from each other, we can build a good team.

① We can't build a good team. Nevertheless, we are different from each other.
② We can build a good team, so we are different from each other.
③ We can build a good team even if we are different from each other.
④ Although we can build a good team, we aren't different from each other.
⑤ We can build a good team if we are different from each other.

21~22 다음 빈칸에 알맞은 말이 바르게 짝지어진 것을 고르시오.

21

• Charles ________ took care of his niece or walked the dog.
• ________ Leo had a headache, he didn't take medicine for it.

① both – Though ② either – Though
③ neither – That ④ either – That
⑤ neither – Since

22

________ octopus and squid live in the sea. __________, they have some differences. An octopus has eight legs ________ a squid has ten legs.

① Both – However – while
② Both – Therefore – though
③ Either – Therefore – while
④ Either – In contrast – since
⑤ Neither – However – though

23 다음 중 어법상 어색한 문장의 개수는?

ⓐ Start your homework right now, or you can finish it on time.
ⓑ Although my grandfather is nearly 80, he is still very active.
ⓒ Leave a piece of cake for her so that she can eat after school.
ⓓ Both Jane and Chris study psychology in college.

① 없음 ② 1개 ③ 2개
④ 3개 ⑤ 4개

24 다음 중 어법상 옳은 문장의 개수는?

ⓐ If they agree or disagree doesn't matter.
ⓑ Treat people as you want to be treated, and they will like you.
ⓒ He describes it as specifically as possible so that everyone can understand.
ⓓ We have hard time talking on the phone because the time differences.

① 없음 ② 1개 ③ 2개
④ 3개 ⑤ 4개

25 다음 중 어법상 옳은 문장끼리 바르게 짝지은 것은?

ⓐ He likes neither playing the piano nor draw pictures.
ⓑ The actor is popular so that hundreds of fans are waiting for him at the airport.
ⓒ This hand cream is good for your skin. In addition, it smells good.
ⓓ Try to be honest at all times, and you will gain trust from everyone.
ⓔ Serena had lived with her parents before she got married.

① ⓐ, ⓑ ② ⓑ, ⓓ ③ ⓑ, ⓔ
④ ⓑ, ⓓ, ⓔ ⑤ ⓒ, ⓓ, ⓔ

〈다음부터는 서술형 주관식 문제입니다.〉

26~28 다음 문장의 밑줄 친 부분이 어법상 맞으면 ○표 하고, 틀리면 바르게 고쳐 쓰시오.

26 Try to think positive, or it will work out as you think.

→ ____________________

27 Whether you turn left at the corner, you will see the sign.

→ ____________________

28 Jackson has been late for school all week. Besides, he didn't even bring his textbooks.

→ ____________________

29~31 다음 문장에서 어법상 어색한 부분을 찾아 바르게 고쳐 쓰시오.

29 It is brilliant which King Sejong created Hangeul.

______________ → ______________

30 Eddie scratched his leg on a branch until he was climbing up the tree.

______________ → ______________

31 Neither she nor her friends is satisfied with the test result.

______________ → ______________

32~35 다음 주어진 문장과 의미가 같도록 빈칸에 알맞은 말을 쓰시오.

32

Neither food nor services of the restaurant were good.

→ ________ food ________ services of the restaurant were not good.

33

Minji drank two cups of coffee so that she could work all night.

→ Minji drank two cups of coffee in ________ ________ ________ all night.

34

Unless he loses more weight, he won't fit into the wedding suit.

→ If ________ ________ ________ more weight, he won't fit into the wedding suit.

35

Not only I but many friends are participating in the play.

→ Many friends as ________ ________ I ________ participating in the play.

36~38 다음 우리말과 같도록 괄호 안의 말을 바르게 배열하시오.

36

그는 충분한 자격을 갖추었음에도 불구하고 상을 받지 못했다. (was, though, win, even, fully, the prize, didn't, he, qualified)

→ He ______________________________.

37

그 감독은 관객들이 자신의 영화를 재미있어할지 궁금했다. (if, would, his, wondered, movie, the audience, enjoy)

→ The director ______________________________
______________________________.

38

그 작가는 이야기를 쓸 뿐 아니라 책의 삽화도 직접 그린다. (not, the author, draws, writes, for the books, only, stories, but, illustrations)

→ ______________________________
______________________________ herself.

39~40 괄호 안의 접속사를 이용하여, 다음 두 문장을 한 문장으로 바르게 연결하시오.

39

(whether) • The researchers don't know. • Should they continue the experiment?

→ The researchers ______________________________
______________________________.

40

(that) • The human body is capable of self-healing. • That's amazing.

→ It ______________________________.

41~42 다음 우리말과 같도록 괄호 안의 말을 활용하여 문장을 완성하시오.

41

그가 화가 났는지 안 났는지는 나에게 큰 의미가 있다. (be angry, not, mean, a lot, me)

→ Whether ______________________________.

42 아무도 그것을 볼 수 없도록, 천으로 덮어라.
(with cloth, no one, so, that, can see)

→ Cover it ______________________.

※ 다음 글을 읽고, 물음에 답하시오.

ⓐ Both hiking and fishing is examples of good outdoor activities. ⓑ More and more people enjoy those activities since they want to experience nature. ⓒ When you go hiking, ⓓ you usually choose either trails and paths. ___(A)___, ⓔ if you want to go fishing, you would choose a place where there is water. ___(B)___, you would have to prepare special tools such as fishing rods and hooks ⓕ whether hiking needs a good pair of training shoes. ⓖ By the way, it is very important that you wear shoes that fit you when hiking. ___(C)___, it is easy to fall or slip.

43~45 위 글의 빈칸 (A)~(C)에 알맞은 말을 |보기|에서 골라 쓰시오.

|보기|

for example	otherwise	nonetheless
thus	moreover	however

43 (A): ______________

44 (B): ______________

45 (C): ______________

46~48 위 글의 밑줄 친 ⓐ~ⓖ 중에서 어법상 어색한 부분을 세 군데 찾아 바르게 고쳐 쓰시오.

46 ______________ → ______________

47 ______________ → ______________

48 ______________ → ______________

49~50 다음 우리말을 주어진 |조건|에 맞게 바르게 영작하시오.

49 문제는 네가 내 수업에 집중을 안 했다는 것이다.

|조건|
1. 접속사 that을 사용할 것
2. 단어 the problem, pay attention to, class를 사용할 것
3. 11단어로 쓸 것

→ ______________________

50 그녀와 나 둘 중 한 명은 그 사고에 책임이 있다.

|조건|
1. 접속사 either를 사용할 것
2. 단어 be responsible for, the accident를 사용할 것
3. she가 문장에 먼저 나오게 할 것
4. 9단어로 쓸 것

→ ______________________

CHAPTER

09 분사구문

UNIT 01 분사구문 만드는 법

부사절(접속사+주어+동사)을 분사를 이용하여 간결하게 줄여 쓰는 방법을 익히세요.

분사구문 만드는 법		
1	부사절의 접속사 생략	~~As~~ Jane got off the bus, she said goodbye.
2	부사절과 주절의 주어가 같다면, 부사절 주어 생략	~~Jane~~ got off the bus, she said goodbye.
3	동사를 현재분사(-ing)로 바꿈	Getting off the bus, she said goodbye.

참고 부사절을 분사구문으로 만들 때 보통은 접속사를 생략하지만, 양보의 경우에는 일반적으로 접속사 although, though, even if를 분사구문 앞에 남겨둔다는 데 유의하세요.

참고 접속사의 의미를 분명하게 하고 싶을 때는, 접속사를 생략하지 않고 쓰기도 해요.

|A| 다음 밑줄 친 부분을 분사구문으로 바꾸어 쓰시오.

주절과 부사절의 주어가 같다면 접속사와 주어를 생략하고 동사원형에 -ing를 붙여서 분사구문을 만들어요. 단, 양보의 접속사(although, though 등)의 경우는 분사구문 앞에 남겨두는 것이 일반적이에요.

01 While he ran in the race, he injured his ankle.

→ ______________________, he injured his ankle.

02 If you turn to the left, you will see the restaurant.

→ ______________________, you will see the restaurant.

03 As he entered the room, he saw her there.

→ ______________________, he saw her there.

04 Because she is a vegetarian, she doesn't eat meat.

→ ______________________, she doesn't eat meat.

05 Although it is expensive, the smartphone sells well.

→ ______________________, the smartphone sells well.

|B| 우리말과 같도록 괄호 안의 말을 활용하여 분사구문을 완성하시오.

01 아파서, Amy는 집에 있어야 했다. (sick)

→ ______________________, Amy had to stay home.

02 음악을 들으면서, 그들은 집을 청소했다. (listen to, the music)

→ ______________________, they cleaned the house.

03 길을 걷다가, 나는 그들이 싸우는 것을 보았다. (walk down, the street)

→ ______________________, I saw them fighting.

04 늦게 일어나서, 그는 서둘러야 했다. (get up, late)

→ ______________________, he had to hurry up.

05 친구들과 이야기를 나누다가, 나는 그 전화를 받았다. (talk to, my friends)

→ ______________________, I answered the phone.

UNIT 02 분사구문의 의미 & 부정

접속사가 없는 분사구문은 주절과의 관계를 파악하여 문맥에 맞게 해석해야 해요.

분사구문	주절과의 관계	의미
Arriving there, she saw Tom.	때	= When she arrived there(도착했을 때)
Being tired, he went to bed.	이유	= Because[Since/As] he was tired (피곤했기 때문에)
Turning right, you will see it.	조건	= If you turn right(우회전하면)
Although being young, she is thoughtful.	양보	= Although she is young(아직 어리지만)
Driving a car, you shouldn't eat.	동시동작	= While[As] you drive a car(운전하는 동안)
He studied hard, passing the exam	연속상황	= and passed the exam(그리고 합격했다)

부사절이 부정문이면, 분사 앞에 not이나 never를 쓰세요.

부정의 부사절	As I didn't know what to say, I kept silent.	뭐라고 말할지 몰라서 나는 침묵을 지켰다.
부정의 분사구문	= Not knowing what to say, I kept silent.	

|A| 다음 밑줄 친 부분을 분사구문으로 바꾸어 쓰시오.

01 Although we left early, we missed the train.

→ ______________________, we missed the train.

02 Because she had some questions to ask, she visited her teacher.

→ ______________________, she visited her teacher.

03 As we don't have anything to eat, we had some food delivered.

→ ______________________, we had some food delivered.

04 When I waited for my friend, I read the article.

→ ______________________, I read the article.

05 While he read a book, he heard someone knock the door.

→ ______________________, he heard someone knock the door.

06 Since she didn't know the answer, she didn't say anything.

→ ______________________, she didn't say anything.

부사절이 부정문이므로 분사 앞에 not을 써서 분사구문의 부정형으로 나타내야 해요.

|B| 우리말과 같도록 괄호 안의 말을 바르게 배열하시오.

01 네 주소를 몰라서 초대장을 보내지 못했다. (your address, knowing, not)

→ ______________________, I couldn't send you an invitation.

02 충분한 돈은 없었지만 우리는 호주를 여행하기로 결정했다. (money, having, not, enough)

→ ______________________, we decided to travel Australia.

03 그것에 대해 이야기하고 싶지 않아서 나는 한 마디도 하지 않았다. (to talk, wanting, about it, not)

→ ______________________, I didn't say a word.

04 가족과 함께 살지 않아서 그녀는 그들을 무척 그리워한다. (with her family, not, living)

→ ______________________, she misses them a lot.

05 나는 그 책을 이해할 수 없어서 그걸 반복해서 읽어야 했다. (the book, understanding, not)

→ ______________________, I had to read it again and again.

|C| 다음 밑줄 친 분사구문을 |보기|에서 알맞은 접속사를 골라 부사절로 바꾸어 쓰시오.

보기
and　　when　　while　　because　　though　　if

01 Going straight for 3 blocks, you'll find the bookstore on your right.

→ ______________________, you'll find the bookstore on your right.

02 Entering the classroom, I saw my friends there.

→ ______________________, I saw my friends there.

03 Having lunch together, we talked about the issue.

→ ______________________, we talked about the issue.

04 Though not being rich, they always help others.

→ ______________________, they always help others.

05 Studying very hard, he is at the top of the school.

→ ______________________, he is at the top of the school.

06 The flight departs from Gimpo at noon, arriving in Jeju-do at 1:00.

→ The flight departs from Gimpo at noon ______________________.

내신기출 우리말과 같도록 괄호 안의 말과 분사구문을 이용하여 문장을 완성하시오.

나는 무엇을 해야 할지 몰라서 선생님께 여쭤보았다. (know, to, do, what)

→ ______________________, I asked the teacher.

실전 TIP

분사구문의 부정형을 만들고, know 뒤에 '무엇을 해야 할지'라는 표현을 넣어야 해요.

UNIT 03 완료형 분사구문

부사절의 시제가 주절의 시제보다 앞서는 경우 〈having+과거분사〉 형태의 완료 분사를 써야 해요.

		부사절	분사구문
단순 분사		As she got off, she said bye.	= Getting off, she said bye.
완료 분사	과거 – 현재	As he had lunch, he can leave.	= Having had lunch, he can leave.
	대과거 – 과거	As he had had lunch, he left.	= Having had lunch, he left.

참고 단순 분사를 썼다는 것은 부사절과 주절의 시제가 같다는 것이고, 완료 분사를 썼다는 것은 부사절의 시제가 주절의 시제보다 과거라는 것을 말해요.

|A| 우리말과 같도록 괄호 안에서 알맞은 것을 고르시오.

01 그녀는 피아노를 치면서 노래했다. → (Playing / Having played) the piano, she sang.

02 나는 코트를 입지 않아서 추웠다. → (Not wearing / Not having worn) a coat, I felt cold.

03 아빠는 운전하면서 내게 이야기했다. → (Driving / Having driven) a car, my dad talked to me.

04 나는 지갑을 잃어버려서 돈이 없다. → (Losing / Having lost) my wallet, I don't have money.

05 그는 음악을 들으면서 요리했다. → (Having listened / Listening) to music, he was cooking.

06 나는 지난밤에 자지 않아서 지금 피곤하다. → (Not having slept / Not sleeping) last night, I'm tired now.

|B| 다음 두 문장의 의미가 같도록 부사절은 분사구문으로, 분사구문은 부사절로 바꾸어 쓰시오.

01 Because I hadn't met him, I didn't know who he was.
→ ______________________, I didn't know who he was.

02 As she lost the key, she can't get the car started.
→ ______________________, she can't get the car started.

03 Because I have heard of his condition, I can understand this situation.
→ ______________________, I can understand this situation.

04 Having saved enough money, they can go to Hawaii.
→ ______________________, they can go to Hawaii.

05 Having cleaned the house, I took a shower.
→ ______________________, I took a shower.

06 As he hadn't learned French, he couldn't understand the song.
→ ______________________, he couldn't understand the song.

부사절이 부정문이고, 부사절의 시제가 주절의 시제보다 과거이므로 〈Not+having+과거분사〉 형태의 완료형 분사구문의 부정형으로 나타내야 해요.

UNIT 04 Being / Having been의 생략

분사구문의 Being이나 Having been을 생략할 수 있는 것에 유의하세요.

보어 앞의	Being 생략	As I was sick with a cold, I stayed home. = (Being) Sick with a cold, I stayed home.
수동태의	Being 생략	As she was given a gift, she felt happy. = (Being) Given a gift, she felt happy.
	Having been 생략	After my bike was repaired at the shop, it works well. = (Having been) Repaired at the shop, it works well.

참고 수동태의 Being은 거의 생략하지만, 보어 앞의 Being은 생략하지 않는 경우도 많아요.

|A| 다음 문장에서 생략 가능한 부분을 찾아 밑줄을 그으시오.

01 Not having been fixed completely, the washing machine broke down again.

02 Being very bored, the students couldn't focus on the lecture.

03 Being so excited, the kids can't calm down.

04 Not being satisfied with the result, you looked down.

05 Not having been written easily, the book doesn't sell well.

06 Having been exhausted, she fell into a deep sleep.

07 Being pleased by the compliment, she seems to be happy.

|B| 다음 밑줄 친 부분을 분사구문으로 바꾸어 쓰시오.

01 Because they were delivered fresh, the oranges are delicious.

→ ______________________, the oranges are delicious.

02 While they flew kites, the kids were running around the park.

→ ______________________, the kids were running around the park.

03 If you are not satisfied with the product, you can return it.

→ ______________________, you can return it.

04 Since they are proud of their son, they look so happy.

→ ______________________, they look so happy.

05 As it was written in haste, the report has some errors.

→ ______________________, the report has some errors.

06 They watched the game as they prayed for the team to win.

→ They watched the game, ______________________.

UNIT 05 독립분사구문

부사절의 주어와 주절의 주어가 다르면, 부사절의 주어를 분사구문 앞에 그대로 써야 해요.

부사절 주어 = 주절 주어	부사절 주어 ≠ 주절 주어
부사절의 주어 생략	부사절의 주어를 그대로 씀
As she got off the bus, she said goodbye. = Getting off the bus, she said goodbye.	As the owner is sick, the store isn't open. = The owner being sick, the store isn't open.
After my bike was repaired, it works well. = (Having been) Repaired, it works well.	As there was no bus, we had to walk. = There being no bus, we had to walk.

참고 위와 같이 주어를 따로 표시해야 하는 분사구문을 독립분사구문이라고 해요. 독립분사구문에서 being은 정확한 의미 전달을 위해 주로 생략하지 않아요.

주의 〈There+be동사 ~〉 구문을 분사구문으로 쓸 때는 There를 분사 앞에 그대로 두세요.

|A| 다음 문장에서 분사구문과 주절의 주어를 찾아 밑줄을 그으시오.

There being ~ 분사구문의 경우 There being 뒤에 나오는 말이 주어예요.

01 It being rainy, we didn't go out.

02 The work being done, you can go home.

03 It being a foggy day, they couldn't look further.

04 Michelle cooking, Andy was washing the car.

05 There being a bench, we sat on it for a while.

06 I entering the room, the phone rang.

07 The test being easy, I solved all the questions quickly.

|B| 다음 밑줄 친 부분을 분사구문으로 바꾸어 쓰시오.

부사절과 주절의 주어가 다르다면 분사구문에서도 주어를 생략할 수 없어요.

01 As the weather was nice, we could enjoy outdoor activities.
→ ______________________, we could enjoy outdoor activities.

02 Since it was Parents' Day, many people bought flowers.
→ ______________________, many people bought flowers.

03 After the sun had set, the moon rose.
→ ______________________, the moon rose.

04 When it got dark, stars began to appear in the sky.
→ ______________________, stars began to appear in the sky.

05 As there are no train stations in that area, I have to fly there.
→ ______________________, I have to fly there.

06 Because the road was wet, drivers had to be more careful.
→ ______________________, drivers had to be more careful.

UNIT 06 비인칭 독립분사구문

주어가 다르지만, 주어 없이 숙어처럼 쓰는 분사구문을 알아 두세요.

frankly speaking	솔직히 말해서	considering ~	~을 고려하면
generally speaking	일반적으로 말해서	compared with[to] ~	~과 비교하면
strictly speaking	엄밀히 말해서	judging from ~	~로 판단해 보면

참고 위의 숙어처럼 쓰는 분사구문은 부사절과 주절의 주어가 다르더라도 주어를 생략하고 쓰며, 이를 비인칭 독립분사구문이라고 해요.

|A| 우리말과 같도록 빈칸에 알맞은 말을 쓰시오.

01 솔직히 말해서, 그 인터넷 서비스는 비싸다. → ______________, the Internet service is expensive.

02 나이를 고려해 보면, 그녀는 매우 예의바르다. → ______________ her age, she's very polite.

03 다른 것들과 비교하자면, 이것은 사용하기가 쉽다. → ______________ others, this is easy to use.

04 일반적으로 말해서, 고양이들은 물을 좋아하지 않는다. → ______________, cats don't like water.

05 엄밀히 말해서, 거미는 곤충이 아니다. → ______________, a spider is not an insect.

06 가격을 고려하면, 그 집은 괜찮은 선택이다.

→ ______________ the price, the house is a good choice.

07 억양으로 판단하건대, 그들은 외국인들이다.

→ ______________ the accent, they are foreigners.

|B| 다음 두 문장의 의미가 같도록 빈칸에 알맞은 말을 쓰시오.

01 If they speak generally, women live longer than men.

→ ______________, women live longer than men.

02 If we compare with cats, dogs are more friendly.

→ ______________, dogs are more friendly.

03 If I judge from my experience, you'd better stay home in this weather.

→ ______________, you'd better stay home in this weather.

04 If I speak strictly, it's your fault.

→ ______________, it's your fault.

05 If we consider his age, Tom Cruise looks young.

→ ______________, Tom Cruise looks young.

06 If you compare with oranges, lemons are sourer.

→ ______________, lemons are sourer.

UNIT 07 with + (대)명사 + 분사

'~한 채로', '~하면서'라는 의미를 문장에 추가할 때 〈with + (대)명사 + 분사〉의 형태로 쓰세요.

형태	〈with+(대)명사+현재분사〉	〈with+(대)명사+과거분사〉
관계	(대)명사와 분사의 관계가 능동	(대)명사와 분사의 관계가 수동
예문	She explained with tears running down. (눈물이 흐르는 채로 설명했다)	He was standing with his eyes closed. (눈을 감은 채 서 있었다)

참고 〈with+(대)명사+분사〉는 동시에 일어나는 일을 표현해요. 따라서 문맥에 맞게 '~한 채로', '~하면서' 등 자연스럽게 해석하세요. 또한 분사는 형용사의 역할을 하는 것으로, 〈with+명사+형용사〉로도 쓸 수도 있어요.
He slept with his mouth open.

|A| 우리말과 같도록 괄호 안에서 알맞은 것을 고르시오.

01 Sam은 팔짱을 낀 채 서 있었다. → Sam was standing with his arms (folding / folded).

02 그 고양이는 한 다리가 부러진 채 걸었다. → The cat walked with one leg (breaking / broken).

03 그녀는 아기가 잠든 채로 책을 읽었다. → She read a book with her baby (sleeping / slept).

04 나는 불을 끈 채로 잔다. → I sleep with the lights (turning / turned) off.

05 그는 심장이 빠르게 뛰는 채로 달렸다. → He ran with the heart (beating / beaten) fast.

|B| 다음 두 문장의 의미가 같도록 with를 이용하여 빈칸을 완성하시오.

01 Eva was waiting for her friend and her arms were folded.
→ Eva was waiting for her friend ______________________.

02 My mom was sleeping and the TV was turned on.
→ My mom was sleeping ______________________.

03 He was listening to the teacher and his book are closed.
→ He was listening to the teacher ______________________.

04 Because his computer was broken, Jim couldn't finish the report.
→ ______________________, Jim couldn't finish the report.

05 He saw the sky and his finger was pointing to the star.
→ He saw the sky ______________________.

내신 기출 다음 빈칸에 괄호 안의 말을 알맞은 형태로 쓰시오.

- We took some rest with our eyes ______________. (close)
- They listened to me with their eyes ______________. (shine)

실전 TIP
눈이 감겼는지, 눈을 반짝이는지 확인하세요.

중간고사·기말고사 실전문제

객관식 (01~25) / 주관식 (26~50)

학년과 반 이름 객관식 / 25문항 주관식 / 25문항

01~03 다음 빈칸에 알맞은 것을 고르시오.

01

__________, the old woman called her daughter to visit her.

① She lonely ② Be lonely
③ Being lonely ④ Is lonely
⑤ Though lonely

02

__________ his pen pal, the man couldn't recognize her.

① Never seen
② Seen never
③ Having seen never
④ Seeing never
⑤ Never having seen

03

__________ a shower, Jerry was singing his favorite song loudly.

① Take ② Taking
③ Taken ④ Being taken
⑤ Be taking

04~05 다음 밑줄 친 우리말과 같도록 괄호 안의 말을 바르게 배열할 때, 세 번째에 오는 것을 고르시오.

04

전에 한 번도 맛본 적이 없기 때문에, I don't know whether I can eat durian or not. (having, before, tasted, never, it)

① having ② before ③ tasted
④ never ⑤ it

05

그 도둑이 그녀의 보석을 훔치는 동안, Nancy was sleeping in her room. (stealing, while, her, jewels, the thief)

① stealing ② while ③ her
④ jewels ⑤ the thief

06~08 다음 우리말을 영어로 바르게 나타낸 것을 고르시오.

06

지갑을 도둑맞아서, 그는 걸어서 집에 와야 했다.

① Stealing, he had to walk home.
② Being stolen, he had to walk home.
③ His wallet stealing, so he had to walk home.
④ His wallet being stolen, he had to walk home.
⑤ His wallet was stolen, he had to walk home.

07

솔직히 말해서, 나는 그의 계획이 의심스럽다.

① Frankly speaking, I doubt his plan.
② Spoken frankly, I doubt his plan.
③ Spoke frankly, I doubt his plan.
④ Frankly to speak, I doubt his plan.
⑤ Frankly spoken, I doubt his plan.

08

그녀는 문을 잠그지 않은 채로 외출했다.

① She went out with the door unlock
② She went out with the door unlocked.
③ She went out with the door unlocking.
④ She went out with the door being unlock.
⑤ She went out with the door be unlocked.

09~10 다음 중 어법상 어색한 것을 고르시오.

09 ① Having recovered from the disease, the man worked harder than before.
② Having lost his old phone, Nick bought a new one.
③ Although not allowed, the detective broke into an empty house.
④ Not having requested to do by anyone, Paul willingly helped the poor.
⑤ When feeling gloomy, people usually want something spicy to eat.

10 ① Breaking into pieces, the vase was delivered to the owner.
② Amusing to everyone, the novel became a best seller.
③ Surprised by the sound, the man looked around the forest.
④ Used so many times, the knife is blunt.
⑤ Before complaining, you should be thankful about what he did.

11 다음 중 어법상 어색한 것을 모두 고르면?
① Having been fixed his watch, Tony wore it all the time.
② Not having read the newspaper, she didn't know what's going on lately.
③ Having heard about him several times, I felt like I already met him.
④ Having left home, Henry headed straight for the hospital.
⑤ Having been never in Europe, Sue is excited about her business trip to London.

12~13 다음 중 어법상 옳은 것을 고르시오.

12 ① Turning left at the corner, you'll see a small church in front of you.
② Though having not many friends, Kevin was always happy at school.
③ Giving one more chance, Max promised me to make it happen the next time.
④ The waiter said hello to us, cleaned the table.
⑤ My mom vacuumed the floor while the coffee making.

13 ① Many people watched, Greg was so nervous in front of them.
② Susan fulfilled her dream with her parents encouraging.
③ The girl wished me a luck with her fingers crossing.
④ With his shoelaces untying, the boy ran after his cat.
⑤ Not admitting your own fault, your friends will be disappointed in you.

14 다음 중 어법상 옳은 것을 모두 고르면?
① Covering with chocolate, the ice cream looked delicious.
② Terrified, the girl cried out for help.
③ Disappointing at the result, she turned off the TV.
④ Pleasing her parents, Judy got a present from them.
⑤ Being finished my work, I asked her if I could go home.

15 다음 문장을 우리말로 바르게 나타낸 것은?

> His wife often uses his car while he working at home.

① 그의 아내는 집에서 일하지만, 그의 차를 종종 사용한다.
② 그의 아내는 그의 차를 종종 사용하지만, 그는 집에서 일한다.
③ 그가 집에서 일할 동안 그의 아내가 그의 차를 종종 사용한다.
④ 그의 아내는 집에서 일하는 동안 그의 차를 종종 사용한다.
⑤ 그의 아내가 그의 차를 종종 사용하기 때문에, 그는 집에서 일한다.

16 다음 밑줄 친 부분을 분사구문으로 잘못 나타낸 것은?

① While Monica felt it easy, Rachel had a hard time in yoga class.(→ While Monica feeling it easy)
② As he didn't leave any trace, the magician disappeared from the stage.(→ Not leaving any trace)
③ If you trust yourself, you will be more successful than expected.(→ Trusting yourself)
④ Since she had nothing to wear to the party, Clare went shopping at the department store.(→ Having nothing to wear to the party)
⑤ Though she was alone, she fully enjoyed her travel to New York.(→ Though having been alone)

17~18 다음 문장을 분사구문으로 바르게 나타낸 것을 고르시오.

17

> As the people disagreed with him, Dan tried to persuade them.

① Disagreed with him, Dan tried to persuade them.
② Disagreeing with him, Dan tried to persuade them.
③ As disagreeing with him, Dan tried to persuade them.
④ People disagreed with him, Dan tried to persuade them.
⑤ People disagreeing with him, Dan tried to persuade them.

18

> Since she had already experienced it, Ann gave the opportunity to someone else.

① Already experienced it, Ann gave the opportunity to someone else.
② Had already experiencing it, Ann gave the opportunity to someone else.
③ Having already experienced it, Ann gave the opportunity to someone else.
④ Already had experiencing it, Ann gave the opportunity to someone else.
⑤ Experiencing it, Ann gave the opportunity to someone else.

19~20 다음 우리말과 같도록 밑줄 친 부분을 부사절로 바르게 나타낸 것을 고르시오.

19

> 옷을 차려입고, Amy는 데이트를 하러 나갔다.
> → Having dressed up, Amy went out on a date.

① Before she has dressed up
② Before she had dressed up
③ After she has dressed up
④ After she had dressed up
⑤ Since she had dressed up

20

> 소포가 너무 늦게 보내져서, 손님들은 크리스마스 전에 받지 못할 것이다.
> → The packages sent too late, customers won't receive them before Christmas.

① Because the packages have sent too late
② Because the packages were sent too late
③ Because the packages sent too late
④ Though the packages had sent too late
⑤ Though the packages were sent too late

21~22 다음 빈칸에 알맞은 말이 바르게 짝지어진 것을 고르시오.

21

> • Though ________ red, the apples were not fully ripe.
> • The sparrow flew into the room with its leg ________.

① turn – broken ② turning – broken
③ turned – broken ④ turning – breaking
⑤ turned – breaking

22

> • ________ exhausted, he soon fell asleep.
> • Our flight departs from Incheon at five, ________ in Tokyo at seven.
> • She knew what was in the box, ________ into it.

① Feeling – arriving – not looking
② Feeling – arrived – looking not
③ Felt – arriving – not looking
④ Felt – arrives – not looked
⑤ Being felt – arrived – looked not

23 다음 중 어법상 어색한 문장의 개수는?

> ⓐ Believing in him, Steve lent money to his colleague.
> ⓑ The driver speeded up at the school zone, got a speeding ticket.
> ⓒ Generally speaking, people over the age of 20 are considered adults.
> ⓓ With the gate open, the mansion remains empty.

① 없음 ② 1개 ③ 2개
④ 3개 ⑤ 4개

24 다음 중 어법상 옳은 문장의 개수는?

> ⓐ Considering he just started to learn Chinese, Jack speaks it quite well.
> ⓑ While her son taking care of by her sister, she went grocery shopping.
> ⓒ The team started to lead the game, with Son scored the first goal.
> ⓓ Growing older, she looks more and more like her grandmother.

① 없음 ② 1개 ③ 2개
④ 3개 ⑤ 4개

25 다음 중 어법상 옳은 문장끼리 바르게 짝지은 것은?

ⓐ Although worn out, he didn't throw away his boots.
ⓑ With Christmas approached, the streets are crowded with people.
ⓒ Looking at each other, they burst into laughter.
ⓓ Frankly speaking, I noticed every time you lied.
ⓔ The experiment went on, costing more and more money.

① ⓐ, ⓑ ② ⓑ, ⓒ ③ ⓒ, ⓔ
④ ⓑ, ⓒ, ⓔ ⑤ ⓒ, ⓓ, ⓔ

〈다음부터는 서술형 주관식 문제입니다.〉

26~27 다음 문장의 밑줄 친 부분이 어법상 맞으면 ○표 하고, 틀리면 바르게 고쳐 쓰시오.

26 My sister liking mint flavor, I don't really like it.

→ ________________

27 Having believed to be a good luck, number seven is always popular.

→ ________________

28~29 다음 빈칸에 괄호 안의 말을 알맞은 형태로 쓰시오.

28 More and more people began to speak up, ________ the situation worse. (make)

29 The birthday song is one of the most famous songs in the world, ________ in many languages. (sing)

30~31 다음 문장에서 어법상 어색한 부분을 찾아 바르게 고쳐 쓰시오.

30 Being a lot of food left, they shared it with neighbors.

________________ → ________________

31 Jack fallen from the tree, his head was damaged.

________________ → ________________

32~33 다음 우리말과 같도록 괄호 안의 말을 활용하여 빈칸을 완성하시오.

32

집 근처에 작은 공원이 있어서, 그는 가끔 거기서 조깅을 한다. (be)

→ ________ ________ a small park near his house, he sometimes goes jogging there.

33

Julie는 학급에서 눈에 띄지 않는 조용한 학생이었다. (notice)

→ Julie was a quiet student, ________ ________ ________ in the class.

34~36 다음 주어진 문장과 의미가 같도록 밑줄 친 부분을 분사구문으로 바꾸어 쓰시오. (단, 생략 가능한 것은 모두 생략할 것)

34

Large machines operate in the factory, and they make loud noises.

→ Large machines operate in the factory, ________________.

35

As the weather is sunny today, we can go swimming in the river.

→ ________________, we can go swimming in the river.

36

If he is elected president, can he solve complicated diplomatic problems?

→ ________________, can he solve complicated diplomatic problems?

37~39 다음 우리말과 같도록 괄호 안의 말을 바르게 배열하시오.

37

어떤 학생들은 음악을 크게 튼 채 공부한다. (music, loudly, students, with, study, some, turned up)

→ ________________

38

임무를 완수하지 못하고, 우주 비행사는 지구로 돌아왔다. (the astronaut, having, to, the mission, completed, not, returned)

→ ________________ ________________ the Earth.

39

요리하는 데 시간이 너무 걸려서, 손님들은 너무 배가 고팠다. (to, cook, it, the guests, too long, very, taking, hungry, were)

→ ________________

40~42 다음 우리말과 같도록 괄호 안의 말을 활용하여 분사구문을 완성하시오. (단, 생략 가능한 것은 모두 생략할 것)

40

시간이 없어서, 나는 그의 사무실에 가지 않기로 결정했다. (have, no time, decide, go, not)

→ ________________ his office.

41 역사에 관심이 있어서, 그녀는 그 강의를 신청했다. (interest, history, apply for)

→ ______________________________
the lecture.

42 지난달과 비교하면, 너의 실력은 많이 향상되었다. (compare, last month, skills, have, improve)

→ ______________________________
______________________________ a lot.

43~45 다음 글의 밑줄 친 ⓐ~ⓒ가 분사구문이면 부사절로, 부사절이면 분사구문으로 바꾸어 쓰시오.

Famous authors have different working habits. ⓐ Since it isn't noisy and bright, some authors write at night. They prefer the time from sunset and to sunrise, ⓑ having flexible work hours. Others write early in the morning ⓒ while they regulate their schedule strictly.

43 ⓐ: ________ ________ ________ noisy and bright

44 ⓑ: as ________ ________ ________ work hours

45 ⓒ: with ________ ________ ________ strictly

46~48 다음 글의 밑줄 친 ⓐ~ⓔ 중 어법상 어색한 부분을 세 군데 찾아 바르게 고쳐 쓰시오.

ⓐ Being Sunday, Suji went to the repair shop to have the tires of her car changed. ⓑ She suddenly got a phone call from her boss, driven to the shop. He told her to come to the office right away. ⓒ Strictly speaking, it is against the law to force workers to work on holidays. ⓓ Though annoyed, she worried if she had made some mistakes. ⓔ So she turned her car to the office with its tires not changing.

46 ______________ → ______________

47 ______________ → ______________

48 ______________ → ______________

49~50 다음 우리말을 주어진 |조건|에 맞게 바르게 영작하시오. (단, 생략 가능한 것은 모두 생략할 것)

49 잘 다뤄진다면, 그 장치는 유용할 것이다.

|조건|
1. 분사구문이 앞에 오도록 쓸 것
2. 단어 handle, well, the device, will, useful을 사용할 것
3. 7단어로 쓸 것

→ ______________________________

50 파티가 끝난 후에, 우리는 집에 갔다.

|조건|
1. 분사구문이 앞에 오도록 쓸 것
2. 단어 the party, have ended, go home을 사용할 것
3. 7단어로 쓸 것

→ ______________________________

CHAPTER

10 관계사

Unit 01 주격 관계대명사
Unit 02 목적격 관계대명사
Unit 03 관계대명사 that을 주로 쓰는 경우
Unit 04 소유격 관계대명사
Unit 05 관계대명사의 생략
Unit 06 관계대명사 what
Unit 07 전치사+관계대명사
Unit 08 관계부사
Unit 09 계속적 용법
Unit 10 복합관계대명사 1
Unit 11 복합관계대명사 2
Unit 12 복합관계부사

UNIT 01 주격 관계대명사

두 문장에 같은 사람 또는 사물이 있을 때, 관계대명사 who, which, that을 써서 두 문장을 연결하세요.

같은 사람	I met a boy. 나는 한 소년을 만났다. He knows you. 그는 너를 안다.	who[that] 연결	I met a boy who[that] knows you. 나는 너를 아는 한 소년을 만났다.
같은 사물	I like the shirt. 나는 그 셔츠를 좋아해. It has no button. 그것은 단추가 없다.	which[that] 연결	I like the shirt which[that] has no button. 나는 단추가 없는 그 셔츠를 좋아해.

참고 a boy, the shirt를 선행사라고 부르며, 관계대명사절이 선행사를 수식하는 형태가 되므로 관계대명사절을 형용사절이라고도 불러요.

다음 관계대명사의 특징들을 알아 두세요.

1	접속사 역할과 절의 대명사 역할 – 주어 역할이면 주격, 목적어 역할이면 목적격 관계대명사라고 불러요.
2	선행사가 사람일 때 주격 관계대명사는 who, 사물이면 which를 쓰고, that은 사람, 사물 모두 쓸 수 있어요.
3	관계대명사절의 동사는 선행사에 맞춰요. I met a boy who[that] knows you.

|A| 괄호 안에서 알맞은 것을 고르시오.

01 The man (who / which) lives on the second floor is a teacher.

02 We want to buy a car (who / which) isn't expensive.

03 Do you see the girl that (wear / wears) jeans?

04 This is a restaurant (that / who) serves Korean food.

05 Ms. Lee is a teacher (who / which) teaches at middle school.

06 These are the books which (help / helps) you study science.

|B| 다음 두 문장을 관계대명사를 이용하여 한 문장으로 쓰시오.

주격 관계대명사가 사람을 받을 땐 who[that], 사물을 받을 땐 which[that]을 써요.

01 The river is the Han River. It runs through Seoul.

→ The river ______________________ is the Han River.

02 Do you know the woman? She has an umbrella in her hand.

→ Do you know the woman ______________________?

03 The parents are looking for a person. The person can take care of their baby.

→ The parents are looking for a person ______________________.

04 They are students. They study economics at university.

→ They are students ______________________.

05 Where are the books? They were on the top of the shelf.

→ Where are the books ______________________?

UNIT 02 목적격 관계대명사

관계대명사가 목적격 대명사의 역할을 할 때는 목적격 관계대명사를 쓰세요.

The boy knows you. 그 소년은 너를 안다.	관계대명사로 연결	The boy who(m)[that] I met knows you. 내가 만난 그 소년은 너를 안다.
I met him. 나는 그를 만났다.		

참고 the boy가 선행사이며, 관계대명사 who(m)[that]은 접속사와 대명사(him, 목적어)의 역할을 하고 있어요.

선행사의 종류에 따른 주격, 목적격 관계대명사를 알아 두세요.

	사람 선행사	사물 선행사	사람 또는 사물
주격 관계대명사	who	which	that
목적격 관계대명사	who(m)	which	

|A| 빈칸에 who, whom, which 중 알맞은 것을 쓰시오.

01 The boy ______________ I like is Matt.

02 This is the bike ______________ he used to ride.

03 Junho has an uncle ______________ drives a taxi.

04 The girl ______________ you saw in the library is Soyun.

05 He's a hairdresser ______________ cuts someone's hair.

06 The car ______________ she bought last month is red.

07 The woman ______________ I met yesterday was my aunt.

|B| 다음 두 문장을 관계대명사를 이용하여 한 문장으로 쓰시오.

목적격 관계대명사가 사람을 받을 땐 who(m)[that], 사물을 받을 땐 which[that]을 써요.

01 This is the cap. I wear it often.
→ This is the cap __________________________________.

02 The bag is on sale. I bought it last week.
→ The bag __________________________________ last week is on sale.

03 He is the man. I have known him for years.
→ He is the man __________________________________.

04 The woman is a famous artist. We met her in the museum.
→ The woman __________________________________ is a famous artist.

05 Do you remember the piano? My parents bought it for me.
→ Do you remember the piano __________________________________?

06 The students were good at math. He taught them last year.
→ The students __________________________________ were good at math.

UNIT 03 관계대명사 that을 주로 쓰는 경우

관계대명사를 who(m)나 which가 아닌, that을 주로 쓰는 경우에 주의하세요.

선행사	사람+사물	Look at the man and his dog that are running.
	최상급이나 서수	This is my best friend that I've known for 15 years.
	the only, the very, the same 등	He is the only child that can make them proud.
	all, much, little, any, no 등	The money was all that she had.
	-thing으로 끝나는 대명사	She gave him everything that she could give.

참고 that의 여러 쓰임에 유의하세요.

that의 쓰임		예문	
관계대명사	선행사(명사) 수식	The movie (that we saw) wasn't good.	우리가 본 그 영화는 좋지 않았다.
접속사	명사 역할	I heard (that it wasn't good).	그것이 좋지 않았다는 것을 들었다.
지시대명사	대명사	That is my bag.	저것은 나의 가방이다.
지시형용사	명사 수식	That bag is mine.	저 가방은 나의 것이다.

|A| 빈칸에 알맞은 관계대명사를 쓰시오.

01 That was the most surprising news ______________ I've heard.

02 He was the drummer ______________ played at the concert.

03 The watch is the only thing ______________ I want to buy.

04 It was the best game ______________ I've ever seen.

05 This is the book ______________ I borrowed from the library.

06 I don't want you to make the same mistake ______________ I made.

|B| 우리말과 같도록 괄호 안의 말과 알맞은 관계대명사를 활용하여 문장을 완성하시오.

01 그는 내가 산 것과 똑같은 신발을 샀다. (buy, the same shoes)

→ He ____.

02 그들은 그들의 아들이 원하는 무엇이든 할 수 있다. (do, everything, want)

→ They can ____.

03 내가 끼고 있는 장갑은 네 것이다. (be wearing, yours)

→ The gloves ____.

04 내가 했던 모든 노력이 소용이 없었다. (all the efforts, make)

→ ____ were useless.

05 거리를 따라 걸어가는 저 소녀와 개를 보아라. (the girl and dog, walk down, the street)

→ Look at ______________________________.

06 작년에 일어난 가장 좋은 일은 내 친구 Lisa를 만난 것이다. (the best thing, happen, last year)

→ ______________________________ was to meet my friend, Lisa.

|C| 괄호 안에서 알맞은 것을 고르시오.

01 Who's (it / that) man talking to Peter?

02 Hana is the smartest person (that / who) I've ever met.

03 She was the one (who / which) welcomed us.

04 You don't need to worry about (that / which).

05 He is the last person (that / who) we can trust.

06 This is the book (who / which) a child can read.

07 The only thing (that / which) mattered to them was money.

08 It is true (this / that) he told us a lie.

|D| 우리말을 참고하여 밑줄 친 that의 쓰임을 |보기|에서 골라 쓰시오.

|보기|

지시형용사　　지시대명사　　관계대명사　　접속사

01 저것은 무엇이니?

→ What's that? ____________

02 기타를 연주하는 저 소년은 누구니?

→ Who's the boy that plays the guitar? ____________

03 그는 그들이 경기에서 이기지 못했다고 말했다.

→ He said that they didn't win the game. ____________

04 저 책이 내 삶을 바꿨다.

→ That book changed my life. ____________

05 나는 너무 졸려서 일찍 잠자리에 들었다.

→ I was so sleepy that I went to bed early. ____________

06 내가 이야기를 나눈 사람들은 친절했다.

→ The people that I spoke to were kind. ____________

내신 기출 다음 밑줄 친 부분의 쓰임이 다른 하나는?

① We couldn't believe that his story was not true.

② They want everything that the politician promised.

③ The second person that finished the work was Helen.

실전 TIP

that절이 완전한 문장인지 무언가가 빠진 문장인지 확인해 보세요.

UNIT 04 소유격 관계대명사

두 문장의 공통된 부분이 소유의 관계일 때, 소유격 관계대명사 whose를 쓰세요.

The boy knows you. 그 소년은 너를 안다.	관계대명사로 연결	The boy whose eyes are big knows you. 눈이 큰 그 소년이 너를 안다.
His eyes are big. 그의 눈은 크다.		
Look at the castle. 성을 봐.		Look at the castle whose roof is covered with gold. 지붕이 금으로 덮여 있는 성을 봐.
Its roof is covered with gold. 그것의 지붕은 금으로 덮여 있어.		

참고 the boy[castle]가 선행사이며, 소유격 관계대명사 whose는 접속사와 소유격 대명사(his, its)의 역할을 하고 있어요.

|A| 다음 문장의 밑줄 친 부분이 어법상 맞으면 ○표 하고, 틀리면 바르게 고쳐 쓰시오.

01 I met a girl whom mother was a nurse. ______

02 We met the actor whose we saw in the movie. ______

03 There was a house whose door was green. ______

04 I know a boy his name is Alex. ______

05 You have a cat which hair is brown. ______

06 It was written by a woman her husband was a sailor. ______

07 Look at the woman's hair is grey. ______

08 There are some dogs whose goal is to help people. ______

|B| 다음 두 문장을 관계대명사를 이용하여 한 문장으로 쓰시오.

관계대명사 소유격은 whose를 써요.

01 Kate is a mother. Her daughter and son are musicians.
→ Kate is a mother ______.

02 I have a classmate. His family is from India.
→ I have a classmate ______.

03 BTS is a boy band. Its songs are very popular.
→ BTS is a boy band ______.

04 The police saved the child. Her life was in danger.
→ The police saved the child ______.

05 Who are the children? Their parents are friendly.
→ Who are the children ______?

06 Do you know the woman? Her dress looks gorgeous.
→ Do you know the woman ______?

UNIT 05 관계대명사의 생략

관계대명사를 생략할 수 있는 경우들을 알아 두세요.

<table>
<tr><td colspan="2">목적격 관계대명사 생략 가능</td><td colspan="2">The boy who(m) I met knows you.</td></tr>
<tr><td>관계대명사의 동사가 진행형일 때</td><td rowspan="2">〈주격관계대명사 + be동사〉 생략 가능</td><td>The boy ~~who is~~ singing is Ben.</td><td rowspan="2">분사가 명사를 후치 수식하는 문장이 됨</td></tr>
<tr><td>관계대명사의 동사가 수동태일 때</td><td>The boy ~~who is~~ invited is Ben.</td></tr>
</table>

|A| 다음 문장에서 생략할 수 있는 부분을 찾아 쓰고, 없으면 ×표 하시오.

01 We have everything that we need. ______________

02 I read the article which was written by you. ______________

03 They bought a table whose legs are made of wood. ______________

04 The boys who are playing basketball are my brothers. ______________

05 He hasn't read anything that the author wrote. ______________

06 Anne is a student whom everyone likes. ______________

07 This is the car which was made in Korea. ______________

08 The girl who has red hair is my classmate. ______________

|B| 괄호 안의 우리말을 참고하여, 다음 두 문장을 관계대명사가 생략된 한 문장으로 쓰시오.

01 He sang a song. Many people love it.

→ He sang a song ______________. (그는 많은 사람들이 좋아하는 노래를 불렀다.)

02 Did you see the movie? It's made by the famous director.

→ Did you see the movie ______________? (너는 그 유명한 감독이 만든 영화를 봤니?)

03 I sent you a letter. You didn't get it.

→ You didn't get a letter ______________. (너는 내가 네게 보낸 편지를 받지 못했다.)

04 I saw a picture. Leonard da Vinci painted it.

→ I saw a picture ______________. (나는 레오나르도 다빈치가 그린 그림을 보았다.)

05 Look at the children. They are dancing on stage.

→ Look at the children ______________. (무대 위에서 춤추는 아이들을 보아라.)

06 We're trying to open the door. It was locked by him.

→ We're trying to open the door ______________. (우리는 그가 잠근 문을 열려고 애쓴다.)

과거분사(locked) 앞에 쓰인 〈주격 관계대명사 + be동사(which was)〉는 생략할 수 있어요.

UNIT 06 관계대명사 what

선행사가 없을 때는 관계대명사 what을 쓰세요.

관계대명사		예문	비교
that	선행사가 있음	The movie (that) I saw was fun. 내가 본 그 영화는 재미있었다.	
what	선행사가 없음	What I saw was fun. 내가 본 것은 재미있었다.	= The one[thing] that I saw was fun.

참고 관계대명사 what은 '~한 것'의 의미로, the thing[one] that/which ~의 문장으로 바꾸어 쓸 수 있어요.

|A| 괄호 안에서 알맞은 것을 고르시오.

01 This is the dictionary (which / what) I was looking for.

02 This is (that / what) they want to get.

03 (Which / What) surprised me was the cold weather.

04 Show me (whose / what) you bought yesterday.

05 Who composed the song (that / what) you like most?

06 I didn't believe (that / what) Sally told me.

07 (That / What) he did was not legal.

|B| 우리말과 같도록 관계대명사 what과 괄호 안의 말을 활용하여 문장을 완성하시오.

01 너는 네 부모님께서 말씀하신 걸 이해했니? (your parents, say)

→ Did you understand ______________________________?

02 네게 필요한 것은 규칙적으로 운동하는 것이다. (need)

→ ______________________________ is working out regularly.

03 야구하는 것은 그가 가장 즐기는 것이다. (enjoy most)

→ Playing baseball is ______________________________.

04 우리는 그녀가 설명하는 것에 귀를 기울였다. (listen to, explain)

→ We ______________________________.

05 너는 네가 말한 것에 대해 사과해야 한다. (should, apologize for, say)

→ You ______________________________.

내신기출 다음 중 빈칸에 들어갈 말이 다른 하나는?

① Nobody knows ________ happened there.

② It is the best movie ________ I have ever seen.

③ Did you see the calendar ________ I put on the table?

실전 TIP

빈칸 앞에 선행사가 있는지 없는지에 따라, 관계사가 달라진다는 데 유의하세요.

UNIT 07 전치사 + 관계대명사

관계대명사가 전치사의 목적어 역할을 할 때, 전치사를 관계사절 끝 또는 관계대명사 앞에 쓰세요.

This is the bed. My dog sleeps on it.	관계대명사로 연결	This is the bed which[that] my dog sleeps on. This is the bed on which~~[that]~~ my dog sleeps.

주의 〈전치사+관계대명사(전치사의 목적어)〉로 쓸 때는 which만 쓸 수 있어요.

전치사의 목적어가 사람일 때, 〈전치사 + whom〉으로 써요.

This is the man. I spoke to him before.	관계대명사로 연결	This is the man whom[who/that] I spoke to before. This is the man to whom~~[who/that]~~ I spoke before.

주의 〈전치사+관계대명사(전치사의 목적어)〉로 쓸 때는 whom만 쓸 수 있어요.

A 괄호 안에서 알맞은 것을 고르시오.

01 He is the teacher about (whom / that) I talked.

02 I can't remember the street (whom / which) I used to live in.

03 This is the experiment (in that / in which) I'm interested.

04 The people with (whom / that) David works are diligent.

05 This is the hospital in (which / what) my sister was born.

06 I liked the city (which / in which) I grew up.

07 It's the room (which / whom) the letter was found in.

08 That is the cafe (that / at which) the author wrote the novel.

B 다음 두 문장을 보기와 같이 관계대명사를 이용하여 한 문장으로 쓰시오.

보기
This is the topic. We are interested in it.
→ It's the topic in which we are interested.
→ It's the topic which[that] we are interested in.

관계대명사가 전치사의 목적어인 경우, 전치사는 관계대명사 앞이나 관계사절 끝에 와야 해요.

01 Are you going to the party? I was invited to it.

→ Are you going to the party ______________________?

→ Are you going to the party ______________________?

02 Did you meet the guy? I talked about him.

→ Did you meet the guy ______________________?

→ Did you meet the guy ______________________?

UNIT 08 관계부사

선행사가 시간, 장소 등인 경우, 〈접속사 + 부사(구)〉의 역할을 하는 관계부사를 쓰세요.

관계부사	두 문장	관계부사가 있는 한 문장	참고
when	25th is the day. We first met on that day.	25th is the day when we first met. = on which	〈접속사+부사구(on the day)〉의 역할
where	This is the park. We had fun in the park.	This is the park where we had fun. = in which	〈접속사+부사구(in the park)〉의 역할
why	That is the reason. He is mad for that reason.	That is the reason why he is mad. = for which	〈접속사 + 부사구(for that reason)〉의 역할
how	I found the way. He solved it in that way.	I found the way ~~how~~ he solved it. I found ~~the way~~ how he solved it. = in which	the way, how 둘 중 하나만 써요.

참고 the time, the place, the day, the reason과 같이 일반적인 선행사는 선행사나 관계부사 둘 중 하나만 써도 돼요.

It is the day when[the day / when] we met.

This is the reason why[the reason / why] he is mad.

|A| 괄호 안에서 알맞은 것을 고르시오.

01 This is a house (in which / in where) we live.

02 It's the office (where / when) my uncle works.

03 He remembers the day (how / when) he entered middle school.

04 You don't know the reason (who / why) I didn't tell the truth.

05 That's (the way how / the way) she sings a song.

06 We remember the time (on when / on which) we won the competition.

07 Andy tried to explain (for which / for why) he was late.

|B| 다음 두 문장을 관계부사를 이용하여 한 문장으로 쓰시오.

선행사가 시간, 장소, 방법, 이유를 나타내는지 잘 파악하여 알맞은 관계부사를 사용해야 해요.

01 Please show me the way. I can get to the airport in that way.

→ Please show me ______________________.

02 December is the month. Nights are long in December.

→ December is the month ______________________.

03 The lecture changed the way. We see the world in that way.

→ The lecture changed ______________________.

04 That is the store. I bought this bike in that store.

→ That is the store ______________________________.

05 Thanksgiving is the day. People eat turkey on that day.

→ Thanksgiving is the day ______________________________.

06 I know the reason. He is so angry for that reason.

→ I know the reason ______________________________.

|C| **다음 문장의 밑줄 친 부분을 생략할 수 있으면 ○, 생략할 수 없으면 ×표 하시오.**

01 Do you remember the time when the storm hit? ____________

02 I remember how my parents took care of me. ____________

03 No one knew the reason why he quit the job. ____________

04 Mina can't figure out the reason why you laughed at her. ____________

05 She saw Tom at the cafe where they used to meet. ____________

06 He explained me the way he finished the job. ____________

|D| **우리말과 같도록 괄호 안의 말을 바르게 배열하시오.**

01 밴쿠버는 내가 살고 싶은 도시다. (Vancouver, where, I, want to live, is, the city)

→ ______________________________

02 월요일은 우리가 축구를 하는 날이다. (on which, Monday, the day, we, is, play soccer)

→ ______________________________

03 그는 그녀가 사라진 이유를 내게 말해 주었다. (disappeared, told, she, me, he, the reason)

→ ______________________________

04 엄마는 내게 수프를 만드는 법을 보여 주셨다. (how, showed, she, my mom, made soup, me)

→ ______________________________

05 나는 고향을 떠났던 날을 기억한다. (the day, I, my hometown, when, I, left, remember)

→ ______________________________

06 너는 공부할 수 있는 조용한 공간이 필요하다. (need, you, can study, you, in which, a quiet place)

→ ______________________________

내신 기출 다음 중 어법상 어색한 것은?

① She explained the way how she solved the problem.

② It was the place where he discovered the hidden treasure.

③ We often talks about the days when we lived in countryside.

실전 TIP

선행사와 관계부사를 함께 쓰지 않는 경우를 생각해 보세요.

UNIT 09 계속적 용법

선행사 뒤에 콤마(,)를 하고 관계사절을 쓰면, 수식 관계가 아닌, 추가적 관계로 해석하는 것에 주의하세요.

관계사	예문	틀린 해석(X)	바른 해석(O)
who	I met Miho, who~~[that]~~ invited me.	나를 초대한 미호	만났는데, 그녀가 나를 초대했다
which	I had pizza, which~~[that]~~ tasted bad.	맛없는 피자	먹었는데, 그것은 맛이 나빴다
when	I went there on Friday, when I met Tom.	내가 Tom을 만난 금요일	금요일에 갔고, 그리고 그때 Tom을 만났다
where	I went to the par, where I lost my bag.	가방을 잃어버린 공원	공원에 갔고, 그리고 거기서 가방을 잃어버렸다

주의 〈콤마(,)+관계사〉를 관계사의 계속적 용법이라고 하며, 선행사가 명사일 수도 있고, 앞 절 전체가 될 수도 있어요.

Miho sent me a message, which I didn't read. *선행사 = a message(명사)

Miho called this morning, which woke me up. *선행사 = Miho called this morning(앞 절)

|A| 빈칸에 알맞은 관계사를 쓰시오.

계속적 용법으로 that을 쓸 수 없다는 점을 유의하세요.

01 I have a brother. ______________ is a soldier.

02 He bought a pair of pants. ______________ was too tight.

03 She moved to Hongkong. ______________ she met her boyfriend.

04 We helped an old lady. ______________ thanked us.

05 They stopped by the cafe. ______________ they often met.

06 All of us like Sumin. ______________ is kind and helpful.

07 He won the gold medal in 2021. ______________ his daughter was born.

08 She passed the exam. ______________ made her parents proud.

|B| 우리말과 같도록 괄호 안의 말과 알맞은 관계사를 활용하여 문장을 완성하시오.

01 그는 새 차를 사고 싶은데, 그것은 비싸다. (expensive)

→ He wants to buy a new car. ______________________.

02 나에게는 운동을 좋아하는 오빠가 있는데, 그는 수영을 잘한다. (like sports)

→ I have a brother. ______________________, is good at swimming.

03 우리는 제주도에서 3일간 머물렀는데, 그곳에서 휴식을 취했다. (relax)

→ We stayed in Jeju-do for 3 days. ______________________.

04 그는 지난 주말에 쇼핑을 갔는데, 그때 그 전화를 받았다. (get the call)

→ He went shopping last weekend. ______________________.

05 Joanne은 유명한 작가인데, 곧 책 한 권을 출간할 것이다. (a famous author)

→ Joanne, ____________________, is going to publish a book.

06 나의 부모님이 내게 선물을 주셨고, 그것이 날 기쁘게 했다. (make me happy)

→ My parents gave me a present, ____________________.

|C| 다음 문장의 밑줄 친 부분이 어법상 맞으면 ○표 하고, 틀리면 바르게 고쳐 쓰시오.

01 I saw Karen on the street, she didn't say hello to me. ____________

02 He visited Geneva, when he attended the conference. ____________

03 We bought a bottle of wine, that was produced in Chile. ____________

04 My brother and I fought, which made my mom angry. ____________

05 The car ran over my dog, that shocked me. ____________

06 George went fishing last week, which he caught a big fish. ____________

07 I bought a jacket, which was too small. ____________

|D| 우리말과 같도록 괄호 안의 말을 콤마(,)를 이용하여 바르게 배열하시오.

01 나에게는 언니가 한 명 있는데, 그녀는 변호사다. (a sister, have, who, is, a lawyer, I)

→ ____

02 그는 개에게 공을 던졌는데, 그것(=개)은 그것(=공)을 놓쳤다. (threw a ball, to his dog, missed, which, he, it)

→ ____

03 그녀는 할리우드를 방문했는데, 거기서 많은 유명인사를 보았다. (saw, many celebrities, she, where, Hollywood, she, visited)

→ ____

04 나의 형은 2002년에 태어났는데, 그때는 월드컵이 열린 때다. (was born, when, was held, my brother, in 2002, the World Cup)

→ ____

05 우리는 엄마를 위해 파티를 준비했고, 그것이 그녀를 깜짝 놀라게 했다. (for my mom, which, we, surprised, prepared, her, a party)

→ ____

내신 기출 다음 두 문장을 주어진 우리말 뜻에 맞게 한 문장으로 쓰시오. (단, 콤마(,)와 관계사를 이용할 것)

They tried to escape from the room. They found it impossible.

→ ____

(그들은 그 방에서 탈출하려고 했지만, 그것이 불가능하다는 것을 알았다.)

실전 TIP

it이 그들이 그 방에서 탈출하는 것을 의미한다는 데 유의하세요.

UNIT 10 복합관계대명사 1

관계대명사 who에 -ever를 붙여서 명사절이나 부사절을 이끄는 접속사로 쓸 수 있어요.

복합관계대명사	명사절: ~하는 사람은 누구나	부사절: 누가[누구를] ~하더라도
whoever	Give it to whoever wants it. = anyone who	Whoever says so, he doesn't believe it. = No matter who
who(m)ever	You can invite who(m)ever you like. = anyone who(m)	Who(m)ever you meet, be honest. = No matter who(m)

|A| 다음 두 문장의 의미가 같도록 빈칸에 알맞은 말을 쓰시오.

01 Whoever comes is welcome. → ________________ comes is welcome.

02 Whoever asks, he won't do it. → ________________ asks, he won't do it.

03 Give these shirts anyone who needs it. → Give these shirts ________________ needs it.

04 We may bring whomever we like. → We may bring ________________ we like.

05 I don't care whoever comes. → I don't care ________________ comes.

06 No matter who comes, they'll be pleased. → ________________ comes, they'll be pleased.

07 Anyone who is responsible for the accident must be arrested.
→ ________________ is responsible for the accident must be arrested.

08 Whoever comes to the house, tell them I'm not here.
→ ________________ comes to the house, tell them I'm not here.

|B| 우리말과 같도록 괄호 안의 말을 바르게 배열하시오.

01 그 수업에 등록한 사람은 누구라도 과제를 제출해야 한다. (anyone, registered for, the class, who)
→ ________________________________ should submit the assignment.

02 이 마을에 사는 누구라도 회의에 참석할 수 있다. (whoever, in this town, lives)
→ ________________________________ can attend the meeting.

03 우리는 당신이 추천한 누구든지 고용할 것이다. (you, hire, whomever, recommend)
→ We'll ________________________________.

04 소비자는 누구든 제품이나 서비스를 사는 사람이다. (who, buys, anyone, a product or service)
→ A consumer is ________________________________.

05 당신은 그곳에 가고 싶어 하는 사람은 누구라도 데리고 갈 것이다. (there, wants, whoever, to go)
→ You'll take ________________________________.

06 네가 누구든지 간에 바르게 행동하는 게 중요하다. (you, are, no matter who)
→ ________________________________, it's important to behave well.

UNIT 11 복합관계대명사 2

선행사가 사물일 때는 whichever와 whatever로 쓰세요.

복합관계대명사	명사절: ~하는 것은 어느 것이든/무엇이든	부사절: 어느 것을/무엇을 ~하더라도
whichever	You can buy whichever you like. = anything which	Whichever he chooses, I will accept it. = No matter which
whatever	She does whatever she likes. = anything that	Whatever happens, he will do it. = No matter what

|A| 다음 두 문장의 의미가 같도록 빈칸에 알맞은 말을 쓰시오.

01 I bought whichever I wanted. → I bought ________________ I wanted.

02 No matter which you choose, you won't be satisfied.

→ ________________, you won't be satisfied.

03 We can do whatever our child wants us to do.

→ We can do ________________ our child wants us to do.

04 Whichever transportation we use, it'll take 2 hours.

→ ________________ transportation we use, it'll take 2 hours.

05 Whatever we suggest, they always disagree.

→ ________________ we suggest, they always disagree.

06 No matter what he decides to do, I'll support him.

→ ________________ he decides to do, I'll support him.

|B| 우리말과 같도록 괄호 안의 말을 활용하여 문장을 완성하시오.

01 그녀가 어느 것을 입을지라도 그녀는 아름다워 보인다. (whichever, wear)

→ ________________________, she looks beautiful.

02 사실인지 (아닌지) 네가 알 수 없는 것은 어느 것이든 절대 말하지 말라. (whichever, not, know)

→ Never say ________________________ to be true.

03 나는 어느 것을 사더라도 쿠폰을 사용할 수 있다. (no matter which, buy)

→ ________________________, I can use the coupon.

04 원하는 것은 무엇이든지 마음껏 드세요. (anything that, want)

→ Help yourself to ________________________.

05 우리는 어느 것이든 다른 사람에게 속한 것은 가져가면 안 된다. (whichever, belong to, others)

→ We should not take ________________________.

06 그가 무엇을 하든, 그녀는 거기서 결점을 찾아낸다. (no matter what, do)

→ ________________________, she finds a fault with it.

UNIT 12 복합관계부사

부사절을 이끄는 〈관계부사+ever〉의 의미도 알아 두세요.

복합관계부사	양보의 부사절 (언제/어디서/어떻게 ~하더라도)	장소, 시간, 방법의 부사절 (언제든/어디든/어떤 방법으로든)
whenever	Whenever you come, I don't care. = No matter when(네가 언제 오더라도)	You can come whenever you want. = at any time(네가 원하는 언제든)
wherever	Wherever you are, I will find you. = No matter where(네가 어디에 있더라도)	You can sit wherever you want. = at any place(네가 원하는 어디든)
however	However she tried, she couldn't win. = No matter how(그녀가 얼마나 노력했더라도)	You can do it however you want. = in any way(네가 원하는 어떤 방법으로든)

|A| 다음 두 문장의 의미가 같도록 빈칸에 알맞은 말을 쓰시오.

01 Sit wherever you want. → Sit ____________ you want.

02 You can call me whenever you need. → You can call me ____________ you need.

03 No matter when he sees us, he smiles. → ____________, he smiles.

04 No matter when I hear the song, it makes me think of you.

→ ____________, it makes me think of you.

05 I want to buy the sneakers, no matter how much they cost.

→ I want to buy the sneakers, ____________ they cost.

06 Wherever the singer goes, thousands of people gather to see him.

→ ____________ the singer goes, thousands of people gather to see him.

|B| 우리말과 같도록 괄호 안의 말을 이용하여 문장을 완성하시오.

양보 부사절을 이끄는 however는 〈however+형용사/부사+주어+동사〉 형태로 써요.

01 우리는 어디에서 물건을 사든 신용카드를 사용할 수 있다. (wherever, shop)

→ ____________, we can use credit card.

02 나는 여기 올 때면 언제든 떠나고 싶어진다. (whenever, come here)

→ I want to leave ____________.

03 그는 아무리 많은 사람이 반대하더라도 의견을 바꾸지 않을 것이다. (however, many, disagree)

→ He won't change his opinion, ____________.

04 그녀는 어디에 갈지라도 사랑받을 것이다. (no matter where, may go)

→ ____________, she'll be loved.

05 너는 아무리 바쁠지라도 끼니를 거르면 안 된다. (however, busy)

→ ____________, you shouldn't skip a meal.

중간고사·기말고사 실전문제

객관식 (01~25) / 주관식 (26~50)

정답과 해설 • 46쪽

학년과 반 　　 이름 　　 객관식 　 / 25문항 　 주관식 　 / 25문항

01~03 다음 빈칸에 알맞은 것을 고르시오.

01

You need to stay still at the spot ________ you stand now.

① which ② that ③ what
④ where ⑤ when

02

They will not forget the moment ________ their first child was born.

① what ② when ③ where
④ why ⑤ which

03

________ I like about the actor is his natural way of acting.

① What ② Which ③ Who
④ Whose ⑤ That

04~06 다음 빈칸에 알맞은 것을 모두 고르시오.

04

It's always a good idea to choose products ________ are popular with many people.

① what ② that ③ who
④ whom ⑤ which

05

Mary used to go to the cafe ________ she could use free Wi-Fi.

① where ② which ③ what
④ at that ⑤ at which

06

The roof of the building leaks ________ it rains.

① what ② when ③ wherever
④ whenever ⑤ that

07~08 다음 우리말을 영어로 바르게 나타낸 것을 고르시오.

07

Harry는 그녀가 만났던 사람 중 가장 위대한 마법사였다.

① Harry was the greatest wizard she had ever met him.
② Harry was the greatest wizard which she had ever met.
③ Harry was the greatest wizard what she had ever met.
④ Harry was the greatest wizard whom she had ever met him.
⑤ Harry was the greatest wizard that she had ever met.

08 피난민들은 그들이 왔던 마을로 돌아갔다.

① The refugees returned to the town where they came.
② The refugees returned to the town that they came.
③ The refugees returned to the town from that they came.
④ The refugees returned to the town which they came.
⑤ The refugees returned to the town what they came.

09~10 다음 중 어법상 어색한 것을 고르시오.

09 ① Commuters in this town who use the subway would have experienced delay in train time.
② Bella can't be satisfied with what she has.
③ I like both the owner and her pets what live across my house.
④ The principal whom many teachers respect will retire next week.
⑤ The scholarship whose amount was about $2,000 was given to Sean.

10 ① Can you give me a hint about how I can get out of the maze?
② February is the month which we celebrate Valentine's Day.
③ India is where Mahatma Gandhi was born.
④ Does anyone understand why he was so upset about the story?
⑤ Mike checked the date he submitted his report.

11~12 다음 중 어법상 옳은 것을 고르시오.

11 ① Clean up the kitchen where baked cookies for the picnic.
② He would like to live a life what he can appreciate small things.
③ He traveled the area where wasn't well-known at all.
④ The guide didn't tell us the time which the cruise departs.
⑤ Employees moved to the building which the company bought.

12 ① Whatever you talk with, you must respect his opinions and listen carefully.
② No matter what she talks to, she tries to smile.
③ Whichever the staff was in the office, his manager called him.
④ No matter what the secretary goes, he carries his laptop with him.
⑤ Mysterious incidents happen wherever the detective appears.

13~15 다음 밑줄 친 단어의 쓰임이 나머지 넷과 다른 것을 고르시오.

13 ① I can't remember the title of the song that she's singing now.
② The fact that she was a female does not affect the results of the fitness test.
③ Plastic bags that are used at the supermarket are not free anymore.
④ The clerk that wore a blue T-shirt showed me another coat.
⑤ Is there anything that we can donate to charity?

14 ① A lot of problems, however, still remain unsolved.
② However hot the room was, they closed the window tightly.
③ However carefully she explains, he won't understand her.
④ The kids couldn't find the answer, however hard they tried.
⑤ Bring my toy back, however you do.

15 ① Watson got an A on social studies, which gave him a lot of confidence.
② My friend likes chocolate mint flavor of which I'm not fond.
③ Ella was confused about which button she had to press.
④ Amy booked the hotel in which she always stays when she goes to Busan.
⑤ They went to his grandfather's funeral which was held in his hometown.

16~18 다음 주어진 문장과 의미가 같은 것을 고르시오.

16

Please let me know the way you were able to succeed in the fashion industry.

① Please let me know what you were able to succeed in the fashion industry.
② Please let me know how you were able to succeed in the fashion industry.
③ Please let me know why you were able to succeed in the fashion industry.
④ Please let me know when you were able to succeed in the fashion industry.
⑤ Please let me know where you were able to succeed in the fashion industry.

17

Citizens admired the mayor, but he was dismissed for taking bribes.

① Citizens admired the mayor whoever was dismissed for taking bribes.
② Citizens admired the mayor, that was dismissed for taking bribes.
③ Citizens admired the mayor, who was dismissed for taking bribes.
④ Citizens admired the mayor, which was dismissed for taking bribes.
⑤ Citizens admired the mayor, whom was dismissed for taking bribes.

18

However rough he reacts, the nurse would handle it well.

① In any way he reacts, the nurse would handle it well.
② In rough way he reacts, the nurse would handle it well.
③ No matter how he reacts rough, the nurse would handle it well.
④ No matter how rough he reacts, the nurse would handle it well.
⑤ No matter however rough he reacts, the nurse would handle it well.

19~20 다음 빈칸에 알맞은 말이 바르게 짝지어진 것을 고르시오.

19

• That is the very issue ________ I disputed with my roommate. • Have you been to the new aquarium, ________ the famous architect designed?

① what – that ② what – which
③ that – which ④ that – where
⑤ which – where

20

- A few men, who ________ as security personnel, are standing at the bank.
- Send her the books on the desk that ________ written in French.
- ________ well they behave, the old man doesn't like children.

① work – are – However
② work – is – No matter how
③ work – are – In any way how
④ works – is – No matter that
⑤ works – are – However

21~22 다음 두 문장을 한 문장으로 쓸 때, 빈칸에 알맞은 것을 고르시오.

21

- The officer took a look at the thing.
- I brought the thing.

→ The officer took a look at ____________.

① which I brought
② that I brought
③ what I brought
④ I brought the thing
⑤ the thing brought

22

- The grocery store is right at the corner.
- We can buy pasta sauce there.

→ The grocery store ____________ is right at the corner.

① where we can buy pasta sauce
② what we can buy pasta sauce
③ which we can buy pasta sauce
④ that we can buy pasta sauce
⑤ whom we can buy pasta sauce

23 다음 중 어법상 어색한 문장의 개수는?

ⓐ The teacher allowed the students to ask which they didn't know.
ⓑ His family brought a stray dog, which he thinks of as his younger brother.
ⓒ The necklace, that Queen Elizabeth put on, is made of gold and diamond.
ⓓ How about having lunch at the place where Jackie recommended?

① 없음　② 1개　③ 2개
④ 3개　⑤ 4개

24 다음 중 어법상 옳은 문장의 개수는?

ⓐ He left it at the library, which he studied.
ⓑ She didn't laugh at that I said.
ⓒ Why he was arrested is not yet known.
ⓓ Can you read us which you wrote?

① 없음　② 1개　③ 2개
④ 3개　⑤ 4개

25 다음 중 어법상 옳은 문장끼리 바르게 짝지은 것은?

ⓐ We visited the college from that our mother graduated.
ⓑ Let's move on to the next chapter whose topic is modern art.
ⓒ This is that the experts say about the vaccine.
ⓓ Is this the snake that bit the child?
ⓔ However route you take, it will take more than 2 hours.

① ⓐ, ⓑ　② ⓑ, ⓓ　③ ⓑ, ⓔ
④ ⓑ, ⓓ, ⓔ　⑤ ⓒ, ⓓ, ⓔ

〈다음부터는 서술형 주관식 문제입니다.〉

26~28 다음 문장의 밑줄 친 부분이 어법상 맞으면 ○표 하고, 틀리면 바르게 고쳐 쓰시오.

26 The residents in this village, which have lived for decades, are suffering from pollution.

→ ______________________

27 Her ugly feet that has numerous wounds show how hard she practiced.

→ ______________________

28 Scarlet clearly recalled the moment where she was awarded.

→ ______________________

29~31 다음 문장에서 어법상 어색한 부분을 찾아 바르게 고쳐 쓰시오.

29 This costume is the same as that he wore last Halloween.

______________ → ______________

30 Despite three hours of long discussion, we have nothing has been settled.

______________ → ______________

31 This parrot can copy a person whoever he says.

______________ → ______________

32~34 다음 괄호 안의 관계사 중 하나를 골라 주어진 두 문장을 한 문장으로 쓰시오. (단, 첫 번째 문장을 주절로 쓸 것)

32 (when / where / how)

- The disaster took place that night.
- People gathered to see the shooting star that night.

→ ______________________________

33 (whose / which / what)

- The boxer became a world champion later.
- His coach was a national champion.

→ ______________________________

34 (whom / which / whose)

- This book introduces the artists.
- Most people are not familiar with them.

→ ______________________________
______________________ familiar.

35~36 다음 주어진 문장과 의미가 같도록 빈칸에 알맞은 말을 쓰시오.

35

No matter what he faces, Russel has an ability to overcome.

→ ________ ________ ________, Russel has an ability to overcome.

36

The charity will support the orphans no matter what happens.

→ The charity will support the orphans ________ ________.

37~39 다음 우리말과 같도록 괄호 안의 말을 바르게 배열하시오.

37

그가 삼킨 커다란 고기 조각이 그를 질식하게 만들었다.
(swallowed, choke, meat, he, him, a large piece of, made)

→ ______________________________

38

언론은 가족이 불법으로 돈을 번 정치인을 비난했다.
(whose, money, the press, the politician, criticized, family, made)

→ ______________________________
______________________ illegally.

39

그 꽃병을 누구나 그것을 볼 수 있는 그 탁자 위에 놔라.
(everyone, it, the table, see, where, on, can)

→ Put the vase ______________________
______________________________.

40~42 다음 우리말과 같도록 괄호 안의 말을 활용하여 문장을 완성하시오.

40

그는 그의 가족을 위해 요리를 할 때는 언제나 행복을 느낀다. (whenever, feel, happy, cook, his family)

→ ______________________________

41 더운 날씨 때문에, 나는 밖에 전혀 나가지 않았는데, 그건 정말 잘 생각한 것이었다. (which, never, go out, a good idea)

→ Due to hot weather, ______________________
______________________.

42 우리는 그가 어떻게 여기서 탈출했는지 궁금했다. (how, wonder, escape from, here)

→ ______________________

43~45 다음 중 어법상 어색한 문장을 찾아 바르게 고쳐 쓰시오. (정답 3개)

ⓐ Many of her friends I've met was pleasant and kind.
ⓑ November is the month which many Americans celebrate Thanksgiving Day.
ⓒ It's not far from the police station where he works.
ⓓ How is that woman you hang out with lately?
ⓔ One hundred degrees is the temperature which water starts to boil.
ⓕ The scientist explained to me why this device was invented.

43 __________ → __________

44 __________ → __________

45 __________ → __________

46~48 다음 글의 밑줄 친 ⓐ~ⓕ 중 어법상 어색한 부분을 세 군데 찾아 바르게 고쳐 쓰시오.

It was a dark night without a single light. Carol left the guesthouse alone to see the sunrise, ⓐ which she had never done before. There was her friend ⓑ who was sleeping in the next room. ⓒ Whatever much she tried, she couldn't wake him up. So she decided to go alone. The guesthouse owner told her ⓓ what she could watch the sunrise. ⓔ It took about an hour from where she stayed. When she got there, the sun began to rise. She will never forget ⓕ that she experienced that day.

46 __________ → __________

47 __________ → __________

48 __________ → __________

49~50 다음 우리말을 주어진 |조건|에 맞게 문장을 완성하시오.

49 그것은 그녀가 꿈꿔오던 일이 아니었다.

|조건|
1. 관계대명사 what을 사용할 것
2. 단어 have, dream of를 사용할 것
3. 문장 전체를 8단어로 쓸 것

→ That ______________________.

50 그 변호사는 그가 왜 범죄를 저질렀는지는 그에게 물어보지 않았다.

|조건|
1. 관계부사 why를 사용할 것
2. 단어 ask, commit, the crime, have를 사용할 것
3. 문장 전체를 11단어로 쓸 것

→ The lawyer ______________________.

내가 가장 취약한 부분에 대해
요점 정리를 해 보세요.

CHAPTER

11 가정법

UNIT 01 가정법 과거 & 가정법 과거완료

현재 사실의 반대를 가정할 때는 가정법 동사(일반동사: 과거형, be동사: were)를 쓰세요.

가정법 과거	현재 사실	He is not here so he can't join.	여기 없어서 합류할 수 없다
	반대 가정	→ is not의 반대/과거형(be동사는 were만 사용) If he were here, he could join. → can't join의 반대/could+동사원형	여기 있다면, 합류할 수 있을 텐데
가정법 과거완료	과거 사실	He wasn't diligent so he failed.	근면하지 않아서 실패했다
	반대 가정	→ wasn't의 반대/had+과거분사 If he had been diligent, he wouldn't have failed. failed의 반대/wouldn't+have+과거분사 ←	근면했다면 실패하지 않았을 텐데

참고 가정법은 단순히 반대를 가정하는 것이 아니라, 안타까움, 후회, 유감을 표현하기 위해 사용해요.

주의 가정법 과거와 가정법 과거완료의 동사 형태에 주의하세요.

구분		if절	주절
단순 조건문		현재	미래
가정법 과거	현재 사실 반대 가정	과거형/were	would/could/might+동사원형
가정법 과거완료	과거 사실 반대 가정	had+과거분사	would/could/might+have+과거분사

|A| 괄호 안에서 알맞은 것을 고르시오.

01 If I (are / were) a bird, I would fly to you.

02 If you (have / had) money, you can buy a new cell phone.

03 What (will / would) you do if you were a magician?

04 If you (wore / had worn) the coat, you wouldn't have caught a cold.

05 If it were sunny, we (can / could) go on a picnic.

|B| 우리말과 같도록 괄호 안의 말을 활용하여 문장을 완성하시오.

01 미나가 내게 크리스마스카드를 보냈다면 나는 기뻤을 텐데. (send, will, pleased)

→ If Mina ______________ me a Christmas card, I ______________.

02 우리가 우주여행을 한다면 나는 달에 갈 수 있을 텐데. (travel, can, go)

→ If we ______________ in space, I ______________ to the moon.

03 그가 나를 봤다면 인사를 했을 텐데. (see, will, say hi)

→ If he ______________ me, he ______________ to me.

04 내가 프랑스어를 이해한다면 그 책을 읽을 수 있을 텐데. (understand, can, read)

→ If I ______________ French, I ______________ the book.

05 그녀가 머리를 자르지 않았다면 그것은 더 길었을 텐데. (cut, will, longer)

→ If she ______________ her hair, it ______________.

06 네가 아프지 않다면 나랑 같이 나갈 수 있을 텐데. (sick, can, go out)

→ If you ______________, you ______________ with me.

|C| 다음 문장이 조건문인지 가정법 문장인지 구분하여 쓰시오.

01 If it rains tomorrow, we'll stay at home. ______________

02 If I were a singer, I could sing for you. ______________

03 If they give me a present, I'll be satisfied. ______________

04 If you take bus, it can take 30 minutes. ______________

05 If he knew her address, he would send an invitation. ______________

06 If I meet Duri, I can pass on the message. ______________

07 If we met together, we could discuss the issue. ______________

08 If it were cloudy, it wouldn't be so hot. ______________

|D| 다음 문장의 밑줄 친 부분이 어법상 옳으면 ○표 하고, 틀리면 바르게 고쳐 쓰시오.

01 If I am taller, I could be a model. ______________

02 If she had arrived on time, they might not be angry. ______________

03 If it snows tomorrow, the kids will play outside. ______________

04 If he had run to the station, he might not have missed the train. ______________

05 If you saved enough money, you could have traveled abroad. ______________

내신 기출 다음 우리말을 바르게 영작한 것은?

그녀가 부자라면, 그녀는 그 호화로운 보트를 살 텐데.

① If she is rich, she would buy the luxurious boat.
② If she were rich, she would buy the luxurious boat.
③ If she was rich, she would have bought the luxurious boat.

실전 TIP

현재 사실의 반대 가정을 표현하는 동사는 if절에는 과거형[were], 주절에는 〈would+동사원형〉을 써야 해요.

UNIT 02 혼합 가정법

가정하려는 일의 시제가 서로 섞여 있는 경우에 주의하세요.

if절		주절	
과거 사실	어젯밤에 끝내지 못했다	**현재 사실**	오늘 못 간다
과거 사실 반대 가정	어젯밤에 끝냈더라면	**현재 사실 반대 가정**	오늘 갈 수 있을 텐데
가정법 과거완료: had+과거분사		가정법 과거: would/could/might+동사원형	
If I **had finished** it yesterday,		I **could go** with you today.	

참고 혼합 가정법은 과거의 어떤 일이 현재에 영향을 미치고 있는 상황에서의 유감, 안타까움을 표현할 때 써요.

|A| 괄호 안에서 알맞은 것을 고르시오.

01 If I (practice / had practiced) harder, I could win the first prize now.

02 If you (had saved / saved) more money before, you could buy the car today.

03 If he (were / had been) injured severely then, he would still be in hospital.

04 If he (had drunk / drinks) coffee in the morning, he wouldn't be sleepy.

05 If we (studied / had studied) harder last week, we could pass the test today.

06 If she (went / had gone) to the party last night, she would be tired now.

07 If they (used / had used) all the money then, they might be very poor now.

08 If you (listened / had listened) to her more carefully, you wouldn't be confused now.

|B| 우리말과 같도록 괄호 안의 말을 활용하여 문장을 완성하시오.

01 그녀가 내 충고를 따랐다면 지금 후회하지 않을 텐데. (follow, will, regret)

→ If she ______________ my advice, she ______________ now.

02 우리가 표를 예매했다면, 오늘 콘서트를 즐길 수 있을 텐데. (reserve, can, enjoy)

→ If we ______________ the tickets, we ______________ the concert today.

03 내가 어제 열심히 공부했다면 지금 모든 문제를 풀 수 있을 텐데. (study, can, solve)

→ If I ______________ hard yesterday, I ______________ all the problems now.

04 네가 그때 거짓말을 하지 않았다면 지금 모두가 널 믿을 텐데. (tell a lie, will, trust)

→ If you ______________ then, everybody ______________ you now.

05 내가 우산을 가져왔다면 지금 빗속을 달리지 않을 텐데. (bring, will, run)

→ If I ______________ an umbrella, I ______________ in the rain now.

06 내가 더 일찍 일어났다면 지금 교통체증을 피할 수 있을 텐데. (get up, can, avoid)

→ If I ______________ earlier, I ______________ a traffic jam now.

UNIT 03 가정법과 직설법의 전환

가정법 문장을 직설법 문장으로 바꾸어 쓸 때 의미와 시제를 잘 판단하여 쓰세요.

가정법 과거	가정법	If he were here, he could join.	여기 있다면, 합류할 수 있을 텐데
	직설법	= Because he is not here, he can't join. = He is not here, so he can't join.	여기 없어서 합류할 수 없다
가정법 과거완료	가정법	If he had been diligent, he wouldn't have failed.	근면했다면 실패하지 않았을 텐데
	직설법	= Because he was not diligent, he failed. = He wasn't diligent, so he failed.	근면하지 않아서 실패했다

|A| 다음 두 문장의 의미가 같도록 괄호 안에서 알맞은 것을 고르시오.

01 If I were tall, I could join the basketball team.
→ Because I (am not / wasn't) tall, I can't join the basket team.

02 If you could drive a car, you could travel a lot.
→ As you (can't / couldn't) drive a car, you can't travel a lot.

03 If he had known my e-mail address, he would have sent me the file.
→ He didn't know my e-mail address, so he (hadn't / didn't) send me the file.

04 If I had slept enough yesterday, I could feel energetic now.
→ As I (didn't sleep / hadn't slept) enough yesterday, I can't feel energetic now.

05 If she had had a camera, she could have taken pictures.
→ Because she (didn't have / hadn't have) a camera, she couldn't take pictures.

|B| 다음 가정법 문장을 직설법 문장으로 쓸 때, 빈칸을 완성하시오.

가정법 과거시제는 직설법 현재로, 가정법 과거완료는 직설법 과거로 바꿔 쓸 수 있어요.

01 If I weren't so busy, I could visit my grandparents.
→ As I am so busy, I ______________________.

02 If she had taken the medicine, she would feel better.
→ She ______________________, so she doesn't feel better.

03 If I didn't have an appointment, I could talk with you.
→ As ______________________, I ______________________.

04 If he had a dog, he would be happy.
→ He ______________________, so he ______________________.

05 If you had had a car, you could have given us a ride.
→ You ______________________, so you ______________________.

UNIT 04 I wish + 가정법

'~라면 …좋(았)을 텐데'라고 할 때는 〈I wish + 가정법〉으로 표현하세요.

가정법 과거	현재 사실	Sujeong is not here.	수정이는 여기 없다.
	유감/아쉬움	I wish Sujeong ~~was~~ were here. → 가정법 과거동사(were)	수정이가 여기 있으면 좋을 텐데.
가정법 과거완료	과거 사실	Sujeong was not here.	수정이는 여기 없었다.
	유감/아쉬움	I wish Sujeong had been here. → 가정법 과거완료(had+과거분사)	수정이가 여기 있었다면 좋았을 텐데.

참고 사실과 반대되는 일에 대한 유감/아쉬움의 표현이므로 가정법 동사를 써요.

|A| 우리말과 같도록 괄호 안에서 알맞은 것을 고르시오.

01 내가 답을 알면 좋을 텐데. → I wish I (know / knew / had known) the answer.

02 내가 더 많이 공부했더라면 좋았을 텐데. → I wish I (study / studied / had studied) more.

03 내가 그 영화를 봤더라면 좋았을 텐데. → I wish I (see / saw / had seen) the movie.

04 내가 부자라면 좋을 텐데. → I wish I (am / were / had been) rich.

05 내가 수영을 잘하면 좋을 텐데. → I wish I (swim / swam / had swum) well.

06 내가 영어를 유창하게 말하면 좋을 텐데. → I wish I (speak / spoke / had spoken) English fluently.

07 내가 박물관을 방문했더라면 좋았을 텐데. → I wish I (visit / visited / had visited) the museum.

|B| 다음 두 문장의 의미가 같도록 빈칸을 완성하시오.

01 I wish I had learned a foreign language.
→ I'm sorry I ______________________.

02 I wish I had more time to exercise.
→ I'm sorry I ______________________.

03 I'm sorry he didn't win the election.
→ I wish ______________________.

04 I wish I had answered the question.
→ I'm sorry ______________________.

05 I'm sorry you didn't apologize to me.
→ I wish ______________________.

06 I wish they had told me the truth.
→ I'm sorry ______________________.

〈I wish + 가정법〉에서도 가정법 과거시제는 직설법 현재(I'm sorry + 현재 사실)로, 가정법 과거완료는 직설법 과거(I'm sorry + 과거 사실)로 바꿔 쓸 수 있어요.

|C| 우리말과 같도록 괄호 안의 말을 활용하여 문장을 완성하시오.

01 내가 키가 좀 더 크면 좋을 텐데. (be, taller)

→ I wish ________________________.

02 네가 TV에 나오면 좋을 텐데. (appear, on TV)

→ I wish ________________________.

03 그녀가 날 이해했다면 좋았을 텐데. (understand, me)

→ I wish ________________________.

04 그들이 좀 더 일찍 왔더라면 좋았을 텐데. (come, earlier)

→ I wish ________________________.

05 그가 우리에게 자기 형을 소개했더라면 좋았을 텐데. (introduce, his brother)

→ I wish ________________________ to us.

|D| 우리말을 참고하여, 밑줄 친 부분이 어법상 옳으면 ○표 하고, 틀리면 바르게 고쳐 쓰시오.

01 네가 어젯밤에 내게 전화했더라면 좋았을 텐데.

→ I wish you called me last night. ________________

02 네가 그렇게 수줍어하지 않으면 좋을 텐데.

→ I wish you weren't so shy. ________________

03 우리가 무대에서 노래를 더 잘했더라면 좋았을 텐데.

→ I wish we sang a song better on stage. ________________

04 그가 금메달을 땄더라면 좋았을 텐데.

→ I wish he had won the gold medal. ________________

05 그들이 좀 더 부지런하면 좋을 텐데.

→ I wish they are more diligent. ________________

내신 기출 다음 우리말을 바르게 영작한 것은?

그가 시험 준비를 더 열심히 했더라면 좋았을 텐데.

① I wish he prepared for the contest harder.
② I wish he had prepared for the contest harder.
③ I wish he would have prepared for the contest harder.

실전 TIP

과거의 사실과는 반대되는 일에 대한 소망은 ⟨I wish+주어+had+과거분사⟩로 써야 해요.

UNIT 05 as if + 가정법

'마치 ~인[이었던] 것처럼'이라고 쓸 때는 〈as if+가정법〉으로 표현하세요.

주절	as if절	as if절의 해석	as if 가정법과 직설법(사실)의 비교
현재	가정법 과거	주절과 같은 시제로 해석	He acts as if he could do it. (할 수 있는 것처럼 행동한다) = In fact, he can't do it.
과거			He acted as if he could do it. (할 수 있었던 것처럼 행동했다) = In fact, he couldn't do it.
현재	가정법 과거완료	주절보다 더 과거로 해석	He talks as if he had seen me. (나를 봤던 것처럼 말한다) = In fact, he didn't see me.
과거			He talked as if he had seen me. (나를 봤었던 것처럼 말했다) = In fact, he hadn't seen me.

참고 가정이 아닌, 실제로 그럴 수도 있는 경우에는 as if절에 직설법을 쓸 수도 있어요.
He looks as if he needs some water. 그는 마치 물이 필요한 것처럼 보인다.

|A| 우리말과 같도록 괄호 안에서 알맞은 것을 고르시오.

01 너는 마치 (지금) 거기 사는 것처럼 말한다.
→ You talk as if you (live / lived) there.

02 너는 마치 (예전에) 거기 살았던 것처럼 말한다.
→ You talk as if you (lived / had lived) there.

03 그녀는 마치 (당시에) 그 답을 아는 것처럼 말했다.
→ She talked as if she (knows / knew) the answer.

04 그녀는 마치 (더 이전에) 그를 만났던 것처럼 말했다.
→ She talked as if she (met / had met) him.

|B| 다음 문장을 as if를 이용하여 가정법 문장으로 쓸 때, 빈칸을 완성하시오.

as if절에 가정법 과거완료는 주절의 시제보다 하나 더 과거의 의미로 해석해요.

01 In fact, we weren't heroes.
→ We felt ______________________________.

02 In fact, Seoyun wasn't a singer.
→ Seoyun sang ______________________________.

03 In fact, they had known me.
→ They behaved ______________________________.

04 In fact, Hana doesn't know the secret.
→ Hana looks ______________________________.

05 In fact, you didn't clean your room.

→ You talk ______________________.

06 In fact, the suspect wasn't innocent.

→ The suspect talked ______________________.

|C| **우리말과 같도록 괄호 안의 말을 활용하여 문장을 완성하시오.**

01 너는 마치 선생님인 것처럼 이야기한다. (a teacher)

→ You talk ______________________.

02 그녀는 마치 그 회사에서 일했던 것처럼 말한다. (work for, the company)

→ She talks ______________________.

03 그는 마치 무엇을 해야 할지 모르는 것처럼 보였다. (know, what to do)

→ He looked ______________________.

04 너는 마치 왕실에서 태어났던 것처럼 행동했다. (be born, in a royal family)

→ You behaved ______________________.

|D| **다음 두 문장을 한 문장으로 쓸 때, 빈칸을 완성하시오.**

01 You don't live in Jeju-do. You talk like you live in Jeju-do.

→ You ____________ as if you ______________________.

02 Tom was Anna's boyfriend. Tom sounds like he wasn't Anna's boyfriend.

→ Tom ____________ as if he ______________________.

03 He hadn't pass the exam. He talked like he had passed the exam last year.

→ He ____________ as if he ______________________.

04 We didn't lose the game. We feel like we had lost the game.

→ We ____________ as if ______________________.

05 He isn't responsible for the accident. He behaves like he is responsible for the accident.

→ He ______________________.

내신기출 다음 우리말을 바르게 영작한 것은?

너는 인생에 대해 모든 것을 아는 것처럼 말하는구나.

① You talk as if you knew everything about life.

② You talked as if you know everything about life.

③ You talk as if you had known everything about life.

실전 TIP

'마치 ~인 것처럼'이라는 뜻의 실제로는 아닌 일을 말할 때는 〈주어+현재동사+as if+주어+과거동사〉 형태로 써야 해요.

UNIT 06 Without[But for] + 가정법

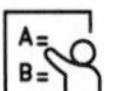

'~가 아니라면[없이는] …할[일] 것이다'라고 할 때는 ⟨Without[But for] ~+가정법 동사⟩로 표현하세요.

가정법 과거	현재 사실	There is water so life can exist.	물이 있어서 생명이 존재할 수 있다.
	반대 가정	Without[But for] water, life couldn't exist. 현재 사실(can)의 반대 가정	물이 없다면, 생명은 존재할 수 없을 것이다.
가정법 과거완료	과거 사실	You were here so I was not sad.	네가 여기 있어서 나는 슬프지 않았다.
	반대 가정	Without[But for] you, I would have been sad. 과거 사실(was not)의 반대 가정	네가 없었다면, 나는 슬펐을 것이다.

⟨Without[But for] ~+가정법 동사⟩를 ⟨If it were not[had not been] for ~⟩와 서로 바꾸어 쓸 수 있도록 하세요.

가정 과거	Without[But for] water, life couldn't exist. = If it were not for water, ~.	물이 없다면, 생명은 존재할 수 없을 것이다.
가정법 과거완료	Without[But for] you, I would have been sad. = If it had not been for you, ~.	네가 없었다면, 나는 슬펐을 것이다.

|A| 괄호 안에서 알맞은 것을 고르시오.

01 If it (is / were) not for oxygen, we would die.

02 If it had not been for you, I (can't / couldn't) have survived.

03 Without your help, I (could / couldn't) have succeeded. You helped me a lot.

04 If it had not been for your advice, I (would fail / would have failed).

05 If it were not for the book, I (couldn't figure out / couldn't have figure out) the answer.

|B| 우리말과 같도록 괄호 안의 말을 바르게 배열하시오.

01 태양이 없다면 아무것도 살 수 없을 텐데. (the sun, not, it, for, if, were)

→ ______________________, nothing could live.

02 중력이 없다면 우리는 걸을 수 없을 텐데. (walk, without, we, gravity, couldn't)

→ ______________________

03 네 도움이 없었다면 나는 실패했을 텐데. (your help, for, but, I, have failed, would)

→ ______________________

04 음악이 없다면 우리는 행복하지 않을 텐데. (for, it, not, if, were, music)

→ ______________________, we wouldn't be happy.

05 친구들이 없었다면 나는 슬픔에서 벗어나지 못했을 텐데. (friends, been, if, for, had, not, it)

→ ______________________, I couldn't have become free from worries.

|C| 다음을 If로 시작하는 문장은 Without으로 시작하는 문장으로, Without으로 시작하는 문장은 If로 시작하는 문장으로 바꾸어 쓰시오.

01 Without her reminder, I couldn't have remembered the deadline.

→ ______________________, I couldn't have remembered the deadline.

02 If it were not for the Internet, we couldn't search information easily.

→ ______________________, we couldn't search information easily.

03 Without electricity, we would be in trouble.

→ ______________________, we would be in trouble.

04 If it had not been for your cooperation, we wouldn't have been successful.

→ ______________________, we wouldn't have been successful.

05 Without a washing machine, there would be a lot of work to do.

→ ______________________, there would be a lot of work to do.

06 Without the ice age, dinosaurs would have still been alive.

→ ______________________, dinosaurs would have still been alive.

|D| 우리말과 같도록 괄호 안의 말을 활용하여 문장을 완성하시오.

01 그 선생님이 안 계셨다면, 나는 영어를 공부하지 않았을 텐데. (without, would, study)

→ ______________ the teacher, I ______________ English.

02 에어컨이 없다면 여름에 무척 더울 텐데. (if, would, be very hot)

→ ______________ an air conditioner, we ______________ in summer.

03 배달 서비스가 없다면 생활이 불편할 텐데. (but for, would, be inconvenient)

→ ______________ the delivery service, life ______________.

04 그가 없었다면 그 팀은 그 경기에서 졌을 텐데. (if, would, lose the match)

→ ______________, the team ______________.

05 그들이 없었다면 아무 일도 일어나지 않았을 텐데. (without, would, happen)

→ ______________, nothing ______________.

06 그 책이 없었다면 내 의견은 바뀌지 않았을 텐데. (if, would, change)

→ ______________ the book, my opinion ______________.

내신기출 다음 밑줄 친 부분이 어법상 어색한 것은?

① But for your advice, I would failed. It was very helpful.

② If it were not for Sora, we couldn't reach the top of the mountain.

③ If it had not been for his encouragement, she couldn't have succeeded.

실전 TIP

가정법의 주절이 현재의 반대인지 과거의 반대인지 파악해야 해요.

UNIT 07 It's time + 가정법

이미 했어야 할 것을 아직 안 한 것에 대한 유감, 불평, 아쉬움은 〈It's time that + 가정법 과거〉로 쓰세요.

It's time that + 과거 동사	It's time + (for + 행위자) + to부정사
~했어야 할 시간이다 (유감, 불평, 아쉬움)	(~가) ~할 시간이다 (할 일을 표현)
It's 12. It's time that he went to bed. 12시다. 그가 잠자리에 들었어야 할 시간이다.	It's 10. It's time (for him) to go to bed. 10시다. 그가 잠자리에 들 시간이다.

참고 가정법 과거 동사를 썼다는 것은 현재 사실과 반대되는 것을 표현하는 것으로, 현재 잠자리에 들지 않은 것에 대한 유감, 불평, 아쉬움을 표현하는 것이에요.

〈It's time that + 가정법 과거〉의 의미를 강조하기 위해 time 앞에 high나 about을 넣을 수 있어요.

It's high time that + 과거 동사	It's about time that + 과거 동사
진즉에 ~했어야 했다	(늦었지만) 이제는 (정말) ~할 시간이다

|A| 괄호 안의 동사를 활용하여 빈칸에 알맞은 말을 쓰시오.

01 It's almost midnight. It's time ____________ she ____________ home. (come)

02 She is over 65 years old. It's time for her ____________ ____________. (retire)

03 It's almost 1. It's ____________ that we ____________ eating. (finish)

04 It has been a week since the fight. It's ____________ that you ____________. (apologize)

05 He is 27 years old. It's time for him ____________ ____________ a job. (get)

06 The bike broke down again. It's time ____________ you ____________ a new bike. (buy)

07 It's 8 in the morning. It's____________ that you ____________ ____________. (get up)

|B| 우리말과 같도록 괄호 안의 말을 활용하여 문장을 완성하시오.

01 이제는 너는 공부할 시간이다. (study, about, time)

→ It's ____.

02 진즉에 너는 그에게 사실을 말했어야 했다. (the truth, high, time, tell)

→ It's ____.

03 이제는 우리가 떠나야 할 시간이다. (about, leave, that)

→ It's ____.

04 진즉에 너는 그 숙제를 했어야 했다. (do, high, time, the homework)

→ It's ____.

05 이제는 너는 너희 부모님들께 그것을 보여 줄 시간이다. (show, about, time, your parents)

→ It's ____.

중간고사·기말고사 실전문제

객관식 (01~25) / 주관식 (26~50)

정답과 해설 • 50쪽

학년과 반 이름 객관식 / 25문항 주관식 / 25문항

01~03 다음 빈칸에 알맞은 것을 고르시오.

01

If Gail had missed the chance to take the course, she __________ regretted it.

① would ② has
③ would have ④ would be
⑤ would been

02

If her mother hadn't told her to take an umbrella, Sue __________ in the rain now.

① is ② was
③ had been ④ would be
⑤ would have been

03

Though he ate a hamburger a while ago, the man is eating pizza __________ at all.

① as if he doesn't eat
② if he didn't eat
③ as if he didn't eaten
④ if he hadn't eaten
⑤ as if he hadn't eaten

04~05 다음 문장을 우리말로 바르게 나타낸 것을 고르시오.

04

I wish I could walk down this way holding your hand.

① 네 손을 잡고 이 길을 걸을 수 있었어.
② 네 손을 잡고 이 길을 걷길 바라고 있었어.
③ 네 손을 잡고 이 길을 걷게 되길 원해.
④ 네 손을 잡고 이 길을 걸었으면 좋을 텐데.
⑤ 네 손을 잡고 이 길을 걸으면 좋을 텐데.

05

Without your care, the patient wouldn't have recovered from his illness.

① 당신의 보살핌 없이도, 그 환자는 그의 병에서 회복될 것입니다.
② 당신의 보살핌 없이도, 그 환자는 그의 병에서 회복되었습니다.
③ 당신의 보살핌이 없다면, 그 환자는 그의 병에서 회복되지 못할 것입니다.
④ 당신의 보살핌이 없어서, 그 환자는 그의 병에서 회복되지 못했습니다.
⑤ 당신의 보살핌이 없었다면, 그 환자는 그의 병에서 회복되지 못했을 것입니다.

06~08 다음 우리말을 영어로 바르게 나타낸 것을 고르시오.

06

만약 그가 슬프다면, 큰 소리로 울 텐데.

① If he is sad, he will cry out loud.
② If he were sad, he would cry out loud.
③ If he were sad, he would have cried out loud.
④ If he had been sad, he would cry out loud.
⑤ If he had been sad, he would have cried out loud.

07 만약 공룡이 멸종하지 않았다면, 지금 지구는 어떤 모습일까?

① What does the Earth look like now if dinosaurs are not extinct?
② What would the Earth look like now if dinosaurs were not extinct?
③ What would the Earth look like now if dinosaurs hadn't been extinct?
④ What would the Earth have looked like now if dinosaurs hadn't been extinct?
⑤ What would the Earth have looked like now if dinosaurs were not extinct?

08 한국 전쟁이 일어나지 않았었다면 좋았을 텐데.

① I wish the Korean War doesn't break out.
② I wish the Korean War didn't break out.
③ I wish the Korean War hadn't broken out.
④ I wish the Korean War won't break out.
⑤ I wish the Korean War hasn't broken out.

09~10 다음 중 어법상 어색한 것을 고르시오.

09 ① But for his donation, many children in Africa can't have been educated.
② Would you mind if I used your computer?
③ I wish my mom could cook some Italian dishes.
④ Some animals acts as if they were dead when in danger.
⑤ If he knew I was here, he would come here right away.

10 ① She would be sleeping by now if her husband had come home earlier.
② If he hadn't met his best friend, Henry would be lonely every day.
③ If her son didn't break the oven, she would have baked you some cookies.
④ His teacher would have helped Jerry if he had asked her.
⑤ They would have gone camping if the weather had been warmer.

11~12 다음 문장의 밑줄 친 부분이 어법상 옳은 것을 고르시오.

11 ① If it had not been repaired, the car would have stopped suddenly on the road.
② If the instruction were clear, the army wouldn't have been confused.
③ If Ben had time, he would have helped me move the box.
④ If you had asked me what to do, you wouldn't make a mistake at that time.
⑤ If she will be with his friends, Karen would be more cheerful.

12 ① If you are me, you would have done the same.
② I wish I am the first to solve the riddle in the class.
③ If she hadn't have surgery, she might not be able to walk now.
④ If I had gotten married in my 20s, I would have a child as old as you now.
⑤ My history teacher explained the historical incident as if she has lived in 1800s.

13 다음 중 밑줄 친 if의 쓰임이 나머지 넷과 다른 것은?

① You would like this book if you had watched the movie first.
② The doctor asked if John could remember his childhood.
③ There would have been no seat left if we hadn't hurried.
④ She would have left the message if someone had answered the phone.
⑤ He could do better now if he had studied it yesterday.

14 다음 문장의 밑줄 친 부분과 바꾸어 쓸 수 있는 것을 모두 고르면?

Without break time, hikers would have been exhausted soon.

① If it were not for break time
② If it had not been for break time
③ But for break time
④ But not for break time
⑤ If there isn't break time

15~16 다음 문장을 가정법 문장으로 바르게 나타낸 것을 고르시오.

15

Since it's midnight, the party needs to be over.

① If it isn't midnight, the party wouldn't need to be over.
② If it was midnight, the party would need to be over.
③ If it weren't midnight, the party wouldn't need to be over.
④ If it had been midnight, the party would need to be over.
⑤ If it hadn't been midnight, the party wouldn't have needed to be over.

16

The stranger smiled at me, but he didn't know me well.

① The stranger smiles at me as if he knows me well.
② The stranger smiles at me as if he knew me well.
③ The stranger smiled at me as if he knew me well.
④ The stranger smiled at me as if he had known me well.
⑤ The stranger smiled at me as if he hadn't known me well.

17~18 다음 가정법 문장을 직설법 문장으로 바르게 나타낸 것을 고르시오.

17

If the train arrived on time, we wouldn't be late for the conference.

① The train arrives on time, so we won't be late for the conference.
② The train doesn't arrive on time, so we will be late for the conference.
③ The train arrived on time, so we aren't late for the conference.
④ The train arrived on time, so we weren't late for the conference.
⑤ The train didn't arrive on time, so we were late for the conference.

18

I wish people didn't keep asking me about the accident.

① I'm sorry that people keep asking me about the accident.
② I'm sorry that people don't keep asking me about the accident.
③ I'm sorry that people kept asking me about the accident.
④ I was sorry that people didn't keep asking me about the accident.
⑤ I was sorry that people kept asking me about the accident.

19 다음 문장을 가정법 문장으로 바르게 나타낸 것을 모두 고르면?

Thanks to his classmates, he could win the prize.

① But for his classmates, he couldn't have won the prize.
② If it hadn't been for his classmates, he couldn't have won the prize.
③ Without his classmates, he couldn't win the prize.
④ If it were not for his classmates, he couldn't win the prize.
⑤ If it is not for his classmates, he can't win the prize.

20 다음 주어진 문장과 의미가 같은 것은?

Without a microscope, many microbes would not have been found.

① But for a microscope, many microbes would not be found.
② If it were not for a microscope, many microbes would not be found.
③ If it were not for a microscope, many microbes would not have been found.
④ If it had not been for a microscope, many microbes would not have been found.
⑤ If it had not been for a microscope, many microbes would have been found.

21~22 다음 빈칸에 알맞은 말이 바르게 짝지어진 것을 고르시오.

21

• If Andy ________ more money, he could afford the house in the city.
• She screamed with fear as if she ________ a ghost that night.
• ________ for his cooperation, they would not have succeeded in this business.

① had – sees – Without
② had had – saw – Without
③ had – had seen – But
④ had had – saw – But
⑤ has – had seen – But

22

- I wish tomorrow ________ come.
- If it ________ not for the Internet, it would be difficult to get in touch with people.

① won't – had　② doesn't – were
③ doesn't – was　④ didn't – were
⑤ won't – was

23 다음 중 어법상 틀린 문장의 개수는?

ⓐ Would you have been more excited if more people had been at the concert?
ⓑ If the book had been written in German, he could have read it.
ⓒ If it have not been for the flashlight, we would have fallen down in the cave.
ⓓ Do you wish you didn't get old?

① 없음　② 1개　③ 2개
④ 3개　⑤ 4개

24 다음 중 어법상 옳은 문장의 개수는?

ⓐ If you were more positive, you would have been more satisfied with your life.
ⓑ Where would you live if you could live in any city in the world?
ⓒ Without electricity, people would be very uncomfortable.
ⓓ The famous actor acts as if he were the king of the world.

① 없음　② 1개　③ 2개
④ 3개　⑤ 4개

25 다음 중 어법상 옳은 문장끼리 바르게 짝지은 것은?

ⓐ He sounded as if he hasn't gotten the message.
ⓑ If they have seen the dancing, they would have laughed a lot.
ⓒ He wouldn't have let her take leave if there hadn't been a family emergency.
ⓓ If it had not been for my coach, I wouldn't have won the gold medal.
ⓔ Why do you wish you hadn't left your hometown?

① ⓐ, ⓑ　② ⓐ, ⓓ
③ ⓒ, ⓔ　④ ⓐ, ⓓ, ⓔ
⑤ ⓒ, ⓓ, ⓔ

〈다음부터는 서술형 주관식 문제입니다.〉

26~28 다음 우리말과 같도록 빈칸에 괄호 안의 말을 알맞은 형태로 쓰시오.

26

그 사진을 찍을 때, 그가 좀 더 웃었더라면 좋았을 텐데. (smile)

→ I wish he ____________ more when taking the picture.

27

그는 집이 없는 것처럼 길에서 자는데, 사실은 백만장자이다. (have)

→ He sleeps on the street as if he ____________ a home, but he's actually a millionaire.

28 TV가 없다면, 내 삶은 더 재미있을지도 몰라. (be)

→ If it ______________ for TV, my life might be more fun.

29~31 다음 문장의 밑줄 친 부분이 어법상 맞으면 ○표 하고, 틀리면 바르게 고쳐 쓰시오.

29 If the rabbit hadn't fallen asleep, the turtle couldn't win the race.

→ ______________________

30 My nephew advised me as if he is older than me.

→ ______________________

31 If it had not for this story, he wouldn't have become a director.

→ ______________________

32~33 다음 직설법 문장을 가정법 문장으로 바꾸어 쓸 때, 빈칸에 알맞은 말을 쓰시오.

32 Because he is on a diet, he won't go to the buffet with us tonight.

→ If he ________ ________ on a diet, he ________ ________ to the buffet with us tonight.

33 I'm sorry that too many disposable products are used in everyday life.

→ I wish too many disposable products ________ ________ ________ in everyday life.

34~35 다음 가정법 문장을 직설법 문장으로 바꾸어 쓸 때, 빈칸에 알맞은 말을 쓰시오.

34 If the price hadn't been reasonable, the goods wouldn't have been sold out.

→ Because the price ______________ reasonable, the goods ______________ ________ ________.

35 If it were not for sunlight, plants couldn't grow.

→ Since there ________ sunlight, plants ________ ________.

36~38 다음 우리말과 같도록 괄호 안의 말을 바르게 배열하시오.

36 만약 내가 이집트에 있다면, 피라미드 안에 들어가 볼 수 있을 텐데.
(if, could, I, I, go, were, in Egypt, inside)

→ ______________________
______________ the pyramid.

37 만약 우리가 어제 소고기를 샀었더라면 오늘 스테이크를 먹을 텐데.
(yesterday, bought, if, had, have, we, we, beef, would, steak)

→ ______________________
______________ today.

38 그 범인은 마치 무죄인 것처럼 말한다.
(speaks, innocent, were, the criminal, as, he, if)

→ ______________________

39~42 다음 우리말과 같도록 괄호 안의 말을 활용하여 문장을 완성하시오.

39 만약 그녀가 당신에게 알리지 않았다면, 당신은 좋은 기회를 놓쳤을 것이다. (inform, miss, a good chance)

→ If ______________________
______________________.

40 우리는 떠났어야 할 시간이다. (leave, time)

→ It's ______________________.

41 진즉에 그것을 네 컴퓨터에 설치했어야 했다.
(install, high, that, time)

→ ______________________
on your computer.

42 아이들이 없다면, 세상은 너무 조용할 것이다.
(but, children, the world, too quiet)

→ ______________________

43~45 다음 대화의 밑줄 친 ⓐ~ⓔ 중 어법상 어색한 부분을 세 군데 찾아 바르게 고쳐 쓰시오.

A: Have you finished your report assignment on environmental protection?
B: No, not yet. ⓐ I wish I had a robot to do my homework for me.
A: ⓑ If there has been such a thing, I would have already spent all my allowance to buy it. Anyway, you need to hurry.
B: I know. Did you finish it?
A: No, not yet.
B: What? But ⓒ why did you talk me as if you had already done it?
A: I did not. ⓓ If I have said I didn't even start, would you believe me?
B: Really?
A: Just kidding. Almost done. ⓔ If it were not for the Internet, it would have been hard.

43 ______________ → ______________

44 ______________ → ______________

45 ______________ → ______________

46~48 다음 글의 밑줄 친 ⓐ~ⓖ 중 어법상 틀린 부분을 세 군데 찾아 바르게 고쳐 쓰시오.

ⓐ If you could go back to a moment in the past, which moment will you go back to? ⓑ Is there anything you would want to change there? Everyone has regrets about the past: ⓒ 'I wish I know the answer to that question.', ⓓ 'If I hadn't spent all that money, I could buy a new cell phone now.' However, ⓔ if you think about it, there's a lot to be thankful for: ⓕ 'If I hadn't worn protective gear, I would be hurt badly when I fell off my bike.' ⓖ 'Without my best friends, school would have been really boring.'

46 ______________ → ______________

47 ______________ → ______________

48 ______________ → ______________

49~50 다음 우리말을 주어진 |조건|에 맞게 바르게 영작하시오.

49 그녀가 수업에서 적극적으로 대답하면 좋을 텐데.

|조건|
1. 〈I wish+가정법〉을 사용할 것
2. 단어 answer, actively, in class를 사용할 것
3. 7단어로 쓸 것

→ ______________________

50 어젯밤 그의 도움이 없었더라면, 그녀는 오늘 바쁠 것이다.

|조건|
1. 혼합 가정법을 사용할 것
2. 단어 if, his help, last night, busy를 사용할 것238
3. 15단어로 쓸 것

→ ______________________

CHAPTER

12 일치와 화법

Unit 01 주의해야 할 수의 일치

Unit 02 시제 일치 & 시제 일치의 예외

Unit 03 간접화법 전환 1

Unit 04 간접화법 전환 2

Unit 05 간접화법 전환 3

UNIT 01 주의해야 할 수의 일치

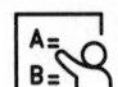 〈부분을 나타내는 명사 + of + 명사〉가 주어일 때, 동사는 of 뒤의 명사의 수에 일치시키세요.

주어			동사
Some / Most / All / Half / ~ percent / 분수(One third / Three fifths) 등	of	단수명사 / 셀 수 없는 명사	단수동사
		복수명사	복수동사

참고 One third of the apple is rotten. 그 사과의 1/3 (단수명사 – 단수동사)
One third of the apples in the basket are rotten. 바구니 안에 있는 사과들의 1/3 (복수명사 – 복수동사)

항상 단수 취급하거나 복수 취급하는 말들을 알아 두세요.

주어	동사	예시
every ~/each ~/each of ~/one of ~/the number of ~ (~의 수)	단수동사	Every rule has its exception. The number of tourists increases every year.
형태는 복수이지만, 의미는 단수인 명사 (과목명, 나라 이름)	단수동사	mathematics(수학) physics(물리학) economics(경제학) the United States(미국) the Philippines(필리핀)
동명사, to부정사, 명사절 주어	단수동사	What they told us was not true.
both ~/a number of ~ (많은 ~)	복수동사	Both sides are clean. A number of tourists are visiting to Korea.
the+형용사	복수동사	the young = young people(젊은 사람들) the poor = poor people(가난한 사람들)

|A| 괄호 안에서 알맞은 것을 고르시오.

01 Half of the cake (was / were) eaten by me.

02 A number of visitors (come / comes) to the city.

03 Mathematics (is / are) my favorite subject.

04 All of the students (attend / attends) the class.

05 The number of visitors (is / are) increasing.

06 Both Seojun and Jaehee (is / are) my classmates.

07 The United States (is / are) the fourth largest country in the world.

08 The young (prefer / prefers) watching movies to reading books.

|B| 빈칸에 괄호 안의 단어를 알맞은 형태로 쓰시오. (단, 현재시제로 쓸 것)

01 Some houses ________________ fire places. (have)

02 The Philippines ________________ located in Southeast Asia. (be)

03 Half of the members ________________ a positive response. (give)

04 Both Yuna and Hayeon ________________ to school. (walk)

05 Two percent of $200 ________________ $4. (be)

06 Each bedroom ________________ its own bathroom. (have)

|C| 다음 문장에서 어법상 어색한 부분을 찾아 바르게 고쳐 쓰시오. (단, 없는 경우 ×표 할 것)

01 Some of the books is mine. ________________

02 Every person has the right to be educated. ________________

03 We think statistics are helpful. ________________

04 All of the machinery has been repaired. ________________

05 It's Sunday and most of the stores is not open. ________________

06 Physics are the most difficult subject to me. ________________

07 The rich is not always happy. ________________

|D| 우리말과 같도록 괄호 안의 말을 활용하여 문장을 완성하시오.

01 10km를 달리는 것은 쉽지 않다. (be, easy)
→ Running 10km ________________.

02 그곳의 피자와 파스타 둘 다 맛있다. (both, be, delicious)
→ ________________ pizza and pasta there ________________.

03 직원 대부분이 운전해서 출근한다. (most, drive)
→ ________________ of the employees ________________ to work.

04 모든 우유가 팔렸다. (all, be, sold out)
→ ________________ milk ________________.

05 그 도시의 학생 수가 증가하고 있다. (the number of, be increasing)
→ ________________ in the city ________________.

06 수하물의 절반이 아직 도착하지 않았다. (half, have arrived)
→ ________________ of the baggage ________________ yet.

07 약자들은 그들 자신의 싸우는 방식을 가지고 있다. (have, weak)
→ ________________ their own way of fighting.

내신 기출 다음 중 어법상 어색한 것은?

① Half of the clothing needs to be washed.
② There was a number of errors in the essay.
③ Every student has to submit the assignment today.

실전 TIP
a number of ~와 the number of ~의 의미 차이에 주의하세요.

UNIT 02 시제 일치 & 시제 일치의 예외

주절의 시제와 종속절의 시제의 기본적인 관계를 알아 두세요.

주절 시제	종속절의 시제	예문	
현재	모든 시제 가능	He knows	that you are honest.
			that you did not tell a lie.
			that you will tell the truth.
과거	과거나 과거완료 가능	He thought	that she was in London.
			that she had gone to London.

항상 현재시제를 쓰는 경우와 항상 과거시제를 쓰는 경우에 유의하세요.

항상 현재	진리, 사실, 속담, 현재의 습관 등	He knew that the earth is round.	둥글다는 것을 알았다
		He told us that he likes to draw pictures.	좋아한다고 말했다
		She said that blood is thicker than water.	더 진하다고 말했다
항상 과거	역사적 사실	I will learn how Armstrong landed on the moon.	어떻게 착륙했는지 배울 거다

|A| 괄호 안에서 알맞은 것을 고르시오.

01 We believed that he (is / was) not guilty.

02 The teacher explained that the Earth (went / goes) around the Sun.

03 I thought you (will / would) come and see me in that afternoon.

04 You said that you always (get / got) up at 7:00.

05 They thought I (can / could) win the first prize.

|B| 다음 문장에서 어법상 어색한 부분을 찾아 바르게 고쳐 쓰시오. (단, 없는 경우 ×표 할 것)

01 I know that you finished washing the dishes. ______________

02 He said that he will play the violin for the concert. ______________

03 I explained that the Pacific was the largest ocean in the world. ______________

04 My mom used to say haste made waste. ______________

05 The World Trade Center in New York was destroyed in 2001. ______________

06 The teacher let us know that Amrok River was the longest river in Korean Peninsula.

____

습관, 진리, 사실, 속담은 반드시 현재시제로, 역사적 사실은 반드시 과거시제로 써요.

|C| 우리말과 같도록 괄호 안의 말을 활용하여 문장을 완성하시오.

01 너는 네 방을 청소할 수 있다고 말했다. (can, clean, your room)

→ You said that you ____________________.

02 나는 '모나리자'가 16세기에 그려진 것을 안다. (be painted)

→ I know that the *Mona Lisa* ____________________ in the 16th century.

03 오늘 우리는 금성이 화성보다 크다고 배웠다. (Venus, large)

→ Today we learned that ____________________ Mars.

04 그는 매일 아침에 우유 한 잔을 마신다고 말했다. (say, drink, a cup of milk)

→ He ____________ that he ____________________ every morning.

05 할머니께서는 반짝이는 모든 것이 금은 아니라고 말씀하셨다. (say, all, that, glitter, be)

→ My grandmother ____________ that ____________________ not gold.

06 선생님께서는 달의 중력이 지구의 중력보다 약하다고 설명하셨다. (explain, weak)

→ The teacher ____________ that the gravity of Moon ____________________ that of the Earth.

|D| 다음 문장을 주절의 시제를 과거시제로 바꾸어 다시 쓰시오.

01 She says she will go to Hawaii someday.

→ ____

02 I learn that oil always floats on water.

→ ____

03 They say they may come earlier than scheduled.

→ ____

04 They learn that East and West Germany united in 1990.

→ ____

내신 기출 다음 중 어법상 어색한 것은?

① He taught his kids that water froze at 0℃.

② She found out that she had lost her wallet.

③ We learned that the Korean War ended in 1953.

실전 TIP

사실이나 진리는 항상 현재로, 역사적 사실은 항상 과거로, 과거 이전의 일은 대과거로 쓴다는 것을 다시 기억하세요.

UNIT 03 간접화법 전환 1

 **직접화법의 문장을 간접화법으로 고쳐 쓸 때, 다음 단계에 따라 고쳐 쓰세요.**

직접화법	Jinsu said to me, "You look so tired now."	
step 1	전달동사 바꾸기(say → say / say to → tell)	said to me → told me
step 2	인용 부호(" ")를 없애고 that절로 쓰기	*that은 생략 가능
step 3	that절의 주어를 전달자의 입장으로 바꾸기	"You" → I
step 4	시제를 전달자 입장으로 바꾸기	"look" → looked *said와 같은 시제
step 5	시간, 장소 부사(구)를 전달자 입장으로 바꾸기	"now" → then
간접화법	Jinsu told me (that) I looked so tired then.	

참고 직접화법은 있는 그대로 전달하는 것이고, 간접화법은 전달자의 입장으로 고쳐 쓴 말이에요.
→ 전달자의 입장에서는 You가 I이며, look이 looked가 돼요.

간접화법으로 고쳐 쓸 때, 주의해야 할 시제 및 부사(구)를 알아 두세요.

전달동사의 시제	현재(say)	인용 부호(" ") 안의 동사 = 간접화법 that절의 동사
	과거(said)	현재 → 과거 / 과거 → 과거완료 / 현재완료 → 과거완료

now → then	today → that day	tonight → that night
this[these] → that[those]	here → there	ago → before
yesterday → the day before, the previous day	tomorrow → the next[following] day	last week → the week before, the previous week

|A| 괄호 안에서 알맞은 것을 고르시오.

01 You (said / told), "I'm not feeling well."

02 I told you that I (will / would) come back later.

03 Susie told me that she (is / was) busy the day before.

04 Harry (said / told) me that he was sorry.

05 Tom said that he (would / had) have lunch at the restaurant the next day.

06 Eunji told her parents she (had done / has done) her homework.

|B| 다음 문장을 간접화법으로 바꾸어 쓸 때, 빈칸에 알맞은 말을 쓰시오.

01 The woman said, "I'm so thirsty now."

→ The woman ______________ that ____.

02 Wendy said to her mom, "I want to buy a bike for my birthday."

→ Wendy ______________ that ____.

03 The man said to us, "I'll meet you in the office tomorrow."

→ The man ____________ that ______________________________.

04 Emma said, "The competition was last week."

→ Emma ____________ that ______________________________.

05 The girl said to me, "I enjoy drawing a picture when I have free time."

→ The girl ____________ that ______________________________.

06 Bill said to us, "I have to finish this work by tomorrow."

→ Bill ____________ that ______________________________.

|C| 다음 문장에서 어법상 어색한 부분을 찾아 바르게 고쳐 쓰시오. (단, 없는 경우 ×표 할 것)

01 He said that his brother has gone to Canada a month before. ____________

02 You told me that you had to return the book that day. ____________

03 She said that she can make a pie with apples. ____________

04 You said that you will go to Bangkok the next week. ____________

05 Matt said that he would be home late that night. ____________

06 She told us that she took a test four days before. ____________

|D| 다음 문장을 직접화법은 간접화법으로, 간접화법은 직접화법으로 바꾸어 쓰시오.

01 You said, "I'm tired and sleepy tonight."

→ ______________________________

02 He said that he would enter the contest the next day.

→ ______________________________

03 She said to me, "I visited my cousin in Busan last week."

→ ______________________________

04 Anne said to me, "I met Jia yesterday."

→ ______________________________

05 Nick told me that he would play soccer there with his friends.

→ ______________________________

06 They said, "We are going to buy this car."

→ ______________________________

내신기출 다음 중 어법상 옳은 문장은?

① He said me that he was going to be late.

② Jack said to us, "I didn't sleep well last night."

③ She told that she had to give a presentation the following day.

실전 TIP

간접목적어가 있는지 없는지에 따라, told를 쓰거나 said를 쓰거나 해야 해요.

UNIT 04 간접화법 전환 2

의문문을 간접화법으로 고쳐 쓸 때, 다음 단계에 따라 고쳐 쓰세요.

직접화법	She said to him, "Where do you live now?"	
step 1	전달동사 바꾸기(say, say to → ask)	said to him → asked him
step 2	인용부호(" ")를 없애고, that을 쓰지 않고 의문사를 접속사로 쓰기	asked him where
step 3	의문사 뒤에 〈주어+동사〉의 어순으로 쓰기	asked him where you live
step 4	의문사 없는 의문문은 if / whether를 쓰기	asked him if / whether ~ (~인지 아닌지 물었다)
step 5	주어, 동사, 부사(구) 등을 전달자 입장으로 바꾸기	"you" → he / "live" → lived / "now" → then
간접화법	She asked him where he lived then.	

주의 의문사가 없는 의문문은 접속사 if나 whether를 쓴다는 것에 주의하세요.

직접화법	He said to me, "Have you been to Busan?" 그는 내게 "부산에 가 본 적 있어?"라고 말했다.
간접화법	He asked me if[whether] I had been to Busan. 그는 내게 부산에 가 본 적이 있냐고 물었다.

|A| 괄호 안에서 알맞은 것을 고르시오.

01 I (said / asked) the kid why he was crying.

02 Jenny asked me if I (am / was) busy.

03 He asked me (where did you live / where I lived).

04 She asked me when he (will / would) come.

05 Last night, my mom asked me what I was doing (now / then).

06 The teacher asked the students if they (had read / have read) the book.

|B| 우리말과 같도록 괄호 안의 말을 바르게 배열하시오.

01 Cindy는 내게 인도에 가 본 적이 있는지 물었다. (had been to, I, India, whether)

→ Cindy asked me ______________________________.

02 그녀는 우리에게 언제 도착할지 물었다. (would, we, when, arrive)

→ She asked us ______________________________.

03 엄마는 내게 그때 뭘 읽고 있는지 물으셨다. (was reading, what, I, then)

→ My mom asked me ______________________________.

04 그는 그녀에게 어디에서 그 노트북 컴퓨터를 샀는지 물었다. (she, the laptop, where, had bought)

→ He asked her ______________________________.

05 민지는 내게 어떻게 그 문제를 풀 수 있었는지 물었다. (could, how, I, solve, the problem)

→ Minji asked me ______________________________.

06 선생님께서는 우리에게 누가 그 전날 교실을 청소했는지 물으셨다. (had cleaned, the day before, the classroom, who)

→ The teacher asked us ______________________________.

|C| **다음 문장을 직접화법은 간접화법으로, 간접화법은 직접화법으로 바꾸어 쓰시오.**

01 Ben said to me, "Do you want to buy this book?"

→ Ben asked me ______________________________.

02 My sister asked me if I could help her then.

→ My sister said to me, "______________________________?"

03 Matt said to her, "Where do you live now?"

→ Matt asked her ______________________________.

04 Sarah asked him what he would do that weekend.

→ Sarah said to him, "______________________________?"

05 Betty said to me, "Have you eaten lunch?"

→ Betty asked me ______________________________.

06 You asked me how you could get to my house.

→ You said to me, "______________________________?"

|D| **다음 문장에서 어법상 어색한 부분을 찾아 바르게 고쳐 쓰시오. (단, 없는 경우 ×표 할 것)**

01 Betty asked Tony what was he doing then. ______________

02 Yunju asked us where we will go for a picnic. ______________

03 Billy asked me whether I have to go home by 9. ______________

04 He asked me when I got the invitation he had sent. ______________

05 She asked me how would I get there. ______________

06 They asked the police officer who was responsible for the accident. ______________

실전 TIP

간접의문문의 의문 접속사가 의미상 올바른지 확인하세요.

내신 기출 다음 밑줄 친 부분이 어법상 어색한 것은?

① John asked Sarah what she attended the class.

② The doctor asked me how long I had felt dizzy.

③ I asked him why he hadn't show up the previous day.

UNIT 05 간접화법 전환 3

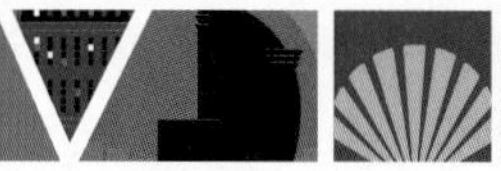

명령문을 간접화법으로 고쳐 쓸 때, 다음 단계에 따라 고쳐 쓰세요.

직접화법	He said to me, "Stop picking your nose."	
step 1	전달동사를 명령문의 내용에 따라 바꾸기	tell(지시), ask(요청), advise(충고), order(명령)
step 2	인용 부호(" ")를 없애고 〈목적어+to부정사〉로 쓰기	told me to stop *5형식 목적격보어: to부정사
step 3	부정명령(Don't ~)일 때는 〈not+to부정사〉로 쓰기	told me not to ~
step 4	기타 목적격 · 소유격 대명사, 부사 등 고치기	"your"→ my
간접화법	He told me to stop picking my nose.	

|A| 우리말과 같도록 괄호 안의 말을 바르게 배열하시오.

01 너는 내게 거기서 기다리라고 말했다. (told, there, wait, me, to)

→ You ______________________________.

02 그는 우리에게 마실 것을 가져와 달라고 요청했다. (bring, us, to, something to drink, asked)

→ He ______________________________.

03 의사는 그 환자에게 너무 많이 먹지 말라고 조언했다. (eat too much, the patient, not, advised, to)

→ The doctor ______________________________.

04 선생님께서는 내게 긴장하지 말라고 말씀하셨다. (be nervous, not, told, to, me)

→ The teacher ______________________________.

05 그녀는 우리에게 학교에 지각하지 말라고 명령했다. (ordered, not, be late for school, us, to)

→ She ______________________________.

|B| 다음 문장을 괄호 안의 말을 활용하여 간접화법으로 바꾸어 쓰시오.

직접화법 명령문을 간접화법으로 바꾸어 쓸 땐 to부정사가 와요.

01 The doctor said to me, "Work out regularly for your health." (advise)

→ The doctor ______________________________.

02 The librarian said to me "Return the book today." (ask)

→ The librarian ______________________________.

03 He said to you, "Take the subway instead of the bus." (tell)

→ He ______________________________.

04 She said to us, "Come to the party tomorrow." (ask)

→ She ______________________________.

05 They said to the children, "Don't ride your bikes in the parking lot." (order)

→ They ______________________________.

중간고사·기말고사 실전문제

객관식 (01~25) / 주관식 (26~50)

정답과 해설 • 54쪽

학년과 반 이름 객관식 / 25문항 주관식 / 25문항

01~03 다음 빈칸에 알맞은 것을 고르시오.

01

Both Alice and I ________ in the department store at that time.

① is ② are
③ was ④ were
⑤ has been

02

________ student has to take turns playing.

① All ② Both
③ Some ④ Each
⑤ Most of

03

Karen ________ me that she would go to sleep early that night.

① says ② tells
③ said ④ told
⑤ had told

04~05 다음 빈칸에 알맞은 것을 모두 고르시오.

04

Sam assumed that the professor ________ him a bad grade.

① gives ② gave
③ can give ④ has given
⑤ might give

05

________ have been used to make breakfast.

① All of the potatoes
② Half of the eggs
③ One fifth of the onion
④ All milk
⑤ Every vegetable

06~07 다음 빈칸에 알맞지 않은 것을 고르시오.

06

________ was really difficult for me.

① Each subject
② Learning French
③ One third of them
④ Buying fruits
⑤ The first half of the work

07

Everyone thought that she ________ angry at the man.

① was ② got ③ gets
④ would get ⑤ might be

08~09 다음 우리말을 영어로 바르게 나타낸 것을 고르시오.

08

Annie는 그에게 어디에서 그 물건을 샀냐고 물었다.

① Annie told him where did you buy the item.
② Annie told him where you bought the item.
③ Annie asked him where do you buy the item.
④ Annie asked him where did he buy the item.
⑤ Annie asked him where he bought the item.

09

회의에 참석한 모든 유권자는 그에게 반대했다.

① Every voter at the meeting was against him.
② Every voters at the meeting was against him.
③ Every voter at the meeting were against him.
④ All of the voter at the meeting were against him.
⑤ All of the voters at the meeting was against him.

10~11 다음 중 어법상 <u>어색한</u> 것을 고르시오.

10 ① Most of the stores are closed on Sundays.
② Some dishes are prepared for vegetarians.
③ The number of people traveling abroad increases every year.
④ A number of errors was found in the report.
⑤ All the paper was used to print the document.

11 ① We learned from him that practice makes perfect.
② The teacher explained that there are eight planets in the solar system.
③ He told me that his house is robbed last night.
④ The announcer reported that there was a big forest fire in California.
⑤ She informed me that he quit his job last month.

12~13 다음 중 어법상 옳은 것을 고르시오.

12 ① Half of the furniture in this room is secondhand.
② Mathematics have bothered many students for a long time.
③ To remember people's names are not easy for me.
④ Four-fifths of this floor are used as a ballroom.
⑤ Not every players were ready to take challenge.

13 ① Robin told his teacher that he will become a scientist.
② They learned from the experience that "The early bird caught the worm."
③ Some people believe that the Nazca Lines in Peru are drawn by aliens.
④ William said that he takes a walk for 30 minutes this morning.
⑤ Amy told me that she always loves to go fishing.

14~16 다음 문장을 간접화법으로 바르게 나타낸 것을 고르시오.

14

Nate said to me, "You have to help me now."

① Nate said that you have to help me now.
② Nate said me that he had to help me then.
③ Nate told me that he had to help me then.
④ Nate told me that I have to help him now.
⑤ Nate told me that I had to help him then.

15

His wife said to him, "Don't take the subway today."

① His wife said him not take the subway today.
② His wife told him not to take the subway that day.
③ His wife asked him not to take the subway today.
④ His wife told him to not take the subway that day.
⑤ His wife asked him to not take the subway that day.

16

No one said to her, "What do you want to have for lunch?"

① No one said what do you want to have for lunch.
② No one told her what did she want to have for lunch.
③ No one asked her what she wanted to have for lunch.
④ No one asked her whether did she want to have for lunch.
⑤ No one asked her whether she wanted to have for lunch.

17~19 다음 문장을 직접화법으로 바르게 나타낸 것을 고르시오.

17

The judge ordered the lawyer to bring the evidence the next day.

① The judge ordered to the lawyer, "To bring the evidence tomorrow."
② The judge ordered the lawyer, "Brought the evidence the next day."
③ The judge said the lawyer, "Bring the evidence today."
④ The judge said to the lawyer, "Bring the evidence tomorrow."
⑤ The judge said to the lawyer, "Bring the evidence today."

18 Charles told his parents he had sent some money to them.

① Charles said his parents, "He had sent some money to you."
② Charles told his parents, "I have sent some money to them."
③ Charles said to his parents, "I sent some money to you."
④ Charles said his parents, "I have sent some money to you."
⑤ Charles told to his parents, "I have sent some money to them."

19 The counselor asked her if she had experienced those symptoms before.

① The counselor asked her, "If she had experienced these symptoms before?"
② The counselor said to her, "If she had experienced these symptoms before?"
③ The counselor said to her, "Had she experienced these symptoms ago?"
④ The counselor asked her, "Had you experienced these symptom ago?"
⑤ The counselor said to her, "Have you experienced these symptoms before?"

20~22 다음 빈칸에 알맞은 말이 바르게 짝지어진 것을 고르시오.

20 The number of ________ in this year's summer camp ________ 500 in total.

① participant – is
② participant – are
③ participants – have
④ participants – are
⑤ participants – is

21
• Half of his family members ________ in another country.
• She believed the saying that no news ________ good news.

① live – were ② live – is
③ lives – is ④ lives – was
⑤ lived – was

22
• About 30 percent of the budget ________ spent on material purchases.
• Yesterday, Hannah told me that she would leave the house ________.
• I wondered if the swimmer ________ swim through the cold sea.

① is – that night – can
② was – that night – could
③ was – that night – can
④ were – last night – could
⑤ were – last night – can

23 다음 중 어법상 어색한 문장의 개수는?

> ⓐ Taking care of babies take a lot of time and energy.
> ⓑ Most of the audience was satisfied with her performance.
> ⓒ My mom used to say that she was the prettiest girl in high school.
> ⓓ The boy always tells everyone that he would be a superstar.

① 없음 ② 1개 ③ 2개
④ 3개 ⑤ 4개

24 다음 중 어법상 옳은 문장끼리 바르게 짝지은 것은?

> ⓐ What he did to people deserve punishment.
> ⓑ All her colleagues working in the same office are having lunch outside.
> ⓒ A number of eggs was used to bake pies.
> ⓓ We wondered if she could come to school tomorrow.
> ⓔ The lifeguard told them did not go into the water yet.

① ⓐ, ⓑ
② ⓑ, ⓓ
③ ⓑ, ⓔ
④ ⓑ, ⓓ, ⓔ
⑤ ⓒ, ⓓ, ⓔ

25 다음 중 어법상 옳은 문장의 개수는?

> ⓐ Some creatures are able to change their gender.
> ⓑ Being a good parents requires patience.
> ⓒ Half of the workers of the factory is from China.
> ⓓ I think both teams who played hard are winners.

① 없음 ② 1개 ③ 2개
④ 3개 ⑤ 4개

〈다음부터는 서술형 주관식 문제입니다.〉

26~28 다음 우리말과 같도록 빈칸에 괄호 안의 말을 알맞은 형태로 쓰시오.

26

> 네덜란드는 풍차와 튤립으로 유명하다. (be)

→ The Netherlands ________ famous for windmills and tulips.

27

> Steve는 보통 주말에 가족들과 등산을 간다고 말했다. (go)

→ Steve said he usually ________ hiking with his family on weekends.

28
> 전체 전력의 20%가 냉장고와 같은 주방가전에 사용되었다. (be)

→ Twenty percent of all electricity ________ used for kitchen appliances like refrigerators.

29~31 다음 문장에서 어법상 어색한 부분을 찾아 바르게 고쳐 쓰시오.

29 More than a fifth of Koreans suffers from indigestion.

________ → ________

30 The number of questions you can ask are only two.

________ → ________

31 Today, she will score as many goals as she does last time.

________ → ________

32~34 다음 문장을 간접화법으로 바꾸어 쓸 때, 빈칸에 알맞은 말을 쓰시오.

32 Last week, my grandpa said to me, "Where are you going tomorrow?"

→ Last week, my grandpa asked me ________ ________ ________ going ________ ________ day.

33 The police officer said to the kid, "Don't go anywhere and stay here."

→ The police officer told the kid ________ ________ ________ anywhere and stay ________.

34 He said, "I can't believe what you are saying now."

→ He said that ________ ________ believe what ________ ________ saying ________.

35~37 다음 문장을 직접화법으로 바꾸어 쓸 때, 빈칸에 알맞은 말을 쓰시오.

35 David told me that he had never been on a merry-go-round before.

→ David said to me, "________ ________ ________ been on a merry-go-round before."

36 Carry asked him whether he had left her a message.

→ Carry said to him, "________ ________ ________ ________ a message?"

37 Her stepmother ordered Cinderella to wash all the clothes that night.

→ Her stepmother said to Cinderella, "________ ________ the clothes ________."

38~40 **다음 우리말과 같도록 괄호 안의 말을 바르게 배열하시오.**

38

길에서 낯선 사람이 나에게 어느 초등학교를 졸업했는지 물어보았다.
(me, graduated, elementary school, asked, a stranger, which, I, from)

→ ________________________
________________ on the street.

39

1인 가구의 수가 1990년대부터 점점 늘어나고 있다.
(single, increasing, households, has, the number of, been, since)

→ ________________________
________________ the 1990s.

40

그 대통령은 정직이 최선의 방책이라고 확신했다.
(that, is, was, honesty, the president, certain, the best policy)

→ ________________________

41~42 **다음 우리말과 같도록 괄호 안의 말을 활용하여 문장을 완성하시오.**

41

가난한 사람들은 점점 더 가난해지고 있다.
(poor, become, poorer, the, be)

→ ________________________
and poorer.

42

인체의 약 3분의 2가 물로 이루어져 있다.
(about, two thirds, the human body, be made up of, water)

→ ________________________

43~45 다음 글의 밑줄 친 ⓐ~ⓕ 중 어법상 어색한 부분을 세 군데 찾아 바르게 고쳐 쓰시오.

> Q: My mom gave me a box of fruits yesterday. ⓐ When I opened the box, I found that there are 30 pieces of fruit inside. ⓑ Half of them were apples. ⓒ One-fifth of the fruits was oranges, ⓓ and ten percent were watermelons. ⓔ One-sixth of all the fruits were bananas. Then, ⓕ what was a number of strawberries in the box?
>
> A: Only one.

43 ______________ → ______________

44 ______________ → ______________

45 ______________ → ______________

46~48 다음 대화의 밑줄 친 ⓐ~ⓕ 중 어법상 어색한 부분을 세 군데 찾아 바르게 고쳐 쓰시오.

> A: When did you get the call?
>
> B: It was yesterday evening. She told me that she is a friend of my son who lives abroad now. And ⓐ she said my son had a car accident and has to have emergency surgery. ⓑ She said, "Send her some money for the surgery right now."
>
> A: So what did you do?
>
> B: ⓒ I told her I would send it right away and hang up the phone. ⓓ Then I checked if it was true. ⓔ It turned out to be voice phishing.
>
> A: ⓕ That is a relief.

46 ______________ → ______________

47 ______________ → ______________

48 ______________ → ______________

49~50 다음 우리말을 주어진 |조건|에 맞게 바르게 영작하시오.

49 우리는 내일 어떻게 세종대왕이 한글을 창제하셨는지 배울 것이다.

|조건|
1. King Sejong, Hangeul을 사용할 것
2. 단어 will, learn, how, create를 사용할 것
3. 9단어로 쓸 것

→ ______________________________

50 세계 인구의 60%가 아시아인이다.

|조건|
1. Sixty로 시작할 것
2. 단어 percent of, the world's population, Asian을 사용할 것
3. 8단어로 쓸 것

→ ______________________________

CHAPTER

13 강조, 부정, 도치, 부정대명사

UNIT 01 조동사 do를 이용한 강조

do는 조동사로도 쓰일 수 있다는 것을 알아 두세요.

do의 쓰임		예문	주의
본동사	~하다	He does his homework.	그는 숙제를 한다.
조동사	강조 (정말)	He does study hard.	주어/시제에 맞게 do/does/did+동사원형
	부정문	He does not study hard.	주어/시제에 맞게 do/does/did+not+동사원형
	의문문	Does he study hard?	주어/시제에 맞게 Do/Does/Did+주어+동사원형 ~?

참고 조동사가 있는 문장에는 항상 동사원형을 써요.

|A| 다음 문장의 밑줄 친 부분이 조동사인지 본동사인지 구분하여 쓰시오.

01 Do you know his name? ______

02 We should do more exercise. ______

03 I didn't go to school yesterday. ______

04 You do look pretty! ______

05 I did the washes after dinner. ______

06 Don't touch the painting. ______

07 Amy does very well at school. ______

08 Did you do your homework? ______

|B| 우리말과 같도록 조동사 do와 괄호 안의 말을 이용하여 빈칸을 완성하시오.

강조의 뜻을 나타내는 조동사 do는 인칭과 시제에 따라 달라짐에 유의해야 해요.

01 그녀는 시를 좋아하지 않았지만, 소설은 정말 많이 읽었다. (read)

→ She didn't like poetry, but she ______ a lot of novels.

02 Amy는 정말 영화를 좋아해서 금요일마다 영화를 보러 간다. (like)

→ Amy ______ movies, so she goes to a movie every Friday.

03 Tom은 정말 열심히 공부해서 그 시험에 합격했다. (study)

→ Tom ______ hard, so he passed the test.

04 나는 정말 진실을 말했지만, 그들은 나를 믿지 않았다. (tell)

→ I ______ the truth, they didn't trust me.

05 나는 정말 개를 좋아하고, 나의 누나는 고양이를 정말 좋아한다. (love, like)

→ I ______ dogs, and my sister ______ cats.

06 길이 얼었어. 제발 조심해! (be)

→ The road is icy. ______ careful!

UNIT 02 <It is[was] ~ that ...> 강조 구문

'~한 것은 바로 …이다[였다]'라고 강조하고 싶을 때는 It is[was]와 that 사이에 강조하고 싶은 말을 넣으세요.

일반 문장	Jack saw a rainbow in the sky yesterday. Jack은 어제 하늘에서 무지개를 보았다.			
〈It is[was] ~ that ...〉 강조 구문	It is[was]	강조하고 싶은 말	that + 나머지 말	의미
	It was	Jack	that ~~Jack~~ saw a rainbow in the sky yesterday.	그건 Jack이었다
		a rainbow	that Jack saw ~~a rainbow~~ in the sky yesterday.	그건 무지개였다
		in the sky	that Jack saw a rainbow ~~in the sky~~ yesterday.	그건 하늘에서였다
		yesterday	that Jack saw a rainbow in the sky ~~yesterday~~.	그건 어제였다

주의 〈It(가주어) ~ that(진주어)〉 구문과의 차이점을 알아 두세요.
It was true that Jack saw a rainbow in the sky yesterday. 〈that절이 완전한 절〉

|A| 다음 문장의 밑줄 친 부분과 쓰임이 같은 것을 |보기|에서 골라 그 번호를 쓰시오.

|보기|
ⓐ It was John that spoke first.
ⓑ It is amazing that she won the prize.

01 It is said that you are smart. ____________

02 It was the picture that he showed me. ____________

03 It is true that I told you a lie. ____________

04 It was Tom that picked up Jerry at the airport. ____________

05 It was Jiseon that I introduced to my friends. ____________

|B| 〈It is[was] ~ that[who] ...〉을 이용하여 밑줄 친 부분을 강조하는 문장으로 바꾸어 쓰시오.

강조하는 말이 사람이면 that 대신 who를 쓸 수 있어요.

01 He met Aena in the museum.
→ ____________________

02 A new cafe opened next to the restaurant.
→ ____________________

03 Hana was born in 2018.
→ ____________________

04 My parents bought me a bike for my birthday.
→ ____________________

05 Hyewon finally solved the problem.

→ ______________________________

06 Jisu made a cake for Yuju.

→ ______________________________

|C| 다음 |보기| 문장을 괄호 안의 지시에 따라 〈It is ~ that[who] ...〉 강조 구문으로 바꾸어 쓰시오.

|보기|
Sumi is waiting for Jian at the bus stop for 30 minutes.

01 (주어 강조) → It is ______________________________.

02 (목적어 강조) → It is ______________________________.

03 (장소 부사구 강조) → It is ______________________________.

04 (시간 강조) → It is ______________________________.

|보기|
We learn tennis on Tuesdays.

05 (주어 강조) → It is ______________________________.

06 (목적어 강조) → It is ______________________________.

07 (시간 부사구 강조) → It is ______________________________.

|D| 우리말과 같도록 괄호 안의 말을 바르게 배열하시오.

01 그가 내게 보낸 것은 바로 초대장이었다. (was, an invitation, he, me, that, it, sent)

→ ______________________________

02 아침에 너에게 전화한 사람은 바로 David였다. (David, called, you, it, who, in the morning, was)

→ ______________________________

03 우리가 그 영화를 본 건 바로 어제였다. (saw, the movie, yesterday, it, we, that, was)

→ ______________________________

04 내가 그 공책을 찾은 곳은 바로 침대 아래였다. (under the bed, I, it, that, was, the notebook, found)

→ ______________________________

05 그들이 지난여름에 방문한 곳은 바로 제주도였다. (visited, Jeju-do, was, they, it, that, last summer)

→ ______________________________

내신기출 다음 밑줄 친 부분의 쓰임이 다른 하나는?

① It is expected that some of them will be late.
② It is certain that many people will lose jobs.
③ It was in the park that I used to jog in the morning.

실전 TIP
that 앞에 있는 말이 that 뒤로 갈 수 있는지 없는지 확인해 보세요.

UNIT 03 전체 부정 & 부분 부정

부정어(not)와 전체를 나타내는 단어(all, every, both, always 등)가 함께 쓰이면 부분 부정으로 해석해야 해요.

전체 부정	~가 아니다	None of us knows the answer.	우리 중 누구도 답을 모름
		Neither of them is here.	둘 중 어느 누구도 여기 없다
		He has never had ramen before.	라면을 결코 먹어 본 적이 없음
부분 부정	모두 ~인 건 아니다	I do not know all of them. ≠ I do not know any of them.	〈부분 부정〉 그들 모두를 아는 것은 아님 〈전체 부정〉 그들 중 누구도 알지 못함
		He does not like both of them. ≠ He does not like either of them.	〈부분 부정〉 둘 다를 싫어하는 건 아님 〈전체 부정〉 둘 다를 싫어함

참고 no one, no-, none, never, nothing, neither, nobody 등이 쓰이면 '아무도 ~않다 / 아무것도[어느 것도] ~ 아니다'의 뜻으로 전체를 부정하는 말이에요.

|A| 우리말과 같도록 빈칸에 알맞은 말을 |보기|에서 골라 쓰시오.

|보기|
all always both neither never none

01 우리가 언제나 그에게 동의하는 것은 아니다. → We don't ___________ agree with him.

02 그녀는 결코 약속을 어기지 않는다. → She ___________ breaks a promise.

03 모든 학생이 숙제를 마친 것은 아니다. → Not ___________ students have finished their homework.

04 부모님 두 분 다 집에 안 계신다. → ___________ of my parents are at home.

05 그들 둘 다 시합에 나가는 것은 아니다. → Not ___________ of them play in the game.

06 소문들 중 어떤 것도 사실이 아니다. → ___________ of the rumors are true.

|B| 우리말과 같도록 괄호 안의 말을 바르게 배열하여 문장을 완성하시오.

01 우리가 언제나 원하는 것을 할 수 있는 것은 아니다. (cannot, we, always, do)
→ ______________________________ what we want to.

02 우리 둘 다 미국에 가 본 적이 없다. (neither, of, have been, us)
→ ______________________________ to USA.

03 손님들 중 누구도 아직 도착하지 않았다. (none, the guests, of, have arrived)
→ ______________________________ yet.

04 선생님의 허락 없이는 어떤 학생도 교실을 나갈 수 없다. (no, student, leave, can)
→ ______________________________ the classroom without the teacher's permission.

05 모든 사람들이 너처럼 운이 좋은 것은 아니다. (not, people, all, are)
→ ______________________________ as lucky as you are.

UNIT 04 도치

장소나 방향을 나타내는 부사(구)나 전치사구를 문두에 쓸 때, 주어, 동사를 도치시키세요.

일반 문장	도치된 문장
His mother sat on a chair.	On a chair sat his mother.
The change is here.	Here is the change.

참고 be, climb, go, hang, lie, sit, stand, come 등의 자동사가 장소/방향 부사구를 수반할 때 도치할 수 있어요.

주의 단, 주어가 대명사일 때는 도치하지 않아요. On a chair sat she. (×) → On a chair she sat. (○)

부정어(not, little, hardly 등)나 only를 문두에 쓸 때, 주어, 동사를 도치시키세요.

	일반 문장	도치된 문장
be동사	He is not only smart but also rich.	Not only is he smart but also rich.
조동사	He will go only when you go.	Only when you go will he go.
일반동사	He knew little about me.	Little did he know about me.

주의 be동사나 조동사가 있을 때는 be나 조동사를 주어 앞에 쓰고, 일반동사만 있는 경우, 조동사 do[does/did]를 주어 앞에 쓰고, 주어 뒤에는 동사원형을 써요.

'~ 또한 그렇다/그렇지 않다'라고 할 때, So/Neither 뒤에 주어와 동사를 도치시키세요.

be동사 문장	A: I am tired.	B: So am I.	나도 그래.
	A: I was tired.	B: So were my sisters.	내 여동생들도 그랬어.
	A: He isn't tired.	B: Neither are we.	우리도 안 그래.
일반동사/조동사 문장	A: I go swimming.	B: So do I.	나도 그래.
	A: I can swim.	B: So can my sister.	내 여동생도 할 수 있어.
	A: I can't swim.	B: Neither can we.	우리도 못 해.

|A| 다음 주어진 문장에 동의하는 대답을 완성하시오.

01 I like apples. → ________________ I.

02 I watched TV last night. → ________________ we.

03 I don't walk to school. → ________________ he.

04 I'm hungry. → ________________ I.

05 They are so busy. → ________________ we.

06 He can speak Spanish. → ________________ she.

07 She's not interested in science. → ________________ I.

08 We didn't clean the house. → ________________ they.

|B| 우리말과 같도록 괄호 안의 말을 바르게 배열하시오.

01 나는 내 이웃들을 거의 알지 못한다. (know, do, my neighbors, I)

→ Hardly ____.

02 나는 그 문제를 거의 알지 못했다. (the problem, was, aware, of, I)

→ Little ____.

03 여기에 책을 읽고 있는 몇몇 학생들이 있다. (reading, books, students, are, some)

→ Here ____.

04 그렇게 놀라운 공연은 결코 본 적이 없다. (such, an, performance, have, amazing, I, seen)

→ Never ____.

have seen에서 have만 주어 앞에 써요.

|C| 다음 문장을 밑줄 친 말로 시작하는 문장으로 바꾸어 쓰시오.

01 Some soldiers march <u>along the street</u>. → ________________________________

02 I slept <u>little</u> last night. → ________________________________

03 She has <u>never</u> felt so ashamed. → ________________________________

04 A big church stood <u>on the hill</u>. → ________________________________

05 I <u>hardly</u> remember what happened then. → ________________________________

|D| 괄호 안의 말을 활용하여 밑줄 친 말로 시작하는 문장을 완성하시오.

01 트럭 한 대가 <u>우리에게</u> 다가왔다. (come, toward us)

→ ____ a truck.

02 나는 <u>결코</u> 거짓말을 하지 않았다. (never, tell)

→ ____ a lie.

03 그는 그녀가 아팠다는 것을 <u>거의</u> 알지 <u>못했다</u>. (little, know)

→ ____ that she was sick.

04 나는 그 소식을 <u>거의</u> 믿을 수 <u>없었다</u>. (hardly, can, believe)

→ ____ the news.

05 그녀는 자기 일에 대해 <u>거의</u> 얘기하지 <u>않는다</u>. (rarely, talk about)

→ ____ her job.

내신기출 다음 중 문장 전환이 올바르지 <u>않은</u> 것은?

① A bird flew freely in the sky. → In the sky flew a bird freely.

② The singer sang on stage. → On stage sang the singer.

③ I never dreamed of seeing you here. → Never dreamed I of seeing you here.

실전 TIP

부정어구 강조일 때는 일반 동사만 있는 경우 조동사 do[does/did]를 주어 앞에 쓰고 주어 뒤에는 동사원형을 써야 해요.

UNIT 05 부정대명사

정해지지 않은 불특정한 사람이나 물건을 가리킬 때는 부정대명사 one을 쓰세요.

부정대명사	정해지지 않은 것을 가리킴	one	I need a shirt. I'll buy one. (정해지지 않은 셔츠)	단수
		ones	I need shoes. I'll buy ones. (정해지지 않은 신발)	복수

주의 정해진 것(그것)을 말할 때는 인칭대명사 it을 써야 해요.

one 이외의 부정대명사를 알아 두세요.

부정대명사		의미	부정대명사		의미
단수	one	하나	복수	some	(여러 개 중) 몇몇
	another	또 다른 하나		others	다른 몇몇
	the other	나머지 하나		the others	나머지 모두

참고 other(그 밖의 다른, 그 밖의 다른 것) 앞에 the가 붙으면 특정한 것이 되므로 '나머지'라는 의미가 돼요.

|A| 빈칸에 one(s)과 it 중 알맞은 말을 쓰시오.

01 I lost my cap. Have you seen ___________?

02 These are too small. I want bigger ___________.

03 That's my bag. Bring ___________ to me.

04 My chopsticks are gone. Get me new ___________.

05 I'll bring an umbrella. You'll need ___________, too.

|B| 빈칸에 알맞은 말을 |보기|에서 골라 쓰시오.

|보기|
one the other another some others the others

01 This ___________ is a little big. Can you show me ___________?

02 She has three aunts. One lives in Korea, and ___________ live in England.

03 There are two books. ___________ is a fiction and ___________ is a non-fiction.

04 She has three sons. ___________ is a Kevin, ___________ is Mark, and ___________ is James.

05 There are many people. ___________ are morning people, and ___________ are night owls.

내신 기출 다음 빈칸에 들어갈 말이 다른 하나는?

① You should always try not to be rude to ___________.
② Some chose to stay while ___________ chose not to.
③ Only two students passed and ___________ failed.

실전 TIP
그냥 '다른 사람들'인지, '나머지 사람들'인지 구분해 보세요.

중간고사·기말고사 실전문제

객관식 (01~25) / 주관식 (26~50)

정답과 해설 • 57쪽

학년과 반 이름 객관식 / 25문항 주관식 / 25문항

01~03 다음 빈칸에 알맞은 것을 고르시오.

01

It was the giraffe ________ we first saw at the zoo last week.

① who ② that
③ where ④ what
⑤ whom

02

Cathy decided not to buy anything because she liked ________ of the items.

① both ② any
③ either ④ neither
⑤ never

03

____________ been closed since last January.

① The store never has
② Has the store never
③ Has never the store
④ Never has the store
⑤ Never the store has

04~05 다음 빈칸에 알맞지 않은 것을 고르시오.

04

The man didn't find ________, he just found one out of two hidden objects.

① all things ② everything
③ anything ④ all
⑤ both of them

05

It was ________ that Sally was supposed to meet her pen pal for the first time.

① noon ② today
③ at school ④ last week
⑤ in the library

06 다음 대화의 밑줄 친 우리말을 바르게 나타낸 것은?

A: My mom won't give me money to buy comic books.
B: 우리도 그럴 거야.

① So will we.
② So won't we.
③ Neither do we.
④ Neither will we.
⑤ Neither won't we.

07~09 다음 우리말을 영어로 바르게 나타낸 것을 고르시오.

07

Jack은 온라인 수업에 좀처럼 익숙해지지 않았다.

① Rarely Jack got accustomed to online classes.
② Rarely got Jack accustomed to online classes.
③ Rarely does Jack get accustomed to online classes.
④ Rarely did Jack got accustomed to online classes.
⑤ Rarely did Jack get accustomed to online classes.

08

대부분의 손님들은 현금을 사용하지 않았고, 우리 가족도 그랬다.

① Most of the customers didn't use cash, and did so my family.
② Most of the customers didn't use cash, and so did my family.
③ Most of the customers didn't use cash, and did neither my family.
④ Most of the customers didn't use cash, and neither did my family.
⑤ Most of the customers didn't use cash, and my family either didn't.

09

모든 동물들이 그들의 새끼를 잘 돌보는 것은 아니다.

① Not any animals take good care of their young.
② All animals never take good care of their young.
③ Not every animal takes good care of their young.
④ None of the animals take good care of their young.
⑤ No animal takes good care of its young.

10 다음 문장을 〈It was ~ that ...〉 강조 구문으로 바꾸어 쓸 때, 강조할 수 <u>없는</u> 것은?

Sara found her lost doll in the basement last night.

① Sara ② found
③ last night ④ her lost doll
⑤ in the basement

11 다음 중 어법상 <u>어색한</u> 것은?

① Hardly ever does he have a headache.
② Across the street gathered the people.
③ Inside the cave they hid during the war.
④ Here are they playing basketball.
⑤ At the train station we started our journey.

12 다음 중 어법상 어색한 것을 모두 고르면?

① It was the girl who was absent from my class today.
② It was April that the tragic accident happened.
③ It was at the bus stop that everyone was waiting for me.
④ It is here that my family stayed during the trip.
⑤ It is a poem what the author is now writing.

13 다음 중 어법상 옳은 것은?

① The population of Seoul did increase a lot over the decade.
② This soup do need a little more salt.
③ She did drank a lot of coffee during the seminar.
④ The old man at the hospital did appears to be in a serious condition.
⑤ The foreigners do felt lonely during the holiday seasons of the year.

14 다음 중 어법상 옳은 것을 모두 고르면?

① Seldom does the windows of her house closed.
② Hardly do your phone ring on weekends.
③ Rarely does my sister drive at night.
④ In front of the statue stood the woman taking pictures.
⑤ Little was the student write on her essay.

15~17 다음 중 밑줄 친 부분을 강조하는 문장으로 바르게 나타낸 것을 고르시오.

15

It hardly snowed last winter.

① Snowed hardly it last winter.
② Hardly it snowed last winter.
③ Hardly snowed it last winter.
④ Hardly did it snowed last winter.
⑤ Hardly did it snow last winter.

16

She got an A on the English exam.

① She does got an A on the English exam.
② She did got an A on the English exam.
③ She do get an A on the English exam.
④ She did get an A on the English exam.
⑤ She does get an A on the English exam.

17

Many crops dried up because of the severe drought.

① It is the severe drought what many crops dried up.
② It is because the severe drought that many crops dried up.
③ It was because the severe drought that many crops dried up.
④ It was because of the severe drought that many crops dried up.
⑤ It was because of the severe drought who many crops dried up.

18 다음 중 밑줄 친 부분의 쓰임이 같은 것끼리 짝지어진 것은?

> ⓐ My supervisor does have a good sense of humor.
> ⓑ Even the owner didn't do his best to attract customers.
> ⓒ Do come and see us on Chuseok.
> ⓓ What kind of music does he usually listen to when he exercises?
> ⓔ They did pay a lot of money to rent a luxurious villa.

① ⓐ, ⓑ, ⓒ
② ⓐ, ⓒ, ⓔ
③ ⓐ, ⓓ, ⓔ
④ ⓑ, ⓒ, ⓓ
⑤ ⓑ, ⓓ, ⓔ

19~20 다음 주어진 문장과 의미가 같은 것을 고르시오.

19

> Andy will leave only when he gets what he wants.

① Only when Andy gets what he wants will he leave.
② Only when Andy gets what he wants he will leave.
③ Only when Andy gets what he wants he leaves.
④ Only when Andy gets what he wants will he leaves.
⑤ Only when Andy gets what he wants will leave he.

20

> Some travelers are wearing sunglasses while the others are not.

① Not any of the travelers are wearing sunglasses.
② Not every traveler is wearing sunglasses.
③ All travelers are not wearing sunglasses.
④ No traveler is wearing sunglasses.
⑤ Neither of the travelers are wearing sunglasses.

21~22 다음 빈칸에 알맞은 말이 바르게 짝지어진 것을 고르시오.

21

> A: I ________ go to his concert last week.
> B: ________ did I.

① won't – So
② couldn't – Neither
③ didn't – Neither
④ did – Neither
⑤ didn't – So

22

> • The tellers at the bank ________ have a lot of work.
> • It was ________ that my uncle found his cell phone.
> • Carl didn't catch ________ of the balls, but only caught the first one.

① do – the car – either
② do – in the car – both
③ does – the car – either
④ does – in the car – both
⑤ did – in the car – neither

23 다음 중 어법상 틀린 문장의 개수는?

ⓐ Hardly do gardener grows any wild flowers in the garden.
ⓑ Not surprisingly, the dentist does has health teeth.
ⓒ Here are my comments about your presentation.
ⓓ As both apples and pears are too hard, babies cannot eat either of them.

① 없음 ② 1개
③ 2개 ④ 3개
⑤ 4개

24 다음 중 어법상 옳은 문장끼리 바르게 짝지은 것은?

ⓐ None of us haven't played tennis, so we'll all be poor at it.
ⓑ On top of the mountain was a huge pine tree.
ⓒ It was the vet which rescued the injured dog on the road.
ⓓ Not only was the movie funny, but it also taught a good lesson.
ⓔ I think your new sweater does look good on you.

① ⓐ, ⓑ
② ⓑ, ⓓ
③ ⓑ, ⓔ
④ ⓑ, ⓓ, ⓔ
⑤ ⓒ, ⓓ, ⓔ

25 다음 중 어법상 옳은 문장의 개수는?

ⓐ In the sky flew the kites.
ⓑ The fisherman did caught a big fish.
ⓒ It was the theater that she first met her husband.
ⓓ No engineer could fix the air conditioner, so he bought a new one.

① 없음 ② 1개
③ 2개 ④ 3개
⑤ 4개

〈다음부터는 서술형 주관식 문제입니다.〉

26~28 다음 문장의 밑줄 친 부분이 어법상 맞으면 ○표 하고, 틀리면 바르게 고쳐 쓰시오.

26 As Sam used to say, he does donate all his fortune before he died.

→ ______________________

27 Both of the team tried their best in the game.

→ ______________________

28 Not only does she like spiders, she also has them as pets.

→ ______________________

29~31 다음 문장에서 어법상 어색한 부분을 찾아 바르게 고쳐 쓰시오.

29 The movie has two different endings, a happy it and a sad ones.

________ → ________

30 The businessman did sold a lot of products to local customers.

________ → ________

31 Not only Harry sings well, but also he can play the guitar.

________ → ________

32~34 다음 문장의 밑줄 친 부분을 강조하는 도치 구문으로 바꾸어 쓰시오.

32 The patient sat by the window.

→ ________

33 She paid little attention to what the guide explained.

→ ________

34 Your bus comes here.

→ ________

35~37 다음 주어진 문장을 밑줄 친 부분을 강조하는 〈It is[was] ~ that ...〉 구문으로 바꾸어 쓰시오.

35 A stranger helped me find the jacket.

→ ________

36 My best friend lent me his favorite book a few days ago.

→ ________

37 Lucy is having a hard time finishing her math homework.

→ ______________________________
____

38~40 다음 우리말과 같도록 괄호 안의 말을 바르게 배열하시오.

38

어제 정말 많이 걸었기 때문에 우리는 지금 모두 지쳤다. (because, are, walk, exhausted, us, we, now, all, did, a lot, of)

→ ______________________________
______________________________ yesterday.

39

나의 조부모님은 전에 록 음악을 결코 들어본 적이 없다. (rock music, listened to, have, my grandparents, before)

→ Never ______________________________
______________________________.

40

고객은 환불도 교환도 원하지 않았다. (or, an exchange, a refund, either, didn't, want)

→ The customer ______________________________
______________________________.

41~43 다음 우리말과 같도록 괄호 안의 말을 활용하여 문장을 완성하시오.

41

이것 대신에 다른 것을 입어 보실래요? (would like to, try)

→ Instead of this one, ______________________________
______________________________?

42

그는 주말에 거의 밖에 나가지 않는다. (go out, on weekends)

→ Rarely ______________________________.

43

나는 7개 중 3개나 먹었으니, 네가 그 나머지를 먹어도 좋다. (can, other, have)

→ I had three out of seven so ______________________________
______________________________.

※ 다음 대화를 읽고, 물음에 답하시오.

Amy: ⓐ Here we finally came to the BTS concert! Actually, ⓑ I have never been to any concert before.
Ben: (A) 나도 그래. I'm so excited! Where is Cathy?
Amy: She hasn't come yet. ⓒ Rarely does she late.
Ben: ⓓ There is she in front of the entrance. Hi, Cathy! We're here.
Cathy: Oh, hi.
Amy: Cathy, what's wrong? You look so tired.
Cathy: I know. (B) 어젯밤에 잠을 거의 못 잤어 because I was so excited about today.
Ben: Is this your first concert, too?
Cathy: Yeah, so ⓔ I did look forward to this concert.
Amy: ⓕ That means any of us have been to a concert.

44~45 위 대화의 밑줄 친 (A), (B)를 영어로 쓸 때, 빈칸에 알맞은 말을 쓰시오.

44 (A): ________ ________ I.

45 (B): Little ________ ________ ________ last night

46~48 위 대화의 밑줄 친 ⓐ~ⓕ 중에서 어법상 어색한 부분을 세 군데 찾아 바르게 고쳐 쓰시오.

46 ________ → ________

47 ________ → ________

48 ________ → ________

49~50 다음 우리말을 주어진 |조건|에 맞게 바르게 영작하시오.

49 그녀는 좀처럼 사람들 앞에서 웃지 않는다.

|조건|
1. Seldom으로 문장을 시작할 것
2. 단어 smile, in front of, people을 사용할 것
3. 8단어로 쓸 것

→ ________________

50 그 파티에서 그들 중 아무도 그를 눈치채지 못했다.

|조건|
1. None으로 문장을 시작할 것
2. 단어 notice, them을 사용할 것
3. 8단어로 쓸 것

→ ________________

CHAPTER

14 문장의 이해

Unit 01 주어 자리에 오는 말
Unit 02 주격보어 자리에 오는 말
Unit 03 목적어 자리에 오는 말
Unit 04 목적격보어 자리에 오는 말
Unit 05 형용사적 수식어 자리에 오는 말
Unit 06 부사적 수식어 자리에 오는 말

UNIT 01 주어 자리에 오는 말

주어 자리에는 명사나 명사 역할을 하는 말들만 써야 해요.

명사, 대명사	The sun is the center of the solar system.	태양은
앞뒤 수식을 받는 명사	The true center of the solar system isn't the earth.	태양계의 진정한 중심은
to부정사(명사적 용법)	To say goodbye is the saddest thing.	안녕이라고 말하는 것은
동명사	Seeing her again is his last wish.	그녀를 다시 보는 것이
명사절	Whether he is smart (or not) doesn't matter.	그가 똑똑한지 아닌지는

주의 주어가 길어질 때는 어디까지 주어인지 잘 파악하는 것이 중요해요.

|A| 다음 문장에서 주어를 찾아 쓰시오.

01 We usually go hiking on Saturdays. ____________________

02 The medicine taste bitter. ____________________

03 The lilies in the vase look beautiful. ____________________

04 To drive fast in the rain can be dangerous. ____________________

05 Wearing safety goggles and protective clothing is required. ____________________

06 It is said that he's kind. ____________________

07 That he decided to study abroad was surprising. ____________________

08 Those who finished completing the form can sign up. ____________________

09 It is important to recycle used bottles. ____________________

|B| 다음 문장에서 어법상 어색한 부분을 찾아 바르게 고쳐 쓰시오.

01 That the thief stole the treasures were true. ____________________

02 Read a book before bedtime is my old habit. ____________________

03 It is important what all students understand what the teacher says. ____________________

04 The old building between skyscrapers were built in 1970. ____________________

05 Some classmates in my class is good at math. ____________________

06 Parents who have a little child prefers to live near a school. ____________________

07 The apples in the basket smells sweet. ____________________

08 Wearing school uniforms are common in Korea. ____________________

09 A new movie about animals are expected to be released next month. ____________________

10 Raise a hand to ask a question is necessary in classroom. ____________________

UNIT 02 주격보어 자리에 오는 말

주격보어 자리에는 명사나 형용사 또는 그 역할을 하는 말들만 써야 해요.

명사	My teacher is a very kind person.	매우 친절한 사람
to부정사(명사적 용법)	Her dream is not to live a normal life.	평범한 삶을 살지 않는 것
동명사 보어	His job is driving a taxi at night.	밤에 택시 운전하기
명사절	The truth is that the earth goes round the sun.	지구가 태양 주위를 돈다는 것
형용사(분사 포함)	Your idea sounds interesting.	흥미롭게 (들린다)

주의 보어 자리에는 부사를 쓸 수 없어요.

|A| 다음 문장에서 주격보어를 찾아 쓰시오.

01 The man living next door is a fire fighter. ____________________

02 Your story sounds very strange. ____________________

03 It looks foggy outside. ____________________

04 What I like to do is to spend quiet time alone. ____________________

05 Their job is organizing and hosting events. ____________________

06 Something on the table smell sweet! ____________________

07 The weather is getting colder and colder. ____________________

|B| 다음 문장에서 어법상 어색한 부분을 찾아 바르게 고쳐 쓰시오.

01 We had to stay wake to study for the test. ____________________

02 The old milk tastes sourly. ____________________

03 Some of the questions still remain unclearly. ____________________

04 He didn't know what to say, so he kept silence. ____________________

05 You sounded confidently when you introduced yourself. ____________________

06 I tried to keep calmly and carry on when I was in trouble. ____________________

07 We should keep warmly in winter. ____________________

08 The fact is whether 70 percent of the Earth's surface is covered with water.

____

내신 기출 다음 중 밑줄 친 부분이 어법상 어색한 것은?

① I should be stay healthy to realize my dream.

② The mystery was how they could find the missing person.

③ The members prepared the presentation will meet this afternoon.

실전 TIP

보어의 형태가 적절한지, 명사를 수식하는 분사의 형태가 적절한지 확인해 보세요.

UNIT 03 목적어 자리에 오는 말

목적어 자리에도 명사나 명사 역할을 하는 말만 써야 해요.

명사, 대명사	He solved the problem.	그 문제를
앞뒤 수식을 받는 명사	I like the handsome boy wearing a suit.	양복을 입고 있는 잘생긴 소년
to부정사(명사적 용법)	He promised to look into the matter.	그 문제를 살펴볼 것을
동명사	They enjoyed swimming in the pool.	풀장에서 수영하는 것을
명사절	People didn't believe that the earth is round.	지구가 둥글다는 것을

주의 4형식 문장은 목적어를 2개 취하는 문장이에요.
He gives his girlfriend flowers. 그는 그의 여자 친구에게 꽃을 준다.

|A| 다음 문장에서 목적어를 찾아 쓰시오.

01 I purchased the concert ticket online. ______

02 He finally gave up smoking according to the doctor's advice. ______

03 They agreed to meet on July 5th. ______

04 Many people used to believe that the Earth was flat. ______

05 We think him a genius. ______

|B| 다음 문장에서 간접목적어와 직접목적어를 찾아 쓰시오.

01 He showed the security guard his identification. ______

02 My mom wrote me a letter full of warm words. ______

03 What did you give her for her birthday? ______

|C| 다음 문장에서 어법상 어색한 부분을 찾아 바르게 고쳐 쓰시오.

01 I like watch baseball. ______

02 They failed rescuing the child. ______

03 You are fond of to cook. ______

04 He made coffee to them. ______

05 Have you considered get a job abroad? ______

06 He suggested to call a taxi instead of walking. ______

07 She wanted to sell her house for us. ______

08 May I ask a question to you? ______

UNIT 04 목적격보어 자리에 오는 말

목적격보어 자리에는 명사, 형용사, to부정사, 원형부정사, 분사 등 다양한 말이 올 수 있어서 주의해야 해요.

명사	They made their son a doctor.	의사로
형용사	He made his parents happy.	행복하게
to부정사	They forced him to enter the military.	군대에 들어가도록
원형부정사	He had the students follow the rules. 〈사역〉	학교 규칙을 따르도록
분사	He saw a big truck running too fast. 〈지각: 능동〉	너무 빠르게 달리고 있는

참고 원형부정사를 목적격보어로 취하는 대표 동사는 사역동사, 지각동사예요.

참고 분사는 목적어와의 관계에 맞게 현재분사(능동) 또는 과거분사(수동)를 쓸 수 있어요.

|A| 다음 문장에서 목적어와 목적격보어를 찾아 쓰시오.

01 I call my daughter my angel. ______

02 The graph made the article more interesting. ______

03 They felt the ground shake severely. ______

04 The mother kept her baby warm with a blanket. ______

05 My parents allow me to play the online game for an hour a day. ______

06 She had her hair cut last weekend. ______

07 My dad has me come home before 8:00. ______

|B| 다음 문장에서 어법상 어색한 부분을 찾아 바르게 고쳐 쓰시오.

01 Your lie made us madly. ______

02 I got my shoes repair. ______

03 Linda heard a car to stop suddenly outside. ______

04 Your letter always makes him laughs. ______

05 The government advised citizens stay indoors. ______

06 The course will help you understanding the theory better. ______

|C| 다음 문장의 밑줄 친 부분을 우리말로 해석하시오.

01 The movie made the actor famous. ______

02 I saw you crying in the room. ______

03 The dress makes me look slim. ______

04 You told the children not to touch anything. ______

UNIT 05 형용사적 수식어 자리에 오는 말

형용사적 수식어는 명사를 수식하는 말로, 다양한 말들이 명사를 수식할 수 있음을 알아 두세요.

명사 앞뒤 형용사	I bought a new book useful for kids.	아이들에게 유용한 새 (책)
명사 뒤 전치사구	The book on the desk is mine.	책상 위에 있는 (책)
명사 앞뒤 분사	Do you know the dog running in the park?	공원에서 달리고 있는 (개)
to부정사(형용사적 용법)	I have some questions to ask you.	너에게 물어볼 (질문들)
관계사절	This is the book that I was talking about.	내가 이야기했던 (책)

|A| 다음 문장의 밑줄 친 부분을 수식하는 말을 찾아 쓰시오.

01 They need someone with new ideas. ______________

02 The big window broken by us will be replaced tomorrow. ______________

03 This is the best painting that I've ever seen. ______________

04 There was a woman standing alone in the corner. ______________

05 She wanted to buy something hot to drink. ______________

06 I saw a tall gentleman with a beard walking down the street. ______________

07 The wide street lined with tall trees runs to the city hall. ______________

08 The girl hid her favorite doll under the bed. ______________

09 The recently built house at the edge of the town is vacant. ______________

10 His book which explains the issue in detail will be published next month.

____

|B| 다음 문장의 밑줄 친 부분을 우리말로 해석하시오.

01 Several roads under construction are closed to traffic. ______________

02 He bought a camera sold at a reduced price. ______________

03 They made the complicated rules to follow. ______________

04 The sleeping baby on the bed looks peaceful. ______________

05 *The Jungle Book* has stories about a boy who was raised by wolves.

____

UNIT 06 부사적 수식어 자리에 오는 말

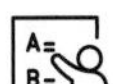

부사적 수식어는 명사 외의 거의 모든 말을 수식하는 말로, 부사적 수식어 역할을 하는 다양한 말들을 알아 두세요.

부사	She always has warm tea with her mom.	항상
전치사구	He often calls her in the morning.	아침에
to부정사(부사적 용법)	He tried hard not to make a mistake.	실수하지 않기 위해
부사절	It started to rain when we left the house.	집을 떠났을 때
분사구문	Getting off the bus, she said goodbye to me.	버스에서 내리면서

|A| 다음 문장에서 부사적 수식어 역할을 하는 말을 모두 찾아 쓰시오.

01 Can you speak more slowly? ______________

02 Suddenly, the dogs started barking. ______________

03 Please call me as soon as you get home. ______________

04 Shocked by the news, we didn't know what to say. ______________

05 They work out every day to stay healthy. ______________

06 Generally, many students think math is very difficult. ______________

07 She was talking on the phone when the bell rang. ______________

08 I studied very hard, so finally I passed the exam. ______________

09 We won't go anywhere if it rains tomorrow. ______________

10 I was terribly sorry to hear the news. ______________

11 He raised a hand to ask a question. ______________

12 Ted and Den often play basketball in the park after school. ______________

13 Wendy was sitting on a sofa with her legs crossed. ______________

내신 기출 다음 밑줄 친 부분이 어법상 어색한 것은?

① Listening to music, I took a shower last night.
② He is emphasizing whether all people are equal.
③ She encouraged everyone to participate in the discussion.
④ Disappointed with the result, I didn't want to do anything.
⑤ The kids picked up red and yellow leaves fallen under the trees.

실전 TIP

분사가 제대로 쓰였는지, 5형식의 목적격보어의 형태가 바른지, 명사절이 제대로 쓰였는지 확인해 보세요.

중간고사·기말고사 실전문제

객관식 (01~25) / 주관식 (26~50)

학년과 반 이름 객관식 / 25문항 주관식 / 25문항

01~04 다음 빈칸에 알맞은 것을 고르시오.

01

A small restaurant at the corner became ______________.

① many visitors from other towns
② so famously after it was aired on TV
③ too crowd with customers
④ well known nationwide
⑤ very busily thanks to SNS

02

The boy didn't want ______________.

① that his father gave him
② the book is about global warming
③ his mom to go out without him
④ taking the medicine
⑤ boring and serious

03

Most teachers at school thought Terry ______________.

① the best student ever
② follow their instructions
③ studying very hard
④ leave the school soon
⑤ not do his best

04

Have you tried the skirt ______________?

① I gave it to you
② that has flower patterns
③ is in my closet
④ very short and tight
⑤ mending yesterday

05~08 다음 빈칸에 알맞지 않은 것을 고르시오.

05

______________ will be the key to solve the case.

① That there was a witness
② The man who lives next door
③ The clue which the victim left
④ That the detective found out
⑤ To read the criminal's mind

06

The little girl believed ______________.

① her brother honestly
② the tooth fairy was real
③ in Santa Claus
④ that she could fly
⑤ her parents love her

07 Ice cream sales decreased ________.

① rapidly
② by five percent this year
③ the freezing winter
④ as the weather got cold
⑤ at the store

08 Please don't make your cat ________.

① run away from the house
② suddenly attack me
③ a bad pet
④ angry by touching its tail
⑤ stealing food

09~10 다음 영어를 우리말로 바르게 나타낸 것을 고르시오.

09 His claim that life exists on Mars doesn't seem right.

① 그는 옳지 않은 방법으로 화성에서 살고 있다.
② 그가 화성에서 산다는 주장은 옳지 않다.
③ 화성에 생명이 산다는 그의 주장은 옳지 않은 것 같다.
④ 그는 화성에 생명이 산다는 것이 옳지 않다고 주장한다.
⑤ 그는 화성에 생명이 산다는 옳지 않은 주장을 들었다.

10 Many people who are tired of their daily lives are planning to travel to relax.

① 여행을 계획하는 많은 사람들이 일상에 지쳐 있다.
② 일상에 지쳐 있는 많은 사람들이 휴식을 위해 여행을 계획하고 있다.
③ 일상에 지쳐 있는 많은 사람들이 여행을 위한 휴식을 계획하고 있다.
④ 계획하는 것에 지친 많은 사람들이 휴식을 위한 여행을 한다.
⑤ 많은 사람들은 휴식을 위한 여행을 계획하는 것에 지쳐 있다.

11~12 다음 우리말을 영어로 바르게 나타낸 것을 고르시오.

11 시험을 준비하는 학생들은 그 강사의 강의가 도움이 된다고 생각했다.

① Students preparing for the test found the instructor's lecture helpful.
② Students prepared for the test find the instructor's lecture helpful.
③ Students who preparing for the test finding the instructor's lecture helpful.
④ Students who were preparing for the test found the instructor's lecture helpfully.
⑤ Students were preparing for the test and finding the instructor's lecture helpfully.

12

캐나다에 살고 있는 나의 이모는 내가 그곳의 대학교에 지원하는 것을 도와주었다.

① My aunt living in Canada helping me applied to the university there.
② My aunt who living in Canada helped me apply the university there.
③ My aunt lives in Canada helped me apply to the university there.
④ My aunt living in Canada helped me apply to the university there.
⑤ My aunt living in Canada helped me applying the university there.

13~16 다음 밑줄 친 부분의 문장 요소를 잘못 나타낸 것을 고르시오.

13

Satellites(ⓐ) send(ⓑ) the Earth(ⓒ) signals(ⓓ) received from space(ⓔ).

① ⓐ: 주어 ② ⓑ: 동사
③ ⓒ: 목적어 ④ ⓓ: 목적격보어
⑤ ⓔ: 형용사적 수식어

14

The man(ⓐ) she interviewed last week(ⓑ) considered(ⓒ) himself(ⓓ) to be a great writer(ⓔ).

① ⓐ: 주어 ② ⓑ: 형용사적 수식어
③ ⓒ: 동사 ④ ⓓ: 목적어
⑤ ⓔ: 부사적 수식어

15

People(ⓐ) who owned the stock(ⓑ) got(ⓒ) furious(ⓓ) as the firm failed in its project(ⓔ).

① ⓐ: 주어 ② ⓑ: 형용사적 수식어
③ ⓒ: 동사 ④ ⓓ: 목적어
⑤ ⓔ: 부사적 수식어

16

It(ⓐ) is going to be(ⓑ) a rule(ⓒ) to turn off the lights(ⓓ) at midnight(ⓔ).

① ⓐ: 가주어 ② ⓑ: 동사
③ ⓒ: 보어 ④ ⓓ: 부사적 수식어
⑤ ⓔ: 부사적 수식어

17 다음 중 어법상 어색한 것은?

① These oranges from his farm taste really sweet.
② What you're saying sounds strangely enough to ask many questions.
③ The book I'm reading now is getting more interesting.
④ One of my wishes for the future is to make as many good friends as possible.
⑤ Her long, blond hair looks soft and beautiful.

18 다음 중 어법상 옳은 것은?

① Her husband encouraged Sarah study for her career.
② The instructor taught how to use the smart phone the old people.
③ Carl made something for his roommate has lived with him for two years.
④ The fact that Jane believed in me gave me strength.
⑤ Jason made everyone in the office surprise by saying he would get married soon.

19~21 다음 주어진 말이 빈칸에 들어갈 수 없는 것을 고르시오.

19

To[to] persuade Simpson

① ____________ can be the hardest thing for me.
② Everyone in his family failed ________.
③ His friends visited him many times ____________.
④ His mom knows a good way ________.
⑤ The counselor trusted by him ________.

20

Behind[behind] the building

① A police officer who looked for a thief went to ____________.
② ____________ lies a beautiful garden.
③ Did you find anyone when you looked ____________?
④ The engineers who came to repair the system are ____________ now.
⑤ ____________, there may be a lot of garbage.

21

That[that] Rebecca died of cancer

① We were surprised to find ____________.
② ____________ brought sadness to many people.
③ No one could cure the disease ________.
④ It can't be true ____________.
⑤ Where did you hear the news ________?

22 다음 빈칸에 알맞은 말이 바르게 짝지어진 것은?

> • The girl ________ on the bench lives next door to me.
> • The old lady heard something ________ last night.

① who sit – broken
② who is sat – breaking
③ who sitting – broke
④ who is sitting – break
⑤ sitting – to break

23 다음 중 문장의 주어(구/절) 부분 전체를 바르게 찾아 밑줄 친 문장의 개수는?

> ⓐ To save money is more crucial than to invest it.
> ⓑ It is not that important whether you understand what was in the book.
> ⓒ What she expected me to do is almost impossible for me.
> ⓓ There are some seats for the elderly.

① 없음 ② 1개 ③ 2개
④ 3개 ⑤ 4개

24 다음 중 문장의 목적어(구/절) 부분 전체를 바르게 찾아 밑줄 친 문장의 개수는?

> ⓐ What kind of flowers do you grow in your garden?
> ⓑ The cruel man forced workers to work long hours without pay.
> ⓒ A handsome boy standing right in front of me asked for directions.
> ⓓ They promised to come back home.

① 없음　② 1개
③ 2개　④ 3개
⑤ 4개

25 다음 중 어법상 옳은 문장끼리 바르게 짝지은 것은?

> ⓐ Living in the area with many trees are very helpful to your health.
> ⓑ All the flight attendants I met on the plane were friendly and thoughtfully.
> ⓒ Does it really matter that we memorize the formulas?
> ⓓ In autumn, the mountains all over the country turn colorful.
> ⓔ The machine that you fixed yesterday still doesn't work.

① ⓐ, ⓑ
② ⓑ, ⓓ
③ ⓑ, ⓔ
④ ⓑ, ⓓ, ⓔ
⑤ ⓒ, ⓓ, ⓔ

〈다음부터는 서술형 주관식 문제입니다.〉

26~29 다음 우리말과 같도록 주어진 말을 활용하여 문장을 완성하시오.

26

> 심해에 사는 엄청나게 많은 물고기가 있다. (tons of, live, there, fish)

→ ______________________________
in the deep sea.

27

> 차별을 당한 사람들을 돕는 것은 용기를 필요로 한다. (who, help, to, discriminate against, the people)

→ ______________________________
needs courage.

28

> 그녀의 가족은 그 도시에 있는 그들의 집에 대한 집세를 지불할 수 없었다. (for, in, their house, the rent, pay, the city)

→ Her family couldn't ______________________________
______________________________.

29

> 지난달에 잡힌 그 죄수는 감옥에서 탈출했다. (catch, escape, the prisoner, last month)

→ ______________________________
from the prison.

30~33 다음 우리말과 같도록 주어진 말을 활용하여 빈칸에 알맞게 말을 쓰시오.

30

그 케이크는 기침약과 같은 맛이 났다. (like, cough syrup, taste)

→ The cake ________ ________ ________ ________.

31

그는 죽음의 공포로 그의 몸이 떨리는 것을 느꼈다. (feel, his body, shake)

→ He ________ ________ ________ ________ with the fear of death.

32

열이 나는 것은 심각한 병의 증상일 수 있다. (have, can, a fever, a symptom)

→ ________ ________ ________ ________ ________ ________ ________ of a serious illness.

33

이 새 재킷은 그것을 입는 모든 사람을 멋지게 만들어 줄 것이다. (make, wear, everyone, stylish, who)

→ This new jacket will ________ ________ ________ ________ ________ ________.

34~37 다음 빈칸에 괄호 안의 단어를 알맞은 형태로 쓰시오.

34 Has anyone ____________ this conference brought the files I sent yesterday? (attend)

35 The little boy, ____________ by kidnappers, is only 9 years old. (take)

36 The girl said hello to the people ________ at her with a shy voice. (look)

37 The artwork ____________ in 1955 earned fame after the artist died in 1993. (complete)

38~41 다음 문장에서 어법상 어색한 부분을 찾아 바르게 고쳐 쓰시오.

38 Even scientists who have studied this field for years cannot explain how is this possible.

_______________ → _______________

39 The two enemies of our health are salty food and sit for a long time.

_______________ → _______________

40 After starving for three days, the person ate the food on the table hurried.

_______________ → _______________

41 The purpose of not helping the trainees are to let them learn how to live on their own.

_______________ → _______________

42~44 다음 우리말과 같도록 괄호 안의 말을 바르게 배열하시오.

42

그 경찰관은 길에서 구조된 개를 훈련시켰다. (from, trained, rescued, the dog, the street)

→ The police officer _______________
_______________.

43

지금까지 진행한 연구는 그것을 밝히지 못했다. (revealed, have, so far, not, conducted, it)

→ Studies _______________
_______________.

44

그녀의 대모가 된 요정은 호박을 마차로 바꾸어 놓았다. (into, godmother, the pumpkin, became, who, a carriage, her, turned)

→ The fairy _______________
_______________.

45~47 다음 중 어법상 어색한 문장을 찾아 바르게 고쳐 쓰시오. (정답 3개)

ⓐ The help received from sponsors to enable us to build educational facilities.
ⓑ The man who stole expensive treasures from the museum quickly disappeared without a trace.
ⓒ Patients should always keep the place cleanly and safely.
ⓓ It was really embarrassed that I wore mismatched shoes.
ⓔ Lying on the grass, Joey looked at the clouds passing by quickly.
ⓕ What ordinary people don't know is that 30% of calories are used in the brain.

45 ______________ → ______________

46 ______________ → ______________

47 ______________ → ______________

48~50 다음 우리말을 주어진 |조건|에 맞게 바르게 영작하시오.

48 너는 그가 방과 후에 누구를 만났는지 들었니?

|조건|
1. Did로 시작할 것
2. 단어 after school, who, meet, hear를 사용할 것
3. 8단어로 쓸 것

→ ______________________

49 나는 그에게 물어볼 중요한 것이 있다.

|조건|
1. 현재분사를 사용할 것
2. 단어 important, ask, something을 사용할 것
3. 7단어로 쓸 것

→ ______________________

50 그녀는 그녀가 만난 그 남자가 그녀를 좋아하는지 궁금했다.

|조건|
1. if가 포함된 명사절을 사용할 것
2. 단어 the man, meet, like, wonder를 사용할 것
3. 9단어로 쓸 것

→ ______________________

내가 가장 취약한 부분에 대해
요점 정리를 해 보세요.

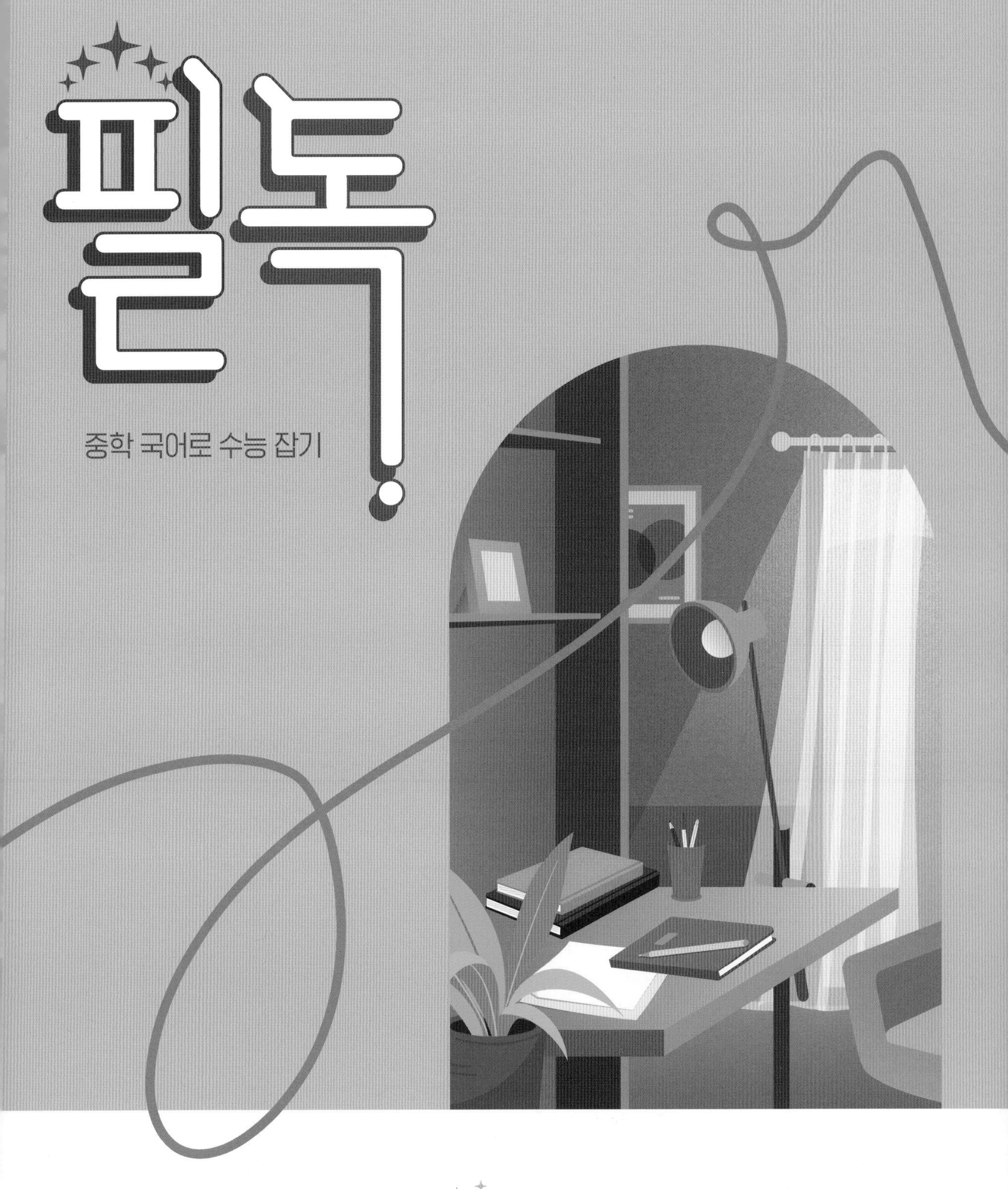

필독 중학 국어로 수능 잡기 시리즈

문학 – 비문학 독해 – 문법 – 교과서 시 – 교과서 소설

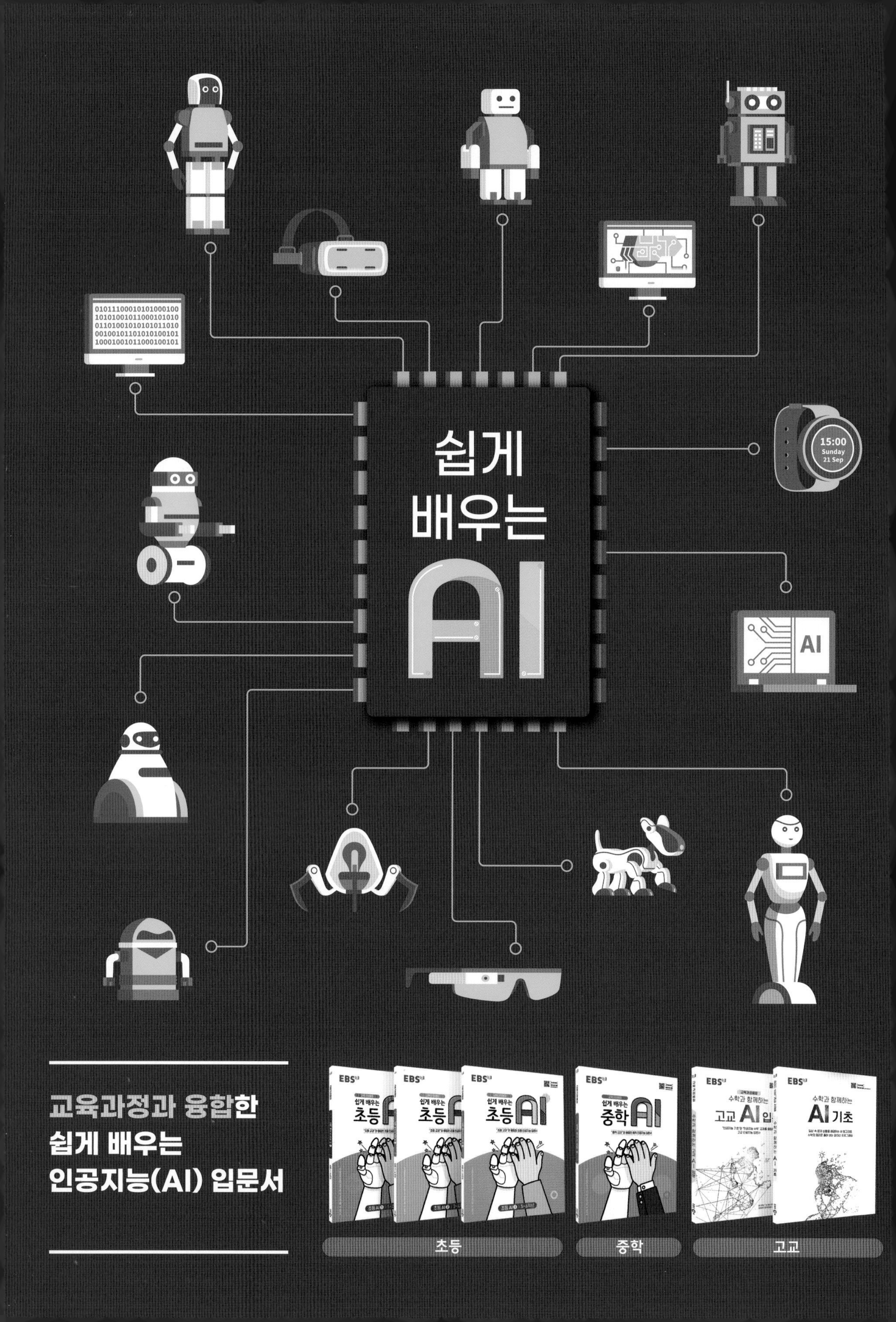

쉽게
배우는
AI
15:00
Sunday
21 Sep
AI
교육과정과 융합한
쉽게 배우는
인공지능(AI) 입문서
EBS
쉽게 배우는
초등 AI
중학 AI
고교 AI 입문
수학과 함께하는
AI 기초
초등
중학
고교

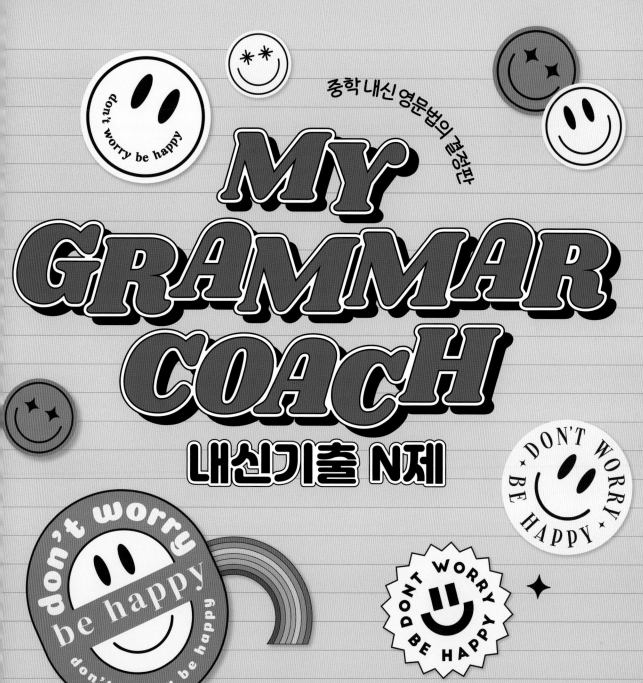

EBS

중 | 학 | 도 | 역 | 시 EBS

중학 내신 영문법의 결정판

MY GRAMMAR COACH

내신기출 N제

don't worry be happy

DON'T WORRY BE HAPPY

Workbook

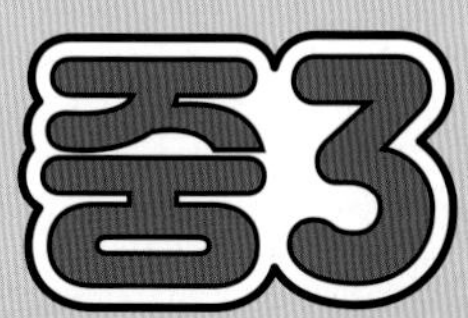

Workbook

CHAPTER

01

문장의 동사

UNIT 01 1형식, 2형식, 3형식 동사

〈주어 + 동사〉 뒤에 어떤 말이 오는가에 따라 1, 2, 3형식으로 구분하세요.

1형식	2형식	3형식
〈주어 + 동사〉	〈주어 + 동사〉 + 보어	〈주어 + 동사〉 + 목적어

참고 부사(구), 전치사구는 구성 요소에서 제외해요.

다음 문장의 문장 요소를 |보기|에서 찾아 표시하시오.

|보기|
주어: S 동사: V 보어: C 목적어: O 수식어: M

01 The baby smiles at her mom.
02 Lots of children like the character.
03 Some people are walking down the street.
04 The Earth goes around the sun.
05 Mr. Johnson is an able lawyer.
06 You should respect yourself.
07 The Second World War broke out in 1939.

UNIT 02 2형식 동사 + 보어

be동사와 감각동사가 취하는 보어의 종류와 그 의미를 파악하세요.

보어를 취하는 동사		보어
be동사	be, am, are, is, was, were	명사, 형용사
감각동사	feel, look, sound, smell, taste	형용사

주의 keep, get, become, turn, remain, appear 등도 보어(명사, 형용사)를 취하는 동사들임에 유의하세요.

참고 감각동사 뒤에 명사를 쓰려면 〈감각동사+like+명사〉로 쓰면 돼요.
He looks smart. → He looks like a smart person.

다음 문장에서 어법상 어색한 부분을 찾아 바르게 고쳐 쓰시오.

01 The online game looks excitingly. → ____________
02 Your vacation plan seems interest. → ____________
03 Try to remain calmly. → ____________
04 Their opinion sounds a good idea. → ____________
05 The dress looks greatly on the bride. → ____________
06 Coffee tastes bitterly. → ____________
07 Many students appeared nervously before the test. → ____________
08 People in the room looked so happiness, but the girl felt sad. → ____________

UNIT 03 3형식 동사+목적어

동사 뒤에 전치사가 필요할 것 같지만, 그렇지 않은 3형식 동사에 주의하세요.

explain(~을 설명하다)	explain it to him	reach(~에 도달하다)	reach the beach
discuss(~을 논의하다)	discuss it	attend(~에 참석하다)	attend a wedding
enter(~에 들어가다)	enter the room	marry(~와 결혼하다)	marry her
mention(~을 언급하다)	mention it to me	resemble(~와 닮다)	resemble him

주의 위의 동사들은 explain about, discuss about, enter to와 같이 전치사와 함께 쓰일 것 같은 의미를 가졌으나, 바로 목적어만 써요.

괄호 안의 말을 바르게 배열하여 3형식 문장으로 완성하시오.

01 (your father / you / don't resemble) → ______________________

02 (discovered / the explorer / the island) → ______________________

03 (how to / knows / he / change tires) → ______________________

04 (the project / she / finished / yesterday) → ______________________

05 (mentioned / the employer / again / the issue) → ______________________

06 (the plan / his brother / with / he / discussed) → ______________________

07 (the conference / last week / attended / he) → ______________________

08 (the station / the next train / soon / will reach) → ______________________

UNIT 04 4형식 수여동사

목적어 두 개, '~에게(간접목적어)'와 '~을/를(직접목적어)'을 취하는 4형식 동사들과 그 어순을 알아 두세요.

4형식 수여동사	give, make, show, send, ask, tell, lend, get, bring, teach, buy, cook 등

참고 목적어가 두 개인 4형식 문장은 3형식 문장으로 바꿔 쓸 수 있어요.

3형식 어순	주어+수여동사+직접목적어+전치사(to/for/of)+간접목적어

다음 4형식 문장을 같은 의미의 3형식 문장으로 바꾸시오.

01 He found me a hotel in Jeju Island. → He found ______________________.

02 Pass me the pen, please. → Pass ______________________, please.

03 The kind man brought me some food. → The kind man brought ______________________.

04 Yuna writes me a letter weekly. → Yuna writes ______________________ weekly.

05 My uncle built us a sand castle. → My uncle built ______________________.

06 Could you lend me the book? → Could you lend ______________________?

07 The chef cooked the guests dishes. → The chef cooked ______________________.

08 The teacher asked the student a question. → The teacher asked ______________________.

UNIT 05 5형식 동사 1

목적격보어로 명사나 형용사를 쓰는 5형식 동사를 알아 두세요.

5형식 어순	명사/형용사를 목적격보어로 쓰는 5형식 동사	목적어	목적격보어
	make, call, name, find, keep, elect, think, believe, consider 등	~을/를, ~이/가	명사, 형용사

주의 만약, 목적어가 to부정사이면, 목적어 자리에 가목적어 it을 쓰고, 진목적어 to부정사를 목적격보어 뒤에 써야 해요.
I think it difficult to talk to him.

괄호 안의 말을 바르게 배열하여 문장을 완성하시오.

01 She ______________________________ on time. (arrive / to / it / impossible / believes)

02 You must ______________________________. (clean / keep / your hands)

03 The teacher ______________________________. (Jian / very smart / found)

04 They ______________________________. (talk with / exciting / found / him / it / to)

05 We ______________________________. (elected / the class president / him)

06 The designer will ______________________________. (the house / green / make)

07 She ______________________________. (the bed / comfortable / found)

08 The nasty boy ______________________________. (his brother / calls / a fool)

09 We ______________________________. (the dog / Winnie / named)

UNIT 06 5형식 동사 2

목적격보어로 to부정사를 쓰는 동사들을 알아 두세요.

5형식 어순	to부정사를 목적격보어로 쓰는 5형식 동사	목적어	목적격보어
	want, ask, tell, expect, enable, encourage, allow, advice, order, get, convince, force 등	~에게, ~이/가	to부정사 (~하기를/~하라고)

참고 to부정사의 부정은 to 앞에 not을 쓰면 돼요.

괄호 안의 말을 활용하여 문장을 완성하시오.

01 Her mother convinced ____________________ a doctor. (she, see)

02 The boss ordered ____________________ the project by next Tuesday. (they, finish)

03 The dentist advised ____________________ sweets. (he, not, eat)

04 I want ____________________ now. (Ian and Mia, leave)

05 My parents forced ____________________ the online game. (we, not, play)

06 My sister told ____________________ the window. (I, open)

07 The safety guard didn't allow ____________________ in the pool. (he, swim)

08 The transportation system enables ____________________ more easily. (citizens, get around)

UNIT 07 5형식 지각동사

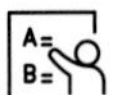

지각동사가 취할 수 있는 목적격보어의 종류와 그 의미를 잘 파악하세요.

	지각동사	목적어	목적격보어	의미
5형식 어순	feel, see, watch, hear, listen to, smell, notice 등	~이/가	원형부정사	목적어가 ~하는 것을(능동)
			현재분사	목적어가 ~하고 있는 것을(진행 강조)
			과거분사	목적어가 ~된/당한 것을(수동)

다음 두 문장을 의미가 같은 한 문장으로 바꿔 쓰시오.

01 They heard a song. It was sung outside. → ______________________

02 I smell the wood. The wood is burning. → ______________________

03 I saw my uncle. He was fishing in the lake. → ______________________

04 He felt someone. He was pushing his back. → ______________________

05 I heard some neighbors. They were arguing. → ______________________

06 He watched his cat. It was chasing a bird. → ______________________

07 He saw his bicycle. It was repaired. → ______________________

08 We felt the ground. It was shaking. → ______________________

09 I noticed a man. He was stealing. → ______________________

UNIT 08 5형식 사역동사

사역동사(~에게 …하도록 시키다)가 취할 수 있는 목적격보어의 종류와 그 의미를 잘 파악하세요.

	사역동사	목적어	목적격보어	의미
5형식 어순	make, have (~가 …하게 시키다)	~이/가	원형부정사	목적어가 …하게 만들다/시키다
			과거분사	목적어가 …되도록 만들다/시키다
	let (~가 …하게 두다)	~이/가	원형부정사	목적어가 …하게 두다
			to be 과거분사	목적어가 …되도록 두다

괄호 안의 말을 알맞은 형태로 넣어 문장을 완성하시오.

01 The teacher makes ______________________ a book every morning. (we, read)

02 My mom let ______________________ the toy. (my sister, buy)

03 Must I have ______________________? (my baggage, check)

04 The coffee made ______________________ awake until 2:00 A.M. (he, stay)

05 We had ______________________ for the party. (some food, deliver)

06 They couldn't make ______________________ crying. (she, stop)

07 Anna had ______________________ on the wall. (the frame, hang)

08 The school rule makes ______________________ at school on time. (we, arrive)

UNIT 09 5형식 동사 help, get

help와 get의 목적격보어에 주의하세요.

	사역동사	목적어	목적격보어	의미
5형식 어순	help (~가 …하도록 돕다)	~이/가	to부정사	목적어가 …하도록 돕다
			원형부정사	
			(to) be 과거분사	목적어가 …되도록 돕다(수동)
	get (~가 …하도록 시키다)	~이/가	to부정사	목적어가 …하도록 시키다
			과거분사	목적어가 …되도록 시키다

다음 문장에서 어법상 어색한 부분을 찾아 바르게 고쳐 쓰시오.

01 We have to get the homework do right now. → ____________

02 The director could get the work to finish. → ____________

03 I helped my brother moved the heavy table. → ____________

04 Get them washing their hands before cooking. → ____________

05 The instructor got Rose practices the violin every day. → ____________

06 Computers help people working efficiently. → ____________

07 You can help Bill fixes the computer. → ____________

08 The hotel workers get the rooms cleaning. → ____________

UNIT 10 목적격보어의 다양한 형태

대표적인 5형식 동사들의 주요 목적격보어의 형태를 전체적으로 확인하세요.

동사	목적격보어	동사	목적격보어
make, call, name, find, keep, elect, think 등	명사, 형용사	make, have, let	원형부정사, 과거분사
want, ask, tell, expect, enable, allow 등	to부정사	help	to부정사, 원형부정사
feel, see, watch, hear, listen to, smell 등	원형부정사, 현재분사, 과거분사	get	to부정사, 과거분사

다음 문장에서 어법상 어색한 부분을 찾아 바르게 고쳐 쓰시오.

01 John got his car check after the accident. → ____________

02 Yunseo made all of us angrily during the game. → ____________

03 My mom let me to help the old lady. → ____________

04 We watched the sun to set into the ocean. → ____________

05 The documentary makes people thinking about the old days. → ____________

06 He helped his daughter riding a bike by herself. → ____________

07 My parents allowed us seeing the scary movie. → ____________

08 Emma had the book to sign by the author. → ____________

중간고사·기말고사 실전문제

객관식 (01~15) / 주관식 (16~30)

정답과 해설 • 65쪽

학년과 반 　　 이름 　　 객관식 　　 / 15문항 　　 주관식 　　 / 15문항

[01~03] 다음 빈칸에 알맞은 것을 고르시오.

01

The girl looks ________ in her dress.

① happily ② awfully
③ comfortably ④ lovely
⑤ beautifully

02

Students asked many questions ________ the teacher.

① for ② of ③ to
④ into ⑤ with

03

Can you make the baby ________ crying?

① stop ② to stop ③ stopping
④ stopped ⑤ stops

[04~05] 다음 우리말을 영어로 바르게 옮긴 것을 고르시오.

04

그 쿠키는 달콤한 향이 났다.

① The cookie smells sweet.
② The cookie smells like sweet.
③ The cookie smelled sweet.
④ The cookie smelled sweetly.
⑤ The cookie smelled like sweetly

05

엄마는 그에게 따뜻한 우유 한 잔을 주셨다.

① My mom gave warm a cup of milk to him.
② My mom gave him to a cup of warm milk.
③ My mom gave a cup of warm milk for him.
④ My mom gave a cup of warm milk him.
⑤ My mom gave him a cup of warm milk.

[06~08] 다음 중 어법상 어색한 것을 고르시오.

06 ① Don't make me angry at you.
② That sounds a good idea.
③ The train arrived at the station.
④ The sun rises in the east.
⑤ Some flowers can grow in the desert.

07 ① John let us swim in the pool.
② Mike helped me moving heavy boxes.
③ She saw the dog running toward her.
④ I heard him call my name.
⑤ My sister bought a present for her friend.

08 ① She looked comfortable in her bed.
② David slept on the sofa yesterday.
③ They called the fire fighter a hero.
④ Jenny resembles with her mom.
⑤ My grandpa always told me to be honest.

[09~11] 다음 중 어법상 옳은 것을 고르시오.

09 ① The pizza tasted well.
② The actress felt confidently on stage.
③ This soap smells flowers.
④ People get tired soon after hiking.
⑤ The clown doesn't look happily.

10 ① The doctor didn't tell to me anything.
② Can you teach me to how to swim?
③ He allowed me to leave the classroom.
④ Let me to help you solve the problem.
⑤ People watched them to play tennis.

11 ① The policeman made her tell him everything.
② That cake tasted sweet chocolate.
③ His son became to a football player.
④ They entered to the ghost house.
⑤ Dad cooked delicious food to my family.

[12~13] 다음 빈칸에 들어갈 말이 바르게 짝지어진 것을 고르시오.

12

- They reached ________ of the mountain.
- This coffee tastes ________.
- He couldn't stay ________ because of the scary dog.

① to the top – bitterly – calmly
② to the top – bitter – calmly
③ for the top – bitterly – calm
④ the top – bitter – calmly
⑤ the top – bitter – calm

13

- My mom didn't let me ________ alone.
- The teacher got me ________ a test.
- She saw a man ________ money.

① travel – to take – steal
② travel – take – stealing
③ travel – to take – to steal
④ to travel – to take – steal
⑤ to travel – take – stealing

[14~15] 다음 빈칸에 알맞지 않은 것을 고르시오.

14

The teacher ________ my brother study hard.

① made ② had ③ let
④ got ⑤ helped

15

David ________ one of the pictures in the gallery to his friend.

① bought ② showed ③ sold
④ gave ⑤ sent

〈다음부터는 서술형 주관식 문제입니다.〉

[16~20] 다음 문장에서 어법상 어색한 부분을 찾아 바르게 고쳐 쓰시오.

16 Many foreign students will attend to the Korean class.

________ → ________

17 Jane made a beautiful dress to her daughter as a birthday present.

________ → ________

18 The boy felt the raindrops to fall on his head.

________ → ________

19 The hotel looks a great place to stay during the holidays.

________ → ________

20 Everyone in this room thought the boy honestly.

________ → ________

[21~23] 다음 밑줄 친 부분이 어법상 맞으면 ○표 하고, 틀리면 바르게 고쳐 쓰시오.

21 We heard the bell ring from his cellphone.

→ ________

22 My uncle had his car repair by the mechanic.

→ ________

23 My mom asked me do laundry.

→ ____________

[24~26] 다음 우리말과 같도록 괄호 안의 말을 바르게 배열하시오.

24

나의 삼촌은 고등학교에서 학생들에게 역사를 가르치신다.
(teaches / high school / history / to / in / students)

→ My uncle ____________
____________.

25

우리는 그녀를 다시 데려오는 것이 가능하다고 믿었다.
(to / believed / bring her / possible / back)

→ We ________ it ________
____________.

26

그 경찰은 아이들에게 안전 규칙을 설명해 주었다.
(explained / the policeman / the safety rules)

→ ____________
____________ to the children.

[27~28] 다음 우리말과 같도록 괄호 안의 말을 활용하여 문장을 완성하시오.

27

그 교수는 이 책이 학생들에게 도움이 된다는 것을 알게 되었다.
(find, helpful, the professor, for)

→ ____________
____

28

더운 날씨가 그 초록 사과를 빨갛게 변하게 했다.
(hot weather, turn, red, green)

→ ____________
____

[29~30] 다음 우리말을 주어진 |조건|에 맞게 바르게 영작하시오.

29 내 친구가 나에게 웃긴 그림 하나를 보여 주었다.

|조건|
1. 3형식 문장으로 쓸 것
2. 단어 show, funny, picture를 사용할 것
3. 8개의 단어로 쓸 것

→ ____________
____

30 그는 내가 그의 집에 방문하기를 원했다.

|조건|
1. 단어 want, visit, house를 사용할 것
2. 필요시 어법에 맞게 단어를 바꿀 것
3. 7개의 단어로 쓸 것

→ ____________
____

CHAPTER

02

시제

UNIT 01 동사 변화형

주어가 3인칭 단수일 때, 현재형

대부분의 동사	-s
-o, -s, -x, -sh, -ch로 끝나는 동사	-es
〈자음+y〉로 끝나는 동사	y를 i로 바꾸고 -es
〈모음+y〉로 끝나는 동사	-s
불규칙 동사	be - am/are/is have - has

동사의 규칙 과거형과 과거분사형

대부분의 동사	-ed
-e로 끝나는 동사	-d
〈단모음+단자음〉으로 끝나는 동사	자음 하나 더 쓰고 -ed
〈자음+y〉로 끝나는 동사	y를 i로 바꾸고 -ed
〈모음+y〉로 끝나는 동사	-ed

* 동사의 불규칙 과거형과 과거분사형은 암기해야 해요.

참고 과거는 과거시제에, 과거분사는 수동태나 완료시제에 쓸 수 있어야 해요.

다음 동사의 과거형과 과거분사형을 쓰면서 외우세요.

01 accomplish – ______ – ______
02 am, is – ______ – ______
03 apply – ______ – ______
04 are – ______ – ______
05 arrange – ______ – ______
06 become – ______ – ______
07 begin – ______ – ______
08 bite – ______ – ______
09 blow – ______ – ______
10 break – ______ – ______
11 breathe – ______ – ______
12 bring – ______ – ______
13 burst – ______ – ______
14 bury – ______ – ______
15 buy – ______ – ______
16 catch – ______ – ______
17 choose – ______ – ______
18 cost – ______ – ______
19 cry – ______ – ______
20 cut – ______ – ______
21 delay – ______ – ______
22 deny – ______ – ______
23 destroy – ______ – ______
24 disagree – ______ – ______
25 display – ______ – ______
26 do – ______ – ______
27 draw – ______ – ______
28 drive – ______ – ______
29 drop – ______ – ______
30 dry – ______ – ______
31 eat – ______ – ______
32 fall – ______ – ______
33 feed – ______ – ______
34 fight – ______ – ______
35 find – ______ – ______
36 fly – ______ – ______
37 forget – ______ – ______
38 forgive – ______ – ______
39 found – ______ – ______
40 freeze – ______ – ______

41 give – ________ – ________
42 go – ________ – ________
43 grab – ________ – ________
44 grow – ________ – ________
45 hear – ________ – ________
46 hide – ________ – ________
47 hit – ________ – ________
48 hold – ________ – ________
49 hurt – ________ – ________
50 keep – ________ – ________
51 know – ________ – ________
52 lay – ________ – ________
53 lead – ________ – ________
54 leave – ________ – ________
55 lend – ________ – ________
56 let – ________ – ________
57 lie(누워 있다) – ________ – ________
58 lie(거짓말하다) – ________ – ________
59 lose – ________ – ________
60 maintain – ________ – ________
61 mean – ________ – ________
62 meet – ________ – ________
63 overcome – ________ – ________
64 pay – ________ – ________
65 prefer – ________ – ________
66 prove – ________ – ________
67 quit – ________ – ________
68 raise – ________ – ________
69 read – ________ – ________
70 regret – ________ – ________
71 ride – ________ – ________
72 ring – ________ – ________
73 rise – ________ – ________
74 run – ________ – ________
75 see – ________ – ________
76 send – ________ – ________
77 set – ________ – ________
78 share – ________ – ________
79 sing – ________ – ________
80 sit – ________ – ________
81 sleep – ________ – ________
82 speak – ________ – ________
83 spend – ________ – ________
84 spread – ________ – ________
85 stand – ________ – ________
86 stay – ________ – ________
87 steal – ________ – ________
88 survive – ________ – ________
89 swim – ________ – ________
90 take – ________ – ________
91 teach – ________ – ________
92 tear – ________ – ________
93 thank – ________ – ________
94 think – ________ – ________
95 throw – ________ – ________
96 understand – ________ – ________
97 wake – ________ – ________
98 wear – ________ – ________
99 win – ________ – ________
100 write – ________ – ________

UNIT 02 기본시제 - 현재, 과거, 미래

기본시제를 표현하는 동사의 형태 및 부정문, 의문문의 어순을 정확히 파악하세요.

시제	동사 형태		시제	동사 형태	
현재	be동사	am, are, is	과거	be동사	was, were
	일반동사	동사원형+(e)s		일반동사	동사원형+(e)d / 불규칙

주의 미래는 조동사 will이나 be going to를 이용해요. (단, 시간, 조건의 부사절에서 미래는 현재시제로 표현하는 것에 주의하세요.)

When he ~~will come~~ comes back, we will start.

괄호 안의 말을 활용하여 문장을 완성하시오.

01 The moon ________________ around the Earth. (go)

02 She ________________ to university next year. (apply)

03 South Korea ________________ 7th at the 2018 Winter Olympics. (rank)

04 It ________________ no use crying over spilt milk. (be)

05 People ________________ the universe in the future. (travel)

06 He finally ________________ their offer last week. (accept)

07 I ________________ my cousins the day after tomorrow. (meet)

08 My father often ________________ at weekends because he has many things to do. (work)

UNIT 03 현재진행 & 과거진행

'~하고 있다'와 같이 진행 중인 동작을 나타낼 때는 진행형 <be동사 + 동사원형-ing>로 써야 해요.

현재진행	am/are/is + 동사원형-ing	현재 진행 중이나 가까운 미래의 예정된 일을 표현
과거진행	was/were + 동사원형-ing	과거에 진행 중이었던 일을 표현

주의 소유, 인식, 감정 상태를 나타내는 동사(have, know, like, exist 등)는 진행형으로 쓸 수 없어요. 하지만 have가 '먹다'라는 의미일 때는 진행형이 가능해요.

괄호 안의 말을 활용하여 진행시제 문장을 완성하시오.

01 She ________________ to the radio when she drove to work. (listen)

02 The train to Gwangju ________________ at 9:00. (leave)

03 The children ________________ soccer in the park now. (play)

04 I saw the girl. She ________________ near the tall tree. (stand)

05 What time ________________ she ________________ this Tuesday? (be, arrive)

06 When you walked into the kitchen, I ________________ dinner. (prepare)

07 We ________________ for the bus when it started raining. (wait)

08 You can't enter the room. The students ________________ a test. (take)

UNIT 04 현재완료 1 - 계속

과거는 과거에 끝난 일을, 현재완료는 과거에 일이 현재까지 영향을 미치는 일을 표현할 때 써요.

	과거	현재완료
예문	He lived here last year. (작년에 살았음 / 현재와는 상관없음)	He has lived here for 5 years. (과거부터 현재까지 5년 동안 살아왔음)

주의 for 또는 since가 있으면 '(과거부터 현재까지 계속) ~해 왔다'는 의미로 현재완료형을 써야 해요.

	for(~동안) + 기간	since(~이후로) + 과거 시점 / 과거 문장
예문	He has lived here for 5 years.	He has lived here since last year. He has lived here since he was born.

괄호 안의 말을 활용하여 과거시제 또는 현재완료시제 문장을 완성하시오.

01 They ______________ the movie together last night. (see)

02 I ______________ several movies since the summer vacation started. (see)

03 It ______________ hot and humid last summer. (be)

04 Ten years ______________ since she left her country. (pass)

05 The weather ______________ very cold and windy recently. (be)

06 They ______________ what the teacher said then. (not, understand)

07 Tom and Jerry ______________ each other for a very long time. (know)

UNIT 05 현재완료 2 - 완료, 경험, 결과

현재완료 〈have[has]+ p.p.〉는 계속의 의미 이외의 다른 의미도 파악하세요.

완료	(과거에 시작한 일을 현재) ~했다	I have just finished the homework. (막 끝냈다) He hasn't read the email yet. (아직 읽지 않았다)
경험	(과거부터 지금까지) ~해 본 적 있다	She has tried Thai food before. (전에 먹어 본 적이 있다) I've never been to Paris. (가 본 적이 전혀[절대] 없다)
결과	(과거에 ~한 결과 현재) ~하다	She has lost her expensive bag. (잃어버려서 지금 가지고 있지 않다) He has gone to the hospital. (병원에 가서 (이곳에) 없다)

괄호 안의 말을 활용하여 현재완료시제 문장을 완성하시오.

01 I __________________ the report yet. (not, do)

02 Yujin __________________ the competition once. (win)

03 Seojun __________________ his wallet on the way to work. (lose)

04 The train from Busan __________________ in Seoul. (arrive, just)

05 Have you __________________ the song before? (hear, ever)

06 I __________________ to the theme park. (be, never)

07 One of my friends __________________ to Miami. (go)

UNIT 06 현재완료 3

자주 쓰이는 부사구와 함께 현재완료의 네 가지 의미와 쓰임을 파악하세요.

계속	for는 '~동안'의 의미로 지속된 기간 / since는 '~이후로, ~부터'의 의미로 시작된 기준 시점
완료	주로 just, already, yet, finally 등과 함께 사용
경험	ever, never, before, often, once 등과 함께 사용
결과	〈have gone to + 장소〉: (~에) 가 버렸다(그래서 지금 여기에 없다)

참고 have been to는 '~에 가 본 적이 있다'는 경험의 뜻인 반면, have gone to는 '~에 가 버렸다(그래서 지금 여기에 없다)'는 결과의 뜻을 나타내요.

다음 문장에서 어법상 어색한 부분을 찾아 바르게 고쳐 쓰시오.

01 The famous author writes many novels so far. → ____________

02 We have gone to Japan a few times. → ____________

03 The patient hasn't eaten anything since 3 days. → ____________

04 Minjun has received the invitation last Monday. → ____________

05 The train has departed for Daejeon at 2:00. → ____________

06 They have already cleans the classroom. → ____________

07 She hasn't drunk coffee when she was in high school. → ____________

08 Danny has been interested in wildlife for he was a little child. → ____________

UNIT 07 현재완료 진행

과거에 시작한 일이 현재까지 진행 중임을 강조할 때는 현재완료 진행형을 사용해야 해요.

	현재완료	현재완료 진행
형태	have[has] + p.p.	have[has] + been + V-ing

참고 현재완료 진행형을 만드는 방법은 동사의 진행형(be동사+V-ing)에서 be동사만 완료형(have[has]+been)으로 만들고 그 뒤에 진행형(V-ing)을 붙여요.

괄호 안의 말을 활용하여 현재완료 진행시제 문장을 완성하시오.

01 He ____________ for the bus for 40 minutes. (not, wait)

02 The men ____________ the fence since noon. (paint)

03 They ____________ around the city for sightseeing. (walk)

04 The announcer ____________ about the issue for 2 hours. (talk)

05 Tom and Jake ____________ on the assignment for a week. (work)

06 Mr. Evans ____________ science since he was 30 years old. (teach)

07 How long ____________ the workers ____________ the bridge? (build)

08 The two teams ____________ the soccer game for more than an hour. (play)

UNIT 08 과거완료

과거 시점을 기준으로 더 앞선 과거(대과거)부터 과거의 어느 한 시점까지에 걸친 일은 과거완료형을 사용해야 해요.

	현재완료	과거완료
형태	have[has]+p.p.	had+p.p.

참고 과거완료(had+p.p.)는 현재완료시제와 마찬가지로 계속, 완료, 경험, 결과를 나타내요.

괄호 안의 말을 활용하여 과거완료시제 문장을 완성하시오.

01 They knew Jenny because they ________________ her once. (meet)

02 My uncle quit his job after he ________________ to go abroad to study. (decide)

03 Kevin realized that he ________________ his homework. (not do)

04 When she entered the room, the presentation ________________. (start)

05 They were angry with their son because he ________________ to them. (lie)

06 I forgot the appointment that I ________________ with Kate. (make)

07 Julie had to go to Yunseo's house because she ________________ her books there. (leave)

08 My friends from Thailand ________________ snow until they visited Korea. (not, see)

09 Jiho ________________ his homework when the teacher came in. (not, complete)

UNIT 09 과거완료 진행

대과거에 시작한 일이 과거까지 진행 중이었음을 강조할 때는 과거완료 진행형을 사용해야 해요.

	과거완료	과거완료 진행
형태	had+p.p.	had+been+V-ing

괄호 안의 말을 활용하여 과거완료 진행시제와 과거시제를 써서 문장을 완성하시오.

01 When he ______________ her, she ______________ for 2 years. (meet, work)

02 The girl ______________ 2km before she ______________ her leg. (walk, break)

03 Laura ______________ it for 5 years before she ______________ here. (learn, move)

04 Jake ______________ on the phone when I ______________ in the door. (talk, knock)

05 They ______________ all day before they ______________ sick. (eat, get)

06 I ______________ there for 30 minutes before the doctor ______________ me. (sit, call)

07 We ______________ for years before we ______________ the house. (save, buy)

08 Scott ______________ there when I ______________ it. (smoke, notice)

09 All of them ______________ for the train before it ______________. (wait, arrive)

중간고사·기말고사 실전문제

객관식 (01~15) / 주관식 (16~30)

학년과 반 이름 객관식 / 15문항 주관식 / 15문항

[01~03] 다음 빈칸에 알맞은 것을 고르시오.

01

What ________ for dinner last night?

① did you eat ② do you eat
③ have you eaten ④ will you eat
⑤ are you eating

02

She has known her colleague ________ last January.

① for ② during ③ to
④ still ⑤ since

03

We ________ throwing a farewell party for our friend tomorrow night.

① are going ② have been ③ are
④ will ⑤ were

[04~05] 다음 문장의 밑줄 친 부분과 용법이 같은 것을 고르시오.

04

She has been to Japan three times.

① I have left my phone on the table.
② He has never gone to Europe.
③ She has worked at the office for 2 years.
④ We have heard about it before.
⑤ They have decided to go abroad.

05

Have you finished the research report yet?

① Have you ever been to New York?
② Has she already sent the message?
③ Has he lost his money by gambling?
④ Since when have they lived in this town?
⑤ I have studied French for a couple of years.

[06~08] 다음 중 어법상 어색한 것을 고르시오.

06
① She bursted into tears.
② The cell phone rang loudly.
③ They founded the company together.
④ He left home right after the fight.
⑤ The storm swept everything away.

07
① Water has become ice.
② She has broken the device.
③ The sun has already rosen today.
④ We haven't spoken to her yet.
⑤ The birds have flown far away.

08 ① Tim usually does exercise after work.
② She is still using her old computer.
③ The Moon revolves around the Earth.
④ How did you feel at this moment?
⑤ I often skip meals these days.

[09~11] 다음 중 어법상 옳은 것을 고르시오.

09 ① The problem seemed serious now.
② Every dog had four legs in general.
③ Many tourists visit the place last year.
④ She won't make the same mistake again.
⑤ The two girls are sharing a house now. They lived together since July.

10 ① I have been short 5 years ago.
② She has gone to her country 3 years ago.
③ He has never driven a car since then.
④ It's still cold. The weather was cold lately.
⑤ They haven't seen each other in 2020.

11 ① What are they having at the restaurant?
② This salad is tasting fresh.
③ She was needing some advices.
④ This coffee is containing too much caffeine.
⑤ What are you knowing about the accident?

[12~13] 다음 빈칸에 들어갈 말이 바르게 짝지어진 것을 고르시오.

12

Simpson ________ his new computer yesterday that he ________ a few weeks ago.

① breaks – has bought
② broke – has bought
③ broke – had bought
④ has broken – has bought
⑤ had broken – bought

13

• Jake ________ a police officer since he was 25 years old. • He hasn't proposed to marry his girlfriend ________. • He ________ buy a ring for her tomorrow.

① was – yet – will
② was – already – is going to
③ has been – yet – will
④ has been – already – is going to
⑤ had been – yet – is going to

[14~15] 다음 빈칸에 알맞지 <u>않은</u> 것을 고르시오.

14

She has been to Seoul ________.

① for 2 days　② last year
③ before　④ since 2020
⑤ once

15

David had ________ the beautiful picture before he went out.

① drew　② chosen　③ hidden
④ found　⑤ hung

〈다음부터는 서술형 주관식 문제입니다.〉

[16~20] 다음 문장에서 어법상 <u>어색한</u> 부분을 찾아 바르게 고쳐 쓰시오.

16 She has enjoyed riding a skateboard during five years.

________ → ________

17 Ms. Scott has completed her training program yet.

________ → ________

18 My parents have known the dentist for last April.

________ → ________

19 Mr. Smith has worked as a vet for ten years, but he retired a month ago.

________ → ________

20 They are owning the mansion with a big pool.

________ → ________

[21~23] 다음 밑줄 친 부분이 어법상 맞으면 ○표 하고, <u>틀리면</u> 바르게 고쳐 쓰시오.

21 Thomas Edison <u>invents</u> the light bulb and many other useful inventions.

____

22 The players will stay home if it <u>will rain</u> tomorrow.

____

23 She has been watching the drama for five hours.

___

[24~26] 우리말과 같도록 괄호 안의 말을 바르게 배열하시오.

24

우리 선생님은 최근에 지갑을 잃어버렸다.
(has / lost / wallet / his / my teacher)

→ ___
___ recently.

25

그의 아들은 초등학교에 가기 전까지 알파벳을 배워 본 적이 없었다.
(his son / the alphabet / had / learned / he / went / before / not / to)

→ ___
___ elementary school.

26

눈보라 때문에, 그들은 2주 동안 그 호텔에 머물러왔다.
(stayed / they / for / the hotel / have / two weeks / at)

→ ___
___ because of the snowstorm.

[27~28] 다음 우리말과 같도록 괄호 안의 말을 활용하여 문장을 완성하시오.

27

학생들은 30분 동안 그 주제에 대해 토론해 오고 있는 중이다.
(discuss, the topic, 30 minutes)

→ Students ___
___.

28

그 남자는 그 문제에 대해 아내가 그에게 했던 말을 기억할 수 없었다.
(remember, tell, about the problem)

→ The man ___ what his wife
___.

[29~30] 다음 우리말을 주어진 |조건|에 맞게 바르게 영작하시오.

29 그 사건이 일어났을 때, 직원들은 이미 빌딩을 떠났다.

|조건|
1. 완료시제를 사용할 것
2. 단어 already, leave, the building을 사용할 것
3. 문장 전체를 10개의 단어로 쓸 것

→ Employees ___
___ when the incident occurred.

30 그들은 3시간 동안 밖에서 축구를 하는 중이다.

|조건|
1. 완료진행시제를 사용할 것
2. 단어 play, soccer, outside를 사용할 것
3. 문장 전체를 9개의 단어로 쓸 것

→ ___
___ for 3 hours.

내가 가장 취약한 부분에 대해
요점 정리를 해 보세요.

CHAPTER

03

조동사

UNIT 01 can, could

조동사 can(~할 수 있다)은 다양한 상황에서 쓰일 수 있으므로 문맥을 파악하는 것이 중요해요.

능력	I can swim.	요청	Can[Could] you wait?
가능	I can help you.	추측	He can be busy.
허가	You can stay here.	금지	You cannot[can't] stay here.

참고 can이 능력/가능을 의미할 때만 be able to와 바꿔 쓸 수 있다는 것을 기억하세요.

다음 문장을 be able to를 이용한 문장으로 바꿔 쓰시오.

01 Could she cook pasta? → ________ she ____________________ pasta?

02 I couldn't open the door. → I ____________________ the door.

03 He could carry it by himself. → He ____________________ it by himself.

04 I can make a snowman. → I ____________________ a snowman.

05 I couldn't solve the problem. → I ____________________ the problem.

06 Could they catch the train? → ________ they ________________ catch the train?

07 We can't live without Internet. → We ____________________ without Internet.

08 Can they eat spicy food? → ________ they ________________ eat spicy food?

UNIT 02 may, might

조동사 may의 다양한 의미를 기억해 두세요.

추측	~일지도 모른다	요청	~해도 될까요?	허가	~해도 된다	금지 may not	~하면 안 된다

참고 might는 may보다 더 불확실한 추측을 나타내요.

괄호 안의 말과 조동사 may를 이용하여 대화를 완성하시오.

01 A: Why does the actress look sad?
B: I don't know. She ____________________ satisfied with her role. (be)

02 A: Why is Jiho so happy?
B: I'm not sure. He ____________________ this song. (like)

03 A: Why didn't Felix call her?
B: He ____________________ her number. (remember)

04 A: ____________________ something here? (eat)
B: No, you may not. You cannot eat or drink anything here.

05 A: Do you know what time they are arriving?
B: They've already left. They ____________________ late. (be)

UNIT 03 must

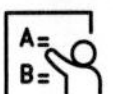

'~해야 한다'라는 의무나, '~임에 틀림없다'라는 강한 추측을 표현할 때 조동사 must를 쓰세요.

의무	강한 추측	강한 금지
~해야 한다	~임에 틀림없다	~하면 안 된다

주의 강한 추측을 나타내는 must의 부정형은 can't[cannot](~일 리가 없다)로 써요. The story can't be true.

괄호 안에서 알맞은 조동사를 고르시오.

01 People under 19 (may / must not) drink alcohol.

02 Jaemin answered all the questions correctly. He (must / cannot) be smart.

03 He (must / must not) study hard nowadays because he had failed the test before.

04 Chris (must / cannot) be Tony's brother. They look totally different.

05 She (must / may not) save money to buy a house.

06 Junho (must / cannot) be crazy to do such a thing.

07 The painting is not that expensive. It (must / cannot) be genuine.

08 Sam (must / cannot) be at home. He usually works at the store until 10 p.m.

UNIT 04 have to

have[has] to는 의미상 must와 바꿔 쓸 수 있지만, 부정문은 서로 다른 의미인 것에 주의해야 해요.

긍정문	의무	We have to pay.	~해야 한다
부정문	불필요	We don't have to pay.	~할 필요가 없다
의문문	의무	Do we have to pay?	~해야 합니까?

주의 주어가 3인칭 단수이면 has to로, 과거(~했어야 했다)는 had to로, 미래(~해야 할 것이다)는 will have to로 써요.

주의 have[has] to의 의문문은 〈Do[Does]+주어+have to+동사원형~?〉의 어순으로 써요.

다음 문장에서 어법상 어색한 부분을 찾아 바르게 고쳐 쓰시오.

01 She must not bring an umbrella. It won't rain. → ________

02 Jimin has to answer the question then. → ________

03 Yuna doesn't have to leaves now. → ________

04 We will must complete the project tomorrow. → ________

05 Somebody has to takes responsibility for the accident. → ________

06 Did you had to stand on the bus? → ________

07 The students must pass the exam last week. → ________

08 You must not wear a coat. It's not cold. → ________

09 Jiho must catch the first train to Busan yesterday. → ________

UNIT 05 should, ought to

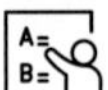 '~해야 한다'라는 의미의 충고나 의무를 나타낼 때 should나 ought to를 쓰세요.

	should	ought to
의미	~해야 한다, ~하는 편이 좋겠다 (충고)	~해야 한다 (should보다 강하고 must보다 약함)
긍정문	You should take the pill.	You ought to take the pill.
부정문	You should not[shouldn't] take the pill.	You ought not to take the pill.
의문문	Should I take the pill?	

괄호 안의 말과 should 또는 ought to를 이용하여 문장을 완성하시오.

01 She ______________________ a table for us in advance. (reserve)

02 Where __________ I __________ the car? (park)

03 He ______________________ for the test next week. (study)

04 __________ I __________ her the truth? (tell)

05 We ______________________ too much sugar for our health. (not, eat)

06 I ______________________ a present for my father. (buy)

07 I ______________________ television after 10 o'clock. (not, watch)

08 All of you ______________________ at least 3 times a week. (exercise)

UNIT 06 had better, would rather

 다음 조동사 표현들을 익히세요.

	had better	would rather
의미	~하는 게 낫다(should보다 강한 충고)	(차라리) ~하겠다
긍정문/축약문	You had better go now. / You'd better	I would rather stay (than leave). / I'd rather
부정문	You'd better not go now.	I would rather not stay.
의문문	Should I go now?	Would you rather stay?

|A| 괄호 안의 말과 had better를 이용하여 문장을 완성하시오.

01 A storm is approaching. You ______________ indoors. (stay)

02 You ______________ on the test, or you'll get an F. (not, cheat)

03 The device is complicated. You ______________ the safety guidelines. (follow)

|B| 괄호 안의 말과 would rather를 이용하여 문장을 완성하시오.

01 I ______________ at home if it rains a lot. (eat)

02 I ______________ music than see a movie. (listen to)

03 You ______________ your time on television if you have many things to do. (not, waste)

UNIT 07 used to, would

'(과거에) ~하곤 했다'와 같이 과거의 반복하던 일은 used to와 would로 쓰세요.

	used to (~하곤 했다)	would (~하곤 했다)
예문	I used to go there on Sunday.	I would go there when it rained.
주의	⟨be used to⟩는 완전 다른 의미가 돼요. be used to + 명사/동명사: ~에 익숙하다 be used to + 동사원형: ~하는 데 사용되다	과거의 상태를 나타낼 때는 would를 못 써요. There would be a tree. (×) → used to be He would live here. (×) → used to live

주의 과거의 습관적 행동을 나타내는 would는 상태 동사인 be, feel, taste, hear, have, live, love, like, want, understand, know, agree, believe 등과 같이 쓸 수 없고 used to를 써야 해요.

괄호 안의 말과 used to 또는 would를 이용하여 문장을 완성하시오.

01 There ______________ a bank behind the church. (be)

02 Mr. and Mrs. Andrews ______________ much money. (have)

03 One of my friends ______________ me after school. (call)

04 My grandmother ______________ for us. (cook)

05 She ______________ to work. (drive)

06 We ______________ my aunt and uncle every month. (visit)

07 The tall building ______________ a hospital. (be)

08 We weren't rich, but we ______________ happy. (be)

UNIT 08 조동사 + have + 과거분사

과거의 추측이나 후회를 나타낼 때는 동사를 ⟨조동사 + have + p.p.⟩의 형태로 쓰세요.

must have p.p.	~했음이 틀림없다 (강한 추측)
cannot have p.p.	~이었을 리가 없다 (강한 부정 추측)
may[might] have p.p.	~했을지도 모른다 (약한 추측)
should have p.p.	~했어야 했다 (후회, 유감)
could have p.p.	~할 수도 있었을 텐데 (후회, 아쉬움)

우리말과 같도록 괄호 안의 말을 활용하여 문장을 완성하시오.

01 지민이는 시합에서 이길 수도 있었다. → Jimin ______________ the competition. (win)

02 너는 더 일찍 도착했음이 틀림없다. → You ______________ earlier. (arrive)

03 그는 교통 체증에 갇혔을지도 모른다. → He ______________ stuck in traffic. (get)

04 그는 시험에서 실수한 것이 틀림없다. → He ______________ mistakes on the test. (make)

05 그녀가 나에게 거짓말을 했을 리 없다. → She ______________ a lie to me. (tell)

06 우리는 더 주의를 기울였어야 했다. → We ______________ more attention. (pay)

중간고사·기말고사 실전문제

객관식 (01~15) / 주관식 (16~30)

학년과 반 이름 객관식 / 15문항 주관식 / 15문항

[01~03] 다음 빈칸에 알맞은 것을 고르시오.

01 Jerry will ________ buy the car if he wins the lottery.

① can ② could ③ must
④ may ⑤ be able to

02 All students ________ take the exam before they become 17.

① must ② have to ③ had to
④ should ⑤ will

03 ________ you like some ice cream for dessert?

① Will ② Would ③ Can
④ Could ⑤ Are

[04~05] 다음 우리말을 영어로 바르게 옮긴 것을 고르시오.

04 그는 오늘 사무실에 돌아가지 않아도 된다.

① He must not return to his office.
② He can't be returning to his office.
③ He doesn't have to return to his office.
④ He has not to return to his office.
⑤ He doesn't return to his office.

05 너는 너무 많은 생각을 하지 않는 것이 낫다.

① You had not better think too much.
② You had better not think too much.
③ You had not better thinking too much.
④ You had better not thinking too much.
⑤ You don't have better think too much.

[06~07] 다음 빈칸에 알맞은 것을 <u>모두</u> 고르시오.

06 He ________ play tennis every Friday, but he stopped playing after he got injured.

① would ② should ③ used to
④ had better ⑤ would rather

07 ________ you please close the window? It's too loud outside.

① Did ② Could ③ Should
④ Might ⑤ Would

[08~09] 다음 중 어법상 어색한 것을 고르시오.

08 ① Jane didn't have to solve the problem.
② Tomorrow is Sunday! You don't have to get up early.
③ I'm not sure how far she will have to go.
④ She will have to be back in the near future.
⑤ Does he must clean his room?

09 ① Could you hand me a towel?
② Andy must go back to school.
③ She has better bring the money back.
④ He should finish his essay by this week.
⑤ They ought not to play the games too long.

[10~11] 다음 중 어법상 옳은 것을 고르시오.

10 ① Sam is able to swimming well.
② It will work if you change the battery.
③ She will can find it easily.
④ May you give me some suggestions?
⑤ You were late. You should take a cab.

11 ① We used to live in the house on the hill.
② I used to baking pies for my family.
③ They used to this tough environment.
④ He used to drive 5 years ago, and he's still driving.
⑤ Ben uses to cry a lot when he was young.

[12~13] 다음 빈칸에 알맞은 것을 고르시오.

12

• We would ________ you for your support.
• My friend lives near here. We ________ meet him on the street.

① to thank – could
② like to thank – should
③ like to thank – might
④ like thanking – could
⑤ like thanking – might

13

• I ________ wait here than go out to find him.
• She ________ along with people, but she preferred to be alone.
• ________ I have your attention, please?

① had better – must have gotten – Can
② had better – must have gotten – Will
③ would like to – could have gotten – Must
④ would rather – could have gotten – May
⑤ would rather – should have gotten – Do

[14~15] 다음 빈칸에 알맞지 않은 것을 고르시오.

14

_______ you give me a hand, please?

① Will ② Would ③ May
④ Can ⑤ Could

15

People _______ smoke cigarettes around the school.

① shouldn't ② must not
③ ought not to ④ can't
⑤ don't have to

〈다음부터는 서술형 주관식 문제입니다.〉

[16~20] 다음 문장에서 어법상 어색한 부분을 찾아 바르게 고쳐 쓰시오.

16 I would like have some fresh orange juice.

_______________ → _______________

17 You had not better go out as it is late now.

_______________ → _______________

18 You have not to transfer to go there.

_______________ → _______________

19 She should tell the truth when the detective asked her a question.

_______________ → _______________

20 We had rather go hiking than go fishing this weekend.

_______________ → _______________

[21~23] 다음 우리말과 같도록 괄호 안의 말과 알맞은 조동사를 이용하여 문장을 완성하시오.

21

Kevin은 뉴욕에 혼자 있는 것이 틀림없다. (be)

→ Kevin _______________ in New York alone.

22

그녀는 사람들 앞에서 노래할 필요가 없었다. (sing)

→ She _______________ in front of people.

23

군인들은 고국으로 돌아가지 못했을지도 모른다.
(return)

→ The soldiers ______________________ to their country.

[24~26] 다음 우리말과 같도록 괄호 안의 말을 바르게 배열하시오.

24

수업 끝나고 따뜻한 커피 한 잔 드릴까요?
(you / coffee / like / would / a cup of / warm)

→ ______________________________________
__________________________ after class?

25

영화는 우리를 상상의 세계로 안내할 수 있다.
(into / world / movies / guide / the / us / imaginary / can)

→ ______________________________________
____

26

그 아이는 며칠 동안 집에 머물러야 할 것이다.
(days / the child / have to / will / stay / at home / a few / for)

→ ______________________________________
____

[27~28] 다음 우리말과 같도록 괄호 안의 말을 활용하여 문장을 완성하시오.

27

그는 그 사실을 믿었어야 했다.
(believe, the fact, should)

→ He ________________________________.

28

그녀가 어렸을 때, 그녀의 집 근처에 호수가 하나 있었다. (지금은 없음)
(there, used to, near, her house, a lake)

→ When she was little, __________________
______________________________________.

[29~30] 다음 우리말을 주어진 |조건|에 맞게 바르게 영작하시오.

29 우리가 어제 만든 그 샌드위치가 상했던 것이 틀림없다.

|조건|
1. 조동사를 사용할 것
2. 단어 make, go bad, sandwiches를 사용할 것
3. 9개의 단어로 쓸 것

→ ______________________________________

30 너는 너의 친구들에게 그 비밀을 말하지 않아야 한다.

|조건|
1. 조동사 ought to를 사용할 것
2. 단어 tell, secret, friends를 사용할 것
3. 9개의 단어로 쓸 것

→ ______________________________________

내가 가장 취약한 부분에 대해
요점 정리를 해 보세요.

CHAPTER

04

수동태

UNIT 01 수동태의 의미와 형태

아래 순서에 따라 수동태 문장을 만드세요.

step 1	목적어를 주어 자리로 옮겨요.	행위자가 인칭대명사라면 주격으로 써야 해요.
step 2	동사를 〈be+p.p.〉로 써요.	be동사는 주어의 인칭, 수에 맞추고 시제도 표현해요.
step 3	문장 끝에 〈by+행위자〉를 써요.	행위자가 인칭대명사라면 by 뒤에 목적격으로 써야 해요. 행위자가 일반인이거나 중요하지 않으면, 생략해요.

주의 목적어가 없는 자동사와 소유나 상태를 나타내는 타동사는 수동태로 쓸 수 없어요.

다음 문장을 수동태 문장으로 바꿔 쓰시오.

01 The factory produces many cars. → ____________________

02 He planned the trip to Taiwan. → ____________________

03 I wrapped the present for her. → ____________________

04 She didn't make the suggestion. → ____________________

05 You didn't break the vase. → ____________________

06 The kid behind me kicks my chair. → ____________________

UNIT 02 by 이외의 다른 전치사를 쓰는 수동태

전치사 by가 아닌 다른 전치사와 자주 사용되는 수동태의 다음 관용 구문을 외우세요.

be made from	~로 만들어지다(재료 성질이 변함)	be excited about	~에 흥분해 있다
be made of	~로 만들어지다(재료 성질이 안 변함)	be worried about	~에 대해 걱정하다
be tired of	~에 싫증이 나다	be covered with	~로 덮여 있다
be known for	~로[때문에] 알려져 있다	be pleased with	~에 기뻐하다
be known to	~에게 알려져 있다	be satisfied with	~에 만족하다
be known as	~로서 알려져 있다	be surprised at	~에 놀라다
be filled with	~로 가득 차 있다 (= be full of)	be interested in	~에 흥미가 있다

다음 문장에서 어법상 어색한 부분을 찾아 바르게 고쳐 쓰시오.

01 The basket is filled of apples. → ____________________

02 The fans are excited with the concert. → ____________________

03 I'm tired by talking to him. → ____________________

04 Few students are interested with advanced math. → ____________________

05 Cheese is made of milk. → ____________________

06 The old car is covered by dust. → ____________________

07 The singer is widely known as many people in Korea. → ____________________

08 He's not satisfied at his appearance. → ____________________

UNIT 03 수동태의 시제

수동태의 시제는 be동사를 이용하여 표현하는 것을 기억하세요.

현재	am/are/is + p.p.	Pengsoo is loved by many people.
과거	was/were + p.p.	The light bulb was invented in the 1880s.
미래	will be + p.p.	A lot of food will be prepared for the party.
진행	am/are/is/was/were + being + p.p.	The artificial lake is being built now.
완료	have/has/had + been + p.p.	The tower has been used as a prison.

다음 문장을 수동태 문장으로 바꿔 쓰시오.

01 We had moved some furniture. → ______

02 They were building a house. → ______

03 We have killed many animals. → ______

04 Our ancestors used shells as money. → ______

05 The team controls the air system. → ______

UNIT 04 조동사가 있는 수동태

수동태의 부정문과 의문문도 모두 be동사만을 이용하지만, 조동사가 있다면 조동사를 이용해야 해요.

	〈be + p.p.〉	〈조동사 + be + p.p.〉
긍정문	The book is loved by all.	The book can be loved by all.
부정문	The book is not loved by all.	The book cannot be loved by all.
의문문	Is the book loved by all?	Can the book be loved by all?

다음 문장을 수동태 문장으로 바꿔 쓰시오.

01 Others might disappoint us.

→ ______

02 Can she recommend a good doctor?

→ ______

03 Can I play the piano for the concert?

→ ______

04 They may not answer calls at night. (by 이하 생략)

→ ______

05 Should I submit the application right now? (by 이하 생략)

→ ______

06 People should not pollute the natural environment. (by 이하 생략)

→ ______

UNIT 05 동사구 수동태

동사구를 수동태로 전환할 때는 동사구를 하나의 단어처럼 취급하여 항상 함께 붙여 써야 해요.

laugh at	~을 비웃다	turn on	~을 켜다
take care of	~을 돌보다	turn off	~을 끄다
turn down	~을 거절하다	put off	~을 미루다, 연기하다
hand in	~을 제출하다	make use of	~을 이용하다
check out	~을 대출하다	look down on	~을 무시하다

다음 문장을 수동태 문장으로 바꿔 쓰시오.

01 Many classmates laugh at me. → ______________________

02 He was turning on the television. → ______________________

03 Some people look down on him. → ______________________

04 You should turn off the lights. → ______________________

05 We can check out five books today. → ______________________

UNIT 06 that절이 뒤에 나오는 수동태

주어가 일반적인 사람들이고 목적어가 that절일 때, 수동태 문장으로 바꿔 쓰는 법을 알아 두세요.

능동태	People/They/We	say	that honesty is the best policy.
수동태	It	is said	that honesty is the best policy.
	Honesty	is said	to be the best policy.

참고 일반적인 사람들 주어와 that절을 목적어로 쓰는 대표적인 동사들을 알아 두세요.
→ say, think, believe, know, consider, report, expect, suppose

주의 that절의 주어를 문장의 주어로 수동태 문장을 쓸 때, that절을 to부정사로 바꿔야 해요.

다음 문장을 두 가지 형태의 수동태 문장으로 바꿔 쓰시오.

01 We suppose that they are guilty.
→ It ______________________.
→ They ______________________.

02 They say Paris is the most attractive city.
→ It ______________________.
→ Paris ______________________.

03 They expect that we will find it soon.
→ It ______________________.
→ We ______________________.

04 Many think he is an honest man.
→ It ______________________.
→ He ______________________.

05 They reported that the child was missing.
→ It ______________________.
→ The ______________________.

UNIT 07 4형식 문장의 수동태

4형식 문장의 목적어 2개(간접목적어, 직접목적어)를 주어로 수동태 문장을 쓸 수 있어야 해요.

	간접목적어(~에게)를 주어로 쓸 때	직접목적어(~을)를 주어로 쓸 때
능동태	She gave them a card.	She gave them a card.
↓ 수동태	They were given a card by her.	A card was given to them by her.
주의	직접목적어는 동사 뒤에 그대로 쓰고, 능동태의 주어는 〈by+행위자〉로 써야 해요.	능동태의 간접목적어(~에게)를 〈전치사+사람〉으로 써야 해요.

직접목적어를 주어로 할 때, 간접목적어 앞의 전치사는 동사에 따라 다르므로 주의하세요.

give, tell, send, show, teach, sell, write 등	to	A card was given to them.
get, make, buy, cook 등	for	Curry was cooked for us.
ask의 직접목적어가 question이나 favor일 때	of	A question was asked of me.

주의 make, buy, get, send, bring, write, cook 등의 동사는 직접목적어만 주어로 써요.

다음 문장을 괄호 안의 지시대로 바꿔 쓰시오.

01 My sister made me a muffler. 〈직접목적어를 주어로 하는 수동태로〉

→ ______________________

02 He showed me the way to the bookstore. 〈두 가지 형태의 수동태로〉

→ I ______________________.

→ The way ______________________.

03 She cooks them a good breakfast every day. 〈직접목적어를 주어로 하는 수동태로〉

→ ______________________

04 Sumi teaches foreign students Korean. 〈간접목적어를 주어로 하는 수동태로〉

→ ______________________

05 The company offered me a new job. 〈두 가지 형태의 수동태로〉

→ I ______________________.

→ A new job ______________________.

06 The police asked him if he possessed a gun. 〈간접목적어를 주어로 하는 수동태로〉

→ ______________________

UNIT 08 5형식 문장의 수동태

5형식 문장에서 목적어를 주어로 하는 수동태 문장을 알아 두세요.

	목적격보어가 명사/형용사/to부정사일 때	
능동태	He made her happy / a doctor.	He told them to save money.
↓ 수동태	She was made happy / a doctor by him.	They were told to save money by him.

참고 능동태의 목적어를 주어로 쓰고, 수동태 동사를 쓴 후, 목적격보어를 그대로 써요.

다음 문장을 수동태 문장으로 바꿔 쓰시오.

01 They saw the suspect entering the bank. → ____________________

02 He found the door unlocked. → ____________________

03 She allowed her children to play. → ____________________

04 The movie made her a star. → ____________________

05 She wants me to take part in the play. → ____________________

UNIT 09 지각동사, 사역동사의 수동태

지각동사나 사역동사의 5형식을 수동태로 쓸 때 목적격보어의 형태에 주의하세요.

	목적격보어가 원형부정사인 지각동사	목적격보어가 원형부정사인 사역동사
능동태	We saw the boys play soccer.	He made the driver stop.
↓ 수동태	The boys were seen to play soccer.	The driver was made to stop by him.

주의 수동태로 쓸 때는 목적격보어가 원형부정사일 때는 to부정사로 쓰고, 분사일 때는 그대로 분사를 써요.
The boys were seen playing soccer.

다음 문장을 수동태 문장으로 바꿔 쓰시오.

01 She made her son play outside. (by 이하 생략)
→ ____________________

02 We heard a girl scream for help. (by 이하 생략)
→ ____________________

03 The teacher made us keep a diary in English.
→ ____________________

04 Eunju saw her friends skate on the frozen pond.
→ ____________________

05 Using a smartphone for a long time makes your eyes feel tired.
→ ____________________

중간고사·기말고사 실전문제

객관식 (01~15) / 주관식 (16~30)

정답과 해설 • 73쪽

학년과 반 이름 객관식 / 15문항 주관식 / 15문항

[01~03] 다음 빈칸에 알맞은 것을 고르시오.

01

This option hasn't ________ by anyone yet.

① choose
② chose
③ be chosen
④ been chosen
⑤ been choosing

02

His research on African animals should ________ by the end of September.

① finish
② be finish
③ be finished
④ is finished
⑤ been finished

03

The baby was ____________ all weekend.

① took care of by his aunt
② took care by his aunt of
③ taken care of by his aunt
④ taken care by his aunt of
⑤ taken by his aunt care of

[04~05] 다음 우리말을 영어로 바르게 옮긴 것을 고르시오.

04

그 노래는 그들에 의해 100년 동안 불려 왔다.

① The song is sang by them for 100 years.
② The song has sang by them for 100 years.
③ The song has been singing by them for 100 years.
④ The song has been sang by them for 100 years.
⑤ The song has been sung by them for 100 years.

05

강아지들을 위한 집이 지금 지어지고 있는 중이다.

① The house for puppies is built now.
② The house for puppies is being built now.
③ The house for puppies is building now.
④ The house for puppies has built now.
⑤ The house for puppies being built now.

[06~08] 다음 중 어법상 어색한 것을 고르시오.

06
① She might be threatened by someone.
② My photo cannot be sending via e-mail.
③ The park will be closed by next month.
④ His car used to be parked here.
⑤ This goal could be achieved by everyone.

07 ① The robbers were catched by the police.
② Their desks were moved somewhere.
③ His opinion was agreed to by everyone.
④ A bunch of flowers is chosen as a gift.
⑤ My books were donated to the preschool.

08 ① A ring was given to Jin by her husband.
② This letter was written to me by her.
③ They are completely satisfied in their results.
④ Cookies were made for the kids by their grandma.
⑤ Money was paid to the cashier by him.

[09~11] 다음 중 어법상 옳은 것을 고르시오.

09 ① The concert will be hold at the stadium.
② Every car ought to be repaired with him.
③ Sentences can was broken up into clauses.
④ The sofa would rather be place here.
⑤ You may be fired because of the mistake.

10 ① Children were disappeared suddenly.
② The fact was lied by the politics.
③ A small accident was happened yesterday.
④ Kittens were raised by their mom.
⑤ This cellphone is costed 500 dollars.

11 ① The man was elected president.
② He's not allowed going out late at night.
③ Jane is called by 'Cutie' by her friends.
④ Everyone was made happily by her smile.
⑤ I was made think about the issue.

[12~13] 다음 빈칸에 들어갈 말이 바르게 짝지어진 것을 고르시오.

12

- The question was asked ________ the policeman by people.
- My dog was heard ________ outside.

① to – bark
② of – bark
③ for – barking
④ to – to bark
⑤ of – to bark

13

- This electronic device for cooking ________ for several years.
- A big package was sent ________ me by my nephew.
- She was asked ________ by the coach.

① used – to – leave
② used – for – leaving
③ is used – of – leaving
④ has been used – to – to leave
⑤ has been used – for – to leave

[14~15] 다음 빈칸에 공통으로 들어갈 말로 알맞은 것을 고르시오.

14

- The gift was given ________ my grandparents by my mom last Monday.
- He was made ________ do exercise by the trainer.

① for ② with ③ to
④ by ⑤ in

15

- Everyone was surprised ________ what he had said last night.
- Many people are angry ________ the director because of the movie.

① as ② at ③ by
④ for ⑤ to

〈다음부터는 서술형 주관식 문제입니다.〉

[16~20] 다음 문장에서 어법상 어색한 부분을 찾아 바르게 고쳐 쓰시오.

16 The expensive necklace with diamonds should never steal.

________ → ________

17 She expected to choose for the role, but the director picked another actress.

________ → ________

18 Your hands will keep warm by these gloves.

________ → ________

19 The players were excited by the result of the game.

________ → ________

20 The brand-new items in the store were sold by many customers by the clerk.

________ → ________

[21~24] 다음 문장을 밑줄 친 부분을 주어로 하는 수동태 문장으로 바꿔 쓰시오.

21 The nurse looked after the critical patients in the hospital.

→ ________

22 The lawyer told his assistant to bring the document.

→ ________

23 Kelly lent her little sister <u>an old blanket</u> she had.

→ ______________________

____

24 The professor made <u>the students</u> finish the assignment by Tuesday.

→ ______________________

____

[25~26] 다음 우리말과 같도록 괄호 안의 말을 바르게 배열하시오.

25

너는 그 영화를 보고 놀란 적이 있니? (you / have / ever / surprised / a movie / at / been)

→ ______________________

____

26

그의 속도는 다른 선수들에게 따라잡힐 수 있었다. (could / the other athletes / surpassed / be / his speed / by)

→ ______________________

____

[27~28] 다음 우리말과 같도록 괄호 안의 말을 활용하여 문장을 완성하시오.

27

우리는 그의 첫 승리에 매우 기뻐했다. (please, very, victory)

→ ______________________

28

그 연극은 아이들을 위해 공연되어 왔다. (the play, children, performed)

→ ______________________

[29~30] 다음 우리말을 주어진 |조건|에 맞게 바르게 영작하시오.

29 그 노래는 많은 인기를 얻을 것으로 예상된다.

|조건|
1. the song을 주어로 할 것
2. 단어 expect, gain, popularity, a lot of를 사용할 것
3. 10개의 단어로 쓸 것

→ ______________________

____

30 그 회의는 20분 동안 지연되고 있다.

|조건|
1. 현재진행시제를 사용할 것
2. 단어 the meeting, delay, for를 사용할 것
3. 8개의 단어로 쓸 것

→ ______________________

____

CHAPTER

05

부정사

UNIT 01 to부정사의 명사적 용법

동사를 명사(~하기, ~하는 것)처럼 사용하려면 〈to + 동사원형〉의 형태로 만들어야 해요.

명사적 to부정사의 역할		주의
주어	To become a scientist takes years. 과학자가 되는 것은 수년이 걸린다.	• to부정사 주어는 단수 취급 • 부정형은 not to부정사
보어	Her dream is to become a scientist. 그녀의 꿈은 과학자가 되는 것이다.	
목적어	He promised not to be late. 그는 늦지 않을 것을 약속했다.	

참고 to부정사가 주어로 쓰일 경우 가주어 It을 문장 앞에 두고 진주어 to부정사는 뒤로 보내요.

우리말과 같도록 괄호 안의 말과 to를 이용하여 문장을 완성하시오.

01 쿠키를 만드는 것은 재미있다. (make) → It is interesting ____________________.

02 편지를 받는 것은 즐거웠다. (receive) → It was a pleasure ____________________.

03 그들은 그 파티를 주최하기 원한다. (host) → They want ____________________.

04 이 숲에서 그 새들을 찾는 것은 흔하다. (find) → ____________________ in this forest is common.

05 나는 그것을 받아들이지 않기로 결정했다. (accept) → I decided ____________________.

06 집을 사는 것은 돈이 많이 드는 일이다. (buy) → It is expensive ____________________.

UNIT 02 to부정사의 의미상 주어

to부정사의 행위를 하는 주체가 다른 경우, 그 행위자의 주체를 표시해야 해요.

〈for + 행위자〉	The book is hard for children to read. 그 책은 아이들이 읽기 어렵다.	to read의 행위자: children
〈of + 행위자〉	It was nice of her to take me home. 나를 집까지 데려다주다니, 그녀는 멋지구나.	to take의 행위자: her

참고 일반적으로 〈for+행위자〉를 사용하나, 사람의 성격이나 성품을 나타내는 형용사(kind, wise, polite, honest, nice, clever, generous, foolish, silly, rude, careless 등)가 오는 경우에는 의미상의 주어로 〈of+행위자〉를 써야 해요.

다음 문장에서 어법상 어색한 부분을 찾아 바르게 고쳐 쓰시오.

01 It's very kind of your to invite us. → ____________________

02 It's important submit the assignment on time. → ____________________

03 It's silly for them to spend a lot of money on that. → ____________________

04 It's not possible of her to finish the homework by Tuesday. → ____________________

05 It's considerate for you to send me the Christmas card. → ____________________

06 It's careless for the boy to break the cup. → ____________________

07 It's easy to me for riding a bike by myself. → ____________________

08 It is comfortable for us listen to relaxing music. → ____________________

09 It's difficulty for them to pass the exam. → ____________________

UNIT 03 의문사+to부정사

의문사 뒤에 to부정사를 써서 하나의 명사처럼 쓸 때, 문맥에 맞게 알맞은 의문사를 써야 해요.

what+to부정사	무엇을 ~할지	when+to부정사	언제 ~할지
which+to부정사	어느 것을 ~할지	where+to부정사	어디에서 ~할지
who+to부정사	누구를 ~할지	how+to부정사	어떻게 ~할지, ~하는 법

참고 〈의문사+to부정사〉는 〈의문사+주어+should+동사원형〉으로 바꿔 쓸 수도 있어요.

I don't know how to get there. (그곳에 가는 방법)
= how I should get there (내가 그곳에 어떻게 가야 하는지)

다음 두 문장의 뜻이 같도록 문장을 완성하시오.

01 John learns how he should play golf. → John learns ____________.

02 He taught me how I can make it. → He taught me ____________.

03 We wondered where to go. → We wondered ____________.

04 Eric asked me when I should leave. → Eric asked me ____________.

05 She advised us what we should choose. → She advised us ____________.

06 Anna told me how I should get there. → Anna told me ____________.

UNIT 04 to부정사의 형용사적 용법

to부정사는 형용사처럼 명사를 꾸밀 수 있는데, 이때 어순에 주의하세요.

어순	형용사	명사	형용사	형용사 역할 to부정사
일반적인 명사의 경우	many	books		to read (~해야 할, ~할)
-thing/-one/-body의 경우		something	interesting	

주의 to부정사가 수식하는 명사가 to부정사구의 전치사의 목적어일 때는 전치사를 함께 써야 해요.

Everyone needs someone to talk with. (모든 사람은 같이 이야기를 나눌 누군가가 필요하다.)

다음 문장에서 어법상 어색한 부분을 찾아 바르게 고쳐 쓰시오.

01 They don't have time playing tennis this weekend. → ____________

02 Some students have much homework completing by tomorrow. → ____________

03 Do you have delicious anything to eat? → ____________

04 Mina and Hana share many things to talk. → ____________

05 They ordered something to drink hot. → ____________

06 Mike reserved a hotel to stay during the break. → ____________

07 I was waiting for a chance introducing myself. → ____________

08 The children want a backyard to play. → ____________

UNIT 05 to부정사의 형용사적 용법 - be to용법

〈be + to부정사〉의 다양한 의미를 알아 두세요.

〈be + to부정사〉	예정	She is to visit the museum.	방문할 예정이다
	운명	Everyone is to die some day.	죽을 운명이다
	의무	We are to finish the project today.	끝내야 한다
	의도, 의지	If you are to get there, leave now.	도착하고자 하면
	가능	No one is to be left alone.	혼자 남겨질 수 없다

우리말과 같도록 괄호 안의 말을 이용하여 〈be + to부정사〉가 포함된 문장으로 완성하시오.

01 올해의 컨퍼런스는 호텔에서 열릴 것이다. (held, be, at the hotel)

→ This year's conference ______________________.

02 그 군인들은 전쟁에서 죽을 운명이었다. (die, the soldiers, were)

→ ______________________ in the war.

03 너는 같은 실수를 다시 하면 안 된다. (make, not, the same mistake)

→ You ______________________ again.

04 테스트에 통과하려면 열심히 공부해야 할 것이다. (pass, the test, are)

→ If you ______________________, you will have to study hard.

05 그 선물은 그의 생일 때까지 열려질 수 없다. (opened, be, not)

→ The gift ______________________ until his birthday.

UNIT 06 to부정사의 부사적 용법

to부정사가 주어, 목적어, 보어가 아니라면, 부사의 역할을 하는 것으로 판단하세요.

목적	~하기 위해서	**판단의 근거**	~하다니 …한	**형용사 수식**	~하기에 …한
결과	~해서 (결국) …하다	**감정의 원인**	~하게 되어 …한		

참고 to부정사가 목적(~하기 위해서)을 나타낼 때는 in order to나 so as to로 바꿔 쓸 수 있어요.

다음 괄호 안의 말을 바르게 배열하여 문장을 완성하시오.

01 We must ______________________. (miss / hurry / not / the flight / to)

02 He wants to go to the USA ______________________. (in / study / order / English / to)

03 Amy studies hard ______________________. (to / a scholarship / get)

04 It is not ______________________. (make / easy / to / new friends)

05 He must be ______________________. (such a question / to / ask / silly)

06 His son ______________________. (become / grew up / to / a firefighter)

07 The online game ______________________. (play / is / to / exciting)

UNIT 07 to부정사의 역할

to부정사가 문장 안에서 명사, 형용사, 부사 중 어떤 역할을 하고 있는지 파악할 수 있어야 해요.

명사 역할	'~하는 것', '~하기'라는 의미로 주어, 보어, 목적어 자리에 쓴다.
형용사 역할	앞의 명사 수식하거나, be동사의 보어(be to 용법)로 쓴다.
부사 역할	목적, 감정의 원인, 형용사 수식, 판단의 근거, 결과의 의미를 표현한다.

우리말과 같도록 괄호 안의 말을 이용하여 to부정사가 포함된 문장으로 완성하시오.

01 학생들은 내일까지 과제를 마무리해야 한다. (be, finish, the assignment)

→ The students ________________ by tomorrow.

02 영어책을 매일 읽는 것은 쉽지 않다. (it, easy, read)

→ ________________ an English book every day.

03 그녀는 이탈리아어를 배우려고 수업을 듣는다. (a class, learn Italian)

→ She attends ________________.

04 Chris는 한국에서 태권도를 배울 계획을 세웠다. (planned, learn Taekwondo)

→ Chris ________________ in Korea.

05 우리는 여기서 소음을 내면 안 된다. (be, make noise)

→ We ________________ here.

06 내 꿈은 에베레스트 산에 오르는 것이다. (dream, climb Mt. Everest)

→ My ________________.

07 보람이는 수업에 늦는 학생이 아니다. (a student, late, for class)

→ Boram is ________________.

UNIT 08 too ~ to부정사 / enough to부정사

〈too ~ to부정사〉와 〈~ enough + to부정사〉를 〈so ~ that〉 구문으로 바꿔 쓸 수 있어야 해요.

too ~ to ...	~ enough to ...	주의
너무 ~해서 …할 수 없다 (= so ~ that ... can't)	…하기에 충분히 ~하다 (= so ~ that ... can)	〈so ~ that ...〉구문에서 that 이하는 시제와 문맥에 맞게 쓰기

다음 문장과 의미가 같도록 빈칸에 알맞은 말을 쓰시오.

01 You are so smart that you can solve this. → You are ________________ this.

02 It is too expensive for her to buy. → It is ________________ it.

03 He was so wise that I couldn't fool him. → He was ________________.

04 It is too cold for us to go camping. → It is ________________ camping.

05 He is so big that he can't wear the shirt. → He is ________________ the shirt.

06 I was too shocked to get up. → I was ________________.

UNIT 09 seem + to부정사

〈seem + to부정사〉를 〈It seems that ~〉 문장으로 바꿀 때 시제에 주의해야 해요.

〈seem + to부정사〉		〈It seems that ~〉 문장을 전환하는 법	
seem(s)	to + 동사원형	seem의 시제는 that 절의 시제와 동일	He seems to know me. (나를 아는 거로 보인다) = It seems that he knows me.
seemed			He seemed to know me. (나를 아는 거로 보였다) = It seemed that he knew me.
seem(s)	to have p.p.	that절의 시제는 seem의 시제보다 과거	He seems to have known me. (나를 알았던 거로 보인다) = It seems that he knew me.
seemed			He seemed to have known me. (나를 알았던 거로 보였다) = It seemed that he had known me.

다음 문장과 의미가 같도록 알맞은 말을 쓰시오.

01 I seem to have left my wallet. → It ______________________.

02 It seemed that he had learned Chinese. → He ______________________.

03 Jeju seems to be a place for holidays. → It ______________________ for holidays.

04 It seemed that the room was cleaned. → The room ______________________.

UNIT 10 목적격보어로 쓰이는 to부정사

목적격보어로 to부정사를 쓰는 동사들을 외워 두세요.

어순	주어	동사	목적어	목적격보어
예문	I	want, ask, tell, expect, enable allow, advice, order, get, help	him	to come.

주의 help는 목적격보어로 to부정사와 원형부정사 둘 다 쓸 수 있어요.

우리말과 같도록 괄호 안의 말을 이용하여 문장을 완성하시오.

01 나는 그 편지가 내일 도착하리라고 예상한다. (expect, arrive, the letter)
→ I ______________________ tomorrow.

02 Tony는 그녀가 자전거 수리하는 것을 도왔다. (repair, helped)
→ Tony ______________________ the bike.

03 그녀는 자신의 말에 주의를 기울이라고 우리에게 명령했다. (order, pay attention to)
→ She ______________________ her words.

04 나는 그 컴퓨터가 작동하게 할 수 없었다. (get, work, the computer)
→ I couldn't ______________________.

05 부모님은 내가 밤늦게 밖에 나가지 않기를 바라신다. (not, go out, want)
→ My parents ______________________ late at night.

UNIT 11 목적격보어로 쓰이는 원형부정사 1 - 사역동사

사역동사는 목적격보어로 to가 없는 원형부정사(동사원형)를 쓴다는 것을 알아 두세요.

어순	주어	사역동사	목적어	목적격보어
예문	I	make, have, let	him	come.

우리말과 같도록 괄호 안의 말을 활용하여 문장을 완성하시오.

01 엄마는 나에게 가끔 애니메이션 영화를 보게 하신다. (let, see)
→ My mom often ______________________ animation movies.

02 그 실수는 그를 시합에서 지게 만들었다. (make, lose the race)
→ The mistake ______________________.

03 그 선생님은 그의 학생들에게 빈칸을 채우도록 시켰다. (have, fill in)
→ The teacher ______________________ the blanks.

04 아빠는 내가 꽃에 물을 주기를 원하신다. (want, water)
→ My dad ______________________ the flowers.

05 그는 그녀가 한 말에 대해 사과하게 했다. (make, apologize)
→ He ______________________ for what she said.

06 그녀는 그녀의 딸이 수프에 소금을 조금 넣도록 했다. (let, add)
→ She ______________________ some salt to the soup.

UNIT 12 목적격보어로 쓰이는 원형부정사 2 - 지각동사

목적격보어로 원형부정사 또는 현재분사(-ing)를 쓰는 지각동사들을 기억하세요.

어순	주어	지각동사	목적어	목적격보어
예문	I	feel, see, watch, hear, listen to, smell 등	him	come / coming.

괄호 안의 말을 활용하여 문장을 완성하시오.

01 He told me ______________ my messy room. (clean)

02 They watched the skater ______________ on the ice. (spin)

03 We make the visitors ______________ their hands. (wash)

04 I could feel my cat ______________ against my legs. (rub)

05 She ordered them ______________ the room. (not, leave)

06 Peter saw Lisa ______________ table tennis. (play)

07 They heard someone ______________ at their child. (shout)

08 The test makes us ______________ 10 hours a day. (study)

09 Jenny could feel something ______________ in the dark. (move)

UNIT 13 독립부정사

독립적인 부사 역할을 하는 to부정사 표현을 기억하세요.

to be honest	사실은	to make matters worse	설상가상으로
to sum up	요약하면	to make a long story short	간단히 말해서
to begin with	우선	so to speak	말하자면
to be sure	확실히	strange to say	이상한 말이지만
to tell the truth	사실을 말하자면	needless to say	말할 필요도 없이
to be frank with you	솔직히 말하면	not to mention ~	~은 말할 것도 없이

우리말과 같도록 빈칸에 알맞은 독립부정사 표현을 쓰시오.

01 말하자면, 그녀는 책벌레다.

→ She is a bookwork, ______________________________.

02 우선, 그의 글은 명확하지 않다.

→ ______________________________, his writing is not clear.

03 사실은, 나는 그를 좋아하지 않는다.

→ ______________________________, I don't like him.

04 사실을 말하자면, 나는 어제 전혀 잘 수 없었다.

→ ______________________________, I couldn't sleep at all yesterday.

05 확실히, 수면 부족은 건강 문제를 일으킬 수 있다.

→ ______________________________, lack of sleep can cause health problems.

06 말할 필요도 없이, 나는 돈보다 가족을 중시한다.

→ ______________________________, I value family above money.

중간고사·기말고사 실전문제

객관식 (01~15) / 주관식 (16~30)

정답과 해설 • 76쪽

학년과 반　　이름　　객관식　　/ 15문항　　주관식　　/ 15문항

[01~03] 다음 빈칸에 알맞은 것을 고르시오.

01

_______ is not hard for him to swim in the ocean.

① It　② That　③ This
④ He　⑤ Which

02

Do you wish _______ the city and live in the countryside?

① leave　② leaving　③ to leave
④ to leaving　⑤ left

03

There is ___________ in my closet.

① nothing to wear suitable
② to wear nothing suitable
③ nothing suitable wearing
④ suitable nothing to wear
⑤ nothing suitable to wear

[04~05] 다음 우리말을 영어로 바르게 옮긴 것을 고르시오.

04

오늘은 너무 더워서 그는 밖에서 축구를 할 수 없다.

① Today is too hot that play soccer outside.
② Today is too hot to play soccer outside.
③ Today is too hot to not play soccer outside.
④ Today is so hot that he plays soccer outside.
⑤ Today is so hot to play soccer outside.

05

사실대로 말하다니, 그는 참 정직하구나.

① It's very honest for him to tell the truth.
② It's very honest of him telling the truth.
③ It's very honest of him to tell the truth.
④ It's very honest to him to tell the truth.
⑤ It's very honest him of telling the truth

[06~08] 다음 중 어법상 어색한 것을 고르시오.

06 ① My plan is to exercise 30 minutes a day.
② It's good to go on a picnic on a sunny day.
③ We all agree to put off the conference.
④ To taking a walk is good for your health.
⑤ Not to eat junk food is my new year's resolution.

07 ① It's not easy of me to like small insects.
② Does he know where to get off the bus?
③ It's wise of you to avoid gossiping.
④ Emily can't choose what she should put on for the event.
⑤ They wish to meet the famous actress in the theater.

08 ① My parents had me finish my dinner.
② She is listening to the boy playing the violin.
③ The owner of the building didn't let the dogs come in.
④ The volunteers helped the people with disabilities take a bath.
⑤ The captain ordered the crew throw away luggage on the ship.

[09~11] 다음 중 어법상 옳은 것을 고르시오.

09 ① We haven't decided the hotel to stay yet.
② I have no one to talk in this room.
③ Is there any question to ask?
④ Kids need someone to play.
⑤ Do you have a notebook to write?

10 ① If you are join, you should know the rule.
② She was enough strong to carry the box.
③ This way is too narrow to getting in.
④ Daniel felt so upset that he couldn't say anything.
⑤ He seems to not find the answer.

11 ① To summing up, being positive is important.
② Being honest, I lied to you the other day.
③ Needless to saying, coffee also contains a lot of caffeine.
④ He works too hard to speak so, he is a workaholic.
⑤ To be sure, this device makes my work much easier.

[12~13] 다음 빈칸에 들어갈 말이 바르게 짝지어진 것을 고르시오.

12

It's clever ___________ her ___________ a new way to solve the problem.

① for – to create ② of – to create
③ for – to creating ④ of – creating
⑤ to – creating

13

• It was so cold ________________ walk the dog at the park.
• Kelly hid the letter ________________ read by anyone.
• Everyone seemed ________________ disappointed at the news.

① that I can't – not to be – to be
② that I could – to not be – that has been
③ that I could – not to be – that has been
④ that I couldn't – not to be – to have been
⑤ that I couldn't – to not be – to have been

[14~15] 다음 문장의 밑줄 친 to부정사의 용법과 다른 것을 고르시오.

14

The concept she explained to us was difficult to understand.

① Farmers work hard to produce good food.
② She has some chores to do today.
③ The boys grew up to be worldwide stars.
④ It's nice to meet my old friend again.
⑤ He turned off the TV to go to bed.

15

His final goal is to be a world champion.

① To be a great writer needs a lot of effort.
② It is uncomfortable to be with a person you haven't met.
③ During the class, kids are to be quiet.
④ They refused to be with the crowd.
⑤ Why do you want to be a flight attendant?

〈다음부터는 서술형 주관식 문제입니다.〉

[16~17] 다음 밑줄 친 부분이 어법상 맞으면 ○표 하고, 틀리면 바르게 고쳐 쓰시오.

16 The teacher let me write a letter to my parents.

____

17 The mayor hopes improving the policies for the city.

____

[18~20] 다음 문장에서 어법상 어색한 부분을 찾아 바르게 고쳐 쓰시오.

18 This musical is interesting enough attracting the audience.

________________ → ________________

19 It's kind for you to share your snacks with friends.

________________ → ________________

20 The passengers didn't know what should do when the train stopped suddenly.

________________ → ________________

[21~22] 다음 우리말과 의미가 같도록 괄호 안의 말을 이용하여 문장을 완성하시오.

21

그 시험을 한 번에 합격하다니, 그는 참 똑똑하구나. (smart)

→ It ________________ to pass the test at once.

22

Tom은 그 임무를 완수하기 위해 최선을 다했다. (complete)

→ Tom did his best ________________ the mission.

[23~24] 다음 두 문장의 의미가 같도록 괄호 안의 말을 이용하여 문장을 완성하시오.

23 Jessy was so busy that she couldn't go to the dentist. (too)

→ Jessy was ______________________ to the dentist.

24 The man seemed to have a complaint about my decision. (that)

→ It seemed ______________________ a complaint about my decision.

[25~26] 다음 우리말과 같도록 괄호 안의 말을 바르게 배열하시오.

25

그 의사는 환자에게 살을 좀 빼라고 조언했다. (advised / the doctor / to / a patient)

→ ______________________
______________ lose some weight.

26

사실을 말하자면, Jane은 그와 친하지 않다. (tell / is / the truth / Jane / not / close / to)

→ ______________________
______________________ to him.

[27~28] 다음 우리말과 같도록 괄호 안의 말을 활용하여 문장을 완성하시오.

27

차가운 마실 것 좀 있나요? (there, cold, something, drink)

→ ______________________

28

그 책은 내가 읽기에는 너무 어려웠다. (the book, hard, too, read)

→ ______________________

[29~30] 다음 우리말을 주어진 |조건|에 맞게 바르게 영작하시오.

29 내 아버지는 나에게 자전거 타는 법을 가르쳐 주셨다.

|조건|
1. 〈의문사+to부정사〉를 사용할 것
2. 단어 father, teach, ride a bike를 사용할 것
3. 9개의 단어로 쓸 것

→ ______________________
____

30 그녀는 매우 속상했던 것 같다.

|조건|
1. She를 주어로 쓸 것
2. 단어 seem, upset, very, have, to를 사용할 것
3. 7개의 단어로 쓸 것

→ ______________________
____

CHAPTER

06

동명사와 분사

UNIT 01 주어, 보어, 목적어로 쓰이는 동명사

to부정사만 목적어로 쓸 수 있는 동사들이 있듯이, 동명사만 목적어로 쓰는 동사를 파악하세요.

enjoy	즐기다	keep	계속 ~하다	imagine	상상하다	practice	연습하다
avoid	피하다	quit	그만 두다	deny	부정하다	give up	포기하다
finish	마치다	mind	신경 쓰다	suggest	제안하다	stop	~하기를 멈추다

참고 stop 뒤에 to부정사가 오면 '~하기 위해 멈추다'라는 의미로 to부정사는 목적어가 아닌, 부사(~하기 위해)의 의미예요.

다음 문장에서 어법상 어색한 부분을 찾아 바르게 고쳐 쓰시오.

01 His hobby is collect sneakers. → ______

02 I enjoy to watch them play. → ______

03 Eat vegetables and fruits is recommended. → ______

04 He kept to think about Yunseo. → ______

05 I suggested to review the notes. → ______

06 She didn't mind to sit with me. → ______

07 By to drink enough water, we can stay healthy. → ______

08 The boy practices to ride a bike. → ______

UNIT 02 동명사 vs. to부정사

동사별로 목적어를 to부정사를 쓸지, 동명사를 쓸지, 아니면 둘 다 쓸 수 있는지를 파악하세요.

to부정사만 목적어로 취하는 동사	want, wish, expect, hope, promise, need, plan, choose, decide, refuse, learn, agree
동명사만 목적어로 취하는 동사	enjoy, keep, imagine, practice, avoid, quit, deny, give up, finish, mind, suggest, stop, consider, stand
둘 다 목적어로 취하는 동사	like, love, hate, prefer, begin, start, continue

주의 목적어가 to부정사일 때와 동명사일 때 의미가 달라지는 동사(remember, forget, try, regret 등)에 주의하세요.

괄호 안의 말을 알맞은 형태로 바꿔 문장을 완성하시오.

01 He tried, but he failed to quit ______. (drink)

02 Jane decided ______ shopping with me. (go)

03 They are considering ______ to a bigger city. (move)

04 You promised ______ a letter every week. (write)

05 I couldn't imagine ______ in a place like this. (live)

06 We didn't expect ______ you. (see)

07 She doesn't mind ______ alone. (be)

08 They planned ______ in Paris for a week. (stay)

UNIT 03 동명사의 의미상 주어 & 부정

동명사의 의미상 주어(행위자)가 문장의 주어와 다를 경우, 의미상 주어를 소유격이나 목적격으로 동명사 앞에 쓰세요.

소유격 의미상 주어	Do you mind my turning on the TV? (내가 TV를 켜는 것)
목적격 의미상 주어	Do you mind me turning on the TV? (내가 TV를 켜는 것)

주의 동명사의 부정은 동명사 바로 앞에 not이나 never를 써야 해요.

우리말과 같도록 괄호 안의 말을 활용하여 문장을 완성하시오.

01 그 비밀을 누구에게도 절대 말하지 않아서 고마워. (tell the secret)
→ Thank you for ______________________ to anyone.

02 그는 그녀가 자신에게 초대장을 보낸 것을 잊었다. (send)
→ He forgot ______________________ him an invitation.

03 그는 건강을 위해서 계속 탄산음료를 마시지 않는다. (not, drink soda)
→ He keeps ______________________ for his health.

04 눈을 쉬게 하지 않는 것은 눈을 건조하게 할 수 있다. (not, rest your eyes)
→ ______________________ can dry them.

05 제가 여기서 피아노를 쳐도 괜찮을까요? (play)
→ Do you mind ______________________ the piano here?

UNIT 04 동명사의 시제와 수동태

동명사의 시제가 문장의 동사 시제보다 과거이면, 〈having + p.p.〉로 써야 해요.

시제	동명사의 형태	예문
동사와 동명사가 같은 시제	+ 단순 동명사 〈V-ing〉	He denied being there. = He denied that he was there.
동명사가 동사보다 이전 시제	+ 완료 동명사 〈having + p.p.〉	He denied having been there. = He denied that he had been there.

주의 동명사의 의미가 수동이면, 〈being+p.p.〉로 써야 해요.

우리말과 같도록 괄호 안의 말을 활용하여 동명사 문장을 완성하시오.

01 그는 그것을 훔쳤다고 인정한다. (admit, steal) → He ______________________ it.

02 그는 거기서 나를 봤었다고 인정했다. (admit, see) → He ______________________ me there.

03 그는 질문 받는 것을 꺼리지 않는다. (mind, ask) → He ______________________.

04 우리는 공격받는 것이 두렵다. (be, attack) → We are afraid of ______________________.

05 그녀는 늦어서 미안해했다. (be, late) → She was sorry for ______________________.

06 그는 차로 여행했던 것을 잊었다. (forget, travel) → He ______________________ by car.

07 그녀는 버스에 치이는 것을 피했다. (avoid, be, hit) → She ______________________ by a bus.

UNIT 05 동명사의 관용 표현

동명사와 자주 쓰이는 관용 표현은 외워야 쓸 수 있어요.

go -ing	~하러 가다	be worth -ing	~할 가치가 있다
How[What] about -ing?	~하는 게 어때?	have trouble -ing	~하는 데 어려움이 있다
be busy -ing	~하느라 바쁘다	feel like -ing	~하고 싶다
spend+시간/돈+-ing	시간/돈을 ~하는 데 쓰다	It is no use -ing	~해 봐야 소용없다
look forward to -ing	~하기를 기대하다	on[upon] -ing	~하자마자 (= as soon as)
when it comes to -ing	~하는 것에 관한 한	cannot help -ing	~할 수밖에 없다
be[get] used to -ing	~에 익숙하다[익숙해지다]	There is no -ing	~할 수 없다

주의 〈be used to+동사원형〉 ~하는 데 사용되다 / 〈used to+동사원형〉 ~하곤 했다

우리말과 같도록 괄호 안의 말을 활용하여 문장을 완성하시오.

01 우리는 집을 청소하느라 바빴다. (busy, clean) → We __________ the house.

02 그는 아빠와 함께 낚시하러 갔다. (go, fishing) → He __________ with his dad.

03 그들은 차를 사는 데 돈을 썼다. (spend, buy) → They ________ money ________ a car.

04 지금 걱정해 봐야 소용없다. (use, worry) → It is __________ now.

05 잠깐 쉬는 게 어때요? (what, have) → __________ a break?

06 그는 그 열쇠를 찾는데 어려움이 있었다. (trouble, find) → He had __________ the key.

UNIT 06 현재분사 vs. 과거분사

동사를 형용사(명사 수식, 보어 역할)처럼 쓰기 위해서는 현재분사나 과거분사로 만들어야 해요.

		현재분사	과거분사
형태		동사원형+-ing	과거분사형 (-ed 또는 불규칙 형태)
의미		~하는 (능동)	~된, ~당한 (수동)
역할	명사 수식	falling leaves (떨어지는)	fallen leaves (떨어진)
	보어	The news is shocking. (충격적인)	People are shocked. (충격받은)

괄호 안의 말을 알맞은 형태로 바꿔 쓰시오.

01 The bottle is __________ with fresh milk. (fill)

02 He avoided __________ a decision. (make)

03 She bought some __________ coffee. (grind)

04 The police rescued the __________ girl. (kidnap)

05 Ben kept __________ about his special plan for summer vacation. (talk)

06 __________ with my friends is my favorite hobby. (sing)

07 Look at the __________ baby! He's so cute. (sleep)

UNIT 07 명사를 앞뒤에서 수식하는 분사

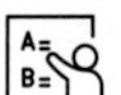

분사는 목적어나 부사(구)를 취할 수 있고, 이때 명사를 뒤에서 수식하는 것을 알아 두세요.

현재분사	명사 앞	Do you know the running dog? (달리고 있는 개)
	명사 뒤	Do you know the dog running in the park? (공원에서 달리고 있는 개)
과거분사	명사 앞	My uncle will fix the broken window. (깨진 창)
	명사 뒤	My uncle will fix the window broken by the boy. (소년에 의해 깨진 창)

괄호 안의 말을 알맞은 분사 형태로 바꿔 쓰시오.

01 The workers ______________ the house are busy. (build)

02 He told me the ______________ news. (shock)

03 We decided to buy a ______________ car. (used)

04 The bike ______________ by a truck was severely destroyed. (hit)

05 The ______________ rumor spread through the town. (interest)

06 I liked their ______________ words. (comfort)

07 The ______________ money was not recovered. (steal)

08 Some houses ______________ by the earthquake haven't been rebuilt. (destroy)

09 The lake ______________ by trees is beautiful. (surround)

UNIT 08 보어로 쓰이는 분사

분사를 형용사처럼 보어로 쓸 때, 주어나 목적어와의 관계가 능동인지 수동인지 파악하세요.

주격 보어	현재분사	The news is surprising. (놀라게 하는, 놀라운)	능동 관계
	과거분사	We are surprised by the news. (놀람을 당한, 놀란)	수동 관계
목적격 보어	현재분사	I heard someone calling my name. (부르는)	능동 관계
	과거분사	I heard my name called. (불려지는)	수동 관계

우리말과 같도록 괄호 안의 말을 활용하여 문장을 완성하시오.

01 그녀는 등이 벽에 눌리는 것을 느꼈다. (press) → She felt her back ____________ against the wall.

02 그 집은 10년 전에 지어졌다. (build) → The house was ____________ 10 years ago.

03 그는 내 이야기가 신난다고 느꼈다. (excite) → He found my story ____________.

04 몇몇 프로그램들이 설치되어 있었다. (install) → Some programs were ____________.

05 그 발표는 매우 지루했다. (bore) → The presentation was very ____________.

06 선수들은 팬들의 응원을 받았다. (cheer) → The players were ____________ on by the supporters.

UNIT 09 감정을 나타내는 동사의 분사

감정 동사를 분사로 만들 때, 감정을 유발하는지 또는 느끼는지를 판단하여 분사의 형태를 결정하세요.

감정을 표현하는 동사	현재분사 (감정을 유발)	과거분사 (감정을 느낌)
interest (흥미를 끌다)	interesting (흥미를 갖게 하는)	interested (흥미를 느끼는)
excite (신나게 하다)	exciting (신나게 하는)	excited (신이 난)

다음 문장을 같은 의미를 지닌 두 개의 문장으로 바꿔 쓰시오.

01 The party will surprise Junsu.
→ Junsu will be ___________ at the party. → The party will be ___________ to Junsu.

02 The movie frightened the audience.
→ The audience was ___________ by the movie. → The movie was ___________.

03 Dolphins fascinate the visitors.
→ The visitors are ___________ by dolphins. → Dolphins are ___________.

04 Your questions embarrassed Mina.
→ Your questions were ___________. → Mina was ___________ by your questions.

05 The Eiffel Tower inspires tourists.
→ The Eiffel Tower is ___________. → Tourists are ___________ by the Eiffel Tower.

06 Your performance satisfied your parents.
→ Your performance was ___________. → Your parents were ___________ with your performance.

UNIT 10 동명사 vs. 현재분사

현재분사와 동명사는 형태가 같아서, 문맥상 그 쓰임과 의미를 구분할 수 있어야 해요.

	현재분사	동명사
명사 앞	running man (뛰고 있는 남자) washing woman (세탁하고 있는 여자)	running shoes (달리기 신발) *뛰고 있는 신발(×) washing machine (세탁기) *세탁하고 있는 기계(×)
be의 보어	The news is surprising. (소식은 놀랍다) The movie was boring. (영화는 지루하다)	My hobby is dancing. (취미는 춤추기이다) The plan is going to Jeju. (계획은 가는 것이다)

〈동사원형+-ing〉가 형용사 역할을 하는지 명사 역할을 하는지에 유의하여 밑줄 친 부분을 우리말로 해석하시오.

01 Susie tried to understand your confusing words. → ___________

02 There are some kids watching TV. → ___________

03 They continued studying after lunch. → ___________

04 The mom took care of the crying baby. → ___________

05 There is no smoking room in this building. → ___________

06 The discussion was very disappointing. → ___________

중간고사·기말고사 실전문제

객관식 (01~15) / 주관식 (16~30)

정답과 해설 • 78쪽

학년과 반 이름 객관식 / 15문항 주관식 / 15문항

[01~03] 다음 빈칸에 알맞은 것을 고르시오.

01

You don't have to worry about ________ mistakes.

① make ② to make ③ making
④ makes ⑤ for make

02

Please, avoid ________ difficult words when you talk to kindergarteners.

① use ② to use ③ from use
④ using ⑤ to using

03

The old lady forgot ________ the medicine this morning and took it again.

① take ② took ③ taken
④ to take ⑤ taking

[04~05] 다음 우리말을 영어로 바르게 옮긴 것을 고르시오.

04

Judy는 그가 큰소리로 노래 부르는 것을 참을 수 없다.

① Judy can't stand him singing out loud.
② Judy can't stand he singing out loud.
③ Judy can't stand him to sing out loud.
④ Judy can't stand he sing out loud.
⑤ Judy can't stand his sang out loud.

05

그 미술관에 방문할 만한 가치가 있었다.

① It was worth visit the gallery.
② It was worth visiting the gallery.
③ It was worth to visit the gallery.
④ It was worth visited the gallery.
⑤ It was worth the gallery to visit.

[06~08] 다음 중 어법상 어색한 것을 고르시오.

06
① I don't feel like to be with someone now.
② The crowd would like to listen to a cheerful song.
③ Are you going to go fishing this Saturday?
④ He has already sent the gift without writing a thank-you card.
⑤ Cathy took a nap instead of taking a walk in her free time.

07
① This class taken by many students is not actually useful.
② There are people lied on the grass at the park.
③ She ate strawberries covered with sugar for a dessert.
④ Riding a roller coaster was a terrifying experience for me.
⑤ The begger ate the food left on the table after the party.

08 ① Zoe prefers using public transportation to driving.
② The students started to clean their classroom.
③ The athlete continued running although his leg was hurt.
④ She suggested to take a break for a minute.
⑤ I hate to be left alone in the dark.

[09~11] 다음 중 어법상 옳은 것을 고르시오.

09 ① My sister enjoys to watch movies on weekends.
② Why do you keep to make such a noise?
③ We haven't finished to paint the wall in our dining room.
④ The clever girl pretended to have a clue.
⑤ She has to practice to speak Spanish every day.

10 ① Mom remembered not turning off the stove, so she had to get back home.
② They decided not inviting their neighbors.
③ We're sorry for not to bring some food for this party.
④ The man promised never showing up again in front of you.
⑤ Thank you for telling not my secret to him.

11 ① Did you shock about the test result?
② Students got interesting in world history after taking her class.
③ Everyone felt the party was bored.
④ Washing a car is a tired job.
⑤ The audience impressed by his performance applauded for a long time.

[12~13] 다음 빈칸에 들어갈 말이 바르게 짝지어진 것을 고르시오.

12

• I don't mind ________ here for a while.
• Did the player choose ________ up the game?

① stand – give
② standing – giving
③ standing – to give
④ to stand – giving
⑤ to stand – to give

13

• ________ can be a serious matter here.
• Try ________ just a bite. You don't need to buy it.
• My sister was ashamed of ________ wearing a huge hat.

① Not being polite – eat – me
② Not being polite – eating – my
③ Being not polite – eating – I
④ Being polite not – to eat – my
⑤ Being not polite – to eat – me

[14~15] 다음 중 밑줄 친 부분의 용법이 나머지 넷과 다른 하나를 고르시오.

14 ① His only wish was going back to his hometown.
② All I did on my vacation was reading books.
③ The next step of the process was checking the errors.
④ The job of the intern was arranging documents.
⑤ Travelers on the beach were taking a nap.

15 ① My son bought a pair of running shoes.
② Please, stay in the waiting room until I call your name.
③ I usually bring a sleeping bag when I go camping.
④ The kids saw a singing bird in the forest.
⑤ She met her husband at a dancing class.

〈다음부터는 서술형 주관식 문제입니다.〉

[16~17] 다음 밑줄 친 부분이 어법상 맞으면 ○표 하고, 틀리면 바르게 고쳐 쓰시오.

16 Because of rain, they put off to go on a vacation.

____

17 The orchestra on the ship continued to play music.

____

[18~20] 다음 문장에서 어법상 어색한 부분을 찾아 바르게 고쳐 쓰시오.

18 All workers needed wearing safety equipment.

______________ → ______________

19 She stopped buying some bread at a bakery. She will have it for breakfast tomorrow.

______________ → ______________

20 The movie was too frightened for the child to watch.

______________ → ______________

[21~22] 다음 우리말과 같도록 괄호 안의 말을 알맞은 형태로 쓰시오.

21

Jack은 겨울에는 보통 스케이트를 타러 간다. (skate)

→ Jack usually goes ______________ in winter.

22

그 예술가가 그린 초상화는 매우 비싸다. (draw)

→ The portraits ______________ by the artist are very expensive.

[23~24] 다음 두 문장의 의미가 같도록 동명사를 사용하여 문장을 완성하시오.

23 Mr. Smith doesn't like that I call him Sir.

→ Mr. Smith doesn't like ________ ________ him Sir.

24 Karen is upset that she failed the driving test yesterday.

→ Karen is upset about ________ ________ the driving test yesterday.

[25~26] 다음 우리말과 같도록 괄호 안의 말을 알맞게 배열하시오.

25

> 그 직원은 회의에 참석하지 않은 것에 대해 모두에게 사과했다.
> (not / apologized / to / attending / for / everyone / the meeting)

→ The staff ________________ ________________.

26

> 그들은 이 사진에 보이는 곳으로 여행을 갈 예정이다.
> (the place / are / to / travel / to / shown / they / going)

→ ________________ ________________ in this picture.

[27~28] 다음 우리말과 같도록 괄호 안의 말을 활용하여 문장을 완성하시오.

27

> 우리는 항상 마스크를 쓰는 것에 익숙해졌다.
> (get, use, wear, masks)

→ ________________ ________________ all the time.

28

> 형은 지난 주말에 내 장난감을 수리해 주었다.
> (repair, had, last weekend, my, toy)

→ My brother ________________ ________________.

[29~30] 다음 우리말을 주어진 |조건|에 맞게 바르게 영작하시오.

29 너는 크리스마스에 선물 받는 것을 고대하고 있니?

|조건|
1. Are로 시작할 것
2. 단어 look forward, get, presents, on Christmas로 사용할 것
3. 9개의 단어로 쓸 것

→ ________________ ________________

30 그녀는 하늘에서 떨어지는 눈을 바라보고 있다.

|조건|
1. 진행 시제와 분사를 사용할 것
2. 단어 watch, fall, snow, the sky를 사용할 것
3. 8개의 단어로 쓸 것

→ ________________ ________________

CHAPTER

07

비교 표현

UNIT 01 원급 비교

'~만큼 …한[하게]'은 〈as + 형용사/부사의 원급 + as〉로 표현하세요.

형용사	She is	as	kind	as	him[he is].
부사	She can swim		well		him[he can].

참고 〈as~ as〉 뒤에는 목적격 대명사(him)나 〈주어(the)+동사(is[can])〉의 형태로 쓸 수 있어요.

주의 부정문(~만큼 …하지 않은[않게])에서는 〈not as[so]+형용사/부사의 원급+as〉로 쓸 수 있어요.

괄호 안의 말과 〈as ~ as〉 구문을 이용하여 문장을 완성하시오.

01 My sister is 10 years old. I am 15 years old.

→ My sister ______________________ I am. (old)

02 The building is 35 meters high. The tree is 10 meters high.

→ The tree ______________________ the building. (high)

03 I get up at 6:00. My mom gets up at 6:00.

→ I ______________________ my mom. (early)

04 Jinsu is 165 cm. Minsu is 165 cm, too.

→ Jinsu ______________________ Minsu. (tall)

05 Science is difficult to me. English is not very difficult to me.

→ English ______________________ science to me. (difficult)

UNIT 02 as + 형용사 / 부사의 원급 + as possible

〈as + 형용사/부사의 원급 + as〉를 이용한 다음 표현을 익혀 두세요.

as ~ as possible (가능한 한 ~하게)	Please call me as quickly as possible.
as ~ as 주어 + can[could] (주어가 …할 수 있는 만큼 ~하게)	Please call me as quickly as you can.

주의 〈as ~ as〉 뒤에 〈주어+can[could]〉을 쓸 때 알맞은 주어와 시제로 쓰세요.

우리말과 같도록 괄호 안의 말을 활용하여 빈칸에 알맞은 말을 쓰시오.

01 그녀는 가능한 한 빨리 그 돈이 필요하다. (soon, possible)

→ She needs the money ______________________.

02 민호는 수진이만큼 중국어를 잘 말할 수 있었다. (well, can)

→ Minho could speak Chinese ________________ Sujin ________________.

03 Tom은 언제나 가능한 한 긍정적으로 생각하려고 노력한다. (positively, possible)

→ Tom always tries to think ______________________.

UNIT 03 비교급과 최상급 만드는 법

 형용사/부사의 비교급과 최상급을 만드는 방법을 알아 두세요.

형용사/부사의 형태		원급	비교급	최상급
대부분	-er / -est	tall	taller	tallest
-e로 끝남	-r / -st	nice	nicer	nicest
-y로 끝남	y를 삭제 -ier / -iest	early	earlier	earliest
〈단모음+단자음〉으로 끝남	자음 추가 -er / -est	hot	hotter	hottest
-ous, -ful, -ive, -ing 등으로 끝남	more / most+원급	famous	more famous	most famous
〈형용사+ly〉 형태의 부사		slowly	more slowly	most slowly

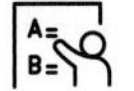 불규칙 변화하는 형용사/부사의 비교급과 최상급은 암기해야 해요.

원급	비교급	최상급
good(좋은) / well(잘)	better(더 좋은, 더 잘)	best(가장 좋은)
bad / ill(나쁜) / badly(나쁘게)	worse(더 나쁜)	worst(가장 나쁜)
many(수가 많은) / much(양이 많은)	more(더 많은)	most(가장 많은)
little(적은)	less(더 적은)	least(가장 적은)

다음 단어들의 비교급과 최상급을 쓰면서 외우시오.

01 능력 있는 able – ________ – ________

02 화난 angry – ________ – ________

03 나쁜 bad – ________ – ________

04 나쁘게 badly – ________ – ________

05 아름다운 beautiful – ________ – ________

06 큰 big – ________ – ________

07 바쁜 busy – ________ – ________

08 편안한 comfortable – ________ – ________

09 호기심이 많은 curious – ________ – ________

10 위험한 dangerous – ________ – ________

11 맛있는 delicious – ________ – ________

12 근면한, 성실한 diligent – ________ – ________

13 더러운 dirty – ________ – ________

14 쉬운 easy – ________ – ________

15 쉽게 easily – ________ – ________

16	뚱뚱한	fat	–	________	–	________
17	상냥한	friendly	–	________	–	________
18	좋은	good	–	________	–	________
19	무거운	heavy	–	________	–	________
20	뜨거운	hot	–	________	–	________
21	아픈	ill	–	________	–	________
22	게으른	lazy	–	________	–	________
23	양이 적은	little	–	________	–	________
24	사랑스러운	lovely	–	________	–	________
25	(수, 양이) 많은	many/much	–	________	–	________
26	예쁜	pretty	–	________	–	________
27	슬픈	sad	–	________	–	________
28	마른	skinny	–	________	–	________
29	느린	slow	–	________	–	________
30	천천히	slowly	–	________	–	________
31	맛있는	tasty	–	________	–	________
32	유용한	useful	–	________	–	________
33	잘	well	–	________	–	________

UNIT 04 비교급

 비교 표현 '~보다 더 …한[하게]'은 〈비교급 + than〉으로 써야 해요.

	예문	의미
비교급 + than(~보다)	She is taller than her mom.	그녀는 그녀의 엄마보다 더 키가 크다.
비교급 강조(훨씬)	She is much taller than her mom.	그녀는 그녀의 엄마보다 훨씬 더 키가 크다.

주의 비교급을 강조할 때는, 비교급 앞에 much, even, far, still, a lot 등을 써요.

참고 very는 원급을 강조할 때만 쓸 수 있으므로 주의하세요.

괄호 안의 말을 활용하여 비교급 문장을 완성하시오.

01 My aunt is ________ ________ my mom. (old)

02 Health is ________ ________ ________ ________ money. (much, important)

03 A cheetah can ________ ________ ________ a rabbit. (run, fast)

04 He gets up ________ ________ ________ before. (far, early)

05 This shirt is ________ ________ ________ that one. (expensive)

06 Greece is ________ ________ South Korea. (large)

UNIT 05 배수사 비교

 '~보다 –배만큼 …한[하게]'은 〈as + 원급 + as〉 또는 〈비교급 + than〉 앞에 배수사를 붙이세요.

주어 + 동사	배수(사)	원급/비교급	비교 대상	의미
Regular pizza is	three times	as thick as	thin pizza.	얇은 피자보다 세 배 더 두꺼운
		thicker than		

다음 두 문장의 의미가 같도록 괄호 안의 말을 이용하여 문장을 완성하시오.

01 This hotel is a hundred times as good as that hotel. (than)
→ This hotel is ________________________ that hotel.

02 I am 10 years and my brother is 20 years old. (as ~ as)
→ My brother is ________________________ me.

03 Lucy works three times as hard as her coworkers. (than)
→ Lucy works ________________________ her coworkers.

04 I studied for an hour and Hana studied for 4 hours. (than)
→ Hana studied ________________________ me.

05 This house is 6 meters tall and that church is 12 meters tall. (as ~ as)
→ That church is ________________________ this house.

06 This plant grows ten times faster than that plant. (as ~ as)
→ This plant grows ________________________ that plant.

UNIT 06 비교급 표현

다음 비교급을 이용한 유용한 표현을 알아 두세요.

형태	〈the + 비교급 ~, the + 비교급 ...〉	〈비교급 + and + 비교급〉
의미	~하면 할수록 더 …하다	점점 더 ~한[하게]

우리말과 같도록 괄호 안의 말을 바르게 배열하시오.

01 늦게 잘수록 우리는 더 피곤해지다. (we go to bed / the more tired / the later / we become)

→ ______________________________

02 열심히 공부할수록 너는 더 좋은 점수를 받는다. (you study / the better grades / the harder / you get)

→ ______________________________

03 그녀는 점점 더 아름다워질 것이다. (more beautiful / more and / will become / she)

→ ______________________________

04 빨리 달릴수록 너는 더 기진맥진해진다. (you become / the faster / the more exhausted / you run)

→ ______________________________

05 집이 더 작을수록 더 저렴하다. (the house is / the cheaper / it is / the smaller)

→ ______________________________

UNIT 07 최상급

다음 최상급 표현을 알아 두세요.

형태	〈the + 최상급〉	〈one of the + 최상급 + 복수명사〉
의미	가장 ~한[하게]	가장 ~한 것들 중 하나

참고 최상급 뒤에는 〈in+단수명사(장소나 집단): ~에서〉, 〈of+복수명사: ~들 중에서〉가 올 수 있어요.

우리말과 같도록 괄호 안의 말을 활용하여 문장을 완성하시오.

01 그들은 우리나라에서 가장 부유한 사람들이다. (wealthy)

→ They are ______________________ in our country.

02 건강이 삶에서 가장 중요하다. (important, thing)

→ Health is ______________________ in life.

03 이것은 이 레스토랑에서 가장 저렴한 요리다. (cheap, dish)

→ This is ______________________ at this restaurant.

04 축구는 가장 인기 있는 스포츠들 중 하나이다. (popular)

→ Soccer is ______________________.

05 그녀는 학교에서 가장 매력적인 학생들 중 한 명이다. (attractive)

→ She is ______________________ in school.

UNIT 08 최상급 표현

원급과 비교급을 이용하여 최상급의 의미를 표현하는 방법을 알아 두세요.

형태	〈No (other) ~ as[so] + 원급 + as〉 = 〈No (other) ~ 비교급 + than〉	〈비교급 + than any other + 단수명사〉 = 〈비교급 + than all the other + 복수명사〉
의미	어떤 사람[사물]도 …만큼 ~하지 않다	다른 누구[무엇]보다도 더 ~하다

우리말과 같도록 괄호 안의 말을 활용하여 문장을 완성하시오.

01 반에서 어떤 학생도 윤수만큼 키가 작지 않다. (short, no other, as)

→ ______________________ as Yunsu in the class.

02 그는 모든 다른 사람들보다 조심히 운전한다. (carefully, all the other)

→ He drives more ______________________.

03 어떤 영화도 이것만큼 지루하지 않다. (boring, no other, as)

→ ______________________ as this one.

04 이 도서관은 도시 안의 다른 어떤 장소보다 더 조용하다. (quiet, any other)

→ This library is ______________________ in the city.

05 어떤 학생도 수미보다 더 부지런하지 않다. (diligent, no other)

→ ______________________ than Sumi.

06 나는 학교의 다른 모든 학생들보다 영어를 더 잘한다. (good, all the other)

→ I'm __________ at English ______________________ in school.

UNIT 09 원급 vs. 비교급 vs. 최상급

형용사/부사의 원급, 비교급, 최상급에 관한 기본 사항을 표에서 확인한 후 종합적으로 연습하세요.

구분	형태	의미	참고
원급	as ~ as ...	…만큼 ~한[하게]	as ~ as 사이에는 원급을 써요.
비교급	-er[more ~] than ...	…보다 더 ~한[하게]	than과 함께 써요.
최상급	the -est[most ~] of/in ...	…에서[중에서] 가장 ~한[하게]	최상급 앞에 the를 붙여요.

다음 문장에서 어법상 어색한 부분을 찾아 바르게 고쳐 쓰시오.

01 He is one of the luckiest person in history. → __________

02 The house is three times old than the school. → __________

03 She ran twice as slowly like me. → __________

04 No other spring was warm than this spring. → __________

05 This lemon is sourer than all other lemon. → __________

06 You play the piano better than I am. → __________

07 No other person can dance better the boy. → __________

중간고사·기말고사 실전문제

객관식 (01~15) / 주관식 (16~30)

학년과 반　　　이름　　　객관식　　/ 15문항　주관식　　/ 15문항

[01~03] 다음 빈칸에 알맞은 것을 고르시오.

01 The movie that the director remade is ________ the original one.

① as not good as　② as good as not
③ not as good as　④ as good not as
⑤ not good

02 This month, the salesman sold ________ as last month.

① as twice much　② so much twice
③ two as much　④ twice as much
⑤ twice more

03 Learning Chinese was ________ for me than learning English because of its intonations.

① very hard　② more hard
③ much hard　④ much hardest
⑤ much harder

[04~05] 다음 우리말을 영어로 바르게 옮긴 것을 고르시오.

04 소비자들은 가능한 한 질 좋은 제품을 저렴하게 구매하기를 원한다.

① Consumers want to purchase quality products as cheaper as possible.
② Consumers want to purchase quality products more cheaply than possible.
③ Consumers want to purchase quality products cheaply possible.
④ Consumers want to purchase quality products as cheaply as possible.
⑤ Consumers want to purchase quality products so cheaply as possible.

05 물이 더 깊을수록 더 많은 물고기가 있다.

① The water goes deeper, there are more fish.
② Deeper the water goes, more fish there are.
③ The deeper the water goes, the more fish there are.
④ The deeper the water goes, the more there are fish.
⑤ The deeper goes the water, the fish there are more.

[06~08] 다음 중 어법상 어색한 것을 고르시오.

06 ① The shirt is as newer as the sweater.
② Her house is twice as big as mine.
③ His thirst grew bigger and bigger.
④ Can I have a cleaner towel than this?
⑤ April was much warmer than average.

07 ① Is your disease as seriously as she has been before?
② They were as skinny as fashion models.
③ The ambitious young man wanted to be as rich as Bill Gates.
④ The bus is going as slowly as a turtle due to the traffic jam.
⑤ Your advice about how to find jobs is as useful as his.

08 ① No employee works as hard as Kelly does.
② No other girl is as athletic than Jenny.
③ No client is more demanding than her.
④ No other friend is more diligent than Dylan.
⑤ No other jewel is as hard as diamond.

[09~11] 다음 중 어법상 옳은 것을 고르시오.

09 ① The more terribly the band performed, more annoyed the audience felt.
② The more money he earns, greedy he turns.
③ The stronger he becomes, the most enemies he will have.
④ The worse the economy gets, the higher the crime rate increases.
⑤ The better you keep the rules, you can be the safer.

10 ① My sister ate the smallest piece of cake.
② Emily takes a fast route than any other players in the race.
③ He was the most smartest student of all.
④ Andy is more energetic of all my friends.
⑤ Who made largest pizza in the world?

11 ① The town along the river is one of the greater places to live in.
② Today is the hottest day in 30 years.
③ This is the less interesting topic we have ever discussed.
④ Loving the one who hurts you would be most difficult thing to do.
⑤ I'm going to wear one of my prettiest dress to their wedding.

[12~13] 다음 빈칸에 들어갈 말이 바르게 짝지어진 것을 고르시오.

12

- Who is ________ student in your class?
- Playing with my nephew was ________ than watching the TV show.

① the tallest – less much boring
② taller than – much less boring
③ tallest – less much boring
④ the tallest – much less boring
⑤ taller than – much boring

13

- I think Spain is the ________ place to travel of all countries.
- These veggie chips are ________ than other snacks.
- The exchange student speaks Korean as ________ as native speakers.

① great – more nutritious – fluent
② greatest – more nutritious – fluently
③ greater – most nutritious – fluent
④ greatest – nutritious – fluently
⑤ greater – nutritious – more fluent

[14~15] 다음 중 주어진 문장과 의미가 같은 것을 고르시오.

14

The sofa Jane bought was not as comfortable as she expected.

① The sofa Jane bought was not most comfortable than she expected.
② The sofa Jane bought was not as comfortable than she expected.
③ The sofa Jane bought was less comfortable than she expected.
④ The sofa Jane bought was so comfortable as she expected.
⑤ The sofa Jane bought was more comfortable than she expected.

15

I think rural life is three times better than city life.

① I think rural life is as three times good than city life.
② I think rural life is three times as better than city life.
③ I think rural life is three times better as city life.
④ I think rural life is better three times as city life.
⑤ I think rural life is three times as good as city life.

〈다음부터는 서술형 주관식 문제입니다.〉

[16~17] 다음 밑줄 친 부분이 어법상 맞으면 ○표 하고, 틀리면 바르게 고쳐 쓰시오.

16 His hands were as coldest as ice when he came home through the snowstorm.

____

17 Please, give me at least half as much money as you gave Kevin.

____

[18~20] 다음 문장에서 어법상 어색한 부분을 찾아 바르게 고쳐 쓰시오.

18 Terry made the most foolish mistakes than all the other players did.

______________ → ______________

19 Most precious moment of my childhood was the night I had a pajama party with my friends.

______________ → ______________

20 My dog is much healthy than when our family first got him.

______________ → ______________

[21~22] 다음 우리말과 의미가 같도록 괄호 안의 말을 활용하여 문장을 완성하시오.

21

이 기계는 사람의 다섯 배 만큼 무거운 짐을 들어 올릴 수 있다. (heavy)

→ This machine can lift loads five times as ________ ________ a person can.

22

> 우리가 더 빨리 떠날수록, 더 일찍 도착할 것이다.
> (early)

→ The sooner we leave, ________ ________ we will arrive.

[23~24] 다음 두 문장의 의미가 같도록 문장을 완성하시오.

23 The firefighters tried to save as many victims as possible.

→ The firefighters tried to save as many victims ________ they ________.

24 Peter was the luckiest boy in his class that day.

→ Peter was ________ than ________ other boy in his class that day.

[25~26] 다음 우리말과 같도록 괄호 안의 말을 알맞게 배열하시오.

25

> 조종사도 승객들만큼이나 겁먹은 것 같았다.
> (as / the passengers / as / frightened)

→ The pilot seemed ________________________.

26

> 시민들은 잘못된 정책을 바꾸는 데 이전보다 더 적극적이다.
> (active / before / changing / than / more / in / the wrong policies)

→ Citizens are ________________________.

[27~28] 다음 우리말과 같도록 괄호 안의 말을 활용하여 문장을 완성하시오.

27

> 그녀의 집은 이 가게보다 두 배는 크다.
> (house, as, large, store)

→ ________________________

28

> 상하이 타워는 중국에서 가장 높은 빌딩이다.
> (the Shanghai Tower, high, building, China)

→ ________________________

[29~30] 다음 우리말을 주어진 |조건|에 맞게 바르게 영작하시오.

29 그는 그 전쟁에서 가장 용감한 군인 중 하나였다.

|조건|
1. He로 문장을 시작할 것
2. 단어 one, brave, soldier, the battle을 사용할 것
3. 10개의 단어로 쓸 것

→ ________________________

30 음식을 빨리 먹을수록, 네 위는 더 나빠질 것이다.

|조건|
1. The로 문장을 시작할 것
2. 단어 fast, eat, worse, stomach, be를 사용할 것
3. 10개의 단어로 쓸 것

→ ________________________

내가 가장 취약한 부분에 대해
요점 정리를 해 보세요.

CHAPTER

08

접속사

UNIT 01 부사절 접속사 1 - 시간

다음의 시간을 나타내는 부사절 접속사를 익혀 두세요.

when	~할 때, ~하면	as	~할 때, ~하면서	since	~한 이후로
while	~하는 동안, ~하면서	until	~할 때까지	as soon as	~하자마자

주의 시간을 나타내는 부사절에서는 현재시제가 미래시제를 대신해요.

밑줄 친 부분이 어법상 옳으면 ○표 하고, 틀린 부분은 바르게 고쳐 쓰시오.

01 While they were out, the thief broke into their house. ______

02 He noticed her as he entered the room. ______

03 I'll visit the Louvre Museum as soon as I'll arrive Paris. ______

04 I watched TV until my parents were sleeping. ______

05 He'll stop studying as soon as he passes the test. ______

06 Let me know when you will get home. ______

07 They talked as they had coffee together. ______

08 Jane met Tom since they were studying in England. ______

UNIT 02 부사절 접속사 2 - 조건

앞뒤 문맥을 확인하여, if를 써야 하는지 반대의 의미인 unless를 써야 하는지를 판단하세요.

if	~한다면	unless	~하지 않는다면(= if ~ not)

주의 조건을 나타내는 부사절에서도 현재시제가 미래시제를 대신해요.

우리말과 같도록 괄호 안의 말을 이용하여 문장을 완성하시오.

01 열심히 공부하지 않는다면, 우리는 시험을 통과할 수 없을 것이다. (unless, study)
→ ______, we can't pass the test.

02 그녀가 서두르지 않는다면, 기차를 놓칠 것이다. (rush, if)
→ ______, she'll miss the train.

03 영어로 된 책을 매일 읽는다면, 내 영어 실력이 향상될 것이다. (read, English books, if)
→ ______, my English will improve.

04 그들이 열심히 연습하지 않는다면, 우승할 수 없을 것이다. (practice, unless, hard)
→ ______, they won't win.

05 네가 그녀에게 안부를 전한다면, 그녀는 기뻐할 것이다. (say hello to, if)
→ ______, she'll be pleased.

06 지나치게 빨리 운전한다면, 교통사고를 낼 것이다. (if, too fast, drive)
→ ______, you'll cause a traffic accident.

UNIT 03 부사절 접속사 3 - 원인과 결과

앞뒤 문맥에 맞게 접속사 so(그래서)를 쓸지, because(~ 때문에)를 쓸지 판단하세요.

so + 결과	그래서 ~	It was very dark, so we couldn't see anything.
because + 원인	~ 때문에	She had to take a taxi because she was too tired. = as[since]

주의 because[as, since]는 접속사로 뒤에 문장을 쓰고, because of는 전치사이므로 뒤에 (동)명사를 써야 해요.
The roads were slippery because[as, since] it snowed.(눈이 내렸기 때문에)
= The roads were slippery because of the snow.(눈 때문에)

우리말과 같도록 괄호 안의 말과 알맞은 접속사를 활용하여 문장을 완성하시오.

01 그녀가 복권에 당첨되었기 때문에 사람들은 그녀가 운이 좋다고 생각한다. (win the lottery)
→ People think she's lucky ________________.

02 그 과학자는 그 발견 때문에 상을 받았다. (the discovery)
→ The scientist won the award ________________.

03 엄마가 식사 준비로 바쁘셔서 내가 설거지를 했다. (do the dishes)
→ My mom was busy preparing the meal. ________________.

04 나는 늦게 일어나서 학교에 지각했다. (be late for)
→ I got up late. ________________.

05 우리는 돈을 모두 써 버렸기 때문에 차를 살 수 없다. (spend all the money)
→ We can't buy a car ________________.

UNIT 04 부사절 접속사 4 - 양보

'비록 ~이지만, 비록 ~일지라도'라는 양보의 표현은 접속사 though를 쓰세요.

though 비록 ~이지만	Though she failed several times, she never gave up. = Although[Even though] she failed several times, she never gave up.

다음 두 문장을 괄호 안의 접속사를 이용하여 한 문장으로 완성하시오.

01 I tried hard. I couldn't do it. → I couldn't do it ________________. (although).

02 It rained. But I went to the beach. → ________________, I went to the beach. (though)

03 We were tired. We kept running. → We kept running ________________. (though)

04 It was cold. We decided to go out. → ________________, we decided to go out. (though)

05 He is rich. He's unhappy. → He's unhappy ________________. (even though)

06 It is not big. It is expensive. → It is expensive ________________. (although)

UNIT 05 so that ~ & so ~ that ...

〈so that ~〉과 〈so ~ that ...〉의 쓰임과 의미를 혼동하지 마세요.

so that ~	~하도록, ~하기 위하여	so + 형/부 + that ...	너무[매우] ~해서 … 하다

참고 〈so that ~(~하도록)〉은 의미상 〈in order that ~ / in order to / so as to〉로 바꿔 쓸 수 있어요.

다음 두 문장을 〈so that ~〉이나 〈so ~ that ...〉을 이용하여 한 문장으로 완성하시오.

01 The oranges were sour. We couldn't eat.

→ The oranges were ________________________________.

02 He went to work early. He could avoid the rush hour.

→ He went to work early ________________________________.

03 Can you help me? I want to finish the homework on time.

→ Can you help me ________________________________?

04 The kids are young. They can't see the movie.

→ The kids are ________________________________.

05 Handle the camera with care. I hope that you don't break it.

→ Handle the camera with care ________________________________.

UNIT 06 여러 의미를 지닌 접속사

다음 접속사들은 한 개 이상의 의미를 지니므로 그 의미를 문맥상 잘 판단하세요.

as	~함에 따라, ~할수록, ~하는 대로, ~ 때문에, ~ 할 때, ~하면서
since	~한 이후로, ~ 때문에
while	~하는 동안, ~하면서, ~하는 반면

우리말과 같도록 괄호 안의 말과 접속사 as, since, while을 활용하여 문장을 완성하시오.

01 그 사진들을 그대로 두시오. (they are)

→ Leave the pictures ____________________________.

02 Tony는 개를 좋아하는 반면, 그의 누나는 고양이를 아주 좋아한다. (like)

→ ____________________________, his sister loves cats a lot.

03 그는 졸업한 이후로 그 회사에서 일했다. (graduate)

→ He has worked for the company ____________________________.

04 네가 책을 읽는 동안 그녀는 숙제를 했다. (be reading)

→ ____________________________ a book, she was doing her homework.

05 너는 숙제를 막 끝냈으니까 나가서 놀아도 된다. (have finished)

→ You may go and play ____________________________.

UNIT 07 명사절 접속사 1 - that

접속사 that(~하는 것) 뒤에 하나의 절(문장)을 써서 하나의 명사처럼 사용하세요.

that절	의미: 그가 늦게 일어난다는 것	주의
주어	That he gets up late is unbelievable.	that절은 단수 취급
목적어	No one knows (that) he gets up late.	목적어 that절의 that은 생략 가능
보어	The truth is that he gets up late.	

참고 주어 자리에 쓰는 that절은 가주어 It을 주어 자리에 쓰고, 진(짜) 주어는 문장 뒤로 옮길 수 있어요.
→ It is unbelievable that he gets up late.

우리말과 같도록 괄호 안의 말과 접속사 that을 활용하여 문장을 완성하시오.

01 그가 아들이 있다는 것은 거짓이다. (son) → ____________ is false.

02 John은 그녀가 옳다고 믿는다. (right) → John believes ____________.

03 진실은 우리가 열심히 노력했다는 것이다. (try hard) → The truth is ____________.

04 나는 그가 부정행위를 한 걸 알았다. (cheat) → I knew ____________.

05 문제는 그가 동의했다는 것이다. (agree) → The problem is ____________.

06 그가 내 이름을 잊어버린 것은 충격적이다. (forget) → It is shocking ____________.

UNIT 08 명사절 접속사 2 - whether/if

'~인지 아닌지'라는 명사절을 만들 때는 접속사 whether 또는 if를 쓰세요.

whether/if절	의미: 그가 늦게 일어나는지(아닌지)	주의
주어	Whether he gets up late is unknown.	주어 자리에는 if를 쓰지 않아요.
목적어	No one knows whether[if] he gets up late.	if를 문장 중간에 쓸 때, 명사절 접속사 if와 조건절의 if를 혼동하지 마세요.
보어	The questions is whether[if] he gets up late.	

참고 whether는 부사절 접속사로 사용될 때는 '~이든 아니든 간에'의 양보의 의미를 지니기도 해요.
Whether you like it or not, you must do it. (네가 좋아하든 아니든)

우리말과 같도록 괄호 안의 말과 접속사 if나 whether를 활용하여 문장을 완성하시오.

01 나는 그녀가 그것을 봤는지가 궁금했다. (see) → I wondered ____________.

02 네가 그걸 받아들일지는 네 선택이다. (accept) → ____________ is your choice.

03 그는 내게 갈 수 있는지 물었다. (could) → He asked me ____________.

04 비가 올지 안 올지는 확실히 모르겠다. (rain) → ____________ is not certain.

05 카페가 있는지는 확실하지 않다. (there is) → I'm not sure ____________.

06 네가 가든 말든, 나는 쇼핑하러 갈 거야. (go) → ____________, I'll go shopping.

UNIT 09 접속부사

문장 앞에 접속부사를 쓸 때, 앞의 문장과의 관계를 파악하여 알맞은 의미의 접속부사를 쓰세요.

앞 문장에 대한	예시를 들어줄 때	for example, for instance (예를 들어)
	반대의 이야기를 할 때	however (하지만), otherwise (그렇지 않으면), on the other hand (반면에) nevertheless, nonetheless (그럼에도 불구하고)
	결과를 말할 때	thus (그래서), therefore, hence (그러므로), as a result (그 결과, 결과적으로)
	추가적인 이야기를 할 때	in addition, besides, moreover (게다가)
	다른 이야기로 전환할 때	anyway, by the way (어쨌든, 그런데)

우리말과 같도록 빈칸에 알맞은 접속부사를 쓰시오.

01 택시를 타라. 그렇지 않으면 지각할 것이다.
→ Take a taxi. ______________________, you'll be late.

02 나는 점심을 먹지 않았다. 하지만 배가 고프지 않다.
→ I didn't eat lunch. ______________________, I'm not hungry.

03 그는 열심히 공부하지 않았다. 그 결과 시험에서 떨어졌다.
→ He didn't study hard. ______________________, he failed the test.

04 태풍이 오는 중이다. 그래서 우리는 집에 있어야 한다.
→ A storm is approaching. ______________________, we must stay home.

05 우리는 숙제가 많다. 게다가 내일 시험도 있다.
→ We have a lot of homework. ______________________, we have a test tomorrow.

06 우리는 그에게 초대장을 보내지 않았다. 그럼에도 불구하고 그는 파티에 왔다.
→ We didn't send him an invitation. ______________________ he came to the party.

UNIT 10 명령문 + and / or

명령문 뒤에 and를 쓸 때와 or를 쓸 때 반대의 의미가 되는 것에 주의해야 해요.

명령문 + and	~해라, 그러면 ~할 것이다	명령문 + or	~해라, 그렇지 않으면 ~할 것이다

빈칸에 and나 if 또는 unless를 써서 같은 의미가 되도록 문장을 완성하시오.

01 If you apologize to him, he'll be glad. → Apologize to him, ________ he'll be glad.

02 Prepare, or you'll fail the test. → ________ you prepare, you'll fail the test.

03 Unless you see a doctor, you'll be sicker. → See a doctor, ________ you'll be sicker.

04 Turn left, and you'll see the school. → ________ you turn left, you'll see the school.

05 Unless you do it now, you can't go out. → Do it now, ________ you can't go out.

06 Drink milk every day, and you'll get taller. → ________ you drink milk every day, you'll get taller.

UNIT 11 상관접속사

 서로 상관이 있는 것들을 묶어 주는 상관접속사의 종류와 의미를 알아 두세요.

상관접속사	의미	상관접속사	의미
both A and B	A와 B 둘 다	not A but B	A가 아니라 B
either A or B	A 또는 B	not only A but (also) B = B as well as A	A뿐만 아니라 B도
neither A nor B	A도 B도 아닌		

참고 〈not only A but also B〉는 〈B as well as A〉로 쓸 수 있어요.

상관접속사로 이루어진 말이 주어질 때 주어와 동사의 수일치에 주의하세요.

상관접속사	수 일치	예문
both A and B	복수 취급	Both Tom and Sara are busy.
either A or B	B에 수 일치	Either I or she has to go.
neither A nor B		Neither his brothers nor his sister knows you. * 모른다(부정)
not A but B		Not Tom but his parents have a car.
not only A but (also) B = B as well as A		Not only Tom but also his sisters are coming. = His sisters as well as Tom are coming

---

우리말과 같도록 빈칸에 알맞은 상관접속사를 쓰시오.

01 그는 잘생겼을 뿐만 아니라 영리하다.

→ He is smart ______________ handsome.

02 그는 선생님일 뿐만 아니라 작가이기도 하다.

→ He's __________ a teacher __________ an author.

03 너는 내게 전화하거나 이메일을 보낼 수 있다.

→ You can __________ call me __________ send me an email.

04 아빠도 엄마도 집에 계시지 않는다.

→ __________ my dad __________ my mom is at home.

05 나는 수학과 과학을 둘 다 못한다.

→ I'm poor at __________ math __________ science.

06 내가 아니라 그가 표 값을 지불할 것이다.

→ __________ I __________ he will pay for the tickets.

중간고사·기말고사 실전문제

객관식 (01~15) / 주관식 (16~30)

학년과 반 　　 이름 　　 객관식 　　 / 15문항 　 주관식 　　 / 15문항

[01~03] 다음 빈칸에 알맞은 것을 고르시오.

01

Greg has been dreaming about being a singer ________ he was in middle school.

① while　② when　③ since
④ until　⑤ unless

02

We might have an accident ________ you drive more carefully.

① whether　② unless　③ if
④ since　⑤ because

03

________ you like it or not doesn't affect my decision.

① If　② Unless　③ Which
④ Though　⑤ Whether

[04~05] 다음 빈칸에 알맞은 것을 모두 고르시오.

04

Please, turn off the light in your room ________ you leave the house.

① since　② when　③ though
④ as　⑤ because

05

Peter forgave their faults ________ he had no other better friends than them.

① as　② if　③ since
④ so that　⑤ as soon as

[06~07] 다음 우리말을 영어로 바르게 옮긴 것을 고르시오.

06

버스가 오지 않아서 우리는 걸어갔다.

① The bus didn't come, we walked.
② The bus didn't come as we walked.
③ We walked, so the bus didn't come.
④ We walked as the bus didn't come.
⑤ We walked so that the bus didn't come.

07

그녀는 겁먹은 것 같지도 불안한 것 같지도 않았다.

① She seemed neither frightened nor anxious.
② She seemed either frightened or anxious.
③ She seemed neither frightened or anxious.
④ She didn't seem neither frightened nor anxious.
⑤ She didn't seem either frightened but anxious.

08 다음 중 어법상 어색한 것을 고르시오.

① Lisa hid the present so that she could surprise her brother.
② The child was so scared that he couldn't even say a thing.
③ Travelers were so that tired they could sleep anywhere.
④ He is cleaning his room so that the guest can stay for a while.
⑤ Karen felt so embarrassed that she wanted to disappear at the moment.

09 다음 중 밑줄 친 접속사의 쓰임이 의미상 옳은 것을 고르시오.

① You can see lots of stars in the sky before the sun sets.
② Dan left the place until he saw the snake.
③ She has worked as a cook when he was 22.
④ I called the ambulance since he got injured.
⑤ The baby kept crying as soon as they were talking on the phone.

[10~11] 다음 중 밑줄 친 접속사의 의미가 나머지 넷과 다른 하나를 고르시오.

10 ① I helped my mom clean the house while my dad was washing the dishes.
② She'd like to go camping while her brother wants to stay at home.
③ While children played, their mom prepared lunch for them.
④ Burglars broke into our house while we were away.
⑤ Please turn on the air conditioner while I work here.

11 ① Amy hasn't eaten anything since she had dinner last night.
② Since I got in here, there has been no one in the room.
③ Harry has loved the girl next door since he became a high school student.
④ The creator has earned lots of money since she was 17 years old.
⑤ The machine needs to be fixed since it has been broken for a long time.

[12~13] 다음 빈칸에 들어갈 말이 바르게 짝지어진 것을 고르시오.

12

________ Jason is all sweaty in the heat, he would like to take a shower ________ possible.

① Since – whether
② Before – until
③ Since – as soon as
④ After – until
⑤ Before – as soon as

13

• Teenagers usually use text message ________ older people prefer phone calls. • You might be cold ________ you put on more clothes. • They had to run so ________ get on the train.

① while – if – that
② until – if – that
③ when – unless – order to
④ until – unless – as to
⑤ while – unless – as to

[14~15] 다음 중 주어진 문장과 의미가 같은 것을 고르시오.

14

The fisherman salted the fish so that he could preserve them.

① The fisherman salted the fish until he could preserve them.
② The fisherman salted the fish in order to preserve them.
③ The fisherman salted the fish when he could preserve them.
④ The fisherman salted the fish not to preserve them.
⑤ The fisherman salted the fish after he could preserve them.

15

If you hesitate, someone else will take your chance.

① Hesitate, and someone else won't take your chance.
② Hesitate, or someone else will take your chance.
③ Don't hesitate, and someone else will take your chance.
④ Don't hesitate, but someone else won't take your chance.
⑤ Don't hesitate, or someone else will take your chance.

〈다음부터는 서술형 주관식 문제입니다.〉

[16~17] 다음 밑줄 친 부분이 어법상 맞으면 ○표 하고, 틀리면 바르게 고쳐 쓰시오.

16 Do not open the test paper since the exam starts.

____

17 The student denied that he had cheated. Moreover, everyone didn't believe him.

____

[18~20] 다음 문장에서 어법상 어색한 부분을 찾아 바르게 고치시오.

18 If he will eat less meat and more vegetables, he will prevent many diseases.

__________ → __________

19 Many other countries as well as Korea enjoys doing Taekwondo.

__________ → __________

20 We may not be able to attend the conference because of the train broke down.

__________ → __________

[21~22] 다음 접속사 중 하나를 골라 빈칸에 쓰시오.

since	because	while	if
as	unless	whether	

21 그는 나이가 들어감에 따라, 작은 것들에 감사하게 되었다.

→ He became grateful for small things __________ he grew older.

22 수입은 점점 줄어드는 반면 지출은 더 늘고 있다.

→ Income is decreasing more and more __________ spending is increasing.

[23~24] 다음 두 문장의 의미가 같도록 문장을 완성하시오.

23 The company developed a new product so as to meet customer needs.

→ The company developed a new product so ________ it ________ meet customer needs.

24 That no one showed up at the party was strange.

→ It ________ ________ ________ no one showed up at the party.

[25~26] 다음 우리말과 같도록 괄호 안의 말을 바르게 배열하시오.

25

그 가수는 무대에 올라가기 전에, 깊은 심호흡을 했다. (before / the stage / breath / went / deep / she / a / on)

→ The singer took ______________________________
______________________________.

26

올바른 절차를 따르지 않으면, 그 프로젝트는 실패할 것이다. (right / you / unless / follow / the / procedure)

→ The project will fail ______________________________
______________________________.

[27~28] 다음 우리말과 같도록 괄호 안의 말을 활용하여 문장을 완성하시오.

27

그녀는 한국어와 일본어 둘 다 말할 수 없다. (speak, can, nor, Korean, Japanese)

→ ______________________________

28

너는 그가 한국으로 돌아올지 아닐지 아니? (know, whether, come back, Korea)

→ ______________________________
______________________________ or not?

[29~30] 다음 우리말을 주어진 |조건|에 맞게 바르게 영작하시오.

29 보트가 세차게 흔들리고 있는 것이 불안했다.

|조건|
1. It~that 구문을 사용할 것
2. 단어 terrifying, the boat, shake, strongly를 사용할 것
3. 9개의 단어로 쓸 것

→ ______________________________
____

30 서울뿐만 아니라 많은 도시들이 위험에 처해 있다.

|조건|
1. Many로 문장을 시작할 것
2. 단어 city, well, Seoul, in danger을 사용할 것
3. 9개의 단어로 쓸 것

→ ______________________________
____

내가 가장 취약한 부분에 대해
요점 정리를 해 보세요.

CHAPTER

09

분사구문

UNIT 01 분사구문 만드는 법

부사절 〈접속사 + 주어 + 동사〉를 분사를 이용하여 간결하게 줄여 쓰는 방법을 익히세요.

1	부사절의 접속사 생략	~~As~~ Jane got off the bus, she said goodbye.
2	부사절과 주절의 주어가 같다면, 부사절 주어 생략	~~Jane~~ got off the bus, she said goodbye.
3	동사를 현재분사(-ing)로 바꿈	Getting off the bus, she said goodbye.

다음 두 문장의 의미가 같도록 분사구문을 완성하시오. (단, 접속사는 생략할 것)

01 While I had chicken, I watched TV. → ______________, I watched TV.

02 As soon as she arrived there, she called us. → ______________, she called us.

03 While he talked to her, he chewed gum. → ______________, he chewed gum.

04 As he had a cold, he went to a doctor. → ______________, he went to a doctor.

05 When he opened the box, he found gloves. → ______________, he found gloves.

UNIT 02 분사구문의 의미 & 부정

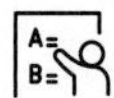

접속사가 없는 분사구문은 주절과의 관계를 파악하여 문맥에 맞게 해석해야 해요.

때	when, while, after, before	조건	if, unless	동시동작	while, as
양보	though, although, even though	이유	because, as, since	연속상황	and

부사절이 부정문이면, 분사 앞에 not이나 never를 쓰세요.

부정의 부사절	As I didn't know what to say, I kept silent.	뭐라고 말할지 몰라서 나는 침묵을 지켰다.
부정의 분사구문	= Not knowing what to say, I kept silent.	

다음 두 문장의 의미가 같도록 분사구문을 완성하시오.

01 As I didn't go to bed early, I was sleepy all day.
→ ______________________, I was sleepy all day.

02 Though it was built a long time ago, the hotel was perfect.
→ Though being ______________________, the hotel was perfect.

03 This bus leaves Seoul at 10:00 and arrives in Daejeon at 11:30.
→ This bus leaves Seoul at 10:00, ______________________.

04 As she doesn't have a car, she takes a bus to work.
→ ______________________, She takes a bus to work.

05 While he played soccer, he broke his leg.
→ ______________________, he broke his leg.

06 Since she never studied hard, Sujin got poor grades.
→ ______________________, Sujin got poor grades.

UNIT 03 완료형 분사구문

부사절의 시제가 주절의 시제보다 앞서는 경우 〈having + p.p.〉 형태의 완료 분사를 써야 해요.

		부사절	분사구문
단순 분사		As she got off, she said bye.	= Getting off, she said bye.
완료 분사	과거 – 현재	As he had lunch, he can leave.	= Having had lunch, he can leave.
	대과거 – 과거	As he had had lunch, he left.	= Having had lunch, he left.

참고 단순 분사를 썼다는 것은 부사절과 주절의 시제가 같다는 것이고, 완료 분사를 썼다는 것은 부사절의 시제가 주절의 시제보다 과거라는 것을 말해요.

다음 두 문장의 의미가 같도록 부사절은 분사구문으로, 분사구문은 부사절로 바꾸어 문장을 완성하시오.

01 After she had been injured, she was moved to a hospital.
→ ______________________, she was moved to a hospital.

02 Since we hadn't bought anything, we couldn't cook well.
→ ______________________, we couldn't cook well.

03 Having run 10 km, I drank a lot of water.
→ As ______________________, I drank a lot of water.

04 Not having been invited, we can't get in.
→ Because ______________________, we can't get in.

UNIT 04 Being / Having been의 생략

분사구문의 Being이나 Having been을 생략할 수 있는 것에 유의하세요.

보어 앞의	Being 생략	As I was sick with a cold, I stayed home. = (Being) Sick with a cold, I stayed home.
수동태의	Being 생략	As she was given a gift, she felt happy. = (Being) Given a gift, she felt happy.
	Having been 생략	After my bike was repaired at the shop, it works well. = (Having been) Repaired at the shop, it works well.

참고 수동태의 Being은 거의 생략하지만, 보어 앞의 Being은 생략하지 않는 경우가 많아요.

다음 두 문장의 의미가 같도록 분사구문을 완성하시오.

01 As we aren't old enough, we can't watch it. → ______________________, we can't watch it.

02 When he was shocked by the news, he cried. → ______________________, he cried.

03 As I had been annoyed by his behavior, I didn't say hello to him.
→ ______________________ I didn't say hello to him.

04 Because it is not used often, the room is usually closed.
→ ______________________, the room is usually closed.

UNIT 05 독립분사구문

부사절의 주어와 주절의 주어가 다르면, 부사절의 주어를 분사구문 앞에 그대로 써야 해요.

부사절 주어 ≠ 주절 주어	부사절의 주어를 그대로 씀	As there was no bus, we had to walk. = There being no bus, we had to walk.

주의 독립분사구문에서 being은 정확한 의미 전달을 위해 주로 생략하지 않아요.
〈There+be 동사 ~〉 구문을 분사구문으로 쓸 때는 There를 분사 앞에 그대로 두세요.

다음 두 문장의 의미가 같도록 분사구문을 완성하시오.

01 As there was much traffic, I took the subway.
→ ______________________, I took the subway.

02 Because it snowed, they built a snowman.
→ ______________________, they built a snowman.

03 When the meeting ended, they went out for lunch.
→ ______________________, they went out for lunch.

04 As it as cold, we stayed at home.
→ ______________________, we stayed at home.

05 Because there were many interesting places, we decided to visit the city.
→ ______________________, we decided to visit the city.

06 While my parents watched TV, I played the game with my brother.
→ ______________________, I played the game with my brother.

UNIT 06 비인칭 독립분사구문

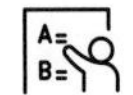

주어가 다르지만, 주어 없이 숙어처럼 쓰는 분사구문을 알아 두세요.

frankly speaking	솔직히 말해서	considering~	~을 고려하면
generally speaking	일반적으로 말해서	compared with~	~과 비교하면
strictly speaking	엄밀히 말해서	judging from~	~로 판단해 보면

다음 두 문장의 의미가 같도록 빈칸에 알맞은 말을 쓰시오.

01 If people speak strictly, that cannot be true. → ______________________, that cannot be true.

02 If I speak frankly, I don't like him. → ______________________, I don't like him.

03 If you consider the costs, don't buy a car. → ______________________, don't buy a car.

04 If they speak generally, buses are cheaper. → ______________________, buses are cheaper.

05 If we judge from his face, he is nervous. → ______________________, he is nervous.

06 If you compare with others, this is better. → ______________________, this is better.

UNIT 07 with + (대)명사 + 분사

'~한 채로', '~하면서'라는 의미를 문장에 추가할 때 〈with + (대)명사 + 분사〉의 형태로 쓰세요.

형태	〈with + (대)명사 + 현재분사〉	〈with + (대)명사 + 과거분사〉
관계	(대)명사와 분사의 관계가 능동	(대)명사와 분사의 관계가 수동
예문	She explained with tears running down her face. 눈물이 흐르는 채로	He was standing with his eyes closed. 눈을 감은 채로

참고 〈with+(대)명사+분사〉는 동시에 일어나는 일을 표현해요. 따라서 문맥에 맞게 '~한 채로', '~하면서' 등 자연스럽게 해석하세요. 또한 분사는 형용사의 역할을 하는 것으로, 〈with+명사+형용사〉로도 쓸 수 있어요.

He slept with his mouth open.

주의 〈with+(대)명사+분사〉에서 (대)명사와 분사의 관계에 따라 현재분사 또는 과거분사를 써요.

다음 두 문장의 의미가 같도록 with를 이용하여 문장을 완성하시오.

01 I was running around the park and my dog was following me.
→ I was running around the park ______________________.

02 They went on a picnic and the sun was shining.
→ They went on a picnic ______________________.

03 You studied in your room and the door was closed.
→ You studied in your room ______________________.

04 We were watching TV and the cat was sleeping on the sofa.
→ We were watching TV ______________________.

05 Tom looked at them and his legs were crossed.
→ Tom looked at them ______________________.

06 She was resting on the bed and her eyes were closed.
→ She was resting on the bed ______________________.

중간고사·기말고사 실전문제

객관식 (01~15) / 주관식 (16~30)

학년과 반　　　　이름　　　　객관식　　　/ 15문항　　주관식　　　/ 15문항

[01~03] 다음 빈칸에 알맞은 것을 고르시오.

01

________ to the beach, they made a big sand castle.

① Go　② Going　③ Gone
④ Went　⑤ Being gone

02

________ sold, the toys were stored in the warehouse.

① Not　② Be not　③ Not be
④ Being not　⑤ Not being

03

________ rainy, the school cancelled the field trip to the zoo.

① Be　② It be　③ Be it
④ It being　⑤ It was

[04~05] 다음 우리말을 영어로 바르게 옮긴 것을 고르시오.

04

우유가 없어서, 그 요리사는 두유를 대신 사용했다.

① Being no milk, the chef used soy milk instead.
② Being there no milk, the chef used soy milk instead.
③ There being no milk, the chef used soy milk instead.
④ There was no milk, the chef used soy milk instead.
⑤ No milk, the chef used soy milk instead.

05

그녀는 다리를 다친 채로 축구 경기를 했다.

① She played soccer with her leg injure.
② She played soccer with her leg injuring.
③ She played soccer with her leg injured.
④ She played the soccer with her leg being injure.
⑤ She played the soccer with her leg having injured.

[06~07] 다음 중 어법상 어색한 것을 고르시오.

06
① While carrying her luggage, she hurt her right arm.
② Cathy was hiding in a closet, waiting for her parents.
③ Folding in half, the note was kept in a book.
④ After eating something, brush your teeth.
⑤ Washed by the owner, the dog became clean.

07
① Feeling excited, we shouted for victory.
② Opening the door, the man wondered what was beyond it.
③ Before turning the stove on, she took the ingredients out of the refrigerator.
④ Not expensive, the product was sold out.
⑤ While being seen by others, the couple pretended to be happy.

[08~09] 다음 중 어법상 옳은 것을 고르시오.

08 ① Being it stormy, the tree fell down by wind.
② Being Friday evening, there's a lot of traffic at this time.
③ Being there no one in the room, she quickly changed her clothes.
④ Flying in the sky, the balloon went up higher and higher.
⑤ Not being far, we can go there on foot.

09 ① To be considered that you are still young, you can be forgiven for once.
② Frankly spoken, I was not interested in this subject.
③ Strictly speaking, it's illegal to have a campfire here.
④ Judged from what he said earlier, he has no intention to hurt you.
⑤ Comparing with coffee, green tea has less caffeine.

[10~11] 다음 문장을 분사구문으로 바르게 바꾼 것을 고르시오.

10

Because she was annoyed with the noise from outside, Patty closed the window.

① She annoyed with the noise from outside, Patty closed the window.
② Annoyed with the noise from outside, the window was closing by Patty.
③ Annoying with the noise from outside, Patty closed the window.
④ Being annoying with the noise from outside, Patty closed the window.
⑤ Annoyed with the noise from outside, Patty closed the window.

11

After he had failed to reach his goal, Paul became very pessimistic.

① Had failing to reach his goal, Paul became very pessimistic.
② Failed to reach his goal, Paul became very pessimistic.
③ Having failed to reach his goal, Paul became very pessimistic.
④ Have failing to reach his goal, Paul became very pessimistic.
⑤ Having failing to reach his goal, Paul became very pessimistic.

12 다음 문장을 부사절 문장으로 바르게 바꾼 것을 고르시오.

성과에 만족한 회사는 직원들의 임금을 인상했다. = Satisfied with the performance, the firm raised the salaries of its workers.

① Before satisfied with the performance, the firm raised the salaries of its workers.
② Because of satisfied with the performance, the firm raised the salaries of its workers.
③ Since it satisfied with the performance, the firm raised the salaries of its workers.
④ As it was satisfied with the performance, the firm raised the salaries of its workers.
⑤ Though it was satisfied with the performance, the firm raised the salaries of its workers.

13 다음 우리말과 같도록 빈칸에 알맞은 것을 고르시오.

그는 용기를 뚜껑이 닫힌 채로 전자레인지에 넣었다.
= He put the container in the microwave
______________________.

① with the lid closes
② with the lid closed
③ with the closing lid
④ with the lid closing
⑤ with the lid was closed

[14~15] 다음 빈칸에 들어갈 말이 바르게 짝지어진 것을 고르시오.

14

- ________ to behave well, the child was very polite to the elderly.
- Carl turned in the test paper with some questions ________.

① Telling – unanswering
② Telling – unanswered
③ Told – unanswer
④ Told – unanswered
⑤ Be told – unanswering

15

- ________ very hot, let's not go out.
- ________ out, Lisa yelled at everybody.
- The car rushed through the building with its engine ________.

① Being – Being stress – burn
② Being – Being stressed – burning
③ It is – Stressing – burned
④ It being – Stressed – burning
⑤ It being – She stressed – burned

〈다음부터는 서술형 주관식 문제입니다.〉

[16~17] 다음 밑줄 친 부분이 어법상 맞으면 ○를 표시하고, 틀리면 바르게 고쳐 쓰시오.

16 Proud of herself, Michelle began her speech.

____

17 Training to bark at strangers, the dog barked violently at my friend.

____

[18~20] 다음 문장에서 어법상 어색한 부분을 찾아 바르게 고쳐 쓰시오.

18 When being very strict, Mr. Kim is one of the best teachers in our school.

______________ → ______________

19 The baby is coming toward his mom, being crying out loud.

______________ → ______________

20 With her son sat next to her, Sandy was writing a story.

______________ → ______________

[21~22] 다음 우리말과 같도록 괄호 안의 말을 이용하여 문장을 완성하시오.

21 그것은 무거웠지만, 그 여자는 쉽게 그 상자를 들 수 있었다. (heavy)

→ Although ________ ________ ________, the woman could lift the box easily.

22 그 자전거는 바퀴들이 망가진 채로 버려져 있었다.

→ The bicycle was abandoned ________ its wheels ________. (break)

[23~24] 다음 주어진 문장과 의미가 같도록 분사구문을 완성하시오.

23

Before she graduated from high school, Angela became a world star.

→ Before ______________________________, Angela became a world star.

24

Since we haven't raised a dog, all of my family don't know how to wash our new pet.

→ __________________, all of my family don't know how to wash our new pet.

[25~26] 다음 우리말과 같도록 괄호 안의 말을 바르게 배열하시오.

25

그 죄수는 교도관이 지켜보는 채로 식사를 끝냈다. (the guard / with / watching / meal / his)

→ The prisoner finished ________________ ______________________________.

26

그의 영어 억양으로 판단해 보면, 그 신사는 영국에서 온 것으로 보인다. (his / the gentleman / be / judging / English accent / from / seems to)

→ ______________________________ ______________________ from England.

[27~28] 다음 우리말과 같도록 괄호 안의 말을 활용하여 분사구문을 완성하시오. (단, 생략 가능한 것은 모두 생략할 것)

27

무엇을 고를지 몰라서, 나는 친구에게 물었다. (not, what, know, choose)

→ ______________________________, I asked my friends.

28

그는 밤에 불을 끈 채 책을 읽었다. (turn off, the light, at night)

→ He read a book ________________ ______________________ at night.

[29~30] 다음 우리말을 주어진 |조건|에 맞게 바르게 영작하시오.

29 줄을 서서 기다리는 동안, 그녀는 휴대폰 게임을 했다.

|조건|
1. 분사구문을 문장 처음에 쓸 것
2. 단어 wait, in line, cell phone games, play를 사용할 것
3. 8개의 단어로 쓸 것

→ ______________________________
____

30 창문이 깨져서, 방에 찬바람이 들어왔다.

|조건|
1. 분사구문을 사용하고 being을 생략하지 말 것
2. 단어 a window, cold wind, break, come을 사용할 것
3. 문장 전체를 10개의 단어로 쓸 것

→ ______________________________
______________________ into the room.

CHAPTER

10

관계사

UNIT 01 주격 관계대명사

두 문장에 같은 사람 또는 사물이 있을 때, 관계대명사 who, which, that을 써서 두 문장을 연결하세요.

같은 사람	I met a boy. 나는 한 소년을 만났다. He knows you. 그는 너를 안다.	who[that] 연결	I met the boy who[that] knows you. 나는 너를 아는 한 소년을 만났다.
같은 사물	I like the shirt. 나는 그 셔츠를 좋아해. It has no button. 그것은 단추가 없다.	which[that] 연결	I like the shirt which[that] has no button. 나는 단추가 없는 그 셔츠를 좋아해.

다음 두 문장을 관계대명사를 이용하여 한 문장으로 완성하시오.

01 I know the girl. She speaks English fluently.
→ I know the girl ______________________.

02 Look at the kids. They play hide and seek.
→ Look at the kids ______________________.

03 He bought a jacket. It is black.
→ He bought a jacket ______________________.

04 The flowers grow in the garden. They smell sweet.
→ The flowers ______________________ smell sweet.

05 Anne is my friend. She is kind and smart.
→ Anne is my friend ______________________.

UNIT 02 목적격 관계대명사

선행사의 종류에 따른 주격, 목적격 관계대명사를 알아두세요.

	사람 선행사	사물 선행사	사물 또는 사람
주격 관계대명사	who	which	that
목적격 관계대명사	who(m)	which	

The boy who(m)[that] I met knows you.
내가 만난 그 소년이 너를 안다.

다음 두 문장을 관계대명사를 이용하여 한 문장으로 완성하시오.

01 The lady has a cat. I met her here. → The lady ______________ has a cat.

02 The box was heavy. He carried it. → The box ______________ was heavy.

03 Look at the picture. She took it. → Look at the picture ______________.

04 The man is from China. I invited him. → The man ______________ is from China.

05 The pen is here. I was looking for it. → The pen ______________ is here.

06 You're wearing a coat. It looks warm. → A coat ______________ looks warm.

UNIT 03 관계대명사 that을 주로 쓰는 경우

that의 여러 쓰임에 유의하세요.

선행사	사람＋사물	최상급이나 서수	the only, the very, the same 등	all, much, little, any, no 등	-thing인 대명사

주의 that의 여러 쓰임에 유의하세요.

that의 쓰임		예문	
관계대명사	선행사(명사) 수식	The movie (that we saw) wasn't good.	우리가 본 그 영화는 좋지 않았다.
접속사	명사 역할	I heard (that it wasn't good).	좋지는 않았다는 것을 들었다.
지시대명사	대명사	That is my bag.	저것은 나의 가방이다.
지시형용사	명사 수식	That bag is mine.	저 가방은 나의 것이다.

우리말과 같도록 괄호 안의 말을 활용하여 문장을 완성하시오.

01 내가 해야 할 일이 많았다. (much work, have to)

→ There was ______________________________.

02 어린이들은 카페인이 들어 있는 어떤 것도 마시지 말아야 한다. (drink, anything, contain caffeine)

→ Children must not ______________________________.

03 의사는 환자를 치료하는 사람이다. (treat a patient)

→ A doctor is someone ______________________________.

04 흥미로워 보이는 것이 아무것도 없었다. (nothing, look exciting)

→ There was ______________________________.

05 우리는 그가 겨우 스무 살이라는 걸 믿을 수 없었다. (believe, only 20 years old)

→ We couldn't ______________________________.

UNIT 04 소유격 관계대명사

두 문장의 공통된 부분이 소유의 관계일 때, 소유격 관계대명사 whose를 쓰세요.

The boy knows you. 그 소년은 너를 안다. His eyes are big. 그의 눈은 크다.	관계대명사로 연결	The boy whose eyes are big knows you. 눈이 큰 그 소년이 너를 안다.

다음 두 문장을 관계대명사를 이용하여 한 문장으로 완성하시오.

01 I have a friend. His father is a teacher. → I have a friend ______________________________.

02 I have a book. Its cover is black. → I have a book ______________________________.

03 Look at the house. Its roof is white. → Look at the house ______________________________.

04 There is a dog. Its tail is short. → There is a dog ______________________________.

05 I have a cousin. Her English is good. → I have a cousin ______________________________.

06 She has a cat. Its name is Cherry. → She has a cat ______________________________.

UNIT 05 관계대명사의 생략

관계대명사를 생략할 수 있는 경우들을 알아두세요.

목적격 관계대명사 생략 가능		The boy ~~who(m)~~ I met knows you.	
관계대명사의 동사가 진행형일 때	〈주격 관계대명사 + be동사〉 생략 가능	The boy ~~who is~~ singing is Ben.	분사가 명사를 후치 수식하는 문장이 됨
관계대명사의 동사가 수동태일 때		The boy ~~who is~~ invited is Ben.	

다음 문장에서 생략할 수 있는 부분을 찾아 쓰고, 생략할 수 없으면 ×표를 하시오.

01 This is the cake that I made for my parents. ______

02 This is the house whose windows were broken. ______

03 Who is the man that is cooking in the kitchen? ______

04 I lost the pen which she lent me. ______

05 The passengers who were injured by the accident were sent to a hospital. ______

06 Do you know the boy who can speak 3 languages? ______

UNIT 06 관계대명사 what

선행사가 없을 때는 관계대명사 what을 쓰세요.

that	선행사가 있음	The movie (that) I saw was fun. 내가 본 그 영화는 재미있었다.	
what	선행사가 없음	What I saw was fun. 내가 본 것은 재미있었다.	= The one[thing] that I saw was fun.

참고 관계대명사 what은 '~한 것'의 의미로, the thing[one] that/which ~의 문장으로 바꿔 쓸 수 있어요.

우리말과 같도록 괄호 안의 말과 관계대명사 what을 이용하여 문장을 완성하시오.

01 너는 네가 보는 것을 믿니? (see) → Do you believe ______?

02 나는 그녀가 했던 일을 기억한다. (do) → I remember ______.

03 그것은 우리가 봤던 것이 아니다. (see) → It is not ______.

04 이 셔츠는 네가 나에게 사준 것이다. (buy) → This shirt is ______.

05 내가 원하는 건 네 이름이다. (want) → ______ is your name.

06 그가 먼저 해야 할 것은 숙제다. (must do) → ______ is the homework.

UNIT 07 전치사+관계대명사

관계대명사가 전치사의 목적어 역할을 할 때, 전치사를 관계사절 끝 또는 관계대명사 앞에 쓰세요.

This is the bed. My dog sleeps on it.	관계대명사로 연결	This is the bed which[that] my dog sleeps on. This is the bed on which~~[that]~~ my dog sleeps.

주의 전치사의 목적어가 사람일 때, 〈전치사+whom〉으로 써요.

다음 두 문장을 |보기|와 같이 관계대명사를 이용하여 한 문장으로 완성하시오.

|보기|
He found the key. I was looking for it.
→ He found the key for which I was looking.
→ He found the key which[that] I was looking for.

01 I love the city. I grew up in the city.
→ I love the city ______________________.
→ I love the city ______________________.

02 This is the boy. I talked about him.
→ This is the boy ______________________.
→ This is the boy ______________________.

UNIT 08 관계부사

선행사가 시간, 장소 등인 경우, 〈접속사+부사(구)〉의 역할을 하는 관계부사를 쓰세요.

when	The 25th is the day when we first met. = on which	접속사+부사구(on the day)의 역할
where	This is the park where we had fun. = in which	접속사+부사구(in the park)의 역할
why	That is the reason why he is mad. = for which	접속사+부사구(for that reason) 역할
how	I found the way ~~how~~ [~~the way~~ how] he solved it.	the way, how 둘 중 하나만 써요.

참고 the time, the place, the day, the reason과 같이 일반적인 선행사는 선행사나 관계부사 둘 중 하나만 써도 돼요.

다음 두 문장을 관계부사를 이용하여 한 문장으로 완성하시오.

01 A library is a place. We look for and read books in a library.
→ A library is a place ______________________.

02 Please tell me the reason. You didn't show up for that reason.
→ Please tell me the reason ______________________.

03 You don't know the time. Your friend will arrive at that time.
→ You don't know the time ______________________.

UNIT 09 계속적 용법

선행사 뒤에 쉼표(,)를 하고 관계사절을 쓰면, 수식 관계가 아닌, 추가적 관계로 해석하는 것에 주의하세요.

관계사	예문	틀린 해석(X)	바른 해석(O)
who	I met Miho, who~~[that]~~ invited me.	나를 초대한 미호	만났는데, 그녀가 나를 초대했다.
which	I had pizza, which~~[that]~~ tasted bad.	맛없는 피자	먹었는데, 그것은 맛이 없었다.
when	I went there on Friday, when I met Tom.	내가 Tom을 만난 금요일	금요일에 갔고, 그리고 그때 Tom을 만났다.
where	I went to the park, where I lost my bag.	가방을 잃어버린 공원	공원에 갔고, 그리고 거기서 가방을 잃어버렸다.

우리말과 같도록 괄호 안의 말과 관계사를 활용하여 문장을 완성하시오.

01 Tom은 부산에 갔는데, 그곳에서 옛 친구를 만났다. (meet an old friend)
→ Tom went to Busan. ______________.

02 그녀는 언제나 주말에 영화를 보는데, 그때는 그녀에게 자유시간이 많다. (have a lot of free time)
→ She always sees a movie on weekends. ______________.

03 이 집에는 방 네 개가 있는데, 그것들은 매우 크다. (very large)
→ This house has four rooms. ______________.

04 그녀는 저녁에 커피 한 잔을 마셨고, 그것이 그녀를 깨어 있게 했다. (keep her awake)
→ She drank a cup of coffee in the evening. ______________.

05 그는 네게 약속이 있다고 했지만, 그것은 거짓말이었다. (a lie)
→ He told you that he had an appointment. ______________.

UNIT 10 복합관계대명사 1

관계대명사 who에 -ever를 붙여서 명사절이나 부사절을 이끄는 접속사로 쓸 수 있어요.

복합관계대명사	명사절: ~하는 사람은 누구나	부사절: 누가[누구를] ~하더라도
whoever	Give it to whoever wants it. = anyone who	Whoever says so, he doesn't believe it. = No matter who
who(m)ever	You can invite who(m)ever you like. = anyone who(m)	Who(m)ever you meet, be honest. = No matter who(m)

우리말과 같도록 빈칸에 알맞은 말을 쓰시오.

01 그 도시에 사는 누구든 세금을 낸다. → Anyone ______________ pays a tax.

02 누가 질문해도, 그는 답하지 않을 거다. → Whoever ______________, he won't answer.

03 내가 누구에게 물어봐도, 답이 없다. → No ______________, there is no answer.

04 여기 있는 누구나 선물을 받을 것이다. → Whoever ______________ will be given a gift.

05 그는 엄마가 선택한 누구라도 결혼할 거다. → He'll marry whomever ______________.

UNIT 11 복합관계대명사 2

선행사가 사물일 때는 whichever와 whatever로 쓰세요.

복합관계대명사	명사절: ~하는 것은 어느 것이든/무엇이든	부사절: 어느 것을/무엇을 ~하더라도
whichever	You can buy whichever you like. = anything which	Whichever he chooses, I will accept it. = No matter which
whatever	She does whatever she likes. = anything that	Whatever happens, he will do it. = No matter what

우리말과 같도록 괄호 안의 단어를 활용하여 문장을 완성하시오.

01 캠핑에 필요한 것은 무엇이든 사세요. (anything that, need)
→ Buy ______________________ for camping.

02 무슨 일이 일어나더라도, 우리는 그곳에 갈 것이다. (no matter what, happen)
→ ______________________, we'll go there.

03 네가 어느 것이 옳다고 생각할지라도, 우리는 동의할 것이다. (agree to, whichever)
→ We ______________________ you think is right.

04 그 아이들은 무엇이든 좋아하는 것을 해도 된다고 허락받았다. (whatever, like)
→ The kids were allowed to do ______________________.

05 네가 어느 것을 선택하든지 그들은 존중할 것이다. (whichever, choose)
→ They will respect you ______________________.

UNIT 12 복합관계부사

부사절을 이끄는 〈관계부사 + ever〉의 의미도 알아 두세요.

복합관계대명사	양보의 부사절	장소, 시간, 방법의 부사절
whenever	Whenever you come, I don't care. = No matter when (네가 언제 오더라도)	You can come whenever you want. = at any time (네가 원하는 언제든)
wherever	Wherever you are, I will find you. = No matter where (네가 어디에 있더라도)	You can sit wherever you want. = at any place (네가 원하는 어디든)
however	However she tried, she couldn't win. = No matter how (그녀가 얼마나 노력했더라도)	You can do it however you want. = in any way (네가 원하는 어떤 방법으로든)

우리말과 같도록 빈칸에 알맞은 말을 쓰시오.

01 그는 언제 도착해도 환영받을 것이다. → No ________ ________ he arrives, he'll be welcomed.

02 편할 때 언제든 와. → Come by ________ it's convenient.

03 내가 아무리 공부해도 충분치 않다. → ________ I study, it isn't enough.

04 그는 내가 가는 곳 어디나 따라온다. → He follows me ________ I go.

05 아무리 목이 마를지라도, 기다려. → No ________ ________ thirsty you are, wait.

중간고사·기말고사 실전문제

객관식 (01~15) / 주관식 (16~30)

학년과 반 이름 객관식 / 15문항 주관식 / 15문항

[01~03] 다음 빈칸에 알맞은 것을 고르시오.

01

> Can you recognize the girl ________ is waving at us now?

① what ② which ③ who
④ whose ⑤ whom

02

> Roses are beautiful flowers ________ scent is often used when making perfume.

① what ② which ③ who
④ whose ⑤ that

03

> Her parents will always be supportive about ________ Katherine tries to do.

① whatever ② whoever ③ wherever
④ whenever ⑤ however

[04~05] 다음 중 밑줄 친 단어의 쓰임이 나머지 넷과 다른 하나를 고르시오.

04 ① Did you get what he's trying to tell you?
② What is unnecessary will be thrown away.
③ What did they expect me to do within such a short amount of time?
④ What I said is not true.
⑤ People often fight over what's not worth much.

05 ① Botanists didn't know exactly when this plant had lived on Earth.
② What do you do when you have free time?
③ Is today when she goes back to her home country?
④ 1988 was when the Olympics were held in Seoul.
⑤ He doesn't seem to remember when he took the medicine.

[06~08] 다음 중 어법상 어색한 것을 고르시오.

06 ① Greg finally met a woman whom he had always wanted.
② Dylan bought a brand-new truck whose wheels are bigger than ordinary cars.
③ We had a chance to chat with the actress whose role was 'The Witch' in the play.
④ The jacket whose pockets are very useful is the one I usually wear.
⑤ This is the chef whose famous for his amazing recipes.

07 ① The bus which you just missed was the last bus today.
② The bike which I gave him a month ago was already broken.
③ Be careful when moving the box which contains glass products.
④ She drove to the airport which her husband arrived.
⑤ The car which I let him drive wasn't actually mine.

08 ① Insects are edible, which mean they can be our food resources in the future.
② Anna has been absent for two days in a row, which is not very usual for her.
③ A gentleman, who looked curious, kept staring at us.
④ Blare, whose dream is to be a ballerina, practices really hard.
⑤ I'm hanging out with my new neighbor, whom I met for the first time yesterday.

[09~11] 다음 중 어법상 옳은 것을 고르시오.

09 ① She purchased that cost more than she earned a month.
② The doorman which was standing right by the front gate helped me carry the luggage.
③ There was nobody what would dance with me in the ballroom.
④ He thought money was all that he needed.
⑤ Gavin was the only one could speak Dutch in the class.

10 ① Whoever you go, you will be welcomed by people.
② John reads comic books wherever he has spare time.
③ How does she know whenever her daughter lies to her?
④ However the owner tried hard, the store went out of business.
⑤ Whatever nervous he may get, Eric should make a speech.

11 ① She left the town on the day why her husband came back.
② Do you have a piece of paper where I can draw something?
③ Can you explain what you were late for the meeting?
④ Let me tell you the way how you can pass the course as fast as possible.
⑤ This is the city when my family used to live.

[12~13] 다음 빈칸에 들어갈 말이 바르게 짝지어진 것을 고르시오.

12

- Do you know anyone ________ is good at computer programming?
- Nancy is one of my colleagues, ________ has met BTS in person.

① who – who
② who – that
③ who – which
④ which – that
⑤ which – who

13

- My family love to go to the beach ________ we can swim and sunbathe.
- He found out ________ caused the fire.
- Lisa brought her cat, ________ tail was hurt, to a vet.

① which – that – its
② which – what – which
③ where – why – which
④ where – what – whose
⑤ when – that – whose

[14~15] 다음 두 문장을 한 문장으로 바르게 연결한 것을 고르시오.

14

- Sarah lost her earrings.
- Her boyfriend bought those earrings.

① Sarah lost her earrings which bought by her boyfriend.
② Sarah lost her earrings that her boyfriend buys.
③ Sarah lost her earrings which her boyfriend bought.
④ Sarah lost that her boyfriend bought those earrings.
⑤ Sarah lost her earrings that her boyfriend bought those.

15

- The inventor needed a note.
- He could write his creative ideas on it.

① The inventor needed a note which he could write his creative ideas.
② The inventor needed a note that he could write his creative ideas.
③ The inventor needed a note on that he could write his creative ideas.
④ The inventor needed a note on which he could write his creative ideas.
⑤ The inventor needed a note where he could write his creative ideas on.

〈다음부터는 서술형 주관식 문제입니다.〉

[16~18] 다음 밑줄 친 부분이 어법상 맞으면 ○를 표시하고, 틀리면 바르게 고쳐 쓰시오.

16 This is the signature menu which our restaurant is famous.

____

17 James described to me that he saw on his way to here.

____

18 The explorer wanted to go to a new land where the treasure was hidden.

____

[19~21] 다음 문장의 어법상 어색한 부분을 찾아 바르게 고쳐 쓰시오.

19 Many people what retire in their early ages are looking for new jobs these days.

______________ → ______________

20 Chris stopped by to see his friend who's office is near his.

______________ → ______________

21 The protesters on the street, which looked furious, marched toward the City Hall.

______________ → ______________

[22~24] 다음 두 문장을 관계사를 이용하여 한 문장으로 고쳐 쓰시오.

22

• Amy was going to apply for a job.
• The job makes her life more relaxed.

→ ______________

23

• Caleb went to the amusement park.
• There are many fun attractions in the amusement park.

→ ______________

24

• Have you ever been to Vienna?
• Schubert was born in Vienna.

→ ______________

[25~26] 다음 우리말과 같도록 괄호 안의 말을 바르게 배열하시오.

25

조종사가 되기를 원하는 누구든 이 학교에 지원할 수 있다.
(a pilot / wants / can / to / be / whoever / apply)

→ ______________
______________ to this school.

26

모든 사람이 투표할 권리가 있고, 그것은 의무이기도 하다.
(is / to / which / also / , / the right / has / vote / a duty)

→ Everyone ______________
______________.

[27~28] 다음 우리말과 같도록 괄호 안의 말을 이용하여 문장을 완성하시오.

27

정직만이 나에게 중요한 단 한 가지이다.
(관계대명사, matters, the only thing, honesty)

→ ______________
______________ to me.

28

Genie는 네가 상상하는 곳이면 어디든 데려다 줄 수 있어.
(복합관계사, take, imagine, you)

→ Genie can ______________
______________.

[29~30] 다음 우리말을 주어진 |조건|에 맞게 바르게 영작하시오.

29 무엇을 먹든 그는 살이 찌지 않는다.

|조건|
1. 복합관계사를 문장 처음에 사용할 것
2. 단어 eat, gain weight를 사용할 것
3. 7개의 단어로 쓸 것

→ ______________________________
____

30 봄은 새싹이 돋아나는 계절이다.

|조건|
1. 〈전치사+관계대명사〉 형태를 사용할 것
2. 단어 season, sprouts, come out를 사용할 것
3. 9개의 단어로 쓸 것

→ ______________________________
____

CHAPTER

11

가정법

UNIT 01 가정법 과거 & 가정법 과거완료

현재나 과거 사실의 반대를 가정할 때는 가정법 동사(일반동사: 과거형, be동사: were)를 쓰세요.

가정법 과거	현재 사실	He is not here so he can't join.	여기 없어서 합류할 수 없다.
	반대 가정	is not의 반대/과거(were만 사용) If he were here, he could join. can't join의 반대/could+동사원형	여기 있다면, 합류할 수 있을 텐데
가정법 과거완료	과거 사실	He wasn't diligent so he failed.	근면하지 않아서 실패했다.
	반대 가정	was not의 반대/과거분사(had+p.p.) If he had been diligent, he wouldn't have failed. failed의 반대/wouldn't have p.p.	근면했다면 실패하지 않았을 텐데

참고 가정법은 단순히 반대를 가정하는 것이 아니라, 안타까움, 후회, 유감을 표현하기 위해 사용해요.

주의 가정법 과거와 가정법 과거완료의 동사 형태에 주의하세요.

구분		if절	주절
단순 조건문		현재형	미래형
가정법 과거	현재 사실 반대 가정	과거형/were	would/could/might+동사원형
가정법 과거완료	과거 사실 반대 가정	had+과거분사형	would/could/might+have+과거분사형

|A| 괄호 안에서 알맞은 말을 고르시오.

01 If I were you, I (won't, wouldn't) do that.

02 If you (have, had) money, you could buy the big house.

03 If he (had known, knew) the answer, he could have told me.

04 If she had had money, she (would lend, would have lent) you some.

|B| 우리말과 같도록 괄호 안의 말을 활용하여 문장을 완성하시오.

01 내기 부자라면 그 차를 살 텐데. (rich, would, buy)

→ If I ________________, I ________________ the car.

02 Tom이 공부를 열심히 했다면 시험이 쉬웠을 텐데. (study, might, easy)

→ If Tom ________________ hard, the test ________________.

03 네가 일찍 일어났다면 학교에 늦지 않았을 텐데. (get up, would, late)

→ If you ________________ early, you ________________ for school.

04 네가 내 주소를 알았다면 나를 찾아올 수 있었을 텐데. (know, could, visit)

→ If you ________________ my address, you ________________ me.

05 그녀가 내 생일을 안다면 축하해 줄 텐데. (know, would, celebrate)

→ If she ________________, she ________________ it.

06 그가 시험을 통과한다면 그는 행복할 텐데. (pass the test, would, happy)

→ If he ________________, he ________________.

UNIT 02 혼합 가정법

가정하려는 일의 시제가 서로 섞여 있는 경우에 주의하세요.

if절		주절	
과거 사실	어젯밤에 끝내지 못했다	현재 사실	오늘 못 간다
과거 사실 반대 가정	어젯밤에 끝냈더라면	현재 사실 반대 가정	오늘 갈 수 있을 텐데
가정법 과거완료: had+과거분사형		가정법 과거: would/could/might+동사원형	
If I had finished it yesterday,		I could go with you today.	

우리말과 같도록 괄호 안의 말을 활용하여 문장을 완성하시오.

01 내가 아침을 먹었다면 지금 배고프지 않을 텐데. (have, would, hungry)

→ If I ________________ breakfast, I ________________ now.

02 그녀가 운동을 규칙적으로 했다면 지금 더 건강할 텐데. (exercise, would, healthier)

→ If she ________________ regularly, she ________________ now.

03 우리가 일찍 출발했다면 지금쯤 도착할 수 있을 텐데. (leave, could, arrive)

→ If we ________________ early, we ________________ by now.

04 그가 숙제를 했다면 오늘 영화를 볼 수 있을 텐데. (do, could, see)

→ If he ________________ his homework, he ________________ a movie today.

05 네가 그 때 그 가방을 사지 않았다면 지금 그 신발을 살 수 있을 텐데. (buy, could)

→ If you ________________ the bag then, you ________________ the shoes now.

UNIT 03 가정법과 직설법의 전환

가정법 문장을 직설법으로 바꿔 쓸 때 의미와 시제를 잘 판단하여 쓰세요.

가정법 과거	가정법	If he were here, he could join.	여기 있다면, 합류할 수 있을 텐데
	직설법	= Because he is not here, he can't join. = He is not here, so he can't join.	여기 없어서 합류할 수 없다
가정법 과거완료	가정법	If he had been diligent, he wouldn't have failed.	근면했다면 실패하지 않았을 텐데
	직설법	= Because he was not diligent, he failed. = He wasn't diligent, so he failed.	근면하지 않아서 실패했다

다음 가정법 문장을 직설법 문장으로 쓸 때, 빈칸을 완성하시오.

01 If I were rich, I could buy the watch. → Because ________________, I can't buy the watch.

02 If you weren't sick, you would see a movie. → As ________________, you won't see a movie.

03 If we had had time, we could have finished it. → We ________________, so we couldn't finish it.

04 If I hadn't lost it, I would have it now. → Because I ____________, I ____________ now.

05 If the weather were fine, we would be there. → The weather ________________, so we aren't there.

UNIT 04 I wish + 가정법

'~라면 …좋(았)을 텐데'라고 할 때는 〈I wish + 가정법〉으로 표현하세요.

가정법 과거	현재 사실	Sujung is not here.	수정이가 여기 없다.
	유감/아쉬움	I wish Sujung ~~was~~ were here. └→ 가정법 과거동사(were)	수정이가 여기 있으면 좋을 텐데.
가정법 과거완료	과거 사실	Sujung was not here.	수정이가 여기 없었다.
	유감/아쉬움	I wish Sujung had been here. └→ 가정법 과거완료(had+과거분사)	수정이가 여기 있었다면 좋았을 텐데.

|A| 다음 두 문장의 의미가 같도록 빈칸을 완성하시오.

01 I wish he were my brother.

→ I'm sorry he ______________________ my brother.

02 I'm sorry I don't know his name.

→ I wish I ______________________ his name.

03 I wish I had more free time.

→ I'm sorry I ______________________.

04 I wish I could go to Mars.

→ I'm sorry I ______________________.

05 I wish you hadn't told me a lie.

→ I'm sorry you ______________________.

06 I'm sorry I skipped the class.

→ I wish I ______________________.

|B| 우리말과 같도록 괄호 안의 말을 활용하여 문장을 완성하시오.

01 우리가 같은 반 친구라면 좋을 텐데. (be, classmates)

→ I wish ______________________.

02 내가 피아노를 잘 치면 좋을 텐데. (play, the piano, well)

→ I wish I ______________________.

03 네가 나에게 편지를 보냈더라면 좋았을 텐데. (send, me, a letter)

→ I wish ______________________.

04 내가 너무 많이 먹지 않았더라면 좋았을 텐데. (eat, too much)

→ I wish ______________________.

UNIT 05 as if + 가정법

'마치 ~인[이었던] 것처럼'이라고 쓸 때는 〈as if + 가정법〉으로 표현하세요.

주절	as if절	as if절의 해석	as if 가정법과 직설법(사실)의 비교
현재	가정법 과거	주절과 같은 시제로 해석	He acts as if he could do it. (할 수 있는 것처럼 행동한다) = In fact, he can't do it.
과거			He acted as if he could do it. (할 수 있었던 것처럼 행동했다) = In fact, he couldn't do it.
현재	가정법 과거완료	주절보다 더 과거로 해석	He talks as if he had seen me. (나를 봤던 것처럼 말한다) = In fact, he didn't see me.
과거			He talked as if he had seen me. (나를 봤었던 것처럼 말했다) = In fact, he hadn't seen me.

|A| 우리말에 맞게 괄호 안에 알맞은 말을 고르시오.

01 그는 마치 (지금) 부자인 것처럼 말한다. → He talks as if he (is, were) rich.

02 그는 마치 (예전에) 부자였던 것처럼 말한다. → He talks as if he (was, had been) rich.

03 그는 마치 (당시에) 부자였던 것처럼 말했다. → He talked as if he (were, has been) rich.

04 그는 마치 (더 이전에) 부자였던 것처럼 말했다. → He talked as if he (has been, had been) rich.

|B| 다음 문장을 as if를 이용하여 가정법 문장으로 바꾸시오.

01 In fact, you don't know everything. → You talk ______________________.

02 In fact, he slept well. → He looks ______________________.

03 In fact, they weren't friends. → They seemed ______________________.

04 In fact, she isn't a teacher. → She feels ______________________.

05 In fact, Minjun doesn't like animals. → Minjun sounds ______________________.

06 In fact, Minsu hadn't won the gold medal. → Minsu talked ______________________.

|C| 우리말과 같도록 괄호 안의 말을 활용하여 문장을 완성하시오.

01 나는 마치 점심을 먹지 않았던 것처럼 느낀다. (have lunch)

→ I feel ______________________________.

02 그는 마치 그 일을 끝냈던 것처럼 보였다. (finish, the job)

→ He seemed ______________________________.

03 그들은 마치 Mr. Anderson을 아는 것처럼 행동했다. (behave, know)

→ They ______________________________.

UNIT 06 Without[But for] + 가정법

'~가 아니라면[없이는] …할[일] 것이다'라고 할 때는 〈Without[But for] ~ + 가정법 동사〉로 표현하세요.

가정법 과거	현재 사실	There is water so life can exist.	물이 있어서 생명이 존재할 수 있다.
	반대 가정	Without[But for] water, life couldn't exist. 현재 사실(can exist)의 반대 가정	물이 없다면, 생명은 존재할 수 없을 것이다.
가정법 과거완료	과거 사실	You were here so I was not sad.	네가 여기 있어서 나는 슬프지 않았다.
	반대 가정	Without[But for] you, I would have been sad. 과거 사실(was not)의 반대 가정	네가 없었다면, 나는 슬펐을 것이다.

〈Without[But for] ~ + 가정법 동사〉를 〈If it were not[had not been] for ~〉와 서로 바꿔 쓸 수 있도록 하세요.

가정법 과거	Without[But for] water, life couldn't exist. = If it were not for water, ~.	물이 없다면, 생명은 존재할 수 없을 것이다.
가정법 과거완료	Without[But for] you, I would have been sad. = If it had not been for you, ~.	네가 여기 없었다면, 나는 슬펐을 것이다.

A 우리말과 같도록 괄호 안의 말을 바르게 배열하시오.

01 그의 도움이 없었다면 나는 수영하는 법을 배우지 못했을 텐데. (had not / if / his help / it / been / for)

→ ______________________, I couldn't have learned how to swim.

02 컴퓨터가 없다면 나는 숙제를 하지 못할 텐데. (a computer / do my homework / I / couldn't)

→ But for ______________, ______________________.

03 팬들이 없었다면 그들은 그렇게 큰 인기를 얻지 못했을 텐데. (so popular / they / have become / couldn't / fans)

→ Without ______________, ______________________.

B 다음 문장을 If는 Without으로, Without은 If로 시작하는 문장으로 바꿔 쓰시오.

01 If it were not for TV, → ______________________, we would have nothing to do.

02 Without a vacuum, → ______________________, it would be dirty.

03 If it hadn't been for you, → ______________________, I would have lost the match.

04 Without the pill, → ______________________, he would have died.

05 Without my dog, → ______________________, I wouldn't feel happy.

06 Without her support, → ______________________, I wouldn't have tried it.

UNIT 07 It's time + 가정법

이미 했어야 할 것을 아직 안 한 것에 대한 유감, 불평, 아쉬움은 ⟨It's time that + 가정법 과거⟩로 쓰세요.

It's time that + 과거 동사	It's time + (for + 행위자) + to부정사
~했어야 할 시간이다 (유감, 불평, 아쉬움)	(…가) ~할 시간이다 (할 일을 표현)
It's 12. It's time that he went to bed. 12시다. 그가 잠자리에 들었어야 할 시간이다.	It's 10. It's time (for him) to go to bed. 10시다. 그가 잠자리에 들 시간이다.

⟨It's time that + 가정법 과거⟩의 의미를 강조하기 위해 time 앞에 high나 about을 넣을 수 있어요.

It's high time that + 과거 동사	It's about time that + 과거 동사
진즉에 ~했어야 했다	(늦었지만) 이제는 (정말) ~할 시간이다

|A| 괄호 안의 말을 활용하여 빈칸에 알맞은 말을 쓰시오.

01 It's almost 11. It's ________ ________ we ________ in bed. (be)

02 He has been working too hard. It's time ________ ________ ________ a rest. (take)

03 They are late. It's ________ that they ________ packing. (start)

04 It's 3:10. It's ________ that the 3 o'clock bus ________. (arrive)

05 Why didn't you go to the doctor? It's time ________ you ________ your doctor. (see)

06 You phone doesn't work. It's time ________ you ________ a new phone. (buy)

07 It's 8 in the morning. It's ________ that you ________ your homework. (finish)

|B| 우리말과 같도록 괄호 안의 말을 활용하여 문장을 완성하시오.

01 자 이제는 뭘 원할지 네가 결정할 때다. (decide, about, time)

→ It's ________________________ what you want to do.

02 진즉에 너는 그것에 대해 내게 말했어야 한다. (tell, high, time)

→ It's ________________________ about it.

03 이제는 우리가 그들을 직접 만날 시간이다. (meet, about, that)

→ It's ________________________ them in person.

04 너는 진즉에 그것을 없애버려야 했다. (get rid of, high, time)

→ It's ________________________ it.

05 이제는 네가 그녀에게 돈을 갚을 시간이다. (pay back, about, time)

→ It's ________________________ the money.

중간고사·기말고사 실전문제

객관식 (01~15) / 주관식 (16~30)

학년과 반 이름 객관식 / 15문항 주관식 / 15문항

[01~03] 다음 빈칸에 알맞은 것을 고르시오.

01

> If Mary ________ a boy, she would be a famous baseball player.

① be ② is ③ was
④ were ⑤ are

02

> Suji wouldn't have given the baby her favorite toy if her dad ________ her to do it.

① don't force ② didn't force
③ wouldn't forced ④ haven't forced
⑤ hadn't forced

03

> I wish he ________ the movie, but I think he's bored.

① enjoy ② enjoys
③ enjoyed ④ has enjoyed
⑤ had enjoyed

[04~05] 다음 우리말을 영어로 바르게 옮긴 것을 고르시오.

04

> 그 소녀는 마치 어른인 것처럼 화장을 하고 학교에 간다.

① The girl goes to school with makeup if she were an adult.
② The girl goes to school with makeup as if she were an adult.
③ The girl goes to school with makeup if she is an adult.
④ The girl goes to school with makeup as if she has been an adult.
⑤ The girl goes to school with makeup as if she had been an adult.

05

> 그의 방해가 없었다면, 그 일은 더 빨리 끝났을 거야.

① Without his interruption, it would end sooner.
② If it were not for his interruption, it would end sooner.
③ If it had not been for his interruption, it would end sooner.
④ If it had not been for his interruption, it would have ended sooner.
⑤ If it were not for his interruption, it would have ended sooner.

[06~07] 다음 중 어법상 어색한 것을 고르시오.

06
① If Jinsu were born in Korea, he could talk with his grandparents in Korean.
② If he hadn't fallen ill, he would have been here with us at this moment.
③ If the mechanic had fixed my car earlier, I would have traveled last week.
④ If she could play the violin, she would play in our school orchestra this coming weekend.
⑤ If it were cheap, he would try to get it.

07
① I wish he could trust the other players more in the game.
② The reporter spoke with excitement as if something big had happened.
③ I wish my teacher were with me.
④ I wish the shoes have been cheaper for me to buy.
⑤ She spoke as if she wouldn't call him.

[08~09] 다음 중 어법상 옳은 것을 고르시오.

08 ① If he is not hurt, he would play with us.
② If the boy not had been so small, he could have ridden the roller coaster.
③ If I have score a goal, our team would have won the game.
④ If my parents live near, I would visit them more often.
⑤ If he hadn't been caught, he would have committed another crime.

09 ① But for her suggestion, we would still be working on the project.
② If it were not for the life jacket, he would have drowned.
③ If it were not for you, the party would have been so boring.
④ Without for his efforts, this company wouldn't have grown like this.
⑤ But it hadn't been for alarm clock, she would have missed her flight.

[10~11] 다음 가정법 문장을 직설법 문장으로 바르게 바꾼 것을 고르시오.

10

If you had been there, you could have seen a monkey dancing on the stage.

① As you are there, you can see a monkey dancing on the stage.
② As you aren't there, you cannot see a monkey dancing on the stage.
③ As you were there, you could see a monkey dancing on the stage.
④ As you weren't there, you couldn't see a monkey dancing on the stage.
⑤ As you had been there, you couldn't see a monkey dancing on the stage.

11

Lisa acts as if she didn't know the password.

① In fact, Lisa knew the password.
② In fact, Lisa knows the password.
③ In fact, Lisa didn't know the password.
④ In fact, Lisa had known the password.
⑤ In fact, Lisa doesn't know the password.

[12~13] 다음 빈칸에 들어갈 말이 바르게 짝지어진 것을 고르시오.

12

• If she had followed directions well, she ________ in the woods. • I wish my dog ________ still alive, but he died a year ago.

① didn't get lost – were
② wouldn't get lost – is
③ wouldn't get lost – was
④ wouldn't have gotten lost – is
⑤ wouldn't have gotten lost – were

13

• If they hadn't sold the house then, they ________ it now at a very high price. • What ________ you do if you could live forever? • The detective told her to confess as if he ________ everything.

① can sell – will – knows
② could sell – will – knew
③ could sell – would – had known
④ could have sold – would – knew
⑤ could have sold – can – had known

[14~15] 다음 직설법 문장을 가정법 문장으로 바르게 바꾼 것을 고르시오.

14 As the tomatoes are rotten, we have to throw them away.

① If the tomatoes aren't rotten, we don't have to throw them away.
② If the tomatoes were rotten, we would have to throw them away.
③ If the tomatoes weren't rotten, we wouldn't have to throw them away.
④ If the tomatoes hadn't been rotten, we would have to throw them away.
⑤ If the tomatoes hadn't been rotten, we wouldn't have to throw them away.

15 I'm sorry that my vacation was put off.

① I wish my vacation isn't put off.
② I wish my vacation wasn't put off.
③ I wish my vacation hadn't been put off.
④ I wished my vacation wasn't put off.
⑤ I wished my vacation hadn't been put off.

〈다음부터는 서술형 주관식 문제입니다.〉

[16~18] 다음 우리말과 의미가 같도록 괄호 안의 말을 활용하여 문장을 완성하시오.

16 Jack이 이 선물을 좋아했다면 좋았을 텐데. (like)

→ I wish Jack ________ this present.

17 그 할머니는 친손자처럼 그 아이를 돌본다. (be)

→ The old lady looks after him as if the child ________ her own grandson.

18 그녀의 격려가 없었다면, 나는 그것을 끝까지 해내지 못했을 거야. (make)

→ Without her encouragement, I ________ ________ it through.

[19~21] 다음 문장에서 어법상 어색한 부분을 찾아 바르게 고쳐 쓰시오.

19 If my parents saw my report card now, they would have been very disappointed.

________ → ________

20 He would have received the letter if it has not been sent to the wrong address.

________ → ________

21 If he wanted to be alone, he won't be here with everyone.

________ → ________

[22~24] 다음 직설법 문장을 가정법 문장으로 바르게 바꿔 문장을 완성하시오.

22 As the kids didn't listen to their teacher, she was angry.

→ The teacher wouldn't have been angry, if the kids ________ ________ ________ her.

23 I'm sorry that there was a flood all over the country.

→ I wish ________ ________ ________ ________ a flood all over the country.

24 In fact, the man can't understand Chinese, but he pretends to understand it.

→ The man pretends as if he ________ ________ Chinese.

[25~26] 다음 우리말과 같도록 괄호 안의 말을 바르게 배열하시오.

25

만약 장영실이 더 오래 살았다면, 더 많은 유용한 발명품들을 만들었을 텐데. (lived / longer / had / created / he / have / would)

→ If Jang Yeong-sil ________________, ________________ more inventions.

26

Dan은 마치 그가 왕자인 것처럼 행동한다. (were, he, prince, a, if, as)

→ Dan acts ________________________________.

[27~28] 다음 우리말과 같도록 괄호 안의 말을 활용하여 문장을 완성하시오.

27

이제는 정말 네 방을 청소해야 할 시간이다. (clean, time, about, that)

→ It's ________________________________.

28

그녀가 트럭을 운전할 수 있다면 좋을 텐데. (wish, can, drive, a truck)

→ ________________________________

[29~30] 다음 우리말을 주어진 |조건|에 맞게 바르게 영작하시오.

29 만약 신을 만난다면 무엇을 요청하겠습니까?

|조건|
1. 가정법을 사용할 것
2. 단어 ask for, meet, God을 사용할 것
3. 문장 전체를 9개의 단어로 쓸 것

→ What ________________________________

________________________________?

30 공기가 없이는, 모든 생물들은 죽을 것이다.

|조건|
1. 가정법을 사용할 것
2. but을 문장 처음에 쓸 것
3. 단어 air, all the living things, die를 사용할 것
4. 9개의 단어로 쓸 것

→ ________________________________

____

내가 가장 취약한 부분에 대해
요점 정리를 해 보세요.

CHAPTER

12

일치와 화법

UNIT 01 주의해야 할 수의 일치

〈부분을 나타내는 명사 + of + 명사〉가 주어일 때, 동사는 of 뒤의 명사의 수에 일치시키세요.

주어			동사
Some / Most / All / Half / ~ percent / 분수(One third / Three fifths) 등	of	단수명사 / 셀 수 없는 명사	단수동사
		복수명사	복수동사

항상 단수 취급하거나 복수 취급하는 말들을 알아 두세요.

주어	동사
every ~ / each ~ / one of ~ / the number of ~(~의 수)	단수동사
형태는 복수이지만, 의미는 단수인 명사(과목명, 나라 이름)	
both ~ / a number of ~(많은 ~) / the + 형용사(~한 사람들)	복수동사

괄호 안의 단어를 알맞은 형태로 쓰시오. (단, 현재형으로 쓸 것)

01 Politics ____________ my brother's major. (be)

02 Two fifths of the students ____________ boys. (be)

03 All of the children ____________ go to school. (have to)

04 The old ____________ to understand the young. (try)

05 Most of the furniture ____________ made of wood. (be)

06 One fourth of year ____________ called a quarter. (be)

UNIT 02 시제 일치 & 시제 일치의 예외

주절의 시제와 종속절의 시제의 기본적인 관계를 알아 두세요.

주절 시제	종속절의 시제	주절 시제	종속절의 시제
현재	모든 시제 가능	과거	과거나 과거완료 가능

항상 현재시제를 쓰는 경우와 항상 과거시제를 쓰는 경우에 유의하세요.

항상 현재	진리, 사실, 속담, 현재의 습관 등	항상 과거	역사적 사실

다음 문장에서 어법상 어색한 부분을 찾아서 바르게 고쳐 쓰시오. (단, 없는 경우 ×표 할 것)

01 We all knew that the Earth is not flat. → ____________

02 They said that they could help me any time. → ____________

03 She said that she has been to Jeju-do several times. → ____________

04 The Pyeongchang Winter Olympic Games are held in 2018. → ____________

05 I learned that water was composed of oxygen and hydrogen. → ____________

06 Koreans know that Hangeul is revealed by King Sejong in 1446. → ____________

UNIT 03 간접화법 전환 1

직접화법의 문장을 간접화법으로 고쳐 쓸 때 다음 단계에 따라 고쳐 쓰세요.

step 1	전달동사 바꾸기 (say → say / say to → tell)	said to me → told me
step 2	인용 부호(" ")를 없애고 that절로 쓰기	*that은 생략 가능
step 3	that절의 주어를 전달자의 입장으로 바꾸기	You → I
step 4	시제를 전달자 입장으로 바꾸기	look → looked *주절의 시제와 맞추기
step 5	시간, 장소 부사(구)를 전달자 입장으로 바꾸기	now → then

Jinsu said to me, "You look so tired now."
→ Jinsu told me (that) I looked so tired then.

간접화법으로 고쳐 쓸 때 주의해야 할 시제 및 부사(구)를 알아 두세요.

now → then / today → that day / tonight → that night / this[these] → that[those]
here → there / ago → before / yesterday → the day before, the previous day
tomorrow → the next[following] day / last week → the week before, the previous week

다음 문장을 간접화법으로 바꿔 쓸 때, 빈칸에 알맞은 말을 쓰시오.

01 I said to you, "I'll take your picture."
→ I ______________ you that ______________ take your picture.

02 My mom said to me, "You have to do your homework tonight."
→ My mom ______________ that ______________________________.

03 My dad said, "I washed my car yesterday."
→ My dad ______________ that ______________________________.

04 Tony said to us, "I can't go see a movie today."
→ Tony ______________ that ______________ go see a movie ______________.

UNIT 04 간접화법 전환 2

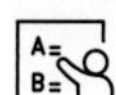
의문사가 있을 때는 의문사를 그대로 쓰지만, 의문문가 없다면 접속사 if나 whether를 쓰세요.

step 1	전달동사 바꾸기 (say, say to → ask)	said to him → asked him
step 2	의문사를 접속사로 쓰기	asked him where
step 3	의문사 뒤에 〈주어+동사〉의 어순으로 쓰기	asked him where you live
step 4	의문사 없는 의문문은 if/whether를 쓰기	asked him if/whether ~ (~인지 아닌지 물었다)
step 5	주어, 동사, 부사(구)등을 전달자 입장으로 바꾸기	you → he / live → lived / now → then

She said to him, "Where do you live now?"
→ She asked him where he lived then.

다음 문장을 직접화법은 간접화법으로, 간접화법은 직접화법 문장으로 바꿔 쓰시오.

01 He said to her, "Can you dance?" → He asked her ________________.

02 She asked me what I was eating. → She said to me, " ________________?"

03 He said to me, "What is your problem?" → He asked me ________________.

04 She asked me who had broken the window. → He said to me, " ________________?"

05 She said to him, "Did you write this?" → She asked him ________________.

06 I asked the chef how he had made it. → I said to the chef, " ________________?"

UNIT 05 간접화법 전환 3

명령문을 간접화법으로 고쳐 쓸 때는 다음 단계에 따라 고쳐 쓰세요.

step 1	전달동사를 명령문의 내용에 따라 바꾸기	tell(지시), ask(요청), advise(충고), order(명령)
step 2	따옴표(")를 없애고 ⟨목적어+to부정사⟩로 쓰기	told me to stop *5형식 목적격보어: to부정사
step 3	부정명령(Don't ~)일 때는 ⟨not+to부정사⟩로 쓰기	told me not to ~
step 4	기타 목적격, 소유격 대명사, 부사 등 고치기	"your"→ my

He said to me, "Stop picking your nose."

→ He told me to stop picking my nose.

다음 문장을 괄호 안의 말을 활용하여 간접화법으로 바꿔 쓰시오.

01 My mom said to us, "Don't make noises at night." (tell)

→ My mom ________________________________.

02 She said to me, "Call me later." (ask)

→ She ________________________________.

03 Sam said to Kate, "Lend me one of these pens." (ask)

→ Sam ________________________________.

04 The police officer said to the drivers, "Don't drive fast in a school zone." (order)

→ The police officer ________________________________.

05 He said to me, "Forgive me for what happened yesterday." (ask)

→ He ________________________________.

06 The teacher said to the students, "Submit the assignment tomorrow." (tell)

→ The teacher ________________________________.

중간고사·기말고사 실전문제

객관식 (01~15) / 주관식 (16~30)

정답과 해설 • 92쪽

학년과 반 　 이름 　 객관식 　 / 15문항 　 주관식 　 / 15문항

[01~03] 다음 빈칸에 알맞은 것을 고르시오.

01

All of the employees in the company usually ________ the office before 8 o'clock.

① leave ② leaves
③ left ④ leaving
⑤ is leaving

02

The explorer claimed that he ________ the treasures on the island.

① find ② finds
③ find ④ had found
⑤ will found

03

From the experiment, students learned that oil ________ lighter than water.

① be ② is
③ are ④ was
⑤ were

[04~05] 다음 빈칸에 들어갈 수 없는 것을 고르시오.

04

They didn't believe that the woman ________ a basketball player.

① was ② has been ③ had been
④ would be ⑤ might be

05

________ the passengers on a plane were not served meals yet.

① Half of ② Some of
③ Most of ④ Both of
⑤ The number of

[06~07] 다음 우리말을 영어로 바르게 옮긴 것을 고르시오.

06

그는 Jane에게 그의 가족이 내일 올 것이라고 말했다.

① He tells Jane that his family will come tomorrow.
② He tells Jane that his family would come tomorrow.
③ He told Jane that his family will come tomorrow.
④ He told Jane that his family would come tomorrow.
⑤ He told Jane that his family had come tomorrow.

07

> 도시 거주자의 3분의 1이 다른 지역으로 출퇴근 한다.

① One-third of the city's resident commutes to other areas.
② One-third of the city's resident commute to other areas.
③ One-third of the city's residents commute to other areas.
④ One-thirds of the city's residents commutes to other areas.
⑤ One-thirds of the city's resident commutes to other areas.

08 다음 중 어법상 어색한 것은?

① He ordered me clean the table after lunch.
② Martin asked me if the necklace on the floor was mine.
③ He asked the woman when the work would be finished.
④ My aunt told me that she was getting married in May.
⑤ She said that they should follow the rule when playing dodge ball.

09 다음 중 어법상 옳은 것은?

① One of the trainees are behind the group.
② Physics has been the most difficult subject for me.
③ Each of puppies were named after four seasons.
④ The number of oranges harvested today are higher than yesterday.
⑤ Shaking hands are not appropriate these days.

[10~11] 다음 문장을 간접화법으로 바르게 바꾼 것을 고르시오.

10

> Clara said to the children, "You have to leave here soon."

① Clara said the children that you have to leave there soon.
② Clara said the children that you had to leave here soon.
③ Clara said to the children they have to leave here soon.
④ Clara told the children that they had to leave there soon.
⑤ Clara told to the children that they had to leave there soon.

11

> The doctor said to her, "Don't eat too much greasy food."

① The doctor said her don't eat too much greasy food.
② The doctor told her not eat too much greasy food.
③ The doctor advised her not eat too much greasy food.
④ The doctor told her to not eat too much greasy food.
⑤ The doctor advised her not to eat too much greasy food.

[12~13] 다음 문장을 직접화법으로 바르게 바꾼 것을 고르시오.

12

The waiter asked us if there is anything else we need.

① The waiter asked us, "If there is anything else we need?"
② The waiter asked us, "There is anything else you need."
③ The waiter said to us, "Is there anything else you need?"
④ The waiter said to us, "Is there is anything else we need?"
⑤ The waiter said to us, "Whether there is anything else you need?"

13

My friend told me that he was preparing dinner for his cousin then.

① My friend said to me, "He was preparing dinner for his cousin then."
② My friend said to me, "He is preparing dinner for his cousin now."
③ My friend said to me, "I was preparing dinner for my cousin now."
④ My friend said to me, "I'm preparing dinner for my cousin now."
⑤ My friend said to me, "I had been preparing dinner for my cousin now.

[14~15] 다음 빈칸에 들어갈 말이 바르게 짝지어진 것을 고르시오.

14

• The police asked them ________ they stole the bicycle.
• The United States ________ composed of 50 states.

① whether – is ② whether – are
③ what – was ④ what – is
⑤ if – are

15

• About two-thirds of South Korea ________ mountainous.
• Each of us ________ to take our own part well.
• He used to say that he ________ be rich someday.

① is – need – could ② is – needs – would
③ are – need – will ④ are – needs – will
⑤ was – need – would

〈다음부터는 서술형 주관식 문제입니다.〉

[16~17] 다음 우리말과 의미가 같도록 괄호 안의 말을 이용하여 문장을 완성하시오.

16

필리핀은 7,000개 이상의 섬으로 이루어져 있다. (consist)

→ The Philippines ______________ of more than 7,000 islands.

17 수박의 반은 냉장고에 넣어졌다. (be)

→ Half of the watermelon ______________ put in the refrigerator.

[18~20] 다음 문장에서 어법상 어색한 부분을 찾아 바르게 고쳐 쓰시오.

18 Most of the homework weren't turned in on time.

______________ → ______________

19 Some concepts of Economics was not easy to understand.

______________ → ______________

20 My uncle promised me that he won't tease me again.

______________ → ______________

[21~22] 다음 문장을 간접화법으로 바꿀 때, 빈칸에 알맞은 말을 써서 문장을 완성하시오.

21 My sister said, "I can invite your friends to my birthday party."

→ My sister said that ________ ________ invite ________ friends to ________ birthday party.

22 He said to me, "Do you have any screw driver at home?"

→ He ________ me ________ ________ ________ any screwdriver at home.

[23~24] 다음 문장을 직접화법으로 바꿀 때, 빈칸에 알맞은 말을 써서 문장을 완성하시오.

23 The fire fighter told me not to light the candles before going to sleep.

→ The fire fighter said to me, "________ ________ the candles before going to sleep."

24 Diana asked her brother whether she could wear his T-shirt.

→ Diana said to her brother, "________ ________ ________ ________ T-shirt?

[25~26] 우리말과 같도록 괄호 안의 말을 알맞게 배열하시오.

25 갈릴레오는 지구가 태양을 돈다고 주장했다. (around / that / revolves / claimed / the Earth / the Sun)

→ Galileo ______________________________.

26 Rachel은 선생님께 조퇴하고 싶다고 말했다. (wanted / that / leave early / her teacher / told / she / to)

→ Rachel ______________________________.

[27~28] 우리말과 같도록 괄호 안의 말을 활용하여 문장을 완성하시오.

27

그 문제에 대한 많은 해결책이 제시되었다. (number, solutions, suggest)

→ ______________________________

______________ to the problem.

28

사람들은 오직 강자만이 살아남는다고 말한다. (strong, survive, only, the)

→ People say that ______________

______________________________.

[29~30] 다음 우리말을 주어진 |조건|에 맞게 바르게 영작하시오.

29 누구나 동등한 권리를 가지고 있다.

|조건|
1. Every로 문장을 시작할 것
2. 단어 man, have, equal rights를 사용할 것
3. 5개의 단어로 쓸 것

→ ______________________________

____

30 그는 나에게 언제 그에게 전화할 것인지 물었다.

|조건|
1. 간접화법을 사용할 것
2. 단어 ask, when, will, call을 사용할 것
3. 8개의 단어로 쓸 것

→ ______________________________

____

내가 가장 취약한 부분에 대해
요점 정리를 해 보세요.

CHAPTER

13

강조, 부정, 도치, 부정대명사

UNIT 01 조동사 do를 이용한 강조

do는 조동사로도 쓰일 수 있다는 것을 알아 두세요.

본동사 do의 쓰임	조동사 do의 쓰임		
~하다	강조(정말)	부정문	의문문

참고 조동사가 있는 문장에는 항상 동사원형을 써요.

우리말과 같도록 괄호 안의 말과 조동사 do를 이용하여 문장을 완성하시오.

01 나는 실수하는 걸 정말 싫어한다. (hate)
→ I ________________ making a mistake.

02 그녀는 어제 정말 멋져 보였다. (look)
→ She ________________ nice yesterday.

03 우리 엄마는 맛있는 쿠키를 진짜 만드신다. (make)
→ My mom ________________ delicious cookies.

04 그는 정말 매일 점심으로 햄버거 하나를 먹는다. (eat)
→ He ________________ a hamburger for lunch every day.

05 너는 말을 많이 하지는 않지만, 정말 친구가 많다. (have)
→ You don't talk a lot, but you ________________ many friends.

UNIT 02 <It is[was] ~ that ...> 강조 구문

'…한 것은 바로 ~이다[였다]'라고 강조하고 싶을 때는 It is[was]와 that 사이에 강조하고 싶은 말을 넣으세요.

	It is[was]	강조하고 싶은 말	that + 나머지 말	의미
〈It is[was] ~ that ...〉 강조 구문	It was	Jack	that ~~Jack~~ saw a rainbow in the sky yesterday.	그건 Jack이었다
		a rainbow	that Jack saw ~~a rainbow~~ in the sky yesterday.	그건 무지개였다
		in the sky	that Jack saw a rainbow ~~in the sky~~ yesterday.	그건 하늘에서였다
		yesterday	that Jack saw a rainbow in the sky ~~yesterday~~.	그건 어제였다

〈It is[was] ~ that[who] ...〉을 이용하여 밑줄 친 부분을 강조하는 문장으로 바꿔 쓰시오.

01 Jiwon likes Brad. → It is ________________________________.

02 I called him last Thursday. → It was ________________________________.

03 I did my sister's homework. → It was ________________________________.

04 We saw the celebrity in the mall. → It was ________________________________.

05 They saw it three days ago. → It was ________________________________.

UNIT 03 전체 부정 & 부분 부정

부정어(not)와 전체를 나타내는 단어(all, every, both, always 등)가 함께 쓰이면 부분 부정으로 해석해야 해요.

부분 부정	모두 ~인 건 아니다	I do not know all of them. ≠ I do not know any of them.	〈부분 부정〉 그들 모두를 아는 것은 아님 〈전체 부정〉 둘 중 누구도 알지 못함
		He does not like both of them. ≠ He does not like either of them.	〈부분 부정〉 둘 다를 싫어하는 건 아님 〈전체 부정〉 둘 다를 싫어함

참고 no one, no-, none, never, nothing, neither of, nobody, not ~ any 등이 쓰이면 '아무도 ~않다 / 아무것도[어느 것도] ~ 아니다'의 뜻으로 전체를 부정하는 말이에요.

우리말과 같도록 괄호 안의 말을 이용하여 문장을 완성하시오.

01 그 게임이 항상 흥미진진한 것은 아니다. (not, always, exciting)

→ The game ______________________.

02 그들 중 누구도 중국어를 말하지 못한다. (None, can, of, speak)

→ ______________________ Chinese.

03 모든 학생들이 영어에 흥미가 있는 것은 아니다. (all, not, students, interested)

→ ______________________ in English.

04 나는 그 노래를 결코 들어본 적이 없다. (never, have, heard)

→ ______________________ the song.

UNIT 04 도치

장소나 방향을 나타내는 부사(구)나 전치사구를 문두에 쓸 때, 주어, 동사를 도치시키세요.

일반 문장	도치된 문장
His mother sat on a chair.	On a chair sat his mother.

주의 주어가 대명사일 때는 도치하지 않아요. On a chair sat she. (×) → On a chair she sat. (○)

부정어(not, little, hardly 등)나 only를 문두에 쓸 때, 주어, 동사를 도치시키세요.

예문	Not only is he smart but also rich.
	Only when you go will he go.
	Little did he know about me.

참고 '~ 또한 그렇다/그렇지 않다'라고 할 때, So/Neither 뒤에 주어와 동사를 도치시키세요.

다음 문장을 밑줄 친 부분을 강조하는 문장으로 바꿔 쓰시오.

01 A little boy sat on the roof. → ______________________.

02 He could hardly believe his ears. → ______________________.

03 I have never been so disappointed. → ______________________.

UNIT 05 부정대명사

정해지지 않은 불특정한 사람이나 물건을 가리킬 때는 부정대명사 one을 쓰세요.

부정대명사	정해지지 않은 것을 가리킴	one	I need a shirt. I'll buy one. (정해지지 않은 셔츠)	단수
		ones	I need shoes. I'll buy ones. (정해지지 않은 신발)	복수

주의 정해진 것(그것)을 말할 때는 인칭대명사 it을 써야 해요.

one 이외의 부정대명사를 알아 두세요.

부정대명사		의미	부정대명사		의미
단수	one	하나	복수	some	(여러 개 중) 몇몇
	another	또 다른 하나		others	다른 몇몇
	the other	나머지 하나		the others	나머지 모두

참고 other(그 밖의 다른, 그 밖의 다른 것) 앞에 the가 붙으면 특정한 것이 되므로 '나머지'라는 의미가 돼요.

우리말과 같도록 빈칸에 알맞은 말을 |보기|에서 골라 쓰시오.

|보기|
one　ones　the other　another　others　the others

01 너는 지난달에 자전거를 샀어. 왜 또 하나를 더 사야 하지?

→ You bought a bike last month. Why do you need to buy __________?

02 그는 다른 사람들이 그에 대해 어떻게 생각하는지 신경 쓰지 않는다.

→ He doesn't care what __________ might think about him?

03 15명 중 10명이 소년이고, 나머지는 소녀다.

→ Ten out of fifteen are boys and __________ are girls.

04 이 장갑들은 좀 작아요. 더 큰 것을 보여 주실 수 있나요?

→ These gloves are a little small. Can you show me bigger __________?

05 그는 두 형이 있다. 하나는 17살이고, 다른 하나는 22살이다.

→ He has two brothers. __________ is 17 years old, and __________ is 22.

06 나는 가방이 세 개가 있다. 하나는 검정, 또 다른 하나는 파랑, 나머지 하나는 흰색이다.

→ I have three bags. __________ is black, __________ is blue, and __________ is white.

중간고사·기말고사 실전문제

객관식 (01~15) / 주관식 (16~30)

정답과 해설 • 93쪽

학년과 반 이름 객관식 / 15문항 주관식 / 15문항

[01~03] 다음 빈칸에 알맞은 것을 고르시오.

01

The choir wasn't perfect but ________ touch the hearts of the audience.

① do ② does ③ did
④ done ⑤ is done

02

________ was their parents who ate all the children's snacks.

① That ② This ③ They
④ It ⑤ Those

03

________, but some people complained about this decision.

① No one ② Nobody ③ Nothing
④ Never ⑤ Not everyone

[04~05] 다음 우리말을 영어로 바르게 옮긴 것을 고르시오.

04

이 조직의 어떤 구성원들도 새로운 제안을 받아들이지 않았다.

① Not any members of this organization accepted the new proposal.
② Not all members of this organization accepted the new proposal.
③ No members of this organization didn't accept the new proposal.
④ Not every member of this organization accepted the new proposal.
⑤ Neither members of this organization didn't accept the new proposal.

05

우리가 작년에 호주를 여행하다가 본 것은 바로 그 코알라였다.

① That was the koala we saw while traveling to Australia last year.
② The koala was it that we saw while traveling to Australia last year.
③ It was the koala that we saw while traveling to Australia last year.
④ It was the koala what we saw while traveling to Australia last year.
⑤ It was the koala we saw that while traveling to Australia last year.

[06~07] 다음 중 어법상 어색한 것을 고르시오.

06
① Everyone in the room did enjoy the party.
② The artist impressed by the scenery did draw a beautiful picture.
③ The man who moved to this town do loves his neighbors.
④ The reporters asking questions do try hard to get answers from the interviewee.
⑤ Ellie does have no money at all.

07
① Nobody has done nothing about the accident.
② The girl hasn't canceled either of the concert tickets yet.
③ Neither of the students are wearing school uniforms.
④ Nothing can be possible without the help of others.
⑤ None are completely satisfied with themselves.

[08~09] 다음 중 어법상 옳은 것을 고르시오.

08 ① It was the desk that he placed his flower pot.
② It was Watson which became assistant of Detective Holmes.
③ It was the big tiger that appeared in her dream last night.
④ It was last weekend what my new training shoes were delivered.
⑤ It was you that we have been looking for a person about half an hour.

09 ① Little did the patient knows about his disease.
② Over the mountain stood the remains of the ancient city.
③ Never did the woman agreed to anything he said.
④ In the doorway her mother stood.
⑤ There was he sweeping the floor of the living room.

[10~11] 다음 대화의 밑줄 친 우리말을 바르게 나타낸 것은?

10

A: I don't think he will stop by the grocery store on his way home.
B: 나도 그래.

① So do I. ② So does he.
③ Neither do I. ④ Neither does he.
⑤ Either does he.

11

A: Scott can finish a whole pizza by himself.
B: 내 아들도 그래.

① So do my son. ② So does my son.
③ So can my son. ④ Neither do my son.
⑤ Neither can my son.

[12~13] 다음 빈칸에 들어갈 말이 바르게 짝지어진 것을 고르시오.

12

• The novelist ________ look delighted when she won the Nobel Prize.
• Not ________ dress is designed by the famous designer.

① do – every ② does – all
③ does – all ④ did – every
⑤ did – either

13

• It is my sister ________ majored in physics.
• He didn't know ________ of the answers, so he wrote nothing on the test paper.
• Tony never likes the pizza with pineapple. – ________ does Kelly.

① that – any – So
② who – any – Neither
③ who – all – Either
④ which – all – Neither
⑤ which – some – So

[14~15] 다음 중 주어진 문장과 의미가 같은 것을 고르시오.

14

Not all the volunteers have arrived at the station yet.

① Any volunteers have never arrived at the station yet.
② None of the volunteers have arrived at the station yet.
③ Not any of the volunteers have arrived at the station yet.
④ No volunteer has arrived at the station yet.
⑤ Not every volunteer has arrived at the station yet.

15

Both Becky and Sean don't understand what the foreigner is talking about.

① Becky doesn't understand what the foreigner is talking about, and so do Sean.
② Becky doesn't understand what the foreigner is talking about, and so does Sean.
③ Becky doesn't understand what the foreigner is talking about, and neither is Sean.
④ Becky doesn't understand what the foreigner is talking about, and neither does Sean.
⑤ Becky doesn't understand what the foreigner is talking about, and neither do Sean.

〈다음부터는 서술형 주관식 문제입니다.〉

[16~18] 다음 밑줄 친 부분이 어법상 맞으면 ○표를 하고, 틀리면 바르게 고쳐 쓰시오.

16 Never has been she to such a wonderful place.

→ ________________

17 Here are some books you can read while waiting.

→ ________________

18 Outstanding scientists does develop many new technologies.

→ ________________

[19~21] 다음 문장에서 어법상 어색한 부분을 찾아 바르게 고쳐 쓰시오.

19 Only then do Kathy know what she had done.

________________ → ________________

20 Not only he raises a dog, but he has two cats.

________________ → ________________

21 The actor memorized some of his lines. But he couldn't memorize any of them.

________________ → ________________

[22~24] 다음 밑줄 친 부분을 강조하는 문장이 되도록 빈칸에 알맞은 말을 쓰시오.

22 The fire fighters tried hard to put out the fire.

→ The fire fighters ________ ________ hard to put out the fire.

23 Trees can hardly survive in the desert.

→ Hardly ________ ________ ________ in the desert.

24 She sat among the celebrities at the party.

→ Among the celebrities ________ ________ at the party.

[25~26] 다음 우리말과 같도록 괄호 안의 말을 바르게 배열하시오.

25

그 나무 아래에는 작은 벤치 하나가 있다. (small / lies / the tree / a / bench)

→ Under ________________________________.

26

세계의 모든 아이들이 적절한 교육을 받고 있는 것은 아니다. (receiving / in the world / not / are / children / all / a proper)

→ ________________________________ education.

[27~28] 다음 우리말과 같도록 괄호 안의 말을 활용하여 문장을 완성하시오.

27

그 파티에서 몇몇 학생들은 노래를 했고, 다른 몇몇은 춤을 췄어. (some, students, sing, dance)

→ At the party, ________________ while ________________.

28

크게 소리를 지른 것은 Sara였다. (who, scream, loudly)

→ It ________________________________.

[29~30] 다음 우리말을 주어진 |조건|에 맞게 바르게 영작하시오.

29 내가 그의 전화를 받은 것은 지난 월요일이었다.

|조건|
1. It으로 문장을 시작할 것
2. 단어 last Monday, get, call을 사용할 것
3. 9개의 단어로 쓸 것

→ ________________________________

30 그 건물에는 그 학교에서 온 아이들이 있었다.

|조건|
1. in으로 문장을 시작하고, 주어 동사는 도치시킬 것
2. 단어 the building, the children, from, the school을 사용할 것
3. 9개의 단어로 쓸 것

→ ________________________________

CHAPTER

14

문장의 이해

UNIT 01 주어 자리에 오는 말

주어 자리에는 명사나 명사 역할을 하는 말들만 써야 해요.

명사, 대명사	The sun is the center of the Solar System.	태양은
앞뒤 수식을 받는 명사	The true center of the Solar System isn't the earth.	태양계의 진정한 중심은
to부정사(명사적 용법)	To say goodbye is the saddest thing.	안녕이라고 말하는 것은
동명사	Seeing her again is his last wish.	그녀를 다시 보는 것이
명사절	Whether he is smart (or not) doesn't matter.	그가 똑똑한지 아닌지는

다음 문장에서 주어를 찾으시오.

01 That the team will win the match is certain.

02 Blaming other people for your problems is useless.

03 Travel to the Mars will be possible in the near future.

04 It may be dangerous climbing the mountain at night.

05 To walk for an hour every day can be good for health.

06 Working from home has become more and more common these days.

07 The business hours of the restaurant are from 11:00 a.m. to 9:00 p.m.

08 The tiny island discovered by the captain is located in the South Pacific ocean.

UNIT 02 주격보어 자리에 오는 말

주격보어 자리에는 명사나 형용사 또는 그 역할을 하는 말들만 써야 해요.

명사	My teacher is a very kind person.	매우 친절한 사람
to부정사(명사적 용법)	Her dream is not to live a normal life.	평범한 삶을 살지 않는 것
동명사 보어	His job is driving a taxi at night.	밤에 택시 운전하기
명사절	The truth is that the earth goes round the sun.	지구가 태양 주위를 돈다는 것
형용사(분사 포함)	Your idea sounds interesting.	흥미롭게 (들린다)

다음 문장에서 보어를 찾으시오.

01 They seemed glad to see us.

02 My cat keeps close to me when we sleep.

03 Yuna and I stayed friends after I moved out of the city.

04 One of my hobbies is cooking for my family.

05 Many buildings in the city remain damaged after the earthquake.

06 That the Sun went around the Earth was proved wrong.

07 The sauce on the chicken tasted sweet and sour.

08 Much about the Great Pyramid remains a mystery.

UNIT 03 목적어 자리에 오는 말

목적어 자리에도 명사나 명사 역할을 하는 말만 써야 해요.

명사, 대명사	He solved the problem.	그 문제를
앞뒤 수식을 받는 명사	I like the handsome boy wearing a suit.	양복을 입고 있는 잘생긴 소년
to부정사(명사적 용법)	He promised to look into the matter.	그 문제를 살펴볼 것을
동명사	They enjoyed swimming in the pool.	풀장에서 수영하는 것을
명사절	People didn't believe that the earth is round.	지구가 둥글다는 것을

참고 4형식 문장은 목적어를 2개 취하는 문장이에요.
He gives his girlfriend flowers. 그의 여자 친구에게 꽃을 준다.

|A| 다음 문장에서 목적어를 찾으시오.

01 My mom is baking some bread and cookies.

02 You pretended to be asleep when I went upstairs.

03 I like taking a walk in the morning.

04 Would you mind opening the window?

|B| 다음 문장에서 간접목적어와 직접목적어를 찾으시오.

01 Mr. Park teaches us Korean.

02 I sent him a present.

03 Sally told him the truth when we met before.

UNIT 04 목적격보어 자리에 오는 말

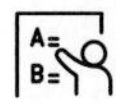

목적격보어 자리에는 명사, 형용사, to부정사, 원형부정사, 분사 등 다양한 말이 올 수 있어서 주의해야 해요.

명사	They made their son a doctor.	의사로
형용사	He made his parents happy.	행복하게
to부정사	They forced him to enter the military.	군대에 들어가도록
원형부정사	He had the students follow the rules. 〈사역〉	학교 규칙을 따르도록
분사	He saw a big truck going too fast. 〈지각: 능동〉	너무 빠르게 달리고 있는

다음 문장에서 목적어와 목적격보어를 찾으시오.

01 He wants me to make a plan for the holidays.

02 We found studying math alone difficult.

03 I heard someone singing a song downstairs.

04 They made me clean the bathroom before my meal.

05 He told her to brush her teeth after every meal.

UNIT 05 형용사적 수식어 자리에 오는 말

형용사적 수식어는 명사를 수식하는 말로, 다양한 말들이 명사를 수식할 수 있음을 알아 두세요.

명사 앞뒤 형용사	I bought a new book useful for kids.	아이들에게 유용한 새 (책)
명사 뒤 전치사구	The book on the desk is mine.	책상 위에 있는 (책)
명사 앞뒤 분사	Do you know the dog running in the park?	공원에서 달리고 있는 (개)
to부정사(형용사적 용법)	I have some questions to ask you.	너에게 물어볼 (질문들)
관계사절	This is the book that I was talking about.	내가 이야기 했던 (책)

다음 문장에서 밑줄 친 명사를 수식하는 말을 괄호로 표시하시오.

01 You bought a new car manufactured in Germany.

02 He gave me a piece of paper to write on.

03 People who have plenty of money can shop here.

04 The famous singer performing on the stage is my cousin.

05 It was time to say good bye.

06 I dropped the large jar filled with honey.

07 She works for a small company founded by her father.

08 My grandfather knows many old stories to tell us.

UNIT 06 부사적 수식어 자리에 오는 말

부사적 수식어는 명사 외의 거의 모든 말을 수식하는 말로, 부사적 수식어 역할을 하는 다양한 말들을 알아 두세요.

부사	She always has warm tea with her mom.	항상
전치사구	He often calls her in the morning.	아침에
to부정사(부사적 용법)	He tried hard not to make a mistake.	실수하지 않기 위해
부사절	It started to rain when we left the house.	집을 떠났을 때
분사구문	Getting off the bus, she said goodbye to me.	버스에서 내리면서

다음 문장에서 부사적 수식어 역할을 하는 말을 모두 찾으시오.

01 Even though it's September, it's still hot.

02 We've never visited Seattle.

03 Knowing that they were saved, we're relieved.

04 Joanne and Heather chatted over a cup of tea.

05 I tried to close the door quietly.

06 Strictly speaking, smoking isn't allowed here.

07 Let me know if you have any problems.

08 Seoeun needs to stop by the library to return a couple of books.

중간고사·기말고사 실전문제

객관식 (01~15) / 주관식 (16~30)

정답과 해설 • 95쪽

학년과 반 이름 객관식 / 15문항 주관식 / 15문항

[01~03] 다음 빈칸에 알맞은 것을 고르시오.

01 What my aunt always wants is ________.

① to work as a teacher
② drive a bus
③ everyone loves her
④ that lives in the city
⑤ be a good mom

02 The researchers found ____________.

① seriously wrong
② what did they miss
③ an amazing effect of the medicine
④ interesting to see the result
⑤ that hasn't been introduced

03 We visited ____________.

① that James beautifully decorated
② where the Statue of Liberty is
③ that many travelers recommended
④ a famous artist once stayed
⑤ spacious enough for a campsite

[04~06] 다음 빈칸에 들어갈 수 없는 것을 고르시오.

04 The girl saw __________ at the park.

① the good-looking boy running
② that someone took a nap
③ a ball that flew fast
④ a lot of people to talk
⑤ her bike stolen

05 __________ influenced his decision.

① The article written by Mr. Park
② Changing the location
③ Too much information
④ That Jessica liked him
⑤ How rich could he be

06 What he said made me ____________.

① less courageous
② much more actively
③ dissatisfied
④ leave his house
⑤ seen as a liar

[07~08] 다음 영어를 우리말로 바르게 옮긴 것을 고르시오.

07 John and Mark sometimes call their older sister mommy.

① John과 Mark는 가끔 그들의 누나와 엄마를 부른다.
② John과 Mark는 가끔 그들의 누나와 엄마에게 전화한다.
③ John과 Mark는 가끔 그들의 누나를 엄마라고 부른다.
④ John과 Mark는 가끔 그들의 누나에게 엄마를 불러준다.
⑤ John과 Mark는 가끔 그들의 누나에게 엄마에게 전화하라고 한다.

08

To recover from a serious disease requires a lot of help from family who support you.

① 가족의 지지로부터 도움을 받아 당신은 심각한 질병에서 회복했다.
② 심각한 질병에서 회복하기 위해서, 가족들로부터 많은 도움을 요청했다.
③ 심각한 질병에서 회복하는 가족의 도움은 당신을 지지해줄 것이다.
④ 심각한 질병에서 회복하는 것은 당신을 지지하는 가족의 많은 도움을 필요로 한다.
⑤ 심각한 질병에서 회복하는 것은 가족들이 당신을 지지하도록 돕는다.

[09~10] 다음 우리말을 영어로 바르게 옮긴 것을 고르시오.

09

별들을 처음 발견한 천문학자가 그 별들의 이름을 '백두'와 '한라'라고 지었다.

① An astronomer first discovered the stars naming 'Baekdu' and 'Halla' of them.
② An astronomer who first discovered the stars to name them 'Baekdu' and 'Halla.'
③ An astronomer who firstly discovered the stars named them by 'Baekdu' and 'Halla.'
④ An astronomer discovered the stars was named by 'Baekdu' and 'Halla.'
⑤ An astronomer who first discovered the stars named them 'Baekdu' and 'Halla.'

10

음악을 들으면서 일하는 것은 내가 하는 일의 효율을 높여준다.

① Work while listening to music increases the efficiency of I do.
② Working while listening to music increases the efficiency of what I do.
③ To work while listen to music increase the efficiency of what I do.
④ To working while listening to music increase the efficiency of what I do.
⑤ Working while listening to music increase the efficiency of I do.

[11~12] 다음 밑줄 친 부분의 문장 요소를 잘못 나타낸 것을 고르시오.

11

The woman next to us (ⓐ 주어) asked (ⓑ 동사) them (ⓒ 목적어) to turn down the volume (ⓓ 형용사적 수식어) a little (ⓔ 부사적 수식어).

① ⓐ ② ⓑ ③ ⓒ ④ ⓓ ⑤ ⓔ

12

The workers (ⓐ 주어) at the factory (ⓑ 형용사적 수식어) should wear (ⓒ 동사) protective gear (ⓓ 목적어) to stay safe (ⓔ 목적격보어).

① ⓐ ② ⓑ ③ ⓒ ④ ⓓ ⑤ ⓔ

13 다음 중 어법상 <u>어색한</u> 것을 고르시오.

① The trainer who owns the gym now helping me stay fit.
② Whether the team wins is a really important matter to me.
③ His knee injury while riding a bicycle was very severe.
④ To write a good story as an author needs constant efforts.
⑤ My sister who loves animals adopted an abandoned dog.

14 다음 중 어법상 옳은 것을 고르시오.

① The man on the subway was kindly gave up his seat for a pregnant woman.
② What should we eat for breakfast to stay healthily?
③ The gift she gave it to me had clearly been made in haste.
④ Simple by adding some salt, you can make better potato soup.
⑤ Everyone must be familiar with the rules before the game starts.

15 다음 빈칸에 들어갈 말이 바르게 짝지어진 것을 고르시오.

• The blind girl felt ____________ when walking down the trail.
• Have you eaten a strawberry ____________?

① fresh – sweet
② freshly – sweet as sugar
③ freshly – sweetly as sugar
④ a breeze – sweet as sugar
⑤ a breeze – sweet

〈다음부터는 서술형 주관식 문제입니다.〉

[16~19] 다음 우리말과 같도록 괄호 안의 말을 활용하여 문장을 완성하시오.

16 아침에 그녀의 몸을 스트레칭하는 것이 그녀의 평소 일과이다. (stretch, be동사)

→ ____________ her body in the morning ________ her ordinary routine.

17 사랑스러운 정원이 있는 집이 결혼한 부부에게 팔렸다. (love, with, garden, a)

→ The house ____________ was sold to the married couple.

18 그 선생님은 그의 학생들에게 포기하지 말라고 말했다. (give up)

→ The teacher told his students ________ ____________.

19 그 연설가는 한 사람을 무대에 올라오도록 했다. (come up to, have)

→ The speaker ____________ one person ____________ the stage.

[20~25] 다음 우리말과 같도록 괄호 안의 말을 바르게 배열하시오.

20

이 계획의 장점은 수정하는 것이 어렵지 않을 것이라는 겁니다. (not / be / will / that / it / difficult)

→ The advantage of this plan is ________ ____________ to modify.

21

Jessica는 그녀 옆에 앉아 있는 그 남자가 무례하다고 생각했다. (next / her / to / rude / to / sitting / man / be / the)

→ Jessica thought ______________________
______________________________________.

22

그 시스템은 그 조직이 다른 사람들과 소통하는 것을 도왔다. (organization / with / the / others / communicate)

→ This system helped ___________________
______________________________________.

23

그의 명령을 따르도록 강요받은 그 군인들은 그 작은 마을을 공격했다. (order / his / the / forced / follow / soldiers / to)

→ ______________________________________
attacked the small village.

24

그 비서는 그녀의 상관에게 제출해야 할 서류를 검토했다. (document / to / the / submit)

→ The secretary checked over ___________
___________________________ to her boss.

25

그가 오늘 목격한 그 새는 세상에서 가장 높이 난다. (that / the / he / today / bird / saw)

→ ______________________________________
flies the highest in the world.

[26~28] 다음 문장에서 어법상 어색한 부분을 찾아 바르게 고쳐 쓰시오.

26 Too much drinking can make your health to worsen.

___________________ → ___________________

27 The bed is compact but very comfortable has a soft mattress filled with memory foam.

___________________ → ___________________

28 After send your application via e-mail, please call the office.

___________________ → ___________________

[29~30] 다음 우리말과 같도록 괄호 안의 말을 활용하여 빈칸에 알맞은 말을 쓰시오.

29

집에서 일하는 나의 상사가 그 프로젝트에 대해 명확한 지시를 내렸다.
(home, give, work, clear, directions)

→ My boss _____________________________
_________________________ on the project.

30

그의 아름다운 연주에 감동한 군중들은 그에게 박수를 보냈다.
(beautiful, move, his, by, crowd, the, performance)

→ ______________________________________
________________________ applauded him.

내가 가장 취약한 부분에 대해
요점 정리를 해 보세요.

내가 가장 취약한 부분에 대해
요점 정리를 해 보세요.

EBS

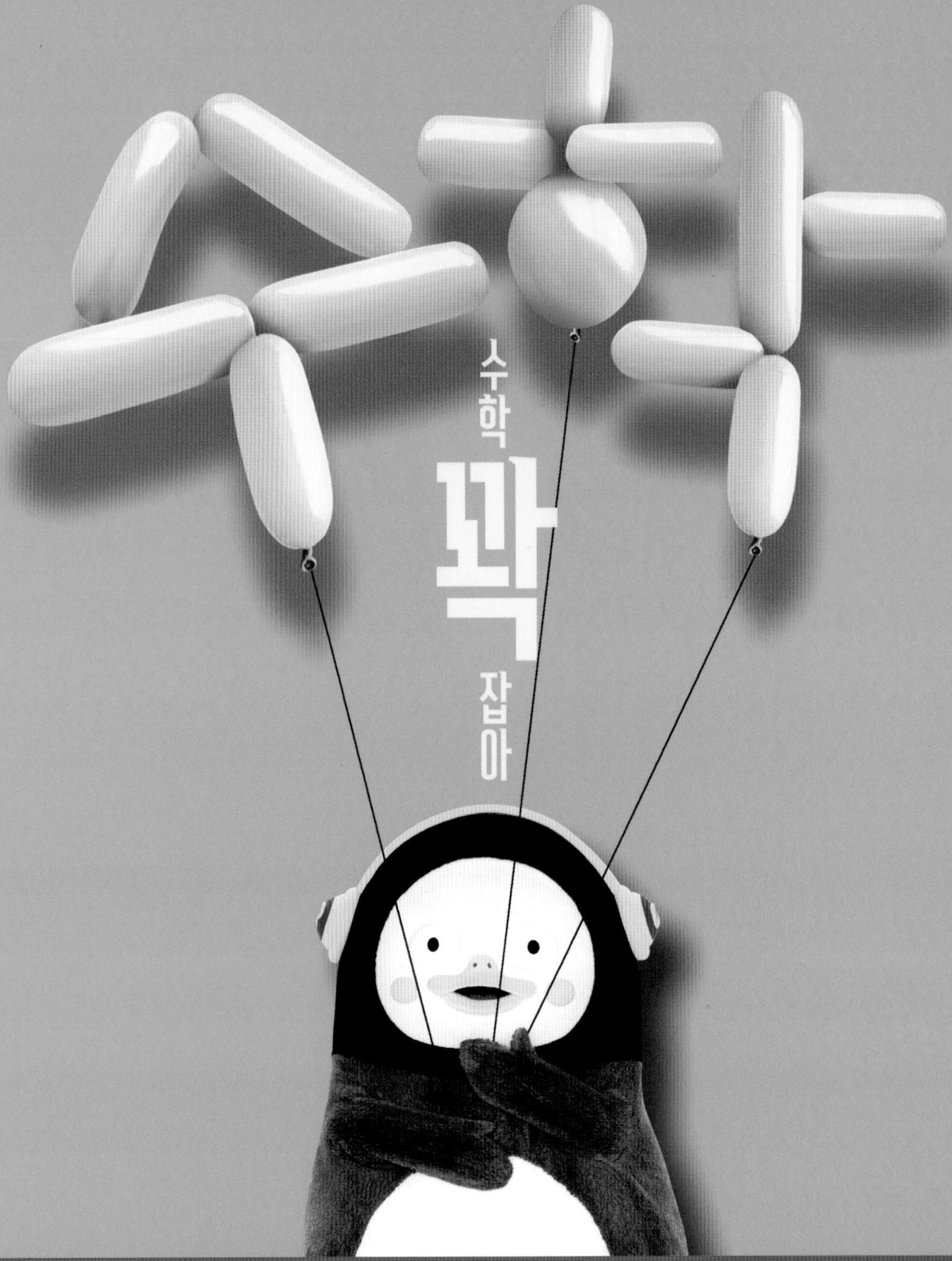
수학
수학 꽉 잡아

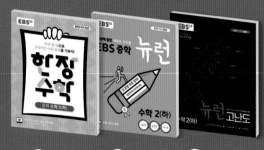

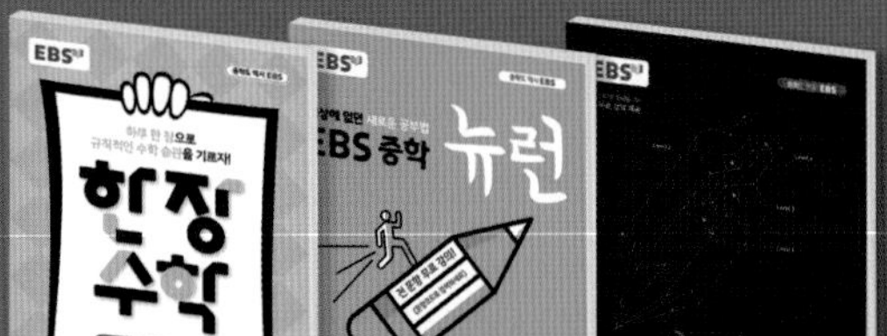
한장 수학
EBS 중학 뉴런
수학 2(하)
뉴런 고난도

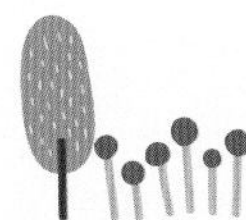

사 뿐

중학 사회
중학 역사

사회를 한 권으로
가뿐하게!

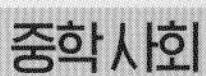

중학 사회

①-1 ②-1 ①-2 ②-2

중학 역사

①-1 ②-1 ①-2 ②-2

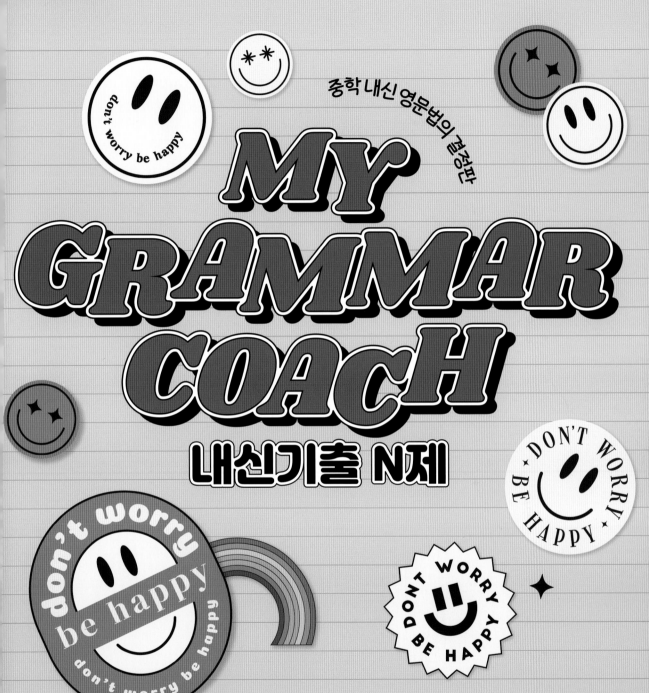

EBS

중 | 학 | 도 | 역 | 시 EBS

중학 내신 영문법의 결정판

MY GRAMMAR COACH

내신기출 N제

don't worry be happy

DON'T WORRY BE HAPPY

정답과 해설

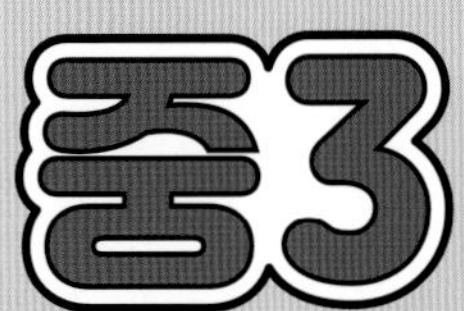

MY GRAMMAR COACH

내신기출 N제 중 3

정답과 해설

CHAPTER 01 문장의 동사

Unit 01
p. 14

A

01 M	**04** M	**07** M	**10** M
02 O	**05** M	**08** C	**11** O
03 C	**06** O	**09** O	**12** M

B

01 My dad works very hard.
S V M

02 She wrote a letter to him.
S V O M

03 The accident happened last night.
S V M

04 We went to the park last weekend.
S V M

05 He became an engineer.
S V C

06 They were standing in the rain.
S V M

07 Gina and Kevin came here by bus.
S V M

08 I saw a bird in the sky.
S V O M

내신기출 ②

Unit 02
p. 15

A

01 turned hot
02 feels rough
03 sounds nice
04 appears rotten
05 tastes good
06 smelled sweet
07 sounds like a good plan
08 looks beautiful

B

01 nicely → nice
02 exhaustedly → exhausted
03 well → good
04 taste like spicy → taste spicy
05 looks an actor → looks like an actor
06 relax → relaxed
07 sourly → sour
08 wonderfully → wonderful
09 smoothly → smooth

Unit 03
pp. 16~17

A

01 O, M	**03** C	**05** O, M	**07** O
02 O	**04** O, M	**06** C, M	**08** O, M

B

01 playing soccer with his friends, 친구들과 함께 축구하는 것을
02 that an accident happened, 사고가 발생했다는 것을
03 a very expensive car, 매우 비싼 차를
04 fighting with her friend yesterday, 어제 친구와 싸웠다는 것을
05 cleaning my room, 내 방을 청소하는 것을
06 to wash their hands before a meal, 식사 전에 손을 씻어야 한다는 것을
07 that the restaurant was open, 그 식당이 문을 열었다는 것을

C

01 explained the rules to us
02 entered the room without asking
03 resembles her sister
04 married a German
05 discussed the problem for two hours
06 had to attend a funeral
07 The boat reached the shore
08 She didn't mention anything to me

내신기출 ④

Unit 04
pp. 18~19

A

01 showed me pictures
02 told stories to us
03 sent Jane e-mails
04 gave him advice
05 bought flowers for her
06 teaches math to them

07 wrote postcards to her
08 cooked us dinner
09 bought them water
10 made pizza for me
11 give you presents
12 pass me the salt

B

01 a card to his friend
02 Korean to us
03 gloves for me
04 a bunch of flowers to her
05 a computer for her son
06 the news to everyone
07 the ticket to me
08 the book to her children
09 a kite for me

C

01 supplies books to the children
02 bought me a new watch
03 provides students with useful information
04 made cookies for us
05 provides medical care for patients
06 supply us with milk

내신기출 ③

Unit 05

p. 20

A

01 true	**06** hard	**11** angry
02 clean	**07** warm	**12** closed
03 the leader	**08** open	**13** fresh
04 bored	**09** happy	**14** healthy
05 sour	**10** Dancing Queen	

B

01 keep the beverage cool
02 it impossible to persuade her
03 leave me alone
04 it hard to believe
05 keep you awake
06 make students nervous
07 it impossible to finish the job
08 keeps the house cool
09 made me excited

Unit 06

p. 21

A

01 My parents want(V) me(O) to study hard(OC).
02 The Internet enables(V) us(O) to contact them(OC).
03 Sumi asked(V) you(O) to go shopping with her(OC).
04 Sophia told(V) her sister(O) not to do so(OC).
05 The doctor advised(V) him(O) not to smoke(OC).
06 Mr. Choi allowed(V) us(O) to enter the room(OC).
07 You want(V) them(O) to stay home after dark(OC).
08 My mom told(V) me(O) to come home early(OC).
09 Many fans expect(V) the team(O) to win(OC).
10 They persuaded(V) him(O) to come to the party(OC).
11 She always told(V) students(O) not to be late(OC).
12 I encouraged(V) Aiden(O) to try again(OC).
13 He warned(V) us(O) not to go there(OC).
14 I asked(V) Lily(O) to play tennis with me(OC).

B

01 you to meet
02 me to study
03 children to grow
04 me to close
05 the tourists not to take
06 her to sing
07 the patient not to drink
08 him to lend

내신기출 ①

Unit 07

p. 22

A

01 dancing **04** play **07** come **10** barking
02 crying **05** baking **08** called **11** running
03 touch **06** sing **09** play **12** watching

B

01 Soyun heard the boy laughing.
02 She watches some birds fly free.
03 They saw the room cleaned completely.
04 I felt my dog licking my hand.
05 She heard her friend crying.
06 We listened to Tommy play the violin.
07 You saw some kids break the window.
08 Hana listened to the singer sing a song.

내신기출 play 또는 playing / washed / burn 또는 burning

Unit 08

p. 23

A

01 made **05** tell **09** had **13** enables
02 has **06** expects **10** lets **14** asked
03 let **07** makes **11** makes **15** lets
04 make **08** had **12** makes **16** have

B

01 me see
02 them smile
03 the door painted
04 her brother borrow
05 the dishes washed
06 them exercise
07 me play
08 your bike fixed
09 me go

Unit 09

p. 24

A

01 do **05** to carry **09** signed **13** study
02 to go **06** fixed **10** to go **14** checked
03 done **07** water **11** lose
04 to be **08** to solve **12** to feel

B

01 stopped → to stop
02 understands → understand 또는 to understand
03 washed → wash 또는 to wash
04 to cut → cut
05 to correct → corrected
06 improving → improve 또는 to improve
07 to repair → repaired
08 looks for → look for 또는 to look for
09 clean → to clean

Unit 10

p. 25

A

01 saw **04** helps **07** had **10** get
02 wanted **05** keep **08** called
03 makes **06** got **09** call

B

01 to fix → fix
02 fixed → to fix
03 leave → to leave
04 left → leave 또는 leaving
05 to sing → sing 또는 singing
06 sing → to sing

내신기출 delivered / stop / to eat / preparing 또는 prepare

중간고사 • 기말고사 실전문제

pp. 26~32

객관식 정답 [01~25]

01 ⑤ **02** ② **03** ② **04** ③ **05** ①
06 ② **07** ③ **08** ③ **09** ⑤ **10** ③, ⑤
11 ④ **12** ⑤ **13** ① **14** ④ **15** ③
16 ①, ④ **17** ④ **18** ② **19** ③ **20** ③
21 ④ **22** ④ **23** ② **24** ④ **25** ③

주관식 정답 [26~50]

26 sound like → sound
27 provides with good health care for workers → provides workers with good health care 또는 provides good health care for workers
28 to → for
29 keep it warm
30 done by her husband
31 stuck somewhere
32 let, use

33 to marry
34 appeared nervous on stage yesterday
35 it difficult to change his mind
36 find it helpful to read the instructions
37 her to oversleep on weekends
38 his secretary to bring the document
39 I couldn't feel the airplane move[moving].
40 My father had me repair his broken camera.
41 Did you hear his name mentioned
42 The doctor advised her to drink lots of warm water.
43 ⓑ going → to go
44 ⓒ differently → different
45 ⓕ gone → go
46 ⓑ wash → washed
47 ⓓ for → to
48 ⓔ drew → draw 또는 to draw
49 This machine will enable us to finish the work fast.
50 She found her wallet stolen.

해설

01 provide A(사람) with B(사물): A에게 B를 제공하다

02 수여동사 get + 직접목적어 + for + 간접목적어

03 4형식: make(수여동사) + 간접목적어(me) + 직접목적어(spicy soup) / 5형식: make(사역동사) + 목적어(her son) + 원형부정사(finish)

04 수여동사 send + 직접목적어 + to + 간접목적어 / ask + 목적어 + 목적격보어(to부정사)

05 get(~해지다)이 2형식 동사로 쓰여 형용사 old를 보어로 갖는다. / 5형식: get + 목적어 + 목적격보어(to think)

06 2형식 문장으로 remain 뒤에는 형용사(calm)가 와야 한다.

07 지각동사 hear의 목적격보어로 원형부정사나 분사가 와야 한다.

08 5형식 문장으로 〈tell + 목적어 + 목적격보어(to부정사구)〉 형태가 되어야 한다.

09 ⑤ speak → to speak / tell의 목적격보어로 to부정사가 와야 한다.

10 ③ cooking → cooked / 목적어(his food)가 '요리되는'이라는 수동의 의미이므로 과거분사(cooked)가 알맞다. ⑤ stared → stare 또는 staring / 목적어(someone)와 능동의 관계를 나타내므로 지각동사(feel)의 목적격보어로 원형부정사(stare)나 현재분사(staring)가 와야 한다.

11 ④ anxiously → anxious / 감각동사(feel) 뒤에는 형용사 보어(anxious)가 와야 한다.

12 ⑤ to → for / 수여동사 get의 간접목적어 앞에는 전치사 for를 쓴다.

13 ② for change → to change / ask + 목적어 + 목적격보어(to부정사) ③ read → to read / get + 목적어 + 목적격보어(to부정사) ④ rang → ring 또는 ringing / 지각동사(hear) + 목적어 + 목적격보어(원형부정사/현재분사) ⑤ falling → fall / 사역동사(make) + 목적어 + 목적격보어(원형부정사)

14 ① usefully → useful / find + 목적어 + 목적격보어(형용사) ② wearing → to wear / encourage + 목적어 + 목적격보어(to부정사) ③ to give → give / 사역동사(let) + 목적어 + 목적격보어(원형부정사) ⑤ to → for / 수여동사 find + 직접목적어 + for + 간접목적어

15 ① going → to go / expect + 목적어 + 목적격보어(to부정사) ② take → to take / advise + 목적어 + 목적격보어(to부정사) ④ polite → to be polite / tell + 목적어 + 목적격보어(to부정사) ⑤ happily → happy / make + 목적어 + 목적격보어(형용사)

16 ②, ③, ⑤ 동사 resemble, attend, marry는 동사 뒤에 전치사를 쓰지 않고 바로 목적어를 쓰는 3형식 동사이다.

17 4형식 문장을 3형식 문장으로 전환 시 수여동사 cook, build는 전치사 for를, offer, read는 to를, ask는 of를 사용한다.

18 ask + 직접목적어 + of + 간접목적어 / ask + 목적어 + 목적격보어(to부정사) / supply A with B: A에게 B를 제공하다

19 목적어(her cellphone)와 목적격보어가 수동의 관계이므로 과거분사 fixed가 알맞다. / 사역동사(let) + 목적어 + 목적격보어(원형부정사) / help + 목적어 + 목적격보어(원형부정사 / to부정사)

20 목적어(the movie)를 설명하는 목적격보어로 형용사 boring(지루한)이 알맞다. / keep + 목적어 + 목적격보어 (형용사: quiet) / consider + 목적어 + 목적격보어(형용사: great)

21 ⓐ calmly → calm / remain+형용사 보어 ⓑ her husband → for her husband / make + 직접목적어 + for + 간접목적어 ⓓ posting → posted / 목적어(me)와 수동의 관계이므로 목적격보어로 과거분사 posted를 쓴다.

22 ⓑ stealing → stolen / 목적어(his bike)와 수동의 관계이므로 목적격보어로 과거분사(stolen)가 와야 한다.

23 ② 수여동사로 쓰인 get(~에게 …를 가져다주다) / ①, ③, ④, ⑤ get(~가 …하도록 시키다) + 목적어 + 목적격보어 (to부정사)

24 ⓑ awfully → awful / taste + 형용사 보어 ⓔ yelled → yell 또는 yelling / 목적어(people)와 능동의 관계이므로 목적격보어로 원형부정사나 현재분사가 와야 한다.

25 ⓓ explained about → explained / explain은 동사 뒤에 전치사 없이 바로 목적어가 오는 3형식 동사이다. ⓔ gave to him → gave him / give + 간접목적어 (him) + 직접목적어(some ~) ⓕ told to him not worry → told him not to worry / tell + 목적어 + 목적격보어(to부정사). to부정사의 부정형은 〈not + to부정사〉이다.

26 감각동사 sound 뒤에 형용사 보어 natural이 왔으므로 전치사 like는 생략한다.

27 provide A with B: A에게 B를 제공하다 / provide B for A: A를 위해 B를 제공하다

28 수여동사 find + 직접목적어 + for + 간접목적어

29 keep + 목적어 + 목적격보어(형용사)

30 목적어가 all the household chores이므로 목적격보어는 수동의 의미인 과거분사(done)가 알맞다.

31 목적어가 himself이므로 '갇힌(수동)'의 의미인 과거분사 (stuck)가 알맞다.

32 사역동사 let이 있는 문장으로 〈let+목적어+목적격보어 (원형부정사)〉 형태가 되어야 한다.

33 permit + 목적어 + 목적격보어(to부정사)

34 동사 appear의 보어로 형용사 nervous가 쓰인 2형식 문장이다.

35 목적어가 to부정사로 가목적어 it을 써서 나타낸다.

36 〈find + 가목적어(it) + 목적격보어(helpful) + 진목적어(to부정사)〉의 어순으로 써야 한다.

37 let의 문장은 〈allow + 목적어 + 목적격보어(to부정사)〉 형태로 바꾸어 쓸 수 있다.

38 〈get + 목적어 + 목적격보어(to부정사)〉 형태로 쓸 수 있다.

39 지각동사(feel) + 목적어(the airplane) + 목적격보어(원형부정사 / 현재분사)

40 사역동사(had) + 목적어(me) + 목적격보어(원형부정사)

41 목적어(his name)와 수동의 관계이므로 〈지각동사 (hear) + 목적어 + 목적격보어(과거분사)〉 형태로 나타낸다.

42 advise + 목적어(her) + 목적격보어(to부정사)

43 ⓑ encourage + 목적어 + 목적격보어(to부정사)

44 ⓒ smell + 형용사 보어

45 ⓕ 목적어(the bee)와 능동의 관계이므로 사역동사(had)의 목적격보어로 원형부정사가 와야 한다.

46 ⓑ 목적어(my dog)와 수동의 관계이므로 get의 목적격보어로 과거분사가 와야 한다.

47 ⓓ write + 직접목적어 + to + 간접목적어

48 ⓔ help + 목적어 + 목적격보어(원형부정사 / to부정사)

49 enable + 목적어 + 목적격보어(to부정사)

50 목적어(her wallet)와 수동의 관계이므로 〈find + 목적어 + 과거분사(stolen)〉의 형태로 나타낸다.

CHAPTER 02 시제

Unit 01

pp. 35~38

A

01 accepted, accepted
02 accomplished, accomplished
03 agreed, agreed
04 allowed, allowed
05 applied, applied
06 arranged, arranged
07 believed, believed
08 borrowed, borrowed
09 breathed, breathed
10 buried, buried
11 carried, carried
12 classified, classified
13 collected, collected
14 copied, copied
15 cried, cried
16 decided, decided
17 delayed, delayed
18 demanded, demanded
19 denied, denied
20 depended, depended
21 destroyed, destroyed
22 disagreed, disagreed
23 displayed, displayed
24 divided, divided
25 dropped, dropped
26 dried, dried
27 enjoyed, enjoyed
28 entered, entered
29 failed, failed
30 founded, founded
31 grabbed, grabbed
32 guessed, guessed
33 hurried, hurried
34 lied, lied
35 laughed, laughed
36 learned, learned
37 maintained, maintained
38 married, married
39 planned, planned
40 played, played
41 preferred, preferred
42 proved, proved
43 pulled, pulled
44 pushed, pushed
45 raised, raised
46 regretted, regretted
47 remembered, remembered
48 shared, shared
49 stayed, stayed
50 stopped, stopped
51 survived, survived
52 thanked, thanked
53 tried, tried
54 worried, worried

B

01 was, been
02 were, been
03 became, become
04 began, begun
05 bet, bet
06 bound, bound
07 bit, bitten
08 bled, bled
09 blew, blown
10 broke, broken
11 brought, brought
12 built, built
13 burst, burst
14 bought, bought
15 caught, caught
16 chose, chosen
17 came, come
18 cost, cost
19 cut, cut
20 did, done
21 drew, drawn
22 drank, drunk
23 drove, driven
24 ate, eaten
25 fell, fallen
26 fed, fed
27 felt, felt
28 fought, fought
29 found, found
30 flew, flown
31 forgot, forgotten
32 forgave, forgiven
33 froze, frozen
34 got, got/gotten
35 gave, given
36 went, gone
37 grew, grown
38 had, had

39 heard, heard
40 hid, hidden
41 hit, hit
42 held, held
43 hurt, hurt
44 kept, kept
45 knew, known
46 laid, laid
47 led, led
48 left, left
49 lent, lent
50 let, let
51 lay, lain
52 lost, lost
53 made, made
54 meant, meant
55 met, met
56 overcame, overcome
57 paid, paid
58 put, put
59 quit, quit
60 read, read
61 rode, ridden
62 rang, rung
63 rose, risen
64 ran, run
65 said, said
66 saw, seen
67 sold, sold
68 sent, sent
69 set, set
70 shot, shot
71 shut, shut
72 sang, sung
73 sat, sat
74 slept, slept
75 spoke, spoken
76 spent, spent
77 spread, spread
78 stood, stood
79 stole, stolen
80 swept, swept
81 swam, swum
82 took, taken
83 taught, taught
84 tore, torn
85 told, told
86 thought, thought
87 threw, thrown
88 understood, understood
89 woke, waken
90 wore, worn
91 won, won
92 wrote, written

내신기출 ③

Unit 02 p. 39

A

01 freezes
02 played
03 opens
04 will[is going to] be
05 invented
06 will[are going to] go
07 is
08 will[am going to] return
09 was

B

01 will[are going to] go
02 has
03 goes
04 meet
05 made
06 invented

Unit 03 p. 40

A

01 is reading
02 is leaving
03 was talking
04 was taking
05 are going
06 was packing

B

01 is taking
02 am eating
03 are coming
04 was cleaning
05 were, drinking
06 was watching
07 were doing

내신기출 ③

Unit 04 p. 41

A

01 for
02 since
03 since
04 for
05 since
06 for

B

01 have lived
02 lived
03 has been
04 was
05 has taught
06 was

내신기출 ②

Unit 05 pp. 42~43

A

01 경험
02 완료
03 결과
04 경험
05 결과
06 경험
07 완료
08 완료
09 결과
10 완료
11 경험

B

01 has just come
02 has just arrived
03 has taught, before
04 have left
05 has lost, twice
06 has already finished
07 has not done, yet
08 has never cleaned, before

C

01 has met Soyun three times

02 Have you already finished

03 have forgotten her number

04 have been to the park before

05 has not called me yet

06 Have you ever tried Spanish food

07 have already seen the movie

08 have never seen a rainbow

09 has gone to Guam

내신기출 ④

Unit 06

pp. 44~45

A

01 ever
02 yet
03 worked
04 have lived
05 has been
06 already
07 Did, visit
08 for
09 before
10 read
11 since
12 just
13 yet

B

01 has just written

02 It hasn't rained since

03 You have already finished

04 not completed the course yet

05 He has lost

06 Have you ever been

07 has never visited

08 Have we ever heard

C

01 for
02 haven't seen
03 has just arrived
04 Have you tried
05 for
06 have never smoked
07 did you go
08 I have ever seen

D

01 I have studied English since 2015.

02 Amy has worked for the company for 2 years.

03 Peter has gone to China to study.

04 Christina has lost her pen.

05 He hasn't finished his homework (yet).

06 We have been friends since we were little kids.

내신기출 ⓒ have been to → have gone to

Unit 07

pp. 46~47

A

01 was reading a book
02 stayed
03 are climbing
04 has been waiting
05 was sleeping
06 has visited
07 have been living
08 was cooking
09 walk
10 has been talking

B

01 have been shopping

02 has been reading

03 has not[hasn't] been raining

04 has been making

05 have been learning

06 have been swimming

07 have been studying

08 have been looking

09 Has, been repairing

10 have been taking

C

01 has been playing, since

02 has been washing, for

03 has been snowing since last Saturday

04 have been playing the online game for an hour

05 has been driving his car for 5 hours

06 has been working for the law firm since she was 27

D

01 have known
02 has been studying
03 since
04 have wanted
05 remember
06 watching
07 for
08 smells

내신기출 ⓑ have been meeting → have met,
ⓔ have been playing → play

Unit 08

p. 48

A

01 had seen
02 were, hadn't eaten
03 had started, entered
04 had borrowed

05 had been injured

06 came, hadn't locked

B

01 had studied

02 had bought

03 had used

04 had lost

05 had not[hadn't] set

06 had seen

07 had eaten

08 had not[hadn't] heard

Unit 09

p. 49

A

01 had been doing

02 had been trying

03 had been snowing

04 had been playing the game

05 had been watching the movie

06 had been cleaning

B

01 had been having, came

02 had been sleeping, woke

03 had been living, graduated

04 had been raining, was

05 had been building, washed

06 had been looking for, found

07 had been playing, got

08 had been working, did not[didn't] want

09 was, had been studying

내신기출 ②

중간고사 • 기말고사 실전문제

pp. 50~56

객관식 정답 [01~25]

01 ⑤	**02** ⑤	**03** ④	**04** ①	**05** ②
06 ①	**07** ④	**08** ①, ②	**09** ④	**10** ①
11 ③, ⑤	**12** ①	**13** ④	**14** ①, ③	**15** ④
16 ②	**17** ③	**18** ②	**19** ⑤	**20** ⑤
21 ③	**22** ②	**23** ③	**24** ④	
25 ①, ④, ⑤				

주관식 정답 [26~50]

26 have you taken → did you take

27 had been wanting → had wanted

28 have raised → raised

29 are preferring → prefer

30 started

31 ○

32 has been

33 has been making

34 has been filming

35 has not[hasn't] chosen

36 How long has the bad weather continued?

37 had already left when we arrived at the bus stop

38 has been living in this town for thirty years

39 has been keeping, for

40 had written, graduated from

41 They haven't begun the race yet.

42 Do you still believe in Santa Claus?

43 Have you ever experienced a war?

44 ⓑ had gone to → went to

45 ⓓ is following → was following

46 ⓔ wasn't realizing → didn't realize

47 ⓑ has been → was

48 ⓒ has been knowing → has known

49 has never been back here since he left

50 had been hiding something, we called her

해설

01 〈for + 기간〉과 현재를 나타내는 still이 함께 쓰였으므로 현재완료(have[has] + 과거분사)가 알맞다.

02 부사 yet(아직)은 완료의 의미로 현재완료의 부정문과 함께 쓰인다.

03 방문한 것(visited)보다 떠난 것(had left)이 먼저 일어난 일이므로 과거완료가 적절하다.

04 주어진 문장과 ①은 경험 ② 완료 ③, ⑤ 계속 ④ 결과

05 주어진 문장과 ②는 완료 ① 결과 ③ 경험 ④, ⑤ 계속

06 코트를 산 것이 버린 것보다 더 이전의 일이므로 코트를 산 것은 과거완료(had bought), 버린 것은 과거시제(threw away)로 나타낸다.

07 어젯밤부터 현재까지 계속 쓰고 있는 중이므로 현재완료 진행형(have[has] been + V-ing)을 써야 한다.

08 과거부터 현재까지 계속 공부해 왔다는 의미의 현재완료의 계속 용법을 나타내는 ⟨for+기간⟩ 또는 ⟨since+과거 시점⟩이 적절하다.

09 ④ seems → seemed / at that time은 과거 시점을 나타내는 부사구로 과거시제를 사용한다.

10 ① had bought → bought / 전화기가 고장난 것(had been broken)이 새 전화기를 산 것보다 먼저 일어난 일이고, 과거 시점을 나타내는 부사구(last week)가 왔으므로 과거시제(bought)로 써야 한다.

11 ③ already get → have already got[gotten] / 상황의 완료를 나타내는 현재완료(have+과거분사)가 알맞다. ⑤ lose → had lost / found out보다 이전의 일이므로 과거완료(had+과거분사)가 적절하다.

12 ① 동사 have가 '먹다'의 의미일 때는 진행형이 가능하다. ②, ③, ④, ⑤ want, belong, smell(냄새가 나다), believe는 진행형으로 쓸 수 없다.

13 ① has → had / 과거(visited) 시점보다 먼저 일어난 일이므로 과거완료 진행형이 알맞다. ② have known → had known / 과거(became) 시점보다 먼저 일어난 일이므로 과거완료가 적절하다. ③ had been loving → had loved / love는 진행형으로 쓸 수 없다. ⑤ had forgotten → forgot, gave → had given / 선생님이 답을 준 것(had given)이 잊어버린 것(forgot)보다 먼저 일어난 일이므로, 시제를 바꾸어 써야 한다.

14 ② finished → had finished, had come out → came out / 의미상 부사절의 finish가 먼저 일어난 일이므로 과거완료로, 주절의 come out을 과거시제로 써야 알맞다. ④ gone → been / have[has] gone to(~에 가 버렸다)는 결과를 나타내며, 경험을 나타낼 때는 have[has] been to(~에 가 본 적이 있다)를 쓴다. ⑤ Have → Had / 과거(started) 시점보다 먼저 일어난 일이므로 과거완료가 알맞다.

15 ④ taste가 '~한 맛이 나다'라는 의미일 때는 진행형으로 쓸 수 없으나, '~의 맛을 보다'라는 의미일 때는 진행형으로 쓸 수 있다. ⟨taste like+명사⟩는 '~와 같은 맛이 나다'라는 의미이다.

16 ① has cut → had cut / before절의 과거(put) 시점보다 먼저 일어난 일이므로 과거완료가 알맞다. ③ don't turn off → hadn't turned off / when절의 과거(left) 시점보다 먼저 일어난 일이므로 과거완료가 알맞다. ④ had hidden → hid / after절이 먼저 일어난 일이므로 과거완료로, 주절은 과거시제를 쓴다. ⑤ were you started → had you started / before절의 과거(arrived) 시점보다 먼저 일어난 일이므로 과거완료가 알맞다.

17 10분 전부터 지금까지 계속 알람이 울리므로 현재완료 진행형으로, 기간 앞에는 전치사 for를 쓴다.

18 캐나다에 여행간 경험이 있고 지금은 서울에 살고 있으므로 현재완료(경험)로 나타내야 한다. has been to(경험) / has gone to(결과)

19 말을 탄(과거완료: had ridden) 것이 이사 온(과거: moved) 것보다 더 과거 시점이다.

20 1시간 전에 방에 들어간 이후로 계속을 나타내는 현재완료시제가 와야 한다.

21 on Saturdays는 현재의 반복을 나타내므로 현재시제를 쓴다. / 미래 부사구(this coming weekend)가 왔으므로 미래시제가 알맞다. / ⟨for+기간⟩이 왔으므로 현재완료시제를 쓴다.

22 ⓒ gone → been / has gone to(결과: ~에 가 버렸다), has been to(경험: ~에 가 본 적이 있다)

23 ⓐ has been → was / 과거 부사 ago가 있으므로 과거시제가 알맞다. ⓑ am clearly remembering → cleary remember / remember는 진행형으로 쓸 수 없다.

24 ⓐ was believing → believed / believe는 진행형으로 쓸 수 없다. ⓒ trust → trusted / 완료시제를 나타내므로 과거분사를 써야 한다. ⓓ fell → will fall 또는 are going to fall / 미래 부사구(sooner or later)가 왔으므로 미래시제를 쓴다.

25 ① are you hating → do you hate / hate는 진행형으로 쓸 수 없다. ④ have met → met / when절이 과거(was) 시점을 나타내므로, 과거시제가 알맞다. ⑤ are → have been / ⟨since+과거 시점⟩이 오므로 현재완료시제가 적절하다.

26 과거를 나타내는 부사 yesterday가 왔으므로 과거시제를 써야 한다.

27 want는 진행형을 쓸 수 없다.

28 과거 부사구(in 2010)가 왔으므로 과거시제가 알맞다.

29 prefer는 진행형을 쓸 수 없다.

30 since 뒤에는 과거시제가 와야 한다.

31 〈for + 기간〉과 함께 현재완료시제가 쓰였다.

32 〈since + 과거 시점〉이 왔으므로 현재완료시제가 와야 한다.

33 so far(현재까지)가 왔으므로 현재완료 진행형이 적절하다.

34 과거 시점(last winter)부터 현재까지 진행 중인 일을 나타내므로 현재완료 진행형이 와야 한다.

35 부사 yet은 완료의 의미를 나타내는 현재완료의 부정문과 함께 쓰인다.

36 과거부터 현재까지 계속됨을 나타내는 현재완료 의문문으로 나타낸다. (How long + have[has] + 주어 + 과거분사 ~?)

37 when절은 과거(arrived), 주절은 과거완료(had left)인 문장을 완성한다.

38 〈for + 기간(for thirty years)〉이 쓰인 현재완료 진행형(has been living) 문장이다.

39 과거에 시작한 일이 현재까지 진행 중임을 나타내므로 현재완료 진행시제(has been keeping)를 쓰며, 전치사 for를 사용하여 기간을 나타낸다.

40 until절의 과거(graduated) 시점까지 진행된 일은 과거완료시제(had written)로 나타낸다.

41 부사 yet은 완료의 의미를 나타내는 현재완료의 부정문과 함께 쓰인다.

42 동사 believe를 진행형으로 쓰지 않는 것에 주의한다.

43 부사 ever와 함께 경험의 의미를 나타내는 현재완료시제를 사용한다.

44 ⓑ 과거 부사구(Last Wednesday)가 왔으므로 과거시제로 나타내야 한다.

45 ⓓ 주절이 과거시제(felt)이므로 과거진행시제를 써야 한다.

46 ⓔ 동사 realize는 진행형으로 쓸 수 없다.

47 ⓑ 과거 부사구 that day는 과거시제와 함께 쓰인다.

48 ⓒ 동사 know는 진행형으로 쓸 수 없다.

49 부사 since가 쓰인 현재완료 문장을 완성한다.

50 when절은 과거(called), 주절은 그 이전에 일어난 일이므로 과거완료 진행시제(had been hiding)로 나타낸다.

[CHAPTER 03 조동사]

Unit 01

p. 58

A

01 능력	05 능력	09 허가	13 추측
02 허가	06 허가	10 요청	14 요청
03 추측	07 금지	11 추측	
04 능력	08 능력	12 금지	

B

01 I am able to ride a bike.
02 Are you able to sing it in French?
03 They are able to speak Russian.
04 Mary is able to run fast.
05 He is not[isn't] able to play the guitar.
06 Chickens are not[aren't] able to fly very high.
07 She was not[wasn't] able to drive a car.
08 Is she able to play the game?

Unit 02

p. 59

A

01 요청	05 추측	09 허가	13 허가
02 추측	06 요청	10 요청	14 추측
03 금지	07 추측	11 추측	15 추측
04 허가	08 요청	12 추측	16 추측

B

01 may	04 may
02 may	05 may not
03 may not	

Unit 03

p. 60

A

01 의무	05 의무	09 추측	13 의무
02 의무	06 추측	10 금지	14 추측
03 추측	07 의무	11 추측	
04 의무	08 금지	12 추측	

B

01 must
02 must not
03 must not
04 must
05 must not
06 must
07 must
08 must
09 cannot

내신기출 ③

Unit 04

p. 61

A

01 had to
02 have to
03 don't
04 must
05 mustn't
06 had to
07 has
08 have to
09 must
10 have to
11 Did
12 have to
13 Do
14 mustn't

B

01 will must → will have to
02 do have not → don't have
03 have → has
04 must helped → had to help
05 doesn't have to → must not[mustn't]
06 have speak → have to speak
07 Do → Does
08 has → have
09 to sing → sing

Unit 05

p. 62

A

01 should take care of my brother
02 ought to listen to my advice
03 ought to tell the truth
04 should fasten your seat belt
05 ought not to stay up late
06 should not behave stupidly
07 ought not to give up hope
08 ought to be careful

B

01 ought not to talk
02 should drink
03 Should, ask
04 ought not to be
05 should see
06 Should, eat
07 ought to quit
08 should not[shouldn't] worry
09 ought not to spend

Unit 06

p. 63

A

01 had better
02 would rather
03 had better not
04 would rather
05 had better not
06 had better
07 would rather
08 had better

B

01 had better take
02 would rather die than show
03 Would, rather eat
04 had better wear
05 had better not eat
06 would rather not get
07 would rather sleep than watch
08 would rather not go
09 would rather walk than take

Unit 07

p. 64

A

01 used to
02 would
03 was used to
04 used to
05 used to
06 is used to
07 was used to
08 would
09 used to
10 would

B

01 used to like
02 used to have
03 used to[would] tell
04 used to wear
05 used to[would] go
06 used to live
07 used to[would] argue
08 used to[would] walk
09 used to[would] read

내신기출 ②

Unit 08

pp. 65~66

A

01 may have stayed
02 must have rained
03 cannot have arrived
04 must
05 may have forgotten
06 should
07 cannot
08 must
09 should have been

B

01 should have washed
02 could have apologized
03 may[might] have seen
04 must have read
05 cannot[can't] have forgotten
06 should have spent

C

01 must have broken
02 should have done
03 must have called
04 cannot[can't] have been
05 could have warned
06 may have been
07 should have been
08 might have been

D

01 should → could
02 could have be → should have been
03 cannot be → may[might] have been
04 could lost → must have lost
05 must had catch → must have caught
06 might not be → cannot[can't] have been
07 can't be → can't have been
08 must know → must have known

내신기출 ③

중간고사 • 기말고사 실전문제

pp. 67~72

객관식 정답 [01~25]

01 ①	**02** ③	**03** ④	**04** ⑤	**05** ①
06 ①	**07** ②	**08** ③	**09** ④	**10** ②
11 ②, ④	**12** ⑤	**13** ③	**14** ①, ②	**15** ③
16 ①	**17** ④	**18** ③	**19** ③	**20** ④
21 ③	**22** ④	**23** ②	**24** ①	**25** ③

주관식 정답 [26~50]

26 is used to be → used to be
27 ought not take → ought not to take
28 must have been tired → must be tired
29 must have been closed
30 should have taken
31 can't have finished
32 must have been written
33 rather dance than sing
34 The assistant should not have made excuses for her mistake.
35 He must have left without us.
36 I would rather wash the dishes than take care of my little sister.
37 able to breathe
38 to earn
39 We may not see polar bears
40 Dinosaurs used to live on Earth
41 Julie could have become a swimmer
42 You had better not take off your mask
43 ⓐ may lose → may have lost
44 ⓓ might left → might have left
45 ⓔ would better → had better

46 ⓐ would → used to
47 ⓒ must been → must have been
48 ⓓ had better to say → had better say
49 shouldn't have lent him her cellphone
50 cannot[can't] have been absent from the meeting

해설

01 의미상 '~일 리가 없다'는 뜻의 cannot이 적절하다.

02 의미상 '~하곤 했다'는 뜻의 would가 알맞다.

03 must: ~해야 한다(의무) / must have+과거분사: ~이었음에 틀림없다(과거의 강한 추측)

04 Could you ~?: ~해 주시겠어요? (정중한 요청) / could have+과거분사: ~했을 수도 있었다 (하지만 하지 않았다)

05 should: ~해야만 한다(의무) / should have+과거분사: ~했어야 했다(후회)

06 ought not to+동사원형: ~해서는 안 된다

07 would rather+동사원형: 차라리 ~하겠다

08 may have+과거분사: ~했을지도 모른다

09 ④ Do you → Can[Could/Will/Would] you / 요청의 의미를 나타내므로 조동사 Can[Could/Will/Would]를 써야 한다.

10 ② would be → used to be / '~이었다'라는 과거의 상태를 나타낼 때는 used to를 쓴다.

11 ② might → must / 확신한다(certain)고 했으므로 강한 추측의 조동사 must가 알맞다. ④ can → can't / 아름다운 목소리를 가지고 있다고 했으므로, '~했을 리 없다'는 뜻의 〈can't have+과거분사〉를 써야 한다.

12 ① seeing → see / be able to+동사원형 ② able to → be able to / will be able to+동사원형 ③ can → can't / 음식 맛이 형편없었으므로 '~일 리 없다'의 의미인 〈can't+동사원형〉을 쓴다. ④ has to → had to / 과거 부사구(last night)가 왔으므로 과거시제가 알맞다.

13 ① has to → must / 의미상 '~임에 틀림없다'라는 뜻의 조동사 must가 알맞다. ② can → be able to / 조동사 두 개를 연달아 쓸 수 없다. ④ must not → don't have to / don't have to+동사원형: ~할 필요가 없다 ⑤ would like listen → would like to listen / would like to+동사원형: ~하고 싶다

14 ③ might → can't / 어제 여기에 없었다고 했으므로, '~했을 리 없다'의 의미인 〈can't have+과거분사〉가 알맞다. ④ should → must / 그녀의 말을 분명히 기억한다고 했으므로, '~했었음이 틀림없다'라는 뜻의 〈must have+과거분사〉가 알맞다. ⑤ should → shouldn't / 또 거짓말을 했다고 했으므로, '~하지 말았어야 했다'의 의미인 〈shouldn't have+과거분사〉가 적절하다.

15 ③ will의 과거형 ①, ②, ④, ⑤ ~하곤 했다(과거의 습관)

16 ① ~임에 틀림없다(추측) ②, ③, ④, ⑤ ~해야 한다(의무)

17 must have+과거분사: ~했음에 틀림없다

18 didn't have to+동사원형: ~할 필요가 없었다

19 would rather not: (차라리) ~ 안 하는 게 낫겠다 / can't have+과거분사: ~이었을 리가 없다

20 shouldn't have+과거분사: ~하지 말았어야 했다 / will be able to+동사원형: ~할 수 있을 것이다

21 과거(melted)의 상황에 대한 후회이므로 〈should have+과거분사(~했어야 했다)〉 / 어렸을 때의 과거 습관을 표현하므로 〈used to+동사원형(~하곤 했다)〉 / will be able to+동사원형: ~할 수 있을 것이다

22 ⓐ overcoming → overcome / be able to+동사원형 ⓒ should come → should have come / 과거(left)의 상황에 대한 후회: should have+과거분사 ⓓ wore → wear / had better+동사원형

23 ⓐ must be → must have been / 과거(took)의 상황에 대한 강한 추측이므로 〈must have+과거분사〉가 알맞다. ⓑ can → could / 과거 시점(last night)으로 보아 과거형(could)이 알맞다. ⓓ should have watched → should watch / 미래 시점(next week)으로 보아 〈should+동사원형〉이 알맞다.

24 ⓑ doesn't ought to → ought not to / ought to의 부정형: ought not to+동사원형 ⓓ might have rained → might rain / 미래 시점(tomorrow)이 왔으므로 〈might+동사원형〉 ⓔ must have been → must be / 곧 연설을 할 거라고 했으므로 〈must+동사원형〉

25 ⓒ vegetables to meat → vegetables than meat / would rather A than B(B보다 차라리 A하겠다) ⓓ should have had → should have / today가 왔

으므로 〈should + 동사원형〉이 알맞다.

26 used to + 동사원형: ~이었다(과거의 상태) / be used to + 동사원형: ~에 사용되다

27 ought to의 부정형: ought not to + 동사원형

28 현재 시점(now)이므로 〈must + 동사원형〉이 알맞다.

29 과거의 상황에 대한 강한 추측이므로 '~했음에 틀림없다'의 의미인 〈must have + 과거분사〉로 나타낸다.

30 과거의 상황에 대한 후회이므로 '~했어야 했다'의 의미인 〈should have + 과거분사〉로 나타낸다.

31 과거의 상황에 대한 부정적 추측이므로 '~했을 리가 없다'의 의미인 〈can't have + 과거분사〉로 나타낸다.

32 과거의 상황에 대한 강한 추측: must have + 과거분사(~했음에 틀림없다)

33 would rather A than B: B보다 차라리 A하겠다

34 should not have + 과거분사: ~하지 말았어야 했다

35 must have + 과거분사: ~했음에 틀림없다

36 would rather A than B: B보다 차라리 A하겠다

37 can = be able to(~할 수 있다)

38 used to + 동사원형: ~이었다(과거의 상태)

39 미래에 대한 추측: may not + 동사원형

40 used to + 동사원형: ~이었다(과거의 상태)

41 could have + 과거분사: ~할 수도 있었다 (하지만 하지 않았다)

42 had better not + 동사원형: ~하지 않는 것이 좋겠다

43 ⓐ 과거의 상황에 대한 약한 추측이므로 〈may have + 과거분사〉: ~했을지도 모른다

44 ⓓ 과거의 상황에 대한 약한 추측이므로 〈might have + 과거분사〉: ~했을지도 모른다

45 ⓔ had better + 동사원형: ~하는 게 좋겠다

46 ⓐ '~이었다'라는 과거의 상태를 나타내므로 used to로 고쳐 써야 한다.

47 ⓒ 과거의 상황에 대한 강한 추측이므로 '~했음에 틀림없다'라는 뜻의 〈must have + 과거분사〉가 알맞다.

48 ⓓ had better + 동사원형: ~하는 게 낫다

49 shouldn't have + 과거분사: ~하지 말았어야 했다

50 can't have + 과거분사: ~했을 리가 없다

CHAPTER 04 수동태

Unit 01

pp. 74~75

A

01 was broken
02 was taken
03 were flown
04 am loved
05 was found
06 were laid

B

01 Spanish is spoken in Argentina.
02 The pianist is loved in Korea.
03 My bike was stolen yesterday.
04 The town was built in 1980.
05 Rice cookers are widely used in Asia.
06 The room was cleaned completely.
07 The guests were welcomed at the party.

C

01 were arrived → arrived
02 was occurred → occurred
03 is appeared → appears
04 is resembled by → resembles
05 was → were
06 are died → died
07 is grown not → is not[isn't] grown
08 is risen → rises

D

01 Many poems were written by the poet.
02 The telephone was invented by Bell in 1876.
03 Fast food is not preferred by them.
04 The Pyramids were built by Egyptians a long time ago.
05 My handwriting is understood only by my sister.
06 Used bottles are recycled by many people.

내신기출 ③

Unit 02 p. 76

A

01 for
02 about
03 in
04 with
05 of
06 from
07 with
08 with
09 as
10 at
11 about
12 of

B

01 of → with
02 of → with
03 to → for
04 on → at
05 with → about
06 of → with
07 to → by
08 from → of

내신 기출 ①

Unit 03 p. 77

A

01 was delivered
02 was being fixed
03 will be cleaned
04 has been polluted
05 is being built
06 will be calculated
07 had been known

B

01 The cups are being washed by me.
02 I have been raised by my grandparents.
03 Curry was being made by the students.
04 The car has been owned by him since 2020.
05 A new medicine is being developed by the researchers.
06 The company will be run by a new management team.

Unit 04 p. 78

A

01 could be solved
02 may be affected
03 Must, be canceled
04 might be used
05 must, be measured
06 should be helped
07 should be followed
08 must not be ignored
09 Can, be accepted
10 may not be removed

B

01 An e-mail should be sent by Seoeun.
02 The disease may be cured by him.
03 A car must not be driven by people under 18.
04 The flowers can be planted next to the tree.
05 Must our homework be done before dinner?
06 Many things could be bought with a hundred thousand won.

Unit 05 p. 79

A

01 was turned down
02 was put off
03 was laughed at
04 was turned off
05 was handed in
06 was made use of
07 was turned on
08 were taken care of
09 was looked down on

B

01 Children should be taken care of by parents.
02 The invitation was turned down by me.
03 The application can be handed in by you.
04 The meeting was put off to next week.
05 Juwon's experience will be made use of.
06 Other people's opinions should not be laughed at.

Unit 06 p. 80

A

01 are said to
02 It is believed
03 It is supposed that
04 is thought to be
05 It was reported that
06 is expected to be
07 It is considered that

B

01 It is known that global warming is serious. / Global warming is known to be serious.
02 It is considered that fire fighters are heroes. / Fire fighters are considered to be heroes.
03 It is said that French is hard to learn. / French is said to be hard to learn.
04 It is believed that he has a talent for teaching. / He is believed to have a talent for teaching.

05 It is thought that she is the best player on the team. / She is thought to be the best player on the team.

Unit 07

pp. 81~82

A

01 to	**04** to	**07** to	**10** to
02 of	**05** for	**08** of	**11** to
03 for	**06** to	**09** to	**12** for

B

01 was asked a hard question by the client, was asked of the lawyer by the client

02 was given a ring by her boyfriend, was given to her by her boyfriend

03 was told her address by Miso, was told to me by Miso

04 was bought for me by Hani

05 were sent to our mom for her birthday by us

06 was got[gotten] for me by my aunt

C

01 was got[gotten] for him by his father

02 was sent to her yesterday

03 were cooked for us by Dad

내신기출 should be shown to

Unit 08

p. 83

A

01 called 'Genius'

02 was told to come

03 asked to move aside

04 elected chairperson

05 encouraged to write the book

06 made interesting

07 helped to choose

08 found boring

B

01 The boy is called 'Bookworm' by them.

02 I am taught to speak politely by my parents.

03 The politician was asked to answer a few questions by the journalist.

04 Her friends were made very surprised by her.

05 All of us were made disappointed by the news.

06 He was elected the mayor by the citizens.

Unit 09

p. 84

A

01 was made to brush

02 were seen to twinkle

03 was seen playing

04 was made to read

B

01 You were seen to wave a flag by me.

02 I will not be allowed to go with you.

03 A car was heard to stop suddenly by him.

04 Something was felt to crawl on my arm.

05 A mechanic was made to fix the washing machine by us.

중간고사 • 기말고사 실전문제

pp. 85~92

객관식 정답 [01~25]

01 ②	**02** ①	**03** ④	**04** ②	**05** ③
06 ③	**07** ①	**08** ③	**09** ④	**10** ①
11 ①, ③	**12** ②	**13** ②	**14** ⑤	**15** ③, ④
16 ③	**17** ①	**18** ②, ⑤	**19** ①, ④	**20** ③
21 ⑤	**22** ④	**23** ③	**24** ②	**25** ④

주관식 정답 [26~50]

26 lain → laid

27 polluting → polluted

28 taught → were taught

29 have, been sold

30 is known for

31 The Olympics was put off by the committee because of the pandemic disease.

32 Jeju Island is thought to be the best vacation site by most people.

33 We were allowed to go outside the school during the lunchtime by the principal.

34 Free bread has been provided by us since we opened this restaurant.

35 The highest building in the world is being constructed

36 She must have been pickpocketed

37 The lobster dishes were cooked for the customers

38 was told to me by my colleague

39 was asked how to get to the station by her

40 was seen sleeping[to sleep] under the tree by me

41 might have been promoted last month

42 is believed that the number 4 is unlucky

43 ⓑ was happened → happened

44 ⓓ dissatisfied by → dissatisfied with

45 ⓕ should built → should be built

46 ⓑ hasn't been arrived → hasn't arrived

47 ⓒ worry for → worried about

48 ⓕ pleasing → pleased

49 It is said that the South Pole is covered with glaciers.

50 This building has been used as a warehouse.

해설

01 get은 직접목적어를 수동태의 주어로 하는 경우 간접목적어 앞에 전치사 for를 쓴다.

02 동사 appear는 수동태로 쓸 수 없다.

03 '기억될 것이다'의 수동의 의미를 나타내므로 조동사 수동태(조동사+be+과거분사)가 와야 한다.

04 be known for: ~로 알려져 있다 / buy는 직접목적어를 수동태의 주어로 할 경우 간접목적어 앞에 전치사 for를 쓴다.

05 be pleased with: ~에 기뻐하다 / be filled with: ~로 가득 차다

06 동사구(laugh at) 수동태는 한 단어처럼 취급하여 수동태를 만든다. (be laughed at by)

07 that절이 목적어로 쓰인 문장의 수동태로 〈It has been known that+주어+동사 ~〉로 나타낸다.

08 offer는 직접목적어를 수동태의 주어로 하는 경우 간접목적어 앞에 전치사 to를 쓴다.

09 ④ are still remained → still remain / remain은 수동태로 쓸 수 없다.

10 ① The girl was brought two kittens ~. → Two kittens were brought to the girl ~. / bring은 수동태를 만들 때, 간접목적어를 주어로 쓸 수 없다.

11 ② has being played → has been played / 현재완료 수동태: have[has]+been+과거분사 ④ was asked to him → was asked of him / ask의 직접목적어(favor)를 수동태의 주어로 하는 경우 간접목적어 앞에 전치사 of를 쓴다. ⑤ will held → will be held / 미래 수동태: will be+과거분사

12 smell, resemble, rise, fit는 수동태로 쓸 수 없다. (① was smelled → smelled ③ is resembled by → resembles ④ was risen → rose ⑤ is fitted → fits)

13 ① That is known → It is known that / that절이 목적어로 쓰인 문장의 수동태: It is+과거분사+that+주어+동사 ③ → A sand castle was made for Dan by his brother. / make는 간접목적어(Dan)를 주어로 수동태를 쓸 수 없다. ④ turn → turned / 완료 수동태: have[has]+been+과거분사 ⑤ participated → to participate / 동사 force의 수동태는 목적격보어로 to부정사를 사용한다.

14 ⑤ wasn't let to buy → wasn't allowed to buy / 사역동사 let은 수동태로 쓰지 않으며, 수동태로 쓸 때는 〈be allowed to ~〉로 나타낸다.

15 ③ for → with / be satisfied with: ~에 만족하다 ④ patrol → to patrol / 지각동사의 목적격보어가 원형부정사일 때는 수동태에서 to부정사를 쓴다.

16 ① are must handled → must be handled / 조동사 수동태: 조동사+be+과거분사 ② have been operating → have been operated / 현재완료 수동태: have[has] been+과거분사 ④ → A new bicycle was bought for her nephew by Anna. / buy는 간접목적어를 주어로 수동태를 쓸 수 없다. ⑤ was heard laugh → was heard to laugh / 지각동사의 목적격보어가 원형부정사일 때는 수동태에서 to부정사를 쓴다.

17 지각동사(saw)의 5형식을 수동태로 쓸 때, 목적격보어가 분사일 때는 그대로 분사를 쓴다.

18 ②는 간접목적어(everyone)를 주어로 한 수동태이다. ⑤는 직접목적어(pictures of her childhood)를 주어로 한 수동태로, show는 간접목적어 앞에 전치사 to를 쓴다.

19 ① that절의 주어가 문장의 주어인 수동태: that절을 to부정사로 쓴다. ④ that절이 목적어로 쓰인 문장의 수동태: It was thought that+주어+동사 ~.

20 be known to: ~에게 알려져 있다 / '그가 쓰인 것'이므로 수동태(be동사+과거분사)가 알맞다.

21 '그려지고 있었다'라는 의미의 과거진행형 수동태: was+being+과거분사 / 조동사 수동태: 조동사+be+과거분사 / '이름 지어지다'라는 수동의 의미를 나타내므로 수동태(be동사+과거분사)가 알맞다.

22 ⓐ finished → be finished / 조동사 수동태: 조동사+be+과거분사 ⓑ been arrived → arrived / arrive는 수동태로 쓸 수 없다. ⓒ that is → to be / that절의 주어가 문장의 주어인 수동태: that절을 to부정사로 써야 한다.

23 ⓑ be occurred → occur / occur는 수동태로 쓸 수 없다. ⓒ covered by → covered with / be covered with: ~로 덮여 있다

24 ⓐ reported → is reported / that절이 목적어로 쓰인 문장의 수동태: It is+과거분사+that+주어+동사 ⓓ die는 수동태로 쓸 수 없다. ⓔ buy는 간접목적어를 주어로 수동태를 쓸 수 없다.

25 ⓐ be hurried → hurry / hurry는 수동태로 쓸 수 없다. ⓒ is known that is → is known to be / that절의 주어가 문장의 주어인 수동태: that절을 to부정사로 써야 한다. ⓓ hasn't finished → hasn't been finished / 주어가 the first page이므로 완료 수동태(have[has] been+과거분사)를 써야 한다.

26 lie–lay–lain(눕다, 있다)은 목적어를 취하지 않으므로, 수동태로 쓰지 않는다. lay–laid–laid(~을 놓다)는 목적어를 취하고 수동태로 쓸 수 있다. 이 문장의 경우 〈by+행위자〉에 의해 놓임을 당하는 수동의 의미로 동사 lay의 수동태 was laid로 써야 한다.

27 현재완료 수동태: have[has] been+과거분사

28 '훈련생들이 강사에게 교육을 받았다'는 수동의 의미가 되어야 하므로 수동태(were taught)로 고쳐 써야 한다.

29 주어(Most of the goods)가 이미 팔렸으므로 완료 수동태(have been+과거분사)로 나타낸다.

30 be known for: ~로 알려져 있다

31 동사구(put off)를 수동태로 전환할 때는 하나의 단어처럼 취급하여 쓴다. (was put off by)

32 that절의 주어가 문장의 주어인 수동태: that절을 to부정사로 써야 한다.

33 사역동사 let을 수동태로 쓸 때는 〈be allowed to ~〉로 나타낸다.

34 완료 수동태(have+been+과거분사)로 만들며, 주어의 수 일치에 주의한다.

35 '지금 건설되고 있다'는 의미의 진행형 수동태(be동사+being+과거분사)로 나타낸다.

36 조동사(must)와 함께 쓰인 완료 수동태(must have been+과거분사)로 나타낸다.

37 '요리되었다'라는 수동의 의미로 〈주어+be동사+과거분사+for 대상+by 행위자〉 형태의 수동태로 나타낸다.

38 간접목적어(I)를 주어로 하는 수동태를 직접목적어(A rumor about my boss)를 주어로 하는 수동태로 바꾸어 쓸 경우, 동사 tell은 간접목적어 앞에 전치사 to를 쓴다.

39 직접목적어(How to ~ station)를 주어로 하는 수동태를 간접목적어(A police officer)를 주어로 하는 수동태로 바꾸어 쓸 경우, 전치사 of를 생략하고, 직접목적어를 동사 뒤에 그대로 쓰고, 〈by+행위자〉가 오도록 해야 한다.

40 지각동사(see)의 목적격보어는 수동태에서 to부정사나 현재분사로 쓴다.

41 '승진되다(수동)'와 '~했을지도 모른다'라는 의미를 나타내야 하므로 might have been promoted로 쓴다.

42 that절이 목적어로 쓰인 문장의 수동태: It is+과거분사+that+주어+동사

43 ⓑ 동사 happen은 수동태로 쓸 수 없다.

44 ⓓ be dissatisfied with: ~에 불만족스럽다

45 ⓕ 주어가 Your self-esteem(자존감)이므로 '세워지다'라는 수동의 의미를 나타내야 한다. (조동사+be+과거분사)

46 ⓑ 동사 arrive는 수동태로 쓸 수 없다.

47 ⓒ be worried about: ~에 대해 걱정하다

48 ⓕ be pleased with: ~에 기뻐하다

49 that절이 목적어로 쓰인 문장의 수동태: It is+과거분사+that+주어+동사

50 현재완료 수동태: have[has] been+과거분사

CHAPTER 05 부정사

Unit 01
pp. 94~95

A

01 to help
02 to be
03 to fight
04 to read
05 To win
06 to build
07 to answer
08 To prepare

B

01 need to take a walk
02 promised not to be late
03 difficult to study English
04 for your health to work out
05 not to disturb

C

01 It is annoying to hear people keep complaining.
02 It is simple to order books online.
03 It is not easy to use public transportation abroad.
04 It is difficult to pronounce some French words correctly.

D

01 planned to retire at the age of 60
02 to sail across the ocean
03 agreed not to use our smart phone
04 To deliver a speech in front of people
05 not fair to treat students differently
06 dangerous to cross the street at the red light

내신기출 ②

Unit 02
p. 96

A

01 for
02 for
03 of
04 of
05 for
06 of
07 of
08 for
09 for
10 for

B

01 for → of
02 wearing → to wear
03 check → to check
04 of → for
05 for → of

내신기출 ②

Unit 03
p. 97

A

01 how to use
02 what to wear
03 where to go
04 when to stop
05 where to visit
06 how to solve
07 what to do
08 when to start

B

01 when to turn off the lights
02 where to shop for Christmas
03 when I should go to bed
04 how to order a meal
05 what I should eat in Italy

Unit 04
p. 98

A

01 a chance to see a lion
02 many things to do right now
03 some friends to help him
04 bought a house to live in
05 something warm to drink
06 old pictures to show us
07 chairs to sit on in the park
08 nothing new to read

B

01 write → write on
02 answer → to answer
03 depend → depend on
04 eat → eat with
05 warm something → something warm
06 attending → to attend
07 of → to
08 what do → what to do
09 take care → take care of

Unit 05 p. 99

A

01 is to arrive
02 are not to smoke
03 were to be singers
04 are to succeed
05 was to be found
06 is to marry Tom
07 are to fasten their seat belts

B

01 is to visit Washington D.C.
02 was to come back home
03 are to be a good pianist
04 are to memorize the poem

내신기출 ②

Unit 06 pp. 100~101

A

01 나는 유럽에 가기 위해서 돈을 저축했다.
02 나는 너를 다시 보게 되어 기쁘다.
03 James 씨는 만족시키기 매우 어렵다.
04 그녀는 그런 해답을 생각해 내다니 똑똑하다.
05 그는 자라서 훌륭한 음악가가 되었다.
06 사람들은 음식을 데우기 위해 전자레인지를 사용한다.
07 우리는 네가 그 경기에서 이겼다는 것을 들어서 기쁘다.
08 그 커피 자판기는 사용하기 쉽다.
09 위험을 무시하다니 너는 부주의했다.

B

01 happy to win the gold medal
02 so as to walk his dog
03 grew up to be a scientist
04 clever to reserve the tickets in advance
05 hard for foreigners to learn

C

01 pleased to meet our cousins
02 lucky to win the lottery
03 very confusing to understand
04 are excited to go to the theme park
05 awoke to find himself famous

D

01 seen → to see
02 improving → to improve
03 to not → not to
04 miss → to miss
05 enjoy → to enjoy
06 remembering → to remember
07 not in order to → in order not to

내신기출 ④

Unit 07 p. 102

A

01 명사	**04** 형용사	**07** 형용사	**10** 명사
02 부사	**05** 명사	**08** 명사	
03 명사	**06** 부사	**09** 부사	

B

01 are to meet
02 decided where to stay
03 something hot to drink
04 a colleague to talk with
05 not to catch a cold
06 It is difficult for you to read

Unit 08 pp. 103~104

A

01 fast enough	**06** can
02 too	**07** careful
03 to run	**08** that
04 too	**09** so
05 enough	**10** too

B

01 clever enough to answer
02 so anxious that he couldn't sleep
03 too tired to clean
04 so selfish that he can't help others
05 too late to get up early
06 so high that she could be

C

01 too exhausted to go up

02 so complicated that they can't follow

03 good enough to win

04 so clear that we could understand

05 too shy to talk to

06 so light that I can carry

D

01 that can't → that he can't

02 too → so

03 freeze → to freeze

04 enough interesting → interesting enough

05 too brave → brave enough

내신 기출 to

Unit 09 pp. 105~106

A

01 to like, like

02 seemed, knew

03 have, studied

04 have, was

05 broken, had

B

01 seem to be nervous

02 seemed that he was sick

03 seemed that the thief had stolen

04 seems that she completed

05 seems that they didn't reach

06 to understand the question

07 have been disappointed with

C

01 seems that you are interested in

02 seems to have something to say

03 seemed that all the servers were busy

04 seems to have found the evidence

05 seemed that the teacher had known what to do

06 seems to have majored in economics

D

01 studied → study

02 She → It

03 tells → told

04 being → to be 또는 being 삭제

05 sleep → have slept

내신 기출 ③

Unit 10 p. 107

A

01 ○

02 to work

03 ○

04 to spend

05 ○

06 ○

07 to start

08 ○

B

01 advised him to lose some weight

02 told us to read

03 doesn't allow the guests to smoke

04 want you to understand

05 advised the children not to eat

06 asked me to turn down

Unit 11 p. 108

A

01 work out

02 to give

03 tell

04 laugh

05 make

06 do

07 show

08 to make

09 look

10 to learn

B

01 made me be late for school

02 had her accept

03 doesn't let us eat

04 you not to meet

05 has her sons mow

06 make us buy

Unit 12 p. 109

A

01 touch

02 take

03 screaming

04 not to leave

05 stand

06 fly

07 burning

B

01 to wash

02 crawl 또는 crawling

03 sneak 또는 sneaking

04 bark 또는 barking

05 to brush

06 ride 또는 riding

07 return

내신기출 shake 또는 shaking / go / to dance

Unit 13

p. 110

A

01 To

02 worse

03 sum

04 Needless

05 with

06 Strange

07 not

08 you

B

01 so to speak

02 To be sure

03 To make a long story short

04 To make matters worse

05 Strange to say

06 To sum up

중간고사 • 기말고사 실전문제

pp. 111~116

객관식 정답 [01~25]

01 ③	**02** ④	**03** ④	**04** ②	**05** ①
06 ③	**07** ⑤	**08** ③	**09** ②, ⑤	**10** ①, ④
11 ③	**12** ①	**13** ⑤	**14** ③	**15** ①
16 ②	**17** ①	**18** ③	**19** ②	**20** ⑤
21 ③	**22** ②	**23** ③	**24** ④	**25** ③

주관식 정답 [26~50]

26 to come

27 ○

28 to take care → to take care of

29 paying → to pay

30 of him → for him

31 to go out

32 to realize

33 too fast to

34 are not to get a cold, you should wear warmer clothes

35 let me know what to choose next

36 sincere to get up early every morning

37 very tricky to pronounce some French words

38 strong that he could save the world

39 have pretended to like me

40 selfish of him not to help others

41 was looking for something to sit on

42 tastes too sour to drink

43 ⓐ how get → how to get

44 ⓒ walking → to walk

45 ⓓ wanted go → wanted to go

46 ⓒ enough brave → brave enough

47 ⓔ proud see → proud to see

48 ⓕ to not mention → not to mention

49 seemed to have been sick

50 You are to turn in the assignment

해설

01 to부정사의 부정형: not+to부정사

02 get+목적어+목적격보어(to부정사)

03 seem+to have+과거분사: ~했던 것 같다(뒤에 yesterday가 쓰인 것에 유의한다.)

04 so+형용사+that+주어+can+동사원형: 너무 ~해서 …할 수 있다 / so to speak: 말하자면

05 help+목적어+목적격보어(to부정사/원형부정사)/지각동사(see)+목적어+목적격보어(원형부정사/현재분사)

06 -one으로 끝나는 대명사+형용사+to부정사

07 when+to부정사: 언제 ~할지(= when+주어+should+동사원형)

08 주어에 수 일치하여 현재 시제를 사용하고, 부사적 용법의 to부정사(~하기 위해)를 사용한다.

09 too+형용사+to부정사: 너무 ~해서 …할 수 없다(= so+형용사+that+주어+can't[couldn't]+동사원형)

10 where + to부정사: 어디에 ~할지(= where + 주어 + should + 동사원형)

11 ③ of you → for you / 형용사 good이 오므로 to부정사의 의미상 주어는 〈for + 목적격〉으로 나타낸다.

12 ① stay → to stay / want + 목적어 + 목적격보어(to부정사)

13 to부정사가 수식하는 명사가 to부정사구의 전치사의 목적어일 때는 전치사를 함께 써야 한다.
① to play → to play with
② to write → to write with
③ to live → to live in
④ to talk → to talk to[with]

14 ① to understanding → to understand / too+형용사+to부정사: …하기엔 너무 ~한 ② to call → call / when+주어+should+동사원형: 언제 ~할지(= when+to부정사) ④ to seeing → to see / 〈be동사+to부정사(예정)〉로 to 다음에 동사원형이 와야 한다. ⑤ enough held → enough to hold / 형용사 + enough + to부정사: …하기에 충분히 ~한

15 〈be동사+to부정사〉로, '~해야 한다(의무)'의 뜻으로 조동사 must로 바꾸어 쓸 수 있다.

16 〈be동사+to부정사〉 문장으로 ②는 '의무', 나머지는 '예정'의 의미를 나타낸다.

17 ① to부정사의 부사적 용법(결과) ②, ③, ④, ⑤ to부정사의 부사적 용법(목적)

18 so + 형용사 + that + 주어 + can + 동사원형: …하기에 충분히 ~한(= 형용사 + enough + to부정사)

19 〈seem(s) + to부정사〉는 〈It seems that절 ~〉로 바꾸어 쓸 수 있다. seems 뒤에 〈to have + 과거분사〉가 왔으므로 that절의 동사는 과거시제(knew)가 와야 한다.

20 strange to say: 이상한 이야기지만 / too + 형용사+to부정사: …하기에 너무 ~하다

21 사람의 성격이나 성품을 나타내는 형용사(polite) 뒤에 to부정사의 의미상 주어는 〈of + 목적격〉을 쓴다. / how + to부정사: ~하는 방법 / seemed + to have + 과거분사: ~했었던 것으로 보였다

22 빈칸 뒤에 더 큰 사이즈가 있는지 묻는 말로 보아 작아서 맞지 않는다는 내용의 말이 와야 알맞다. (too + 형용사+to부정사: 너무 ~해서 …할 수 없다)

23 ⓐ to talk → to talk about / to부정사가 수식하는 명사가 to부정사구의 전치사의 목적어이므로 전치사를 함께 쓴다. ⓒ are → is / to부정사 주어는 단수 취급한다.

24 ⓒ to lying → to lie / 보어로 쓰인 to부정사로, to 다음에 동사원형이 와야 한다.

25 ⓐ what to make → how to make / 의미상 '파스타를 만드는 방법'이 적절하므로 〈how + to부정사〉가 알맞다. ⓒ chose to not → chose not to / to부정사의 부정: not+to부정사 ⓓ to move → to move in / to부정사가 수식하는 명사가 to부정사구의 전치사의 목적어이므로 전치사를 생략하지 않는다.

26 invite + 목적어 + 목적격보어(to부정사)

27 '~할 운명이다'라는 의미의 〈be동사+to부정사〉로 쓰였다.

28 to부정사구로 수식하는 명사가 to부정사구의 전치사의 목적어이므로 전치사를 함께 써야 한다.

29 tell + 목적어 + 목적격보어(to부정사)

30 일반 형용사(important) 뒤에는 to부정사의 의미상 주어로 〈for + 목적격〉을 쓴다.

31 allow + 목적어 + 목적격보어(to부정사)

32 to부정사의 부사적 용법 '~해서 결국 …하다(결과)'의 의미로 사용되었다.

33 too + 부사 + to부정사: 너무 ~해서 …할 수 없다

34 '~하려면'이라는 의도 · 의지를 나타내는 〈be동사+to부정사〉 형태로 to부정사의 부정형은 to부정사 앞에 not을 쓴다.

35 what + to부정사: 무엇을 ~할지

36 '~하다니 …한(판단의 근거)'의 의미를 나타내는 to부정사의 부사적 용법으로 쓰인 문장이다.

37 주어로 쓰인 to부정사구(To pronounce some French words)를 가주어 it을 사용하여 〈가주어(It) ~ 진주어(to부정사구)〉 문장으로 나타낸다.

38 형용사 + enough + to부정사: …하기에 충분히 ~한 (= so + 형용사 + that + 주어 + can + 동사원형)

39 주절의 동사가 seemed, that절의 동사가 had pretended이므로 〈seemed + to have + 과거분사〉로 바꾸어 쓸 수 있다.

40 〈It is+사람의 성격이나 성품을 나타내는 형용사+of+목적격+to부정사〉 형태로 나타낸다.

41 sit on something이므로 수식하는 명사가 to부정사구의 전치사의 목적어이므로 전치사를 함께 써야 한다. (-thing+to부정사)

42 too+형용사+to부정사: …하기에 너무 ~하다

43 ⓐ how+to부정사: ~하는 방법

44 ⓒ it takes+시간+to부정사: ~하는데 (시간)이 … 걸리다

45 ⓓ 동사 want는 to부정사를 목적어로 취한다.

46 ⓒ 형용사+enough+to부정사: …하기에 충분히 ~한

47 ⓔ '~하다니 …한(판단의 근거)'의 의미를 나타내는 부사적 용법으로 쓰인 to부정사로 써야 한다.

48 ⓕ not to mention ~: ~은 말할 것도 없이

49 '보였던 것'은 과거시제(seemed), '아팠던 것'은 더 이전의 일이므로 〈to have+과거분사〉를 사용해서 나타낸다.

50 '~해야 한다(의무)'라는 의미를 나타내는 〈be동사+to부정사〉를 사용해서 나타낸다.

CHAPTER 06 동명사와 분사

Unit 01

pp. 118~119

A

01 S **02** C **03** O **04** S **05** O **06** P.O. **07** O **08** O **09** S **10** P.O. **11** P.O. **12** O

B

01 매일 아침 조깅하는 것은
02 외국에서 공부하는 것을 고려했다
03 우주를 여행하는 것이다
04 거짓말을 했다는 것을 부인했다
05 기사를 쓰는 것이다
06 대중교통을 이용하는 것을 꺼리지 않는다
07 우승자가 되는 것을 상상할 수 있었다
08 너를 설득하려고 애쓰는 것을 포기했다
09 불평하는 것을 멈추지 않았다

C

01 cook → cooking
02 get → getting 또는 to get
03 learned → learning
04 are → is
05 to make → making
06 played → playing
07 go → going
08 say → saying

D

01 prevented, from dying
02 being chosen 또는 to be chosen
03 didn't mind waiting
04 sorry for being
05 talk about protecting the environment

내신기출 ②

Unit 02

pp. 120~121

A

01 traveling by car
02 to learn
03 to cry
04 increasing

05 to read **06** to work

B

01 playing
02 designing
03 using
04 to reduce
05 cheating
06 to eat
07 to start

C

01 don't remember talking
02 tried not to cry
03 stopped to rest
04 forgot to lock
05 stopped digging
06 remember to go
07 tried taking part in

D

01 to quit → quitting
02 to post → posting
03 staying → to stay
04 to snow → snowing
05 to drive → driving
06 informing → to inform

내신기출 ④

Unit 03

p. 122

A

01 not being
02 not finishing
03 you
04 winning
05 not going
06 his
07 Her
08 their
09 my

B

01 your[you] being rude
02 not having
03 not polluting the air
04 your[you] completing the course
05 not applying to a university

Unit 04

p. 123

A

01 is
02 was
03 did not[didn't]
04 had not[hadn't]
05 stole
06 had stolen

B

01 enjoy taking pictures
02 Being served
03 hate being laughed at
04 being chosen
05 prefer not being helped

Unit 05

pp. 124~125

A

01 went
02 reading
03 teaching
04 looking
05 worth
06 finding
07 doing
08 use
09 reading
10 couldn't

B

01 is worth visiting
02 feel like drinking
03 couldn't help loving
04 looking forward to going
05 is used to drinking
06 Upon arriving

C

01 inviting → invited
02 find → finding
03 to listen → listening
04 Who → When
05 stay → staying
06 to prepare → preparing

D

01 couldn't help telling the secret
02 don't feel like going out
03 is worth seeing
04 a plan to go swimming
05 spend too much time playing

06 is used to being with
07 It was no use calming down

내신기출 ②

Unit 06
p. 126

A

01 동명사 03 현재분사 05 진행형 07 현재분사
02 수동태 04 동명사 06 완료형

B

01 speaking
02 finished
03 interesting
04 arrested
05 waiting
06 Reading[To read]
07 closed
08 looking, hearing

Unit 07
p. 127

A

01 baby, 자고 있는 아기
02 parts, 망가진 부분들
03 door, 닫힌 문
04 car, 도난당한 차
05 a baby, 침대에서 자고 있는 아기
06 insects, 날고 있는 곤충들
07 skin, 탄 피부
08 the car, 지난주에 도난당한 그 차

B

01 leading, The man
02 deleted, files
03 surrounding, The fence
04 relaxing, vacation
05 making, The homework
06 gathering, People
07 composed, The song
08 interested, Anyone

내신기출 ①

Unit 08
p. 128

A

01 The new online game
02 He
03 the song
04 the boy
05 We
06 someone
07 Our achievement
08 a tree
09 one box
10 She
11 some bees
12 They

B

01 crowded, the beach
02 thrilling, Their adventure
03 taking, the suspect
04 talking, my mom
05 discovered, The missing child

Unit 09
pp. 129~130

A

01 tiring
02 moved
03 disappointed
04 shocked
05 disappointing
06 excited
07 shocking
08 tired
09 exciting

B

01 confusing
02 confused
03 bored
04 boring
05 amazing
06 amazed
07 exhausted
08 exhausting
09 depressed
10 depressing

C

01 pleased
02 satisfying
03 moved
04 surprised, shocking

D

01 were embarrassed when we got the test result
02 This book has touching stories.
03 were disappointed because the trip was canceled

내신기출 ②

Unit 10
p. 131

A

01 현재분사 04 동명사 07 현재분사
02 현재분사 05 동명사 08 동명사
03 동명사 06 현재분사

B

01 경찰관이 되는 것
02 대기실
03 흰 재킷을 입은 여자
04 마실 물
05 매혹적인 이야기
06 충격적인 소식
07 운동화 한 켤레
08 달려가는 중이었다

내신기출 ①

중간고사 • 기말고사 실전문제 pp. 132~138

객관식 정답 [01~25]

01 ②	**02** ③	**03** ④	**04** ②	**05** ③
06 ③	**07** ①	**08** ⑤	**09** ⑤	**10** ③
11 ③, ④	**12** ③	**13** ①	**14** ④, ⑤	**15** ②
16 ③	**17** ⑤	**18** ④	**19** ②	**20** ②
21 ③	**22** ④	**23** ③	**24** ②	**25** ⑤

주관식 정답 [26~50]

26 taking
27 ○
28 taken
29 to charge
30 singing → sung
31 to open → opening
32 turned on
33 having
34 not being punished
35 turning up
36 There is no parking here before 11 a.m.
37 about a boy finding his mom was really moving
38 She is sorry about having ignored her son's words.
39 Does he remember to visit the nursing home
40 is proud of his father being a musician
41 was fascinated by the exotic scenery
42 The police found a clue hidden
43 ⓐ embarrassing → embarrassed
44 ⓔ bored → boring
45 ⓕ to read → reading
46 ⓐ give → gives
47 ⓑ to watch → watching
48 ⓕ use → using
49 He prefers cooking at home to eating out.
50 We can't help watching her amazing performance.

해설

01 remember+동명사: ~했던 것을 기억하다

02 be worth -ing: ~할 가치가 있다

03 '날고 있는'이라는 능동의 뜻을 나타내는 현재분사가 와야 한다.

04 enjoy는 동명사를 목적어로 취한다.

05 refuse는 to부정사를 목적어로 취한다.

06 regret+to부정사: ~하게 되어 유감이다

07 '신나는'이라는 감정을 유발하는 것이므로 현재분사(exciting)가 알맞다. / keep+동명사: 계속 ~하게 하다

08 be used to -ing: ~에 익숙하다

09 ⑤ to drink → drinking / quit은 동명사를 목적어로 취한다.

10 ③ to collect → collecting / be busy -ing: ~하느라 바쁘다

11 ③ to camp → camping / go -ing: ~하러 가다 ④ to buy → buying / spend+시간[돈]+-ing: 시간[돈]을 ~하는 데 쓰다

12 ① to visit → to visiting / look forward to -ing: ~하기를 고대하다 ② go → going / drinking과 병렬 구조를 이루므로 동명사로 고쳐 써야 한다. (What about -ing?: ~하는 게 어때?) ④ to love → loving / cannot help -ing: ~하지 않을 수 없다 ⑤ to hike → hiking / go -ing: ~하러 가다

13 ② embarrassed → embarrassing / 당황스러운 감정을 유발하는 것이므로 현재분사가 알맞다. ③ interested → interesting / 흥미를 유발하는 것이므로 현재분사가 알맞다. ④ confused → confusing / 혼란스러운 감정을 유발하는 것이므로 현재분사가 적절하다. ⑤ boring → bored / 지루한 감정을 느끼는 것이므로 과거분사가 알맞다.

14 ① stood → standing / '서 있는'이라는 능동의 의미로 현재분사가 알맞다. ② writing → written / '쓰인'이라는 수동의 의미를 나타내므로 과거분사가 알맞다. ③ breaking → broken / '깨진'이라는 수동의 의미를 나타내므로 과거분사가 알맞다.

15 remember+to부정사: ~할 것을 기억하다(미래의 일)

16 ③ 현재분사 ①, ②, ④, ⑤ 동명사

17 ⑤ 동명사 ①, ②, ③, ④ 현재분사

18 동명사의 완료형(having cried)으로 보아, 과거의 일을 부인하고 있는 것이므로 주절은 현재시제, that절은 과거시제가 되어야 한다.

19 동명사의 의미상 주어가 him이므로, 그(he)가 질문하는 것이라는 의미를 가진 ②가 적절하다.

20 enjoy는 동명사를 목적어로 취하며, '떨어진'이라는 수동의 의미인 과거분사를 사용한다.

21 동명사구 주어는 단수 취급한다. / 수동태 문장으로 imagine은 동명사만을 목적어로 취하므로 동명사 수동태(being+과거분사)가 알맞다. / '결함이 있는'이라는 수동의 의미로 goods를 설명하는 과거분사(damaged)가 적절하다.

22 remember+to부정사: ~할 것을 기억하다(미래의 일), 앞 문장에서 좌회전하라고 했음에 유의한다.

23 ⓐ fascinated → fascinating / '매력적인'이라는 감정을 유발하는 것이므로 현재분사가 알맞다. ⓒ accepting → to accept / refuse는 to부정사를 목적어로 취한다.

24 ⓐ to play → playing / practice는 동명사를 목적어로 한다. ⓑ burned → burning / '타는'이라는 능동의 의미를 나타내는 현재분사가 적절하다. ⓒ exhausting → exhausted / '지친'이라는 감정을 느끼는 것이므로 과거분사가 알맞다.

25 ⓐ deal → dealing / when it comes to -ing: ~하는 것에 관한 한 ⓑ choosing → chosen / 주어(The lady)가 '선택되는'이라는 수동의 의미를 나타내므로 과거분사가 알맞다.

26 동사 suggest는 동명사를 목적어로 취한다.

27 동명사의 의미상 주어는 동명사 앞에 소유격이나 목적격을 쓴다.

28 '병원으로 이송된'이라는 수동의 의미를 나타내므로 과거분사(taken)로 써야 한다.

29 forget+to부정사: ~할 것을 잊다(미래의 일)

30 'Lady Gaga에 의해 불려진'이라는 수동의 의미를 나타내므로 과거분사(sung)로 고쳐 써야 한다.

31 regret+동명사: ~했던 것을 후회하다(과거의 일)

32 '불이 켜진'이라는 수동의 의미를 나타내므로 과거분사(turned on)로 써야 한다.

33 on -ing: ~하자마자

34 동명사의 부정형: not+동명사 / 동명사 수동태: being+과거분사

35 mind는 동명사를 목적어로 취한다.

36 There is no -ing: ~할 수 없다

37 '엄마를 찾는 소년'이라는 의미가 되도록 현재분사구(finding his mom)가 a boy를 수식하며, 감정을 느끼게 하는 과거분사(moving)가 보어로 쓰였다.

38 과거에 있었던 일에 대해 말하는 시점이 현재이므로 〈현재시제+전치사+완료 동명사(having+과거분사)〉의 형태로 나타낸다.

39 remember+to부정사: ~할 것을 기억하다

40 전치사 of 뒤에 〈의미상 주어+동명사〉를 쓴다.

41 Everyone이 느끼는 감정을 설명하므로 과거분사를 쓴다.

42 a clue를 설명하므로 수동의 의미(숨겨진)인 과거분사를 사용한다.

43 ⓐ 주어(You)가 감정을 느끼는 것이므로 과거분사(embarrassed)가 알맞다.

44 ⓔ '지루하게 만드는' 감정을 유발하는 것이므로 현재분사(boring)가 적절하다.

45 ⓕ give up은 동명사를 목적어로 한다.

46 ⓐ 동명사구(Not driving ~ to work)는 단수 취급한다.

47 ⓑ enjoy는 동명사를 목적어로 취한다. 앞에 나온 reading과 병렬 구조를 이룬다.

48 ⓕ get used to -ing: ~에 익숙해지다

49 prefer A to B: B하는 것보다 A하는 것을 선호하다

50 cannot help -ing: ~할 수밖에 없다

CHAPTER 07 비교 표현

Unit 01
p. 140

A

01 is as cold as
02 is as hot as
03 are not[aren't] as[so] rich as
04 is as tall as
05 is not[isn't] as[so] heavy as
06 are as bright as
07 is as smart as
08 is not[isn't] as[so] thick as

B

01 is as popular as
02 is not[isn't] as[so] warm as
03 is not[isn't] as[so] expensive as
04 cannot[can't] go as[so] fast as
05 is not[isn't] as[so] famous as
06 are not[aren't] as[so] friendly as

Unit 02
p. 141

A

01 get up as early as possible
02 arrive as soon as you can
03 eat as much as possible
04 walk as fast as you can
05 respond as quickly as possible
06 visited as often as you could
07 study as hard as possible

B

01 as you can
02 as I could
03 as, as possible
04 as she could
05 as often as

내신기출 can → could

Unit 03
pp. 142~145

A

01 abler, ablest
02 angrier, angriest
03 worse, worst
04 worse, worst
05 more beautiful, most beautiful
06 bigger, biggest
07 more boring, most boring
08 braver, bravest
09 brighter, brightest
10 busier, busiest
11 more careful, most careful
12 more carefully, most carefully
13 cheaper, cheapest
14 cleaner, cleanest
15 colder, coldest
16 more comfortable, most comfortable
17 more curious, most curious
18 more dangerous, most dangerous
19 darker, darkest
20 deeper, deepest
21 more delicious, most delicious
22 more difficult, most difficult
23 more diligent, most diligent
24 dirtier, dirtiest
25 easier, easiest
26 more easily, most easily
27 more exciting, most exciting
28 more expensive, most expensive
29 more famous, most famous
30 faster, fastest
31 fatter, fattest
32 more fluently, most fluently
33 more foolish, most foolish
34 fresher, freshest
35 friendlier, friendliest
36 better, best
37 greater, greatest

38 more handsome, most handsome
39 happier, happiest
40 harder, hardest
41 healthier, healthiest
42 heavier, heaviest
43 more helpful, most helpful
44 higher, highest
45 hotter, hottest
46 worse, worst
47 more important, most important
48 more interesting, most interesting
49 kinder, kindest
50 larger, largest
51 lazier, laziest
52 lighter, lightest
53 less, least
54 longer, longest
55 lovelier, loveliest
56 lower, lowest
57 luckier, luckiest
58 more, most
59 more, most
60 nicer, nicest
61 noisier, noisiest
62 older, oldest
63 politer, politest
64 poorer, poorest
65 more popular, most popular
66 prettier, prettiest
67 more quickly, most quickly
68 quieter, quietest
69 ruder, rudest
70 sadder, saddest
71 safer, safest
72 more serious, most serious
73 shallower, shallowest
74 skinnier, skinniest
75 slower, slowest
76 more slowly, most slowly
77 smaller, smallest
78 stronger, strongest
79 sunnier, sunniest
80 tastier, tastiest
81 more terrible, most terrible
82 thicker, thickest
83 thinner, thinnest
84 uglier, ugliest
85 more useful, most useful
86 weaker, weakest
87 better, best
88 wider, widest
89 wiser, wisest
90 younger, youngest

Unit 04

p. 146

A

01 more important
02 ○
03 a lot
04 much[even / far / still / a lot]
05 more expensive
06 ○
07 we could
08 cheaper

B

01 better than
02 is worse than
03 better than
04 still more
05 a lot more careful than
06 am taller than
07 is even longer than
08 is far more crowded than

내신기출 ③

Unit 05

p. 147

A

01 twice as many as
02 three times longer than

03 ten times as large as
04 twice as often as
05 a hundred times easier than
06 five times as much as
07 twice as fast as
08 three times more expensive than
09 six times higher than

B
01 three times as long as
02 five times heavier than
03 four times shorter than
04 three times more expensive than
05 ten times as light as

Unit 06 p. 148

A
01 hotter and hotter
02 The older, the wiser
03 The smaller, the lighter
04 The younger, the faster
05 more and more expensive
06 The fresher, the more delicious
07 faster and faster
08 The more, the better
09 The heavier, the cheaper

B
01 The earlier I get up, the sooner I'll arrive.
02 The more you have, the more you want.
03 The nights are getting longer and longer
04 Children get taller and taller
05 The more often they meet, the closer they become.
06 The finer the weather is, the more people go outside.

Unit 07 p. 149

A
01 the tallest
02 the most beautiful
03 movies
04 cafes
05 the highest
06 the coldest
07 the fastest
08 the worst
09 family
10 one

B
01 the longest river
02 one of the most serious issues
03 is the most useful
04 the most popular spot
05 one of the ablest employees

Unit 08 p. 150

A
01 taller, as tall
02 student, all
03 the fastest, faster

B
01 more dangerous
02 No other person was braver
03 more fluently than any other person
04 more difficult than all the other subjects
05 No other chair is as comfortable
06 larger than any other lake

Unit 09 p. 151

A
01 longer
02 colder and colder
03 the newest
04 even
05 much
06 better than
07 The tastier, the happier
08 can

B
01 the one → one
02 old → older
03 like → as
04 warm → warmer
05 all other lemon → all the other lemons
06 am → do

07 more louder → louder
08 did → could

내신기출 ④

중간고사 • 기말고사 실전문제 pp. 152~158

객관식 정답 [01~25]

01 ⑤	02 ③	03 ①	04 ②	05 ④
06 ⑤	07 ④	08 ①	09 ③	10 ①
11 ③, ⑤	12 ⑤	13 ③	14 ③, ④	15 ③
16 ④	17 ③	18 ①	19 ⑤	20 ③
21 ⑤	22 ④	23 ③	24 ④	25 ②

주관식 정답 [26~50]

26 lazier
27 most quickly
28 quieter
29 best
30 more and more highly → higher and higher
31 of → in
32 as, can
33 times, than
34 honest than any
35 less diligent
36 The more often the volunteers visit, the happier the kids will be.
37 No other mother can be more devoted to her son than Maria.
38 of friendship are even more stressful than those of family
39 has twice as many books as his friend
40 became thinner and thinner because of his illness
41 No other dog is cleverer than my dog.
42 The whistle didn't sound so loud as I thought.
43 faster than
44 three times longer
45 much time as
46 ⓒ view → views
47 ⓔ the dangerous → the more dangerous
48 ① twice much → twice as much
49 Your safety is the greatest concern
50 She scored three times higher than

해설

01 비교급+and+비교급: 점점 더 ~한[하게]

02 as quickly as he could: 그가 할 수 있었던 만큼 빠르게

03 not as+원급(부사)+as ...: …만큼 ~하지 않다

04 very는 비교급을 강조할 수 없다. (비교급 강조 부사: even, much, far, still, a lot 등)

05 뒤에 than이 오므로 최상급 least는 쓸 수 없다.

06 less+원급+than: ~보다 덜 …한[하게] / cheap(값이 싼)의 비교급은 cheaper이다.

07 one of the+최상급+복수명사: 가장 ~한 것들 중 하나

08 비교급을 이용한 최상급 표현: No (other)+주어+동사+비교급 than ~

09 ③ loudlier → more loudly / 부사 loudly의 비교급은 앞에 more를 붙인다.

10 ① that → those / leaves를 가리키므로 복수형 those가 알맞다.

11 ③ so → as / as ~ as possible: 가능한 한 ~하게 ⑤ very → much[even, far, still, a lot 등] / very는 비교급을 강조할 수 없다.

12 ① more ill → worse / ill의 비교급: worse ② more lighter → lighter / light의 비교급: lighter ③ less sweeter → less sweet / less+원급+than: ~보다 덜 …한[하게] ④ easilier → more easily / easily의 비교급: more easily

13 ① terriblest → most terrible / terrible의 최상급: most terrible ② hardly → hard / '열심히'라는 의미의 부사는 형용사와 같은 형태의 hard이다. (hardly: 거의 ~않다) ④ more worse → worse / 형용사 bad[ill]의 비교급: worse ⑤ very → (much) more / 뒤에 than이 나오므로 비교급 문장임을 알 수 있다. (difficult의 비교급: more difficult)

14 ① helpfuller and helpfuller → more and more helpful / helpful의 비교급: more helpful(more and

more+형용사: 점점 더 ~한) ② greatest → the greatest / one of the+최상급+복수명사: 가장 ~한 것들 중 하나 ⑤ not as smarter than → not smarter than / 〈not 비교급+than ...〉 형태의 비교급 문장으로 as는 생략한다.

15 ③ as+원급+as ①, ②, ④, ⑤ 최상급의 의미

16 ④ 수성보다 덜 작은 게 없다(수성이 가장 크다는 의미)

①, ②, ③, ⑤ 수성이 가장 작다

17 not as+원급+as ~: ~만큼 …하지 않은(= less+원급+ than ~)

18 〈비교급+than+any other+단수명사〉는 최상급 표현이다.

19 '너는 더 적은(less) 시간과 노력으로 수업을 더 쉽게(more easily) 이해할 수 있다'는 의미를 표현해야 한다.

20 비교급+than+any other+단수명사 / '두 배'라는 뜻의 배수사 표현에는 twice를 사용한다. / 두 대상을 비교하는 비교급으로, 동사의 형태를 일치시킨다.

21 ⑤ 3배(three times)가 아니라 3살 더 많다.

22 ④ Andy의 집은 Betty보다는 학교에서 가깝지만 Clare보다는 멀다.

23 ⓑ scary as → as scary as / as+원급+as: ~만큼 …한 ⓓ more and more good → better and better / 〈비교급+and+비교급〉 문장으로 good의 비교급은 better이다.

24 ⓑ more → much / as를 이용한 원급 비교로 much가 적절하다.

25 ⓐ more competitive and competitive → more and more competitive / 앞에 more가 붙는 비교급은 '점점 더 ~한'의 의미를 만들 때, 〈more and more 형용사〉의 형태로 쓴다. ⓒ as → than / less+원급+than: ~보다 덜 …한 ⓔ mountain → mountains / one of the+최상급+복수명사: 가장 ~한 것들 중 하나

26 -y로 끝나는 경우: y를 i로 고치고, -er를 붙인다.

27 부사 quickly의 최상급은 앞에 most를 붙인다.

28 뒤에 than이 나오므로 비교급(quieter)이 와야 한다.

29 앞에 the가 있고 뒤에 of all ~이 나오므로 최상급 문장이다. good의 최상급은 best이다.

30 〈비교급+and+비교급〉 문장으로 '높게'라는 의미의 부사는 형용사와 같은 형태의 high이다.

31 the+최상급+in+단수명사(장소나 집단) / the+최상급+of+복수명사

32 as+형용사/부사의 원급+as possible: 가능한 한 ~하게(= as+형용사/부사의 원급+as+주어+can[could])

33 배수사(~ times)+as+원급+as: –의 ~배 …한(= 배수사(~ times)+비교급+than)

34 최상급 = 비교급+than+any other+단수명사

35 not so[as]+원급+as ~: ~만큼 …하지 않은(= less+원급+than ~)

36 the+비교급+주어+동사, the+비교급+주어+동사: ~하면 할수록 더 …하다

37 비교급을 이용한 최상급 표현: No (other)+주어+동사+비교급+than ~

38 〈비교급+than ~〉 구문으로, 비교급을 강조하는 부사 even은 비교급 앞에 쓴다.

39 배수사(twice)+as+원급+as: ~의 두 배 …한

40 비교급+and+비교급: 점점 더 ~한

41 비교급을 이용한 최상급 표현: No (other)+주어+동사+비교급+than ~

42 not so[as]+원급+as ~: ~만큼 …하지 않은

43 No (other)+주어+동사+비교급 than ~ = 최상급

44 배수사(three times)+비교급 than ~: ~보다 세 배 …한

45 not as+원급+as ~: ~만큼 …하지 않은

46 ⓒ one of the+최상급+복수명사: 가장 ~한 것들 중 하나

47 ⓔ the+비교급 ~, the+비교급 ...: ~하면 할수록 더 …하다

48 ⓕ 배수사(twice)+as+원급+as: ~의 두 배 …한

49 the 최상급+of 복수명사

50 배수사(three times)+비교급 than ~: ~보다 세 배 …한

CHAPTER 08 접속사

Unit 01 p. 160

A

01 while
02 until
03 when
04 as
05 since
06 when
07 when
08 as

B

01 ○
02 ○
03 we pick you up
04 since
05 ○
06 until
07 ○
08 we hear

Unit 02 p. 161

A

01 If
02 Unless
03 If
04 Unless
05 Unless
06 If

B

01 If you eat too much
02 Unless I leave now 또는 If I don't leave now
03 If you work out regularly
04 Unless you apologize 또는 If you don't apologize
05 Unless they concentrate on 또는 If they don't concentrate on
06 If we sing loudly

내신기출 ②

Unit 03 p. 162

A

01 so
02 as
03 because
04 since
05 because of
06 so
07 as soon as
08 so

B

01 so many people recognize
02 because[as, since] he had his hair cut
03 because[as, since] I'm poor at science
04 because of the heavy rain
05 so I bought a bunch of flowers
06 because of the new medicine

Unit 04 p. 163

A

01 Though
02 because
03 but
04 though
05 because
06 though

B

01 although I tried hard
02 Though it rained a lot
03 even though we were tired
04 Although it was very cold
05 though it is not big

내신기출 ②

Unit 05 p. 164

A

01 in order to
02 so that
03 to be cleaned
04 so that
05 so interesting that
06 so foggy that I couldn't
07 so that

B

01 so that you can contact me
02 so comfortable that I can sit on it all day
03 so slippery that the drivers must be careful
04 so that they could understand the problem
05 so that we could travel to Europe
06 so high that the child couldn't reach it

Unit 06 p. 165

A

01 as
02 while
03 as
04 As

05 While
06 as
07 since

B
01 as[while] she came out of
02 as he gets older
03 since I was a child
04 While she wanted to study abroad
05 while it is hot
06 As[Since] they were interested in

Unit 07 p. 166

A
01 S
02 O
03 S
04 C
05 O
06 C

B
01 That you came up with the solution
02 that they won the gold medal
03 that I was nervous
04 that oil floats on water
05 that Picasso was born in Spain

내신기출 ③

Unit 08 p. 167

A
01 I/W
02 I/W
03 I
04 W
05 I/W
06 W
07 I

B
01 Whether you will leave tomorrow
02 if[whether] you were born in Korea
03 Whether we succeed or fail
04 if[whether] we need new sources
05 Whether we are ready or not

Unit 09 p. 168

A
01 However
02 Thus
03 Besides
04 Thus
05 However
06 Thus
07 Besides

B
01 On the other hand
02 In addition
03 Thus
04 However
05 For example
06 Nonetheless

내신기출 ③

Unit 10 p. 169

A
01 and
02 or
03 or
04 and
05 and
06 or

B
01 and
02 or
03 If
04 Unless
05 and

내신기출 ②

Unit 11 pp. 170~171

A
01 both
02 not only
03 neither
04 well
05 and
06 but
07 or

B
01 have to
02 teach
03 are going to
04 go to school
05 has
06 are
07 is supposed to
08 are

C
01 nor, is
02 Both, are
03 as well as
04 not only
05 either, or
06 not, but

D
01 dancing
02 ○
03 have to
04 nor
05 strength
06 are

내신기출 ①

중간고사 • 기말고사 실전문제 pp. 172~178

객관식 정답 [01~25]

01 ③	**02** ④	**03** ②	**04** ③	**05** ⑤
06 ①, ④	**07** ③, ⑤	**08** ①	**09** ④	**10** ⑤
11 ②	**12** ④	**13** ①	**14** ③	**15** ③
16 ⑤	**17** ①	**18** ②	**19** ③	**20** ③
21 ②	**22** ①	**23** ②	**24** ③	**25** ⑤

주관식 정답 [26~50]

26 and
27 If
28 ○
29 which → that
30 until → while[as/when]
31 is → are
32 Both, and
33 order to work
34 he doesn't lose
35 well as, are
36 didn't win the prize even though he was fully qualified
37 wondered if the audience would enjoy his movie
38 The author not only writes stories but draws illustrations for the books
39 don't know whether they should continue the experiment
40 is amazing that the human body is capable of self-healing
41 he is angry or not means a lot to me
42 with cloth so that no one can see it
43 However
44 Moreover
45 Otherwise
46 ⓐ is → are
47 ⓓ and → or
48 ① whether → while
49 The problem is that you didn't pay attention to my class.
50 Either she or I am responsible for the accident.

해설

01 의미상 '부화할 때까지'가 되도록 시간의 접속사 until(~할 때까지)이 와야 한다.

02 보어 역할을 하는 명사절을 이끄는 접속사 that이 알맞다.

03 명령문, or: ~해라, 그렇지 않으면 …할 것이다

04 의미상 앞 내용의 결과를 나타내는 접속사가 와야 한다. (③ otherwise: 그렇지 않으면)

05 의미상 '코미디언이 무대에 올라왔을 때'라는 뜻이 되도록 시간의 접속사가 와야 한다. (⑤ unless: ~하지 않는다면)

06 의미상 '그것이 너무 복잡했기 때문에'라는 뜻이 되도록 이유의 접속사가 와야 한다.

07 의미상 '경기에서 이기기 위해'라는 '목적'의 의미를 나타내는 말이 와야 한다.

08 as: ~할 때(시간의 접속사)/as: ~ 때문에(이유의 접속사)

09 while: ~하는 동안(시간의 접속사) / while: ~하는 반면에(역접의 접속사)

10 '~할 때까지'라는 뜻의 시간의 접속사 until이 적절하다.

11 주어 역할을 하는 접속사 that이 이끄는 명사절이 오며, that절은 단수 취급한다.

12 '~인지 아닌지'의 의미를 가진 명사절 접속사 whether를 사용하며, 같은 의미의 접속사 if는 주어 자리에 쓸 수 없다.

13 ① is → are / 〈either A or B〉가 주어로 쓰일 때, 동사의 수는 B에 일치시킨다.

14 ③ because → because of / 뒤에 명사구가 오므로 because of가 와야 한다. (because+절)

15 ① so that could → so that she could / so that+주어+동사 ~: ~하도록 ② If → Whether / '~인지 아닌지'의 의미를 가진 명사절 접속사 whether가 알맞다. 같은 의미의 접속사 if는 주어로 쓸 수 없다. ④ I didn't → that I didn't / 〈가주어(it) ~ 진주어(that절)〉 문장이다. ⑤ because of → because / 뒤에 완전한 절이 오므로, 접속사 because가 알맞다. (because of+구)

16 ① is → are / 〈both A and B〉가 주어로 쓰일 때 복수 취급한다. / 〈either A or B〉, 〈not only A but (also) B〉, 〈not A but B〉, 〈B as well as A〉가 주어로 쓰일 때, 동사의 수는 B에 일치시킨다. (② is → are ③ is → are

④ have → has)

17 ① 만약 ~라면(조건의 접속사) ②, ③, ④, ⑤ ~인지 아닌지(명사절 접속사)

18 ② ~때문에(이유의 접속사) ①, ③, ④, ⑤ ~할 때(시간의 접속사)

19 명령문, or = Unless = If ~ not

20 양보의 접속사 though: 비록 ~일지라도(= although, even though, even if)

21 either A or B: A와 B 둘 중 하나 / though: 비록 ~일지라도

22 both A and B: A와 B 둘 다 / however: 하지만 / while: ~인 반면에

23 ⓐ or → and / 의미상 '~해라. 그러면 …할 것이다'라는 뜻의 〈명령문, and ...〉가 알맞다.

24 ⓐ If → Whether / '~인지 아닌지'의 의미로 쓰인 if절은 주어로 쓸 수 없다. ⓓ because → because of / 뒤에 명사구가 오므로 because of가 적절하다. (because +절)

25 ⓐ draw → drawing / 〈neither A nor B〉 구문으로, A와 B는 형태를 일치시켜야 한다. ⓑ popular so that → so popular that / so+형용사+that ...: 너무 ~해서 …하다

26 의미상 '~해라. 그러면 …할 것이다'라는 뜻의 〈명령문, and ...〉가 적절하다.

27 의미상 명사절 또는 양보절을 이끄는 Whether가 아닌, '~하면'이라는 의미의 부사절 If가 적절하다.

28 의미상 '게다가'의 의미를 가진 Besides는 적절하다.

29 〈가주어(It) ~ 진주어(that절)〉 구문이다.

30 의미상 시간의 접속사 while[as/when]이 적절하다.

31 〈Neither A nor B〉가 주어로 쓰일 때, 동사의 수는 B에 일치시킨다.

32 의미상 '음식도 서비스도 좋지 않다'는 뜻이므로 〈both A and B (A와 B 둘 다)〉를 사용해서 부정문으로 나타낸다.

33 so that ~: ~하도록(= in order to)

34 unless: 만약 ~하지 않는다면(= if ~ not)

35 not only A but (also) B: A뿐만 아니라 B도(= B as well as A)

36 '~에도 불구하고'의 의미를 가진 접속사 even though를 사용한다.

37 '~인지 아닌지'의 의미를 가진 명사절 접속사 if를 사용한다.

38 'A뿐만 아니라 B도'의 의미를 가진 〈not only A but (also) B〉 형태로 나타낸다.

39 '~인지 아닌지'의 의미를 가진 명사절 접속사 whether를 사용하여 연결한다.

40 접속사 that을 사용하여 〈It(가주어) ~ that절(진주어)〉 구문으로 나타낸다.

41 whether ~ or not: ~인지 아닌지

42 so that+주어+동사 ~: ~하도록

43 하이킹에 대한 앞의 내용과 다른 낚시에 대한 내용이 빈칸 뒤에 오므로, However(그러나)가 와야 한다.

44 낚시에 대한 앞 내용의 추가적인 설명이 나오므로, Moreover(게다가)가 적절하다.

45 하이킹 때 잘 맞는 운동화를 신지 않으면 넘어지거나 미끄러지기 쉽다라고 연결되는 것이 적절하므로 빈칸에는 Otherwise(그렇지 않으면)가 오는 것이 알맞다.

46 ⓐ 〈both A and B〉가 주어로 쓰일 때 복수 취급한다.

47 ⓓ either A or B: A와 B 둘 중 하나

48 ⓕ 의미상 '~인 반면에'라는 의미의 접속사 while이 알맞다.

49 보어 역할을 하는 명사절을 이끄는 접속사 that을 사용한다.

50 'A와 B 둘 중 하나'의 의미로 〈either A or B〉를 사용하며, B에 동사의 수를 일치시킨다.

CHAPTER 09 분사구문

Unit 01 p. 180

A

01 Running in the race
02 Turning to the left
03 Entering the room
04 Being a vegetarian
05 Although being expensive

B

01 Being sick
02 Listening to the music
03 Walking down the street
04 Getting up late
05 Talking to my friends

Unit 02 pp. 181~182

A

01 Although leaving early
02 Having some questions to ask
03 Not having anything to eat
04 Waiting for my friend
05 Reading a book
06 Not knowing the answer

B

01 Not knowing your address
02 Not having enough money
03 Not wanting to talk about it
04 Not living with her family
05 Not understanding the book

C

01 If you go straight for 3 blocks
02 When I entered the classroom
03 While we had lunch together
04 Though they are not rich
05 Because he studies very hard
06 and (it) arrives in Jeju-do at 1:00

내신기출 Not knowing what to do

Unit 03 p. 183

A

01 Playing
02 Not wearing
03 Driving
04 Having lost
05 Listening
06 Not having slept

B

01 Not having met him
02 Having lost the key
03 Having heard of his condition
04 Because[Since/As] they saved enough money
05 After I had cleaned the house
06 Not having learned French

Unit 04 p. 184

A

01 having been
02 Being
03 Being
04 being
05 having been
06 Having been
07 Being

B

01 (Having been) Delivered fresh
02 Flying kites
03 Not (being) satisfied with the product
04 (Being) Proud of their son
05 (Having been) Written in haste
06 praying for the team to win

Unit 05 p. 185

A

01 It, we
02 The work, you
03 It, they
04 Michelle, Andy
05 a bench, we
06 I, the phone
07 The test, I

B

01 The weather being nice

02 It being Parents' Day

03 The sun having set

04 It getting dark

05 There being no train stations in that area

06 The road being wet

Unit 06 p. 186

A

01 Frankly speaking

02 Considering

03 Compared with[to]

04 Generally speaking

05 Strictly speaking

06 Considering

07 Judging from

B

01 Generally speaking

02 Compared with cats

03 Judging from my experience

04 Strictly speaking

05 Considering his age

06 Compared with oranges

Unit 07 p. 187

A

01 folded

02 broken

03 sleeping

04 turned

05 beating

B

01 with her arms folded

02 with the TV turned on

03 with his book closed

04 With his computer broken

05 with his finger pointing to the star

내신기출 closed, shining

중간고사 • 기말고사 실전문제 pp. 188~194

객관식 정답 [01~25]

01 ③	**02** ⑤	**03** ②	**04** ③	**05** ①
06 ④	**07** ①	**08** ②	**09** ④	**10** ①
11 ①, ⑤	**12** ①	**13** ②	**14** ②, ④	**15** ③
16 ⑤	**17** ⑤	**18** ③	**19** ④	**20** ②
21 ②	**22** ①	**23** ②	**24** ③	**25** ⑤

주관식 정답 [26~50]

26 ○

27 Having believed → (Having been) Believed to be a good luck

28 making

29 sung

30 Being → There being 또는 Being a lot of food left → A lot of food being left

31 fallen → falling

32 There being

33 not being noticed

34 making loud noises

35 The weather being sunny today

36 Elected president

37 Some students study with music turned up loudly.

38 Not having completed the mission, the astronaut returned to

39 It taking too long to cook, the guests were very hungry.

40 Having no time, I decided not to go to

41 Interested in history, she applied for

42 Compared with[to] last month, your skills have improved

43 It not being

44 they have flexible

45 their schedule regulated

46 ⓐ Being Sunday → It being Sunday

47 ⓑ driven → driving

48 ⓔ changing → changed

49 Handled well, the device will be useful.

50 The party having ended, we went home.

해설

01 의미상 이유를 나타내는 분사구문이 와야 적절하다. (= Because she was lonely=Being lonely)

02 주절의 시제보다 과거이므로 완료형 분사구문(having+과거분사)이 적절하며, 부정문일 경우 분사 앞에 never[not]를 쓴다.

03 의미상 시간을 나타내는 분사구문이 와야 한다. (=While he was taking)

04 Never having tasted it before: 완료형 분사구문 부정형(never[not] having+과거분사)

05 While the thief stealing her jewels: 분사구문의 의미상 주어가 주절의 주어와 다르므로 분사 앞에 주어를 그대로 쓴다.

06 분사구문의 의미상 주어(His wallet)가 주절의 주어(he)와 다르므로 분사구문 앞에 주어를 써준다. (=As his wallet was stolen → His wallet being stolen)

07 frankly speaking: 솔직히 말해서(비인칭 독립분사구문)

08 with+(대)명사+분사(~한 채로): the door와 수동의 관계이므로 과거분사(unlocked)가 알맞다.

09 ④ having requested → having been requested / 분사구문에서 생략된 주어와 수동의 관계이므로 〈having been+과거분사〉를 쓴다.

10 ① Breaking → Broken / 분사구문에서 생략된 주어와 수동의 관계이므로 과거분사를 쓴다.

11 ① Having been fixed → Having fixed / 분사구문에서 생략된 주어와 능동의 관계이므로 현재분사를 쓴다. ⑤ Having been never → Never having been / 분사구문의 부정형은 분사 앞에 never[not]를 쓴다.

12 ② having not → not having / 분사구문의 부정형은 분사 앞에 not[never]을 써야 한다. ③ Giving → Given / 생략된 주어와 수동의 관계이므로 과거분사를 쓴다. ④ cleaned → cleaning / 생략된 주어와 능동의 관계이므로 현재분사를 쓴다. ⑤ making → being made / 분사구문의 주어와 수동의 관계이므로 과거분사를 쓴다.

13 ① watched → watching / 분사구문의 주어와 능동의 관계이므로 현재분사를 쓴다. ③ crossing → crossed / 〈with+(대)명사+분사(~한 채로)〉 형태로, her fingers와 수동의 관계이므로 과거분사를 쓴다. ④ untying → untied / his shoelaces와 수동의 관계이므로 과거분사를 쓴다. ⑤ Not → You not / 분사구문의 의미상 주어가 주절의 주어(your friends)와 다르므로 분사구문 앞에 주어를 써 주어야 한다.

14 ① Covering → Covered / 분사구문에서 생략된 주어와 수동의 관계이므로 과거분사를 쓴다. ③ Disappointing → Disappointed / 분사구문에서 생략된 주어와 수동의 관계이므로 과거분사를 쓴다. ⑤ Being finished → Finishing / 생략된 주어와 능동의 관계이므로 현재분사가 알맞다.

15 접속사 while이 '~하는 동안'의 의미로 쓰인 분사구문이며, 주절의 주어(His wife)와 다른 것에 유의한다.

16 ⑤ → Though being alone / 부사절과 주절의 주어가 같으므로 주어는 생략하고, 시제도 과거시제로 동일하므로 being으로 고쳐 써야 한다.

17 부사절의 주어(the people)가 주절의 주어(Dan)와 다르므로 분사구문 앞에 그대로 쓴다.

18 부사절의 시제는 과거완료이고 주절의 시제는 과거이므로 완료형 분사구문(having+과거분사)을 써야 한다.

19 시간을 나타내는 분사구문으로, 의미상 접속사 after(~한 후에)를 사용하여 나타낸다.

20 이유를 나타내는 수동형 분사구문으로 sent 앞에 being이 생략되어 있다. 접속사 because를 사용하여 수동태 문장으로 나타내야 한다.

21 주어(the apples)가 변하는(능동) 것이므로 현재분사(turning)가 알맞다. / 〈with+(대)명사+분사〉 형태의 분사구문으로 its leg와 수동의 관계이므로 과거분사가 알맞다.

22 주어(he)가 느끼는(능동) 것이므로 현재분사(Feeling)가 알맞다. / 주어(Our flight)가 도착하는(능동) 것이므로 현재분사(arriving)가 알맞다. / 분사구문의 부정형으로 분사 앞에 not을 쓰고, 주어(she)가 들여다보는(능동) 것이므로 현재분사(looking)가 적절하다.

23 ⓑ got → getting / 분사구문에서 생략된 주어(the driver)와 능동의 관계이므로 현재분사(getting)로 고쳐 써야 한다.

24 ⓑ taking → taken / 분사구문의 주어(her son)와 수동

의 관계이므로 과거분사가 적절하다. / ⓒ scored → scoring / 〈with+(대)명사+분사〉 형태의 분사구문으로, Son과 능동 관계이므로 현재분사가 알맞다.

25 ⓐ Although worn out → Although they[his boots] worn out / 분사구문의 의미상 주어와 주절의 주어가 다르므로 분사 앞에 주어를 그대로 쓴다. ⓑ approached → approaching / 분사구문의 의미상 주어와 능동의 관계이므로 현재분사를 쓴다.

26 My sister liking mint flavor, ~. = While my sister likes mint flavor, ~.

27 수동태 분사구문으로 (Having been) Believed to be a good luck으로 고쳐 써야 한다.

28 분사구문에서 생략된 주어와 능동의 관계이므로 현재분사(making)가 와야 한다.

29 분사구문에서 생략된 주어와 수동의 관계이므로 과거분사(sung)가 알맞다.

30 Because there was a lot of food left 또는 Because a lot of food was left라는 의미가 되어야 하므로, Being → There being으로 고치거나, Being a lot of food left → A lot of food being left로 고쳐서 주절의 주어와 일치하지 않는 독립분사구문으로 써야 한다.

31 분사구문의 의미상의 주어와 주절의 주어가 다른 분사구문으로, 주어(Jack)와 능동 관계이므로 현재분사(falling)로 고쳐 써야 한다.

32 As there is a small park near his house → There being a small park near his house: 〈There+be동사 ~〉 구문을 분사구문으로 쓸 때는 There를 분사 앞에 쓴다.

33 분사구문의 부정형으로 분사 앞에 not을 쓰며, 분사구문에서 생략된 주어와 수동의 관계이므로 〈being+과거분사〉를 쓴다.

34 주절과 부사절의 주어가 같으므로 주어를 생략하고, 동사를 현재분사(making)로 바꾸어 쓴다.

35 부사절의 주어(the weather)와 주절의 주어(we)가 다르므로 분사 앞에 주어를 그대로 쓰고, 동사(is)를 현재분사(being)로 바꾸어 쓴다.

36 부사절과 주절의 주어가 같으므로 주어를 생략하고, 수동태 분사구문이므로 (Being) Elected president로 바꾸어 쓴다.

37 with+(대)명사+과거분사: ~한 채로

38 완료형 분사구문의 부정형: Not having+과거분사 ~

39 분사구문의 의미상 주어(It)와 주절의 주어(the guests)가 다르므로 분사 앞에 주어가 와야 한다.

40 분사구문의 의미상 주어(I)와 주절의 주어(I)가 같으므로 접속사와 주어를 생략하고, 동사를 현재분사(Having)로 바꾸어 쓴다.

41 분사구문의 의미상 주어(she)와 주절의 주어(she)가 같으므로 접속사와 주어를 생략하고, 수동태 분사구문이므로 (Being) Interested in history, ~.로 쓴다.

42 '~와 비교하면'이라는 의미의 비인칭 독립분사구문 〈compared with[to] ~〉를 사용하여 나타낸다.

43 분사구문의 의미상 주어(it)가 주절의 주어와 다르므로 분사 앞에 주어를 그대로 써 주어야 한다.

44 이유를 나타내는 분사구문으로 〈접속사(as)+주어(they)+동사(have) ~〉 형태로 나타낸다.

45 '~하면서'라는 뜻의 〈with+(대)명사+분사〉 형태로 명사와 수동 관계이므로 과거분사(regulated)를 써야 한다.

46 ⓐ 분사구문의 주어(it)가 주절의 주어(Suji)와 다르므로 분사 앞에 주어(It)를 써야 한다.

47 ⓑ 분사구문의 생략된 주어(she)와 능동 관계이므로 현재분사(driving)로 고쳐 써야 한다.

48 ⓔ 〈with+(대)명사+분사〉 형태의 분사구문으로 its tires와 수동 관계이므로 과거분사(changed)가 알맞다.

49 주절의 주어와 일치하는 분사구문의 의미상 주어(the device)를 생략하고, 수동태 분사구문인 (Being) Handled로 나타낸다.

50 분사구문의 주어(The party)가 주절의 주어(we)와 다르므로 분사 앞에 주어를 써 주고, 완료형 분사구문인 having ended로 나타낸다.

CHAPTER 10 관계사

Unit 01 p. 196

A

01 who **02** which **03** wears **04** that **05** who **06** help

B

01 which[that] runs through Seoul
02 who[that] has an umbrella in her hand
03 who[that] can take care of their baby
04 who[that] study economics at university
05 which[that] were on the top of the shelf

Unit 02 p. 197

A

01 who(m) **02** which **03** who **04** who(m) **05** who **06** which **07** who(m)

B

01 which[that] I wear often
02 which[that] I bought
03 who(m)[that] I have known for years
04 who(m)[that] we met in the museum
05 which[that] my parents bought for me
06 who(m)[that] he taught last year

Unit 03 pp. 198~199

A

01 that **02** who[that] **03** that **04** that **05** which[that] **06** that

B

01 bought the same shoes that I bought
02 do everything that their son wants
03 which[that] I am wearing are yours
04 All the efforts that I made
05 the girl and dog that walk down the street
06 The best thing that happened last year

C

01 that **02** that **03** who **04** that **05** that **06** which **07** that **08** that

D

01 지시대명사 **02** 관계대명사 **03** 접속사 **04** 지시형용사 **05** 접속사 **06** 관계대명사

내신기출 ①

Unit 04 p. 200

A

01 whose **02** who(m) 또는 that **03** ○ **04** whose **05** whose **06** whose **07** the woman whose hair **08** ○

B

01 whose daughter and son are musicians
02 whose family is from India
03 whose songs are very popular
04 whose life was in danger
05 whose parents are friendly
06 whose dress looks gorgeous

Unit 05 p. 201

A

01 that **02** which was **03** × **04** who are **05** that **06** whom **07** which was **08** ×

B

01 many people love
02 made by the famous director
03 I sent you
04 Leonard da Vinci painted
05 dancing on stage
06 locked by him

Unit 06
p. 202

A

01 which **03** What **05** that **07** What
02 what **04** what **06** what

B

01 what your parents said
02 What you need
03 what he enjoys most
04 listened to what she explained
05 should apologize for what you said

내신기출 ①

Unit 07
p. 203

A

01 whom **05** which
02 which **06** in which
03 in which **07** which
04 whom **08** at which

B

01 to which I was invited, which[that] I was invited to
02 about whom I talked, who(m)[that] I talked about

Unit 08
pp. 204~205

A

01 in which **05** the way
02 where **06** on which
03 when **07** for which
04 why

B

01 how I can get to the airport
02 when nights are long
03 how we see the world
04 where I bought this bike
05 when people eat turkey
06 why he is so angry

C

01 ○ **03** ○ **05** ○
02 × **04** ○ **06** ×

D

01 Vancouver is the city where I want to live.
02 Monday is the day on which we play soccer.
03 He told me the reason she disappeared.
04 My mom showed me how she made soup.
05 I remember the day when I left my hometown.
06 You need a quiet place in which you can study.

내신기출 ①

Unit 09
pp. 206~207

A

01 who **03** where **05** where **07** when
02 which **04** who **06** who **08** which

B

01 which is expensive
02 who likes sports
03 where we relaxed
04 when he got the call
05 who is a famous author
06 which made me happy

C

01 who **03** which **05** which **07** ○
02 where **04** ○ **06** when

D

01 I have a sister, who is a lawyer.
02 He threw a ball to his dog, which missed it.
03 She visited Hollywood, where she saw many celebrities.
04 My brother was born in 2002, when the World Cup was held.
05 We prepared a party for my mom, which surprised her.

내신기출 They tried to escape from the room, which they found impossible.

Unit 10

p. 208

A

01 Anyone who
02 No matter who
03 whoever
04 anyone whom
05 no matter who
06 Whoever
07 Whoever
08 No matter who

B

01 Anyone who registered for the class
02 Whoever lives in this town
03 hire whomever you recommend
04 anyone who buys a product or service
05 whoever wants to go there
06 No matter who you are

Unit 11

p. 209

A

01 anything which
02 Whichever you choose
03 anything that
04 No matter which
05 No matter what
06 Whatever

B

01 Whichever she wears
02 whichever you do not[don't] know
03 No matter which I buy
04 anything that you want
05 whichever belongs to others
06 No matter what he does

Unit 12

p. 210

A

01 at any place
02 at any time
03 Whenever he sees us
04 Whenever I hear the song
05 however much
06 No matter where

B

01 Wherever we shop
02 whenever I come here
03 however many people disagree
04 No matter where she may go
05 However busy you are

중간고사 • 기말고사 실전문제

pp. 211~217

객관식 정답 [01~25]

01 ④	**02** ②	**03** ①	**04** ②, ⑤	**05** ①, ⑤
06 ②, ④	**07** ⑤	**08** ①	**09** ③	**10** ②
11 ⑤	**12** ⑤	**13** ②	**14** ①	**15** ③
16 ②	**17** ③	**18** ④	**19** ③	**20** ①
21 ③	**22** ①	**23** ③	**24** ②	**25** ②

주관식 정답 [26~50]

26 who have lived
27 that have numerous wounds
28 when she was awarded
29 that → what
30 nothing has → nothing that has
31 whoever → whatever
32 The disaster took place that night when people gathered to see the shooting star.
33 The boxer, whose coach was a national champion, became a world champion later.
34 The book introduces the artists with whom most people are not
35 Whatever he faces
36 whatever happens
37 A large piece of meat he swallowed made him choke.
38 The press criticized the politician whose family made money
39 on the table where everyone can see it
40 He feels happy whenever he cooks for his family.
41 I never went out, which was a good idea
42 We wondered how he escaped from here.
43 ⓐ was → were

44 ⓑ which → when 또는 in which
45 ⓔ which → where 또는 at which
46 ⓒ Whatever → However
47 ⓓ what → where
48 ⓕ that → what
49 was not what she had dreamed of
50 didn't ask him why he had committed the crime

해설

01 선행사가 장소(the spot)를 나타내므로 관계부사 where가 알맞다.

02 선행사가 시간(the moment)을 나타내므로 관계부사 when이 알맞다.

03 선행사가 없는 관계대명사절로 What을 써야 한다.

04 선행사가 사물(products)이므로 which나 that이 와야 한다.

05 선행사가 장소(the cafe)를 나타내므로 관계부사(where)나 〈전치사+관계대명사(at which)〉가 적절하다.

06 의미상 '비가 올 때(when)' 또는 '비가 올 때는 언제든(whenever)'이 되어야 알맞다.

07 선행사에 최상급(the greatest)이 왔으므로 관계대명사 that을 쓴다.

08 선행사가 장소(the town)이므로 관계부사 where나 from which(전치사+관계대명사)로 나타낸다.

09 ③ what → that / 선행사가 〈사람+동물〉이므로 관계대명사 that을 써야 한다.

10 ② which → when 또는 in which / 선행사가 시간(the month)이고, 뒤에 완전한 절이 오므로 관계부사 when이나 in which(전치사+관계대명사)가 와야 한다.

11 ① where → where you / 관계부사 뒤에 주어가 생략되었다. ② what → where 또는 in which / 선행사(a life)가 있고, 뒤에 완전한 절이 오므로 관계부사 where나 in which로 고쳐 써야 한다. ③ where → which / the area를 선행사로 하는 주격 관계대명사 which가 알맞다. ④ which → when 또는 at which / 선행사가 시간(the time)을 나타내며, 뒤에 완전한 절이 오므로 관계부사 when이나 at which로 써야 한다.

12 ① Whatever → Whoever / Whoever you talk with(네가 누구와 이야기를 하더라도) ② what → who(m) / No matter who(m) she talks to (그녀가 누구에게 말을 걸더라도) ③ Whichever → Whenever / Whenever the staff was in the office(그 직원이 사무실에 있었을 때마다) ④ what → where / No matter where the secretary goes(그 비서는 어디에 가더라도)

13 ② The fact와 동격의 접속사 ①, ③, ④, ⑤ 관계대명사

14 ① 접속부사 ②, ③, ④, ⑤ 복합관계부사

15 ③ 의문사(어떤) ①, ②, ④, ⑤ 관계대명사

16 선행사가 the way(방법)을 나타내므로 관계부사 how와 바꾸어 쓸 수 있다.

17 선행사가 사람(the mayor)인 관계대명사의 계속적 용법이므로 who를 사용한다.

18 복합관계부사 however+형용사[부사]: 아무리 ~ 하더라도(=No matter how+형용사[부사])

19 선행사에 the very가 오므로 관계대명사 that을 써야 한다. / 선행사가 사물(the aquarium)인 계속적 용법이므로 관계대명사 which가 알맞다.

20 선행사가 복수형(A few men)이므로 복수동사 work가 알맞다. / 선행사가 복수형(the books)이므로 복수동사 are가 적절하다. / '아무리 ~하더라도'의 양보의 의미를 나타내는 복합관계부사 However가 와야 한다.

21 〈선행사+관계대명사(that)〉을 써서, a look at the thing that I brought로 쓰거나, 선행사를 포함하는 관계대명사 what을 써서 a look at what I brought로 써야 한다.

22 선행사가 장소(the grocery store)이므로 관계부사 where를 사용한다.

23 ⓐ which → what / 선행사를 포함하는 관계대명 what이 와야 한다. ⓒ that → which / 관계대명사 that은 계속적 용법으로 쓸 수 없다.

24 ⓐ which → where / 뒤에 완전한 절이 오고, 장소를 선행사로 하는 관계부사 where이 적절하다. ⓑ that → what / '내가 말한 것'이라는 의미로 선행사를 포함하는 관계대명사 what이 적절하다. ⓓ which → what / '네가 쓴 것'이라는 의미로 선행사를 포함하는 관계대명사

what이 적절하다.

25 ⓐ that → which / 관계대명사 that 앞에는 전치사를 쓸 수 없다. ⓒ that → what / 선행사가 없으므로 관계대명사 what이 적절하다. ⓔ However → Whichever 또는 whatever / 의미상 '어느 길을 선택하든'이라는 뜻의 복합관계대명사 Whichever나 Whatever가 알맞다.

26 선행사가 사람(The residents)이므로 관계대명사 who로 고쳐 써야 한다.

27 선행사가 복수형(Her ugly feet)이므로 복수동사 have로 고쳐 써야 한다.

28 선행사가 시간(the moment)을 나타내므로 관계부사 when으로 고쳐 써야 한다.

29 선행사를 포함하는 관계대명사 what으로 고쳐 써야 한다.

30 선행사 nothing 뒤에 주어가 없는 절이 오므로 관계대명사 that이 와야 한다.

31 의미상 '무엇을 ~하든지'라는 의미의 복합관계대명사 whatever가 알맞다.

32 선행사가 시간(that night)을 나타내므로 관계부사 when을 쓴다.

33 소유격 대명사 His를 대신하는 관계대명사 whose를 사용한다.

34 관계대명사가 전치사의 목적어 역할을 하므로 〈전치사+관계대명사〉 형태로 나타낸다.

35 '무엇을 ~하더라도' 의미의 〈no matter what+주어+동사〉는 〈복합관계부사 whatever+주어+동사〉로 바꾸어 쓸 수 있다.

36 '무슨 일이 일어날지라도'라는 의미로 no matter what을 복합관계대명사 whatever를 써서 나타낸다.

37 목적격 관계대명사가 생략된 문장으로 관계사절(he swallowed)이 선행사(a large piece of meat)를 수식한다.

38 선행사 the politician을 소유격 관계대명사 whose로 연결하여 나타낸다.

39 선행사 the table과 뒤에 문장 everyone can see it을 관계부사 where로 연결하여 나타낸다.

40 '~할 때마다'라는 의미의 복합관계부사 whenever가 쓰인 문장이다.

41 앞 문장 전체가 선행사인 관계대명사 which가 쓰인 계속적 용법의 문장이다.

42 방법을 나타내는 선행사(the way)가 생략된 경우로 관계부사 how가 쓰인 문장이다.

43 ⓐ 선행사가 복수형(Many of her friends)이므로 복수동사 were가 알맞다.

44 ⓑ 선행사가 시간(the month)을 나타내며, 뒤에 완전한 절이 오므로 관계부사 when 또는 in which(전치사+관계대명사)가 알맞다.

45 ⓔ 뒤에 완전한 절이 오므로 관계부사 where 또는 at which(전치사+관계대명사)로 고쳐 써야 한다.

46 ⓒ 복합관계부사 however+형용사[부사]: 아무리 ~하더라도

47 ⓓ 장소를 나타내는 관계부사 where가 알맞다. 관계부사는 선행사를 생략할 수 있다.

48 ⓕ 선행사가 없으므로 관계대명사 what이 적절하다.

49 선행사를 포함하는 관계대명사 what을 사용하여 나타낸다.

50 이유를 나타내는 관계부사 why를 사용하여 나타낸다. 관계부사는 선행사를 생략할 수 있다.

CHAPTER 11 가정법

Unit 01 pp. 220~221

A

01 were
02 have
03 would
04 had worn
05 could

B

01 had sent, would have been pleased
02 traveled, could go
03 had seen, would have said hi
04 understood, could read
05 hadn't cut, would have been longer
06 weren't sick, could go out

C

01 조건문 **02** 가정법 **03** 조건문 **04** 조건문 **05** 가정법 **06** 조건문 **07** 가정법 **08** 가정법

D

01 were
02 might not have been
03 ○
04 ○
05 had saved

내신기출 ②

Unit 02 p. 222

A

01 had practiced
02 had saved
03 had been
04 had drunk
05 had studied
06 had gone
07 had used
08 had listened

B

01 had followed, would not regret
02 had reserved, could enjoy
03 had studied, could solve
04 hadn't told a lie, would trust
05 had brought, wouldn't run
06 had got up, could avoid

Unit 03 p. 223

A

01 am not
02 can't
03 didn't
04 didn't sleep
05 didn't have

B

01 can't visit my grandparents
02 didn't take the medicine
03 I have an appointment, can't talk with you
04 doesn't have a dog, isn't happy
05 didn't have a car, couldn't give us a ride

Unit 04 pp. 224~225

A

01 knew
02 had studied
03 had seen
04 were
05 swam
06 spoke
07 had visited

B

01 didn't learn a foreign language
02 don't have more time to exercise
03 he had won the election
04 I didn't answer the question
05 you had apologized to me
06 they didn't tell me the truth

C

01 I were taller
02 you appeared on TV
03 she had understood me
04 they had come earlier
05 he had introduced his brother

D

01 had called
02 ○
03 had sung
04 ○
05 were

내신기출 ②

Unit 05
pp. 226~227

A

01 lived
02 had lived
03 knew
04 had met

B

01 as if we were heroes
02 as if she were a singer
03 as if they hadn't known me
04 as if she knew the secret
05 as if you had cleaned your room
06 as if he were innocent

C

01 as if you were a teacher
02 as if she had worked for the company
03 as if he didn't know what to do
04 as if you had been born in a royal family

D

01 talk, lived in Jeju-do
02 sounds, hadn't been Anna's boyfriend
03 talked, had passed the exam last year
04 feel, we had lost the game
05 behaves as if he were responsible for the accident

내신기출 ①

Unit 06
pp. 228~229

A

01 were
02 couldn't
03 couldn't
04 would have failed
05 couldn't figure out

B

01 If it were not for the sun
02 Without gravity, we couldn't walk.
03 But for your help, I would have failed.
04 If it were not for music
05 If it had not been for friends

C

01 If it had not been for her reminder
02 Without the Internet
03 If it were not for electricity
04 Without your cooperation
05 If it were not for a washing machine
06 If it had not been for the ice age

D

01 Without, wouldn't have studied
02 If it were not for, would be very hot
03 But for, would be inconvenient
04 If it had not been for him, would have lost the match
05 Without them, would have happened
06 If it had not been for, wouldn't have changed

내신기출 ①

Unit 07
p. 230

A

01 that, came
02 to retire
03 time, finished
04 time, apologized
05 to get
06 that, bought
07 time, got up

B

01 about time that you studied
02 high time that you told him the truth
03 about time that we left
04 high time that you did the homework
05 about time that you showed it to your parents

중간고사 • 기말고사 실전문제
pp. 231~238

객관식 정답 [01~25]

01 ③	**02** ④	**03** ⑤	**04** ⑤	**05** ⑤
06 ②	**07** ③	**08** ③	**09** ①	**10** ③
11 ①	**12** ④	**13** ②	**14** ②, ③	**15** ③
16 ④	**17** ②	**18** ①	**19** ①, ②	**20** ④
21 ③	**22** ④	**23** ②	**24** ④	**25** ⑤

주관식 정답 [26~50]

26 had smiled

27 didn't have

28 were not

29 couldn't have won

30 he were older

31 it had not been for

32 were not, would go

33 were not used

34 was, were sold out

35 is, can grow

36 If I were in Egypt, I could go inside

37 If we had bought beef yesterday, we would have steak

38 The criminal speaks as if he were innocent.

39 she had not informed you, you would have missed a good chance

40 time that we left

41 It's high time that you installed it

42 But for children, the world would be too quiet.

43 ⓑ has → had

44 ⓓ have said → said

45 ⓔ were not → had not been

46 ⓐ will → would

47 ⓒ know → had known

48 ⓕ would be → would have been

49 I wish she answered actively in class.

50 If it had not been for his help last night, she would be busy today.

해설

01 if절의 동사가 had missed(had+과거분사)이므로 가정법 과거완료 문장임을 알 수 있다. 그러므로 주절의 동사는 〈would have+과거분사〉 형태가 와야 한다.

02 '~였다면(과거) …일 텐데(현재)'의 의미를 나타내는 혼합 가정법 문장으로, if절은 가정법 과거완료(had+과거분사), 주절은 가정법 과거(would+동사원형)가 와야 한다.

03 as if+가정법 과거완료(주어+had+과거분사): 마치 ~했었던 것처럼(주절보다 더 이전의 과거)

04 I wish+가정법 과거(주어+과거동사): ~라면 좋을 텐데(현재 사실에 대한 유감)

05 주절의 동사가 〈would have+과거분사(wouldn't have recovered)〉 형태이므로 〈Without+가정법 과거완료(~이 없었다면)〉 문장임을 알 수 있다.

06 '~라면 …일 텐데'라는 의미의 가정법 과거로 if절에는 과거동사, 주절에는 〈would+동사원형〉이 와야 한다.

07 '~였다면(과거) …일 텐데(현재)'의 의미를 나타내는 혼합 가정법으로, if절은 가정법 과거완료(had+과거분사), 주절은 가정법 과거(would+동사원형)가 알맞다.

08 I wish+가정법 과거완료: ~했었다면 좋았을 텐데(과거 사실에 대한 유감)

09 ① can't → couldn't / 〈But for+가정법 과거완료〉로 couldn't have been educated가 알맞다.

10 ③ didn't break → hadn't broken / 가정법 과거완료 문장으로 if절의 동사는 〈had+과거분사〉가 와야 한다.

11 ① 주절의 동사가 〈would+have+과거분사〉 형태의 가정법 과거완료로, if절의 동사는 〈had+과거분사〉가 알맞다.

12 '~였다면(과거) …일 텐데(현재)'의 의미를 나타내는 혼합 가정법 문장으로, if절은 가정법 과거완료(had+과거분사), 주절은 가정법 과거(would+동사원형)가 와야 한다.

13 ② 명사절 접속사 if(~인지 아닌지) ①, ③, ④, ⑤ 부사절 접속사 if(만약 ~라면)

14 주절에 가정법 과거완료(would have+과거분사)가 왔으므로, Without ~ = But for ~ = If it had not been for ~(~이 없었다면)로 바꾸어 쓸 수 있다.

15 직설법 현재시제 문장으로 현재 사실에 반대를 나타내는 가정법 과거로 나타낸다.

16 직설법 과거시제 문장으로 과거 사실에 반대를 나타내는 〈as if+가정법 과거완료(주어+had+과거분사)〉로 나타낸다.

17 가정법 과거로, 현재 사실에 반대를 나타내므로 직설법 현재시제 문장으로 나타낸다.

18 〈I wish+가정법 과거〉로, 현재 사실에 대한 유감을 나타내므로 직설법 현재시제 문장으로 나타낸다.

19 '~이 없었다면'이라는 과거 사실의 반대를 나타내는 〈But for[Without/If it had not been for] ~,+가정법 과거

완료〉 형태로 나타낼 수 있다.

20 Without ~+가정법 과거완료: ~이 없었다면(= But for[If it had not been for] ~, 주어+would+have+과거분사)

21 주절의 동사가 could afford인 가정법 과거로 if절의 동사는 과거동사(had)가 와야 한다. / as if+가정법 과거완료: 마치 ~했던 것처럼 / But for ~+가정법 과거완료: ~이 없었다면

22 I wish+가정법 과거(주어+과거동사): ~라면 좋을 텐데 / if it were not for ~: ~이 없다면

23 ⓒ have → had / if it had not been for ~: ~이 없었다면

24 ⓐ would have been → would be: 가정법 과거: If+주어+과거동사 ~, 주어+would+동사원형 …

25 ⓐ hasn't → hadn't / as if+가정법 과거완료(과거 사실의 반대) ⓑ have → had / 가정법 과거완료: If+주어+had+과거분사 ~, 주어+would+have+과거분사 …

26 I wish+가정법 과거완료(주어+had+과거분사): ~했다면 좋았을 텐데(과거 사실에 대한 유감)

27 as if+가정법 과거(주어+과거동사): 마치 ~인 것처럼(현재 사실의 반대)

28 If it were not for ~: ~가 없다면(현재 사실의 반대)

29 가정법 과거완료: If+주어+had+과거분사 ~, 주어+could[would]+have+과거분사 …(~했다면 …했을 텐데)

30 as if+가정법 과거(주어+과거동사): 마치 ~인 것처럼(현재 사실의 반대)

31 If it had not been for ~: ~이 없었다면

32 직설법 현재시제 문장으로 현재 사실에 반대를 나타내는 가정법 과거(If+주어+과거동사 ~, 주어+would+동사원형 …)으로 나타낸다.

33 현재 사실에 대한 유감을 나타내는 직설법 현재시제 문장으로 〈I wish+가정법 과거(주어+과거동사)〉로 나타낸다.

34 과거 사실에 반대를 나타내는 가정법 과거완료로 직설법 과거시제 문장으로 나타낸다.

35 현재 사실에 반대를 나타내는 가정법 과거로 직설법 현재시제 문장으로 나타낸다.

36 가정법 과거: If+주어+과거동사 ~, 주어+could+동사원형 …(~라면 …일 텐데)

37 '~였다면(과거) …일 텐데(현재)'의 의미를 나타내는 혼합 가정법 문장으로, if절은 가정법 과거완료(had+과거분사), 주절은 가정법 과거(would+동사원형)가 와야 한다.

38 as if+가정법 과거(주어+과거동사): 마치 ~인 것처럼(현재 사실의 반대)

39 가정법 과거완료: If+주어+had+과거분사, 주어+would+have+과거분사 …(~했다면 …했을 텐데)

40 It's time that+주어+과거동사: ~할 시간이다

41 It's high time that+주어+과거동사: 진즉에 ~했어야 했다

42 But for ~+가정법 과거(주어+과거동사): ~이 없다면(현재 사실의 반대)

43 ⓑ 가정법 과거완료: If+주어+had+과거분사 ~, 주어+would+have+과거분사 …(~했다면 …했을 텐데)

44 ⓓ 가정법 과거: If+주어+과거동사 ~, 주어+would+동사원형 …(~라면 …일 텐데)

45 ⓔ If it had not been for ~: ~이 없었다면(과거 사실의 반대)

46 ⓐ 가정법 과거: If+주어+과거동사 ~, 주어+could[would]+동사원형 …(~라면 …일 텐데)

47 ⓒ I wish+가정법 과거완료(주어+had+과거분사): ~했다면 좋았을 텐데(과거 사실에 대한 유감)

48 ⓕ If절의 동사가 과거완료(hadn't worn)인 가정법 과거완료이므로 주절에는 〈would+have+과거분사〉 형태가 와야 한다.

49 '~하면 좋을 텐데'라는 의미의 현재 사실에 대한 유감을 나타내는 〈I wish+가정법 과거(주어+과거동사)〉로 나타낸다.

50 if절은 가정법 과거완료(had+과거분사), 주절은 가정법 과거(would+동사원형) 형태의 혼합 가정법으로 나타낸다. (if it had not been for ~: ~이 없었다면)

CHAPTER 12 일치와 화법

Unit 01 pp. 240~241

A

01 was **03** is **05** is **07** is
02 come **04** attend **06** are **08** prefer

B

01 have **03** give **05** is
02 is **04** walk **06** has

C

01 is → are **04** × **07** is → are
02 × **05** is → are
03 are → is **06** are → is

D

01 is not[isn't] easy
02 Both, are delicious
03 Most, drive
04 All, was sold out
05 The number of students, is increasing
06 Half, has not[hasn't] arrived
07 The weak have

내신 기출 ②

Unit 02 pp. 242~243

A

01 was **03** would **05** could
02 goes **04** get

B

01 × **04** made → makes
02 will → would **05** ×
03 was → is **06** was → is

C

01 could clean your room
02 was painted
03 Venus is larger than
04 said, drinks a cup of milk
05 said, all that glitters is
06 explained, is weaker than

D

01 She said she would go to Hawaii someday.
02 I learned that oil always floats on water.
03 They said they might come earlier than scheduled.
04 They learned that East and West Germany united in 1990.

내신 기출 ①

Unit 03 pp. 244~245

A

01 said **04** told
02 would **05** would
03 was **06** had done

B

01 said, she was so thirsty then
02 told her mom, she wanted to buy a bike for her birthday
03 told us, he would meet us in the office the next[following] day
04 said, the competition had been the week before[the previous week]
05 told me, she enjoyed drawing a picture when she had free time
06 told us, he had to finish that work by the next[following] day

C

01 has → had **04** will → would
02 × **05** ×
03 can → could **06** took → had taken

D

01 You said (that) you were tired and sleepy that night.
02 He said, "I'll enter the contest tomorrow."
03 She told me (that) she had visited her cousin in Busan the week before[the previous week].
04 Anne told me (that) she had met Jia the day before[the previous day].

05 Nick said to me, "I'll play soccer here with my friends."
06 They said (that) they were going to buy that car.

내신기출 ②

Unit 04 pp. 246~247

A

01 asked	04 would
02 was	05 then
03 where I lived	06 had read

B

01 whether I had been to India
02 when we would arrive
03 what I was reading then
04 where she had bought the laptop
05 how I could solve the problem
06 who had cleaned the classroom the day before

C

01 if[whether] I wanted to buy that book
02 Can you help me now
03 where she lived then
04 What will you do this weekend
05 if[whether] I had eaten lunch
06 How can I get to your house

D

01 was he → he was	04 ×
02 will → would	05 would I → I would
03 have → had	06 ×

내신기출 ①

Unit 05 pp. 248

A

01 told me to wait there
02 asked us to bring something to drink
03 advised the patient not to eat too much
04 told me not to be nervous
05 ordered us not to be late for school

B

01 advised me to work out regularly for my health
02 asked me to return the book that day
03 told you to take the subway instead of the bus
04 asked us to come to the party the next[following] day
05 ordered the children not to ride their bikes in the parking lot

중간고사 • 기말고사 실전문제 pp. 249~256

객관식 정답 [01~25]

01 ④	02 ④	03 ④	04 ②, ⑤	05 ①, ②
06 ③	07 ③	08 ⑤	09 ①	10 ④
11 ③	12 ①	13 ⑤	14 ⑤	15 ②
16 ③	17 ④	18 ③	19 ⑤	20 ⑤
21 ②	22 ②	23 ③	24 ②	25 ④

주관식 정답 [26~50]

26 is
27 goes
28 was
29 suffers → suffer
30 are → is
31 does → did
32 where I was, the next[following]
33 not to go, there
34 he couldn't, I was, then
35 I have never
36 Did you leave me
37 Wash all, tonight
38 A stranger asked me which elementary school I graduated from
39 The number of single households has been increasing since
40 The president was certain that honesty is the best policy.
41 The poor are becoming poorer
42 About two thirds of the human body is made up of water.
43 ⓐ are → were
44 ⓒ was → were

45 ① a number of → the number of

46 ⓐ has to → had to

47 ⓑ her → me

48 ⓒ hang up → hung up

49 We will learn how King Sejong created Hangeul tomorrow.

50 Sixty percent of the world's population is Asian.

해설

01 〈Both+주어+복수동사〉로 사용하며, at that time이 과거를 나타내므로 과거형 were가 알맞다.

02 빈칸 뒤에 단수명사와 단수동사가 왔으므로 Each가 알맞다.

03 종속절의 시제(과거)와 일치시키며, 전치사가 필요한 said는 사용할 수 없다.

04 주절의 시제가 과거(assumed)이므로 과거시제가 알맞다.

05 빈칸 뒤에 복수동사가 왔음에 유의한다. 〈All of+복수명사〉와 〈Half of+복수명사〉는 복수 취급한다.

06 ③ 분수 표현(one third of) 뒤에 복수명사가 왔으므로 복수동사가 와야 한다.

07 주절의 시제가 과거(thought)이므로 현재시제는 올 수 없다.

08 의문사가 있는 의문문의 간접화법은 〈의문사+주어+동사〉의 순서로 쓰며, 대명사를 대상에 알맞게 바꾼다.

09 〈every+단수명사〉는 단수 취급한다.

10 ④ was → were / '많은 ~'의 의미의 〈a number of+복수명사〉는 복수 취급한다.

11 ③ is → was / 주절의 동사와 종속절의 동사의 시제를 일치시킨다.

12 ② have → has / mathematics는 과목명이므로 단수 취급한다. ③ are → is / to부정사구 주어는 단수 취급한다. ④ are → is / 〈분수 of+단수명사〉는 단수 취급한다. ⑤ players were → player was / 〈every+단수명사〉는 단수 취급한다.

13 ① will → would / 주절의 시제(told)에 일치시킨다. ② caught → catches / 속담은 현재시제를 쓴다. ③ are → were / 과거의 사건이나 역사를 기술할 때는 과거시제를 쓴다. ④ takes → took / 주절의 시제(said)와 일치시킨다.

14 전달동사 said to는 told로 바꾸고, that절의 주어와 시제는 전달자의 입장으로 바꾸어 써야 한다.

15 전달동사 said to는 asked나 told로 바꾸고, 부정명령문은 〈not+to부정사〉로 바꾸어 쓴다.

16 의문사가 있는 의문문의 간접화법으로 전달동사 said to는 asked로 바꾸고, 〈의문사+주어+동사〉의 어순으로 쓰며, 주어와 시제는 전달자의 입장으로 바꾸어 써야 한다.

17 명령문의 직접화법으로 전달동사 ordered는 said to로, to부정사(to bring)는 동사원형(Bring)으로, 부사구 the next day는 tomorrow로 바꾸어 써야 한다.

18 평서문의 직접화법으로 전달동사 told는 said to로, 주어 he는 I로, had sent는 sent로, to them는 to you로 바꾸어 쓴다.

19 의문사가 없는 의문문의 직접화법으로 접속사 if를 없애고, had experienced를 have experienced로, those를 these로 쓴다.

20 '~의 수'라는 의미로 〈The number of+복수명사〉라고 쓰며, 단수로 취급한다.

21 〈Half of+복수명사〉는 복수 취급한다. / 속담은 항상 현재시제를 쓴다.

22 〈~ percent of+단수명사〉는 단수 취급한다. / 간접화법으로 서술하였으므로 that night을 사용해야 한다. / 주절의 시제(wondered)와 일치시킨다.

23 ⓐ take → takes / 동명사구 주어는 단수 취급한다. ⓓ would → will / 주절의 시제(tells)와 일치시킨다.

24 ⓐ deserve → deserves / 관계대명사 what이 이끄는 관계대명사절이 주어로 왔으므로 단수 취급한다. ⓒ was → were / 〈a number of+복수명사〉는 복수 취급한다. ⓔ did not go → not to go / 부정명령문의 간접화법은 〈not+to부정사〉의 형태로 쓴다.

25 ⓒ is → are / 〈Half of+복수명사〉는 복수 취급한다.

26 나라 이름(the Netherlands)은 단수 취급한다.

27 현재의 습관은 주절의 시제와 상관없이 항상 현재시제를 쓴다.

28 〈~ percent of+단수명사〉는 단수 취급한다.

29 〈분수 of+복수명사〉는 복수 취급한다.

30 〈The number of + 복수명사〉는 단수 취급한다.

31 과거를 나타내는 last time이 왔으므로 과거시제가 알맞다.

32 의문사가 있는 의문문의 간접화법은 〈의문사+주어+동사〉의 형태로 만들고, 부사 tomorrow는 the next [following] day로 바꾸어 쓴다.

33 부정명령문의 간접화법은 〈not + to부정사〉의 형태로 쓰고, 부사 here는 there로 바꾸어 쓴다.

34 평서문의 간접화법으로 that절의 주어와 시제를 전달자의 입장으로 바꾸어 쓰고, 부사 now는 then으로 바꾸어 쓴다.

35 평서문의 직접화법으로 주어 he는 I로, had been은 have been으로 바꾸어 쓴다.

36 의문사가 없는 의문문의 직접화법으로 whether를 생략하고, 과거완료 시제는 과거시제로 바꾸어 쓴다.

37 명령문의 직접화법으로 〈to + 동사원형〉은 〈동사원형 ~〉으로, 부사 that night은 tonight으로 바꾸어 쓴다.

38 의문사가 있는 의문문의 간접화법은 〈의문사+주어+동사〉의 형태로 만든다.

39 '~의 수'라는 의미로 〈The number of + 복수명사〉 형태로 쓰고, 단수 취급한다.

40 속담이나 격언은 현재시제로 쓴다.

41 주어진 말에 the가 있으므로, '가난한 사람들'은 the poor라고 쓰고, 동사는 현재진행형(are becoming)으로 쓴다. 〈비교급 + and + 비교급〉으로 '점점 더 가난한'으로 표현한다.

42 〈분수(two thirds) of + 단수명사〉는 단수 취급한다.

43 ⓐ 주절의 시제(found)와 종속절의 시제를 일치시킨다.

44 ⓒ 〈분수(One-fifth) of + 복수명사〉는 복수 취급한다.

45 ⓕ 의미상 '~의 수'라는 뜻의 〈the number of + 복수명사〉가 와야 적절하며, 단수 취급한다.

46 ⓐ 주절의 시제(said)와 일치시킨다.

47 ⓑ 명령문의 직접화법으로 전화를 건 자신을 지칭하므로 her는 적절하지 않다.

48 ⓒ 주절의 시제(told)와 일치시킨다.

49 주절이 미래시제(will learn)이지만, 역사적 사실은 과거시제(created)를 사용함에 유의해야 한다.

50 〈~ percent of + 단수명사〉는 단수 취급한다.

CHAPTER 13 강조, 부정, 도치, 부정대명사

Unit 01 p. 258

A

01 조동사 **04** 조동사 **07** 본동사
02 본동사 **05** 본동사 **08** 조동사, 본동사
03 조동사 **06** 조동사

B

01 did read **04** did tell
02 does like **05** do love, does like
03 did study **06** Do be

Unit 02 pp. 259~260

A

01 ⓑ **03** ⓑ **05** ⓐ
02 ⓐ **04** ⓐ

B

01 It was Aena that[who(m)] he met in the museum.

02 It was a new cafe that opened next to the restaurant.

03 It was in 2018 that Hana was born.

04 It was my parents that[who] bought me a bike for my birthday.

05 It was Hyewon that[who] finally solved the problem.

06 It was a cake that Jisu made for Yuju.

C

01 Sumi that[who] is waiting for Jian at the bus stop for 30 minutes

02 Jian that[who(m)] Sumi is waiting for at the bus stop for 30 minutes

03 at the bus stop that Sumi is waiting for Jian for 30 minutes

04 for 30 minutes that Sumi is waiting for Jian at the bus stop

05 we that[who] learn tennis on Tuesdays

06 tennis that we learn on Tuesdays
07 on Tuesdays that we learn tennis

D
01 It was an invitation that he sent me.
02 It was David who called you in the morning.
03 It was yesterday that we saw the movie.
04 It was under the bed that I found the notebook.
05 It was Jeju-do that they visited last summer.

내신 기출 ③

Unit 03

p. 261

A
01 always
02 never
03 all
04 Neither
05 both
06 None

B
01 We cannot always do
02 Neither of us have been
03 None of the guests have arrived
04 No student can leave
05 Not all people are

Unit 04

pp. 262~263

A
01 So do
02 So did
03 Neither does
04 So am
05 So are
06 So can
07 Neither am
08 Neither did

B
01 do I know my neighbors
02 was I aware of the problem
03 are some students reading books
04 have I seen such an amazing performance

C
01 Along the street march some soldiers.
02 Little did I sleep last night.
03 Never has she felt so ashamed.
04 On the hill stood a big church.
05 Hardly do I remember what happened then.

D
01 Toward us came
02 Never did I tell
03 Little did he know
04 Hardly could I believe
05 Rarely does she talk about

내신 기출 ③

Unit 05

p. 264

A
01 it
02 ones
03 it
04 ones
05 one

B
01 one, another
02 the others
03 One, the other
04 One, another, the other
05 Some, others

내신 기출 ③

중간고사 • 기말고사 실전문제

pp. 265~272

객관식 정답 [01~25]

01 ②	**02** ④	**03** ④	**04** ③	**05** ①
06 ④	**07** ⑤	**08** ④	**09** ③	**10** ②
11 ④	**12** ②, ⑤	**13** ①	**14** ③, ④	**15** ⑤
16 ④	**17** ④	**18** ②	**19** ①	**20** ②
21 ③	**22** ②	**23** ③	**24** ④	**25** ③

주관식 정답 [26~50]
26 did donate
27 Both of the teams
28 ○
29 a happy it and a sad ones → a happy one and a sad one
30 sold → sell
31 Not only Harry sings → Not only does Harry sing
32 By the window sat the patient.

33 Little did she pay attention to what the guide explained.
34 Here comes your bus.
35 It was a stranger that helped me find the jacket.
36 It was a few days ago that my best friend lent me his favorite book.
37 It is her math homework that Lucy is having a hard time finishing.
38 All of us are exhausted now because we did walk a lot
39 have my grandparents listened to rock music before
40 didn't want either a refund or an exchange
41 would you like to try another
42 does he go out on weekends
43 you can have the others
44 Neither have
45 did I sleep
46 ⓒ does → is
47 ⓓ is she → she is
48 ⓕ any → none
49 Seldom does she smile in front of people.
50 None of them noticed him at the party.

해설

01 ⟨It is[was] ~ that ...⟩ 강조 구문으로, 강조하는 대상이 the giraffe(동물)임에 유의한다.

02 '어느 것도 ~가 아닌'의 전체 부정의 의미인 ⟨neither of ~⟩를 사용한다.

03 부정어 Never가 문장의 앞으로 나가면서 주어와 동사가 도치된 경우로, 조동사가 있는 경우는 조동사를 주어 앞에 써준다.

04 둘 중 하나를 찾았으므로, 전체 부정의 의미를 나타내는 anything은 쓸 수 없다.

05 전치사구(at noon)를 강조할 때는 전치사를 포함한 구 전체를 함께 써야 한다.

06 부정문에 대한 동의로 조동사 will이 왔으므로 ⟨Neither + 조동사(will) + 주어⟩ 형태로 나타낸다.

07 부정어 Rarely가 문장의 맨 앞으로 나가면 주어와 동사가 도치되어 주어 앞에 조동사 did가 와야 한다. (Rarely+조동사(did)+주어+동사원형)

08 부정문에 대한 동의로, 조동사 do가 왔으므로 ⟨neither + 조동사(do) + 주어⟩ 형태로 나타낸다.

09 부분 부정을 나타내므로 부정어(not)와 전체를 나타내는 단어를 함께 써서 나타낸다.

10 동사 found는 강조할 수 없다.

11 ④ Here are they → Here they are / 주어가 대명사일 때는 도치시키지 않는다.

12 ② April → in April / 전치사구를 강조할 때는 전치사를 포함한 구 전체를 함께 써야 한다. ⑤ what → that / ⟨It is[was] ~ that ...⟩ 강조 구문으로, a poem을 강조하고 있다.

13 조동사 do를 사용하여 강조한 경우에는 주어와 시제에 맞게 ⟨do[does / did] + 동사원형⟩의 형태로 나타낸다.

② do → does ③ drank → drink ④ appears → appear ⑤ do felt → did feel

14 ① does → are / 도치된 문장이 수동태 문장으로 be동사를 쓴다. ② do → does / 주어가 your phone이므로 동사의 수를 일치시킨다. ⑤ was → did / 부정어(Little)가 문장 앞으로 나가면서 주어와 동사가 도치된 문장으로 주어 앞에 조동사 did를 써야 한다.

15 부정어(Hardly)를 문장의 맨 앞으로 보내고, 과거 시제임을 유의하여 주어와 동사를 도치시켜 ⟨Hardly + 조동사(did) + 주어 + 동사원형⟩의 형태로 나타낸다.

16 과거시제의 일반동사를 강조하므로 ⟨did + 동사원형⟩의 형태로 나타낸다.

17 ⟨It was ~ that ...⟩ 강조 구문으로 전치사구를 강조하므로 전치사를 포함한 구 전체를 함께 써야 한다.

18 ⓐ, ⓒ, ⓔ 강조의 do ⓑ 일반동사 do(do one's best: 최선을 다하다) ⓓ 의문문을 만드는 조동사 do

19 only when he gets what he wants를 문장의 맨 앞으로 보내면 주어와 동사가 도치되어 주어 앞에 조동사 will이 와야 한다.

20 '모두가 ~인 것은 아니다'라는 의미의 부분 부정을 나타내는 문장으로 바꾸어 쓸 수 있다. (not every + 단수명사)

21 빈칸 뒤의 go, did로 보아, 부정문(didn't go)에 대한 동

의로 〈Neither + did + 주어〉 형태로 나타낸다.

22 주어(The tellers)가 복수형이므로 do가 와야 한다. / 〈It was ~ that ...〉 강조 구문으로 전치사구를 강조하므로 전치사를 포함한 구 전체를 함께 써야 한다. / 첫 번째 공은 잡았다고 했으므로 부분 부정을 나타내는 말이 와야 한다. (not ~ both: 둘 다 ~인 것은 아니다)

23 ⓐ do gardener grows → does gardener grow / 주어가 3인칭 단수이므로 〈does + 주어 + 동사원형〉 형태로 쓴다. ⓑ has → have / 주어가 3인칭 단수인 일반동사 has를 강조하므로 〈does + 동사원형〉으로 나타낸다.

24 ⓐ None → Any 또는 haven't → have / 문장에 부정어가 두 번 사용되어 이중 부정이 된다. ⓒ which → who 또는 that / 강조하는 대상이 사람(the vet)이므로 which를 쓸 수 없다.

25 ⓑ did caught → did catch / 과거동사를 강조하므로 〈did + 동사원형〉 형태로 쓴다. ⓒ the theater → in the theater / 〈It is[was] ~ that ...〉 강조 구문으로, 장소를 나타내는 전치사구를 강조하므로 전치사를 함께 써 줘야 한다.

26 종속절의 과거시제와 일치시킨다.

27 〈Both of + 복수명사〉의 형태로 나타낸다.

28 부정어 Not only가 문장 앞으로 와서 주어와 동사가 도치된 경우로, 〈does + 주어 + 동사원형〉으로 나타낸 것은 적절하다.

29 정해지지 않은 막연한 것을 가리키는 경우 one을 쓴다.

30 과거 시제의 일반동사를 강조하므로 〈did + 동사원형〉의 형태로 나타낸다.

31 부정어 Not only가 문장의 맨 앞으로 왔으므로 주어와 동사를 도치시켜 does Harry sing이라고 써야 한다.

32 전치사구가 문장 앞에 나왔으므로, 주어와 동사를 도치시킨다.

33 부정어(little)를 문장의 맨 앞으로 보내고, 과거시제임을 유의하여 주어와 동사를 도치시켜 〈Little + 조동사(did) + 주어 + 동사원형)〉의 형태로 나타낸다.

34 장소를 나타내는 부사(here)를 문장의 맨 앞으로 보내고, 주어(your bus)와 동사(comes)를 도치시킨다.

35 사람(a stranger)을 강조하므로 〈It was + 강조 대상 + that[who] ...〉 형태로 나타낸다.

36 〈It was + 강조 대상 + that ...〉 형태로 나타낸다.

37 〈It is + 강조 대상 + that ...〉 형태로 나타낸다.

38 과거시제의 일반동사를 강조하므로 〈did + 동사원형〉의 형태로 나타낸다.

39 부정어 never가 문장의 앞으로 나가서 주어와 동사가 도치된 문장으로 〈Never + 조동사(have) + 주어 + 동사원형)〉의 형태로 나타낸다.

40 not + either A or B: A도 B도 ~이 아닌(전체 부정)

41 '또 다른 하나'를 나타낼 때는 another를 쓴다.

42 부정어 Rarely가 문장의 맨 앞에 왔으므로, 주어와 동사가 도치되어 〈Rarely + does + 주어 + 동사원형〉의 형태로 써야 한다.

43 정해진 나머지 모두를 나타낼 때는 the others를 사용한다.

44 부정문에 대한 동의로, 조동사 have가 왔으므로 〈Neither + have + 주어〉 형태로 나타낸다.

45 부정어 Little이 문장의 맨 앞에 왔으므로, 주어와 동사가 도치되어 〈Little + did + 주어 + 동사원형〉의 형태로 써야 한다.

46 ⓒ 부정어 Rarely가 문장 앞에 와서 주어와 동사가 도치된 문장으로 주어(she) 뒤에 late가 왔으므로 does를 is로 고쳐 써야 한다.

47 ⓓ 주어가 대명사일 때는 도치시키지 않는다.

48 ⓕ 아무도 콘서트에 가 본 적이 없으므로 전체 부정을 나타내는 〈none of ~〉로 고쳐 써야 한다.

49 부정어(seldom)를 문장의 맨 앞으로 보내고, 주어와 동사를 도치시켜 〈Seldom + does + 주어(she) + 동사원형(smile) ~〉의 형태로 나타낸다.

50 '그들 중 아무도 ~않다'라는 전체 부정의 의미로 None of them ~으로 시작한다.

CHAPTER 14 문장의 이해

Unit 01
p. 274

A

01 We
02 The medicine
03 The lilies in the vase
04 To drive fast in the rain
05 Wearing safety goggles and protective clothing
06 It, that he's kind
07 That he decided to study abroad
08 Those who finished completing the form
09 It, to recycle used bottles

B

01 were → was
02 Read → To read 또는 Reading
03 what all → that all
04 were → was
05 is → are
06 prefers → prefer
07 smells → smell
08 are → is
09 are → is
10 Raise → To raise 또는 Raising

Unit 02
p. 275

A

01 a fire fighter
02 strange
03 foggy
04 to spend quiet time alone
05 organizing and hosting events
06 sweet
07 colder and colder

B

01 wake → awake
02 sourly → sour
03 unclearly → unclear
04 silence → silent
05 confidently → confident
06 calmly → calm
07 warmly → warm
08 whether → that

내신기출 ③

Unit 03
p. 276

A

01 the concert ticket
02 smoking
03 to meet on July 5th
04 that the Earth was flat
05 him

B

01 간접목적어: the security guard / 직접목적어: his identification
02 간접목적어: me / 직접목적어: a letter full of warm words
03 간접목적어: her / 직접목적어: What

C

01 watch → to watch 또는 watching
02 rescuing → to rescue
03 to cook → cooking
04 to → for
05 get → getting
06 to call → calling
07 for → to
08 to → of

Unit 04
p. 277

A

01 목적어: my daughter / 목적격보어: my angel
02 목적어: the article / 목적격보어: more interesting.
03 목적어: the ground / 목적격보어: shake severely
04 목적어: her baby / 목적격보어: warm
05 목적어: me / 목적격보어: to play the online game for an hour a day
06 목적어: her hair / 목적격보어: cut
07 목적어: me / 목적격보어: come home before 8:00

B

01 madly → mad
02 repair → repaired
03 to stop → stop 또는 stopping
04 laughs → laugh
05 stay → to stay
06 understanding → understand 또는 to understand

C

01 그 배우를 유명하게 만들었다

02 네가 방에서 울고 있는 것을 봤다

03 내가 날씬해 보이게 한다

04 아이들에게 아무것도 만지지 말라고 말했다

Unit 05

p. 278

A

01 with new ideas

02 broken by us

03 that I've ever seen

04 standing alone in the corner

05 hot to drink

06 with a beard walking down the street

07 lined with tall trees

08 under the bed

09 The recently built, at the edge of the town

10 which explains the issue in detail

B

01 공사 중인 몇몇 도로들

02 할인 가격에 판매된 카메라

03 따라야 할 복잡한 규칙들

04 침대 위에서 자고 있는 아기

05 늑대들에게 키워진 소년

Unit 06

p. 279

A

01 more slowly

02 Suddenly

03 as soon as you get home

04 Shocked by the news

05 everyday, to stay healthy

06 Generally, very

07 on the phone, when the bell rang

08 very hard, finally

09 anywhere, if it rains tomorrow

10 terribly, to hear the news

11 to ask a question

12 often, in the park after school

13 on a sofa, with her legs crossed

내신기출 ②

중간고사 • 기말고사 실전문제

pp. 280~287

객관식 정답 [01~25]

01 ④	**02** ③	**03** ①	**04** ②	**05** ④
06 ①	**07** ③	**08** ⑤	**09** ③	**10** ②
11 ①	**12** ④	**13** ④	**14** ⑤	**15** ④
16 ④	**17** ②	**18** ④	**19** ⑤	**20** ①
21 ③	**22** ④	**23** ②	**24** ③	**25** ⑤

주관식 정답 [26~50]

26 There are tons of fish living

27 To help the people who are discriminated against

28 pay the rent for their house in the city

29 The prisoner caught last month escaped

30 tasted like cough syrup

31 felt his body shake[shaking]

32 Having a fever can be a symptom

33 make everyone who wears it stylish

34 attending

35 taken

36 looking

37 completed

38 is this → this is

39 sit → sitting

40 hurried → hurriedly

41 are → is

42 trained the dog rescued from the street

43 conducted so far have not revealed it

44 who became her god mother turned the pumpkin into a carriage

45 ⓐ to enable → enables

46 ⓒ cleanly and safely → clean and safe

47 ⓓ embarrassed → embarrassing

48 Did you hear who he met after school?

49 I have something important to ask him.

50 She wondered if the man she met liked her.

해설

01 보어 자리에는 명사, 형용사가 오며, 의미상 ④가 적절하다.

02 want는 목적어나 목적격보어로 to부정사가 올 수 있다.

03 think는 목적어 뒤 목적격보어로 명사, 형용사, to부정사의 형태가 올 수 있다.

04 명사 the skirt의 형용사적 수식어는 분사, to부정사, 전치사구, 관계사절을 사용한다.

05 주어 자리에는 명사구나 절, to부정사, 동명사를 사용할 수 있다. ④는 That을 What으로 고쳐 써야 한다.

06 목적어 자리에는 명사구나 절, to부정사, 동명사를 사용할 수 있으며, 목적격보어로 부사를 사용할 수 없다.

07 자동사 decrease를 수식하는 부사적 수식어가 와야 한다.

08 make의 목적격보어는 명사, 형용사, 원형부정사를 쓴다.

09 주어는 His ~ Mars, 동사는 doesn't seem이다.

10 주어는 Many ~ lives, 동사는 are planning이다.

11 주어 Student를 현재분사구가 뒤에서 꾸며 주며, 동사 find는 부사가 아닌 형용사를 목적격보어로 쓴다.

12 주어 My aunt를 현재분사구가 뒤에서 꾸며 주며, 동사 help는 원형부정사를 목적격보어로 쓸 수 있다.

13 ⓐ는 직접목적어이다.

14 ⓔ는 목적격보어이다.

15 ⓓ는 보어이다.

16 ⓓ는 진주어이다

17 ② strangely → strange / sound+형용사 보어

18 ① study → to study / 동사 encourage는 목적격보어로 to부정사를 쓴다. ② the old people → to the old people / teach+직접목적어+to+간접목적어 ③ has → who has / 명사 roommate를 관계사절이 뒤에서 꾸며 준다. ⑤ surprise → surprised / 목적어 everyone과 수동의 관계이므로 과거분사 형태로 목적격보어를 사용한다.

19 ⑤는 동사가 없는 문장이므로, 동사구가 들어가야 한다.

20 ①은 전치사 to 뒤에 바로 전치사구가 들어갈 수 없다.

21 ③은 선행사 the disease를 수식하는 관계사절이 와야 하므로 that 명사절은 들어갈 수 없다.

22 ⓐ The girl을 수식하는 관계사절(who is sitting) 또는 분사(sitting)가 가능하다. ⓑ 동사 hear의 목적격보어는 원형부정사 또는 분사가 알맞다.

23 ⓑ 보어 ⓒ What ~ to do까지가 주어구 ⓓ 도치 문장의 유도부사 there

24 ⓑ 목적격보어 ⓒ 명사 boy를 꾸며 주는 형용사적 수식어구

25 ⓐ are → is / 동명사구가 주어로 쓰였으므로 단수 취급한다. ⓑ thoughtfully → thoughtful / be동사가 쓰인 2형식 문장으로 형용사 보어를 쓴다.

26 유도부사 there이 문장 앞에 나와서 주어와 동사가 도치되었다.

27 '~하는 것'의 의미로 to부정사구를 주어로 쓴다.

28 동사 pay 뒤에 목적어 the rent가 온다.

29 주어 prisoner를 과거분사가 뒤에서 꾸며 준다.

30 2형식 동사 taste는 보어로 형용사 또는 〈like+명사〉의 형태를 쓴다.

31 동사 feel의 목적격보어는 원형부정사 또는 분사를 쓴다.

32 '~하는 것'의 의미로 동명사구 주어를 사용한다.

33 목적어 everyone을 관계사절이 뒤에서 꾸며 주고, 동사 make의 목적격보어로 형용사를 사용한다.

34 주어 anyone을 현재분사(능동)가 뒤에서 꾸며 준다.

35 주어 The little boy를 수식하는 과거분사구가 온다.

36 the people을 현재분사(능동)가 뒤에서 꾸며 준다.

37 주어 The artwork를 과거분사(수동)가 뒤에서 꾸며 준다.

38 동사 explain의 목적어로 〈의문사+주어+동사〉 형태의 명사절이 와야 한다.

39 의미상 보어의 역할을 하는 동명사가 와야 한다.

40 동사(ate)를 수식하기 위해 부사가 와야 한다.

41 주어 The purpose와 동사의 수를 일치시킨다.

42 the dog를 과거분사(수동)가 뒤에서 꾸며 준다.

43 주어 Studies를 과거분사(수동)가 뒤에서 꾸며 주며, have not revealed가 동사로 쓰였다.

44 주어 The fairy를 관계사절이 뒤에서 꾸며 주며, turned가 동사로 쓰였다.

45 ⓐ 문장의 동사가 없으므로 주어 The help의 수에 일치하여 동사로 쓴다.

46 ⓒ 동사 keep의 목적격보어로 부사를 쓸 수 없다.

47 ⓓ that절이 문장의 진주어로 현재분사를 사용한다.

48 〈의문사+주어+동사〉 형태의 명사절을 목적어로 쓴다.

49 -thing+형용사+to부정사(형용사적 용법)

50 〈if+주어+동사〉 형태의 명사절을 목적어로 쓴다.

MY GRAMMAR COACH

내신기출 N제 중 3

Workbook

정답과 해설

CHAPTER

01 문장의 동사

Unit 01

p. 4

01 The baby / smiles / at her mom.
S V M

02 Lots of children / like / the character.
S V O

03 Some people / are walking / down the street.
S V M

04 The Earth / goes / around the sun.
S V M

05 Mr. Johnson / is / an able lawyer.
S V C

06 You / should respect / yourself.
S V O

07 The Second World War / broke out / in 1939.
S V M

Unit 02

p. 4

01 excitingly → exciting
02 interest → interesting
03 calmly → calm
04 sounds → sounds like
05 greatly → great
06 bitterly → bitter
07 nervously → nervous
08 happiness → happy

Unit 03

p. 5

01 You don't resemble your father.
02 The explorer discovered the island.
03 He knows how to change tires.
04 She finished the project yesterday.
05 The employer mentioned the issue again.
06 He discussed the plan with his brother.
07 He attended the conference last week.
08 The next train will reach the station soon.

Unit 04

p. 5

01 a hotel in Jeju Island for me
02 the pen to me
03 some food to me
04 a letter to me
05 a sand castle for us
06 the book to me
07 dishes for the guests
08 a question of the student

Unit 05

p. 6

01 believes it impossible to arrive
02 keep your hands clean
03 found Jian very smart
04 found it exciting to talk with him
05 elected him the class president
06 make the house green
07 found the bed comfortable
08 calls his brother a fool
09 named the dog Winnie

Unit 06

p. 6

01 her to see
02 them to finish
03 him not to eat
04 Ian and Mia to leave
05 us not to play
06 me to open
07 him to swim
08 citizens to get around

Unit 07

p. 7

01 They heard a song sung outside.
02 I smell the wood burning.
03 I saw my uncle fishing in the lake.
04 He felt someone pushing his back.
05 I heard some neighbors arguing.
06 He watched his cat chasing a bird.
07 He saw his bicycle repaired.
08 We felt the ground shaking.
09 I noticed a man stealing.

Unit 08

p. 7

01 us read
02 my sister buy
03 my baggage checked
04 him stay
05 some food delivered
06 her stop
07 the frame hung
08 us arrive

Unit 09

p. 8

01 do → done
02 to finish → finished
03 moved → (to) move
04 washing → to wash
05 practices → to practice
06 working → (to) work
07 fixes → (to) fix
08 cleaning → cleaned

Unit 10

p. 8

01 check → checked
02 angrily → angry
03 to help → help
04 to set → set 또는 setting
05 thinking → think
06 riding → (to) ride
07 seeing → to see
08 to sign → signed

중간고사 • 기말고사 실전문제

pp. 9~12

객관식 정답 [01~15]

01 ④ **02** ② **03** ① **04** ③ **05** ⑤
06 ② **07** ② **08** ④ **09** ④ **10** ③
11 ① **12** ⑤ **13** ① **14** ④ **15** ①

주관식 정답 [16~30]

16 attend to → attend
17 to her → for her
18 to fall → fall 또는 falling
19 looks a great place → looks like a great place
20 honestly → honest
21 ○
22 repaired
23 to do
24 teaches history to students in high school
25 believed, possible to bring her back
26 The policeman explained the safety rules
27 The professor found this book helpful for students.
28 Hot weather turned the green apple(s) red.
29 My friend showed a funny picture to me.
30 He wanted me to visit his house.

해설

01 2형식 동사 look 뒤에는 형용사인 lovely만 가능하다. ①, ②, ③, ⑤는 모두 부사이므로 사용할 수 없다.

02 4형식 동사 ask를 3형식으로 쓸 때 간접목적어 앞에 전치사 of를 사용한다.

03 사역동사 make는 목적격보어로 동사원형(원형부정사)을 사용한다.

04 2형식 동사 smell 뒤에는 형용사 sweet를 써야 한다. ①은 현재시제가 쓰였으므로 우리말 해석과 맞지 않다.

05 4형식 동사 give는 전치사 없이 뒤에 간접목적어(him), 직접목적어(a ~ milk)가 순서대로 나온다.

06 ② 〈감각동사 + like + 명사〉 형태로 써야 한다.

07 ② help는 목적격보어로 동사원형 또는 to부정사를 사용한다.

08 resemble은 목적어가 필요한 3형식 타동사로 전치사 with가 필요 없다.

09 ① 2형식 동사 taste 뒤에는 형용사 good을 써야 한다. ② 2형식 동사 feel 뒤에는 형용사 confident를 써야 한다. ③ 감각동사 smell 뒤에 명사를 쓰려면 〈smell + like + 명사〉형태가 되어야 한다. ⑤ 2형식 동사 look 뒤에는 형용사 happy를 써야 한다.

10 ① tell to me → tell me / 〈tell + 간접목적어 + 직접목적어〉의 형태이므로 전치사 to는 필요 없다. ② to how → how / 〈teach + 간접목적어 + 직접목적어(how~)〉의 형태이므로 전치사 to는 필요 없다. ④ to help → help / 사역동사 let의 목적격보어로 동사원형(원형부정사) help를 사용한다. ⑤ to play → play[playing] / 지각동사 watch의 목적격보어로 동사원형 또는 현재분사를 사용한다.

11 ② tasted sweet chocolate → tasted sweet 또는 tasted like sweet chocolate / 2형식 동사 taste의 보어로 명사인 chocolate이 올 수 없다. ③ became to → became / 2형식 동사 become의 보어로 명사 또는 형용사가 오며 전치사 to는 필요 없다. ④ enter to → entered / enter는 전치사가 필요 없는 타동사이다. ⑤ food to → food for / 3형식 동사 cook은 전치사 for를 사용한다.

12 reach는 타동사로 전치사가 필요 없다. / taste 뒤에는 보어로 형용사가 나온다. / stay 뒤에는 보어로 형용사가 나온다.

13 사역동사 let은 목적격보어로 동사원형(원형부정사)이 나온다. / get은 목적격보어로 to부정사가 나온다. / 지각동사 see는 동사원형 또는 분사 형태의 목적격보어를 쓴다.

14 목적격보어가 동사원형(study)이므로 사역동사 make, let, have, help는 가능하지만, get은 사용할 수 없다.

15 수여동사 show, sell, give, send는 3형식 문장 전환시, 간접목적어 앞에 전치사 to를 쓰지만, buy는 전치사 for를 사용한다.

16 attend는 목적어가 필요한 3형식 타동사로 전치사 to가 필요 없다.

17 make는 목적어 뒤에 전치사 for를 사용한다.

18 지각동사 feel은 목적격보어로 동사원형 또는 분사를 사용한다.

19 감각동사 뒤에 명사가 나올 경우, 〈감각동사+like+명사〉 형태로 사용한다.

20 think의 목적격보어로 형용사인 honest를 사용한다.

21 지각동사 hear의 목적격보어로 동사원형(원형부정사) 또는 분사를 사용한다.

22 사역동사 have의 목적격보어가 목적어와 수동의 관계일 때는 과거분사의 형태를 사용한다.

23 ask가 '요청하다'의 의미인 5형식 동사이므로 목적격보어로 to부정사를 사용한다.

24 전치사 to가 있으므로 〈주어+수여동사(teach)+(직접)목적어+to 대상〉 형태의 3형식 문장을 만든다.

25 〈주어+believe+가목적어 it+목적격보어(possible) 진목적어(to부정사)〉 어순으로 써야 한다.

26 〈주어+explain+목적어〉 형태의 문장을 만든다. explain은 전치사가 필요 없는 3형식 타동사이다.

27 〈주어+find+목적어+목적격보어(형용사)〉 형태의 문장을 만든다. find의 목적격보어가 부사가 아닌 형용사가 오는 것에 주의한다.

28 〈주어+turn+목적어+목적격보어(형용사)〉 형태의 문장을 만든다. turn의 목적격보어가 부사가 아닌 형용사가 오는 것에 주의한다.

29 〈주어+수여동사(show)+(직접)목적어+to 대상〉 형태의 문장을 만든다. 3형식 문장으로 전환 시, show는 전치사 to를 사용하는 것에 주의한다.

30 〈주어+want+목적어+목적격보어(to부정사)〉 형태의 문장을 만든다. 동사 want의 목적격보어는 to부정사를 사용하는 것에 주의한다.

CHAPTER 02 시제

Unit 01

p. 14

01 accomplished, accomplished
02 was, been
03 applied, applied
04 were, been
05 arranged, arranged
06 became, become
07 began, begun
08 bit, bitten
09 blew, blown
10 broke, broken
11 breathed, breathed
12 brought, brought
13 burst, burst
14 buried, buried
15 bought, bought
16 caught, caught
17 chose, chosen
18 cost, cost
19 cried, cried
20 cut, cut
21 delayed, delayed
22 denied, denied
23 destroyed, destroyed
24 disagreed,

disagreed
25 displayed, displayed
26 did, done
27 drew, drawn
28 drove, driven
29 dropped, dropped
30 dried, dried
31 ate, eaten
32 fell, fallen
33 fed, fed
34 fought, fought
35 found, found
36 flew, flown
37 forgot, forgotten
38 forgave, forgiven
39 founded, founded
40 froze, frozen
41 gave, given
42 went, gone
43 grabbed, grabbed
44 grew, grown
45 heard, heard
46 hid, hidden
47 hit, hit
48 held, held
49 hurt, hurt
50 kept, kept
51 knew, known
52 laid, laid
53 led, led
54 left, left
55 lent, lent
56 let, let
57 lay, lain
58 lied, lied
59 lost, lost
60 maintained, maintained
61 meant, meant
62 met, met
63 overcame, overcome
64 paid, paid
65 preferred, preferred
66 proved, proved
67 quit, quit
68 raised, raised
69 read, read
70 regretted, regretted
71 rode, ridden
72 rang, rung
73 rose, risen
74 ran, run
75 saw, seen
76 sent, sent
77 set, set
78 shared, shared
79 sang, sung
80 sat, sat
81 slept, slept
82 spoke, spoken
83 spent, spent
84 spread, spread
85 stood, stood
86 stayed, stayed
87 stole, stolen
88 survived, survived
89 swam, swum
90 took, taken
91 taught, taught
92 tore, torn
93 thanked, thanked
94 thought, thought
95 threw, thrown
96 understood, understood
97 woke, waken
98 wore, worn
99 won, won
100 wrote, written

Unit 02

p. 16

01 goes
02 will[is going to] apply
03 ranked
04 is
05 will[are going to] travel
06 accepted
07 will[am going to] meet
08 works

Unit 03

p. 16

01 was listening
02 is leaving
03 are playing
04 was standing
05 is, arriving
06 was preparing
07 were waiting
08 are taking

Unit 04

p. 17

01 saw
02 have seen
03 was
04 have passed
05 has been
06 didn't understand
07 have known

Unit 05

p. 17

01 have not[haven't] done
02 has won
03 has lost
04 has just arrived
05 ever heard
06 have never been
07 has gone

Unit 06
p. 18

01 writes → has written
02 gone → been
03 since → for
04 has received → received
05 has departed → departed
06 has already cleaned → cleaned
07 hasn't drunk → didn't drink
08 for → since

Unit 07
p. 18

01 has not[hasn't] been waiting
02 have been painting
03 have been walking
04 has been talking
05 have been working
06 has been teaching
07 have, been building
08 have been playing

Unit 08
p. 19

01 had met
02 had decided
03 had not[hadn't] done
04 had started
05 had lied
06 had made
07 had left
08 had not[hand't] seen
09 had not[hadn't] completed

Unit 09
p. 19

01 met, had been working
02 had been walking, broke
03 had been learning, moved
04 had been talking, knocked
05 had been eating, got
06 had been sitting, called
07 had been saving, bought
08 had been smoking, noticed
09 had been waiting, arrived

중간고사 • 기말고사 실전문제
pp. 20~23

객관식 정답 [01~15]

01 ①	**02** ⑤	**03** ③	**04** ④	**05** ②
06 ①	**07** ③	**08** ④	**09** ④	**10** ③
11 ①	**12** ③	**13** ③	**14** ②	**15** ①

주관식 정답 [16~30]

16 during → for
17 has → has not[hasn't]
18 for → since
19 has worked → had worked
20 are owning → own **21** invented
22 rains **23** ○
24 My teacher has lost his wallet
25 His son had not learned the alphabet before he went to
26 They have stayed at the hotel for two weeks
27 have been discussing the topic for 30 minutes
28 couldn't remember, had told him about the problem
29 had already left the building
30 They have been playing soccer outside

해설

01 last night는 과거의 특정한 시점을 나타내므로 과거시제를 사용한다.

02 계속의 의미로 쓰인 현재완료시제일 때, 과거의 특정한 시점을 나타내는 last January 앞에는 전치사 since를 사용한다.

03 멀지 않은 미래(tomorrow night)를 나타낼 때는 현재진행시제가 미래시제를 대신할 수 있다.

04 〈보기〉 문장과 ④는 경험(~해 본 적 있다)의 의미로 쓰인 현재완료시제이다. ①, ②는 결과, ③은 계속 ⑤는 완료의 의미로 쓰였다.

05 〈보기〉 문장과 ②는 완료(이미~했다)의 의미로 쓰인 현재완료시제이다. ①은 경험, ③은 결과 ④, ⑤는 계속의 의미로 쓰였다.

06 ① bursted → burst / burst의 과거형은 burst이다.

07 ③ rosen → risen / rise가 '오르다', '(해가) 떠오르다)' 의미일 때 과거분사형은 risen이다.

08 ④ did → do / at this moment는 현재를 나타내는 부사구이므로 현재시제를 사용한다.

09 ① seemed → seems / now는 현재 시점이므로 현재시제를 사용한다. ② had → has / in general은 일반적 사실을 나타내므로 현재시제를 사용한다. ③ visit → visited / 부사구 last year가 과거를 나타내므로 과거시제를 사용한다. ⑤ lived → have lived / 〈since+특정 시점〉은 과거부터 현재까지 계속되는 상황을 나타내므로 현재완료시제를 사용한다.

10 ① have been → was / ago는 과거의 특정한 시점을 나타내므로 과거시제를 사용한다. ② has gone → went / 과거 특정 시점(3 years ago)이 나오므로 과거시제를 사용한다. ④ was → has been / 최근(lately)의 현상이 현재(still)까지도 지속되므로 현재완료시제를 사용한다. ⑤ in → since / 계속적 의미의 현재완료시제가 사용되었으므로 〈since+특정 시점〉을 사용한다.

11 ② taste(맛이 나다), ③ need(필요로 하다), ④ contain(함유하다), ⑤ know(알다)는 진행형으로 쓸 수 없다.

12 컴퓨터를 구입한 것이 고장 난 것보다 더 과거 시점이므로 broke, had bought가 알맞다.

13 〈since+특정 시점〉은 과거부터 현재까지 계속되는 상황을 나타내므로 현재완료시제를 사용한다. / 현재완료시제 부정문이므로 부사 yet(아직)을 사용한다. / 미래 시점을 나타내는 부사 tomorrow가 나오므로 미래시제를 사용한다.

14 ② last year는 과거의 특정한 시점을 나타내므로 현재완료시제와 함께 쓸 수 없다.

15 ① 과거완료시제는 〈had+p.p.〉이며, draw의 과거분사형은 drawn이다.

16 계속의 의미로 사용된 현재완료시제 뒤에 기간(five years)이 나오면 전치사 for를 사용한다.

17 부사 yet은 완료의 의미로 사용된 현재완료시제 부정문과 함께 쓰인다.

18 계속의 의미로 사용된 현재완료시제 뒤에 특정 시점(last April)이 나오면 전치사 since를 사용한다.

19 과거 특정 기간 일했고(had worked), 한 달 전 과거 시점에 은퇴했으므로(retired) 과거완료시제를 사용한다.

20 own(소유하다)은 진행형으로 쓸 수 없다.

21 과거에 있었던 역사적 사실을 기술하고 있으므로 과거시제를 사용한다.

22 미래시제의 조건절에서는 현재시제를 사용한다.

23 일정기간(for five hours)에 이어 현재(now)까지 계속되므로 현재완료 진행시제를 사용한다.

24 지갑을 잃어버려서 (현재) 지갑이 없기 때문에 결과를 나타내는 현재완료시제를 사용한다.

25 초등학교에 간 것(went to~)보다 알파벳을 배우지 않은 것(had not learned)이 먼저 일어난 일이므로 〈과거완료+before+과거〉 형태를 사용한다.

26 일정기간(for two weeks)동안 호텔에 머물고 있으므로 계속의 의미를 나타내는 현재완료시제를 사용한다.

27 토론이 일정기간(for 30 minutes)에 이어 현재까지 진행되고 있으므로 현재완료 진행시제를 사용한다.

28 기억할 수 없었던 것(couldn't remember)은 과거의 일이고, 아내가 그에게 말했던 것(had told him~)은 그 이전에 일어난 일이므로 과거시제와 과거완료시제를 사용한다.

29 사건이 일어났을 때는(occurred) 과거의 일이고, 직원들이 떠난(had left~) 상황은 그 이전에 일어난 일이므로, 과거시제와 과거완료시제를 사용한다.

30 축구를 일정기간(for 3 hours)에 이어 현재까지 계속하는 중이므로 현재완료 진행시제를 사용한다.

CHAPTER 03 조동사

Unit 01 p. 26

01 Was, able to cook
02 was not[wasn't] able to open
03 was able to carry
04 am able to make
05 was not[wasn't] able to solve
06 Were, able to
07 are not[aren't] able to live
08 Are, able to

Unit 02 p. 26

01 may not be
02 may like
03 may not remember
04 May I eat
05 may not be

Unit 03 p. 27

01 must not
02 must
03 must
04 cannot
05 must
06 must
07 cannot
08 cannot

Unit 04 p. 27

01 must not → doesn't have to
02 has to → had to
03 leaves → leave
04 will must → will have to
05 takes → take
06 had → have
07 must → had to
08 must not → don't have to
09 must → had to

Unit 05 p. 28

01 should[ought to] reserve
02 should, park
03 should[ought to] study
04 Should, tell
05 should not[shouldn't] eat/ought not to eat
06 should[ought to] buy
07 should not[shouldn't] watch/ought not to watch
08 should[ought to] exercise

Unit 06 p. 28

A
01 had better stay
02 had better not cheat
03 had better follow

B
01 would rather eat
02 would rather listen to
03 would rather not waste

Unit 07 p. 29

01 used to be
02 used to have
03 used to[would] call
04 used to[would] cook
05 used to[would] drive
06 used to[would] visit
07 used to be
08 used to be

Unit 08 p. 29

01 could have won
02 must have arrived
03 may[might] have got
04 must have made
05 cannot have told
06 should have paid

중간고사 • 기말고사 실전문제 pp. 30~33

객관식 정답 [01~15]

01 ⑤	02 ②	03 ②	04 ③	05 ②
06 ①, ③	07 ②, ⑤	08 ⑤	09 ③	10 ②
11 ①	12 ③	13 ④	14 ③	15 ⑤

주관식 정답 [16~30]

16 would like → would like to

17 had not better → had better not

18 have not to → don't have to

19 should tell → should have told

20 had rather → would rather

21 must be

22 didn't have to sing

23 may[might] not have returned

24 Would you like a cup of warm coffee

25 Movies can guide us into the imaginary world.

26 The child will have to stay at home for a few days.

27 should have believed the fact

28 there used to be a lake near her house

29 The sandwiches (that) we made yesterday must have gone bad.

30 You ought not to tell your friends the secret.

해설

01 가능을 나타내는 can의 미래시제는 will be able to로 써야 한다.

02 '해야 한다'는 의미이므로 have to가 알맞다.

03 '~를 원하니?'의 의미를 나타낼 때는 〈Would you like + 명사 ~? 〉 형태로 써야 한다.

04 ③ '~하지 않아도 된다(불필요)'의 의미를 나타낼 때는 〈don't[doesn't] have to + 동사원형〉 형태로 써야 한다.

05 ② '~하는 게 낫다'의 의미를 나타낼 때는 〈had better + 동사원형〉으로 쓰며, 부정형은 had better 다음에 not이 나온다.

06 과거의 습관적인 행위를 나타낼 때는 would와 used to를 사용한다.

07 상대방에게 정중하게 무엇을 요청할 때는 Would[Could] you~ ? 표현을 사용한다.

08 ⑤ Dose he must clean~? → Must he clean~? / 조동사가 있는 문장을 의문문으로 만들 때에는 조동사를 문장 앞에 위치시킨다.

09 ③ '~하는 게 낫다'의 의미를 나타낼 때는 〈had better + 동사원형〉 형태로 쓴다.

10 ① swimming → to swim / '~을 할 수 있다'는 가능의 표현인 be able to 다음에는 동사원형을 써야 한다. ③ will can → will be able to / 가능을 나타내는 can의 미래시제는 will be able to로 써야 한다. ④ May → Would[Will] 또는 Could[Can] / 요청이나 허가를 나타낼 때 의문문의 주어가 you이면 조동사 may를 사용할 수 없다. ⑤ should take → should have taken / 과거에 대한 후회나 유감을 나타낼 때는 should have p.p.를 사용한다.

11 ② baking → bake / used to 뒤에는 동사원형을 써야 한다. ③ They used to → They are[were] used to / '~에 익숙하다'는 be used to를 사용한다. ④ used to drive → drove / used to는 과거에 반복하던 행동을 지금은 더 이상 하지 않을 때 사용한다. ⑤ uses to → used to / used to는 항상 과거 시점을 나타내므로 현재시제를 사용하지 않는다.

12 '~하고 싶다'는 〈would like to + 동사원형〉 형태이다. / '~일지도 모른다'라는 추측의 의미를 나타내므로 조동사 might를 사용한다.

13 '…보다 (차라리) ~하겠다'의 의미를 나타낼 때는 〈would rather + 동사원형 + than...〉 형태를 사용한다. / '~할 수 있었다(하지만 하지 못했다)'를 나타낼 때 could have p.p.를 사용한다. / 허가나 요청을 나타낼 때는 may 또는 can을 사용한다.

14 상대방에게 요청하는 의문문에서는 may를 사용하지 않는다.

15 '학교구역에서는 담배를 피우면 안 된다'는 의미이므로 의무, 금지의 표현이 알맞다. ⑤ don't have to는 '~할 필요 없다(불필요)'의 의미이므로 적절하지 않다.

16 '~하고 싶다'는 의미를 나타낼 때는 〈would like to + 동사원형〉 형태로 써야 한다.

17 had better의 부정형은 had better not이다.

18 '~하지 않아도 된다', '~할 필요가 없다'의 의미를 나타낼 때는 〈don't[doesn't] have to + 동사원형〉 형태로 써야 한다.

19 과거에 대한 후회나 아쉬움을 나타낼 때는 should have p.p.를 사용한다.

20 '…보다 (차라리) ~하겠다'의 의미를 나타낼 때는 〈would rather+동사원형+than ...〉으로 써야 한다.

21 '~하는 것이 틀림없다'라는 현재의 '강한 추측'의 의미를 나타낼 때는 〈must+동사원형〉 형태로 써야 한다.

22 '~할 필요가 없었다'라는 과거의 의미를 가진 조동사 표현은 〈didn't have to+동사원형〉이다.

23 '~하지 않았을지도 모른다'라는 과거의 추측의 의미를 가진 조동사 표현은 may[might] not have p.p.로 나타낸다.

24 '~를 드릴까요?'의 의미를 표현할 때는 〈Would you like+명사~?〉 형태로 써야 한다.

25 가능의 의미를 표현할 때는 〈can+동사원형〉 형태로 써야 한다.

26 미래의 의무를 표현할 때는 〈will+have to+동사원형〉 형태로 써야 한다.

27 과거에 대한 후회나 유감을 나타낼 때는 〈should have p.p.〉 형태를 사용한다.

28 과거의 습관이나 상태를 나타낼 때는 〈used to+동사원형〉 형태를 사용한다.

29 과거의 강한 추측을 나타낼 때는 must have p.p. 형태를 사용한다.

30 부정의 의무를 나타낼 때는 〈ought not to+동사원형〉 형태를 사용한다.

CHAPTER 04 수동태

Unit 01

p. 36

01 Many cars are produced by the factory.
02 The trip to Taiwan was planned by him.
03 The present for her was wrapped by me.
04 The suggestion was not[wasn't] made by her.
05 The vase was not[wasn't] broken by you.
06 My chair is kicked by the kid behind me.

Unit 02

p. 36

01 of → with
02 with → about
03 by → of
04 with → in
05 of → from
06 by → with
07 as → to
08 at → with

Unit 03

p. 37

01 Some furniture had been moved by us.
02 A house was being built by them.
03 Many animals have been killed by us.
04 Shells were used as money by our ancestors.
05 The air system is controlled by the team.

Unit 04

p. 37

01 We might be disappointed with others.
02 Can a good doctor be recommended by her?
03 Can the piano be played by me for the concert?
04 Calls may not be answered at night.
05 Should the application be submitted right now?
06 The natural environment should not be polluted.

Unit 05

p. 38

01 I am laughed at by many classmates.
02 The television was being turned on by him.
03 He is looked down on by some people.
04 The lights should be turned off (by you).
05 Five books can be checked out today (by us).

Unit 06

p. 38

01 is supposed that they are guilty, are supposed to be guilty

02 is said that Paris is the most attractive city, is said to be the most attractive city

03 is expected that we will find it soon, are expected to find it soon

04 is thought that he is an honest man, is thought to be an honest man

05 was reported that the child was missing, child was reported to be missing

Unit 07
p. 39

01 A muffler was made for me by my sister.

02 was shown the way to the bookstore by him, to the bookstore was shown to me by him

03 A good breakfast is cooked for them every day by her.

04 Foreign students are taught Korean by Sumi.

05 was offered a new job by the company, was offered to me by the company

06 He was asked if he possessed a gun by the police.

Unit 08
p. 40

01 The suspect was seen entering the bank by them.

02 The door was found unlocked by him.

03 Her children were allowed to play by her.

04 She was made a star by the movie.

05 I am wanted to take part in the play by her.

Unit 09
p. 40

01 Her son was made to play outside.

02 A girl was heard to scream for help.

03 We were made to keep a diary in English by the teacher.

04 Her friends were seen to skate on the frozen pond by Eunju.

05 Your eyes are made to feel tired by using a smartphone for a long time.

중간고사 • 기말고사 실전문제
pp. 41~44

객관식 정답 [01~15]

01 ④	**02** ③	**03** ③	**04** ⑤	**05** ②
06 ②	**07** ①	**08** ③	**09** ⑤	**10** ④
11 ①	**12** ⑤	**13** ④	**14** ③	**15** ②

주관식 정답 [16~30]

16 steal → be stolen

17 to choose → to be chosen

18 will keep → will be kept

19 excited by → excited about

20 sold by → sold to

21 The critical patients were looked after in the hospital by the nurse.

22 His assistant was told to bring the document by the lawyer.

23 An old blanket she had was lent to her little sister by Kelly.

24 The students were made to finish the assignment by Tuesday by the professor.

25 Have you ever been surprised at a movie?

26 His speed could be surpassed by the other athletes.

27 We were very pleased with his first victory.

28 The play has been performed for children.

29 The song is expected to gain a lot of popularity.

30 The meeting is being delayed for 20 minutes.

해설

01 'option(옵션)이 선택되지 않았다'의 수동의 의미이므로 부정형 완료 수동태 hasn't been p.p.를 써야 한다.

02 수동의 의미이고 조동사 should가 있으므로 should be p.p.를 써야 한다.

03 두 개 이상의 동사구는 한 단어로 취급하여 수동태로 전환해야 하므로 be taken care of by로 써야 한다.

04 '노래가 그들에 의해 불려 왔다'의 의미가 되므로 완료 수동태 have[has] been p.p.를 사용한다. sing의 과거분사형은 sung이다.

05 집이 (현재) 지어지고 있는 중이므로 진행형 수동태 be being p.p.를 사용한다.

06 ② sending → sent / '사진이 이메일로 보내지지 않는다'의 의미이므로 cannot be sent가 되어야 한다.

07 ① were catched → were caught / catch의 과거분사형은 caught이다.

08 ③ satisfied in → satisfied with / be satisfied with(~에 만족하다)

09 ① be hold → be held / hold의 과거분사형은 held이다. ② with him → by him / 일반적인 동사의 수동태 문장에서 행위의 주체를 나타낼 때는 전치사 by를 사용한다. ③ can was → can be / 조동사가 있는 문장의 수동태는 〈조동사+be+p.p.〉 형태로 나타낸다. ④ be place → be placed / 주어 sofa(소파)가 여기에 위치되는 것이 좋겠다는 의미이므로 수동태인 be+p.p.를 사용한다.

10 ① were disappeared → disappeared / 자동사 disappear(사라지다)는 수동태로 만들 수 없다. ② The politics lied about the fact / 자동사 lie(거짓말하다)는 수동태로 만들 수 없다. ③ was happened → happened / 자동사 happen(일어나다)은 수동태로 만들 수 없다. ⑤ is costed → costs / 자동사 cost(비용이 들다)는 수동태로 만들 수 없다.

11 ② allowed going → allowed to go / allow는 전치사 to를 사용하여 수동태를 만든다. ③ called by 'Cutie' → called 'Cutie' / call(부르다)의 목적격보어 'Cutie'는 전치사를 사용하지 않고 수동태를 만든다. ④ was made happily → was made happy / make는 목적격보어로 부사를 사용할 수 없으며, 수동태로 변형할 때도 형용사인 목적격보어는 그대로 사용된다. ⑤ was made think → was made to think / 사역동사 make 문장을 수동태로 만들 때, 목적격보어는 동사원형(원형부정사)에서 to부정사로 바뀐다.

12 수여동사 ask는 수동태 전환 시, 전치사 of를 사용한다. / 지각동사 hear를 수동태로 만들 때, 목적격보어는 동사원형에서 to부정사로 바뀐다.

13 '전자기기가 요리에 사용되어 왔다'는 의미이므로 현재완료형 수동태 has been used가 알맞다. / 수여동사 send는 수동태를 만들 때 전치사 to를 사용한다. / ask(요청하다)를 수동태로 만들 때, 목적격보어로 쓰인 to부정사는 그대로 유지한다.

14 수여동사 give는 전치사 to를 사용하여 수동태를 만든다. / 사역동사 make를 수동태로 만들 때, 목적격보어는 동사원형에서 to부정사로 바뀐다.

15 be surprised at(~에 놀라다) / be angry at~(~에 화가 나다)

16 '값비싼 목걸이가 절대 도난당해서는 안 된다'는 의미이므로 조동사가 있는 문장의 수동태 should be p.p.를 사용한다.

17 '그녀가 그 역할에 선택되기를 기대했다'는 의미이므로 목적어로 쓰인 to부정사를 수동의 형태로 바꿔야 한다.

18 '손이 장갑에 의해 따뜻하게 될 것이다'는 의미이므로 미래형 수동태 will be kept가 알맞다.

19 be excited about(~에 대해 흥분하다)는 by이외의 전치사를 사용하는 관용구문이다.

20 '물건들이 많은 손님들에게 팔렸다'는 의미이므로 many customers 앞에 전치사 to를 쓴다.

21 수동태를 만들 때, 동사구 look after는 하나의 단어로 취급하여 분리하지 않는다.

22 to부정사를 목적격보어로 하는 5형식 동사 tell의 문장을 수동태로 만들 때, to부정사의 형태를 변형하지 않고 그대로 쓴다.

23 4형식 동사 lend의 직접목적어를 주어로 하는 수동태 문장을 만들 때, 〈주어(직접목적어)+be p.p.+to+간접목적어+(by 행위자)〉의 형태를 사용한다.

24 사역동사 make의 문장을 수동태로 만들 때, 목적격보어는 동사원형(원형부정사)에서 to부정사로 바꾼다.

25 경험을 나타내는 현재완료 수동태 의문문이므로 Have you ever been p.p. ~?를 사용한다.

26 '그의 속도는 따라잡힐 수 있었다'는 의미이므로 조동사의 수동태 could be p.p.를 사용해야 한다.

27 be pleased with(~에 기뻐하다)는 by 이외의 전치사를 사용하는 관용구문이다.

28 '연극이 공연되어 왔다'는 의미이므로 현재완료 수동태 have been p.p.를 사용한다.

29 '그 노래는 ~예상된다'는 의미이므로, expect를 사용한 수동태 문장이 되어야 하며 목적격보어로 쓰인 to부정사(to gain)는 바꾸지 않고 그대로 쓴다.

30 '회의가 일정 시간 동안 지연되고 있다'는 의미이므로 현재완료형 수동태 have been p.p.를 사용한다.

CHAPTER 05 부정사

Unit 01 p. 46

01 to make cookies
02 to receive a letter
03 to host the party
04 To find birds
05 not to accept it
06 to buy a house

Unit 02 p. 46

01 your → you
02 submit → to submit
03 for → of
04 of → for
05 for → of
06 for → of
07 to me for riding → for me to ride
08 listen to → to listen
09 difficulty → difficult

Unit 03 p. 47

01 how to play golf
02 how to make it
03 where we should go
04 when to leave
05 what to choose
06 how to get there

Unit 04 p. 47

01 playing → to play
02 completing → to complete
03 delicious anything → anything delicious
04 to talk → to talk about
05 to drink hot → hot to drink
06 to stay → to stay in
07 introducing → to introduce
08 to play → to play in

Unit 05 p. 48

01 is to be held at the hotel
02 The soldiers were to die
03 are not to make the same mistake
04 are to pass the test
05 is not to be opened

Unit 06 p. 48

01 hurry not to miss the flight
02 in order to study English
03 to get a scholarship
04 easy to make new friends
05 silly to ask such a question
06 grew up to become a firefighter
07 is exciting to play

Unit 07 p. 49

01 are to finish the assignment
02 It is not easy to read
03 a class to learn Italian
04 planned to learn Taekwondo
05 are not to make noise
06 dream is to climb Mt. Everest
07 not a student to be late for class

Unit 08 p. 49

01 smart enough to solve
02 so expensive that she can't buy
03 too wise for me to fool him
04 so cold that we can't go
05 too big to wear
06 so shocked that I couldn't get up

Unit 09 p. 50

01 seems that I left my wallet
02 seemed to have learned Chinese
03 seems that Jeju is a place
04 seemed to be cleaned

Unit 10 p. 50

01 expect the letter to arrive
02 helped her (to) repair
03 ordered us to pay attention to
04 get the computer to work
05 want me not to go out

Unit 11 p. 51

01 lets me see
02 made him lose the race
03 had his students fill in
04 wants me to water
05 made her apologize
06 let her daughter add

Unit 12 p. 51

01 to clean
02 spin[spinning]
03 wash
04 rub[rubbing]
05 not to leave
06 play[playing]
07 shout[shouting]
08 study
09 move[moving]

Unit 13 p. 52

01 so to speak
02 To begin with
03 To be honest
04 To tell the truth
05 To be sure
06 Needless to say

중간고사 • 기말고사 실전문제 pp. 53~56

객관식 정답 [01~15]

01 ①	**02** ③	**03** ⑤	**04** ②	**05** ③
06 ④	**07** ①	**08** ⑤	**09** ③	**10** ④
11 ⑤	**12** ②	**13** ④	**14** ②	**15** ③

주관식 정답 [16~30]

16 ○
17 to improve
18 attracting → to attract
19 for you → of you
20 what should do → what to do 또는 what they should do
21 is smart of him
22 in order to[so as to] complete
23 too busy to go
24 that he had
25 The doctor advised a patient to
26 To tell the truth, Jane is not close
27 Is there something cold to drink?
28 The book was too hard for me to read.
29 My father taught me how to ride a bike.
30 She seems to have been very upset.

해설

01 가주어 It, 진주어 to부정사(to swim~)를 사용한 문장이다.

02 wish는 목적어로 to부정사(~하는 것)를 사용한다.

03 -thing으로 끝나는 명사 뒤에서 〈형용사+to부정사〉가 수식하는 문장이다.

04 '너무 ~해서 …할 수 없다'의 의미를 나타낼 때, 〈too+형용사+to부정사〉 형태를 사용한다.

05 〈It's+사람의 성격, 성품을 나타내는 형용사+of+목적격+to부정사〉를 사용한 문장이다.

06 ④ To taking → To take / to부정사가 주어로 쓰인 문장으로 〈to+동사원형〉 형태로 써야 한다.

07 ① of me → for me / to부정사의 의미상 주어는 〈for+행위자〉를 사용한다.

08 ⑤ throw → to throw / order의 목적격보어로 to부정사를 써야 한다.

09 ① to stay → to stay at ② to talk → to talk to[with] ④ to play → to play with ⑤ to write → to write on

10 ① are join → are to join / '~하려면'의 의미로 '의도[조건]'을 나타내는 〈주어+be to부정사〉를 써야 한다. ② enough strong → strong enough / '…하기에 충분히 ~한'의 의미로 〈형용사+enough+to부정사〉를 써야 한다. ③ to getting → to get / '너무 ~해서 …할 수 없다' 의미로 〈too+형용사+to부정사〉를 써야 한다. ⑤ seems to not → doesn't seem to / '~한 것 같지 않다'의 의미로 〈don't[doesn't] seem+to부정사〉를 써야 한다.

11 ① To summing up → To sum up(요약하자면) ② Being honest → To be honest(사실은) ③ Needless to saying → Needless to say(말할 필요도 없이) ④ to speak so → so to speak(말하자면)

12 〈It's+사람의 성격, 성품을 나타내는 형용사+of+목적격+to부정사〉를 사용한 문장이다.

13 '너무 ~해서 …할 수 없었다' 의 의미로 〈so+형용사+that+주어+couldn't+동사원형〉 형태를 사용한다.

/ to부정사의 부정 표현은 ⟨not+to부정사⟩의 형태로 쓴다. / '…했었던 것 같았다'의 의미로 ⟨seemed(과거)+to have p.p.(대과거)⟩ 형태를 사용한다.

14 ⟨보기⟩ 문장과 ①, ③, ④, ⑤는 to부정사의 부사적 용법으로 쓰였고 ②는 앞의 명사 chores를 수식하므로 to부정사의 형용사적 용법으로 쓰였다.

15 ⟨보기⟩ 문장과 ①, ②, ④, ⑤는 to부정사의 명사적 용법으로 쓰였고 ③은 ⟨be+to부정사⟩로 '의무'를 나타내는 형용사적 용법으로 쓰였다.

16 사역동사 let은 목적격보어로 원형부정사(동사원형)를 사용한다.

17 hope는 목적어로 to부정사를 사용한다.

18 '…하기에 충분히 ~한'의 의미를 나타낼 때, ⟨형용사+enough+to부정사⟩를 사용한다.

19 ⟨It's+사람의 성격, 성품을 나타내는 형용사+of+목적격+to부정사⟩ 형태를 사용한 문장이다.

20 '무엇을 ~할지'의 의미로 ⟨what+to부정사⟩ 또는 ⟨what+주어+should+동사원형⟩을 사용한다.

21 ⟨It's+사람의 성격, 성품을 나타내는 형용사+of+목적격+to부정사⟩의 형태를 사용한다.

22 '하기 위해서'의 의미를 나타낼 때 부사적 용법의 to부정사를 사용한다. ⟨in order to/so as to+동사원형⟩도 가능하다.

23 ⟨so+형용사+that+주어+can't[couldn't]+동사원형⟩은 ⟨too+형용사+to부정사⟩의 형태로 바꿀 수 있다.

24 ⟨주어+seemed+to부정사(동사원형)⟩는 ⟨It seemed that+주어+과거시제 동사⟩의 형태로 바꿀 수 있다.

25 advise(조언하다)는 목적격보어로 to부정사를 사용한다.

26 to tell the truth는 '사실을 말하자면'의 의미를 가진 독립부정사이다.

27 -thing으로 끝나는 명사 뒤에서 ⟨형용사+to부정사(형용사적 용법)⟩가 앞의 명사를 수식한다.

28 ⟨too+형용사+to부정사⟩를 사용한다.

29 '~하는 방법'의 의미로 ⟨how+to부정사⟩를 사용한다.

30 '~했던 것 같다'라고 과거의 상황을 현재 추측하여 말하고 있으므로 seem은 현재시제(seems)로, to부정사는 과거를 나타내는 완료시제(to have been)로 쓴다.

CHAPTER 06 동명사와 분사

Unit 01 p. 58

01 collect → collecting[to collect]
02 to watch → watching
03 Eat → Eating[To eat]
04 to think → thinking
05 to review → reviewing
06 to sit → sitting
07 to drink → drinking
08 to ride → riding

Unit 02 p. 58

01 drinking
02 to go
03 moving
04 to write
05 living
06 to see
07 being
08 to stay

Unit 03 p. 59

01 not[never] telling the secret
02 her sending
03 not[never] drinking soda
04 Not resting your eyes
05 my[me] playing

Unit 04 p. 59

01 admits having stolen
02 admitted having seen
03 doesn't mind being asked
04 being attacked
05 being late
06 forgot having traveled
07 avoided being hit

Unit 05 p. 60

01 were busy cleaning
02 went fishing
03 spent, buying
04 no use worrying
05 What about having
06 trouble finding

Unit 06 p. 60

01 filled
02 making
03 ground
04 kidnapped
05 talking
06 Singing[To sing]
07 sleeping

Unit 07 p. 61

01 building
02 shocking
03 used
04 hit
05 interesting
06 comforting
07 stolen
08 destroyed
09 surrounded

Unit 08 p. 61

01 pressed
02 built
03 exciting
04 installed
05 boring
06 cheered

Unit 09 p. 62

01 surprised, surprising
02 frightened, frightening
03 fascinated, fascinating
04 embarrassing, embarrassed
05 inspiring, inspired
06 satisfying, satisfied

Unit 10 p. 62

01 너의 혼란스러운 말(을)
02 TV를 보는 몇몇 아이들(이)
03 공부하기를 계속했다
04 울고 있는 아기(를)
05 흡연실
06 매우 실망스러운

중간고사 • 기말고사 실전문제 pp. 63~66

객관식 정답 [01~15]

01 ③	02 ④	03 ⑤	04 ①	05 ②
06 ①	07 ②	08 ④	09 ④	10 ①
11 ⑤	12 ③	13 ②	14 ⑤	15 ④

주관식 정답 [16~30]

16 going
17 ○
18 wearing → to wear
19 buying → to buy
20 frightened → frightening
21 skating
22 drawn
23 my[me] calling
24 having failed
25 apologized to everyone for not attending the meeting
26 They are going to travel to the place shown
27 We got used to wearing masks
28 had my toy repaired last weekend
29 Are you looking forward to getting presents on Christmas?
30 She is watching snow falling from the sky.

해설

01 전치사 about의 목적어로 동명사가 나온다.

02 avoid는 동명사를 목적어로 취하는 동사이다.

03 〈forget+동명사〉는 '(과거에) ~했던 것을 잊다'의 의미이다.

04 '…가 ~하는 것을 참다'의 의미를 나타낼 때 stand 뒤에 〈의미상 주어(소유격[목적격])+동명사〉형태를 쓴다.

05 〈be worth+동명사〉는 '~할 가치가 있다'의 의미이다.

06 ① to be → being / 〈feel like+동명사〉: ~하고 싶다

07 ② lied → lying / '눕다'의 의미인 자동사 lie는 현재분사로만 사용할 수 있다.

08 ④ to take → taking / suggest는 동명사를 목적어로 취한다.

09 ① to watch → watching ② to make → making ③ to paint → painting ⑤ to speak → speaking

10 ② inviting → to invite ③ to bring → bringing ④ showing → to show ⑤ telling not → not telling

11 ① Did you shock → Were you shocked / you가 감정을 느끼는 대상이 되므로 과거분사를 써야 한다.
② interesting → interested / students가 감정을 느끼는 대상이 되므로 과거분사를 써야 한다.
③ bored → boring / the party가 감정을 유발하는 주체가 되므로 능동의 의미인 현재분사를 써야 한다.

④ tired → tiring / job이 감정을 유발하는 주체가 되므로 능동의 의미인 현재분사를 써야 한다.

12 mind는 동명사를 목적어로 취하는 동사이다. / choose는 목적어로 to부정사를 취하는 동사이다.

13 동명사의 부정형은 〈not + 동명사〉이다. / 〈try + 동명사〉: 시험 삼아 ~ 해보다 / 동명사의 의미상 주어는 소유격이나 목적격을 쓴다.

14 ⑤는 과거진행시제에 쓰인 현재분사이고 ①, ②, ③, ④는 동명사이다.

15 ④는 형용사의 역할을 하는 현재분사이고 ①, ②, ③, ⑤는 동명사이다.

16 put off는 동명사를 목적어로 취한다.

17 continue는 목적어로 동명사와 to부정사를 모두 사용한다.

18 need는 목적어로 to부정사를 사용한다.

19 '~하기 위해 멈추다'의 의미로 〈stop + to부정사(부사적 용법)〉를 사용한다.

20 movie가 감정을 유발하는 주체이므로 현재분사인 frightening이 되어야 한다.

21 '~하러 가다'의 의미로 〈go + 동명사〉를 사용한다.

22 The portraits를 꾸며주는 분사이므로 '그려진' 의미의 과거분사를 사용한다.

23 '…가 ~하는 것을 좋아하지 않다'의 의미로 doesn't like 뒤에 〈의미상 주어(소유격[목적격]) + 동명사〉를 써야 한다.

24 과거에 있었던 일에 대해 말하는 시점이 현재일 때, 〈현재시제 + 전치사 + 완료동명사(having p.p.)〉를 써야 한다.

25 전치사 for의 목적어로 동명사(attending)를 사용하며, 동명사의 부정형은 〈not + 동명사〉이다.

26 place를 꾸며주는 분사이므로 과거분사를 사용하여 명사 뒤에서 수식해준다.

27 '~에 익숙해지다'의 의미로 〈be[get] used to + 동명사〉를 사용한다.

28 my toy와 수동의 관계이므로 과거분사(repaired)를 사용한다.

29 '~하기를 고대하다'의 의미로 〈look forward to + 동명사〉를 사용한다.

30 '떨어지는 눈'의 의미이므로 현재분사(falling)를 사용한다.

[CHAPTER 07 비교 표현]

Unit 01

p. 68

01 isn't as[so] old as
02 isn't as[so] high as
03 get up as early as
04 is as tall as
05 isn't as[so] difficult as

Unit 02

p. 68

01 as soon as possible
02 as well as, could
03 as positively as possible

Unit 03

p. 69

01 able, ablest
02 angrier, angriest
03 worse, worst
04 worse, worst
05 more beautiful, most beautiful
06 bigger, biggest
07 busier, busiest
08 more comfortable, most comfortable
09 more curious, most curious
10 more dangerous, most dangerous
11 more delicious, most delicious
12 more diligent, most diligent
13 dirtier, dirtiest
14 easier, easiest
15 more easily, most easily
16 fatter, fattest
17 friendlier, friendliest
18 better, best
19 heavier, heaviest
20 hotter, hottest
21 worse, worst

22 lazier, laziest
23 less, least
24 lovelier, loveliest
25 more, most
26 prettier, prettiest
27 sadder, saddest
28 skinnier, skinniest
29 slower, slowest
30 more slowly, most slowly
31 tastier, tastiest
32 more useful, most useful
33 better, best

Unit 04 p. 71

01 older than
02 much more important than
03 run faster than
04 far earlier than
05 more[less] expensive than
06 larger than

Unit 05 p. 71

01 a hundred times better than
02 twice as old as
03 three times harder than
04 four times longer than
05 twice as tall as
06 ten times as fast as

Unit 06 p. 72

01 The later we go to bed, the more tired we become.
02 The harder you study, the better grades you get.
03 She will become more and more beautiful.
04 The faster you run, the more exhausted you become.
05 The smaller the house is, the cheaper it is.

Unit 07 p. 72

01 the wealthiest people
02 the most important thing
03 the cheapest dish
04 one of the most popular sports
05 one of the most attractive students

Unit 08 p. 73

01 No other student is as short
02 carefully than all the other people
03 No other movie is as boring
04 quieter than any other place
05 No other student is more diligent
06 better, than all the other students

Unit 09 p. 73

01 person → people[persons]
02 old → older
03 like → as
04 warm → warmer
05 all other lemon → all the other lemons
06 am → do
07 better the boy → better than the boy

중간고사 • 기말고사 실전문제 pp. 74~77

객관식 정답 [01~15]

01 ③	02 ④	03 ⑤	04 ④	05 ③
06 ①	07 ①	08 ②	09 ④	10 ①
11 ②	12 ④	13 ②	14 ③	15 ⑤

주관식 정답 [16~30]

16 cold
17 ○
18 the most → more
19 Most → The most
20 healthy → healthier
21 heavy as
22 the earlier
23 as, could
24 luckier, any

25 as frightened as the passengers

26 more active in changing the wrong policies than before

27 Her house is twice as large as this store.

28 The Shanghai Tower is the highest building in China.

29 He was one of the bravest soldiers in the battle.

30 The faster you eat, the worse your stomach will be.

해설

01 '~만큼 …하지 않은'의 의미로 ⟨not as[so]+원급(형용사)+as ~⟩가 사용된다.

02 '~보다 두 배만큼 …한[하게]'의 의미로 ⟨twice as+원급(부사)+as ~⟩가 사용된다.

03 '~보다 훨씬 더 …한'의 의미로 ⟨much+비교급(형용사)+than ~⟩이 사용된다.

04 '가능한 ~하게'의 의미로 ⟨as + 원급(부사) + as possible⟩이 사용된다.

05 '~하면 할수록, 더 …하다'의 의미로 ⟨the+비교급~, the+비교급 ...⟩이 사용된다.

06 ① newer → new / 원급을 비교할 때는 ⟨as+원급(형용사)+as⟩를 써야 한다.

07 ① seriously → serious / 동사 is의 보어로 형용사를 써야 한다.

08 ② than → as / 원급을 이용한 최상급 표현으로 ⟨No other ~ as+원급+as ...⟩를 사용한다.

09 ① more annoyed → the more annoyed ② greedy → the greedier ③ the most → the more ⑤ you can be the safer → the safer you can be

10 ② fast → faster / ⟨비교급+than any other+단수명사⟩의 형태로 쓴다. ③ the most smartest → the smartest / 형용사 smart의 최상급은 단어 뒤에 -est를 붙여 만든다. ④ more → the most 또는 of → than / ⟨the+최상급+of+복수명사⟩ 또는 ⟨비교급+than+비교대상⟩ 형태로 쓴다. ⑤ largest → the largest / 형용사의 최상급 앞에는 항상 the를 써야 한다.

11 ① greater → greatest / '가장 ~한 것들 중 하나'의 의미로 ⟨one of the+최상급+복수명사⟩를 사용한다. ③ the less → the least / '가장 덜 ~한'의 의미로 최상급을 나타낼 때는 the least로 쓴다. ④ most → the most / 형용사의 최상급 앞에는 항상 the를 써야 한다. ⑤ dress → dresses / '~한 것들 중 하나'의 의미로 ⟨one of the+최상급+복수명사⟩를 사용한다.

12 '가장 ~한'의 의미로 ⟨the+최상급+of[in] ...⟩를 사용한다. / '~보다 훨씬 덜 …한'의 의미로 ⟨much+ less 형용사+than ~⟩을 사용한다.

13 '가장 ~한'의 의미로 ⟨the+최상급+of[in] ...⟩를 사용한다. / '~보다 더 …한'의 의미로 ⟨비교급+than ~⟩을 사용한다. / 원급을 비교할 때는 ⟨as+원급(부사)+as ...⟩를 사용한다.

14 ⟨not as+원급(형용사)+as ~⟩는 ⟨less+형용사+than ~⟩으로 바꿔 쓸 수 있다.

15 ⟨배수사+비교급+than ...⟩은 ⟨배수사+as+원급+as ...⟩로 바꿔 쓸 수 있다.

16 '~만큼 …한'의 의미로 ⟨as+원급+as ~⟩로 써야 한다.

17 '~의 반만큼 …한'의 의미로 ⟨half as+원급+as ~⟩로 써야 한다.

18 최상급을 표현할 때는 ⟨비교급+than all the other+복수명사⟩를 써야 한다.

19 형용사의 최상급 앞에는 항상 the를 쓴다.

20 '~보다 훨씬 더 …한'의 의미로 ⟨much+비교급(형용사) than ~⟩을 사용한다.

21 '~보다 –배 만큼 …한'의 의미로 ⟨배수사+as+원급+as ~⟩를 사용한다.

22 '~할수록 더 …하다'의 의미로 ⟨the+비교급 ~, the+비교급 ...⟩ 형태를 써야 한다.

23 ⟨as+원급+as possible⟩은 ⟨as+원급+as+주어+can[could]⟩ 형태로 바꿔 쓸 수 있다.

24 비교급을 이용하여 최상급을 표현할 때는 ⟨비교급+than any other+단수명사⟩를 사용한다.

25 '~만큼 …한'의 의미로 ⟨as+원급+as ~⟩를 사용한다.

26 '이전보다 더 적극적'이라고 했으므로 ⟨비교급(more active)+than+비교대상(before)⟩의 형태로 쓴다.

27 '~보다 –배 만큼 …한'의 의미로 〈배수사+as+원급+as ~〉를 사용한다.

28 '가장 ~한'의 의미로 〈the+최상급〉을 사용하며 뒤에 장소가 제시되었으므로 〈in+단수명사(장소)〉가 나온다.

29 '가장 ~한 것들 중 하나'의 의미로 〈one of the+최상급+복수명사〉 형태가 사용된다.

30 '~하면 할수록, 더 …하다'의 의미로 〈the+비교급 ~, the+비교급 ...〉 형태가 사용된다.

CHAPTER 08 접속사

Unit 01 p. 80

01 ○
02 ○
03 as soon as I arrive Paris
04 while
05 ○
06 when you get home
07 ○
08 when[while]

Unit 02 p. 80

01 Unless we study hard
02 If she doesn't rush
03 If I read English books every day
04 Unless they practice hard
05 If you say hello to her
06 If you drive too fast

Unit 03 p. 81

01 because[as/since] she won the lottery
02 because of the discovery
03 so I did the dishes
04 so I was late for school
05 because[as/since] we spent all the money

Unit 04 p. 81

01 although I tried hard
02 Though it rained
03 though we were tired
04 Though it was cold
05 even though he is rich
06 although it is not big

Unit 05 p. 82

01 so sour that we couldn't eat
02 so that he could avoid the rush hour
03 so that I can finish the homework on time
04 so young that they can't see the movie
05 so that you don't break it

Unit 06 p. 82

01 as they are
02 While Tony likes dogs
03 since he graduated
04 While you were reading
05 since[as] you've finished your homework

Unit 07 p. 83

01 That he has a son
02 that she's right
03 that we tried hard
04 that he cheated
05 that he agreed
06 that he forgot my name

Unit 08 p. 83

01 if[whether] she saw it
02 Whether you accept it
03 if[whether] I could go
04 Whether it will rain
05 if[whether] there is a cafe
06 Whether you go or not

Unit 09 p. 84

01 Otherwise
02 However
03 As a result
04 Thus[Therefore/Hence]
05 Besides[In addition/Moreover]
06 Nevertheless[Nonetheless]

Unit 10 p. 84

01 and
02 Unless
03 or
04 If
05 or
06 If

Unit 11 p. 85

01 as well as
02 not only, but (also)
03 either, or
04 Neither, nor
05 both, and
06 Not, but

중간고사 • 기말고사 실전문제 pp. 86~89

객관식 정답 [01~15]

01 ③	**02** ②	**03** ⑤	**04** ②, ④	**05** ①, ③
06 ④	**07** ①	**08** ③	**09** ④	**10** ②
11 ⑤	**12** ③	**13** ⑤	**14** ②	**15** ⑤

주관식 정답 [16~30]

16 until
17 However[Nevertheless/Nonetheless/On the other hand]
18 will eat → eats
19 enjoys → enjoy
20 because of → because
21 as
22 while
23 that, could
24 was strange that
25 a deep breath before she went on the stage
26 unless you follow the right procedure
27 She can speak neither Korean nor Japanese.
28 Do you know whether he will come back to Korea
29 It was terrifying that the boat was shaking strongly.
30 Many cities as well as Seoul are in danger.

해설

01 주절의 시제가 현재완료 진행시제이므로 '~한 이후로'의 의미를 가진 접속사 since를 사용한다.

02 '~하지 않으면'의 의미를 가진 접속사 unless를 사용한다.

03 '~인지 아닌지'의 의미를 가진 접속사 whether를 사용한다. 같은 의미의 접속사 if는 주어 자리에 쓸 수 없다.

04 '~할 때'의 의미를 가진 접속사 when, as를 사용한다.

05 '~하기 때문에'의 의미를 가진 접속사 as, since를 사용한다.

06 '~하기 때문에'의 의미를 가진 접속사 as를 사용하여 원인과 결과를 기술한다.

07 'A도 B도 아닌'이라는 뜻의 〈neither A nor B〉 형태로 쓴다.

08 ③ so that tired → so tired that / '너무 ~해서 …하다'의 의미는 〈so+형용사+that ...〉의 형태로 쓴다.

09 ① before → after / 일몰 후에, 별을 볼 수 있으므로 after가 알맞다. ② until → when / '뱀을 봤을 때, 떠났다'는 것이 의미상 적절하다. ③ when → since / 주절의 시제가 현재완료 진행시제이므로 since를 쓰는 것이 알맞다. ⑤ as soon as → while / '통화하는 동안에' 이므로 while이 적절하다.

10 ②는 '~하는 반면에'의 의미로 사용되었고, ①, ③, ④, ⑤는 '~하는 동안에'의 의미로 사용되었다.

11 ⑤는 '~ 때문에'의 의미로 사용되었고, ①, ②, ③, ④는 '~한 이후'의 의미로 사용되었다.

12 '땀이 났기 때문에 가능한 빨리 샤워하고 싶었다'이므로 since와 as soon as possible이 적절하다.

13 '~하는 반면에'의 의미인 while을 사용한다. / '~하지 않으면'의 의미인 unless를 사용한다. / '~하기 위해서'의 의미인 〈so as to ~〉를 사용한다.

14 〈so that ~ (~하도록)〉은 〈in order to부정사〉로 바꿔 쓸 수 있다.

15 If 조건절 문장은 〈명령문, or ...〉의 형태로 바꿔 쓸 수 있다.

16 '~할 때까지'의 의미인 접속사 until을 사용한다.

17 '그러나'의 의미를 가진 접속부사 However를 사용한다. 의미상 Nevertheless, Nonetheless, On the other hand도 가능함.

18 조건절의 동사는 현재시제가 미래시제를 대신한다.

19 〈B as well as A〉가 주어로 사용될 때, 동사의 수는 B에 일치시킨다.

20 뒤에 완전한 절이 오므로, 접속사 because를 사용한다.

21 '~함에 따라'의 의미를 가진 접속사 as를 사용한다.

22 '~하는 반면에'의 의미를 가진 접속사 while을 사용한다.

23 〈so as to부정사〉는 〈so+that+주어+can[could]〉으로 바꿔 쓸 수 있다.

24 주어 자리에 쓰는 that절은 가주어 it을 사용하여 바꿔 쓸 수 있다.

25 '~하기 전에'의 의미는 〈before+주어+동사〉의 형태로 쓴다.

26 '~하지 않으면'의 의미는 〈unless+주어+동사〉의 형태로 쓴다.

27 'A도 B도 아닌'이라는 뜻의 〈neither A nor B〉 형태를 사용한다.

28 '~인지 아닌지'라는 뜻의 〈whether+주어+동사+or not〉의 형태로 쓴다.

29 주어 자리에 that절이 쓰이면 가주어 it을 주어 자리에 쓰고 진짜 주어는 문장 뒤로 옮긴다.

30 'A뿐만 아니라 B도'의 의미로 〈B as well as A〉 형태를 사용하며, 동사의 수는 B에 일치시킨다.

CHAPTER 09 분사구문

Unit 01 p. 92

01 Having chicken
02 Arriving there
03 Talking to her
04 Having a cold
05 Opening the box

Unit 02 p. 92

01 Not going to bed early
02 built a long time ago
03 arriving in Daejeon at 11:30
04 Not having a car
05 Playing soccer
06 Never studying hard

Unit 03 p. 93

01 Having been injured
02 Not having bought anything
03 I had run 10 km
04 we were not invited

Unit 04 p. 93

01 Not (being) old enough
02 (Being) Shocked by the news
03 (Having been) Annoyed by his behavior
04 Not (being) used often

Unit 05 p. 94

01 There being much traffic
02 It snowing
03 The meeting ending
04 It being cold
05 There being many interesting places
06 My parents watching TV

Unit 06
p. 94

01 Strictly speaking
02 Frankly speaking
03 Considering the costs
04 Generally speaking
05 Judging from his face
06 Compared with others

Unit 07
p. 95

01 with my dog following me
02 with the sun shining
03 with the door closed
04 with the cat sleeping on the sofa
05 with his legs crossed
06 with her eyes closed

중간고사 • 기말고사 실전문제
pp. 96~100

객관식 정답 [01~15]

01 ②	**02** ⑤	**03** ④	**04** ③	**05** ③
06 ③	**07** ④	**08** ④	**09** ③	**10** ⑤
11 ③	**12** ④	**13** ②	**14** ④	**15** ④

주관식 정답 [16~30]

16 ○
17 Trained
18 When → Though[Although/Even though]
19 being crying → crying
20 sat → sitting
21 it being heavy
22 with, broken
23 graduating from high school
24 Not having raised a dog
25 his meal with the guard watching
26 Judging from his English accent, the gentleman seems to be
27 Not knowing what to choose,
28 with the light turned off
29 Waiting in line, she played cell phone games.
30 A window being broken, cold wind came

해설

01 부사절 When they went~가 분사구문 Going~ 으로 바뀐 문장이다.

02 분사구문의 부정형은 분사 앞에 not을 써야 한다.

03 분사구문의 의미상 주어가 주절의 주어와 다른 경우, 분사구문에 주어를 따로 표시한다.

04 유도부사 there가 사용된 부사절의 분사구문은 〈There+분사 ~〉의 순서로 쓴다.

05 〈with+(대)명사+분사〉형태를 사용하며 명사와 수동의 관계이므로 과거분사를 쓴다.

06 ③ Folding → Folded / 주어가 note이므로 수동의 의미인 과거분사를 쓴다.

07 ④ Not expensive → Not being expensive / 분사구문의 부정문에서 be동사는 생략할 수 없다.

08 ① Being it stormy → It being stormy / 독립분사구문은 〈주어 + 분사 ~〉의 순서이다. ② Being Friday → It being Friday / 주절의 주어가 다르므로 생략할 수 없다. ③ Being there → There being / 유도부사 there가 사용된 부사절의 분사구문은 〈There+분사 ~〉의 순서이다. ⑤ Not being far → It not being far / 주절의 주어가 다르므로 생략할 수 없다.

09 ① To be considered → Considering / Considering(~을 고려하면) / ② spoken → speaking / Frankly speaking(솔직히 말해서) / ④ Judged → Judging / Judging from(~로 판단해 보면) / ⑤ Comparing → Compared / Compared with(~와 비교하면)

10 주절과 부사절의 주어가 일치하므로, 접속사, 주어, being을 생략하여 분사구문을 만든다.

11 완료시제의 분사구문은 Having p.p. ~의 형태이다.

12 인과관계를 설명하므로 접속사 as, since, because 등을 사용하며, '~에 만족한'을 의미하는 be satisfied with를 써야 한다.

13 '뚜껑이 닫힌 채'의 의미이므로 〈with+명사+과거분사〉의 형태를 사용한다.

14 주어 child가 듣는 상황이므로 과거분사를 사용한다. / some questions는 답해지지 않은 상황이므로 수동의 의미인 과거분사를 사용한다.

15 분사구문의 의미상 주어가 주절의 주어와 일치하지 않으므로 주어를 생략할 수 없다. / 주어인 Lisa가 스트레스를 받는(수동) 상황이므로 과거분사를 사용한다. / engine이 타고 있는(능동) 상황이므로 현재분사를 사용한다.

16 부사절 As she was proud~를 분사구문으로 알맞게 바꾸었다.

17 The dog이 훈련받는(수동) 상황이므로 과거분사가 적절하다.

18 문맥상 양보의 의미가 어울리므로, 접속사 When을 Though[Although/Even though]로 바꿔야 한다.

19 진행시제로 분사구문을 만들 때 being은 생략한다.

20 with를 사용한 분사구문이며, 능동의 상황이므로 현재분사로 고친다.

21 주절의 주어와 일치하지 않으므로, 분사구문으로 고칠 때, 주어를 생략하지 않는다.

22 with를 사용한 분사구문이며, 수동의 상황이므로 과거분사를 써야 한다.

23 분사구문을 만들 때, 주절과 부사절의 주어가 같으면 접속사와 주어를 생략하고 동사를 분사형태로 바꾼다. 의미를 분명하게 하기 위해 접속사는 생략하지 않을 때도 있다.

24 완료시제의 분사구문은 Having p.p. ~ 형태이고, 분사구문의 부정은 분사 앞에 not을 쓴다.

25 〈with+(대)명사+분사〉 형태를 사용하며 명사와 능동의 관계이므로 현재분사를 쓴다.

26 Judging from ~은 '~로 판단해 보면'의 의미를 가진 독립분사구문이다.

27 분사구문의 부정은 분사 앞에 not을 써야 한다.

28 〈with+(대)명사+분사〉 형태를 사용하며 명사와 능동의 관계이므로 과거분사를 쓴다.

29 분사구문을 만들 때, 주절과 부사절의 주어가 같으면 접속사와 주어를 생략하고 동사를 분사 형태로 바꾼다.

30 분사구문을 만들 때, 주절과 부사절의 주어가 다르면, 주어를 생략할 수 없다.

CHAPTER 10 관계사

Unit 01 p. 102

01 who[that] speaks English fluently
02 who[that] play hide and seek
03 which[that] is black
04 which[that] grow in the garden
05 who[that] is kind and smart

Unit 02 p. 102

01 who(m)[that] I met here
02 which[that] he carried
03 which[that] she took
04 who(m)[that] I invited
05 which[that] I was looking for
06 which[that] you're wearing

Unit 03 p. 103

01 much work that I had to do
02 drink anything that contains caffeine
03 who[that] treats a patient
04 nothing that looked exciting
05 believe (that) he is only 20 years old

Unit 04 p. 103

01 whose father is a teacher
02 whose cover is black
03 whose roof is white
04 whose tail is short
05 whose English is good
06 whose name is Cherry

Unit 05 p. 104

01 that
02 ×
03 that is
04 which
05 who were
06 ×

Unit 06
p. 104

01 what you see
02 what she did
03 what we saw
04 what you bought (for) me
05 What I want
06 What he must do first

Unit 07
p. 105

01 in which I grew up, which[that] I grew up in
02 about whom I talked, whom[that] I talked about

Unit 08
p. 105

01 where we look for and read books
02 why you didn't show up
03 when your friend will arrive

Unit 09
p. 106

01 where he met an old friend
02 when she has a lot of free time
03 which are very large
04 which kept her awake
05 which was a lie

Unit 10
p. 106

01 who lives in the city
02 asks a question
03 matter whom I ask
04 is here
05 his mom chooses

Unit 11
p. 107

01 anything that you need
02 No matter what happens
03 agree to whichever
04 whatever they liked
05 whichever you choose

Unit 12
p. 107

01 matter, when
02 whenever
03 However
04 wherever
05 matter, how

중간고사 • 기말고사 실전문제
pp. 108~112

객관식 정답 [01~15]

01 ③	**02** ④	**03** ①	**04** ③	**05** ②
06 ⑤	**07** ④	**08** ①	**09** ④	**10** ③
11 ②	**12** ①	**13** ④	**14** ③	**15** ④

주관식 정답 [16~30]

16 for which
17 what
18 ○
19 what → who
20 who's → whose
21 which → who
22 Amy was going to apply for a job which [that] makes her life more relaxing.
23 Caleb went to the amusement park where [in which] there are many fun attractions.
24 Have you ever been to Vienna where[in which] Schubert was born?
25 Whoever wants to be a pilot can apply
26 has the right to vote, which is also a duty
27 Honesty is the only thing that matters
28 take you wherever you imagine
29 Whatever he eats, he doesn't gain weight.
30 Spring is the season in which sprouts come out.

해설

01 선행사가 사람(the girl)이고 is의 주어 역할을 하는 관계대명사 who가 사용된다.

02 명사 scent가 이어지므로 소유격 관계대명사가 사용된다.

03 '~는 무엇이든지'의 의미를 가진 복합관계대명사는 whatever이다.

04 ①, ②, ④, ⑤는 선행사가 없는 관계대명사로 쓰였으며, ③은 '무엇'을 의미하는 의문사로 쓰였다.

05 ①, ③, ④, ⑤는 선행사가 생략된 관계부사로 명사절을 이끌며, ②는 접속사(~할 때)로 쓰였다.

06 ⑤ whose → who's[who is] / 관계대명사 뒤에 주어와 동사가 없으므로, 〈주격관계대명사+동사〉가 들어가야 한다.

07 ④ which → where / 뒤에 완전한 절이 나오므로 관계부사를 사용한다.

08 ① mean → means / 앞 문장 전체를 부가 설명하는 계속적 용법의 관계대명사는 단수로 수를 일치시킨다.

09 ① that → what / 선행사가 없는 관계대명사절은 what을 써야 한다. ② which → who[that] / 선행사가 사람이므로 who나 that을 써야 한다. ③ what → who[that] / 선행사가 있는 관계대명사절은 what을 쓸 수 없다. ⑤ one could → one that could / 주격 관계대명사 that은 생략할 수 없다.

10 ① Whoever → Wherever[Whenever] / 의미상 '어디를[언제] 가든지'가 자연스럽다. ② wherever → whenever / 의미상 '~할 때마다'라는 의미의 복합관계사를 써야 한다. ④ However the owner tried hard → However hard the owner tried / 〈however+형용사+주어+동사〉의 순서로 쓴다. ⑤ Whatever → However / 〈however+ 형용사+주어+동사〉 형태를 써야 한다.

11 ① why → when / 선행사가 시간이므로 관계부사 when을 사용한다. ③ what → why / 이유를 나타내는 관계부사 why를 사용한다. ④ the way how → the way 또는 how / the way와 관계부사 how는 동시에 사용할 수 없다. ⑤ when → where / 선행사가 장소이므로 관계부사 where를 사용한다.

12 선행사가 사람이므로 관계대명사 who를 사용한다. / 선행사가 사람이며, 콤마(,)와 쓰인 계속적 용법의 관계대명사이므로 who를 사용한다.

13 뒤에 완전한 절이 오므로 관계부사를 사용한다. / 선행사가 없으므로 관계대명사 what을 사용한다. / 명사 tail이 이어지므로 소유격 관계대명사를 사용한다.

14 두 번째 문장의 목적어를 꾸며주는 목적격 관계대명사절이 필요하며, 선행사가 사물이므로 which 또는 that을 사용한다. 또한, 앞 문장과의 시제일치(과거형)에 주의한다.

15 선행사가 장소 혹은 위치(a note)이므로 관계부사 where가 사용되며 이때, 관계부사는 〈전치사(on)+관계대명사〉로 바꿔 쓸 수 있다.

16 뒤에 전치사가 생략된 불완전한 문장이 나오므로 〈전치사+관계대명사〉의 형태가 되어야 한다.

17 '그가 본 것'을 설명했다는 의미이며 선행사가 없으므로 관계대명사 what이 적절하다.

18 뒤에 완전한 절이 나오므로 관계부사 또는 〈전치사+관계대명사〉를 사용한다.

19 people을 선행사로 하는 주격 관계대명사 who를 사용한다.

20 명사 office가 이어지므로 소유격 관계대명사를 사용한다.

21 선행사가 사람이며, 콤마(,)와 쓰인 계속적 용법의 관계대명사이므로 who를 사용한다.

22 a job을 선행사로 하는 관계대명사 which 또는 that을 사용한다.

23 선행사가 장소(the amusement park)이므로 관계부사 where를 사용한다.

24 선행사가 장소이며, 두 번째 문장의 동사가 자동사이므로 〈전치사+관계대명사〉의 형태가 되어야 한다.

25 '~는 누구든(지)'를 의미하는 복합관계대명사 〈whoever+동사 ~〉 형태를 사용한다.

26 앞 문장 전체를 부가 설명하고 있으므로 계속적 용법의 관계대명사를 사용한다.

27 선행사가 –thing이 올 때 관계대명사 that을 사용한다.

28 '~은 어디든지'를 의미하는 복합관계부사 〈wherever+주어+동사 ~〉 절을 사용한다.

29 '~은 무엇이든지'를 의미하는 복합관계대명사 〈whatever+주어+동사 ~〉 절을 사용한다.

30 관계대명사 which를 사용하여, 선행사 season을 꾸며 주는 관계대명사절을 만들며, 전치사 in을 쓰는 것에 주의한다.

CHAPTER 11 가정법

Unit 01 p. 114

A

01 wouldn't
02 had
03 had known
04 would have lent

B

01 were rich, would buy
02 had studied, might have been easy
03 had got up, wouldn't have been late
04 had known, could have visited
05 knew my birthday, would celebrate
06 passed the test, would be happy

Unit 02 p. 115

01 had had, would not be hungry
02 had exercised, would be healthier
03 had left, could arrive
04 had done, could see
05 hadn't bought, could buy

Unit 03 p. 115

01 I'm not rich
02 you're sick
03 didn't have time
04 lost it, don't have it
05 isn't fine

Unit 04 p. 116

A

01 isn't
02 knew
03 don't have more free time
04 can't go to Mars
05 told me a lie
06 hadn't skipped the class

B

01 we were classmates
02 played the piano well
03 you had sent me a letter
04 I hadn't eaten too much

Unit 05 p. 117

A

01 were
02 had been
03 were
04 had been

B

01 as if you knew everything
02 as if he hadn't slept well
03 as if they were friends
04 as if she were a teacher
05 as if he liked animals
06 as if he had won the gold medal

C

01 as if I hadn't had lunch
02 as if he had finished the job
03 behaved as if they knew Mr. Anderson

Unit 06 p. 118

A

01 If it had not been for his help
02 a computer, I couldn't do my homework
03 fans, they couldn't have become so popular

B

01 Without TV
02 If it were not for a vacuum
03 Without you
04 If it had not been for the pill
05 If it were not for my dog
06 If it had not been for her support

Unit 07

p. 119

A

01 time, that, were
02 that, he, took
03 time, started
04 time, arrived
05 that, saw
06 that, bought
07 time, finished

B

01 about time that you decided
02 high time that you told me
03 about time that we met
04 high time that you got rid of
05 about time that you paid back

중간고사 • 기말고사 실전문제

pp. 120~123

객관식 정답 [01~15]

01 ④	**02** ⑤	**03** ③	**04** ②	**05** ④
06 ②	**07** ④	**08** ⑤	**09** ①	**10** ④
11 ②	**12** ⑤	**13** ③	**14** ③	**15** ③

주관식 정답 [16~30]

16 had liked
17 were
18 couldn't have made
19 would have been → would be
20 has → had
21 won't → wouldn't
22 had listened to
23 there had not been
24 could understand
25 had lived longer, he would have created
26 as if he were a prince
27 about time that you cleaned your room
28 I wish she could drive a truck.
29 would you ask for if you met God
30 But for air, all the living things would die.

해설

01 현재 사실과 반대되는 가정법 과거 문장은 if절에서 과거 시제를 사용한다.

02 과거 사실과 반대되는 가정법 과거완료 문장은 if절에서 과거완료 시제를 사용한다.

03 '~라면 좋을 텐데'라는 현재 사실에 대한 유감의 의미로 〈I wish+주어+과거시제〉를 사용한다.

04 '마치 ~인 것처럼'의 의미로 현재 사실과 반대되는 일을 가정할 때는 〈as if+주어+과거시제〉를 사용한다.

05 '~가 없었다면'의 의미로 과거 사실과 반대되는 일을 가정할 때는 〈If it had not been for ~, 주어+가정법 과거완료〉를 사용한다.

06 ② would have been → would be / 현재시제를 나타내는 부사(at this moment)가 있으므로 현재 사실에 반대되는 일을 가정하는 가정법 과거를 사용한다.

07 ④ have → had / I wish 가정법 과거완료는 〈I wish+주어+had p.p.〉를 사용해야 한다.

08 ① is not → were not / '~라면 …일 텐데'라는 의미의 현재 사실과 반대되는 일을 가정하는 가정법 과거는 if절에서 과거시제를 사용한다. ② If the boy not had been → If the boy had not been / 과거완료 시제의 부정문은 had not p.p. 형태로 쓴다. ③ have score → had scored / 가정법 과거완료는 if절에서 과거완료 시제(had p.p.)를 사용해야 한다. ④ live → lived / '~라면 …일 텐데'라는 의미의 현재 사실과 반대되는 일을 가정하는 가정법 과거는 if절에서 과거시제를 사용한다.

09 '~가 없었다면'의 의미로 과거 사실과 반대되는 일을 가정할 때는 〈Without[But for]/If it had not been for ~, 주어+과거완료 시제〉를 사용하며, '~가 없다면'의 의미로 현재 사실과 반대되는 일을 가정할 때는 〈Without [But for]/If it were not for ~, 주어+과거시제〉를 사용한다. ② were not → had not been ③ were not → had not been ④ Without for → Without[But for] ⑤ But → If

10 가정법 과거완료는 직설법 과거로 바꿔 쓸 수 있다.

11 가정법 과거는 직설법 현재로 바꿔 쓸 수 있다.

12 조건절이 가정법 과거완료이므로, 〈주어+조동사의 과거형+have p.p.〉를 사용한다. / '~라면 좋을 텐데'라는 현

재 사실에 대한 유감을 나타낼 때는 〈I wish+주어+과거시제〉를 사용한다.

13 '~라면(과거) …일 텐데(현재)'의 의미를 나타내는 혼합 가정법 문장일 때, 조건절은 과거완료 시제, 주절은 과거 시제를 사용한다. / '~라면 …일 텐데'라는 의미의 현재 사실과 반대되는 가정문은 과거시제를 사용한다. / '마치 ~했던 것처럼'의 의미로 과거 사실에 대해 반대되는 일을 가정할 때는 〈as if +주어+과거완료 시제〉를 사용한다.

14 직설법 현재는 가정법 과거로 바꿀 수 있다.

15 직설법 과거는 가정법 과거완료로 바꿀 수 있다.

16 '~했다면 좋았을 텐데'라는 과거 사실에 대한 유감의 의미로 〈I wish+주어+과거완료 시제〉를 사용한다.

17 '마치 ~한 것처럼'라는 의미로 현재 사실에 반대되는 일을 가정할 때는 〈as if+주어+과거시제〉를 사용한다.

18 '~가 없었다면'이라는 과거 사실의 반대인 의미로 〈Without ~, 주어+과거완료 시제〉를 사용한다.

19 '~라면 …일 텐데'라는 의미의 현재 사실과 반대되는 가정문은 과거 시제를 사용한다.

20 가정법 과거완료는 과거완료 시제(had p.p.)를 사용해야 한다.

21 '~라면 …일 텐데'라는 의미의 현재 사실과 반대되는 가정문은 주절에서 〈조동사의 과거형+동사원형〉을 사용한다.

22 직설법 과거는 가정법 과거완료로 바꿔 쓸 수 있다.

23 직설법 과거는 가정법 과거완료로 바꿔 쓸 수 있다.

24 직설법 현재는 가정법 과거로 바꿔 쓸 수 있다.

25 과거 사실에 대한 아쉬움을 나타날 때는 가정법 과거완료를 사용한다.

26 '마치 ~인 처럼'의 의미로 현재나 미래에 반대되는 일을 가정할 때는 〈as if+주어+과거시제〉를 사용한다.

27 '~이제는 (정말) ~할 시간이다'의 의미로 〈It's about time that+과거 동사〉를 사용한다.

28 '~하면 좋을 텐데'라는 현재 사실에 대한 유감의 의미로 〈I wish+주어+과거시제〉를 사용한다.

29 '~라면 …일 텐데'라는 의미의 현재 사실과 반대되는 가정문은 if절에서 과거시제를 사용한다.

30 '~가 없다면'의 의미로 현재 사실에 대해 반대되는 일을 가정할 때는 〈But for ~, 주어+과거시제〉를 사용한다.

CHAPTER 12 일치와 화법

Unit 01

p. 126

01 is
02 are
03 have to
04 try
05 is
06 is

Unit 02

p. 126

01 ×
02 ×
03 has → had
04 are → were
05 was → is
06 is → was

Unit 03

p. 127

01 told, I would
02 told me, I had to do my homework that night
03 said, he had washed his car the day before[the previous day]
04 told us, he couldn't, that day

Unit 04

p. 128

01 if[whether] she could dance
02 What are you eating
03 what my problem was
04 Who broke the window
05 if[whether] he had written that
06 How did you make it

Unit 05

p. 128

01 told us not to make noises at night
02 asked me to call her later
03 asked Kate to lend him one of those pens
04 ordered the drivers not to drive fast in a school zone
05 asked me to forgive him for what had happened the day before[the previous day]
06 told the students to submit the assignment the next[following] day

중간고사 • 기말고사 실전문제 pp. 129~133

객관식 정답 [01~15]

01 ①	**02** ④	**03** ②	**04** ②	**05** ⑤
06 ④	**07** ③	**08** ①	**09** ②	**10** ④
11 ⑤	**12** ③	**13** ④	**14** ①	**15** ②

주관식 정답 [16~30]

16 consists **17** was
18 weren't → wasn't **19** was → were
20 won't → wouldn't **21** she, could, my, her
22 asked, if[whether], I had
23 Don't light **24** Can I wear your
25 claimed that the Earth revolves around the Sun
26 told her teacher that she wanted to leave early
27 A number of solutions were suggested
28 only the strong survive.
29 Every man has equal rights.
30 He asked me when I would call him.

해설

01 〈All of+복수명사〉는 복수로 취급하여 동사의 수를 일치시키며, usually가 있으므로 현재시제를 쓴다.

02 주절(과거)보다 먼저 일어난 일을 나타내므로 과거완료 시제를 쓴다.

03 과학적 사실은 현재시제를 사용한다.

04 주절(과거)과 시제를 일치시키거나 한 시점 이전으로 나타내야 하므로 현재완료 시제는 사용할 수 없다.

05 '~의 수'라는 의미의 〈The number of+복수명사〉는 단수로 취급한다.

06 ④ 주절의 동사와 종속절 동사의 시제를 일치시키기 위해 조동사 will을 과거형으로 써야 한다.

07 ③ 〈분수+of+복수명사〉는 복수로 취급한다.

08 ① clean → to clean / 명령문을 간접화법으로 바꿀 때, 〈주어+동사(order)+목적어+to부정사〉의 형태로 쓴다.

09 ① are → is / 〈one of the+복수명사〉는 단수로 취급한다. ③ were → was / 〈each of+복수명사〉는 단수로 취급한다. ④ are → is / 〈The number of+복수명사〉는 단수로 취급한다. ⑤ are → is / 동명사 주어는 단수로 취급한다.

10 평서문을 간접화법으로 바꿀 때, said to는 told로, here는 there로 바꿔야 한다.

11 전달동사 said to는 충고의 의미인 advised로 바꾸고, 부정문은 to 앞에 not을 써야 한다.

12 의문사가 없는 의문문을 직접화법으로 바꿀 때, 접속사 if를 없애고, asked는 said to로, 간접의문문을 직접의문문으로, we는 you로 바꾼다.

13 평서문을 직접화법으로 바꿀 때, 접속사 that을 없애고, 전달동사 told는 said to로, he는 I로, his는 my로, then은 now로 바꿔야 한다.

14 의문사가 없는 의문문의 간접화법은 접속사 whether 또는 if를 사용하여 만든다. / 나라 이름이므로 단수로 취급한다.

15 〈분수+of+단수명사〉는 단수로 취급한다. / 〈each of+복수명사〉는 단수로 취급한다. / 주절(과거)과 시제를 일치시킨다.

16 나라 이름은 단수로 취급한다.

17 〈Half of+단수명사〉는 단수로 취급한다.

18 〈Most of+단수명사〉는 단수로 취급한다.

19 〈Some+복수명사〉는 복수로 취급한다.

20 주절(과거)과 시제를 일치시킨다.

21 평서문을 간접화법으로 바꿀 때 that절의 인칭대명사와 시제는 전달자의 입장으로 바꿔 써야 한다.

22 의문사가 없는 의문문을 간접화법으로 바꿀 때, 접속사 whether 또는 if를 사용하며, 전달동사 said to는 asked로, 직접의문문을 간접의문문으로 바꾼다.

23 명령문을 직접화법으로 바꿀 때, 〈not+to부정사〉는 〈Don't+동사〉로 바꿔야 한다.

24 의문사가 없는 의문문을 직접화법으로 바꿀 때, 접속사 whether를 없애고, asked는 said to로, 간접의문문을 직접의문문으로, She는 I로, his는 your로 바꾼다.

25 과학적 사실은 현재시제를 사용한다.

26 평서문 간접화법을 사용한다.

27 '많은 ~'이라는 의미의 〈A number of+복수명사〉를 사

용한다.

28 '강자들'은 the strong이라고 쓰고, only를 그 앞에 붙인다. 주어가 복수이므로 동사는 survive로 써야 한다.

29 〈every+단수명사〉는 단수로 취급한다.

30 의문사가 있는 의문문의 간접화법은 〈의문사+주어+동사〉의 형태로 만든다.

CHAPTER 13 강조, 부정, 도치, 부정대명사

Unit 01 p. 136

A

01 do hate
02 did look
03 does make
04 does eat
05 do have

Unit 02 p. 136

01 Jiwon that[who] likes Brad
02 last Thursday that I called him
03 my sister's homework that I did
04 in the mall that we saw the celebrity
05 three days ago that they saw it

Unit 03 p. 137

01 is not always exciting
02 None of them can speak
03 Not all students are interested
04 I've never heard

Unit 04 p. 137

01 On the roof sat a little boy
02 Hardly could he believe his ears
03 Never have I been so disappointed

Unit 05 p. 138

01 another
02 others
03 the others
04 ones
05 One, the other
06 One, another, the other

중간고사 • 기말고사 실전문제 pp. 139~142

객관식 정답 [01~15]

01 ③	**02** ④	**03** ⑤	**04** ①	**05** ③
06 ③	**07** ①	**08** ③	**09** ②	**10** ③
11 ③	**12** ④	**13** ②	**14** ⑤	**15** ④

주관식 정답 [16~30]

16 Never has she been
17 ○
18 do[did]
19 do → did
20 he raises → does he raise
21 any → all
22 did try
23 can trees survive
24 she sat
25 the tree lies a small bench
26 Not all children in the world are receiving a proper
27 some students sang, others danced
28 was Sara who screamed loudly
29 It was last Monday that I got his call.
30 In the building were the children from the school.

해설

01 과거시제의 일반동사를 강조하므로 〈did+동사원형〉의 형태를 쓴다.

02 〈It is[was] ~ that[who] ...〉 형태의 강조 구문이다.

03 '모두가 ~인 것은 아니다'라는 의미의 부분 부정으로 〈not every+단수명사〉를 쓴다.

04 '어떤 ~도 …가 아니다, 모두가 아니다'라는 의미의 전체 부정으로 〈not any ~〉를 쓴다.

05 〈It is[was] ~ that...〉 형태의 강조 구문을 쓴다.

06 ③ do loves → does love / 주어인 the man에 강조 동사 do의 수를 일치시킨다.

07 ① Nobody → Anybody 또는 nothing → anything / 문장에 부정어가 두 번 사용되어 이중 부정이 된다.

08 ① the desk → on the desk / 전치사구를 강조할 때는 전치사를 포함한 구 전체를 함께 써야 한다. ② which → who 또는 that / 강조 대상이 사람이므로 which를 쓸 수 없다. ④ what → that / 〈It is[was] ~ that...〉 형태의 강조 구문이다. ⑤ 목적어 자리의 a person을 삭제한다.

09 ① knows → know / 도치된 조동사 did가 앞에 있으므로 동사원형을 써야 한다. ③ agreed → agree / 도치된 조동사 did가 앞에 있으므로 동사원형을 써야 한다. ④ her mother stood → stood her mother / 전치사구가 문장 앞에 나왔으므로, 주어와 동사를 도치시킨다. ⑤ was he → he was / 주어가 대명사일 때는 도치시키지 않는다.

10 부정문에 대한 동의는 〈Neither+Be/조동사+주어〉 형태이다.

11 긍정문에 대한 동의는 〈So+Be/조동사+주어〉 형태이다.

12 과거시제의 일반동사를 강조할 때는 〈did+동사원형〉을 쓴다. / 〈not+every+단수명사〉의 형태이다.

13 〈It is ~ that[who] ...〉 강조 구문이다. / 전체 부정을 의미하는 〈not ~ any〉를 사용한다. / 부정문에 대한 동의는 〈Neither+Be/조동사+주어〉를 쓴다.

14 '모두가 ~인 것은 아니다'의 부분 부정형 〈not every+단수명사〉는 〈not all+복수명사〉로 바꿔 쓸 수 있다.

15 부정문에 대한 동의는 〈Neither+Be/조동사+주어〉 형태이다.

16 부정어(Never)가 문장 앞에 나오면 〈Never+Be/조동사+주어 (+동사)〉의 형태로 쓴다.

17 장소부사(Here)가 문장 앞에 나오면 〈Here+Be동사+주어〉의 형태로 쓴다.

18 주어에 수일치시키며, 현재형과 과거형으로도 가능하다.

19 과거시제의 일반동사를 강조하므로 〈did+동사원형〉의 형태로 쓴다.

20 부정어가 문장 앞에 나오면 〈Not only+Be/조동사+주어 (+동사)〉의 형태로 쓴다.

21 '모두가 ~인 것은 아니다'라는 의미의 부분 부정은 〈not ~ all〉을 쓴다. 〈not ~ any〉는 '아무 것도[전혀] ~가 아니다'라는 의미의 전체 부정이 된다.

22 과거시제의 일반동사를 강조하므로 〈did+동사원형〉의 형태를 쓴다.

23 부정어를 문장 앞에 쓰면, 〈Hardly+조동사(can)+주어+동사원형〉의 형태로 쓴다.

24 주어가 대명사일 때는 도치시키지 않는다.

25 전치사구가 문장 앞에 나왔으므로, 주어와 동사를 도치시킨다.

26 '모두가 ~인 것은 아니다'라는 부분 부정을 나타낼 때는 〈not+all+복수명사〉를 쓴다.

27 '(여러 명 중에) 몇몇'이라는 의미의 some과 '다른 몇몇'이라는 의미의 others를 사용한다.

28 〈It is[was] ~ that[who] ...〉 형태의 강조 구문을 사용하여 Sara를 강조한다.

29 〈It was ~ that ...〉 형태의 강조 구문을 사용하여 last Monday를 강조한다.

30 전치사구가 문장 앞에 나왔으므로, 주어와 동사를 도치시킨다.

CHAPTER 14 문장의 이해

Unit 01

p. 144

01 That the team will win the match

02 Blaming other people for your problems

03 Travel to the Mars

04 가주어: It / 진주어: climbing the mountain at night

05 To walk for an hour every day

06 Working from home
07 The business hours of the restaurant
08 The tiny island discovered by the captain

Unit 02
p. 144

01 glad
02 close to me
03 friends
04 cooking for my family
05 damaged
06 wrong
07 sweet and sour
08 a mystery

Unit 03
p. 145

A
01 some bread and cookies
02 to be asleep
03 taking a walk in the morning
04 opening the window

B
01 간접목적어: us / 직접목적어: Korean
02 간접목적어: him / 직접목적어: a present
03 간접목적어: him / 직접목적어: the truth

Unit 04
p. 145

01 목적어: me / 목적격보어: to make a plan for the holidays
02 목적어: studying math alone / 목적격보어: difficult
03 목적어: someone / 목적격보어: singing a song downstairs
04 목적어: me / 목적격보어: clean the bathroom before my meal
05 목적어: her / 목적격보어: to brush her teeth after every meal

Unit 05
p. 146

01 (manufactured in Germany)
02 (to write on)
03 (who have plenty of money)
04 (performing on the stage)
05 (to say good bye)
06 (filled with honey)
07 (founded by her father)
08 (many old), (to tell us)

Unit 06
p. 146

01 부사절: Even though it's September / 부사: still
02 부사: never
03 분사구문: Knowing that they were saved
04 부사구: over a cup of tea
05 부사: quietly
06 분사구문: Strictly speaking
07 부사절: if you have any problems
08 to부정사: to return a couple of books

중간고사 • 기말고사 실전문제
pp. 147~150

객관식 정답 [01~15]

01 ①	**02** ③	**03** ②	**04** ④	**05** ⑤
06 ②	**07** ③	**08** ④	**09** ⑤	**10** ②
11 ④	**12** ⑤	**13** ①	**14** ⑤	**15** ④

주관식 정답 [16~30]

16 Stretching[To stretch], is
17 with a lovely garden
18 not to give up
19 had, come up to
20 that it will not be difficult
21 the man sitting next to her to be rude
22 the organization communicate with others

23 The soldiers forced to follow his orders
24 the document to submit
25 The bird that he saw today
26 to worsen, worse 또는 worsen
27 is, that is 또는 which is
28 send, sending
29 working at home gave me clear directions
30 The crowd moved by his beautiful performance

해설

01 보어 자리에는 명사구 또는 명사 역할의 to부정사 또는 동명사가 올 수 있다. ②, ⑤ 동사 ③ 접속사 없는 문장 ④ 관계대명사절이 이어지므로 보어 자리에 올 수 없다.

02 동사 find의 목적어 자리에는 명사구 또는 명사 역할의 to부정사 또는 동명사가 올 수 있다. ①, ④ 형용사 ② 직접의문문 ⑤ 관계대명사절이 이어지므로 목적어 자리에 올 수 없다.

03 동사 visit의 목적어로 (대)명사, 명사절이 가능하다. where the Statue of Liberty is는 '자유의 여신상이 있는 곳'이란 의미로 명사절을 이끄므로 visited의 목적어가 될 수 있다.

04 ④ 동사 see는 목적어로 that절을 취할 수도 있고, 목적어와 목적격보어도 취할 수 있다. 단, 목적격보어로 to부정사를 사용할 수 없다.

05 ⑤ 간접의문문 How rich he could be로 바꾸면 명사절 주어로 사용이 가능하다.

06 ② 동사 make의 목적격보어는 원형부정사, 명사, 형용사, 과거분사만 가능하다. 부사는 사용할 수 없다.

07 〈call A B〉는 'A를 B라고 부르다'라는 의미이며 5형식 문장을 만든다.

08 to부정사를 주어로 사용하였고 requires가 문장의 동사로 사용되었다.

09 〈name A B〉는 'A를 B라고 이름 짓다'라는 의미의 5형식 문장을 만든다.

10 '~하는 것'이라는 의미를 나타낼 때, to부정사 또는 동명사를 주어로 사용할 수 있으며, while 뒤에 주어가 없으므로 분사구문을 사용한다.

11 ⓓ는 목적격보어이다.

12 ⓔ는 부사적 수식어(~하기 위해) 이다.

13 ① helping → helps / 문장에 동사가 없으므로 주어의 수와 일치하는 동사를 써야 한다.

14 ① was 삭제 / 동사 gave up이 있으므로 was를 쓸 수 없다. ② healthily → healthy / '~하게 유지하다'라는 의미의 stay 뒤에는 형용사만 올 수 있다. ③ it 삭제 또는 gave me / 수여동사 give 뒤에는 〈간접목적어+직접목적어〉의 형태가 오거나 〈목적어+to 대상〉이 올 수 있다. ④ Simple → Simply / '간단히'라는 의미로 부사가 와야 한다.

15 동사 feel 뒤에는 목적어 또는 형용사 보어가 올 수 있다. / 형용사구가 길어지면 명사 a strawberry를 뒤에서 수식 할 수 있다.

16 '~하는 것'이라는 의미를 나타낼 때 to부정사 또는 동명사를 주어로 사용한다.

17 주어 The house를 전치사구(with ~ garden)가 뒤에서 꾸며준다.

18 told의 목적격보어로 to부정사가 나오며, 부정문은 to 앞에 not을 쓴다.

19 사역동사의 목적격보어로 동사원형이 나온다.

20 that이 이끄는 명사절이 보어로 사용되었다.

21 동사 thought 뒤에 the man sitting next to her가 목적어로, to be rude가 목적격보어로 사용되었다.

22 동사 helped 뒤에 the organization이 목적어로, communicate with others가 목적격보어로 사용되었다.

23 주어 The soldiers를 과거분사구가 뒤에서 꾸며 준다.

24 목적어 the document를 to부정사가 뒤에서 꾸며 준다.

25 주어 The bird를 관계대명사절이 뒤에서 꾸며 준다.

26 동사 make는 목적격보어로 형용사 또는 원형부정사를 쓸 수 있다.

27 관계사가 없으면, 접속사 없이 두 개의 동사(is, has)를 가진 비문이 된다.

28 전치사 After의 목적어로는 동명사를 사용한다.

29 주어 My boss를 현재분사구가 뒤에서 꾸며 준다.

30 주어 The crowd를 과거분사구가 뒤에서 꾸며 준다.

EBS

MY GRAMMAR COACH

내신기출 N제 중3